CORPVS VASORVM ANTIQVORVM

GREAT BRITAIN, FASCICULE 17

BRITISH MUSEUM, FASCICULE 9

For Martin Robertson

UNION ACADÉMIQUE INTERNATIONALE

CORPVS
VASORVM ANTIQVORVM

GREAT BRITAIN
THE BRITISH MUSEUM

DYFRI WILLIAMS

Published for
THE TRUSTEES OF THE BRITISH MUSEUM
by
BRITISH MUSEUM PRESS
1993

Great Britain, Fascicule 17 *British Museum, Fascicule 9*

Published by British Museum Press
A division of British Museum Publications Ltd
46 Bloomsbury Street
London WC1B 3QQ

ISBN 0 7141 2201 7

British Library Cataloguing in Publication Data
A catalogue reference for this book is available
from the British Library

Designed by Andrew Shoolbred
Illustration and plate sections designed by Susan Bird

Printed in Great Britain by Henry Ling Ltd, Dorchester, Dorset

CONTENTS

PREFACE

The seven early fascicules of the *Corpus Vasorum Antiquorum (CVA)* produced by the British Museum between 1925 and 1932 contained, by and large, small illustrations and only brief descriptions, but they did attempt to chart most of the collection of Greek and Italian pottery. R. M. Cook's fascicule of 1954 was a new departure. It concentrated almost entirely on one area, that of the notoriously difficult East Greek fabrics, and provided both good illustrations and detailed text with discursive introductory sections. In returning to the format of the *CVA* nearly forty years later, it has been decided to endeavour to follow Robert Cook's example. One group of vases omitted in the early fascicules of the *CVA* was the red-figured cups. Since the British Museum's collection is probably large enough to fill three fascicules on this group, the author decided to follow his own particular expertise and produce a fascicule dedicated to red-figured cups of the Late Archaic period.

The recent move away from loose packs of plates to a more normal, and cheaper, book format, together with the coherence of the vases included in this fascicule, has provided further opportunities to modify the normal *CVA* scheme. Firstly, it has been decided to give each vase a running number, rather than rely wholely on a complex system of plate numbers of the type found in most fascicules of the *CVA*. Secondly, the best way to organise the vases has proved to be by painter, which has enabled the author to follow Cook's use of introductory comments to sections, by giving brief introductory bibliographies and remarks on each painter or group of painters. It is hoped that, thanks to the breadth of the British Museum's collection, such an arrangement will allow this fascicule of the *CVA* to serve as some sort of a conspectus of Late Archaic red-figured cups and their painters.

A NOTE ON THE BIBLIOGRAPHY AND TERMINOLOGY

Almost all of the vases included in this fascicule have been illustrated many times over in one form or another. It has been decided, therefore, to be severely selective in the bibliographic sections of the entries, omitting many references to publications that have little more than an illustration, for Beazley's lists provide many of these. The bibliographic sections, therefore, concentrate on early mentions, important discussions or listings, and more recent references, not to be found in Beazley's own lists or in the *Beazley Addenda.*

All measurements are in centimeters. The width is measured from the extremity of one handle to the extremity of the other. The diameter of the tondo includes the tondo border. The diameter of the exterior ground line does not include the border.

The terminology for border patterns was carefully worked out by Beazley in his early articles (esp. J.D. Beazley, *JHS* 31 [1911] 279). More recently, D.C. Kurtz, *Athenian White Lekythoi* (Oxford 1975) figs. 4–5, has drawn out many of them in a very useful manner. The most common elements are the maeander and the key. The distinction between the two lies in whether the line is continuous or interrupted at the centre: if there is an interruption the pattern is a maeander. A variation is the so-called false maeander, a term coined by Beazley (C.B. iii 21) and explained by him as a 'maeander in one line that penetrates to the middle of the maze but does not come out again.' Running maeander, a term used by Kurtz and many others, is a helpful abbreviation of Beazley's original usage, maeander 'running in twos' (C.B. ii 31). The place at which the painter started and finished his border pattern may sometimes be observed, either because he has omitted a unit altogether or because he has added an extra one or because one can be seen to be defective: the term that Beazley used for the last, 'odd man' (see C.B. ii 23–4), is adopted here.

LIST OF ABBREVIATIONS

Agora xii
B.A. Sparkes and L. Talcott, *The Athenian Agora xii: Black and Plain Pottery of the 6th, 5th and 4th Centuries B.C.* (Princeton, New Jersey 1970)

Amsterdam Colloquium
H.A.G. Brijder, *Ancient Greek and Related Pottery: Proceedings of the International Vase Symposium Amsterdam 1984* (Amsterdam 1984)

Archaic into Classical
C.G. Boulter (ed.), *Greek Art: Archaic into Classical* (Leiden 1985)

A. H. S.
P.E. Arias, M. Hirmer and B.B. Shefton, *A History of Greek Vase Painting* (London 1962)

ARV
J.D. Beazley, *Attic Red-figure Vase-painters* (Oxford 1942)

ARV²
J.D. Beazley, *Attic Red-figure Vase-painters* (2nd edn, Oxford 1963)

AV
J.D. Beazley, *Attische Vasenmaler des rotfigurigen Stils* (Tübingen 1925)

Baker *Furniture*
H.S. Baker, *Furniture in the Ancient World* (London 1966)

Beazley Add²
T.H. Carpenter (comp.), *Beazley Addenda: Additional references to ABV, ARV² & Paralipomena* (2nd edn, Oxford 1989)

Beazley *CF*
J.D. Beazley, *Campana Fragments in Florence* (Oxford 1933)

Beazley *Kleophrades-Maler*
J.D. Beazley, *Der Kleophrades-Maler* (Berlin 1933)

Beazley Lectures
D.C. Kurtz (ed.), *Greek Vases: Lectures by J.D. Beazley* (Oxford 1989)

Beazley *RG*
J.D. Beazley, 'Un realista greca' in *Adunanze Straordinarie per il conferimento dei premi della Fondazione A. Feltrinelli* 1, 3 (Rome 1966) 53–60

Beazley *VP*
J.D. Beazley, *Greek Vases in Poland* (Oxford 1928)

Bloesch *FAS*
H. Bloesch, *Formen attischer Schalen* (Berne 1940)

BM Cat Glass i
D.B. Harden, *Catalogue of Greek and Roman Glass in the British Museum* i (London 1981)

BM Cat Terracottas
R.A. Higgins, *Catalogue of the Terracottas in the Department of Greek and Roman Antiquities British Museum* i (London 1969)

BM Cat Vases
C.H. Smith, *Catalogue of the Greek and Etruscan Vases in the British Museum* iii (London 1896)

BM Old Cat Vases
S. Birch and C.T. Newton, *A Catalogue of the Greek and Etruscan Vases in the British Museum* i (London 1851)

Boardman *ARFV Archaic*
J. Boardman, *Athenian Red Figure Vases: The Archaic Period* (London 1975)

Brommer *V³*
F. Brommer, *Vasenlisten zur griechischen Heldensage* (3rd edn, Marburg 1973)

Buitron-Oliver *Douris*
D. Buitron-Oliver, *Douris* (Kerameus series, forthcoming)

Cabinet Durand
J. de Witte, *Description des Antiquités et Objets d'Art qui composent le Cabinet de feu M. le Chevalier E. Durand* (Paris 1836)

Cambitoglou *Brygos Painter*
A. Cambitoglou, *The Brygos Painter* (Sydney 1968)

Carpenter *Art and Myth*
T.H. Carpenter, *Art and Myth in Ancient Greece* (London 1991)

C.B. i, ii, iii
L.D. Caskey and J.D. Beazley, *Attic Vase Paintings in the Museum of Fine Arts, Boston* i (Boston 1931), ii (1954), iii (1963)

Cité des Images
J.-P. Vernant (ed.), *La Cité des Images* (Paris 1984)

Copenhagen Colloquium
J. Christiansen and T. Melander (eds.), *Proceedings of the 3rd Colloquium on Ancient Greek and Related Pottery* (Copenhagen 1988)

de Witte *Fabricants*
J. de Witte, *Noms des fabricants et dessinateurs de vases peints* (Paris 1848)

Dohrn Festschrift
H. Blanck and S. Steingräber (eds.), *Miscellanea Archeologica Tobias Dohrn dedicata* (Rome 1982)

Euphronios
Euphroniox: peintre à Athenes au VIe siècle avant J.-C. (Paris 1990)

Euphronios Peintre
M. Denoyelle (ed.), *Euphronios Peintre* (Rencontres de l'École du Louvre, Paris 1992)

Eye of Greece
D.C. Kurtz and B.A. Sparkes (eds.), *The Eye of Greece. Studies in the Art of Athens* (in honour of Martin Robertson; Cambridge 1982)

Ferrari *Tarquinia*
G. Ferrari, *I Vasi Attici a Figure Rosse del Periodo Arcaico* (Rome 1988)

Festschrift Bloesch
M. Schmidt in H.P. Isler and G. Seiterle (eds.), *Zur griechischen Kunst* (*AntK* 9th Beiheft, Bern 1973)

Festschrift Schauenburg
E. Böhr and W. Martini (eds.), *Studien zur Mythologie und Vasenmalerei. Festschrift für Konrad Schauenburg* (Mainz 1986)

Froehner *Collection van Branteghem*
W. Froehner, *Collection van Branteghem: Catalogue des Monuments antiques, vases peints, terres quites* (Paris sale, 30 May – 1 June 1892 [a small, unillustrated cat. gives date as 16–18 June])

Frucht *Duris*
H. Frucht, *Die signierten Gefässe des Duris* (Munich 1914)

F.R. i, ii, iii
A. Furtwängler and K. Reichhold (et al.), *Griechische Vasenmalerei. Auswahl hervorragender Vasenbilder* i (Munich 1904), ii (Munich 1909), iii (Munich 1932)

Gardiner *AAW*
E.N. Gardiner, *Athletics of the Ancient World* (Oxford 1930)

Getty Vases
Greek Vases in The J. Paul Getty Museum (*Occasional Papers on Antiquities*, Malibu)

Ginouvès *Balaneutikè*
R. Ginouvès, *Balaneutikè. Recherches sur le bain dans l'antiquité grecque* (Paris 1962)

Glories of the Past
D. von Bothmer (ed.), *Glories of the Past: Ancient Art from the Shelby White and Leon Levy Collection* (New York 1990)

Guy *Followers of Douris*
J.R. Guy, 'The Late Manner and Early Classical Followers of Douris', Oxford D.Phil thesis, 1982

Hartwig *M*
P. Hartwig, *Die Griechischen Meisterschalen der Blüthezeit des strengen rotfigurigen Stiles* (Stuttgart and Berlin 1893)

Hirschmann Collection
H. Bloesch (ed.), *Greek Vases from the Hirschmann Collection* (Zurich 1982)

Hoppin i & ii
J.C. Hoppin, *A Handbook of Attic Red-figured Vases* (Cambridge, Mass. 1919)

Immerwahr *Attic Script*
H.R. Immerwahr, *Attic Script. A Survey* (Oxford 1990)

Johnston *Trademarks*
A.W. Johnston, *Trademarks on Greek Vases* (Warminster 1979)

Keuls *Phallus*
E.C. Keuls, *The Reign of the Phallus* (New York 1985)

Klein *L*
W. Klein, *Die griechischen Vasen mit Lieblingsinschriften* (Vienna 1890)

Klein *L²*
W. Klein, *Die griechischen Vasen mit Lieblingsinschriften* (2nd edn, Leipzig 1898)

Klein *M*[2]
W. Klein, *Die griechischen Vasen mit Meistersignaturen* (2nd edn, Vienna 1887)

Knauer *Foundry Painter*
E.R. Knauer, *A Red-Figure Kylix by the Foundry Painter: Observations on a Greek Realist* (Indiana University Art Museum Occasional Paper 1; Bloomington, Indiana 1987)

Koch-Harnack
G. Koch-Harnack, *Knabenliebe und Tiergeschenke* (Berlin 1983)

Korshak *Frontal Faces*
Y. Korshak, *Frontal Faces in Attic Vase Painting of the Archaic Period* (Chicago 1987)

Leonard *Hieron*
F. Leonard, *Über einige Vasen der Werkstatt des Hieron* (Greifswald 1912)

LIMC
Lexicon Iconographicum Mythologiae Classicae (Zurich and Munich 1981 continuing)

Lissarrague *Flot d'Images*
F. Lissarrague, *Un Flot d'Images: une esthétique du banquet grec* (Paris 1987)

Lissarrague *L'autre guerrier*
F. Lissarrague, *L'autre guerrier: archers, peltastes, cavaliers dans l'imagerie attique* (Paris and Rome 1990)

Looking at Greek Vases
T. Rasmussen and N. Spivey (eds.), *Looking at Greek Vases* (Cambridge 1991)

Maas and McIntosh Snyder
M. Maas and J. McIntosh Snyder, *Stringed Instruments of Ancient Greece* (New Haven 1989)

Morrow *Greek Footwear*
K.D. Morrow, *Greek Footwear and the Dating of Sculpture* (Madison, Wisconsin 1985)

Murray *DGV*
A.S. Murray, *Designs from Greek Vases in the British Museum* (London 1894)

Mus. Étrusque
Museum Étrusque de Lucien Bonaparte Prince de Canino, fouilles de 1828 à 1829: Vases peints avec inscriptions (Viterbo 1829)

Nachbaur *Makron*
G. Nachbaur, *Schalen des Makron aus der Werkstatt des Hieron* (Dissertation, Graz, 1978)

New Perspectives
D. Buitron-Oliver (ed.), *New Perspectives in Early Greek Art* (Washington 1991)

Ninagawa Museum
E. Simon, *The Kurashiki Ninagawa Museum* (Mainz 1982)

Open Univ.
Fifth Century Athens: Democracy and City-State (Open Univ., Rainham 1989)

Para
J.D. Beazley, *Paralipomena: Additions to Attic Black-figure Vase-painters and to Attic Red-figure Vase-painters [second edition]* (Oxford 1971)

Peschel *Hetäre*
I. Peschel, *Die Hetäre bei Symposion und Komos in der attisch-rotfigurigen Vasenmalerei des 6.-4. Jahrh. v. Chr.* (Frankfurt 1987)

Poliakoff *Combat Sports*
M.B. Poliakoff, *Combat Sports in the Ancient World* (New Haven 1987)

RE
Paulys Real-Encyclopädie der klassischen Altertumswissenschaft (new edn, by G. Wissowa; Stuttgart 1894–1972)

Reinsberg *EHK*
C. Reinsberg, *Ehe, Hetärentum und Knabenliebe im antiken Griechenland* (Munich 1989)

Richter *Survey*[2]
G.M.A. Richter, *Attic Red-figured Vases. A Survey* (2nd edn, New Haven 1958)

Richter and Hall
G.M.A. Richter and L.F. Hall, *Red-figured Athenian Vases in The Metropolitan Museum of Art* (New York 1936)

Robertson *Art of Vase-painting*
M. Robertson, *The Art of Vase-painting in Classical Athens* (Cambridge 1992)

Robertson *HGA*
M. Robertson, *A History of Greek Art* (Cambridge 1975)

Robertson *Shorter HGA*
M. Robertson, *A Shorter History of Greek Art* (Cambridge 1981)

Schefold *GkhK*
K. Schefold, *Die Göttersage in der klassischen und hellenistischen Kunst* (Munich 1981)

Schefold *GuH*
K. Schefold, *Götter und Heldensagen der Griechen in der spätarchaischen Kunst* (Munich 1978)

Schefold *Sagen*
K. Schefold and F. Jung, *Die Sagen von den Argonauten, von Theben und Troia in der klassischen und hellenistischen Kunst* (Munich 1989)

Schefold *Urkönige*
K. Schefold and F. Jung, *Die Urkönige, Perseus, Bellerophon, Herakles und Theseus in der klassischen und hellenistischen Kunst* (Munich 1988)

Seki *U*
T. Seki, *Untersuchungen zum Verhältnis von Gefässform und Malerei attischer Schalen* (Berlin 1985)

Studies Robinson
G.E. Mylonas and D. Raymond (eds.), *Studies Presented to David Moore Robinson* ii (Saint Louis, Missouri 1953)

Sweet *Sport and Recreation*
W.E. Sweet, *Sport and Recreation in Ancient Greece* (Oxford and New York 1987)

Sympotica
O. Murray (ed.), *Sympotica: A Symposium on the Symposion* (Oxford 1990)

Tonks *Brygos*
O.S. Tonks, *Brygos – His Characteristics* (*Memoirs of the American Academy of Arts and Sciences* xiii, 2, 1904) 65–117

VA
J.D. Beazley, *Attic Red-figured Vases in American Museum* (Cambridge, Mass. 1918)

Wegner *Brygosmaler*
M. Wegner, *Brygosmaler* (Berlin 1973)

Wegner *Duris*
M. Wegner, *Duris* (Münster 1968)

Williams *Greek Vases*
D. Williams, *Greek Vases* (London 1985)

Abbreviations of periodicals follow those used by the Deutsches Archäologisches Institut, but add

Princeton Record
Record of The Art Museum Princeton University

Other Abbreviations

fr.: fragment
frr.: fragments
retr.: retrograde
U: upper exterior side when viewed from correctly poised tondo
L: lower exterior side when viewed from correctly poised tondo
gt. dim: greatest dimension

ACKNOWLEDGEMENTS

I owe a debt of gratitude to many friends and colleagues for help and advice. First and foremost, I should like to mention Dietrich von Bothmer who has added to my burden of debt and friendship to him by reading the whole text with great thoroughness and speed. He offered many suggestions and improvements: the mistakes that remain are all the author's fault. Brian Cook also kindly undertook to read the text and did so with his customary care and attention. In addition, I should like to thank others who have faithfully answered questions or provided information, in particular, Diana Buitron-Oliver, for allowing me to consult her forthcoming book on Douris, Robert Guy, for permission to consult and quote his unpublished Oxford D.Phil. thesis, Norbert Kunisch, for help in consulting Nachbaur's thesis on Makron and on other Macronian matters, Donna Kurtz, for help in the Beazley Archive and for supplying the photograph of the missing Leipzig fr. that joins **2** (E 46), Cornelius Vermeule for photographs of the fr. in the collection of his daughter that joins the same cup, Michael Vickers for the photographs of the Oxford fr. that joins **25** and V. M. Strocka for the photographs of the Freiburg fr. that belongs to the same piece; also Lucilla Burn, the late Peter Corbett, Hero Grainger-Taylor and Ian Jenkins.

I should also like to record my gratitude to the members of the Ceramic Section of the British Museum Department of Conservation, especially the late Nigel Williams, and the photographers of the Photographic Department, especially P. E. Nicholls: they have all been so patient. In addition, I am very grateful to Miss Susan Bird for all the drawings and the lay-out of the plates and for constant encouragement.

Finally, I should like to dedicate this book to Martin Robertson, a friend, a gentle critic and a constant inspiration.

CATALOGUE

Nos. 1–6 Onesimos

For Onesimos see, in addition to Beazley's lists (especially his comments in *ARV*[2] 313–14), the following: A. Furtwängler in F.R. ii 110–12, 134; Buschor *GV* 171–2; *VA* 82–8 and 88–9; *VP* 22–3; J.D. Beazley in *Commemorative Studies in Honor of Theodore Leslie Shear* (*Hesperia 8th Suppl.*, 1949) 3–5; J.D. Beazley in C.B. ii 21–36, nos. 71–81; Richter *Survey*[2] 76–8; Robertson *GP* 103–6; J.D. Beazley, *AJA* 66 (1962) 235–6; A.H.S. 333–5 (nos. 134 and 149); G. von Lücken in G. von Lücken and K. Zimmerman (eds.), *Die Griechische Vase* (Rostok 1967) 485–90; E. Vermeule, *AJA* 71 (1967) 311–14; Boardman *ARFV Archaic* 133–4; D. Williams, *JbBerlMus* 18 (1976) 9–23; M. Ohly-Dumm, *GettyMusJ* 9 (1981) 5–21; B.A. Sparkes in *Archaic into Classical* 18–39; Immerwahr *Attic Script* 83–5; D. Williams, *Getty Vases* 5 (1991) 41–64; Robertson *Art of Vase-painting* 43–55.

Onesimos was a pupil of the painter Euphronios and was the most important of the artists that Euphronios gathered around him when he began to turn from painting to potting. These earlier phases of Onesimos, the Leagran (*c.* 505–500 BC) and Panaetian (*c.* 500–495 BC), have been much discussed in recent years, and the British Museum's holdings concentrate on them. His later works (*c.* 495 until after 490 BC) are characterised by the *kalos* name Lykos and an increased delicacy of drawing. To this period belongs his only signed work, the cup in the Louvre (*ARV*[2] 324, 60). There is also a brief very late phase which goes down to about 485 BC. After about 490 BC Onesimos' style begins to show the influence of his pupil, the Antiphon Painter.

Onesimos seems to have worked exclusively for the potter Euphronios: see Bloesch *FAS* 7–80; *ARV*[2] 313–14; D. Williams in *Euphronios* 33–7 and in *Getty Vases* 5 (1991) 41–2. Onesimos was chiefly a cup-painter, but he also decorated kyathoi, three covered and spouted skyphoid cups (Getty 81.AE.214 A and B; also frr. of a third, later), a pair of kantharoi (Getty 87.AE.82 and 83), a phiale (M.P. Baglione in *Copenhagen Colloquium* 18 fig. 1, attributed there to the Brygos Painter) and a plate.

1 (pl. 1 and fig. 4a)

Cup: GR 1901.7–11.2 frr.
From Rhodes.
Presented by Sir Alfred Biliotti.

Bibliography: H.B. Walters, *JHS* 41 (1921) 124 no. 2.

Dimensions: width *c.* 24.5; diam. *c.* 18.5; diam. of tondo 12.5.

Condition: one large fr. and one smaller; foot missing (stem has been keyed for plaster and was restored with an alien Acrocup foot, now removed); glaze at rim on exterior badly flaked.

Description
INTERIOR: komast at a krater.
A youth moves to the left, both his knees bent in a pose sometimes associated with running, sometimes with dancing (right knee and left ankle and foot missing). He holds up in his right hand a large skyphos, slightly tipped towards him as if he has just finished the last drop. The skyphos is decorated with groups of lines at the rim and on the body, but has only a small stub of a handle. In his left hand (missing) the youth held a knotty stick and over his arms is draped a plain chlamys. He has a red wreath on his head and there is a large patch of fuzzy hair on his cheek (dilute glaze), his *ioulos*. On the left, partly obscured by the frame of the scene, is a calyx-krater.

INSCRIPTIONS: HO[ΓAIΣ] (retr.), KAΛO[Σ](retr.) and N[AI+I]
Border: two reserved lines.

Relief contour throughout (except hair); dilute glaze for minor interior markings; added red for inscriptions.

c. 510–500 BC.

Comment: Attributed by Walters to the Panaitios Painter, but never included by Beazley in any of his published lists, although there is a drawing of it in the Beazley Archive. It is, indeed, a very early work of Onesimos. It compares extremely closely in details of eye, nose, ear and stomach muscles with the pieces discussed in D. Williams, *JbBerlMus* 18 (1976) 18–23, including the two London cups (**3** [E 45] and **2** [E 46]). It is a simple piece, but the drawing is full of life and power.

The krater on the left suggests an excerpt from a symposium, but kraters are also sometimes seen being lifted or carried by one of the revellers in *komos* processions and even put down for use *en route*. The youth may be dancing at the krater or even refilling his skyphos. On the imagery of the symposium see Lissarrague *Flot d'Images* 23–40 and *Sympotica* 196–209.

2 (pls. 2–3 and fig. 4b)

Cup: GR 1892.7–18.7 (*BM Cat Vases* E 46) and 1924.7–18.1 and 2 (by exchange, from Leipzig, noticed by H. Nachod and A. Rumpf). One fr. remained in the Antikenmuseum der Karl-Marx-Universität, Leipzig, as Beazley pointed out (not located by author in 1991; Lady Beazley's photograph supplied by the Beazley Archive, Oxford), and a second has been noted by J.R.

Guy in the collection of Miss E.D.B. Vermeule in Boston (photograph kindly supplied by C.C. Vermeule).
From Cerveteri; A. van Branteghem collection.
Bought at the van Branteghem sale, 1892.

Bibliography: A. Furtwängler, *Gazette Archéologique* 1888, 173; W. Fröhner, *Burlington Fine Arts Catalogue of Objects of Greek Ceramic Art* (London 1888) 15 no. 12; Klein *L* 40 no. 13; Froehner *Collection van Branteghem* no. 53 with pls. 15–16; Hartwig *M* 102–4 and 684 no. 11, pl. 8; *VA* 87 no. 3; Hoppin i, 425 no. 52; F. Studniczka, *Disjecta Membra griechischer Vasen* (Leipzig 1919) 2; *AV* 166 no. 7; Bloesch *FAS* 75 no. 24, pl. 21, 1; *ARV* 210 no. 1; *ARV*² 315–16, 1; I. Scheibler in K. Schefold (ed.), *Die Griechen und ihre Nachbaren* (*Propyläen Kunstgeschichte* i, Berlin 1967) fig. 201 (I), with p. 222; H.A.G. Brijder, *BABesch* 50 (1975) 173, 13a; D. Williams *JbBerlMus* 18 (1976) 16–17 figs. 8–10; *Beazley Add*² 213.

Dimensions: width 29.8; diam. 23.3; diam. of tondo 16.5; ht. 9.4; diam. of exterior ground line 11.3; diam. of foot plate 10.6.

Condition: Broken and mended from frr.; some rim and wall frr. missing, together with one from the foot plate.

Description

INTERIOR: a youth coursing a hare.
The youth is naked except for a red hair-band and a red anklet on his left leg. His sideburns are shown by a patch of dilute glaze on his cheek. He seems to have been crouching and to have just let the hare loose. The hare leaps forward: dilute glaze strokes on its skin and a thin red collar around its neck.

INSCRIPTIONS: ᒪEAΛROΣ (retr.) KAᒪOΣ (retr.);
HOΓAIΣ KAᒪOΣ
Border: stopt maeanders (four-stroke, anticlockwise).

EXTERIOR: komasts.
Side A (L): On the left, a komast dances between two skyphoi that rest on the ground, one behind and one in front. Only his right leg and his raised left foot are preserved. In the centre a youth leans forward as he plays the pipes, a cloak over his shoulders (line border) – his face, arms and pipes were preserved on a fr. once in Leipzig (now missing). On the right a youth rests his right hand on top of a knotty stick as he kicks up his left leg. He has a red wreath on his head and a cloak (line border) over his right upper arm and shoulder. The Vermeule fr. completes this figure and the thigh of the central youth. Almost under the handle is a skyphos.

Side B (U): On the left a youth wearing a red wreath leans forward holding a skyphos low in front of him; behind him a knotty stick (top missing) leans against the handle. In the centre dances a youth, his legs splayed outwards, head bowed (most of head and groin missing). On the right is a third youth wearing a red wreath and holding a skyphos up in front of his head, his left arm back, hand probably on top of a knotty stick against the handle.

INSCRIPTION: [ᒪ]EAΛR[OΣ] KA[ᒪ]OΣ
Border: stopt maeanders (four-stroke, anticlockwise).

Relief contours throughout (except hair); dilute glaze for minor interior markings; added red for inscriptions; no reserved lines at lip.

c. 510–500 BC.

Comment: Furtwängler (*apud* Hartwig), Hartwig and others attributed the cup to Euphronios. Beazley placed it in the first section of his Proto-Panaetian Group (i.e. 'especially close to Onesimos'). He also commented that "the forerunners of these komasts are those on the neck of the volute-krater by Euphronios in Arezzo" (*ARV*² 316 top; cf. Beazley in C.B. ii 24). Although the dancer with splayed legs has connections with the bearded dancer on the back of the Arezzo krater, there are even closer ties between two new cups, one in Berlin (*Beazley Add*² 397, Leagros kalos), the other once in Fort Worth (*Beazley Add*² 394, Epidromos kalos) and the krater. The Berlin cup is clearly an early work of Onesimos, and the Fort Worth piece might be too. The Arezzo dancer itself derives from figures such as the satyr on Euphronios' Dionysiac calyx-krater (*ARV*² 14, 4; *Euphronios* no. 11); compare also the komasts on Smikros' psykter in the Louvre (*ARV*² 21, 6) – see further D. Williams in *Euphronios Peintre* 92; and the pelike Louvre Cp 10785, recently attributed to Smikros by M. Denoyelle and, independently, by Dietrich von Bothmer. See further on **54**. The London cup has been attributed to Onesimos himself as a very early work (Williams, *op. cit.* 17–18). Bloesch has attributed the potting to Euphronios.

On hares as love-gifts, both to serve as pets and to be let loose for the hounds to chase, see especially A. Schnapp in *Cité des Images* 77–82. Brijder's idea (*op. cit.* 161–2) of linking the scene with Philostratos' comment that runners were trained by competing with horses and hares is not completely convincing.

On Leagros *kalos* see *ARV*² 1591–4 and *Beazley Add*² 396. See also J.K. Davies, *Athenian Propertied Families 600–300 BC* (Oxford 1971) 90–2, no. 3027; M. Vickers, *Proceedings of the Cambridge Philological Society* 207 (1981) 97–136; R. Tölle-Kastenbein, *AA* (1983) 573–84; R.M. Cook, *JHS* 109 (1989) 167.

3

(pls. 4–5 and fig. 4c)

Cup: GR 1836.2–24.101 (*BM Cat Vases* E 45).
From Vulci; Durand collection.
Bought at the Durand sale, 1836.

Bibliography: *Cabinet Durand* (1836) 96–7, lot 293; Hartwig *M* 118–20, 684 no. 17 and pl. 13 (I, A-B); Murray *DGV* pl. 7 no. 28 (I) and p. 11 fig. 5; Hoppin i, 409 no. 25; *AV* 167 no. 24; Beazley *CF* 9 on pl. 3, 15; Bloesch *FAS* 78 no. 38 and pl. 21, 4; *ARV* 212 no. 13; F. Brommer, *Herakles* (Münster/Köln 1953) 89 no. C 10; D. von Bothmer, *Amazons in Greek Art* (Oxford 1957) 132 no. 8, 138 and pl. 69, 4 (A and B); *ARV*² 316 no. 8 and p. 1645; Brommer *V*³ 23 no. B 15; D. Williams, *JbBerlMus* 18 (1976) 22; D. Williams, *JHS* 97 (1977) 161; *LIMC* i *sv* Amazones no. 67 and pl. 449 (A); K. Hoffelner, *AM* 103 (1988) 117 fig. 41 (A); *Beazley Add*² 214; *LIMC* v *sv* Herakles, p. 72.

Dimensions: width 29.7; diam. 23.1; diam. of tondo 15.9; ht. 8.3; diam. of exterior ground line 10.2; diam. of foot plate 10.2.

Condition: made up from frr.; centre of side B broken and repaired in antiquity – remains of four pairs of rivet holes; two rim frr. and two flakes missing.

Description

INTERIOR: Two Amazons run to the left, side by side, keeping step.

The further Amazon, ʘEPO (retr.), is an archer and wears a long jacket and trousers decorated with zip pattern and, in dilute glaze, zigzags. The deep 'V' neckline has a 'z' pattern border, the lower hem of the jacket a continuous maeander. On her head is a high-domed hat with long side-flaps and a spiral decoration. In her right hand she holds an arrow, in her left a 'Scythian' bow, the red string of which is wrongly continued across the other Amazon's torso. At her waist is a quiver, the flap with cut-out waves hanging between her legs. Her mouth is open (dilute glaze for extension of lower lip). The nearer Amazon, H]I[Γ]OᒪVTE (retr.), is armed as a hoplite in corslet, greaves and a 'Chalcidian' helmet with cheek-guard raised, showing her hair over her ear and the leather lining (black). She also wears a short chiton with scalloped folds and decorated with dilute glaze crosses. She has a spear in her right hand, resting on her right shoulder in a 'shoulder arms' position, and a shield (device: winged dolphin – in silhouette with wing in outline). The missing flake has damaged her name and the right legs of both Amazons. Border: stopt maeanders (four-stroke, anticlockwise); odd man at 3 o'clock (extra single vertical line).

EXTERIOR: Herakles and the Amazons.

Side A (L): Herakles and Andromache. In the centre Herakles, HEPAKᒪEϟ (retr.), looms over a fallen Amazon hoplite, who sinks back, vainly trying to draw her sword from its scabbard, her left leg tucked under her – thigh seen from above (shield device: wheel with two pairs of wings attached as a whirligig). Herakles wears his lion-skin over his head and shoulders, tied at the neck, and a scabbard. He wields a club in his right hand and clutches at the *pteryges* of the Amazon's corslet. Herakles' right lower leg (apart from the tips of his toes) is lost (flake). The Amazon, like her comrades, wears a short chiton, cuirass, helmet (here of 'Attic' type) and greaves. On the right another Amazon hoplite advances, spear at the ready, her shield seen in profile (device: tripod); she wears an 'Attic' helmet. In front of her and behind, we read ANΔPOMA+E, written from left to right and balancing Herakles' name, so no doubt the name of the fallen Amazon, his opponent. On the left another Amazon hoplite runs to the left. She carries a spear in the 'shoulder arms' position and a shield (device: chariot box). Her chiton has scalloped folds and is decorated with dots; her helmet is of 'Attic' type. Her name, HIΓO (retr.), runs under the handle root. Part of her right hand and wrist lost (rim frr.).

Side B (U): Amazons. On the left, an Amazon hoplite, KAᒪI[.], runs to the left, but turns her head back to the right (shield device: flying bird). Her short chiton has wavy horizontal folds and is decorated with crosses. In the centre an Amazon archer runs to the left holding a horse by its red reins in her right hand and her 'Scythian' bow in her left (red bowstring). She wears a leather cap with rolled down peak and long flaps with wave-like cut-out edges and a striped shirt under a long jacket and trousers. The 'V' neck of the jacket and its lower hem are decorated with a 'z' pattern. She has a quiver with a spiral pattern at her hip. Horse's head missing (rim fr.). On the right, an Amazon hoplite, EVOΓE (retr.) runs to the left. She holds a spear in the 'shoulder arms' position and carries a shield (device: five lobed leaf). Her short chiton has wavy folds and is decorated with crosses.

Ground line: stopt maeander border (four-stroke, anticlockwise).

Relief line contours throughout; dilute glaze for minor interior markings; added red for inscriptions; thick reserved line inside lip, thin outside.

c. 510–500 BC.

Comment: Attributed to Euphronios by Hartwig, who was followed by E. Radford (*JHS* 35 [1915] 118) and Hoppin. Murray (*DGV* 11) was rather more hesitant. Beazley at first gave it to the Panaitios Painter, while he still kept that artist separate from Onesimos, but later to his Proto-Panaetian Group (section i, 'specially akin to early Onesimos ['Panaitios Painter']'). It goes very closely with a number of other pieces from Beazley's Proto-Panaetian Group and from his Eleusis Painter, and is in fact an early work of Onesimos himself (see further D. Williams, *JbBerlMus* 18 [1976] 18 and 22; and B. Sparkes in *Archaic into Classical* 20 and 24). The potting has been attributed by Bloesch to Euphronios.

On Herakles' fight with the Amazons see most recently J. Boardman in *Eye of Greece* 1–28; F. Brommer, *Getty Vases* 2 (1985) 183–9; J. Boardman in *LIMC* v, 71–2. For a list of Amazon names see *LIMC* i, 653. Since there was probably only room for one letter over the horse's head (for there are some touches of the relief line contours of its muzzle before the break), *KALI[.]* may be restored either as Kalie for Kallie (as on Louvre E 875: *ABV* 104 no 123; *LIMC* i, 589 no. 16) or Kalis, the latter appearing, along with Thero, as a name for a maenad on Oltos' contemporary, colossal cup in Tarquinia (*ARV*² 60 no. 66). The Amazon on side A who seems to flee from Herakles may in fact have been running to join the Amazons on the other side, as Bothmer suggests (*Amazons in Grek Art* 138).

For the costume of Amazon archers in general see M. F. Vos, *Scythian Archers in Archaic Attic Vase-Painting* (Groningen 1963) 40–51; and now R. Rolle, *The World of the Scythians* (London 1989) 57–61. On their leather or felt caps note J. D. Beazley, *The Lewes House Collection of Ancient Gems* (Oxford 1920) 82–3 and figs. 1–3 (of Beazley himself), as well as A. Bovon, *BCH* 87 (1963) 594–5. For the motif of Amazon reinforcements, paired as hoplite and archer, and the close relationship with an early cup by Douris in Baltimore (*ARV*² 442, 215), see D. Williams, *JHS* 97 (1977) 161–3.

Short chitons with scalloped or wavy folds are to be found among the works of many artists in the first half of the fifth century. They are probably the result of careful tucking of the chitons at the waist. For the shield device of a leaf see J.D. Beazley, *BSA* 46 (1951) 13–14; cf. also **53**.

4 (pl. 6 and fig. 4d)

Cup, type B or C: GR 1888.6–1.757, 1888.6–1.758 and 1905.1–26.1 (*BM Cat Vases* D 1)
Excavated at Naukratis, Egypt.

Bibliography: W.M. Flinders Petrie, *Naukratis I, 1884–5* (London 1886) 52–3; C. Smith, *Classical Review* 2 (1888) 233; Hartwig *M* 494–9 and 684 no. 41, with pl. 50; H. Lorimer, *JHS* 25 (1905) 122 with pl. 6, 4 (additional fr.); *AV* 200, 10; *ARV* 281, 18; H. Philippart, *Les Coupes Attiques à Fond Blanc* (Brussels 1936) 11–12, pl. 2 (I); Bloesch *FAS* 137 no. 2; *ARV*^{2} 429, 20; Wegner *Duris* 133; Brommer *V*^{3} 516 no. B 6 and 45 no. B 28; J. Mertens, *MetrMusJ* 9 (1974) 101 figs. 21–2 (I and A); J. Mertens, *Attic White-Ground* (New York 1977) 164 no. 27, 170–1, pl. 29, 2–3; D. von Bothmer in U. Höckmann and A. Krug [eds.], *Festschrift für Frank Brommer* [Mainz 1977] 54 no. 48; I. Wehgartner, *Attisch weissgrundige Keramik* (Mainz 1983) 56 no. 21, 81–2, pl. 16, 1–2; *LIMC* iv *sv* Europe I no. 37, pl. 35 (I); *Beazley Add*^{2} 236.

Dimensions: a) (Europa's head) gt. dim. 4.2; b) GR 1888.6–1.757 (Europa's body) gt. dim. 7.0; c) (bull's body) gt. dim. 6.0; d) (bull's legs) gt. dim. 5.0; e) GR 1905.1–26.1 (rim fr.) length at rim 4.3; f) GR 1888.6–1.758 (rim fr. with head) length at rim 2.9. Estimated diam. 26.0.

Condition: six frr., two rim and four wall frr.

Description: All decoration on a white ground; offset lip inside.
INTERIOR: Europa and the bull.
Of Europa only the face, neck, left shoulder, part of the right upper arm, part of the torso, right arm and the frontal knee, bent up in front, are preserved (frr. a–b). She wears a sakkos and a disc earring. Her hair is done with a dilute wash over black wavy relief lines, her nostril in dilute glaze. She also wears a chiton with tiny crosses on it (between the groups of folds in relief line there are long curving strokes in dilute glaze) and a dark cloak with folds rendered in added white and decorated with tiny white crosses and a border of added red. Of Zeus, as the bull, only parts of the shoulder and neck (many dilute glaze wrinkles on neck and on top of shoulder) and two legs bent up below the body are preserved (frr. c–d). The bull seems to have been kneeling for Europa either to mount or dismount: she was probably shown sitting side-saddle on the bull's back. Below is an exergue bordered above with an ovolo pattern.
Border: there is a black band before the black offset rim.
On the interior of fr. e, on the offset rim, there is a trace of a graffito, no doubt part of a dedication to a deity: ...]I A[.. ?

EXTERIOR: Herakles and the Tripod; fight.
Side A (U): Herakles and Apollo struggle for the Tripod. From the extreme left (fr. c) comes the sandalled right foot of a figure in long chiton (wavy dilute glaze lines; tiny black cross) moving to the right. Behind this figure, and under the handle, is the head of a dolphin. On the left of fr. e is the tip of a spear, suggesting that this first figure was Athena. Above the point of the spear is written HE[PAKLES] (retr.). Herakles' head is covered by a lion-skin, which is tied around his neck (dilute glaze strokes on skin and for claws). He wields his club up in his right hand, while one leg of the tripod crosses diagonally in front of his chest. Over his right shoulder passes the strap of his sword belt; the hilt of the sword in its scabbard are visible in front of his stomach. Fr. a preserves the end of the scabbard, his frontal left knee and, to the left, part of the lion's tail and, to the right, one of its paws. Fr. b gives his pointed frontal left foot. To the right of him was Apollo, whose sandalled feet and lower legs are preserved on fr. b, and part of his thigh on fr. a, together with the end of his name: [AΓOLL]ON (retr.). Fr. f preserves the back of a blond head with a touch of an ear, probably Apollo's. Beyond the legs of Apollo on fr. b are the right foot of a figure to the left that wears a long chiton with tiny crosses and a himation with a black border. This was probably Artemis.

Side B (L): fight. Fr. d preserves a section of the centre of the scene with parts of two warriors. On the left are the end of a scabbard (to left) and a curved object, seemingly the upper contour of a thigh of a figure to the right. On the right are the knee and parts of the thigh and calf of a figure to the left, with the point of a spear above and the tip of a sword above that again. The spear presumably belongs to a third figure.
Ground line: two black bands with a dilute glaze line between.

All contours done with relief line; dilute glaze for minor interior markings; inscriptions in black.

c. 500 BC.

Comment: Hartwig attributed the frr. to Euphronios; he was followed by Smith and Philippart. Beazley gave it to Douris as an early work (period 1). The attribution to Douris has been followed by Buitron-Oliver, but she places it in her Transitional I period (Buitron-Oliver *Douris* no. 33). This would be the only white-ground cup by Douris, although he decorated three white-ground lekythoi (see most recently D.C. Kurtz, *Getty Vases* 4 [1989] 118–25).

Details of style, however, suggest that this cup is really an early work of Onesimos. For example, the form of Europa's mouth and nostril are Onesimos' (cf. e.g. Polyxene on the Getty Iliupersis cup: D. Williams, *Getty Vases* 5 [1991] 51 fig. 8f); Herakles' lion-skin compares very closely with that on the exterior of **3** (E 45. Cf. also Boston, E.D.B. Vermeule frr.: *Beazley Add*^{2} 397, Leagros kalos); the curved folds within Europa's drapery match those on Hermes on **6** (E 44); Apollo's elaborate sandals might be compared to those worn by a figure on frr. in a Centre Island collection (*Para* 360 add as 93 *ter*); and, finally, the form of Herakles' frontal knee-cap and foot are Onesiman not Dourian.

Bloesch placed the frr. in his Eleusis Class (*FAS* 137–8, no. 2), a rather amorphous assembly of pieces with a long time-span (see also J. Mertens, *HSCP* 76 [1972] 275–6). It is perhaps best to class the London frr. with other cups that are lipped inside only: these can be of type B or C. The idea occurs in the works of the potters Euergides (Bloesch *FAS* 52 no. 11), Pamphaios (Bloesch *FAS* 64 no. 14 and 65 no. 23) and Chachrylion (Thasos frr.: J.-J. Maffre in *Euphronios Peintre* 61–4). None have been associated with the potter Euphronios, but it seems likely that the following were his: Tarquinia 696 (type B: *ARV*^{2} 352, 2, Colmar Painter; Ferrari *Tarquinia* no. 33), Louvre G 122 (type B: *ARV*^{2} 428, 10, Douris; Bloesch *FAS* 138), Baltimore, Johns Hopkins Univ. 1780 (type B: *ARV*^{2} 442, 215, Douris), Eleusis 618 frr. (type B or C: *ARV*^{2} 314, 3; Onesimos), Getty 86.AE.313 (type B or C: D. Williams *Getty Vases* 5 (1991) 42 fig. 1, Onesimos), Louvre G 290 (type B or C: *ARV*^{2} 401, 9, Foundry Painter; Bloesch *FAS* 137 no. 3). It also seems possible that Brygos continued the tradition, as he may have done with regular type C cups (cf. Williams, *op. cit.* 47–9): Leipzig T 582 frr. (*ARV*^{2} 370, 9), Princeton 1990–2 (type B or C: *Princeton Record* 50, 1 (1991) 57 lower, Brygos Painter), New York, private (type B or C: *Festschrift Bloesch* pl. 36, 3; now augmented by Bothmer and attributed to the Dokimasia Painter), **58** (E 73, type B or C: *ARV*^{2} 192, 106, Kleophrades Painter; Bloesch *FAS* 137 no. 4) and Oxford 1911.617 (*ARV*^{2} 314, 3, Pan Painter; Bloesch *FAS* 137 no. 5).

On Europa and the bull see M. Robertson in *LIMC* iv *sv* Europe I, 76–92 (no. 37). The way that the bull kneels is unique on Attic vases: it recurs in Roman representations (Robertson *loc. cit.* 90). For scenes of Herakles and the Tripod see most recently *LIMC* v, 133–42 (S. Woodford and J. Boardman). The composition follows the scheme set out by Bothmer (*Festschrift für Frank Brommer* 54 nos. 33–52). The scene on the other side of the exterior is too fragmentary to interpret.

The three frr. excavated in the first season (a, c and d) appear never to have been registered; fr. b, found in the second season was registered in 1888. Fr. f, also seemingly found in the second season, was not illustrated by Hartwig but was included by Smith and Philippart. It was separated as alien in July 1956 because the colour and curvature were judged not to correspond. It is included here since neither of these reasons seem correct or sufficient. Fr. e was bought on the site of Naukratis by Dr. F.W. von Bissing and presented to the Antikensammlungen in Munich. It was acquired for the British Museum in 1905 in exchange for pottery from Enkomi. Unfortunately, no information is preserved concerning the precise find-spots of any of the frr.

5 (pls. 7–8 and fig. 4e)

Cup: GR 1894.3–14.1 (*BM Cat Vases* E 47)
From Orvieto.
Bought of Dr. P. Hartwig, 1894.

Bibliography: P. Hartwig, *AM* 1894, 155 (note of talk); *VA* 86 no. 4; Hoppin i, 425 no. 53; *AV* 168 no. 40; *ARV* 213 no. 2; F. Vian, *Repertoire des Gigantomachies figurées dans l'art grec et romain* (Paris 1951) 72–3 no. 333; *ARV*^{2} 319 no. 3 and p. 1645; Brommer *V*^{3} 65 no. B 13; B.A. Sparkes in *Archaic into Classical* 27 with pl. 27; Schefold *GkhK* 92–3; *LIMC* iv *sv* Euryalos I no. 2, pl. 48 (detail of A), *sv* Gigantes no. 301, *sv* Hephaistos no. 206; *Beazley Add*^{2} 214.

Dimensions: diam. *c.* 32.0; diam. of tondo *c.* 23.0; diam. of exterior ground line *c.* 13.0.

Condition: Made up from frr., with one floating fr. that can be positioned with some confidence; remains of four pairs of ancient repair holes; right handle, right half of tondo and foot missing.

Description

INTERIOR: A god killing a giant.
On the left is the right leg of the god (the foot would have overlapped the border) and on the right edge of the fr. is the rear contour of his advancing lower left leg and heel. The ends of his chlamys with a two-line border are preserved, as well as part of the fingers of his right hand and the butt of his spear or the like. On the ground, below and to the left, are the greaved right leg of the giant and a trace of his knee bent up under him, the top of his thigh seen frontally. He has a red greave-pad with red ties at the back. Preliminary sketch indicates earlier thoughts of a higher, more extended position for the giant's right leg (see fig. 1a).
Inscriptions: AΘENOΔ[OTOϟ]; and on a strip below the ground line KA[ΛOϟ]
Border: running maeander in twos (anticlockwise, five- to six-stroke core).

EXTERIOR: gigantomachy.
Side A (U): Only the extreme right hand side is preserved: a giant in full hoplite armour (shield, helmet, cuirass and greaves) and wearing a chlamys (border: two widely spaced lines) strides past a fallen fellow who collapses under the handle. The standing giant is named Φ[O]ΦVRIO[ϟ], and we may, therefore, presume that further to the left was his opponent, Zeus. The giant's right arm was raised beside his head and must have held a spear. The fallen giant, who is naked and bearded, struggles to draw his sword; his Attic helmet has a swan's head crest-holder, his shield the device of a flying eagle, and his scabbard a double red strap.

Side B (L): On the extreme left Hephaistos (HEΦAIϟTOϟ) lunges down at a fallen giant named Euryalos ([E]VRVA[ΛOϟ]) with a red lump of red-hot metal held in a pair of tongs in his left hand; his other hand is back, holding another pair of tongs (most of his torso is missing; red sparks above left thigh show that he held another red-hot lump). He wears helmet, cuirass, short chiton and greaves. The fallen giant already has a red patch on either thigh, probably burns from Hephaistos' weapons. He wears the skin of a feline (*pardalis*) over his shoulders and his hair is looped up in a *krobylos* at the back of his head and held in place by a double red tie, the triple ends of which fall down his back. He topples backwards, his bearded chin and his nose obscured by the back of his shoulder. Above his raised left arm are remains of a preliminary sketch (a rough circle, drawn twice: see fig. 1b),

probably for a rock tumbling from his grasp. In the centre, another giant in a similar animal skin retreats to the left before an advancing god. He has a particularly wild hair-do (upward combed fringe) and has an arrow stuck in his shoulder through the animal skin. Above his right knee is what seems to be the head of another arrow, pointing downwards. All that remains of the god is his shield (device: ithyphallic donkey) and his name, ARES (retr.).
Ground line: two closely set reserved lines.

Relief line contour throughout (except hair); dilute glaze for minor interior markings; added red for inscriptions; thick reserved line inside lip, thin outside.

c. 500 BC.

Comment: Attributed by Hartwig to Euphronios (letters in the archive of the Greek and Roman Department, British Museum, indicate that he wanted to publish the cup in the *JHS* but his article was refused by the editor, and that Furtwängler disagreed with the attribution). He was followed by Smith. Beazley placed it among the early (Panaetian) works of Onesimos.

This is a particularly large and finely potted cup and it may well have been the work of the potter Euphronios, although, without the stem and foot, any attribution can only be rather tentative.

On giants in general see most recently F. Vian (with M.B. Moore) in *LIMC* iv, 191–270. The god on the interior is normally identified as Hermes (Smith, Vian and Sparkes), but he does not wear the winged boots of that god and he does not seem to have been carrying his *kerykeion*. It might be better to identify him as Poseidon on the analogy of the name vase of the Painter of the Paris Gigantomachy (*ARV*[2] 417, 1), where the god's foot also breaks the border, and imagine him wielding a trident against Polybotes or Ephialtes.

The scene on side A may have shown either Zeus on foot attacking Porphyrion with his thunderbolt and Athena further to the left finishing off another giant in the company of Herakles, or Zeus in his chariot accompanied by Herakles and Athena. The pairs on side B of Hephaistos with Euryalos and Ares with his opponent must have been completed by a third pair, perhaps Dionysos or Hermes with a giant.

The theme of the gigantomachy occurs on four Late Archaic cups: a fr. of an elaborate zone cup by Onesimos from Odos Marathonos in Athens (J.-J. Maffre, *RA* 1972, 223 fig. 1 and 225 fig. 2; attribution – D. Williams, *JbBerlMus* 18 [1976] 12), the cup in Berlin by the Brygos Painter (*ARV*[2] 370 no. 10), the name piece of the Painter of the Paris Gigantomachy in the Cabinet des Médailles (*ARV*[2] 417 no. 1) and a fragmentary piece by Makron from the Athenian Acropolis (*ARV*[2] 461 no. 23). There does seem to be some connection between Onesimos' piece and the two Brygan cups: the missing part of the London cup, the earliest of the group, would, no doubt, have done much to clarify the precise relationship. If its tondo did show Poseidon, then it may have served as a prototype for the Paris tondo, just as Onesimos' very early white-ground tondo from Eleusis with Athena and a giant may well have been an indirect model for Makron's tondo.

As Brian Sparkes has noted (*op. cit.* 27), Onesimos seems to have drawn a clear contrast between giants as hoplites on one side and as savages on the other. The only other artist to have depicted giants as savages dressed in skins at this period is Euthymides, on his fragmentary coral-red cup from the Acropolis (*ARV*[2] 29 no. 20): the Kleophrades Painter's and the Tyszkiewicz Painter's stamnoi (*ARV*[2] 187 no. 55 and *ARV*[2] 292 no. 29) are later. The combed-up hair style of one of the giants is, in fact to be found on monsters (e.g. Sinis – **18** [E 48]), heroes (e.g. **43** [E 69]) and men (e.g. athlete – *ARV*[2] 407, 11).

On Athenodotos *kalos* see *ARV*[2] 1567–8 and *Beazley Add*[2] 393. He is praised on cups from the Proto-Panaetian Group, by Onesimos, by the Colmar Painter (see on **13** [GR 1897.10–28.1]), by Peithinos and by Douris. His name is coupled on two pieces with Leagros.

6 (pls. 9–10 and fig. 4f)

Cup: GR 1836.2–24.25 (*BM Cat Vases* E 44).
From Vulci; Durand collection.
Bought at the Durand sale, 1836.

Bibliography: *Cabinet Durand* 22–4, lot 61; De Witte *Fabricants* 42 xxvi no. 4; W. Klein, *Euphronios* (Vienna 1886) 86–104; Klein *M*[2] 139 no. 4; Hartwig 444–9, 684 no. 3; Murray *DGV* no. 27 (I), p. 10 fig. 4 (A); FR i 110–13, pl. 23; *VA* 85 no. 2; Hoppin i 389; *AV* 168 no. 39; *ARV* 214, 11; Bloesch *FAS* 70 no. 4, pl. 20, 2 (drawing of the foot); *ARV*[2] 318, 2; K. Schefold, *AM* 77 (1962) 133–5 and Beil. 36 (A–B); *Para* 358; Brommer *V*[3] 53 no. B 2; Boardman *ARFV* fig. 222 (I); E. Simon, *Die Griechischen Vasen* (Munich 1976) pl. 134 with p. 108; S. Waetzoldt et al. (eds.), *Bilder von Menschen in der Kunst des Abendlandes* (Berlin 1980) 58 no. 11 (I); E. Keuls, *MNIR* 44–5 (1983) pl. 6, 15 (I); Seki *U* pl. 47, 3 (underneath); Williams *Greek Vases* fig. 48 (I); B. Sparkes in *Archaic to Classical* (1985) pl. 21 (B); Keuls *Phallus* 189 fig. 172; Peschel *Hetäre* 195 and fig. 132; D. Harvey in *Copenhagen Colloquium* 249 and 251 fig. 6; Maas and McIntosh Snyder 118 and 134 fig. 12 (I); *Beazley Add*[2] 214; B. Cohen, *MetrMusJ* 26 (1991) 66 and figs. 28–30 (A and signature).

Dimensions: width 42.3; diam. 33.6; diam. of tondo 20.0; ht. 12.6; diam. of exterior ground line 14.1; diam. of foot plate 13.8.

Condition: fr. of rim over left handle broken and repaired in antiquity (eight pairs of rivet holes); two rim frr. missing; some flakes lost from tondo; interior slightly burnt.

Description

INTERIOR: hetaira and man.
On the left stands a hetaira, fully frontal but for her head, which is turned down to the right. Her hands are busy tying the *zone* around her waist, the *kolpos* of her transparent chiton held up over her forearms (dilute glaze folds above waist). She also wears a sakkos (decorated with waves and dots in dilute glaze) and a disc earring. On a stool on the right is seated a bearded man with receding hair-line; three dilute glaze creases on his brow. He stretches out his left hand towards the hetaira's groin, as his right

hand grips a knotty stick; his legs seem to surround her. Over his legs is draped a cloak (two line warp border; one line weft border); he wears shoes and there is a red wreath in his hair. Between the heads of the two figures hangs a basket with red ties above, a cover and a foot, and in the lower left hand corner of the tondo is a *barbiton* lyre (relief line for the seven strings). There is a small reserved exergue into which protrudes the man's frontal left foot.

INSCRIPTION: ΓΑΝΑΙΤΟϟ ΚΑΛΟϟ
Border: running maeander (anticlockwise, six-stroke core); odd man at nine o'clock.

EXTERIOR:
Side A (U): Herakles and the boar. In the centre Eurystheus has taken refuge in a pithos, most of which is buried below ground and on the rim of which is written his name, ΕVΡVϟΘΕVϟ. He has his arms raised in defence, as Herakles approaches from the left with the Erymanthian boar on his shoulders. Herakles wears his lion-skin (outer side has dilute glaze wash) and has a sword in a scabbard at his waist. The boar is held upside-down so that its rear is towards Eurystheus while its fierce head faces a tree with red leaves. Next to it hangs Herakles' bow and quiver (scale pattern) held by long red ties. To the right of Eurystheus is another tree with red leaves from beyond which comes a woman dressed in chiton (dilute glaze folds above waist) and cloak (line border), her arms outstretched to beg, it would seem, for mercy to be shown to Eurystheus. Her hair is tied up with a double red band and she wears a disc earring. Behind her is an elderly man in long chiton (dilute glaze folds above waist), himation with two line border and shoes, who leans on a knotty stick and holds the top of his head with his right hand. His hair is given a thinning look by using dilute glaze and his hair line is receding. In addition, there are three furrows on his brow done with dilute glaze.

INSCRIPTION: ΚΑΛΕ

Side B (L): Hermes and the chariot of Odysseus (?).
A four-horse chariot is driven by a long-haired, youthful charioteer, dressed only in a cloak with a line border that hangs over his shoulders and is looped down his back, although there is a sword in a scabbard at his hip. The chariot is carefully represented, but the felloe is hand-drawn, rather than compass-drawn. The linchpin is visible as it passes through the rectangular end of the axle. The reins are red beyond the yoke. The horses have elaborate chest-bands (linked trefoils and zs). Their teeth are bared and their tails slightly raised (dilute glaze waves in manes). On the far side of the chariot a bearded warrior moves rapidly forward. He is dressed in short chiton, corslet, greaves and helmet (the tip of his helmet crest crosses his back) and carries a shield of Boeotian type and a spear. There is a scabbard hung at his hip. On the far right stands Hermes, dressed in short chiton (dilute glaze folds above waist), chlamys (black border) fastened at the neck with a brooch decorated with a cross, winged boots and petasos (red ties). His hair is tied up with a double red band. His left hand rests lightly on his left hip, just above the falcon's head pommel of his machaira; his right hand holds his *kerykeion*, which points down at the ground in front of the horses.

INSCRIPTIONS: [Κ]ΑΛΟϟ; [Κ]ΑΛΟϟ
Border: stopt maeanders (anticlockwise, four-stroke).
Graffito under foot: see fig. 3h
Incised signature on the handle: ΕVΦΡΟΝΙΟϟ ΕΓΟΙΕϟΕΝ (see fig. 3e)

Relief line contour throughout (except hair); dilute glaze for minor interior markings; added red for inscriptions; wide reserved band inside lip, narrow outside.

500–490 BC.

Comment: Attributed by Klein, Hartwig and others to Euphronios (see *BM Cat Vases* 68); by Furtwängler to his Panaitios Painter (F.R. i 110; cf. ii 177–8); and finally by Beazley to Onesimos as an early ('Panaetian') work. Signed by Euphronios as potter on one handle. On incised signatures see B. Cohen *op. cit.* 49–95.

For the action of the tondo see Williams *Greek Vases* 43: Keuls (*Phallus* 189–90), and Maas and McIntosh Snyder have misunderstood it (cf. Harvey *op. cit.* 249). The chiton has been hitched up over the forearms in order to allow the *zone* to be tied up: on other representations the chiton is held up in the teeth (e.g. London E 719: *ARV*² 1560, Alexomenos kalos). For the *barbiton* see most recently Maas and McIntosh Snyder 113–138. For hetairai see Peschel *Hetäre*.

For representations of Herakles and the boar see Brommer *V*³ 47–54; Schefold *GuH* 96–100; W. Felten in *LIMC* v, 43–8. This is the only preserved occurrence of the theme on Late Archaic cups. The woman and man behind Eurystheus are presumably his parents, Kalliphobe and Sthenelos. These two are named on a cup by Oltos (Louvre G 17: *ARV*² 62, 83), a piece which also has a very similar chariot scene on the other side (cf. C. Robert, *Die griechische Heldensage* [Zurich 1921] 1188) where the warrior is identified as Odysseus. The representation of Odysseus as a hoplite and the presence of his chariot suggests that the scene should be set in the Trojan War. Hermes, as the messenger of the gods, is perhaps stopping Odysseus from joining the fray at a moment when he might have upset their plans – certainly the downward pointing *kerykeion*, the bared teeth and raised tails of the horses and the raised right hand of the warrior all suggest that Hermes wishes to bring the chariot to a halt. Schefold (*op. cit.* 133–4), however, suggests that the scene should be linked with the other side of the cup and posits that the charioteer is Iolaos and the warrior Likymnios, Alkmene's stepbrother.

For the *kalos* name Panaitios see *ARV*² 1604–5 and *Beazley Add*² 398. The graffito under the foot is listed by Johnston as type 20 B no. 3 (*Trademarks* 105 and 198). The other members of the list seem unrelated and Johnston remains uncommitted as to whether it is a trader's mark or an Etruscan owner's mark.

Nos. 7–9 Proto-Panaetian Group

Beazley collected together a number of pieces that he referred to as the Proto-Panaetian Group (*ARV*^{2} 314–18; Beazley in C.B. ii 21–5 [nos. 71–3]; Immerwahr *Attic Script* 83–4; Robertson *Art of Vase-painting* 45–6) – they belong to the last years of the sixth century BC. Beazley isolated one artist, whom he dubbed the Eleusis Painter, and assembled some sixteen or more pieces in his Proto-Panaetian Group, which he subdivided into two, those in the first section being 'specially akin to early Onesimos', those in the second being 'less near him'.

Some of the pieces in all three of Beazley's sections seem, in fact, to be works of Onesimos himself (see above, and D. Williams, *JbBerlMus* 18 [1976] 16–23 and *Getty Vases* 5 [1991] 41–4), but others are not. One further individual can be recognised (see on **7** [E 816]), whose *oeuvre* incorporates members of both Beazley's Eleusis Painter and the Proto-Panaetian Group, but there remain other unplaced pieces.

Some other artists isolated by Beazley, but placed elsewhere in his lists, in fact belong in the general sphere of the Proto-Panaetian Group and, for convenience, have been included here. These are the Ashby Painter and the Carpenter Painter.

7 (pl. 11 and fig. 5a)

Cup: GR 1865.11–18.46 (*BM Cat Vases* E 816)
From Vulci, Cucumella area C ('fam. Fepia') March 1829; Canino, Pourtalès and Witt collections.
Presented by George Witt, 1865.

Bibliography: *Mus. Étrusque* no. 1510; L.J.J. Dubois, *Galerie Pourtalès* (sale, Paris 1865) no. 393; Hartwig *M* 109–11, 684 no. 14; Hoppin i 409 no. 26; *AV* 166 no. 4; *ARV* 21 no. 1; *ARV*^{2} 315 no. 2; Boardman *ARFV Archaic* fig. 219 (Beazley's drawing); Keuls *Phallus* 178 fig. 158; Peschel *Hetäre* fig. 88; *Beazley Add*^{2} 213.

Dimensions: width 30.0, diam. 22.7, diam. of tondo 15.6.

Condition: made up from frr.; foot missing (keyed for alien foot, now removed); two rim frr., one major wall fr. and other chips missing.

Description

INTERIOR: love-making.
A naked woman lies face down on a bench or couch, her left arm curled round her head as it rests on a folded cushion (black stripes and dilute glaze lines). Her hair is tied up behind in a *krobylos* with a red band. A man kneels between her legs behind her. She grips his erect penis with her right hand. The fingers of his right hand are spread; his left hand is on the far side of her torso. His beard is characterised by the use of dilute glaze as thin or greying; there are two dilute glaze creases on his brow and a dilute glaze line marking the edge of his cheek bone. He has a red garland on his head. Above on the right is a food-basket (red ties above).

INSCRIPTION: ᒪΕΑΛΡΟϟ ΚΑᒪΟϟ
Border: continuous maeander (anticlockwise, four-stroke core).

Hair contours incised around added relief dots; all other contours done with relief line; dilute glaze for minor interior markings; added red for inscriptions.

510–500 BC.

Comment: Hartwig, followed by Hoppin, attributed this cup to Euphronios. Beazley placed it, along with a fr. in Herbert Cahn's collection in Basel (101: *ARV*^{2} 315 no. 2), near his Eleusis Painter. The London piece, however, is superior to the Cahn fr. and clearly by a different hand. Indeed, to the same painter as the London cup may be attributed the following pieces:

a. Athens, Kerameikos fr.: *Para* 358 (P-P Grp.).
b. Manila, Zobel de Ayala fr.: *ARV*^{2} 315 no. 5 (Eleusis Ptr.).
c. Basel, Cahn 423 fr. (ex Langlotz): *ARV*^{2} 315 no. 7 (Eleusis Ptr.).
d. Boston 10.196: *ARV*^{2} 315 no. 6 (Eleusis Ptr.).
e. Munich 8703 frr.: *ARV*^{2} 1582 no. 1 (Hektor kalos).
f. Würzburg H 5344 frr.: *CVA* 2, pl. 37, 1–2.

This artist, who belongs to the general sphere of the Proto-Panaetian Group, might be dubbed the Painter of London E 816 after the London love-making cup.

For possible interpretations of some scenes of *symplegma* see most recently Keuls *Phallus* 153–86. For Leagros *kalos* see on **2** (E 46).

8 (pls. 12–13 and fig. 5b)

Cup: GR 1867.5–8.1061 (*BM Cat Vases* E 64)
From Vulci; Raoul-Rochette, (Basseggio) and Blacas collections.
Bought from the estate of the Duc de Blacas, 1866.

Bibliography: E. Braun, *AdI* 1839, 251–5; *Collection D. Raoul-Rochette* (sale, Paris 30 April – 1 May 1855) 12 no. 47; anonymous sale (?Basseggio), Paris, 30 April, 1, 3 and 4 May 1857, lot 316; Murray *DGV* no. 42; Hartwig *M* 330 and 688 no. 27; Hoppin i, 131 no. 59; Tonks *Brygos* 109 no. 23; *AV* 54, lower no. 2; *ARV* 299 no. 7; *ARV*^{2} 455 no. 9 and p. 1654; S. Kaempf-Dimitriadou, *Die Liebe der Götter in der attischen Kunst des 5. Jahrhunderts v. Chr.* (11th Beiheft *AntK*, Bern 1979) 32–3 (no. 314), pl. 24, 2–4; Schefold *GkhK* 205–7; *Beazley Add*^{2} 243; Korshak *Frontal Faces* fig. 65 (A).

Dimensions: width 37.0; diam. 29.6; diam. of tondo 23.8; ht. 11.5; diam. of exterior ground line 14.1; diam. of foot 11.2.

Condition: made up from frr. Interior surface much rubbed.

Description

INTERIOR: Apollo and a woman (? Daphne or Kreusa).
On the left Apollo, who wears a chlamys with a black border, covering his left shoulder and right upper arm, and has a 'Cretan' bow and quiver on his right shoulder, moves rapidly to the right in attempt to catch a woman. She flees to the right, but turns her head back to the left. Both her feet are off the ground. She wears

a chiton and a himation (two- and one-line borders) and with her left hand raises part of the himation above her left shoulder. The fingers of Apollo's left hand clutch her himation, just below her raised hand. The positions of their right hands cannot be determined for certain, but he may well have been gripping her wrist. His hair is tied up behind his head in a *krobylos*, hers hangs down free but she does wear a reserved stephane. He has a red wreath in his hair. There is a reserved ground-line with a black exergue below.

INSCRIPTION: HOΠΑΙΣΚΑΛΟΣ (in large thick letters)
Border: running maeander (clockwise, six-stroke core) surmounted by a frieze of addorsed palmettes with long pointed central fronds and lyre-form surrounding tendrils that extends to the rim (see fig. 3a).

EXTERIOR: symposium.
Side A (U): three symposiasts.
On the left a bearded symposiast reclines to the left (all are bearded and recline to the left), but looks back right. He holds a *barbiton* lyre in his left hand and a red *plektron* (red cord attached to lyre) in his right; his mouth is open. He has a red wreath in his hair and wears a himation around his waist and over his legs. His chest is fully frontal and he leans against a cushion decorated with a band framed by lines and with zip patterns. On the left of him hangs a spotted flute-case. In the centre the head and chest of the symposiast are fully frontal and he has a himation with a black border draped around his waist and legs. He plays a pair of pipes and there is a dilute glaze line on either side of his nose, marking the inflated cheeks: he is actually blowing. On the right, the symposiast has thrown back his head, his mouth open and right hand to his forehead. He holds a cup in his left hand and wears a himation with a black border around his waist and legs and a red wreath in his hair. His left arm rests on a cushion with stripes, lines and a comb pattern.

INSCRIPTION: HOΠΑΙΣΚΑΛΟΣ

Side B (L): three symposiasts and a serving-boy.
On the left stands a naked boy, a red apicate fillet in his hair, holding an oinochoe in his lowered right hand. His left arm is outstretched: perhaps he has just returned the cup freshly filled to the symposiast in front of him. This symposiast holds out the cup in his right hand: the cup is level, suggesting that it is full. He has a long thick red fillet around his head, a himation with a line border and he leans against the bent right leg of his companion behind him. His mouth is slightly open, as if talking to the boy, perhaps thanking him. In the centre the symposiast looks back to the right. He wears a himation with a line border round his waist and over his legs, a red wreath in his hair. He holds a black cup with a reserved stripe in his left hand: as it is tipped, it must be empty. Between the heads of the first two symposiasts a food-basket with red tassles hangs from red ties. On the right, the third symposiast, a long red fillet tied round his head and a red wreath in his hair, holds out a skyphos in his right hand. He leans against a cushion with comb pattern and T-maeanders.

INSCRIPTION: HOΠΑΙΣΚΑΛΟΣ
Predella: a frieze of silhouette vessels (three cups, a skyphos, a skyphos with offset lip, a skyphos with a phallos spout, two jugs on their sides, two pairs of boots and a footstool), with a line above and below.

Relief line contours throughout (except for hair); dilute glaze for minor interior markings; added red for inscriptions; wide reserved band inside lip, narrow line outside.

c. 500 BC.

Comment: Hartwig gave the vase to Brygos; he was followed by Hoppin. Beazley attributed it to his Ashby Painter. Beazley's Ashby Painter seems to have two definite phases – the early pieces (*ARV*² 454–5 nos. 1–6 and 12) in a spare, almost early Oltan style, and the mature works in a powerful 'Panaetian' manner (*ARV*² 455 nos. 7–11) – the early vases were only added by Beazley to his list in *ARV*². The name vase itself, the Castle Ashby cup, now New York 1993.11.5, is properly Proto-Panaetian and thus something of a transitional piece. To the artist's mature phase should be added a cup once on the Philadelphia market (photographs in the Beazley Archive). The black glaze is badly flaked, but the splendid drawing is clear. It has two young warriors in the tondo and a very musical symposium outside with several impassioned listeners. There is also below the scene a frieze of vessels that includes a basket, a stick, and boots. Robertson (*Art of Vase-painting* 52) calls the Ashby Painter a pupil of Euthymides, but without explanation.

The shape of the London cup was not commented on by Bloesch, but the richly profiled edge of the foot and the prominent stand-ring recall the Berlin Peithinos cup (*ARV*² 115, lower no. 2; Bloesch *FAS* 54). The New York vase has a similarly profiled edge to the foot, but lacks the stand-ring (*CVA Castle Ashby* drawing no. 58).

The tondo of the London cup is particularly large, recalling two of Onesimos' very early cups (Berlin F 2280–2281 and Vatican frr. [*ARV*² 19 nos. 1–2] and Basel, Cahn 106 [*ARV*² 316 no. 3]; for both see D. Williams, *JbBerlMus* 18 [1976] 11, 13–14 and 19) that have palmette borders. A similar palmette border is found on the interior of the fragmentary phiale from Pyrgi, also by Onesimos (see M.P. Baglione in *Copenhagen Colloquium* 18 fig. 1, there attributed to the Brygos Painter). These and other large tondi may well have been prompted by the decoration of such elaborate phialai (for others of the same type see the phiale by Douris, M. Robertson, *Getty Vases* 5 [1991] 75–98).

The tondo is the earliest occurrence of a god involved in an erotic pursuit scene. Unfortunately, there are no clear iconographic indications as to Apollo's prospective victim. Braun called her Boline (personification of a town in Achaia), but Smith was more cautious, preferring to label her simply a nymph. More recently, Schefold has argued for Daphne (*GkhK* 205–7) and he has been followed by Robertson (*Art of Vase-painting* 52). Nevertheless, the date and the very lack of attributes might be thought to exclude Daphne, as well as Marpessa and Kyrene. An alternative would be Kreusa, the future mother of Ion, a very Athenian figure whose story might well have suddenly become popular at the time of the Ionian Revolt. On divine pursuit scenes see further Kaempf-Dimitriadou *op. cit.*; on Apolline pursuits, O.Palagia and G. Kokorou-Aleuras in *LIMC* ii (*sv* Apollon) 313 (this vase no. 1085) and 321; on erotic pursuits in general, C. Sourvinou-Inwood, *'Reading' Greek Culture* (Oxford 1991) 29–98.

For friezes of vessels see Hartwig *M* 329–31; *CVA Berlin* 2, 21; *Agora xii* 15, note 28; J. Boardman in A. Cambitoglou (ed.), *Studies in Honour of Arthur Dale Trendall* (Sydney 1979) 35; C. Weiss, *CVA Karlsruhe* 3, 71–2. Most occur on cups, but there are some exceptions. Examples include (cups unless otherwise indicated): *ARV*[2] 132 middle (kantharos); 188 no.6 (psykter); 1647, add as 344 no. 55 *bis*; 344 no. 56 with New York 1976.20.3, (added by Bothmer); 355 no. 39; 364 no. 52; 372 no. 30; 421 no. 78 (**56** [E 70]); 421 no. 80 (now attributed by Guy to the Triptolemos Painter); 801 no. 22; 831 no. 13 *bis*; 834 no. 1; 871 no. 9; 1612 (Florence PD 315 and Göttingen fr.); 1612 (once Hamilton Grey). Also Cambridge 37.19 (*CVA* pl. 7, 2); Berlin 2299 (*CVA* pl. 95); Karlsruhe 69/35 (*CVA* 3, pl. 120, 2); Centre Island, private, frr. (with letters, as *ARV*[2] 1612); Basel, Cahn 620 fr. (Painter of the Paris Gigantomachy); Lugano market (Painter of the Paris Gigantomachy); Chamay frr. (Painter of the Paris Gigantomachy); Basel BS 1417 (Hermonax); Zurich Arch. Inst. (Hermonax: *AntK* 27 [1984] pl. 23); Philadelphia market (Ashby Painter: see above); Princeton Univ. y1989–69 (psykter; Kleophrades Painter: *Princeton Record* 49, 1 [1990] 46); Cerveteri frr. (F. Gilotta, *Prospettiva* 46 [1986] 42–5, solid dais with silhouette vessels on one side only). This scheme seems to have first been thought of in the last decade of the sixth century; it continues until almost the middle of the fifth. In addition to vessels, there are also boots, shoes, flute-cases, sticks, baskets and footstools. On the Princeton psykter there is a silhouette dog and on the Aberdeen cup (*ARV*[2] 871 no. 9) a particularly pleasing conceit, a silhouette Ethiopian. Most of the vessels are of normal type, except for the phallos-skyphos, which also appears as a silhouette on *ARV*[2] 427 no. 2 and 364 no. 52. A vessel of this shape is seen in use on *ARV*[2] 450 no. 22 (see further J. Boardman, *AA* 1976, 289). The Princeton psykter has a phallos-rhyton.

The frontal headed piper is known in both his human and satyr forms (see Korshak *op. cit.* figs. 59–66). The Ashby Painter's cup is the only one to have a bearded human figure. The *plektron*, with its spoon-like depression, is drawn with particular clarity. On these see most recently F. Jurgeit in *Dohrn Festschrift* 53–62.

The figure with his head thrown back in passionate song recalls Ekphantides on Euphronios' calyx-krater in Munich (see most recently, *Euphronios* no. 5) and is repeated many times thereafter. The type is discussed by F. Hauser in FR ii, 230, by P. Jacobstahl, *Göttinger Vasen* (Berlin 1912) 59–60 and by J.D. Beazley in *Studies Robinson* ii 75. Some examples are also mentioned in Lissarrague *Flot d'Images* 124–6.

9 (pl. 14 and fig. 5c)

Cup: gr 1836.2–24.231 (*BM Cat Vases* E 23)
From Vulci (or Chiusi); Durand collection.
Bought at the Durand sale, 1836.

Bibliography: J. de Witte, *BdI* 1832, 117 no. 9; *Cabinet Durand* 279 lot 875; H. Blümner, *Technologie und Terminologie der Gewerbe und Knste* (2nd edn, Leipzig 1912) ii, 339 fig. 53; *VA* 22; *ARV* 90, middle 1; Bloesch *FAS* 60 no. 5; Baker *Furniture* 283 fig. 446; *ARV*[2] 179, 1; N.I. Sokolskij, *Derevoobrabatyvajuschee remeslo v antichnyh-gosudarstvah Severnogo Pricernomorja* (Moscow 1971) pp. 176 and 178, fig. 49 (I); Boardman *ARFV Archaic* fig. 124; G.F. Pinney, *AJA* 85 (1981) 146 with pl. 29 fig. 1; D. von Bothmer, *GettyMusJ* 14 (1986) 12 fig. 7 (I); *Beazley Add*[2] 185.

Dimensions: width 26.2; diam. 20.5; diam. of tondo 10.5; ht. 7.6; diam. of foot 8.6.

Condition: Made up from frr.; six pairs of ancient repair holes.

Description

INTERIOR: carpenter at work.
A youth wearing a chlamys with a two-line border tied around his waist and a red wreath in his hair holds a long-handled adze (*skeparnon*) in his right hand as he steadies a beam with his left hand. The cord lashing the head of the tool onto the shaft is carefully marked with relief line.
Border: single reserved line.
Incised hair contour; relief line for all other contours; dilute glaze for minor interior markings.

c. 510–500 BC.

Comment: Attributed by Smith to Epiktetos; Beazley, however, made it the name-piece of his Carpenter Painter. This artist has received two recent studies, G. Ferrari-Pinney, *AJA* 85 (1981) 146–51 and D. von Bothmer, *GettyMusJ* 14 (1986) 5–20. He belongs in the general area of the Proto-Panaetian Group. Some additions and refinements to Ferrari-Pinney's and Bothmer's discussions are possible. A revised list of the artist's works is given below.

(Cups)
a. London E 23: see above (**9**)
b. Boston 00.336: *ARV*[2] 180, middle.
c. Orvieto, Faina 2542 (101): *ARV*[2] 179 no. 2
d. Louvre G 11: *ARV*[2] 180, top.
e. Basel, Cahn frr.: *Para* 507, add as 1592 Leagros kalos no. 20 *bis*.
f. Getty 85.AE.25: *GettyMusJ* 14 (1986) 6–7.
g. Munich 2636: *ARV*[2] 317 no. 16 (Proto-Panaetian Group).
h. Basel BS 489: *ARV*[2] 454 no. 1 (H.P. Painter).
i. Athens 1666: *ARV*[2] 1567 Athenodotos kalos no. 13; (later).
j. Basel, Cahn 451 fr.: (later).
k. Velia: *RM* 86 (1979) pl. 38; (later).
l. Brunswick 527 and Florence 7 B 6–7 frr.: *ARV*[2] 1567 Athenodotos kalos no. 1; (late).
(Hydriae)
m. Vatican 16548: *ARV*[2] 179, lower no. 3.
n. Rouen 24: *ARV*[2] 179, bottom; (later).

The object on which the carpenter is working consists of a thick beam of indeterminable length with a square projection below that is cut to take a tenon joint. One may reconstruct, therefore, a second beam at right angles to the run of the first beam and set at a lower level. This might indicate that the piece of furniture under production was a couch, if it had some horizontal tie-beams or slatting as well as criss-cross interlacing under the mattress. Although this seems a sensible system on a large solid couch, no illustration of a Greek couch confirms it (see further C.L. Ransom, *Studies in Ancient Furniture* [Chicago 1905] 62–5 and G.M.A. Richter, *The Furniture of the Greeks Etruscans and Romans* (London 1966) 52–3). If the carpenter was not a *klinopoios* (cf. Plato, *Republic* X, 597b), but was rather working on part of some larger structure, one might consider the possibility of him being a shipwright.

De Witte gave the find-spot of the London cup as Chiusi in his article of 1832, but in his catalogue of the Durand collection of 1836 he wrote Vulci.

Nos. 10–12 Apollodoros Group

This group has been discussed or referred to on a number of recent occasions: M. Dumm, *MüJbK* 22 (1971) 7–22; K. Schefold, *AK* 17 (1974) 137-42; Boardman *ARFV Archaic* 62; R. Blatter, *HefteABern* 2 (1976) 5–9; D. Williams, *JHS* 97 (1977) 160–8; R. Blatter, *AW* 1978, 59–60; Robertson *Art of Vase-painting* 111–12. Beazley identified a closely knit group of artists, the Epidromos Painter, the Elpinikos Painter, the Kleomelos Painter and Apollodoros (*ARV*^{2} 117–21). He wondered if all might not be phases of one and the same artist. Martha Dumm suggested that the Kleomelos and Elpinikos Painters were one and the same, but Williams went further and argued that Beazley's suggestion was correct in its entirety: the Epidromos Painter being the earliest phase, followed by the Kleomelan and Elpinikan phases, with the signed works that praise Euryptolemos coming at the end. Despite a considerable number of new vases and frr., especially in the J. Paul Getty Museum and a Centre Island private collection, this 'unitarian' solution still seems preferable. Of the Getty pieces note especially the following: 83.AE.238 (*Beazley Add*^{2} 394), 85.AE.377 (*Beazley Add*^{2} 396), 84.AE.38 (*Beazley Add*^{2} 396), 83.AE.323 (old man with goat), 81.AE.114.17 (youth with vessel on shoulder), 82.AE.41.4 (feet of one presumably seated to right, knotted stick).

The potter work of all the cups in this group is very close: see Bloesch *FAS* 127–8, Apollodoros Class. Some of the earlier pieces, however, are rather different (e.g. **3**) and Bloesch even attributed one to Hieron as a very early work (*FAS* 94 no. 25). Apollodoros, however, also decorated in his various phases a mug (A. Adriani [ed.], *Odeon ed altri 'monumenti' archeologici* [Palermo 1971] pl. 46 a–d), aryballoi and an oinochoe.

10 (pl. 15 and fig. 5d)

Cup, type C: GR 1892.7–18.6 (*BM Cat Vases* E 43).

From Città della Pieve (nr. Chiusi); van Branteghem collection. Bought at the van Branteghem sale, 1892

Bibliography: Fröhner *Van Branteghem Collection* no. 31, pl. 4; Hartwig *M* pl. 3, 3 with p. 50 and 683 no. 14; *AV* 51, lower no. 4; Bloesch *FAS* 121 no. 35; *ARV* 88 no. 12; *ARV*^{2} 118 no. 13 and 1627; Boardman *ARFV Archaic* fig. 114; R. Blatter, *HefteABern* 2 (1976) 5–9, pl. 2, 4; *Beazley Add*^{2} 174.

Dimensions: width 26.4; diam. 19.8; diam. of tondo 12.8; ht. 7.4; diam. of foot plate 8.0.

Condition: made up from frr.; unglazed surface damaged, especially around breaks.

Description

INTERIOR: fight.

A youthful warrior, wearing a black Attic helmet (reserved zigzag and two rows of dots on crest-holder; spiral on cheek piece) and greaves, with a chlamys (two-line border) draped over his shoulders and holding his striped scabbard with its red strap in his left hand, almost straddles his opponent as he plunges his sword into his belly. The dying warrior sinks to his knees on the left. He is bearded and wears a short chiton and cuirass, as well as being equipped with a double-crested Chalcidian helmet with a black caul, a shield (decorated with an ivy wreath) and greaves. His head and torso are frontal, his legs in profile. Red blood pours from the wound in his stomach. His teeth are shown and his eyes are beginning to turn up into his head; his sword arm seems to have lost its strength.

INSCRIPTION: ΕΓΙΔΡΟΜΟΣΚΑLΟΣ

Border: two reserved lines.

Relief contours throughout; dilute glaze for minor interior markings; added red for inscription.

c. 500 BC.

Comment: Hartwig attributed the cup to Chachrylion; Beazley gave it to his Epidromos Painter. Williams has argued that it is, together with the other works of Beazley's Epidromos Painter, an early work of Apollodoros (*JHS* 97 [1977] 163–4). Bloesch placed this cup type C in his 'fortschrittliche Richtung', but the shape also recalls his Apollodoros Class (*FAS* 127).

The helmet worn by the fallen warrior is of particular interest. Crests mounted widthways on helmets are fairly common, especially in the western Greek world, but double lengthways crests are much rarer (e.g. Oxford, Guy frr.: Onesimos). The crest-holders here have a series of short lines on one side of a vertical dividing line that suggests that they are intended to be horns, while below them are what can only really be large ears. Helmets with horns and ears are known on Athenian vases from the sixth century (e.g. C. Blinkenberg, *Lindos: Fouilles de l'acropole 1902–1914. 1 Les Petits Objets* [Berlin 1931] pl. 127 no. 2618, Corinthian type with feathers and bull's horns – see further R.M. Cook, *Clazomenian Sarcophagi* [Mainz 1981] 124 note 108) and the fifth century (e.g. *ARV*^{2} 185, 36, Corinthian type with central crest and ram's horns; 364, 43, Corinthian type with central crest and bull's horns; *Beazley Add*² 393, Chairestratos, Geneva market, Corinthian type with central crest and bull's horns and ears [attributed to Douris by Bothmer]; once Basel market, *Eye of Greece* 37 no. 142 A, as last; 860, 5, Attic-Phrygian type, with bull's horns and ears; Berlin 1970.9 [Triptolemos Painter], Corinthian type with central crest and bull's horns and ears). They are also found on Clazomenian sarcophagi (Cook *op. cit.* 124) and on a marble relief fragment from the Archaic Artemision at Ephesos (F.N. Pryce, *Catalogue of Sculpture in the Department of Greek and Roman Antiquities of the British Museum* [London 1928] no. B 174). Some actual helmets also survive: H. Pflug, *Schutz und Zier* (Basel 1981) no. 81 (seventh-century Corinthian); W. Wrede et al., *Olympiabericht* 1 (Berlin 1937) pl. 12 (fr.: seventh-century Corinthian); P. Gercke (ed.), *Funde aus der Antike. Sammlung Paul Dierichs* (Kassel 1981) no. 45 (fifth-century Corinthian). None of them, however, show the arrangement seen here, where the crests are attached to the horns.

For other frontal-headed warriors see Korshak *Frontal Faces* 60–3 and especially figs. 30 and 44. For Epidromos *kalos* see on **12** (E 25).

The find-spot, Città della Pieve, is given in the manuscript copy of the van Branteghem catalogue in the Department of Greek and Roman Antiquities, British Museum.

11 (pl. 16 and fig. 5e)

Cup, type C: GR 1836.2–24.230 (*BM Cat Vases* E 57).
From Vulci; Durand collection.
Bought at the Durand sale, 1836.

Bibliography: *Cabinet Durand* 279, lot 874; Hartwig *M* 299 no. 15 and 687 no. 41; Hoppin ii 93 no. 37; *AV* 53, 8; Bloesch *FAS* 127 no. 3, pl. 34, 6; *ARV* 87, 8; *ARV*² 120, 9 and 1627; Boardman *ARFV Archaic* fig. 117; *Beazley Add*² 175.

Dimensions: width 26.2; diam. 19.5; diam. of tondo 13.2; ht. 7.8; diam. of foot plate 7.8.

Condition: made up from frr.; one rim fr. missing and other small chips.

Description

INTERIOR: man leading a cheetah to the left.
The man is bearded and wears a himation and an apicate red fillet. His hair has a relief line fringe at the front and three horizontal relief lines over the neck. His beard has, as well as a relief line fringe, a spiral curl in relief line under the front. In his left hand he carries a knotty stick and in his right hand the red lead attached by a ring to the collar of a spotted cheetah. In the field on the left hangs a sponge and a scraper (the aryballos presumably obscured).

INSCRIPTION: HOΓAIϟKAΛOϟ
Border: single reserved line.

Relief line contour throughout (except hair); dilute glaze for minor interior markings; added red for inscription.

c. 490 BC.

Comment: The cup was attributed by Hartwig to Hieron, even though he had already isolated Apollodoros as an artistic personality (*M* 628–40), beginning with the signed cup fr. formerly in Castle Ashby, now in the collection of Herbert Cahn in Basel (*ARV*² 120, 4; *Beazley Add*² 175). Smith saw more of a connection with Douris (*BM Cat Vases* iii p. 80). Beazley corrected these attributions by including the cup in his first listing of vases by Apollodoros.

This piece belongs to the final phase of the artist's career, if the merging of Beazley's Epidromos, Elpinikos and Kleomelos Painters with Apollodoros is correct. His style at this point echoes that of Douris in his 'early middle' period, but some pieces reach on into his Hippodaman phase. The relief line curl at the tip of the man's beard imitates a Dourian characteristic (cf. **21** [E 52] and **22** [E 54]). Bloesch placed the cup in his Apollodoros Class.

For discussions of the keeping of exotic felines as pets by rich Athenians see W.L. Brown, *Etruscan Lion* (Oxford 1960) 170–4; A. Ashmead, *Expedition* 20 (1978) 39, 45, 47; Koch-Harnack 105–15.

12 (pl. 17 and fig. 6a)

Cup, type C: GR 1848.3–20.1 (*BM Cat Vases* E 25)
Purchased of Mrs. Badham, 1848

Bibliography: Klein *M*² 133, Epidromos kalos no. 4; Klein *L* 45 lower no. 3; Hartwig *M* pl. 3, 1 with p. 44 and 46–7, 683 no. 12; Klein *L*² 83 no. 3; Bloesch *FAS* 127, 4; *ARV* 922, 11; *ARV*² 1577, 13.

Dimensions: width 25.0; diam. 18.9; diam. of tondo 11.2; ht. 7.0; diam. of foot plate 7.5.

Condition: made up from frr.

Description

INTERIOR: youth.
A youth crouches to the right, a chlamys with a two-line border over his extended left arm, a thin knotty stick held back in his right hand. He has a red wreath.
Inscriptions: EΓIΔPOMOϟ KAΛOϟ; NAI+I (retr.).
Border: single reserved line.

Incised hair contour, relief line for all other contours; dilute glaze for minor interior markings; added red for inscriptions.

c. 500 BC.

Comment: Hartwig attributed this cup to Chachrylion, but Beazley left it unattributed, merely listing it with vases bearing the *kalos* name Epidromos. Bloesch placed the cup in his Apollodoros Class.

The drapery closely recalls the earliest work of Apollodoros ('Epidromos Painter'), but little else does. The treatment of the chest recalls some pieces near early Douris and the Magnoncourt

Painter (*ARV*^{2} 456), but the head does not correspond. The hip might be compared with that of the runner on the lost Epidromos *kalos* cup noted below.

The youth crouches with left arm covered by his cloak as if he were meeting the onrush of a boar or the like, but the knotted stick suggests he is really a komast: perhaps he is to be thought of as dancing, more specifically crouching before jumping.

On Epidromos *kalos* see *ARV*^{2} 1577–8 and *Beazley Add*^{2} 394. The *kalos* name occurs not only on works by Beazley's Epidromos Painter (e.g. above **10** [E 43]), but also on a number of other cups: a lost piece with a runner at the start (*ARV*^{2} 1577, 12); a cup attributed to the Salting Painter (*ARV*^{2} 1577, 14 = 178, 1; really a work of the Carpenter Painter, see on **9** [E 23]); a piece by the Kiss Painter (*ARV*^{2} 1577, 15 = 177, 3); and two Proto-Panaetian cups (*ARV*^{2} 1577, 16 = 317, 9; and *Beazley Add*^{2} 394).

Nos. 13–14: The Colmar Painter

For the Colmar Painter see, in addition to Beazley's lists, the following accounts and publications: *VA* 81–2; Richter and Hall 58–9 (nos. 36–7); D.K. Hill, *AJA* 49 (1945) 503–7; Richter *Survey*^{2} 85; A.-B. Follmann, *CVA Hannover* 1, 45–8; N. Kunisch, *Antiken der Sammlung Julius C. und Margot Funcke* (Bochum 1972) 98–9 (no. 86); Boardman *ARFV Archaic* 134–5; R. Lullies in E. Berger and R. Lullies, *Antike Kunstwerke aus der Sammlung Ludwig* I (Basel 1979) 101–4; Ferrari *Tarquinia* 115–16 (no. 34); Robertson *Art of Vase-painting* 109–10.

Beazley labelled seven of the pieces in his list 'very early' and a further three 'early', although one of the former seems rather to be the work of the Bonn Painter (*ARV*^{2} 352–7: very early, nos. 1–3, 25 and 61–3; early, nos. 20, 26 and 27; no. 61 is by the Bonn Painter). This grouping is perhaps a little awkward, for the works appear to fall more naturally into a large early group with a few pieces standing out in front as very early (very early: *ARV*^{2} 354, 25–6 and 20).

The painter clearly had an extremely long career. His earliest surviving works belong to the time of Euphronios' maturity, when he worked in what one might call a sub-Oltan circle on the fringes of Euphronian influence. He then moved more firmly into this area, when Euphronios began to pot some of his cups and he gradually came under the influence of Onesimos. His early works are related to Onesimos' Panaetian phase; his middle period corresponds to Onesimos' later, Lykan phase. His long late phase reveals the influence of Onesimos' pupil, the Antiphon Painter. His career even continued into the 470s, for Beazley's Painter of Würzburg 487 (*ARV*^{2} 836) must be his latest, Early Classical phase.

He decorated cups almost entirely, but there is a donkey-head rhyton in Paris (*ARV*^{2} 357, 74) and a fr. of a mug from Olympia (acontist and diskobolos: attributed by Martin Robertson).

Recent additions of particular interest to the Colmar Painter's *oeuvre* include two large cups with komos scenes (Rouen 450: *Hommes, Dieux et Héros de la Grèce* [Rouen 1982] no. 75. Centre Island, private [attributed by D. von Bothmer]), an early cup on the New York Market bearing the *kalos* name Leagros and with an extract from the Judgement of Paris on the interior (seated Athena making a libation and a woman with jug and mirror; outside, komos) and a late cup with mythological scenes (London market: J.-L. Zimmermann, *Collection de la Fondation Thétis* [Geneva 1987] no. 107 [attributed by Bothmer]).

13 (pls. 18 and 19 a-b, fig. 6b)

Cup: GR 1897.10–28.1
From Falerii.
Bought of P. Hartwig, 1897.

Bibliography: Klein *L*^{2} 92 no. 10; *VA* 87, bottom; H.B. Walters, *JHS* 41 (1921) 123–4, pl. 3, II, 1 with p. 123–4; *AV* 228 no. 9; Bloesch *FAS* 76 no. 26; *ARV* 227 no. 9; *ARV*^{2} 354 no. 24.

Dimensions: width 31.0; diam. 24.3; diam. of tondo 15.0; ht. 9.3; diam. of exterior ground line 10.4; diam. of foot ring 11.0.

Condition: made up from frr.; ancient repair holes (parts of eight pairs); two rim frr. missing and three other frr.

Description

INTERIOR: warrior.
A young warrior in chiton (dilute glaze folds; two-line border) and Thracian cloak (battlement, strokes, rays bordered by dots, zigzag, dots; zip, black band bordered on either side by a dilute glaze line), equipped with an Attic helmet, a peltast's shield (pair of eyes separated by a strip of continuous maeander) and a spear, moves rapidly to the left. He is in three-quarter back view.

INSCRIPTION: ΑΟΕΝΔΟΤΟΣ (for Athenodotos; very thin lettering).
Border: two closely set reserved lines.

EXTERIOR: warriors.
Side A (L): three naked warriors move in crouching pose to the left. Each has an Attic helmet, a shield and a spear and is in three-quarter back view with long hair falling down on to right shoulder. The shield devices are, from left to right, a wheel, a horse (only the rear part seen) and ΛΕΑΓΡΟΣ written retrograde.

INSCRIPTIONS: ΛΕΑΓΡ[ΟΣ] ΚΑΛΟΣ

Side B (U): as side A, but the shield devices are different. They are, from left to right, a bull's head with a circle enclosing a dot above and below (head and shoulders of this warrior missing), a tripod and ΚΑΛΟΣ written retrograde.

INSCRIPTION: ΚΑΛΟΣ (retrograde)
Ground line: single reserved line.

Relief line contour throughout; dilute glaze for minor interior markings; added red for inscriptions; thick reserved band inside lip, thin line outside.

c. 510–500 BC.

Comment: Beazley attributed the cup to his Colmar Painter. The lone warrior seen in three-quarter back view is a favourite motif of the Colmar Painter in his early period (e.g. *ARV*^{2} 353–4 and 356, 8, 21, 26, 27 and 61). This pose is also enjoyed by Beazley's Bonn Painter (*ARV*^{2} 351, 1, 6, 10, 11): the artists are connected but they are not identical. The files of warriors on the exterior are repeated on New York 14.105.9 (*ARV*^{2} 354, 23). The double reserved line border is found on the very early cup in Washington (*ARV*^{2} 354, 25), a fragmentary cup in a Centre Island collection (attributed by D. von Bothmer) and a cup on the New York market (inside, seated Athena making a libation and a woman with jug and mirror, perhaps an extract from the Judgement of Paris; outside, komos).

Beazley does not mark the cup as 'early', although it is clearly connected with the early group, which bear the *kalos* names Leagros and Antias. Traces of influence from the young Onesimos are just beginning to become apparent and Bloesch placed the cup in his list of works by the potter Euphronios. The *kalos* names Athenodotos and Leagros are also coupled on a very early work of Onesimos (Boston 10.179: *ARV*^{2} 327 no. 110). On Leagros see further on **2** (E 46); on Athenodotos see further on **5** (E 47).

Pairs of eyes appear on a number of peltai (list kindly supplied by D. von Bothmer): *ARV*^{2} 156, 55; 444, 231; 885, 95–6; 1624, 24 *ter*; *CVA Robinson* ii, pl. 10; Siena fr. (satyr with trumpet, pelta on ground); Centre Island, private frr. Single eyes also occur (e.g. *ARV*^{2} 155, 43; 156, 52–4; 157, 88; 1629, 57 *bis*). On Thracian peltasts see most recently Lissarrague *L'autre guerrier* 151–6. It is not clear whether the scenes on the exterior represent warriors in actual ambush or in some sort of athletic or ritual training exercise – the absence of greaves and other armour might favour the latter. For a general discussion of this sort of scene see F. Lissarrague in *Cité des Images* 37–9 and his book, noted above, 170.

The find-spot of this cup is given by Beazley (*ARV* 227, 9; *ARV*^{2} 345, 24) and appears as such in his notes in the Beazley Archive, Oxford – he may have got the information from a drawing done for Hartwig. There is no confirmation, however, in the Greek and Roman Department Register, nor among the letters of Hartwig, nor in early publications.

14

(pl. 19 c)

Cup: GR 1952.12–2.6
Once E.P. Warren collection.
Bought of Mrs. Redfern-Loades, 1952.

Bibliography: *ARV*^{2} 354 no. 29.

Dimensions: length at rim 3.6; ht. 3.1; diam. of rim c. 22.0.

Condition: single fr.; relief line flaking slightly; fired greenish. The broken edge at the bottom of the fr. seems relatively fresh.

Description
EXTERIOR: head of youth playing pipes to left, presumably from a symposium scene, since there is no trace of drapery on his shoulder.

Relief line contour throughout (except for hair); reserved line outside lip.

c. 500–490 BC.

Comment: Attributed by Beazley to the Colmar Painter. The scale of the figure is large. The cup may be still early, but it could equally come from early in his middle phase. His later symposium scenes show the influence of the Antiphon Painter.

A youth playing the pipes at a symposium recurs on two pieces (*ARV*^{2} 355 no. 35; *Para* 363). A cup by the painter decorated with a symposium was recently on the London market (Christie's Dec. 1986, lot 221).

No. 15: The Antiphon Painter

On the Antiphon Painter and his Group see *VA* 111–12; *ARV*^{2} 336–50; Richter *Survey*^{2} 85–6; M. Bazzari, *StEtr* 26 (1958) 259–65; I. Raumschüssel, *Dresdener Kunstblätter* 8 (1964) 59–64; K. Peters, *AA* 1967, 174–5; R. Blatter, *AA* 1968, 640–52; A.M. Tamassia, *Bollettino d'Arte* 1974, 147–51; Boardman *ARFV Archaic* 135; G. Riccioni in A. Cambitoglou (ed.), *Studies in Honour of Arthur Dale Trendall* (Sydney 1979) 125–8; R. Blatter, *HefteABern* 10 (1984) 5–7; D. Williams in *Festschrift Schauenburg* 75–81; D. Williams in *Copenhagen Colloquium* 674–83; D. Williams in *New Perspectives* 294–7; Robertson *Art of Vase-painting* 106–7.

The Antiphon Painter was almost exclusively a painter of cups, although he did also decorate some skyphoi (*ARV*^{2} 341, 90 with *Beazley Add*^{2} 219; 347, 115 – by the painter himself; Centre Island private, frr., attributed by D. von Bothmer). His name-piece, the splendid stand in Berlin that praises Antiphon (*ARV*^{2} 335, 1), is a remarkable exception to this series of drinking vessels. He was a pupil of Onesimos and his earliest works date to around 495 BC or shortly before (*ARV*^{2} 342, 5; Basel, Cahn 422 fr.; *ARV*^{2} 337, 30 *bis*). There then follows an early phase that clearly runs parallel to Onesimos' later, Lykan phase (*c.* 495–490 BC). The Antiphon Painter, however, quickly begins to add a new sense of volume and solidity to his figures and also experiments with the form of the naked male chest. By his early middle period his style has fully matured. His later middle works are characterised by the *kalos* name Lysis. Many of his late works bear the name Laches and at this time he sometimes he employs an old-fashioned feature, the incised hair-contour. He was still painting after 480 BC.

The potting of many of the Antiphon Painter's cups has been attributed by Bloesch to Euphronios (*FAS* 79–80 nos. 48, 52, 57, 59, 61, 71): one appears to have been signed (*ARV*^{2} 330, 5: attribution by Williams). There is, however, an exception, a large cup clearly potted by Python, Douris' regular potter (*ARV*^{2} 340, 71 with p. 1646): perhaps the Antiphon Painter was asked to step in and complete an urgent order.

15 (pl. 19 d)

Cup: GR 1993.4–5.1
Presented by Dr. D. von Bothmer

Dimensions: preserved ht. 5.8; greatest width 8.0

Condition: single fr. with part of tondo, stem and turn into foot

Description
INTERIOR: two males, probably komasts
On the left are the upper thighs, groin, hips left side of chest and extended left arm of a naked male in profile moving to the right. There is a touch of a black object on the palm of his left hand, very probably a black skyphos. On the right are the upper thighs, groin, hips and lower abdomen of a male in three-quarter front view, a chlamys (two-line border) draped over his right upper, which must have been extended to the left. A small part of his right arm is preserved between the edge of his drapery and the left shoulder of his companion.

c. 485 BC.

Comment: This fr. comes from a fine, mature middle work by the Antiphon Painter, as the treatment of the extended median line (for a discussion of this see especially D. Williams in *New Perspectives* 294–7), the drapery and the genitals indicate.

The scene probably showed two komasts. Two figure tondo compositions are rarely attempted by the Antiphon Painter and his group. The fragment once in Bloesch's collection (*ARV*^{2} 336, 14 *bis*) is not decorated outside and is a late piece; the Oxford cup is much more impressive (*ARV*^{2} 340, 70). The London fr. probably comes from a comparable piece. It may also be compared with the painter's name-piece.

No. 16: The Cage Painter

Beazley's Cage Painter was named after the subject of the London cup (see further *ARV*^{2} 348–9). He related him to the Antiphon Painter, a pupil of Onesimos: for the Antiphon Painter see on **15**. Beazley's list of the Cage Painter's works contains two pieces (nos. 5–6) that are really earlier works by another follower of the Antiphon Painter, Beazley's Adria Painter (*ARV*^{2} 349), whose oeuvre may now be augmented by some twenty or more pieces. The remaining pieces in Beazley's list of the Cage Painter may similarly be increased with, among others, the following pieces:

a. Oxford 518: *ARV*^{2} 336, 22
b. Basel market: *Münzen und Medaillen AG Auktion* 40 (Basel 1969) no. 92
c. Villa Giulia, Boston 03.840 and Vatican, Astarita 511: *ARV*^{2} 342, 10 plus
d. Boston 62.613: *ARV*^{2} 1701, add as 342, 19 *bis*
e. Vienna 107 b fr.: *ARV*^{2} 339, 52 – Adria Bc 101 fr. (*ARV*^{2} 1671, add to 816) may belong
f. Acrop. 281 fr.: *ARV*^{2} 337, 31
g. Louvre C 11366 and C 12513 frr.: *ARV*^{2} 343, 35 (the latter added by Giroux)
h. Louvre C 250 frr.: *ARV*^{2} 341, 86
i. Centre Island, New York, priv.: A – head of youth leaning to right, head and shoulders of a heavily wrapped boy seated to left.

The Cage Painter was a pupil of the Antiphon Painter in his later years and his work runs parallel to the master's late period. He decorated only cups.

16 (pls. 20–1 and fig. 6c)

Cup: GR 1901.5–14.1
From Orvieto; Bourguignon collection.
Bought at the Bourguignon sale, 1901.

Bibliography: A. Sambon and C. and E. Canessa, *Collection d'antiquités* (Bourguignon collection, sale 18 March 1901, Paris) p. 18, lot 52 (I); Hoppin i, 283 no. 77; H.B. Walters, *JHS* 41 (1921) 125–6 (I); *ARV* 237, 1; *ARV*^{2} 348, 2; Boardman *ARFV* fig. 244 (I); *Beazley Add*^{2} 220.

Dimensions: diam. 24.0; diam. of tondo 14.5; diam. of exterior ground line 10.0.

Condition: made up from frr.; ancient repair holes (parts of three pairs); foot missing (stem shaved flat) and right handle.

Description
INTERIOR: seated youth with a bird-cage.
A youth wearing a himation (black border) draped over his left shoulder and around his waist and legs sits on a stool to the right. He has a red apicate fillet in his hair. On his knees he holds a cylindrical bird-cage with a conical top. He puts the thumb and forefinger of his right hand (awkwardly twisted, palm outwards, so that one wonders if the artist really meant to paint the left hand) through the apertures of the cage, above and below the central band, perhaps to open the door of the cage. Inside is a bird, painted in silhouette but with four reserved flashes on the wings. Above is a stick with a cross set against it. The cross has a central hole, through which the stick does not pass, and a dilute glaze line runs down the centre of each arm.

INSCRIPTION: HOΠAI[Σ]KAΛOΣ
Border: stopt maeanders (four-stroke, anticlockwise).

EXTERIOR: youths and boys in conversation.
Side A (U): in the centre a boy, close wrapped in his himation (black border), sits on a stool to the right; above him hangs a phormiskos bag and a cross without a stick. He may have had his hands around his right knee, lifting that foot off the ground. His headband is reserved. On the left stands a youth with hair done with a dilute wash and a red headband, leaning on a knotty stick and clad in a himation (line border). In front of him hangs a pair of sandals with red ties below. On the right stands another male, leaning on a knotty stick and also wearing a himation (black

vertical border). His right hand is visible with its fingers curled up behind his back, the left holds out a writing case with the top open (red tie dangling from it). The front of his red wreath is visible.

INSCRIPTION: HOΓ]AIΣKA[Λ]OΣ

Side B (L): In the centre sits a youth or a boy on a stool to the right. He wears a himation (black border) over his left shoulder and around his waist and legs. His headband is reserved and the hair below it is done with small relief dots over a wash of dilute glaze. His left hand, still draped in his garment, grasps the upper end of a knotty stick. The fingers of his right hand are spread beside his thigh. In front of him hangs a closed writing case with a black stylus tucked into the ties at the side: it hangs from red ties. Behind him, on the left, stands a youth in a himation. He leans on a stick and holds out an opened writing case in his right hand (red tie dangling from top). He has a red wreath in his hair. Hung up behind him is another cross. The third figure, that on the far right of the scene, is completely missing.

INSCRIPTION: HOΓA[I]ΣKA[ΛOΣ]
Ground line: single reserved line.

Relief line contour throughout; dilute glaze for minor interior markings; added red for inscriptions; rim worn (reserved line on outer top edge of lip only ?).

c. 485–480 BC.

Comment: Sambon, Hoppin and Walters attributed the cup to Douris. Beazley made it the name-piece of his Cage Painter, whom he related to the Antiphon Painter.

Pet birds are seen in cages on only a few other vases: Agora P 17531 (*ARV*^{2} 355, 50); London GR 1907.5–19.1 (*JHS* 41 [1921] pl. 3); Oxford 321 (*ARV*^{2} 561, 9); Leningrad 1791 (*ARV*^{2} 1476, 3); Paris, Cab. Méd 361. (*ARV*^{2} 651, 16); New York market (Andre Emmerich Gallery, *Masterpieces of Greek Vase Painting*, 1964, no. 37); California market (Summa: *Catalogue 1: Ancient Art*, 1976, no. 19). The bird on the Cabinet des Médailles vase, which is in outline technique and is quite large in proportion to its cage, is described by Beazley as a partridge; that on the Leningrad lekanis is also in outline and quite large; that on the late fifth-century chous once on the New York market is in red-figure (speckled body) and quite large in relation to its cage – it is out and trying to eat a worm. Those on the Agora fr., the London vases, the Oxford lekythos and the California market pelike are much smaller and are in silhouette: the London birds are called quails by Walters, so, too, the Oxford bird by Beazley. Both partridges and quails were kept by the Greeks as pets and for fighting (in general see most recently J. Pollard, *Birds in Greek Life and Myth* [London 1977]; for water birds Koch-Harnack 124–8 and, for a heron as love-gift, L. Burn in *Copenhagen Colloquium* 103).

On one side of a Brygan cup recently on the London market (ex Hesperia Arts Auction, Ltd, 27 November 1990, part I, no. 121) there is a scene of bird-selling, apparently in the palaistra: there are two birds in a large net bag, over which is bent a youth holding a third bird, while a fourth flies away (note that there is a cross-shaped object on the far left). On bird catching see most recently E. Böhr, *AA*, 1992, 573–83.

There is a cage on the kantharos in Boston potted by Nikosthenes (95.61: *ARV*^{2} 132; E. Vermeule *AntK* 12 [1969] 12–13 with pl. 9), but the bird has flown. Hares are also seen in or out of cages: *ARV*^{2} 20 and *ARV*^{2} 866, 1 (*Hirschmann Collection* no. 3).

The cross-shaped instrument that appears on both the inside and the outside of this cup was identified by Walters (*JHS* 41 [1921] 126) as a bird-clapper. Various other interpretations have been proposed, including a toy windmill, a torch (e.g. H.R.W. Smith in *CVA University of California* on pl. 36, p. 41–2) and a set-square: for a fairly full list see F.A.G. Beck, *Album of Education* (Sydney 1975) 17; see also K. Schauenburg, *Kunst in Hessen und am Mittelrhein* 6 (1967) 123–4 and C. Isler-Kerenyi, *AntK* 27 (1984) 154 n. 8. On the interior the tapering stick does render the object very similar to the cross-type torches commonly seen on South Italian vases, and terracottas, but this is probably misleading since it is regularly seen without such an attachment (even on some early South Italian vases: e.g. A.D. Trendall, *The Red-figured Vases of Lucania, Campania and Sicily* [Oxford 1967] 17 no. 19; A.D. Trendall and A. Cambitoglu, *The Red-figured Vases of Apulia* [Oxford 1978] 16 no. 55) and the stick does not pass through the cross.

In its simple cross form it appears on a number of vases, often in the context of youths and boys at their lessons or near the palaistra, but sometimes simply in conversation; it is also seen on a few vases with women making music (e.g. *ARV*^{2} 1060, 147 and 1046, 7. Cf. also *ARV*^{2} 1190, 30). On only one vase is one of these objects actually being held – a red-figured pyxis with two women with lyres and a third with pipes (*ARV*^{2} 777, upper 1; *Beazley Add*^{2} 288) – and the woman holds it by one end, low down, as she moves rapidly.

Lullies describes the object as a tuning fork (R. Lullies, *Eine Sammlung griechischer Kleinkunst* [Munich 1955] no. 65), but this seems unlikely. Wegner suggested that it was an instrument for adjusting the tension of the strings of a lyre by inserting into the tops of the tuning pegs (M. Wegner, *Das Musikleben der Griechen* [Berlin 1949] 38), but the sheer size as well as the shape seem unlikely for such a function (the tops of extant Roman tuning pegs are triangular in section, for which the circular hole seen in the centre of the crosses is clearly unsuitable). The object remains an enigma.

No. 17: The Triptolemos Painter

On the Triptolemos Painter see in addition to Beazley's lists: E. Buschor, *JdI* 31 (1916) 74–6; *VA* 98–9 note 1; J.D. Beazley, *BSA* 46 (1951) 7–15; J.D. Beazley in K. Schauenburg (ed.), *Charites* (Festschrift für Ernst Langlotz, Berlin 1957) 136–9; *ARV*^{2} 360–7; M. Schmidt in P. Zazoff (ed.), *Opus Nobile: Festschrift zum*

60. Geburtstag von Ulf Jantzen (Wiesbaden 1969) 141–52; E.R. Knauer, *Ein Skyphos des Triptolemosmalers* (Berlin 1973); J.R. Guy, 'The Triptolemos Painter', Cincinnati MA thesis, 1974; Boardman *ARFV Archaic* 139–40; E.R. Knauer, *GrRomByzSt* 17 (1976) 209–16; C. Isler-Kerenyi, *Stamnoi* (Lugano 1977) 43–8; J.R. Guy, *Arts in Virginia* 21:2 (1981) 2–15; Robertson *Art of Vase-painting* 112–15.

The Triptolemos Painter seems to have begun life as a cup-painter in the 'workshop' of Euphronios, as Bloesch's attribution of five of his cups to Euphronios suggests (*ARV*² 363, 35; 364, 43 and 45 and 50–51). His early style has much in common with the early products of other painters in this group, including Onesimos, Douris, and Makron. The Triptolemos Painter was an independent spirit, but he clearly kept in close touch with Douris (cf. *ARV*² 360), while also having connections with the Brygan workshop (*ARV*² 364, 49: Bloesch *FAS* 85 no. 21; also stylistic connections). His earlier vases are all cups; later he decorated a wide variety of larger shapes, collaborating occasionally with the Flying-angel Painter and decorating a white-ground alabastron for the potter Hermotimos (*ARV*² 363, 29 – signed on mouth). Beazley also suggested that, when decorating a stamnos, he sat for a time in the same workshop as the Pan Painter (cf. *Charites* 138–9). He clearly continued to work into the Early Classical period and J.R. Guy has argued that Beazley's Painter of London E 99 represents his very latest phase, when he turned back to smaller shapes (*Arts in Virginia* 11 and 15 note 80; cf. his *Followers of Douris* 125–6; he also now adds to this phase Beazley's Painter of the Leningrad Herm Mug, see *ARV*² 311 – no. 1 is now BM GR 1956.10–20.2). This is the only phase represented in the collections of the British Museum.

Two cups decorated by the Triptolemos Painter bear the signature of Douris as painter (see most recently Guy, *Arts in Virginia* 10–11 and 14 notes 69–70). Immerwahr (*Attic Script* 86) has argued that these signatures are 'in Douris' handwriting, although in his less neat style'. Whether Douris actually signed the cup or the Triptolemos Painter both borrowed Douris' name and imitated his handwriting remains unclear, as does the motive for either scenario.

17 (pls. 22–3 and fig. 6d)

Cup: GR 1864.10–7.81 (*BM Cat Vases* E 99)
Excavated on Rhodes, Kamiros Tomb F 199.

Bibliography: *ARV* 568; *ARV*² 788, 1.

Dimensions: width 30.8; diam. 25.5; diam. of tondo 13.0; ht. 9.2; diam. of exterior ground line 9.7; diam. of foot plate 9.2.

Condition: made up from frr.; one rim fr. and three small wall frr. missing.

Description
INTERIOR: a youth at a wash basin.
A youth wearing a himation (dilute glaze selvage) pulled up over the back of his head stands frontally, his right arm pointing down at a wash basin on the left and his head turned in the same direction. On the right is a Doric pillar, unfluted but with a base.
Border: stopt maeander (four-stroke, anticlockwise) interrupted in four places by a dotted cross square.

EXTERIOR: men, youths and boys.

Side A (U): youth, boy and man. On the left, stands a youth in a himation with a knotty stick in his left hand; in the field in front of him is hung a sponge, aryballos and scraper. In the centre a boy clad in a himation stands to the right, a lyre in his left hand. In front of the boy, on the right, a bearded man in a himation leans on a knotty stick to the left, his right hand back on his hip, his left hand out in front. He is in three-quarter back view.

Side B (L): men and a boy. On the left, stands a bearded man, clad in a himation. He leans on a knotty stick tucked under his left arm, his right hand on his hip, his left arm out in front of him. In the centre stands a himation-clad boy (head missing) to the right, a lyre in his left hand. On the right is a bearded man, as on side A.
Ground line: single reserved line.
Under the handles: palmette with long pointed central leaf enclosed by lyre-form tendrils; growing from the handle roots a tendril with a spiral (see fig. 8b).

No relief line contours; wide reserved band inside lip.

c. 470 BC.

Comment: The cup is the name-piece of Beazley's Painter of London E 99, the only other attributed work being a cup in the Petit Palais (*ARV*² 788, 2), although two other works were also related (*ARV*² 788, middle and 803, 47). Guy has convincingly suggested (*Arts in Virginia* 21, 2 [1981] 11 and 15 note 80; cf. also his *Followers of Douris* 125–6) that this artist is really the latest, Early Classical, phase of the Triptolemos Painter (*ARV*² 360–367).

The underside of the foot is very flat and the turn into the cone in the centre unusually sharp. The form bears a vague relation to some of the smaller late cups decorated by the Brygos Painter (e.g. Bloesch *FAS* pl. 24, 3).

Beazley (*VP* 26) suggested that a similar scene on the interior of an athletic cup by the Painter of the Paris Gigantomachy represents a youth dipping his hand in a laver as he enters the palaistra. The outside of the London cup mixes music (boys with lyres) and athletics (scraper, etc.), thus suggesting that some music lessons might have taken place in one of the rooms of the palaistra.

The lyre-form palmettes under the handles have been compared with those by the Sabouroff Painter (Guy, *Arts in Virginia* 15 n. 80).

For the tomb group see *BM Cat Glass* i 158. It included the red-figured hydria London E 188 (*ARV*² 1048, 42) and the red-figured lekythos GR 1864.10–7.1646, as well as four other pieces of pottery, *BM Cat Glass* 257, four spindle whorls and two bronze scrapers – seemingly a mix of female and male accoutrements.

Nos. 18–29: Douris

In addition to Beazley's lists see also the accounts and publications in the following: Hartwig *M* 200–30, 582–627, 657–80; Furtwängler in F.R. i, 246–8 and 262–75; E. Pottier, *Douris et les peintres des vases grecs* (Paris 1904); Furtwängler in F.R. ii, 85–6; Buschor *GV* 173; Frucht *Duris*; E. Buschor, *JdI* 31 (1916) 74–95; *VA* 97–100; J.D. Beazley, *JHS* 39 (1919) 84–7; S. Papaspyridi and N. Kyparissis, *ADelt* 11 (1927–8) 91–110; Richter *Survey*[2] 83–5; A.H.S. 339–43; J.D. Beazley in C.B. iii, 17–28 (nos. 125–35); Wegner *Duris*; B. Philippaki in M. Andronikos (ed.), *Kernos. Timetike prosphora ston kathegete Georgio Bakalake* (Thessaloniki 1972) 197–202; Boardman *ARFV Archaic* 137–9; D.C. Kurtz, *Athenian White Lekythoi* (Oxford 1975) 25–32; D. von Bothmer, *RLouvre* 27 (1977) 218–20; A. Lezzi-Hafter in *Greek Vases from the Hirschmann Collection* (Zurich 1982) 66–73 (nos. 32–4); Guy *Followers of Douris* (unpublished thesis); J.R. Guy in C. Bérard, C. Bronn and A. Pomari (eds.), *Images et Société en Grèce ancienne* (Lausanne 1987) 223–5; D.C. Kurtz, *Getty Vases* 4 (1989) 118–125; Immerwahr *Attic Script* 85–7; D. Buitron-Oliver, *Getty Vases* 5 (1991) 64–74; M. Robertson, *Getty Vases* 5 (1991) 75–98; Robertson *Art of Vase-painting* 84–93; Buitron-Oliver *Douris* (forthcoming).

The chronology of Douris' career has been fully set out by Beazley *ARV*[2] 425–7 and C.B. iii 17–18 (Buitron-Oliver offers slight adjustments). He began work shortly before 500 BC in the Euphronian circle and was from the start influenced by Euphronios and the young Onesimos. There are no examples of this inventive period (period 1: very early and early) among the cups in the British Museum. Period 2 (early middle: *c.* 500–490 BC or soon after) is characterised by a more settled style and rather bare decoration. The long middle period (period 3: *c.* 485–475 BC) is typified by richer decoration (maeander and cross-square tondo border, handle palmette complex) and the use of the *kalos* name Hippodamas. Late in period 3 the tondo border begins to be modified (now paired maeander units). Douris' late phase (period 4; down to about 470 BC or soon after) sees both elaboration and simplification, while attribution is complicated by the presence of pupils.

Douris had two major Late Archaic pupils, the Painter of London E 55 (recognised by J.R. Guy, see further on **26**) and the Oedipus Painter: the former begins in Douris' middle phase, just about the time when he apparently stops signing his cups, the latter starts slightly later, after 480 BC. The Dourian school, however, continued down towards the middle of the century.

Douris was primarily a cup-painter, but he also decorated other shapes: phiale, skyphos, kantharos, rhyton, psykter, neck-amphora, oinochoe, lekythos, pyxis, and aryballos. He also signed as potter on two pieces (kantharos and aryballos). Most of his cups were the work of the potter Python (Bloesch *FAS* 96–101; *ARV*[2] 426–7), but three early pieces have been attributed to Euphronios (*ARV*[2] 427–8, 1, 2, 13; Bloesch *FAS* 70–77 nos. 2, 9, 33), one to Brygos (*ARV*[2] 442, 213; Bloesch *FAS* 83 no. 12) and two are signed by Kleophrades (*ARV*[2] 429, 21; Bloesch *FAS* 58 no. 2; add Getty 83.AE.217: D. Buitron-Oliver, *Getty Vases* 5 [1991] 64–74). Two new early middle works bear signatures, one of Phaidrias (Getty 87.AE.46 etc. frr.: signature noted by J.R. Guy), the other very fragmentary (M. Robertson, *Getty Vases* 5 [1991] 95 – ...kros or ...chros). A middle work bears the potter's signature of Kalliades (*ARV*[2] 434, 74; Bloesch *FAS* 134 no. 3).

18 (pls. 24–5 and fig. 6e)

Cup: GR 1867.5–8.1060 (*BM Cat Vases* E 39)
From Vulci; Canino, Raoul-Rochette and Blacas collections
Bought of the estate of the Duc de Blacas, 1867.

Bibliography: M. Buonocore, *Codices Vaticani Latini: Codices 9734–9782 (Codices Amatiani)* (Vatican 1988) no. 9770 (list of Canino vases written by Amati in 1831) f. 35 v., no. 3498; L.J.J. Dubois, *Notice d'une collection de vases du prince de Canino* (Paris 1843) no. 214; De Witte *Fabricants* 32 no. xviii, 4; *Collection D. Raoul-Rochette* (sale, Paris 30 April–1 May 1855) p. 28 no. 129; Klein *M*[2] 152 no. 1; Hartwig *M* 685 no. 1; Murray *DGV* no. 24; Frucht *Duris* 11 no. 1 and 17–18; Hoppin i, 236–7 no. 15; *AV* 201, 22; *ARV* 282, 29; Bloesch *FAS* pl. 27, 1, p. 96, no. 1; *ARV*[2] 430, 29 and p. 1653; Wegner *Douris* 30 and 41, figs. 6–7 (A-B) and 8 (I); *Beazley Add*[2] 236; Korshack fig. 43 (detail of A); Buitron-Oliver *Douris* no. 49.

Dimensions: width 34.5; diam. 27.1; diam. of tondo 13.9; ht. 9.9; diam. of exterior ground line 11.5; diam. of foot 9.2.

Condition: made up from frr.; four pairs of ancient repair holes; three major rim frr. missing, one large chip from the centre of the tondo and other smaller chips.

Description

INTERIOR: athlete at altar.
A naked athlete bends forward towards an altar. His right hand is outstretched over the altar, his left is behind his back and holds a boxer's thong (red) – preliminary sketch shows the thongs close up against his buttocks. His trunk is shown in three-quarter back view, with the head inclined, thus obscuring the lower part of his face. The altar has a volute corner.

INSCRIPTION: +AIRESTRATOSKALOS
Border: single reserved line.

EXTERIOR: boxers.
Side A (L): two pairs of boxers fighting and a trainer. Of the pair of boxers on the left, the one on the right is seen in back view, with a fully foreshortened view of the right foot. The boxers' left arms cross, their right hands are held back for a blow; both have red thongs tied round their hands and wrists. The bearded trainer in the centre, clad in a himation, holds a trainer's forked stick in his right hand, while with his left hand he signals to the boxers on the right, presumably to stop the contest. Of this pair, the one on the left has his arms outstretched as he towers over his fallen opponent. This defeated boxer is down on his left knee, his face, torso and right leg all frontal. He has raised one finger of his right hand in a gesture of surrender.

INSCRIPTION: ΔORIՏ[EΛ]RAΦՏEN

Side B (U): pair of boxers fighting, a trainer and two boxers with their thongs. Of the fighting boxers, the one on the extreme left has a frontal right leg, the other is seen from the back with his right foot fully foreshortened. The difference between this pair and the similar pair on side A lies chiefly in the position of the arms of the boxer on the left (right hand missing). In the centre, a bearded trainer moves to the right but turns his head (face very damaged) back and down to the left, towards the fighting boxers. He is clad in a himation and holds a trainer's forked stick in his right hand. To the right of the trainer stands an athlete straightening one of his red thongs. His right arm is extended and his right leg is shown fully frontal. On the extreme right another athlete holds a red thong in either hand.

INSCRIPTION: KALOՏ
Ground line: a single reserved line.

Relief line contours throughout (except hair); dilute glaze for minor interior markings; added red for inscriptions; reserved line outside lip only.

c. 500–490 BC.

Comment:
Signed by Douris as painter. Beazley placed the cup in his 'early middle' phase (period 2) with its typical 'bare' decoration; Buitron-Oliver allocates it to her Transitional II. Potting attributed by Bloesch to Python.

Of the several athletic cups from Douris' early middle period the fragmentary cup divided between the Louvre, Amsterdam and perhaps Erlangen (see *Beazley Add*² 236 on *ARV*² 430, 37 etc.) is the closest in terms of the exterior subject, for there pairs of boxers are also divided by trainers. The figure of the boxer on the tondo seems to be offering a prayer either before drawing his lot (cf. Lucian, *Hermotimus* 40) or before his turn in the competition (since there is no boar on the altar, the scene does not seem to be connected with the swearing of the oath, see Pausanias v, 24, 9 and, for a representation of the cult statue, D. Bailey, *Jewellery Studies* 5 [1991] 33–4 no. 2). It is a quiet scene of private communion and the use of the three-quarter back view with the lower part of the face obscured helps to evoke this. Lone athletes are rare in the tondi of Douris' larger athlete cups – he seems normally to prefer to place a draped figure of a trainer or admirer (but for an exception: *Beazley Add*² 393–4).

For boxing techniques see most recently Poliakoff *Combat Sports* 80–5. For the pair of boxers on the right of side A compare the fragmentary cup by Onesimos in a Centre Island collection (*Para* 360, 28 *bis*; Poliakoff 30 fig. 14).

For the *kalos* name Chairestratos see *ARV*² 1569–70 and *Beazley Add*² 393–4. It occurs only on Dourian vases and only in periods 1 and 2.

19 (pls. 26–7 and fig. 7a)

CUP: GR 1843.11–3.13 (*BM Cat Vases* E 48)

From Vulci, Cavalupo area E ('fam. Ania'), December 1828; Canino collection.
Bought of the Principessa di Canino, 1843.

Bibliography:
Mus. Étrusque no. 183; De Witte *Fabricants* 32 no. xviii, 1 and 6; Klein *M*² 158 no. 16; Hartwig *M* 613–14, 686 no. 25; Murray *DGV* no. 29; Frucht *Duris* 14 no. 18 and 49–53; Pottier *Douris* 53 fig. 11 and p. 75; Hoppin i, 238–9 no. 16; *AV* 202, 40; *ARV* 283, 46; Bloesch *FAS* 98, no. 13; *ARV*² 431, 47 and p. 1653; Brommer *V*³ 211 etc.; Wegner *Duris* 106–16, figs. 23–5; Seki *U* 74 no. 335, p. 79 with note 172, pl. 48, 3 (underside) and pl. 57, 4 (detail of Phaia); J. Neils, *The Youthful Deeds of Theseus* (Rome 1987) pl. 9, figs. 43–5; *Beazley Add*² 236; Carpenter *Art and Myth* figs. 238–9 (A–B); *LIMC* vi pl. 62, Krommyo no. 1, and pl. 319, Minotauros no. 23; Buitron-Oliver *Douris* no. 87.

Dimensions: width 41.0; diam. 32.9; diam. of tondo 21.5; diam. of exterior ground line 14.6.

Condition: made up from frr.; five rim frr. missing and other chips; alien foot removed.

Description
INTERIOR: Theseus and the Minotaur.
On the left is Theseus dressed in a short, transparent chiton with a red fillet round his head (loop at back), a petasos with red ties over his shoulder and a scabbard at his left hip suspended from a baldric drawn with a triple relief line. His hair is drawn with vertical wavy relief lines over his brow and horizontal wavy relief line contours over his neck; there is a dilute glaze line above and below his eye. With his left hand he restrains the Minotaur's left wrist; in his right hand is a sword with which he thrusts at the creature. The Minotaur is almost down on his right knee; his raised left hand holds a small stone, his right reaches for Theseus' sword arm. He has a bull's head (rippling strokes in dilute glaze on face) and tail and a skin covered with dotted circles. There is a dilute line at both wrists and ankles which marks off the decorated skin from the hands and feet as if it was a leotard. There is a reserved exergue.

INSCRIPTION: ΛORIՏEΛPAΦՏEN
Border: false maeanders (alternately clockwise and anticlockwise, ten- to twelve-stroke) alternating with blackened cross-squares.

EXTERIOR: the deeds of Theseus.

Side A (L): sow and Sinis.
On the left the wild sow of Krommyon is at bay before Theseus. She is already wounded by Theseus' spear, which passes through her shoulders (the end of the spear is not drawn and one may presume that it has broken off in the beast's charge). She has five teats and the curl of her tail serves double duty for the spiral at the end of the floral decoration under the handle. In the background behind the sow is a woman. She wears a peplos (the dots on it are perhaps intended to indicate the roughness of the fabric) with a black border incised with sigmas and zs, which is fastened at her waist with a belt also decorated with sigmas, and

a cloak over her shoulders (two line border). She tears at her hair, which is drawn with separate strands presumably to indicate that it is grey or streaked with grey, with her right hand and stretches out her left towards Theseus in supplication (most of arm missing). Theseus wears a transparent short chiton and has a cloak (line border) wrapped round his left arm in hunting fashion. His left hand (now missing) held the scabbard of the sword that he wields in his right. He is seen in back view so that the tip of his chin is hidden by his left shoulder and has a red hair-band with a loop at the back (relief lines in his hair as on I).

Towards the right are Sinis, the pine-bender, and Theseus. Sinis is down, his left leg outstretched and frontal, his right bent up sharply under him. His left wrist is pinioned by Theseus, his right vainly grips a stone on the ground. His mouth is open and his teeth bared. His hair is combed upwards over his brow (relief lines). In the background is a tree with red leaves; in it are hung his cloak (line border) and pilos (brim vertical on the left). Theseus, clad in transparent short chiton and a red hair-band and with a petasos with red ties on his shoulders and a sword and scabbard at his left hip (hilt perhaps in the form of a bird's head; red strap), pulls down the branch of a pine tree (scaly bark in dilute glaze) with red leaves in his left hand as he holds Sinis with his right. Theseus' torso and right leg are shown as frontal.

Side B (U): Skiron and Kerkyon.

On the left Athena moves away to the left, her right arm raised, but turns her head back to the right to look at the scene. She wears a transparent long chiton, a himation with a line border, a scaly aegis with black snake fringe (dilute glaze dot in each scale) and a helmet, and cradles a spear in her left arm. The frontlet of her helmet has a tiny pattern of crossed squares, set alternately up and down; the metal spear head and butt are carefully rendered. Theseus wears a transparent short chiton and a double red hair-band (hair as on I). He has a petasos with red ties on his shoulder and a sword with a duck's head pommel in its scabbard hung at his left hip from a triple relief line strap. He is attempting to loosen Skiron's grip on the rock by pulling his right leg and the wrist of his right arm that passes round the back of the rock. In the shallow water at the base of the rock waits a turtle. Skiron is drawn with frontal right leg, torso and rather awkward three-quarter face. His teeth are shown; he has relief lines in his hair and two furrows of dilute glaze on his brow. The wavy dilute wash at the base of the rock is no doubt intended to represent the sea. It goes over Skiron's left hand and wrist, thereby suggesting perhaps that they are already under water. The top right of the rock and part of his right arm are missing. Partly obscured, at the bottom left of the rock, is Skiron's *podanipter*.

On the right Theseus and Kerkyon wrestle. The beardless Theseus bends forward (red hair-band; hair as on I), his arms locked around Kerkyon's body as he lifts him off the ground. The bearded Kerkyon (hair as I) similarly has his arms round Theseus, but in vain. His right leg is seen in back view with the sole of the foot showing. Behind Theseus is a tree with red leaves on which he has hung his cloak and sword. The ends of the branches on the right and the back of Theseus' head, together with the hump of his shoulders, are missing.

At either handle: floral complex with a circumscribed palmette either side of the handles and a large and a small palmette addorsed under the handles; spiral terminals and dots (see fig. 2a).

Ground line: single reserved line.

Relief line contours throughout (double for hair); dilute glaze for minor interior markings; reserved line inside and outside lip; added red for inscriptions.

c. 485–480 BC.

Comment: Signed by Douris as painter. Beazley placed the cup in his middle period (period 3: Hippodaman), Buitron-Oliver in her Middle I. Bloesch attributed the potter work to Python.

For the deeds of Theseus see most recently F. Brommer, *Theseus* (Darmstadt 1982); Schefold *Urkönige* 230–51; and Neils *op. cit.* This is the only Theseid cycle cup decorated by Douris. The combination of the cycle with the death of the Minotaur recurs on a number of roughly contemporary cups (*ARV*[2] 413, 25; 192, 107) and is echoed on some much later cups when it usually occurs as the tondo surrounded by a zone. The Minotaur's apparently eye-covered skin, which is reminiscent of Argos and was already noted by Smith (*BM Cat Vases* iii p. 73), might suggest inspiration from dramatic costume.

Douris repeats the struggle with Skiron on the tondi of two late cups (*ARV*[2] 438, 129 and 130). Here the scheme remains basically the same, only the head of Skiron is now drawn fully frontal. Kerkyon is being lifted off the ground in a waist-lock (see Poliakoff *Combat Sports* 40), which is presumably the manoeuvre that he is said to have invented (Eustathios on *Iliad* 23, 730) and was used on him in turn by Theseus (cf. *ARV*[2] 115, 3; and, probably, 191, 104). Apollodoros (*Epitome* I, 1) records that the sow of Krommyon was called Phaia after her aged nurse (see now E. Simantoni-Bournia in *LIMC* VI 139–142). A woman is often seen in representations of the scene, regularly elderly (on Douris' cup the grey or greying hair might allude to the name Phaia which means grey) and wearing a peplos, but on a cup in Madrid painted by Aison (*ARV*[2] 1174, 1) she is named Krommyo, perhaps the local nymph (see Brommer *Theseus* 9–13, but see Simantoni-Bournia *loc. cit.*). The pilos shown in the branches above Sinis is a regular attribute of Theseus; here, however, one should perhaps think of it as Sinis' since Theseus already has a petasos on his back.

Douris' arrangement of the adventures encountered by Theseus on his way from Troizene does not quite follow the geography reconstructed by Brommer (*Theseus* 76 fig. 11), but Sinis and the sow should occur before Skiron and Kerkyon, hence the allotment of A and B here. Athena's presence on the later side of the cup, moving away from the events suggests that she should be thought of as leading Theseus on to Athens, his destination.

For the podanipter in general see Ginouvès *Balaneutikè* 61–75; in connection with Theseus and Skiron p. 71.

20 (pls. 48–9 and fig. 7b)

Cup: GR 1843.11–3.15 (*BM Cat Vases* E 49) and Rome, Villa Giulia fr.
From Vulci, Cavalupo area E ('fam. Ania'), March 1829; Canino collection.
Bought of the Principessa di Canino, 1843.

Bibliography:
Mus. Étrusque no. 1184; De Witte *Fabricants* 32 xviii no. 2; Klein *M*[2] 154 no. 7; Hartwig *M* 605–6, 685 no. 18; Murray *DGV* no. 30; Frucht *Duris* 15 no. 23 and 58–61; Hoppin i 240–1 no. 17; *AV* 203, 51; *ARV* 283, 50; Beazley *CF* 33 no. 11, Villa Giulia fr., pl. Z, 25; Bloesch *FAS* 98 no. 15; *ARV*[2] 432, 52; Wegner *Duris* 95–7, fig. 30 a–b (A–B); Robertson *HGA* 232 and pl. 78 c (A); M. Robertson, *MüJb* 27 (1976) 40 and 37 fig. 11; J. Bazant, *Les Citoyens sur les Vases Athéniens* (Prague 1985) pl. 39 fig. 65 (A); Open Univ. ii figs. 44 (I), 45 (A–B) and 46 (detail B); *Beazley Add*[2] 237; Robertson *Art of Vase-painting* 87 with fig. 79 on p. 89; Buitron-Oliver *Douris* no. 96.

Dimensions: width 39.6; diam. 31.5; diam. of tondo 20.4; ht. 12.5; diam. of exterior ground line 15.0; diam. of foot plate 11.5.

Condition: made up from frr.; missing fr. under one handle recognized by Beazley in the Villa Giulia.

Description
INTERIOR: komast.
A bearded komast moves to the right with head turned back to left. He wears a chlamys over his upper arms and a red apicate fillet in his hair. He holds a cup back in his right hand and a knotty stick across his body in his left. Relief line for vertical strokes of fringe over forehead and for horizontal lines of hair tied up at back (relief line fringe for beard); dilute glaze line above and below eye. Preliminary sketch indicates that the chlamys was intended to be longer on the right.

INSCRIPTION: ΛΟRIϟΕΛΡΑΦϟΕΝ (retr.)
Border: alternating false maeander (twelve-stroke, alternately clockwise and anticlockwise) and blackened cross-square.

EXTERIOR: symposium.
Side A (L): three banqueters on couches attended by two boys. On the couch on the left a bearded man reclines to the left, his head turned back to the right. He wears a himation over his left shoulder and around his waist and legs and a red apicate fillet in his hair. He rests against a folded cushion decorated with pairs of stripes, while he grips a cup in his left hand and holds out his right hand palm upward as if holding another. Above him hang two cups, seen from underneath, and a flat-bottomed oinochoe. His couch rests on a dais, the corner of which is visible on the left, and in front of it (ie. alongside) is a three-legged table on which are three red garlands.

In front of the left hand end of the central couch stands a naked boy with a red fillet in his hair. He holds an oinochoe in his right hand and stretches out his left hand towards the symposiast on the central couch. Here a bearded man reclines to the left (cushion decorated with a pair of stripes and a stripe flanked by pairs of lines). He holds out a cup high in his right hand; his left hand is empty. He wears a himation in the same manner as the first symposiast, but has a thick reserved fillet (alternately vertical line and rows of dots at each bunching) in his hair. Above him and the boy hang two footless oinochoai and a cup seen from underneath. Alongside his couch is a three-legged table over which hang three red garlands.

The couch on the right is seen in end view from the back. On it reclines a bearded man with a himation round his waist and a red apicate fillet in his hair. He is seen from the back, his left elbow resting on his cushion and his raised right knee splayed out to the right. He holds a cup up to his lips in his left hand and gestures with his right to the boy who stands between him and the central couch. Either side of the end of the couch project the ends of his striped cushion. Alongside the couch is a three-legged table, also seen from the end, the two legs in profile in the foreground, the third in back view beyond. The naked boy attendant who stands on the left of the couch, behind the table, has a frontal torso and left leg. His hair has a long straight fringe of relief lines over his neck. He holds an oinochoe in his left hand, tipped down so that the trefoil mouth is shown foreshortened. He gestures with his right hand as he looks at the symposiast. Above these two figures are two cups seen from underneath and a small footless oinochoe.

INSCRIPTIONS: ΚΑLΟϟ ΚΑLΟϟ

Side B (U): three couches and one boy attendant.
The couch and its occupant on the left repeats the form of the central couch on side A, although the symposiast's himation has a line border and his cushion pairs of lines. As on the first couch on side A, the corner of the dais is visible. Above this couch hang two cups seen from underneath and a footed oinochoe.

At the left hand end of the central couch stands a naked boy with a red hair-band, holding a small chytra in his right hand as he holds up his left hand. The bearded man on this couch repeats the scheme of the central couch on side A, save that here he holds a cup in his *left* hand and extends his *right* arm out towards the boy. From the fingers of his right hand hangs a red circlet. Above hang a footless oinochoe, a cup seen from underneath and a small chytra.

The couch on the right is seen from behind, as on side A. The man here, however, holds a cup in his left hand as he leans on his left elbow, and his right hand is held out further to the left (no hair-band). The corner of the dais is visible and there is a three-legged table alongside the couch, but no attendant, nor are there any red garlands on the table and the cushion is plain. Above hang two cups seen from underneath and a small footless oinochoe.

INSCRIPTIONS: ΚΑLΟϟ ΚΑLΟϟ

At either handle: floral complex with a circumscribed palmette either side of the handles and a large and a small palmette addorsed under the handles; spiral terminals and dots (see fig. 2b).
Ground line: single reserved line.
Graffiti under foot: see fig. 3j.

Relief line contours throughout (double for hair, except on A1); dilute glaze for minor interior markings; reserved line inside and outside lip; added red for inscriptions.

c. 485–480 BC.

Comment: Signed by Douris as painter; placed by Beazley in his middle period (period 3, Hippodaman) and by Buitron-Oliver in her Middle I. Attributed by Bloesch to the potter Python.

All the cups held by the symposiasts have offset lips and the stem of the foot does not continue the contour of the bowl. They may be of metal or of clay, if of clay perhaps of the so-called Acrocup type (see most recently K. Vierneisel and B. Kaeser [eds.], *Kunst der Schale – Kultur des Trinkens* [Munich 1990] 180–1). The presence of chytra is also ambiguous, for, although chytra are regularly cooking pots of coarse fabric, they were sometimes imitated in black glaze and bronze (e.g. GR 1864.10–7.336 [black glaze]; GR 1882.10–19.18 [bronze]). See further *Agora xii* 224–6. Chytra are also held by the servant boys on three other Dourian symposia (*ARV*^{2} 432, 55 and 58; 438, 140; 792, 53) and are to be seen hung up on a head kantharos, a late work of Douris (Swiss priv., ex Holger Termer, Galerie Neuendorf: *Kunst der Antike* [Hamburg 1978] no. 10; see also J.R. Guy, *Arts in Virginia* 21:2 [1981] 6 and 8). The appearance of these small chytra at symposia suggests the serving of warmed wine, perhaps heavily spiced.

Cups hung up and viewed from underneath seem to have been particularly liked by Douris. They recur in symposium and komos scenes on a good number of Dourian cups: see **23** (E 50) and **22** (E 53); and *ARV*^{2} 432, 53–6; 436, 98; 438, 140; Centre Island, private. They also occur in a school scene (*ARV*^{2} 431, 48), in scenes involving warriors (*ARV*^{2} 435, 92–3 and 436, 110) and in what seems to be a mixed conversation scene (*ARV*^{2} 800, 7). The idea is sometimes imitated by contemporary painters (e.g. **56** [E 70]) and Early Classical artists (e.g. *ARV*^{2} 258, 21, Copenhagen Painter; *ARV*^{2} 567, 3, Leningrad Painter), but it also recurs later (e.g. Vienna IV 824: *CVA* 2 pl. 89, 1–3). There can be no doubt that cups were in fact hung up on hooks on the wall (cf. the Tomba dei Rilievi, where even the hooks are shown: H. Blanck and G. Proietti, *La Tomba dei Rilievi di Cerveteri* [Rome 1986] pl. 6a, 15 c).

The symposium is first represented by Douris on the very early cup in the Vatican (*ARV*^{2} 427, 2; compare also frr. in a Centre Island private collection, attributed by D. von Bothmer) and here the participants recline on the ground-line in the manner of many late sixth-century symposium scenes. Participants reclining on a couch set on a dais and accompanied by a table first appear in the works of Douris on a 'bare' cup in the Louvre (*ARV*^{2} 43c, 36 with 345, 68 and 434, 82; see *Beazley Add*^{2} 236). This becomes the norm on middle cups (e.g. *ARV*^{2} 432, 53 and 55 and 57) and was imitated by Douris' followers (e.g. *ARV*^{2} 432, 58 and *ARV*^{2} 438, 140; both now attributed by J.R. Guy to his Painter of London E 55; and two earlyish works of the Euaion Painter, *ARV*^{2} 792, 48 and 51).

For the motif of the couch seen from one end compare **23** (E 50), with commentary, and Florence 3922 (*ARV*^{2} 432, 55). For the thick reserved headbands see on **24** (E 54). On boys at symposia see J. Bremmer in *Sympotica* 135–48.

The graffiti appear to be Etruscan: they may have recorded ownership.

21

(pls. 30–1 and fig. 7c)

Cup: GR 1843.11–3.53 (*BM Cat Vases* E 52)
From Vulci, Cucumella area C ('fam. Fepia'), March 1829; Canino collection.
Bought of the Principessa di Canino, 1843.

Bibliography:
Mus. Étrusque no. 1435; Hartwig *M* 620 no. 3, 686 no. 45; Murray *DGV* no. 32; Hoppin i, 282 no. 71; *AV* 202, 37; *ARV* 284, 58; Bloesch *FAS* 97 no. 6; *ARV*^{2} 432, 59; Wegner *Duris* 176–9; *Beazley Add*^{2} 237; Buitron-Oliver *Douris* no. 105.

Dimensions: width 38.5; diam. 30.2; diam. of tondo 20.3; ht. 11.8; diam. of exterior ground line 12.7; diam. of foot plate 11.1.

Condition: made up from frr.; foot was mended in antiquity with four pairs of rivets; one small rim fr. and one wall fr. missing, together with a couple of chips.

Description
INTERIOR: a standing man.
A bearded man stands to the left, but turns his head back to the right. Relief lines over brow and along neck contour; relief line curl under front of beard. His chest is shown frontal. He wears a himation which is draped over his left shoulder and a red apicate fillet in his hair. He holds a knotty stick in his right hand; his left arm, probably akimbo, is hidden in his himation. On the right a sponge, aryballos and, in front, a net bag with a tail hang from a red loop.

INSCRIPTION: HOΓAIΣKAΛOΣ (retr.)
Border: alternating spiral maeander (twelve-stroke core; alternately clockwise and anticlockwise; additional unit at one o'clock) and blackened cross-square.

EXTERIOR: victor, youths, boys and men.

Side A (U): victor, youth, boy and two men. On the left a youth in a himation holds out a red circlet in his hands towards a boy. The youth has a red apicate fillet in his own hair (relief line strokes over brow and neck) and a plain stick rests loosely against his arm and chest. The naked boy facing him already has a long red fillet with loop and ties in his hair (relief lines over brow) and a second, longer and thicker one, a *tainia*, is tied round the biceps of his left arm and trails on the ground. In either hand he holds a red branch, perhaps of olive. In the centre stands a himation-clad man leaning to the right on a plain stick and holding out a small red flower in his right hand to a boy. The latter figure, also clad in himation holds out a small red flower too. Both figures have red apicate fillets in their hair (relief lines in hair as A1). On the far right is a man in a himation leaning on a knotty stick. Under his left arm is tucked a pad of drapery that loops over his forearm, and his back is shown in three-quarter view. He holds a small red flower in his left hand and has a red apicate fillet in his hair (relief lines in hair as on A1).

INSCRIPTION: HOΓAIS KAΛOS

Side B (L): three youths and two boys. On the left a youth in a himation stands to the left but with his head turned back to the right (front of head missing; relief lines in hair as I). He has a red fillet in his hair and holds a knotty stick in his right hand. In front of him hang a sponge, an aryballos and a net bag. A boy, closely wrapped in a himation, faces him, a red apicate fillet in his hair (relief lines in hair as I). In the centre stands a youth, his right leg and torso frontal, his head turned to the left. He wears a himation and a red apicate fillet in his hair (relief lines in hair as I) and in his left hand holds a plain stick that crosses his body. He holds up his right hand with fingers spread. A boy moves towards him, but turns his head back to the right. A himation is draped over his left shoulder, but his right hand holds a bunch of folds so that most of his body is revealed. He has a red apicate fillet in his hair (relief lines in hair as I). On the far right stands a youth in a himation and red apicate fillet, holding a plain stick in his right hand.

INSCRIPTION: HOΓAIS KAΛOSNAI+I

At either handle: floral complex with a circumscribed palmette either side of the handles and a large and a small palmette addorsed under the handles; spiral terminals and dots (see fig. 2c).
Ground line: single reserved line.
Graffiti under foot: see fig. 3l.

Relief line contour throughout (double for hair); dilute glaze for minor interior markings; reserved line inside and outside lip; added red for inscriptions.

c. 485–480 BC.

Comment: Attributed by Hartwig to Douris; placed by Beazley in that artist's middle period (period 3, Hippodaman) and by Buitron-Oliver in her Middle I. Bloesch attributed the potting to Python – see further on **26** (E 51).

The presence of sponges and aryballoi place the scenes inside and out in the *palaistra*. The boy on the left of side A is adorned with a victor's trappings. The two bearded men who surround the boy on the right are probably courting him by attempting to exchange flowers (cf. Koch-Harnack 160–1). This theme appears to continue on side B, as is suggested by the movement of the himation by the boy on the right: compare the boy on the left of one side of a cup by Makron (*ARV*^{2} 471, 196). This mixture of *palaistra* and courting is to be found on a number of other cups by Douris. On two earlier cups (*ARV*^{2} 430, 33; Wegner *Duris* figs. 14 and 16. *ARV*^{2} 431, 38–42, associated by Wegner [*Duris* 135], Guy adding another Villa Giulia fr.) a boy victor also appears. On the later examples (*ARV*^{2} 436, 99 with *Beazley Add*^{2} 238; *ARV*^{2} 437, 114; *ARV*^{2} 437, 128, side B), and on one by a follower (*ARV*^{2} 432, 60 with *Beazley Add*^{2} 237, now attributed by J.R. Guy to his Painter of London E 55) the attraction of a victor is omitted. If all the iconographic clues are taken literally, the occurrence of a victory ceremony of some sort within the palaistra may suggest that the competition was not associated with one of the Athenian festivals.

For attributes of victors (Olympic) see W.W. Hyde, *Olympic Victor Monuments and Greek Athletic Art* (Washington 1921) 148–61. A number of scenes on vases showing victors have been collected in T.B.L. Webster, *Potter and Patron in Classical Athens* (London 1972) 152–7: branches, tainiai and wreaths are common adornments (rarer are the special helmets on *ARV*^{2} 446, 263 and 455, 10).

Empty net bags are sometimes seen hung up with sponge, aryballos and scraper (or being carried with them) on Dourian cups (*ARV*^{2} 431, 40; 432, 60; 437, 114; 441, 187. Cf. also *ARV*^{2} 326, 93 [Onesimos] and *ARV*^{2} 348, 3 [Antiphontic]). They are probably being used to hold or carry equipment for the palaistra, see further on **38** (E 62).

Graffito (a), a ligature of *M* and *Z*, is probably mercantile (Greek or Etruscan); (b) seems Etruscan and is perhaps part of a name.

22 (pls. 32–3 and fig. 7d)

Cup: GR 1843.11–3.45 (*BM Cat Vases* E 53)
From Vulci, Cucumella area C ('fam. Fepia'), April 1829; Canino collection.
Bought of the Principessa di Canino, 1843.

Bibliography: *Mus. Étrusque* no. 1538; Murray *DGV* no. 33; Hartwig *M* 622 no. 9, 686 no. 51; Hoppin i 282 no. 72; *AV* 203, 49; *ARV* 283, 76; Bloesch *FAS* 99 no. 29; *ARV*^{2} 435, 87; Wegner *Duris* 174–6; *Beazley Add*^{2} 238; Buitron-Oliver *Douris* no. 131.

Dimensions: width 37.0; diam. 29.1; diam. of tondo 19.2; diam. of exterior ground line 10.9

Condition: made up from frr.; one large and two small frr. missing; alien foot removed.

Description

INTERIOR: seated man at altar.
A bearded man sits to the right on a plain stool clad in a himation (black border). With his right hand he pours a libation from a phiale over an altar, his left rests on the crutch of a plain stick. He wears a reserved apicate fillet and has high relief dots for the curls of his hair below it. His mouth is slightly open, suggesting the prayer that goes with a libation. The phiale is of the lobed or bossed type (relief line lobes, dilute glaze dashes within): the wine of the libation being poured is shown by a splash of red that

covers the end of the phiale and the edge of the altar. The altar has two further splashes of red on it, presumably from an earlier sacrifice. Its top has an ovolo moulding above which is a volute-ended crown and a fire-brick. In the field on the right hangs a cup, seen from underneath. On the left of the man are hung a sponge, aryballos (circumscribed cross) and net bag with a loop at the bottom. Reserved exergue with a line at the top.

INSCRIPTION: HOΓAIϟ KAΛOϟ
Border: alternating false maeander (twelve-stroke, alternately clockwise and anticlockwise; repeated clockwise unit at three o'clock) and blackened cross-square.

EXTERIOR: komos.
Side A (U): four dancing komasts and another. On the far left, a man moves to the right, but with his head turned back and down to the left. He wears a himation with a black border (as all the other komasts on the exterior) over his shoulders, his left hand holding up a bunch of folds above his left shoulder. His right hand must have held the plain stick (fr. with hand, shoulder and touch of forehead, with palmette, missing), which crosses his body. He, like all the other komasts, wears a thick reserved headband decorated with wavy dilute glaze lines and has relief dots over neck and forehead. The next komast moves to the right, but again looks back and down to the left. He has his himation over his shoulders and similarly picks at the folds on his left shoulder. He holds a large black skyphos in his right hand in front of his chest. It has a reserved lip and a reserved band below handle level. His right leg is shown in an awkward three-quarter view and his torso is frontal. In the centre a dancing man is shown in a particularly lively pose. He wears a himation over his shoulders and up over the back of his head. His legs are splayed, the right one bent up high; his torso frontal. His hands are clasped together on the right, the fingers and thumbs clearly entwined, index fingers raised. To the right of him a man moves to the left, head turned back to the right and up. His left arm and shoulder are covered with a himation; his right arm is bent up with the fingers slightly spread. His torso is frontal and his left foot seen in three-quarter frontal view. On the far right a man wearing a himation in the normal fashion moves to the left. He holds a cup in his left hand, handle towards the viewer. His right arm is raised, as if directing the dancers.

Side B (L): five komasts, one with frontal head. On the far left is a man moving to the right, but with his head turned back and down to the left. He has a himation over his shoulders (his left shoulder is missing) and holds a cup by its handle in his left hand (index finger pointed). He puts his right hand up to his thick reserved headband. To the right of him a man moves to the right, seen fully in profile, with a himation over his right upper arm and left shoulder. He holds a cup out in his right hand. His left hand is also outstretched, as if to catch any drips. In the centre a man with a himation round his shoulders moves to the left. He holds a skyphos in his left hand, which he seems to look down at with intense concentration, and holds up his right hand. His penis is infibulated. On the right a man moves away to the right, but looks back and down to the left, his torso frontal. He holds a black cup in his left hand and holds his right up in the air. On the far right a man moves to the left, a himation round his shoulders. His head is fully frontal. He holds a cup in his left hand by the foot (handle outwards) and his right hand reaches up to his thick headband.

At either handle: floral complex with a circumscribed palmette either side of the handles and a pair of addorsed palmettes under the handles; spiral terminals and dots (see fig. 2d).
Ground line: single reserved line.

Relief line contour throughout (double for hair); dilute glaze for minor interior markings; reserved line inside and outside lip; inscriptions in added red.

c. 480 BC.

Comment: Attributed by Hartwig to Douris. Beazley placed the cup in that artist's middle period (period 3, Hippodaman); Buitron-Oliver puts it in her Middle II. Bloesch attributed the potting to Python.

Douris seems to have depicted the *komos* rather less frequently than many of his contemporary cup-painters. The members of this *komos* are solely bearded men: this restriction recurs on three other cups of the same period (**23** [E 54]; *ARV*[2] 435–6, 95; Tarquinia 87784, Ferrari *Tarquinia* no. 53, pl. 76, 2) and on one early middle piece (*ARV*[2] 431, 45, also with a frontal-headed komast at the end of the queue). On a transitional, period 4, cup (*ARV*[2] 438, 133) two youths are included.

The two figures on the left of side A seem to be dancing in unison. The central figure is a real *tour de force*. The pose of the legs, splayed with one raised, can be traced back to Euphronios (see on **2** [E 46]); for a contemporary occurrence compare a cup by Makron (Getty S.80.AE.251 [Bareiss 51]: *Bareiss Checklist* no. 158). The motif of the clasped hands is probably taken from the dance called the *oklasma*: see F. Wege, *Der Tanz in der Antike* (Halle 1926) 97–8, figs. 148–56; A.E. Kalpaxis in H.A. Cahn and E. Simon (eds.), *TAINIA. Festschrift für Roland Hampe* (Mainz 1980) 299. It recurs on a Dourian cup in Basel (*ARV*[2] 1653 add as 10 *bis*; *CVA Basel* 2, pls. 21–2).

For the net bags see on **21** (E 52) etc. For cups seen from underneath see on **20** (E 49). For fire-bricks see on **45** (E 65). For infibulation by athletes see on **53** (E 818). Komasts, however, are also, on occasion, to be seen infibulated (e.g. **24** [E 54]). Sweet *Sport and Recreation* (132 fig. 44) suggests that this is because the komast was 'in training'. Satyrs too are sometimes shown infibulated (*ARV*[2] 446, 262, satyrs cavorting; 501, 35, satyr arming).

23

(pl. 34 and fig. 8a)

Cup: GR 1892.5–18.1 (*BM Cat Vases* E 50)
From Falerii (Scavi Perez).
Bought of P. Hartwig, 1892.

Bibliography: Hartwig *M* 608–10 and 686 no. 41, pl. 67, 4; Hoppin i 282 no. 69; *AV* 203, 44; *ARV* 291, 174; Bloesch *FAS* 100, no. 37; *ARV*² 443, 227 and p. 1653; Wegner *Duris* 83–4; *Para* 375; *Beazley Add*² 240; Buitron-Oliver *Douris* no. 102.

Dimensions: diam. 19.7; diam. of tondo 14.4; restored ht. 9.0; diam. of foot plate 8.0.

Condition: made up from frr.; stem modern, foot may belong; left handle missing, together with two rim frr.; surface weathered.

Description

INTERIOR: symposiast.

A youth reclines on a couch seen from the back. He is shown in back view with his raised right knee splaying to the right. He wears a himation (two line border) around his waist and legs and has a red fillet in his hair. He rests on his left elbow, with a bunch of drapery tucked under his arm and showing on the left. He holds out a small cup in his right hand: it is seen from underneath, the foot in his hand, the body black, the handles and rim reserved. On either side of the head of the couch projects the end of the cushion against which the youth leans. On the left is a three-legged table, underneath which is suspended a food basket (red tassels below). Above the youth hangs a cup, seen from underneath; on the left hangs a footed oinochoe. The couch rests on a large reserved exergue.

INSCRIPTION: KAΛOΣ HIΓOΔAMAΣ

Border: alternating false maeander (ten-stroke, alternately clockwise and anticlockwise) and blackened cross-square (cross-square omitted at 3 o'clock).

Relief line contour throughout (double for hair); added red for inscriptions.

c. 485–480 BC.

Comment: Attributed by Hartwig to Douris; placed by Beazley in that artist's middle period (period 3, Hippodaman) and by Buitron-Oliver in her Middle I. Potting attributed by Bloesch to Python. The foot is certainly a Python foot, but it is possible that it does not belong.

For early discussions of the rear view of the couch see Beazley in *Studies Robinson* ii 75 with note. It is seen on two other cups by Douris (**20** [E 49]; and Florence 3922, *ARV*² 432, 55). It is also found on some Brygan cups (e.g. *ARV*² 372, 38; 402, 12). A rear view of a couch is seen on an earlier cup by Epiktetos in the British Museum (E 38: *ARV*² 72, 16; M. Robertson, *MüJb* 27 [1976] 37 fig. 10 with p 40–1) and on one of the frr. of a very early calyx-krater by the Kleophrades Painter (Copenhagen 13365 frr.: *ARV*² 185, 32; *CVA Copenhagen* p. 259, fig., the missing fr.). There are still earlier frr. in the collection of Dr. H.A. Cahn that also preserve a couch seen in rear view (Basel, Cahn 680 frr.; *Attische Meisterzeichnungen: Vasenfragmente der Sammlung Herbert A. Cahn, Basel* [Freiburg, Oct. 1988 – March 1989] 8 no. 25; see further D. Williams *New Perspectives* 292 with fig. 8 [one fr. only]). It is possible that the idea was developed by a Pioneer like Euphronios.

A second cup decorated inside only with the figure of a symposiast (not end-on) is to be found in a Centre Island private collection (attributed by D. von Bothmer).

The drawing of the cup that the symposiast holds out is particularly unusual. Cups with black bodies and reserved lips are occasionally seen in the works of other artists (e.g. *ARV*² 339, 57, Antiphon Painter). For cups seen from underneath see on **20** (E 49).

On Hippodamas see *ARV*² 1585 and *Beazley Add*² 395–6: he is praised on cups by both Douris and Makron and is usually presumed to be the *strategos* of 459/8 BC.

24 (pls. 35 and 36 a-b, fig. 8b)

CUP: GR 1843.11–3.4 (*BM Cat Vases* E 54)

From Vulci, Cucumella area C ("fam. Fepia"), March 1829; Canino collection.

Bought of the Principessa di Canino, 1843.

Bibliography: *Mus. Étrusque* no. 1525; Hartwig *M* 622 no. 10, 686 no. 52; Murray *DGV* no. 34; Hoppin i 282 no. 73; *AV* 205, 76; *ARV* 286, 85; Bloesch *FAS* 100 no. 30; *ARV*² 436, 96; Wegner *Duris* 170, figs. 32 (A) and 33 (I); Robertson *HGA* 231–2, pl. 78d; M. Robertson, *MüJb* 27 (1976) 35, 37 figs. 8, 10–11 (I, A-B); Robertson *Shorter HGA* 68 fig. 100 (I); Sweet *Sport and Recreation* 132 fig. 44; *Beazley Add*² 238; Robertson *Art of Vase-painting* 87 with fig. 76; Buitron-Oliver *Douris* no. 144.

Dimensions: width 37.7; diam. 33.0; diam. of tondo 21.0; ht. 10.7; diam. of exterior ground line 10.6; diam. of foot plate 10.5

Condition: made up from frr.; three rim frr. and small chips missing.

Description

INTERIOR: two komasts.

On the left a bearded komast moves to the right, a himation (black border) over his shoulders, a thick reserved fillet decorated with vertical zigzags in dilute glaze in his hair (relief dots in his hair over brow and relief lines over neck) and his penis infibulated. He holds a black skyphos (relief line just below handle level) out in front of him in his left hand and a black oinochoe down in his right hand. On the right another bearded komast with a himation over his shoulders and a thick reserved fillet decorated with vertical zigzags in dilute glaze in his hair (relief dots over brow and neck) moves to the right but turns back to the left to look at his companion and to put his right hand behind his back, perhaps to steady him: he holds a plain stick low in his left hand. There is a small reserved exergue.

INSCRIPTION: HOΓAIΣ KAΛOΣ

Border: pair of false maeander units (nine- to ten-stroke; one anticlockwise, the other clockwise) alternating with blackened cross-square (cross-square omitted at 6 o'clock).

EXTERIOR: komos.

Side A (L): five bearded komasts with drinking vessels, one cup is black. On the left a man fully draped in a himation (black border) and wearing a thick reserved fillet (decorated with vertical zigzags and pairs of dots in dilute glaze) moves to the right (line of relief dots over brow and neck). With his covered left hand he raises his skyphos; his right is raised inside his drapery up towards the back of his head. On the right of him another man similarly clad (only the himation is plain) moves to the right but turns back to look at his companion. Both hands are free of drapery and are raised, one towards his head. In the centre another man dressed in a himation with a black border and a thick reserved fillet (as A1) moves to the right, holding a cup up by the foot in either hand, handle outwards. He has a row of relief dots over his brow and a relief line over his neck. To the right of him stands a man in a plain himation and a thick red fillet (hair as A1, but with a relief line curl at tip of beard). His torso and left leg are frontal, his right leg is to the left and his head turned back to the right. He holds a black cup in his right hand and gestures with his left hand up to the right. On the far right is a man fully wrapped in a himation with a black border and wearing a red fillet (hair as A1). He moves to the right but turns his head and shoulders back to the left, as he holds a cup out in his right hand, handle outwards.

Side B (U): five bearded komasts.
On the left a komast, who wears a thick reserved fillet (as A1) and a himation with a black border draped over both shoulders, moves to the right (relief dots over brow, relief lines over neck). He holds a skyphos out in his left hand (the top is missing, along with the nose of this figure and the tips of the fingers of the next) and a cup close to his chest in his right, handle outwards. On the right another komast moves to the right but turns his head back to the left (hair as B1). He wears a plain himation and thick reserved fillet (decorated with vertical zigzags in dilute glaze) and his chest is frontal. He holds a cup out to the right in his left hand, handle outwards, while his right hand is outstretched to the left. In the centre is a komast, who has a himation (black border) draped over both shoulders and a thick reserved fillet (as B1) in his hair, and bends very slightly forward. He holds a deep cup-skyphos in his left hand, handle outwards, and gestures with his right up in front of his head (row of relief dots over brow and neck). On the right a komast with a plain himation over both shoulders and a thick reserved fillet (as B1) moves to the right, slightly swaying backwards, a cup in either hand, handles outwards (hair as B3; relief line curl at tip of beard). On the far right is a komast closely wrapped in a himation with a black border (hair as B3). He wears a thick reserved fillet (as I) and holds a cup in his drapery-covered left hand. His right hand is curled up inside his drapery in front of his chest.

At either handle: floral complex with a circumscribed palmette either side of the handles and a large and a small palmette addorsed under the handles; spiral terminals and dots (see fig. 2e).
Ground line: single reserved line.

Relief line contours throughout (double for hair); dilute glaze for minor interior markings; reserved band inside and outside lip; added red for inscriptions.

c. 480–475 BC.

Comment: Attributed by Hartwig to Douris; placed by Beazley in that artist's middle period (period 3, Hippodaman; the double maeander unit making it late in the period) and by Buitron-Oliver in her Middle III. Attributed by Bloesch to the potter Python.

For comments on the make-up of the *komos* see **22** (E 53). In addition, one might note that the motif of a man holding two cups recurs on a fr. in Tarquinia attributed to Douris by Ferrari (87784: Ferrari *Tarquinia* no. 53, pl. 76, 2). The 'calyx composition' of the tondo is particularly well balanced: it has been commented on by Robertson. Outside, the attention is drawn to the different drinking vessels being carried by the komasts, their different poses and the variation in their drapery.

For the thick reserved headbands with decoration in dilute glaze see most recently M. Blech, *Studien zum Kranz bei den Griechen* (Berlin 1982) 45–6, who argues that they are made of many small flowers. Visually, they appear to be some sort of textile, probably woollen, that can be pulled tight with drawstrings (cf. A. Krug, *Binden in der griechischen Kunst* [Hösel 1968] 15–19; E.R. Knauer, *Getty Vases* 2 (1986) 99 fn. 22). Cf. also **20** (E 49). For infibulation by komasts see on **22** (E 53), by athletes see on **53** (E 818).

25 (pl. 36 c–f)

Cup: GR 1952.12–2.11, Oxford 1927.4607 and Freiburg S 181 frr. From Orvieto. London fr. ex E.P. Warren, bought of Mrs. G. Redfern-Loades, 1952; Oxford part on loan from H. Stuart-Jones since 1903, given 1927.

Bibliography: London fr.: *ARV*[2] 437, 124; Buitron-Oliver *Douris* no. 166. Oxford fr.: *CVA Oxford* 2, pl. 57 nos. 16 and 27; *ARV* 535, 12; *ARV*[2] 801, 22.

Dimensions: diam. *c.* 20.0; length of London fr. 9.2.

Condition: rim and wall frr.

Description
INTERIOR: (Oxford and Freiburg frr.) part of a head, feet of a figure to the right and end of a stick; large reserved exergue.
Border: stopt maeander (five-stroke core, clockwise).

EXTERIOR: symposium.
A bearded man with a thick red hair-band reclines to the left, holding a *barbiton* lyre (one arm and edge of the box preserved). His himation is shown bunched under his left arm, as he leans against a striped cushion. Draped knees, a touch of hair contour and red hair-band from a second figure appear on the right. Above, and between the two figures, hangs a food basket with red hooped ties above and triple tassels below. The Freiburg fr. adds more of the cushion and more of the draped legs of the symposiast to the right, as well as the line of the couch and a touch of the ground line. The Oxford fr. is from the other side and shows a chalice under the couch.

Relief line contour throughout (only inner hair contour); dilute glaze for minor interior markings; reserved line inside lip only.

c. 480–475 BC.

Comment: The London fr. was attributed to Douris by Beazley and listed between his middle (period 3) and late (period 4) works. Buitron-Oliver calls it Middle to Late Transitional. The Oxford fr. was described by Beazley in *CVA Oxford* 2, p. 111, as being from the 'Following of Douris: near the painter of Munich 2660.' In *ARV* and *ARV*² he placed it in his list of unascribed pieces by followers of Douris. The association of the London fr. with that in Oxford is by Williams, the Freiburg part by Bothmer; the join is by Williams.

The scheme was clearly not as on **20** (E 49) with only one figure to a couch, but more like Florence V 48 (*ARV*² 432, 58, now attributed by J.R. Guy to his Painter of London E 55. Cf. also *ARV*² 438, 138 and 140) with two men on each couch. The chalice on the ground is a shape rarely found in pottery, except for the earlier Chiot series (see most recently A. Lemos, *Archaic Pottery of Chios* [Oxford 1991] 10–11 and 80–4): it should probably be thought of as being of metal.

The sickle form of the beard is rather unexpected in the work of Douris, as is the failure to use the double relief line contour for the hair. The form of the interior border, is to be found on some small, late cups by Douris himself (e.g. *ARV*² 444, 248), but on larger cups it appears more regularly among the works of the Oedipus Painter, both those attributed by Beazley and those added by Guy (for the Oedipus Painter see further on **28** [E 56]).

The provenance of the frr. is given by the Oxford part.

26 (pls. 37–8 and fig. 8c)

Cup: GR 1843.11–3.94 (*BM Cat Vases* E 51)
From Vulci; Canino collection.
Bought of the Principessa di Canino, 1843.

Bibliography:
Mus. Étrusque no. 2023; Hartwig *M* 620 no. 2, 686 no. 44; Murray *DGV* no. 31; Hoppin i 282 no. 70; *AV* 208, 115; *ARV* 296, 10; Bloesch *FAS* 98 no. 19, pl. 28, 1; *ARV*² 449, 4 and p. 1653; *Para* 376; T.B.L. Webster, *Athenian Culture and Society* (London 1973) pl. 10 (I); M. Meyer, *JdI* 103 (1988) 95 fig. 4 (I) and 104 fig. 8 (A).

Dimensions: width 37.3; diam. 28.7; diam. of tondo 18.9; ht. 12.5; diam. of exterior ground line 11.0; diam. of foot 10.5.

Condition: damage to left handle area only (one small rim fr. missing) and slight damage to centre of B, otherwise excellent condition.

Description

INTERIOR: woman

A woman, clad in a chiton, a himation with a black border and an ornate headscarf (decorated with double key-hole pattern, dots and linked triple dots), stands to the left, smelling the large rosebud that she holds up in her right hand. The bud is surrounded by tendrils drawn only with relief lines (see fig. 1c). Her left hand, within her himation, catches up a bunch of material. She wears a hoop earring, has relief dots in her hair and a dilute glaze line above and below her eye (dilute glaze nostril). Behind her, on the right, a kalathos (decorated with spiral maeanders and zs) rests on the ground and above it is hung a mirror with a graffito *G* or *L* on it. On the left of the woman is the end of a couch with a mattress decorated with dotted cross-hatching.

INSCRIPTION ΗΕΓΑΙϟΚΑΛΟϟ

Border: alternating false maeander (twelve-stroke; 11 o'clock to 7 o'clock clockwise, rest anticlockwise) and blackened saltire-square (saltire-square omitted at 7 o'clock).

EXTERIOR (L): men, youths and women in conversation.

Side A: three bearded men and two women. On the left a man in himation rests his right hand on top of a knotty stick as he holds out a purse to a woman. His hair has relief dots over the brow and relief line strokes over the neck; he has a red hair-band. The woman is dressed in chiton, himation and headscarf (relief lines in her hair over her brow) and holds an alabastron in her left hand. Her right hand is raised as if holding a flower. In the centre, a man stands to the right closely wrapped in his himation, a knotty stick leaning against his left arm. He holds out his left hand as if holding a flower, but with all fingers spread (hair as A1). Facing him is another woman in chiton, himation and headscarf. She also holds up her right hand, her fingers spread, but her thumb tucked in. On the far right is a man in a himation, his right hand holding a knotty stick, his left clutching a purse (hair as A1).

Side B (U): three youths and two women. On the left is a youth in a himation holding a knotty stick in his left hand (relief dots over brow and neck; red hair-band). Before him is a woman in chiton and himation who holds an alabastron in her left hand and gestures with her right hand. Her hair hangs down on her shoulders, but the ends are turned up in a bag (relief lines along hair below hair-band). In the centre, a himation-clad youth stands to the right (hair as on B1). He holds a knotty stick in his left hand and has raised his right hand up behind his head. In front of him hangs a mirror and facing him stands a woman. She is dressed in chiton and himation and gestures with her right hand. Her hair is held up in a loose bun by a red fillet (relief lines along hair below fillet). She seems to wear a hoop earring. On the far right is a youth in a himation holding a knotty stick in his right hand (hair as A1; red band).

At either handle: floral complex with a circumscribed palmette either side of the handles and a large and a small palmette addorsed under the handles; spiral terminals and dots (see fig. 2f).

Ground line: single reserved line.

Relief contour throughout (double for hair); dilute glaze for minor interior markings; reserved band inside and outside lip; added red for inscriptions.

c. 480–470 BC.

Comment: Hartwig attributed the cup to Douris; Smith followed this for the interior, but gave the exterior to 'some artist working under his influence' (*BM Cat Vases* iii p. 75). It was placed by Beazley in the manner of Douris with the additional comments 'as London E 55' (**27**) and 'with these two compare also the Harvard cup (p.436 no. 112)'. Beazley also compared a cup in Cleveland and a fr. in the Louvre with the Harvard piece (*ARV*[2] 436, 111; 437, 113 with *Beazley Add*[2] 239). Under London E 55 (**27**) Beazley wrote 'stiff imitation, late middle period'. Following on from these indications, J.R. Guy has convincingly attributed these pieces and others to his Painter of London E 55 (Guy *Followers of Douris* 8–11 and 25–8; see also the list in Buitron-Oliver *Douris*). Guy calls this cup 'still early'.

Bloesch attributed the potting to Python. He notes, however, that it does not have the characteristic step under the foot. This is also found on London E 52 (**21**) and Florence V 497 and V 48 (Bloesch nos. 3, 6 and 9; cf. also no. 23; Bloesch no. 21, **28** [E 56], is mistaken, the foot is alien). On London E 55 (**27**), which is lacking its foot, he comments that it has a comparable bowl and handles to London E 51 (**26**). The form of the foot of these cups, which also compares with that used by Bloesch's 'Nachahmer des Python', makes one wonder if they might also be the work of a follower of Python rather than by the master himself, just as they were painted by followers of Douris not by himself.

The women on this cup are all presumably hetairai; the men on the exterior are attempting to buy their services. The men on one side are all bearded, while the women they approach all wear headscarves; on the other side the youths approach women with uncovered heads. This differentiation appears quite deliberate, but its significance is unclear: perhaps the women with headscarves are older. It is also noticeable that only the men hold purses. For recent discussions of hetairai see D. Williams in A. Cameron and A. Kuhrt (eds.), *Images of Women in Antiquity* (London 1983) 92–106; D. Harvey in *Copenhagen Colloquium* 242–54. On purses see Koch-Harnack 161–71 and M. Meyer, *Jb* 103 (1988) 87–125.

It has been suggested that the hetairai on the exterior are bargaining with the men over a suitable price for their services, the arrangement of the fingers indicating the actual prices in obols (*BM Cat Vases* iii, 76; cf. also G. Neuman, *Gesten und Gebärden in der griechischen Kunst* [Berlin 1965] 13 with note 38; M. Price, *British Museum Society Bulletin* 52 [1986] 9, caption to upper fig. – Price inflates the price to drachmae!). The arrangement of the fingers of the man in the centre and the woman facing him do match regular positions for the numbers three and four (cf. H.A. Cahn in H. Froning, T. H. Hölscher [eds.], *Kotinos. Festschrift für Erika Simon* [Mainz 1992] 214–7 with pl. 45, 4). For an example of coins actually being held by prospective lovers compare the scene on the outside of a cup by Makron in Bochum (*ARV*[2] 1654 add as 472, 206 *bis*; N. Kunisch, *Antiken der Sammlung Julius C. und Margot Funcke* [Bochum 1972] no. 87; Bothmer in *Eye of Greece* 30, and 42).

The hair-bag recurs on two other Dourian cups (*ARV*[2] 441, 185 and 186). This fashion, which seems to have begun in the Early Classical period, involved tucking the ends of long hair into a bag and then folding the hair up once and tying the bag to the hair (the method is well shown on *ARV*[2] 441, 186, although here the bag has been folded up). The bag is sometimes shown as plain; sometimes it has what looks like a crossed fillet. The ties fastening the bag to the hair can be done in black or added red. One vase seems to show the fashion without the bag (*ARV*[2] 604, 47, Niobid Painter). Some examples of the hair-bag: Berlin Painter (*ARV*[2] 208, 158, late); Copenhagen Painter (*ARV*[2] 257, 17; 258, 26; Zurich Univ., *ARV*[2] 1656 add as 496, 2 *bis*, re-attributed by C. Isler-Kerenyi; German private, H.A. Cahn in *Copenhagen Colloquium* 107–15; New York, White-Levy, *Glories of the Past* no. 121); Painter of Munich 2413 (*ARV*[2] 495, 1); Painter of the Yale Oinochoe (*ARV*[2] 503, 23); Aegisthus Painter (*ARV*[2] 504, 1); Pan Painter (*ARV*[2] 550, 1); Niobid Painter (*ARV*[2] 590, 11); Altamura Painter (*ARV*[2] 594, 56); P.S. Painter (*Para* 353, 1); Achilles Painter (*ARV*[2] 993, 84); unattributed (Athens, Acrop. 513, Achilles Painter); Phiale Painter (*Para* 441, add as 1021, 117 *bis*); unattributed (London E 87). Sometimes the bag is tucked right up under a hair-band (e.g. on two of the pieces by the Copenhagen Painter; also *ARV*[2] 644, 134, now *CVA Berlin DDR* 1, fig. 22).

27 (pls. 39–40 and fig. 8d)

Cup: GR 1843.11–3.16 (*BM Cat Vases* E 55)
From Vulci, Cavalupo area D ('fam. Fuesca'), January 1829; Canino collection.
Bought of the Principessa di Canino, 1843.

Bibliography: *Mus. Étrusque* no. 589; Hartwig *M* 623 no. 12, 686 no. 54; Murray *DGV* no. 35; Hoppin i 282 no 74; *AV* 208, 114; *ARV* 296, 9; Bloesch *FAS* 98, no. 18; *ARV*[2] 449, 3; Open Univ. ii figs. XIII (A-B) and 31 (I).

Dimensions: width 36.5; diam. 29.0; diam. of tondo 18.8; diam. of exterior ground line 11.1.

Condition: made up from frr.; alien foot removed; one fr. over left handle missing and some minor chips.

Description

INTERIOR: maenad.

A maenad clad in chiton and himation (line border) moves to the right but turns her head back to the left. She holds an empty oinochoe in her left hand and, in her right, a thyrsos which crosses her body almost horizontally. Her hair is tied up with a red fillet in a droopy bun at the back (relief lines on bun and wavy relief lines on lower margin of hair). The preliminary sketch shows the left hand raised up by the head, holding a tendril (see fig. 1d).

INSCRIPTION: ΚΑΛΟΣ (large letters).

Border: alternating false maeander unit (ten-stroke, alternately clockwise and anticlockwise) and blackened saltire-square.

EXTERIOR (U): Dionysos with satyrs and maenads.
Side A: Dionysos with a satyr and three maenads.
On the left stands a maenad in chiton and himation (line border). She holds a thyrsos low in her right hand and the fingers of her raised left hand are in the gesture of holding a flower. Her hair is tied up in a bun behind her head with a red fillet (relief lines as on I). On the right a satyr moves to the right. His long hair is tied up in a *krobylos* at the back of his head with a red fillet (relief lines on bun, and for bristles of beard and forehead hair) and he has dilute glaze strokes for hair around his pectorals (as do the other satyrs on the exterior). He holds an empty oinochoe low in his right hand and gestures with his left towards Dionysos, who is in the centre. Dionysos moves to the right but turns his head back to the left. He wears a chiton and a himation (line border) and has a red fillet in his hair (relief dots over brow; relief lines on small bun at back). He holds a vine branch in his left hand with two red bunches of grapes and three red leaves and a large kantharos low in his right. The vine branch is done with relief lines only; beyond the extended hand of the satyr on the left there is a preliminary sketch for a further vine leaf (see fig. 1e). On the right stands a maenad facing Dionysos. She wears a chiton and himation (line border) and a red fillet holds up her hair at the back of her head (relief lines as on I). She carries a thyrsos in her left hand against her shoulder and has her right hand raised as if holding a flower. On the far right stands a maenad in chiton and himation (line border). Her body is frontal, feet to the right and head back to the left. She holds a thyrsos in her right hand and a black pair of krotala low in her left. She wears a headscarf decorated with linked trefoils over her hair (arcing relief lines on forehead hair).

Side B (L): two satyrs and three maenads.
On the left a satyr moves to the right, a red fillet in his hair (relief lines as on A2) and an oinochoe horizontal in his right hand. His left hand seems to reach for the himation of the maenad in front of him. This maenad moves to the right, but turns her head back to the left. She wears a chiton and himation (line border) and a headscarf decorated with linked trefoils (hair as on A5), and holds a thyrsos in her right hand and her left up as if holding a flower. In the centre a satyr dances to the right, his left leg raised and his hands gesturing in the dance. His long hair flows up at the back with his movement (relief lines as on A2). In front of him is a maenad in chiton and himation (line border) who carries a thyrsos low in her left hand and has her right up as if holding a flower. Her hair is held up at the back with a red fillet (relief lines in hair as on I). On the far right is a maenad in chiton and himation (line border): she stands to the right but has turned her head back to the left, as she holds up an oinochoe in her right hand. She carries a thyrsos in her left and has a red fillet in her hair (relief lines in hair as on I).

At either handle: floral complex with a circumscribed palmette either side of the handles (the spiral terminals end with a small lotus-palmette) and three small palmettes (two on their sides) addorsed to one larger one under the handles, on either side of which is a large lotus-palmette; surrounding tendrils with spiral terminations and small circles (see fig. 2g).

Ground line: single reserved line.

Relief line contours throughout (double for hair); dilute glaze for minor interior markings; reserved line inside and outside lip; added red for inscription.

c. 480–470 BC.

Comment: Attributed by Hartwig to Douris himself but placed in his manner by Beazley with the additional comment 'stiff imitation, late middle period: as London E 51 (no. 4)'. This piece has been made the name vase of J.R. Guy's Painter of London E 55, see further on **26** (E 51). The drapery is very stiffly drawn and the thyrsoi have lollipop-like heads. The same features are particularly clear on the Cleveland and Harvard cups (*ARV*[2] 436, 111 and 112). Guy calls **27** (E 55) 'early'.

Bloesch noted that the foot was alien, but commented that the bowl and handle were comparable to those of London E 51 (**26**: see there for further comments). Perhaps by a follower of Python rather than by the master himself.

The style and subject matter follows in a very tame fashion middle works by Douris like the cup in Boston (Boston 00.499: *ARV*[2] 435, 89). Other details, such as the decoration of the headscarves, can also be seen on Douris' middle works (e.g. *ARV*[2] 434, 74), as well as on other pieces now attributed to the Painter of London E 55 (e.g. the Harvard and Cleveland cups noted in commentary on **26** [E 51]).

The particular elaboration of the Dourian handle-palmette complex is unparalleled, although the addition of ivy leaves and lotus-buds does occur on a number of Douris' late grand works (e.g. *ARV*[2] 438, 133, 139 and 141; *Hirschmann Collection* no. 34).

28 (pls. 41–2 and fig. 8e)

Cup: GR 1843.11–3.61 (*BM Cat Vases* E 56)
From Vulci, Cucumella area C ('fam. Fepia'), April 1829; Canino collection.
Bought of the Principessa di Canino, 1843.

Bibliography: *Mus. Étrusque* no. 1534; Murray *DGV* no. 36; Hartwig *M* 621 no. 6, 686 no. 48, and p. 600 note; Hoppin i 283 no. 75; *AV* 204, 60; *ARV* 287, 107; Bloesch *FAS* 99 no. 21; *ARV*[2] 441, 180; *Para* 375; Brommer *V*[3] 343 no. 12; *Beazley Add*[2] 240.

Dimensions: width 40.0; diam. 32.4; diam. of tondo 19.2; diam. of exterior ground line 12.2.

Condition: made up from frr.; two pairs of ancient rivet-holes in stem (alien foot removed); only small chips missing.

Description

INTERIOR: Achilles and Odysseus.
On the left Achilles sits on a plain stool, closely wrapped in a himation that covers the back of his head, and with head bent forward, his left hand supporting his forehead (relief lines for forehead hair and lower fringe of beard). Behind him his sword in its striped scabbard is suspended from a red loop and above

him is his shield wrapped in its cover (*sagma*). On the right stands Odysseus clad in a himation and leaning on a knotty stick. He has a red fillet in his hair and gestures with the thumb and fingers of his right hand as he speaks to Achilles: his mouth is shown slightly open. Behind him on the ground is the corner of a stool with a plain cushion. There is a large reserved exergue.

INSCRIPTION: HOΠAIΣ KAΛOΣ
Border: stopt maeanders (five-stroke, clockwise) interrupted at irregular intervals by nine dotted cross-squares.

EXTERIOR: departure of warriors and conversation scene.

Side A (U): departure of three warriors.
On the left a bearded warrior moves away to the left, but turns his head back to the right (relief strokes on beard). He wears an Attic type helmet with the cheek flaps up (crest holder decorated with zigzag and triangles), cuirass, greaves and a himation and carries a spear in his left hand. Behind him an elderly bearded man with thinning hair (and relief strokes on beard and hair over neck) stands to the left. He wears a himation and shoes, and has a red fillet in his hair. His right hand rests on the top of a plain stick; his left is under his cloak. In the centre a woman stands to the left but turns her head back to the right. She wears a chiton (upper folds in dilute glaze), a himation and a headscarf and holds an oinochoe with a black foot out in her right hand and a bossed phiale (lobes in dilute glaze) low in her left. On the right stands a young warrior in an Attic type helmet with the cheek flaps up (dotted crest holder), cuirass and himation. He holds out a bossed phiale (lobes in dilute glaze) in his right hand, while his left grips a spear against his body. Behind him is a second young warrior, similarly clad and accoutred, but gesturing with his right hand. On the far right is a woman in chiton and himation and with a red fillet in her hair (wavy relief lines over forehead) and a bun at the back. She has her right hand up as if holding a flower, her left is hidden in her drapery.

Side B (L): men and youths in conversation, together with a young warrior.
On the left is a bearded man in himation, seen in three-quarter back view, to the right. He holds a knotty stick on the far side of his body and gestures with his right hand. There is a thick reserved fillet in his hair. In front of him a bearded man in himation and with a red fillet in his hair (relief line fringe in beard and hair, both over brow and neck) stands to the right but turns his head back to the left, so that his chest is frontal. His left hand rests near the top of a knotty stick. In the centre, a youth dressed in cuirass and himation, stands to the right, his head turned back. His left hand holds a staff (perhaps a sceptre) and there is a red fillet in his fringed hair (relief lines). On the right is a bearded man in three-quarter back view, wearing a himation that is caught up under his left armpit. He also has a red fillet in his hair (relief lines over brow). His right hand reaches out towards and behind the young warrior in the centre, his left arm hangs down. To the right of this man a youth in himation stands to the left but turns back to the right. His right hand is raised and he has a red fillet in his hair. Behind him, on the far right, is a bearded man in a himation who holds out his right hand. He too has a red fillet in his hair.

At either handle: floral complex with a circumscribed palmette either side of the handles and a large and a small palmette addorsed under them; spiral terminals and dots (see fig. 2h).
Ground line: single reserved line.

Relief line contours throughout (inner hair contour only); dilute glaze for minor interior markings; added red for inscriptions; reserved line inside and outside lip.

c. 470 BC.

Comment: Attributed by Hartwig to Douris and placed by Beazley in that artist's latest period. Guy has now reattributed it to Beazley's Oedipus Painter (*ARV*² 451–2), as an early work: see his comments in his *Followers of Douris* 37, and in N. Leipen (ed.), *Glimpses of Excellence: A Selection of Greek Vases and Bronzes from the Elie Borowski Collection* (Toronto 1984) 17 on no. 13. Buitron-Oliver has made the same reattribution (*Douris* no. O 5).

Bloesch attributed the potting to Python, with the comment that the foot is like that of London E 51 (**26**). The foot, however, was alien (although it comes from another cup by Python).

The figures on the tondo are not named but their actions identify them as Odysseus on his mission to persuade the sulking Achilles to return to the fray. For this *presbeia* see further A. Kossatz-Deissmann, *LIMC* i 107–14; Schefold *Sagen* 196–200. The figures on the exterior are not so easily identified, although their combination with a Trojan tondo tempts one to see them as epic rather than every day events. The departure of three warriors to battle, a bearded man and two youths, could well be Trojan in subject, while the conversation or even argument, seemingly being arbitrated by a youth in armour, on the other side, a scene that echoes the argument and vote over the arms of Achilles, might represent some other moment of strife in the Greek camp or in Troy. For warriors wearing himatia over their armour cf. five cups by Douris, three with non-mythological scenes (*ARV*² 435, 92 and 93; 436, 110) and two with representations of the Greeks voting over the arms of Achilles (*ARV*² 433, 71 and 72).

29

(pls. 43 and 44 a–b, fig. 9a)

CUP: GR 1843.11–3.10 (*BM Cat Vases* E 60)
From Vulci; Canino collection.
Bought of the Principessa di Canino. 1843.

Bibliography: *Mus. Étrusque* no. 644; Murray *DGV* no. 39; *AV* 208, 121; *ARV* 296, 23; Bloesch *FAS* 100 no. 33; *ARV*² 449, 7.

Dimensions: width 40.1; diam. 32.5; diam. of tondo 18.6; ht. 13.1; diam. of exterior ground line 12.0; diam. of foot 11.3.

Condition: made up from frr.; one wall and one rim fr. missing (foot belongs, *pace* Bloesch).

Description

INTERIOR: boy on horseback.

A naked boy rides a stallion to the left. The boy grasps the reins in both hands, although only his left hand is visible, a red loop falling down over his thigh. He has a red fillet in his hair and strands of hair fall down the back of his neck. The horse has an S-shaped cheek-piece and the reins are attached to a hook or the like hidden behind. There is an oval brand mark (dilute glaze strokes) on the horse's rear thigh. In the background behind the horse is a tree with red leaves. A reserved ground line provides a large black exergue.
Border: false maeander units (rectangular shape, eight-stroke; clockwise between 11 o'clock and 7 o'clock, paired alternately clockwise and anticlockwise between 8 o'clock and 11 o'clock) interrupted by six dotted cross-squares and one dotted saltire-square; odd man at 3 o'clock.

EXTERIOR: arming and a fight.

Side A (L): arming of two warriors.
On the extreme left is a balding man with a short beard, done with thinned glaze and dots to render thinning or greying. He wears a long chiton (fringed selvage; dilute glaze dots above; folds over arms in dilute glaze) and himation and stands to the right in three-quarter back view. His right hand rests on top of a plain stick. He has three dilute glaze creases on his brow. Next to him, a woman in chiton (upper folds in dilute glaze), himation and sakkos, also seen in three-quarter back view, holds out a plain phiale in her right hand, towards a bearded man, in the centre, whose torso and left leg are frontal, while his head is turned to the right. He is in the process of putting on a cuirass over his short belted chiton, his right hand holding one shoulder-flap over his shoulder, his left gripping the side of the cuirass itself. He wears greaves decorated with gorgoneia on the knee-caps. On his right stands a youth, torso frontal, head to the right, feet, in shoes, to the left. He wears a himation with a black border and holds the warrior's spear, the tip of which is not shown. On the right another youth in a himation to the left stoops slightly, his right hand pointing downwards, his left holding the spear of the figure on the extreme right, a naked youth, who bends to the left to snap on his second greave.

Side B (U): fight.
On the far left, on the ground, is a fallen young warrior with a long reserved headband, short chiton and cuirass. His torso and left leg are frontal, his right leg turned back and up behind the left and his head turned up to the right. He supports himself very awkwardly on his right hand and holds up his shield, seen in profile, on his left arm in vain defence. In the background behind him a youth, naked but for a soft skin hat with one flap tucked up at the back and a cloak over his left arm, escapes to the left. He is seen in three-quarter back view and holds a sword back in his right hand and its striped scabbard out in his left. The assailant of the fallen warrior is equipped with a Thracian helmet, cuirass, short chiton and greaves. He has a shield over his left arm, seen in profile, and a sword back in his right. In the centre, seen in three-quarter back view, a young warrior equipped with only an Attic helmet with raised cheek guards, a shield and a sword moves to the left. He wears a plain short chiton. On the right another young warrior moves to the left, but looks back to the right. He is seen in three-quarter back view and wears a raised Corinthian helmet, a cuirass with *pteryges* and a short chiton. He holds a sword in his right hand. On the far right a bearded warrior moves away fast to the right, but turns his head back to the left. He has an Attic helmet with raised cheek guards, a short chiton and a shield, seen in profile, but no sword. His right leg is seen in three-quarter front view.

At either handle: floral complex with a circumscribed palmette either side of the handles and a pair of addorsed palmettes under the handles; spiral terminals and dots (see fig. 2i).
Ground line: single reserved line.

Relief contours throughout (inner hair contour only, and not all figures); dilute glaze for minor interior markings; reserved band inside and outside lip.

c. 470 BC.

Comment: Attributed by Murray to Onesimos; Smith was more cautious, calling it 'a somewhat lifeless imitation of a good original, possibly by Onesimos' (*BM Cat Vases* iii p. 82). Beazley placed it in the manner of Douris, but it has now been attributed by J.R. Guy to the Akestorides Painter, whom he sees as a pupil of the Oedipus Painter (Guy *Followers of Douris* 65–6), as a very early work. The drawing is certainly incompetent, but it seems to lack all the charm of the Akestorides Painter and does not compare well with the other cup that Guy gives to the painter as a very early work (Basel BS 401: *ARV*^{2} 1653 add as 10 *bis*; *CVA Basel* 2, pls. 21–2). The scheme of the handle palmettes is particularly stiff. It is best at present, therefore, to reserve judgement, keeping it in the manner of late Douris. Douris himself painted very few horses (Centre Island, private, frr. [attributed by D. von Bothmer]; cf. also *ARV*^{2} 448, 1).

Bloesch attributed the potting to Python. He thought that the foot, although by Python, was alien and wondered if it might belong to **19** (E 48). The foot, in fact, belongs.

Smith (*BM Cat Vases* 82–3) suggested that the scene on the tondo might be an excerpt from the death of Troilos and that the fight on side B was between Greeks and Amazons. There is, however, rather more of the racehorse about the steed on the tondo and the idea of the naked warrior with a skin hat being an Amazon seems unlikely. Birch and Newton (*BM Old Cat Vases* no. 840, p. 294–5) identified the figures on side A as Hektor and Paris arming, with Priam and Hekabe on the left, and those on side B as coming from a Trojan War battle scene. On arming scenes in general see F. Lissarrague in *Cité des Images* 41–4 and his *L'autre guerrier* (Paris and Rome 1990) 35–53.

The drawing of the bit and cheek-piece is very detailed. There is an S-shaped cheek-piece with the ends turned up and down. An actual example of this type and of the early fifth century is known from Olympia: see J.K. Anderson, *Ancient Greek Horsemanship* (Berkeley 1961) p. 74–5 with pl. 33b, lower left – i.e. 'd') and now P.B. Faklaris, *ADelt* 41 (1986) 1–58, esp. 44–9. On greaves with gorgoneia on the knees see most recently D. Williams, *AA* 1989, 543–4.

Nos. 30–41: Makron

On the painter Makron see, in addition to Beazley's lists, the following discussions and publications: Hartwig *M* 270–306 ('Hieron'); Furtwängler in F.R. ii 129–31; Leonard *Hieron*; F. Leonard in *RE sv* Hieron no. 23, 1516–29; Buschor *GV* 173 and 176; G.M.A. Richter, *AJA* 21 (1917) 1–7; *VA* 101–6; J.D. Beazley, *AJA* 25 (1921) 325–36; J.D. Beazley, *BSA* 29 (1927–8) 187–215; Richter and Hall 72–80 (nos. 52–8); J.D. Beazley, *BABesch* 29 (1954) 12–15; J.D. Beazley in *Beazley Lectures* 84–97 (given in 1955/56); Richter *Survey*² 81–3; B.B. Shefton in Arias and Hirmer *HGVP* 332–3; J.D. Beazley in C.B. iii, 30–41 (nos. 137–43); Boardman *ARFV Archaic* 140 with figs. 308–18; Nachbaur *Makron*; M. Stadler, *HefteABern* 7 (1981) 29–35; D. von Bothmer in *Eye of Greece* 29–52; S. Karouzou, *AM* 98 (1983) 57–64; G. Nachbaur, *ÖJh* 54 (1983) 33–45; C. Isler-Kerenyi, *AntK* 27 (1984) 156–9; N. Kunisch, *Jahrbuch 1984 der Ruhr-Universtät Bochum* 19–27; N. Kunisch in M. Schmidt (ed.), *Kanon: Festschrift Ernst Berger* (*AntK* 15th Beiheft, Basel 1988) 305–9, pl. 87; Immerwahr *Attic Script* 89–90; J.R. Guy, *Princeton Record* 50, 1 (1991) 57 upper; M. Denoyelle, *RLouvre* 5/6 (1991) 13–20; Robertson *Art of Vase-painting* 100–6; N. Kunisch, *AntK* 36 (1993) 11–23. Norbert Kunisch promises a monograph on Makron.

Beazley's lists and his entries in C.B. iii give a framework for the painter's career. Nachbaur's dissertation proffers a fuller chronology but is not reliable (essentials in *ÖJh* 54 [1983] 41–5); Isler-Kerenyi also addresses the problem, especially in relation to early Hermonax. Makron's earliest works indicate an origin in the circle of Onesimos, when he was in his Panaetian phase; his early works (*c.* 495–490 BC) betray the influence of the later style of Onesimos (see further on GR 1952.2–12.8). Makron's mature works, however, have a greater monumentality: this was a particularly prolific phase (*c.* 490–485 BC). In the late period, which goes down to *c.* 480 BC and perhaps beyond, his cups tend to be slighter in both scale and quality.

Makron was primarily a painter of cups, but in addition to skyphoi, Beazley also listed examples of the following shapes: askos, aryballos, plate and pyxis. To these we might add an unpublished fragmentary tripod-pyxis in the Brauron Museum (inv. 75).

Although the potting of one of Makron's very early cups has been attributed by Bloesch to Euphronios (*FAS* 77 no. 32), Makron regularly worked for the potter Hieron (see *ARV*² 481–2; Bothmer in *Eye of Greece* 45–9): for his cups see Bloesch *FAS* 91–6, for his skyphoi Beazley in C.B. iii 33 and E.R. Knauer, *Ein Skyphos des Triptolemosmalers* (Berlin 1973) 21 note 8; and for a kantharos, decorated by the Amphitrite Painter (*ARV*² 832, 36) see Beazley in C.B. iii no. 152. The latter records Hieron's father as Medon, suggesting, perhaps, that Hieron was a citizen: the inscription, however, has been doubted (see most recently Robertson *Art of Vase-painting* 152–4).

30 (pl. 44 c)

Cup: GR 1952.12–2.8
E.P. Warren collection.
Bought of Mrs. G. Redfern-Loades, 1952.

Bibliography: *ARV*² 464, 75.

Dimensions: diam. *c.* 24.0; length at rim 8.5; ht 4.5.

Condition: before cleaning there was much black shellac on the fr. filling pits and blemishes in the surface. This might suggest that the fr. was originally attached to more pieces.

Description

EXTERIOR: komast. A bearded man moves to the left, holding a black skyphos in his left hand. His right hand is raised with the fingers spread. He wears a chlamys over his upper arms and round his back, and there is a red fillet around his head with a large loop at the back.

Relief line contour throughout (except hair); lip worn.

c. 500–495 BC.

Comment: Attributed by Beazley to Makron and labelled 'early'. He marked a number of other pieces in his list as early (*ARV*² 460–80, 16, 22, 36–8, 76–80, 117, 131–3, 186–8, 319 and 338) and one, an Acropolis fr., as 'very early' (*ARV*² 461, 29). In addition, he placed three cups, one in Munich, one in Palermo and one in Tarquinia, after his main list with the comment that he took them to be 'early work by Makron' (*ARV*² 480, 1–3; cf. also C.B. iii p. 31 on no. 138).

A number of these cups have only a line border in the tondo (Palermo; Munich; *ARV*² 461, 36; 467, 131; add a cup in Japan [*Palladion Antike Kunst: Katalog 1976* (Basel 1976) no. 30; *Ninagawa Museum* 79–83, no. 34]. See also Bothmer in *Eye of Greece* 35 no. 36A): they seem very early. With them probably goes the Tarquinia cup, which is already showing a more elaborate border (Ferrari *Tarquinia* no. 56, pls. 96–8), and the London fr. There then follow a good number of early pieces (*ARV*² 460, 16 and 22; 461, 29, 34–5 and 38; 464, 76–80; 466, 117; 468, 137–8; 471, 186; 478, 319; **30** [E 58]).

The potting of the Munich cup was attributed by Bloesch to Hieron, but the Palermo piece to Euphronios (Bloesch *FAS* 94, Hieron no. 27 and 77, Euphronios no. 32; Beazley in C.B. iii 31 commented that he thought the foot of the Palermo cup alien). The foot of the Boston cup is probably alien. No comments have been published on the potting of the Tarquinia and Kurashiki cups.

For other comments on the problems of early Makron see Bothmer in *Eye of Greece* 49–50; and Ferrari *Tarquinia* 162–3.

Black vases appear on a number of other pieces by Makron: *ARV*² 464, 74; 465, 85; 467, 122 and 129; Vatican, Astarita 750 fr., *ARV*² 1648, removed from the Triptolemos Painter and given to Makron by Guy; Centre Island, private fr., attributed by Bothmer to Makron, see Bothmer in *Eye of Greece* 35 no. 79A.

31 (pls. 45–6 and fig. 9b)

Cup: GR 1883.12–8.1 (*BM Cat Vases* E 58)
From Vulci. Collection of James Thomson
Presented by Mr. Belt, 1883.

Bibliography: E. Braun, *AdI* 1846, 228–38 (with *MdI* 4, pl. 33); Murray *DGV* no. 37 (I); *VA* 106 no. 101; Hoppin ii 99 no. 63; *AV* 220, 148; *ARV* 307, 93; Bloesch *FAS* 91 no. 3; *ARV*² 467, 133 and p. 1654; *Para* 378; Nachbaur *Makron* 34, 99 and 166 (cat. M. 8); *Beazley Add*² 245.

Dimensions: width 38.0; diam. 29.2; diam. of tondo 15.2; diam. of exterior ground line 14.0.

Condition: made up from many frr.; surface rubbed; foot missing; one large rim fr. and several wall frr. missing.

Description
INTERIOR: Hermes.
Hermes flies to the right in a running pose, his head turned back to the left and down. He holds a lyre (red *plektron* attached with red cord) in his left hand and a *kerykeion* up over his shoulders in his right. The god wears a peaked cap, short chiton (dilute glaze folds above waist), *chlamys* (two line border) tied at the neck (brooch decorated with a cross) and winged boots. Beneath his feet is the sea, represented by a reserved area with a wavy upper contour.
Border: complex running maeander (eight-stroke core, anticlockwise).

EXTERIOR: athletes.

Side A (U): three athletes and a trainer.
On the left an athlete moves to the right holding a *halter* in either hand (right hand missing, but end of *halter* visible). He has a red band in his hair, as do all the other athletes on this cup. In front of him an athlete moves to the right holding an *akontion* in either hand, red loops attached to both (*agkulai*). On the right of the centre a youthful trainer in himation (black border) moves away to the right, but looks back to the left. He holds a forked stick low in his right hand and has a red wreath in his hair. On the far right an athlete holding a discus in his lowered left hand moves to the left.

Side B (D): three athletes and a trainer.
On the left an athlete with a *halter* in either hand moves to the right. In front of him an athlete moves to the left, a discus with a silhouette owl on it low in his left hand. On the right of the centre a youthful trainer wearing a himation (black border) moves to the left, his right hand raised and his left holding a forked stick up to the right, parallel to his forearm. He has a red wreath in his hair. On the far right an athlete moves away to the right, holding a pair of halters back in his right hand and an akontion with a red loop down in his left. His chest is frontal and his head, now misssing, was probably turned back to the left.
Ground line: single reserved line.
Relief contour throughout (except hair); dilute glaze for minor interior markings; reserved line inside and outside lip.

c. 495–490 BC.

Comment: Placed in the style of Douris by Murray; Smith repeated this, but with a question mark. Attributed by Beazley to Makron as an 'early' work (cf. comment on **30** [GR 1952.12–2.8]). Nachbaur places it in the second phase of her early group (500–490 BC). It is a bare work of Makron's early period. Bloesch attributed the potting to Hieron.

The bareness of the decoration on the exterior links this piece with other early works (see Beazley in C.B. iii 31 on no. 138). Of other athletic cups, the Copenhagen cup (*ARV*² 467, 131) should be earlier, while the Louvre frr. (*ARV*² 468, 137–8) should be contemporary. The athletes on the exterior recall similar groups on works of Douris' early middle period (e.g. *ARV*² 430, 29–35).

In addition to Hermes, Makron treats the female divine messenger, Iris, on two tondi (*ARV*² 460, 15 and 478, 307). For the owl, and other symbols, on diskoi see J.D. Beazley, *JHS* 28 (1908) 316–7: he suggests the owl on this vase is 'the short-bodied *Athene noctua*'. The bird also occurs on the earlier cup in Copenhagen, noted above.

32 (pls. 47–8 and 49 a–k, fig. 9c)

Cup: GR 1893.11–15.2 (*BM Cat Vases* E 63) and 1893.11–15.2, 1–13
From Orvieto.
Bought of P. Hartwig, 1893.

Bibliography: *VA* 106 no. 98; Hoppin ii 100 no. 66; *AV* 220, 152; *ARV* 307, 95; *ARV*² 468, 139; *Para* 378; *Beazley Add*² 245.

Dimensions: diam. of tondo 14.8; diam. of exterior ground line 11.5; diam. of foot 9.9.

Condition: made up from frr. with a number of loose frr.; right handle, most of bowl and rim missing; remains of eleven pairs of ancient repair holes.

Description
INTERIOR: trainer and two athletes.
On the left a young boxer binds a red thong round his left wrist and hand. In the centre a bearded trainer stands frontally, his head to the left. He wears a himation and leans his left forearm on the top of a knotty stick. In his right hand he holds a trainer's forked branch. His hair is done with dilute glaze waves and he has a red garland in his hair. On the right a youth attends to the thong on his left wrist. He is presumably to be thought of as sitting on the ground, right knee raised, left thigh probably seen from above. The tondo border cuts off part of his left arm and hip.
Border: continuous maeander (six-stroke, anticlockwise).

EXTERIOR: parade of boxers.

Side A (U): From the right comes a parade of five boxers. Each holds his thongs (relief lines) down in his left hand, while his right hand is raised in a special gesture. On the left are two figures facing to the right who receive the procession. Of the first only the feet are preserved. The second figure (far left) wore a himation and leant on a knotty stick. Under the handle behind the reception committee is a large tripod podanipter (presumably of metal and for the athletes to wash in) with elaborate handle and tripod support with animal feet on a block base. Under the handle behind the parade of boxers a pick (*dikella*).

Loose frr.:

a) (GR 1893.11–15.2,1) Parts of three heads of youths to left, their right hands raised. The central youth has a dilute line around his cheek bone. Length at rim, 6.5; ancient repair hole on right.
b) (GR 1893.11–15.2,2) Chest of youth to left with right arm raised. Greatest dimension 4.1.

Side B (L): On the extreme left was a figure seated on a stool to the right – he wore a himation round his waist and knees and sat on a striped cushion. On the extreme right was a standing male in himation (right foot frontal, left foot to right). There is also the left foot of a figure moving to the left and a thick stroke of added red that splits into four strokes at the end, perhaps the end of a long fillet.

Loose frr.:

c) (GR 1893.11–15.2,3) Right hand raised, but low on the wall, tip of red wreath of a figure to right, probably seated. There is the square end of something up on right with a trace of relief line going almost vertically downwards on the extreme edge of the fr., which is supplanted further down by a touch of the 'eighth-of-an-inch stripe'. Length at rim 4.1. Remains of three pairs of ancient repair holes. Probably from the figure on the extreme left.
d) (GR 1893.11–15.2,4) Upper legs, right knee and belly of athlete moving to the right. The swollen belly indicates a boxer. Greatest dimension 4.3.
e) (GR 1893.11–15.2,5) Genitals and upper legs of a naked figure to the left, stooping slightly forward. Greatest dimension 3.7. Ancient repair hole.

Ground line: single reserved line.

The following loose frr. could belong to side A or B:

f) (GR 1893.11–15.2,6) Bearded head of a standing figure in himation to the right. He has a red wreath and has his head slightly bent. Length at rim 4.3. Probably to Side A, first figure on left.
g) (GR 1893.11–15.2,7) Hooked end of stick, with a trace of a hand holding it. Length at rim 1.5. Might not belong.
h) (GR 1893.11–15.2,8) Shoulder, himation and upper right arm of standing figure to right. Ht. 3.2.
i) (GR 1893.11–15.2,9) Shoulder, neck and drapery of standing figure in himation to right. The head was slightly bent and there is a touch of the back of his beard. On the extreme left a touch of relief line and a vertical stretch of the 'eighth-of-an-inch stripe', perhaps from the right side of a stick. Width 4.4.
j) (GR 1893.11–15.2,10) Forearm and hand holding a stylus or a marker from a standing figure to the right. Width 2.5.
k) (GR 1893.11–15.2,11) Part of himation of a standing figure to the right. Greatest dimension 3.4. Could belong to Side A, the first figure on the left.
l) (GR 1893.11–15.2,12) Rim and reserved handle patch fr. (made up of two frr.) with the beginning of the handle root. Length at rim 5.4. Might not belong.
m) (GR 1893.11–15.2,13) Reserved handle patch fr. Greatest dimension 3.0. Might not belong.

Relief line contour throughout (except hair); dilute glaze for minor interior markings; reserved line inside and outside lip.

c. 490 BC.

(Four further frr. acquired with this group clearly do not belong to the same cup, although three were painted by Makron: they are described separately, see below. A fifth fr. is by another hand – GR 1934.11–5.4: *ARV*² 817, 14)

Comment: Attributed by Hartwig to Peithinos (letter of 26.2.1893 in Greek and Roman Department, British Museum); given by Smith to Hieron (*BM Cat Vases* iii 85–6) and, finally, by Beazley to Makron. It is an early mature work of much interest.

Side A seems to have consisted of a parade of five young boxers towards two officials. This is the only certain parade of boxers, although other pieces show the occasional boxer with one hand raised and holding his thongs in the other (e.g. *ARV*² 401, 10). Smith and E.N. Gardiner (*Greek Athletic Sports and Festivals* [London 1910] 404–5) connected the scene with the taking of the oath to obey the rules of the games (Pausanias v 24, 9).

Side B had a further group of officials on the left, one of them seated and apparently agitated. There were perhaps as many as three officials here, but more probably only two. There was a further draped official on the extreme right. The red stroke with four long tails that crosses his legs suggests the end of a victory fillet tied around an athlete (cf. **21** [E 52]; cf. also New York 1979.11.9 – *Eye of Greece* pls. 7 d and 13 a-b). The theme may, therefore, have been centred on the presentation of the insignia of victory.

Fr. (j) shows a standing figure holding a stylus – it is unlikely to be a marker for recording the distance of a throw (for markers cf. *ARV*² 165, 2; *ARV*² 322, 38; *Beazley Add*² 393, Chairestratos, Stuttgart 79.2), given the apparent lack of any throwers among the athletes represented. It suggests, rather, that some writing was required in the proceedings on either A or B. If it belongs to one of the officials on A, it might indicate that the names of those swearing the oath had to be recorded (cf. the *dokimasia* of the Athenians and their horses: H.A. Cahn, *RA* 1973, 3–22; G.R. Bugh, *The Horsemen of Athens* [Princeton 1988] 14–19). A somewhat similar scene by Makron occurs on a fragmentary, later cup in the Louvre (*ARV*² 468, 136). On one side four athletes with one hand raised surround a draped man who holds the back of his head with his left hand, as he holds out a stylus in his right; on the other side were two boxers fighting and a trainer. Beazley described the first scene as 'athletes answering their names'. Their physique suggests that they are boxers, even though there are no thongs. The official's obvious distress is unexplained.

If fr. (j) belongs to side B (perhaps less likely), then the official might have been recording the name of the victor, rather as Athena seems to be entering the distance of a victorious acontist's throw into the Panathenaic 'record-book' (*ARV*[2] 362, 14. Cf also *ARV*[2] 321, 23 – agitated recorder inside, acontists outside).

For recent additions to athlete cups by Makron see D. von Bothmer in *Eye Of Greece* 36–7. For the podanipter in general see M.J. Milne, *AJA* 48 (1944) 26–63 (the London cup is no. 12 on p. 53). A cup in Godalming, not listed by Milne, shows a woman at a podanipter of exactly the same type (*ARV*[2] 479, 330).

33 (pl. 49 n)

Cup: GR 1893.11–15.2, 14 (removed from *BM Cat Vases* E 63 [**32**])
From Orvieto.
Bought of P. Hartwig, 1893.

Bibliography: *ARV*[2] 468, 140.

Dimensions: max. dim. 7.1.

Condition: single fr.

Description
EXTERIOR: right leg of naked (?) figure to the right; trace of handle root above, to the left of the leg.

Relief line contour throughout; dilute glaze for minor interior markings.

c. 490 BC.

Comment: Attributed by Beazley to Makron.
Probably from an athlete rather than a komast, since there is no trace of drapery. If it were from an athletic scene, one might compare the Copenhagen cup (*ARV*[2] 467, 131).
Cannot belong to **32** (E 63), as Beazley saw.

34 (pl. 49 o)

Cup: GR 1893.11–15.2, 15 (removed from *BM Cat Vases* E 63 [**32**])
From Orvieto.
Bought of P. Hartwig, 1893.

Dimensions: length at rim 3.7

Condition: single fr.

Description
EXTERIOR: bearded head of a draped man wearing a red wreath and probably a himation. Head close up on rim.

Relief line contour throughout (except dotted hair contour); thin reserved line inside lip, thicker one outside.

c. 490 BC.

Comment: Perhaps from a *komos* or courting scene. Painted by Makron, an early mature work.
Style, height of figure and interior wheel marks suggest that this fr. does not belong to **32** (E 63).

35 (pl. 49 p)

Cup: GR 1893.11–15.2, 16 (part of *BM Cat Vases* E 63 [**32**])
From Orvieto.
Bought of P. Hartwig, 1893.

Dimensions: width 2.6.

Condition: single fr.

Description
EXTERIOR: Bearded head to right with red garland. He was looking slightly downwards.

Relief line contour throughout (except hair); lip damaged.

c. 490–480 BC.

Comment: Painted by Makron: a mature work. The reserved surface is paler and the black is duller than on **32** (E 63).

36 (pl. 49 q)

Cup: GR 1893.11–15.2, 17 (part of *BM Cat Vases* E 63 [**32**])
From Orvieto.
Bought of P. Hartwig, 1893.

Dimensions: length of handle 7.0.

Condition: single fr.

Description
Handle fr.: right half of handle, no trace of decoration on right.

Comment: Cannot belong to **32** (E 63). Attribution impossible.

37 (pls. 50–1 and fig. 9 d)

Cup: GR 1867.5–8.1063 (*BM Cat Vases* E 61)
From Vulci; Canino, Durand and Blacas collections.
Bought from the estate of the Duc de Blacas, 1866.

Bibliography: J. de Witte and T. Panofka, *BdI* 1832, 114; *Cabinet Durand* lot 758; De Witte *Fabricants* 52 xxxv no. 4; Klein *M*[2] 165–6 no. 6; Murray *DGV* no. 40 (I), p. 14 fig. 7 (B); Klein *M*[2] 165, 6; Hartwig *M* 279 and 687 no. 6; Leonard *Hieron* 12 no. 15; F. Leonard in *RE sv* Hieron, 1523, 7; *VA* 104 no. 62; Hoppin ii 59 no. 12; *AV* 217, 88; *ARV* 307, 101; Bloesch *FAS* 92, no. 22, pl. 25, 4 (B and foot); *ARV*[2] 468, 145 and p. 1654; Baker *Furniture* 276 fig. 434 (I); Boardman *ARFV Archaic* fig. 317 (part of I); Nachbaur *Makron* 68–9, 169–70 (cat. M 29); M. Meyer, *JdI* 103 (1988) 105 with figs. 9–10 (A–B); *Beazley Add*[2] 245.

Dimensions: width 40.9; diam. 32.7; diam. of tondo 15.0; ht. 13.0; diam. of exterior ground line 14.0; diam. of foot plate 12.0.

Condition: made up from frr.; four pairs of ancient rivet holes to hold centre of tondo (with foot) in place; five other main areas of chipping and fracture on the bowl.

Description

INTERIOR: woman playing pipes and girl dancing.

On the left sits a woman on a folding stool. She wears a transparent chiton and a himation (line border) around her hips and legs and plays a pair of pipes – dilute wash on pipes and for indication of holes. She wears a disc earring; her hair has two reserved lines at the back and there are traces of a double red band in her hair with a loop and long ties at the back. There is a relief line down from her nose towards her chin to indicate that her lips are pursed. The stool has an elaborately decorated seat with running maeander, circular end-pieces and cross-over; the feet are in the form of animal paws. The long cushion is decorated with zip patterns separated by zs, line-battlement and zigzag. On the right a girl in a transparent chiton (wavy lines in dilute glaze above waist), tied at the waist with a red cord, dances to the left, a pair of krotala in either hand (right low in front, left up over head). She kicks her left leg off the ground behind her. Her hair is tied up with a red band with a loop and long ties at the back. She wears a disc earring and a necklace.

Border: complex running maeander (five-stroke core, anticlockwise).

EXTERIOR: men, youths and women.

Side A (L): three bearded men with two women playing pipes.

On the left a man in a himation (line border) and with a red wreath in his hair leans on a knotty stick to the right, right leg and foot frontal. His right hand rests on his hip (little finger doubled up) and he holds out a purse in his left. In front, a woman in chiton and himation (line border) stands to the right playing a pair of pipes. Her hair is cut short (relief line arcs over brow and nape), but has a red band with a loop and triple tassels at the back. In the centre, stands a man to the left. He wears a himation (line border) and has his left hand on top of a knotty stick, almost leaning on it, as he holds a red flower up to his nose with his right hand. He has a red wreath in his hair and the whole of his chest is lavishly stippled with dilute glaze to indicate hair. Back to back with him sits a woman on a stool. She plays a pair of pipes and wears a chiton and a himation (line border) round her hips and legs. Her hair is tied up with a double red band (loop and tassels at the back). On the far right is a man with the same accoutrements and in the same pose as the man in the centre.

Side B (U): three youths and two women.

On the left a youth, wearing a himation and with a red wreath in his hair, leans on a knotty stick, right leg and foot frontal. His right hand rests on his hip and he holds out a purse in his left hand. In front of him a woman sits on a folding stool with a cushion (compare that on the interior), holding out a red wreath in both hands. She wears a chiton and has a himation around her hips, while her hair is tied up with a double red band with triple tassels and there is a disc earring in her ear. In the centre stands a youth with a red wreath in his hair, a himation round his back and tucked up under his right armpit, as he leans on a knotty stick, and falling over his left forearm, his body thus exposed. His left hand rests on his hip and he gestures with his right at the lap of the seated woman. On the right stands a woman in a transparent chiton and a himation. Her chest and right leg are frontal, her head is turned to the left and she has a red band with large blooms in her short cut hair (relief line arcs over brow and neck). She holds a pipe up in either hand. On the far right stands a youth who wears a himation. His left hand rests on top of a knotty stick and his right hand holds a red flower up to his nose.

Under the handles: a palmette with enclosing tendrils ending above in spirals (see fig. 3c).

Ground line: single reserved line.

Incised on one handle: HIEPON EΓOIEΣEN (see fig. 3f)

Relief line contour throughout (sometimes for hair, sometimes not); dilute glaze for minor interior markings; reserved line inside and outside lip.

c. 490–485 BC.

Comment: Hartwig attributed the cup to Hieron. Furtwängler, by implication, gave it to Makron (FR ii 129–31) and in this he was followed by Leonard and Beazley. Nachbaur places it in her middle phase (480–475 BC); Isler-Kerenyi (*AntK* 27 [1984] 157) puts it in her early phase (*c.* 490–480 BC). It is a mature work of the painter. Signed by Hieron as potter; for the incised signature see Bothmer in *Eye of Greece* 45, Immerwahr *Attic Script* 89–90 and B. Cohen, *MetrMusJ* 26 (1991) 70 fig. 37. The error in Hieron's name (*P* for *R*) recurs on *ARV*^{2} 472, 209.

The women on the interior and exterior are all presumably hetairai and the men are come to purchase their services. The sections of the cup seem deliberately organised: the hetairai have the tondo to themselves, while on one side the visitors are mature men and on the other they are youths. Beazley suggested that the seated woman with the wreath was actually twining it and that the plant is smilax, our bindweed (*AJA* 25 [1921] 334).

For purses see Koch-Harnack 161–71 and M. Meyer, *JdI* 103 (1988) 87–125. For the pose of the dancing girl on the tondo compare the maenad on the cup in the Faina collection (*ARV*^{2} 461, 39). The little bunch of drapery on the shoulders of three of the women has been explained by Beazley as the result of a draw-cord in the neck of the garment (CB iii p. 32 on no. 139). The stippling of the whole of the mature male chest occurs on a number of pieces by Makron (e.g. *ARV*^{2} 459, 11; 460, 13; 461, 39 [satyr]; 463, 52 [satyr]; 466, 102; 468, 146; 469, 148; 470, 182; Vatican, Astarita 750 fr., *ARV*^{2} 1648, removed from the Triptolemos Painter and given to Makron by Guy).

Makron painted a large number of cups with courting scenes, among which the Cambridge cup is quite early (*ARV*^{2} 468, 144). For a girl holding pipes in such a setting, compare a figure on the

Vatican cup (*ARV*² 469, 154; cf. also the Louvre fr. *ARV*² 465, 98). The New York cup (*ARV*² 468, 146) takes the events one stage further.

For the palmettes under the handles see Bothmer in *Eye of Greece* 42–3: he notes that the type on this cup recurs on **37** (E 62), on *ARV*² 468, 146 (with lotus bud) and on a piece in Centre Island (*loc. cit.* no. 187A).

38 (pls. 52 and 53 a-b and fig. 10a)

Cup: gr 1843.11–3.44 (*BM Cat Vases* E 62)
From Vulci; Canino collection.
Bought of the Principessa di Canino, 1843.

Bibliography: *Mus. Étrusque* no. 1267; Murray *DGV* no. 41; Hartwig *M* 295 no. 7, 687 no. 33; F. Leonard in *RE sv* Hieron 1528, 11; *VA* 105 no. 73; Hoppin ii 99, 65; *AV* 216, 82; *ARV* 307, 137; Bloesch *FAS* 92, 20; *ARV*² 471, 194; Nachbaur *Makron* 79–80, 172 and 174 (cat. M 34).

Dimensions: width 41.1; diam. 33.2; diam. of tondo 17.0; ht. 13.7; diam. of exterior ground line 13.9; diam. of foot 12.7.

Condition: made up from frr.; two wall frr and two small chips missing.

Description

INTERIOR: seated man and boy.
On the left a bearded man sits on a stool topped by a cushion decorated with stripes, zigzags and dots. He wears a himation around his hips and legs and has a red fillet with large red leaves in his hair. His left hand rests on top of a knotty stick, his index finger raised, and he gestures with his right hand. His mouth is open and there are three creases on his brow done with dilute glaze. His hair is wavy and seems to be thinning over the forehead. On the right stands a naked boy to the left. He holds a leg (cloven hoof) of meat out in his right hand and a dish of food on his left arm. He has a red wreath in his hair. His left foot is obscured by the border. There is a small reserved exergue as a ground line.
Border: complex running maeander (four-stroke, anticlockwise).

EXTERIOR: men and a youth.

Side A (U): three men and a youth.
On the far left stands a man leaning on a knotty stick. He wears a himation and has a red wreath in his hair (as do all the figures on the exterior). The stick goes under his left armpit and there is a wad of drapery over the top of it. His left forearm and hand are raised (all but the curled tips of four fingers missing) and his right held down low. In his right hand is the end of a red fillet – it must have been held between his two hands. Behind him hangs a net bag with fourteen black balls in it. In front of him hangs a sponge, aryballos and probably a scraper. Facing him sits a man on a stool without a cushion. He wears a himation around his hips and legs. He holds a flower in his right hand up near his nose and plays with a hare on his lap. The skin of the hare is done with dilute glaze. Facing to the right sits a man on a stool with a cushion decorated with a dotted cross-hatched pattern. He wears a himation round his hips and his legs and hugs his left knee with both hands. In front of him is a knotty stick. On the far right, facing to the left, sits a youth on an elaborately decorated folding stool with animal feet and with a cushion with a dotted chequer pattern on top. He wears a himation around his hips and legs and holds a red flower down in his left hand, while his right grips the upper shaft of a plain stick, thumb and index finger seeming to adjust his red wreath. In front of him hangs a sponge, aryballos and scraper.

Side B (L): four men.
On the far left sits a man on a stool with a cushion decorated with a dotted cross-hatched pattern. He wears a himation around his hips and legs. His right hand is raised and his left grips the shaft of a knotty stick. Behind him and in front of him hang a sponge, aryballos and scraper. Facing him sits a man on a stool to the left. He wears a himation around his hips and legs and holds a red flower in his left hand, while his right grips the shaft of a plain stick. The cushion on his stool is decorated with rows of dots and strokes. Behind him hangs a sponge, aryballos and scraper. To the right sits a man on a stool with a cushion decorated with pairs of lines and zigzags. He wears a himation round his waist. He strokes the end of his beard with the fingers of his right hand and his left hand grips the shaft of a knotty stick. On the far right stands a man wearing a himation, who stoops slightly forward, his right hand on the top of a knotty stick, his left hand holding up a red flower to his nose.

Under the handles: a large enclosed palmette with spiral tendrils (see fig. 3d).
Ground line: a single reserved line.
Graffito under foot: see fig. 3i.

Relief line contour throughout (except for hair); dilute glaze for minor interior markings; reserved line inside and outside lip.

c. 490–485 BC.

Comment: Attributed by Hartwig to Hieron; by Leonard and Beazley to Makron. Nachbaur places it in her late group (*c.* 460 BC). It is, rather, a fully mature work of the painter. The potting has been attributed by Bloesch to Hieron.

For the meat held by the boy on the interior as a gift see Koch-Harnack 134–42; J.L. Durand in M. Detienne and J.P. Vernant (eds.), *La cuisine du sacrifice en pays grec* (Paris 1979); and Reinsberg *EHK*. For the dish and its contents one is reminded of some special bread in a *tapsi* – the bread is sometimes seen without the dish on a symposiast's table (e.g. *ARV*² 781, 5–6). The scene is repeated on the tondi of three other cups by Makron: an earlier piece in the Borowski collection (N. Leipen [ed.], *Glimpses of Excellence: A Selection of Greek Vases and Bronzes from the Elie Borowski Collection* (Toronto 1984) no. 10), frr. in the Getty Museum (D. von Bothmer in *Eye of Greece* 38 no. 194A, without the meat) and Centre Island, private (without the bread; attributed by Bothmer). The combination of dish and meat recurs on a number of vases by other artists: a pelike by the Tyszkiewicz Painter (*ARV*² 293, 47), a neck-amphora (Basel market, *MuM*

Auktion 56 no. 92, paired with Hermes), lekythos (Freiburg market, Puhze 1981, no. 161, Eros), and an askos by the Clinic Painter (*ARV*² 814, 99, Eros).

The presence of a hare and flowers on the exterior suggests that the subject of the scenes on the exterior are also erotic, while the aryballoi, sponges and scrapers indicate a setting in the palaistra. For a similar conversation scene by Makron with seated figures compare the Berlin cup (*ARV*² 471, 195). For the gesture of stroking the beard in a courting context compare the cup attributed to Makron now in Bochum (*ARV*² 1654 add as 472, 206 *bis*; N. Kunisch, *Antiken der Sammlung Julius C. und Margot Funcke* [Bochum 1972] no. 87; Bothmer in *Eye of Greece* 30, and 42); see also G. Neumann, *Gesten und Gebärden in der griechischen Kunst* (Berlin 1965) 109–12; and Agathias in *Anth. Pal.* 11, 354, 11–12 (quoted by Beazley in C.B. iii 72, end of fn. from previous page). For the pose of holding one knee up compare Hartwig *M* 349–50 with note 1 on p. 350; for the hare on the man's knee compare the tondo of a cup by Douris (*Beazley Add*² 403; *Hirschmann Collection* no. 33).

Net bags with black balls are to be found on a number of Macronian pieces: *ARV*² 471, 195 and 197; 474, 244 and 248; 475, 260; 1654 add as 206 *bis*; Toledo 72.55 (*CVA Toledo* 1, pl. 54); New York 1979.11.8 (Bothmer in *Eye of Greece* pl. 9b); Villa Giulia 50508 (*ARV*² 814, 1); Boston 95.28 etc. (*ARV*² 816, 1). The black balls are sometimes called knucklebones (e.g. most recently J. Neils, *AJA* 96 [1992] 232 n. 28 and 234 n. 43), although it seems clear that the closed leather bags with a flap at the side, regularly called *phormiskoi*, are what were usually employed to hold them (these should be differentiated from money pouches: see M. Meyer, *Jb* 103 [1988] 112–13). Beazley, in connection with the unexplained scene on a cup by the Telephos Painter (*ARV*² 816, 1; C.B. iii 58), where they appear in a bag carried with a scraper and an aryballos, suggests that they are fruit or vegetables; on a Louvre fr. (*ARV*² 474, 244) he simply calls the object a 'ball-bag' (cf. also *BSA* 29 [1927–8] 189). Empty net bags are regularly seen hung up with sponge, aryballos and scraper on Dourian cups (see further on **21** [E 52]) and on some Macronian pieces (*ARV*² 471, 193 and 198; 475, 265 and 267–8; 480, 337; 811, 51. Cf. also *ARV*² 380, 167 and *ARV*² 340, 65). On one cup by Makron a man holds out an empty bag to a youth (*ARV*² 472, 200). The function of the black balls might, therefore, perhaps best be sought in the sphere of the palaistra – are they *harpasta* (see Gardiner *AAW* 230–8)? The name for the bag was presumably *diktydion* (Pollux 7, 179). Such bags could, of course, also be used for other purposes – e.g. transporting birds (London market: *Hesperia Arts Auction*, Ltd, 27 November 1990, part I, no. 121).

For the large leaves attached to the headband of the man on the interior see on **23** (E 54). For the simple *G* or *L* graffito see Johnston *Trademarks* p. 70 add to p. 239 type 13 A note 4. For the palmettes under the handles see on **37** (E 61).

39 (pl. 53 c)

Cup: gr 1893.11–15.3 (*BM Cat Vases* E 134, 3)
From Orvieto.
Bought of P. Hartwig, 1893.

Bibliography: Hartwig *M* 303 note 1; *ARV*² 477, 293.

Dimensions: greatest dimension 10.7.

Condition: fr. from centre of tondo; made up from two frr.

Description

INTERIOR: satyr and maenad. On the left a maenad moves away to the left, her head turned back to the right. She wears a chiton (folds on sleeve in dilute glaze), through which her breasts and legs are visible, and a spotted panther-skin tied around her neck and hanging over her back. Her hair is loose and flows down on either side of her neck and shoulders. On the lower left is the end of a thyrsos, probably held in the maenad's right hand. On the right are the beard, left arm and one knee and thigh (presumably the left) of a satyr to the left, who is attempting to catch the maenad around the waist: his right arm would have been reaching around her back.

Relief line contour throughout; dilute glaze for minor interior markings.

c. 490–485 BC.

Comment: Attributed by Hartwig to Makron, followed by Smith and Beazley. It is a mature work of the painter.

For the pair on the tondo compare Munich 2654 (*ARV*² 462, 47), where, however, the maenad makes more of an attempt to defend herself. Compare also New York 06.1152 (*ARV*² 463, 52). A small fr. in Florence (*ARV*² 476, 279), without find-spot, so possibly from Orvieto, comes from a similar tondo – it might even belong.

On Makron's Dionysiac scenes see J.D. Beazley in *Beazley Lectures* 93–5. Compare also D. von Bothmer in *Eye of Greece* 34–5.

40 (pl. 53 d)

Cup: gr 1952.12–2.9
From Orvieto; E.P. Warren collection.
Bought of Mrs. G. Redfern-Loades, 1952.

Bibliography: *ARV*² 462, 46.

Dimensions: diam. *c.* 29.0; length at rim 5.6; height 8.8.

Condition: rim fr. made up from two joining pieces. Smears of glue on left of fr. Paper label (presumably Warren's): 1923 with an underlined O below, for Orvieto.

Description

EXTERIOR: satyr and maenad.
On the left, left hand holding drinking horn, knees and left calf of a satyr to right. On the right, a maenad moving rapidly to right, head turned back to the left and right hand raised to protect herself. She wears a transparent chiton and she carries a thyrsos (only the butt preserved). Her hair is tied up in a bun at the

back with a red double band and her chiton is fastened with a red girdle. The folds on the upper part of her chiton are done in dilute glaze. She has a disc earring. No trace of decoration inside.

Relief line contour throughout (except hair); dilute glaze for minor interior markings; reserved line inside lip.

c. 490–485 BC.

Comment: Attributed by Roberston to Makron (see *ARV*² 462). It is a mature work of the painter. Bothmer (in *Eye of Greece* 38) wondered whether the fr. might belong to the cup in the Faina collection (Orvieto, Faina 36: *ARV*² 461, 39). This association, which is supported by the find-spot, has, in fact, been confirmed by Norbert Kunisch. The London fr. joins the less well preserved side supplying the rest of the drinking horn of the satyr on the left (the smear of glue on the London fr. here indicates that it was found at the same time as the rest of the cup). There were two more figures to the right of the London maenad, a satyr and a maenad. The better preserved side has two satyrs, one with pipes, and two maenads with thyrsoi. There is a trace of a circumscribed palmette under one handle. The tondo is filled with the lone dancing figure of a maenad, one arm above her loose flowing hair.

In addition to regular thiasoi with both satyrs and maenads, such as this fr. depicts, Makron painted some with just satyrs (*ARV*² 462, 49) and some with just maenads (*ARV*² 463, 50 and 53). For a satyr with a horn in a thiasos compare, in addition, Harvard 1972.41 (*ARV*² 462, 45) and New York 1979.11.11 (*Eye of Greece* pl. 10 b). For Dionysiac scenes see also on **39** (E 134, 3).

41 (pls. 54–5 and fig. 10b)

Cup: GR 1867.5–8.1012 (*BM Cat Vases* E 59)
From Nola; Blacas collection.
Purchased from the estate of the Duc de Blacas, 1866.

Bibliography: Murray *DGV* no. 38 (I); *VA* 105 no. 86; Hoppin ii 99 no. 64; *AV* 219, 119; *ARV* 312, 190; Bloesch *FAS* 95, 40; *ARV*² 475, 266; Nachbaur *Makron* 94–5, 102–3, 168 (cat. M 47).

Dimensions: width 29.4; diam. 23.0; diam. of tondo 11.6; ht. 8.6; diam. exterior ground line 8.8; diam. of foot 8.8.

Condition: made up from frr.: remains of six pairs of large repair holes (5 on body, 1 on foot); three small rim frr. missing; some filing of black-glazed surface near joins.

Description

INTERIOR: boy with hare.
A boy with a himation over his right shoulder and over his left forearm moves to the right. He looks back to the left and holds a hare by its ears in his right hand. The boy has a red fillet in his hair and the hare's skin is done with dilute glaze strokes.
Border: complex running maeander (five-stroke, anticlockwise); odd man at 6 o'clock.

EXTERIOR: youths.

Side A (L): three youths, one playing the pipes.
On the left a youth leans on a knotty stick to the right. He is clad in himation and has a red fillet in his hair. The stick supports him under his left armpit; his left arm is wrapped round the front of his body and he gestures with his right hand. In the centre a youth sits on a *klismos* and plays a pair of pipes. He wears a himation and has a red fillet in his hair; a relief line under his nose indicates that his lips are pursed. In front of him hangs a flute-case with red tassels. On the far right is a youth in three-quarter back view leaning on a stick. He wears a himation and has a red fillet in his hair.

Side B (U): three youths, one holding a wreath.
On the left stands a youth with a red fillet in his hair and a himation. He leans on a stick and holds out a purse in his left hand, his right hand no doubt resting on his hip under the drapery. In front of him hangs a flute-case with red ties. In the centre sits a youth on a plain block topped by a cushion decorated with pairs of stripes flanking a zigzag line, holding out a red wreath with both hands. He wears a himation and has a red fillet around his hair. On the far right a youth in a himation and with a red fillet in his hair stoops to the left, his left hand on the top of a stick. He holds a flower up to his nose in his right hand. Ground line: single reserved line.

Relief line contour throughout (except hair); dilute glaze for minor interior markings; reserved line inside and outside lip.

c. 480 BC.

Comment: Placed by Murray in the style of Douris and more tentatively so by Smith ('later style of Duris'). Attributed by Beazley to Makron. Placed by Nachbaur in her early to middle phase (?490–480 BC); C. Isler-Kerenyi (*AntK* 27 [1984] 156–9) seems to place it *c.* 480–475 BC. A plain, later work with many comparable pieces in Beazley's list (e.g. *ARV*² 466, 107; 475, 260–2, 265, 267–9; cf. also Beazley's comment in C.B. iii 41 on no. 143). Bloesch has attributed the potting to Hieron.

For purses and hares see Koch-Harnack *passim*; Reinsberg *EHK* passim. For similar conversation scenes with music, compare the outside of a cup now in the Louvre (*ARV*² 475, 261: M. Denoyelle, *RLouvre* 5/6 [1991] 13–20).

Nos. 42–46: The Brygos Painter

The Brygos Painter is the name given to the painter of the finest cups signed by the potter Brygos. In addition to Beazley's lists, see the following accounts and publications: Hartwig *M* 307–74; Tonks *Brygos*; Buschor *GV* 172–3; *VA* 89–93; Beazley *VP* 23–5; J.D. Beazley in C.B. i 13–26 (nos. 17–29); Richter and Hall 63–71 (nos. 40–50); J.D. Beazley in *Studies Robinson* ii 74–83; Richter *Survey*² 78–81; Robertson *GP* 106–9; A.H.S. 336–9; Cambitoglou *Brygos Painter*; Wegner *Brygosmaler*; A.M. Tamassia, *BdA* 52 (1976)

1–9; Boardman *ARFV Archaic* 135–6; D. Williams, *JbBerlMus* 24 (1982) 17–40; M. True, *Getty Vases* 1 (1983) 73–84; J.-J. Maffre in *Amsterdam Colloquium* 113–16; Immerwahr *Attic Script* 88–9; *Princeton Record* 50, 1 (1991) 57 lower; Robertson *Art of Vase-painting* 93–100.

Beazley commented on the problem of isolating the early phase of the Brygos Painter (J.D. Beazley, 'Potter and Painter in Ancient Athens', *Proceedings of the British Academy* 30 [1944] 33 = *Beazley Lectures* 57): he noted that the artist's style seemed fully formed on even the earliest looking piece (*ARV²* 371, 14). In his lists he also marked a number of cups as 'late' (*ARV²* 379, 142, 145–58; 380, 160–70), together with a neck-amphora (*ARV²* 383, 201), some lekythoi (*ARV²* 383, 203; 384, 209, 211–16 and 222) and a squat lekythos (*ARV²* 385, 224). He also labelled some larger scale works 'very late' (*ARV²* 381, 174–5; 385, 228).

It is, in fact, possible to isolate an early phase in the Brygos Painter's career: this belongs to the second half of the 490s (see on **42** [E 71]). His middle, fully mature phase dominates the 480s. His late pieces may be placed at the end of the decade, with some late or very late pieces falling after 480. These last works are a mixture of rather simply decorated cups and much more ambitious large-scale pieces. The Brygos Painter decorated mainly cups, but also turned his hand to other symposiac vessels such as skyphoi, kantharoi, rhyta (an important series), kyathoi, mugs and plates. In addition, he painted neck-amphorae and lekythoi. Finally, two very unusual shapes are also represented – a kalathoid psykter (*ARV²* 385, 228) and a pair of stamnoid psykters in the Getty (81.AE.217.7–52 and 64–82). See also on **53**.

For the potter Brygos see also Bloesch *FAS* 81–90 and *ARV²* 398–9. On the name see on **43** (E 68).

42 (pls. 56–7 and fig. 10c)

Cup: GR 1866.8–5.4 (*BM Cat Vases* E 71)
From Vulci (?).
Presented by Mr. T.S. Smith, 1866 (acquired from G. Basseggio).

Bibliography: *AZ* 1870, pl. 39 with p. 106; Murray *DGV* no. 49; Hartwig *M* 327 and 687 no. 19; Tonks *Brygos* 108 no. 16; *VA* 91; Hoppin i, 133 no. 65; *AV* 178 no. 26; *ARV* 248, 25; *ARV²* 372, 29; Wegner *Brygosmaler* 129–35, pls. 30 a (I), 1 (A–B) and 33 a (detail of A); Sweet *Sport and Recreation* 202 fig. 76 (B); *Beazley Add²* 225; D. Williams in *New Perspectives* 293 fig. 10 (A); D. Williams in *Looking at Greek Vases* 108 fig. 43 (A).

Dimensions: width 31.4; diam. 23.7; diam. of tondo 13.4; diam. of exterior ground line 9.6.

Condition: made up from frr.; three rim frr. missing and one large area from right of tondo; foot missing (alien foot removed).

Description

INTERIOR: youth playing pipes.
A youth moves to the right, bending forward as he plays a pair of pipes. He has a dotted chlamys with a black border draped over his left shoulder and a red band in his hair with three large blossoms at the front. On the right leans a knotty stick; from which hangs by a red tie a food basket with red tassels (much of the basket is missing together with the youth's left foot).

INSCRIPTION: ΗΟΓΑ[Ι≶], ΔΕ[.]Ι (retr., perhaps nonsense)
Border: stopt maeander (four-stroke, anticlockwise).

EXTERIOR: symposium.
Side A (U): symposiast, flute girl and komast.
On the left a youth with a himation (black border) around his waist and legs reclines to the left on a couch with a backrest. He turns his head to the right and gestures with his right hand (the hand is missing), his left resting on the back of the flute girl in the centre. There is a red band with three large leaves at the front round his head. His cushion is a wineskin and a skyphos rests on the ground under his couch. A food basket with red ties hangs from a red tie up on the left, while a plain stick leans against the handle-root. In the centre stands a woman playing the pipes to the right. She is dressed in a chiton, shoes and a plain sakkos. On the right is a komast in an extraordinary pose. He is bent over and seen from behind so that, in extreme foreshortening, between his splayed legs appear his anus, his testicles and penis, and his belly, and to the left his shoulders and the back of his head. His left hand is on the ground, his right on his right buttock. He wears a pair of shoes and has a red band around his head with blossoms on either side. On the left a dotted chlamys with a black border, presumably his, is wrapped around a plain stick. A food basket with red tassels hangs from red ties up on the right.

INSCRIPTIONS (nonsense): ΝΑΝ, ΗΗΝΟΝΟ (?)

Side B (L): youth kneeling on a couch, youth dancing and youth playing the pipes.
On the left a youth kneels on a couch with a backrest, as he wields a wineskin over his head. He has a red band in his hair with large leaves at the front. On the couch is his dotted himation (black border). Hanging up on the right is a food basket with red ties (most missing). In the centre dances a naked youth. He kicks up his right foot and swings his arms to keep his balance, his right behind him, his left above his head. He has a red band around his head with two large blossoms at the front. On the right hangs a spotted flute-case. On the far right a youth leans to the left on a knotty stick as he plays the pipes, a chlamys (black border) draped over his lower back and the crutch of the stick under his right armpit. He has a red hair-band with five large leaves at the front; a relief line indicates that his cheeks are puffed. On the extreme right a food basket with red tassels hangs from red ties.

INSCRIPTION (nonsense): ΝΝΟΝΝ
Under one handle, a *kados* inscribed ΚΑΛΟ≶
Ground line: two reserved lines.

Relief contour throughout (except hair); dilute glaze for minor interior markings; thick reserved line inside lip, thin outside; added red for inscriptions.

c. 495–490 BC.

Comment: Attributed by Hartwig to Brygos and given to the Brygos Painter by Beazley. It is an early work and should be compared with a number of other cups (e.g. *ARV*^{2} 369, 6; 372, 34; 375, 70 (now Munich 8956); 376, 88; Getty 86.AE.287 [ex Bareiss 85; *Para* 367]; 390, 39 (*CVA Amsterdam* 1, pl. 31, 3); 402, 14 [NFA Classical Auctions, 11 December 1991 no. 82]; 405, lower i [Mannheim]) and the skyphos in Boston (*ARV*^{2} 381, 173). These follow on from the Faina athlete cup (*ARV*^{2} 404, 9), probably the Brygos Painter's earliest surviving work, which may be closely compared with athlete cups by Onesimos (especially *ARV*^{2} 322, 38).

For the lone piper on the tondo see Beazley in C.B. i 23 (on no. 24). For a recent discussion of the transition from *symposion* to *komos* see C. Bron in *Copenhagen Colloquium* 71–9. The fistfights and disorderly conduct that result from passing beyond Dionysos' recommended three kraters of wine (Euboulos *apud* Athenaeus ii 36b) at a symposium are sometimes shown, especially as it merges into an ensuing komos: *Beazley Add*^{2} 393 (Karlsruhe 70/395); *ARV*^{2} 325, 77. For wineskins as cushions see H. Moebius, *AA* 1964, 294–9; compare also the Brygos Painter's kantharos in New York (*ARV*^{2} 382, 183), as well as some pieces by the Foundry Painter (*ARV*^{2} 401, 11; 402, 12; 382, 184) and Onesimos (*ARV*^{2} 326, 86 *bis*; 328, 121). For the motifs of the chlamys wrapped around a stick and the basket tied to a stick compare the Brygos Painter's cup in Orvieto (*ARV*^{2} 372, 33). The motif of stick and chlamys also appears on Florence 3921 (*ARV*^{2} 372, 31; cf. also on *ARV*^{2} 413, 15 and Adria B 711 – *CVA* pl. 20, 6), while that of stick and basket might be compared with the tondo of a cup in Boston by Onesimos (*ARV*^{2} 324, 65) and the stick and flute-case on the White/Levy cup by the Foundry Painter (*Glories of the Past* no. 119). For the *kados* under the handle see Beazley in C.B. ii 35: add Copenhagen inv. 3880 (*ARV*^{2} 373, 36 with *Para* 372) and the White/Levy cup. For the back view of the head compare **47** (E 67) and the Mannheim cup (*ARV*^{2} 405 middle); for the view of the anus compare a fragmentary cup in a Centre Island private collection attributed to Onesimos by Bothmer with a satyr, seen from behind, bending over at a well-head. On spectacular foreshortening in the Late Archaic period see in general Williams in *New Perspectives* 292–3 and in *Looking at Greek Vases* 108–9. The large leaves at the front of some of the hair-bands are not detailed enough for identification.

43 (pls. 58–9 and fig. 10d)

Cup: GR 1848.6–19.7 (*BM Cat Vases* E 68)
From Vulci
Bought of G. Basseggio, 1848.

Bibliography: S. Birch, *AZ* 1851, 367; Hartwig *M* 319–24, 687 no. 14, pls. 35, 1 (I) and 34 (A–B); Murray *DGV* no. 46, with p. 16; *VA* 93 fig. 61 (detail of A); Hoppin i, 132 no. 62; *AV* 177, 18; Tonks *Brygos* 108 no. 18; *ARV* 247, 21; Bloesch *FAS* 85 no. 22, pl. 23, 4; *ARV*^{2} 371, 24; Cambitoglou *Brygos Painter* 10–11, pl. 2, figs. 1 and 3–4; *Para* 365 and 367; Wegner *Brygosmaler* 119–24, pls 8 (I and B), 27c (detail I) and 36e (detail I); Peschel *HSK* figs. 62 (I), 60 (A) and 61 (B) with p. 101–4; Sweet *Sport and Recreation* 207 fig. 79 (A);Open Univ. ii fig. 5 (A); *Beazley Add*^{2} 225; Immerwahr *Attic Script* 88 no. 548; *Sympotica* pl. 11 a-b (A-B); Robertson *Art of Vase-painting* 96–7, fig. 91.

Dimensions: width 39.7; diam. 31.9; diam. of tondo 17.3; ht. 12.7; diam. of exterior ground line 13.9; diam. of foot 12.0.

Condition: made up from frr.; one wall fr. missing, together with some chips.

Description

INTERIOR: symposiast and girl dancer.

A youth reclines against a large striped cushion on a couch (only the horizontal board shown) to the left. He is named ΓΙLΙΓΟΣ (retr.; for Philippos). He wears a dotted himation with a black border on his left shoulder and over his lower body and has a red wreath in his hair. He grips a pair of pipes in his left hand and holds his right arm out straight to the left in what might be a gesture to stop. His mouth is open. In front of the couch, to the left, dances a very young girl, named KALLIΣTO, who has straight short-cut hair and wears a transparent chiton and a red wreath in her hair. She lifts up her chiton with both hands so that it is slightly raised, either to facilitate her dance or to reveal her ankles. Her left foot is off the ground and she looks downwards. To the right the narrow end of a three-legged table is shown (the rest being cut off by the tondo frame) on which are a skyphos (black handle outwards) and four red garlands. In the background behind the youth his spotted flute-case (*sybene*) is suspended and his knotty stick leans against the border.

Border: groups of three units of stopt maeander (four-stroke, anticlockwise) alternating with dotted cross-squares.

EXTERIOR: symposium.

Side A (U): two symposiasts accompanied by two hetairai and a youth with a *barbiton*.

On the left a youth dressed in a himation (black border) and shoes leans against a fluted column with a plain block base and a Doric capital over a collar of ovolos. He has a red wreath in his blond hair (dilute glaze used) and holds out a *barbiton* (seven strings done in relief line) with both hands: a *plektron* (reserved handle; red end) is attached to its frame by a red cord (his chest and upper arms are lost). At the foot of the first couch sits a blond-haired hetaira wearing chiton, dotted himation with a battlement border, plain sakkos and disc earring, her feet resting on a plain block. She has a red wreath around her head and holds a large cup by the stem and one handle: on it is written KALE. She seems to look at the full cup with great concentration and her mouth is slightly open. Over the girl is written ΓΙLON KALOΣ (for Philon). On the couch a youth reclines to the left, but turns his head back to the right, his mouth open. He wears a himation (battlement border at waist) and a thick reserved fillet, the tail of which he holds in his right hand. He leans against a striped cushion, his elbow actually on the turned post of the couch (all the couches on the exterior have dilute glaze strokes to indicate the grain of the wood). In front of his couch is a three-legged table. On the wall above his knee a footed food basket with red ties is suspended by a red loop. Over his head is written: ΔΕΜΟΝΙΚΟΣ. On the right stands a blond-haired woman wearing a chiton (dilute glaze folds on sleeves), a sakkos decorated with zigzags, a disc earring and a red wreath. She plays the pipes, a relief line to show that her cheeks are puffed. On the far right a bearded man reclines to the left. He wears a dotted himation and a red wreath. His left arm dangles down but his right holds a skyphos out to the right: his little finger juts out stiffly. In front of the couch is a three-legged table. Behind the pipe-player a knotty stick rests against the cushion of the first symposiast. Above his companion a footed food basket with red ties is hung from a red loop. Above him is written: ARISTOKRATES.

Side B (L): two symposiasts accompanied by two hetairai and a youth with a dipper and a strainer.

On the extreme left is a fluted column with a plain block base and a Doric capital over an ovolo collar. A naked boy with a red wreath in his hair leans against it, his right leg flexed, his weight on his frontal left leg. He looks to the left, but his torso and left leg are frontal; his right leg is flexed behind so that it rests only on the toes. He holds a dipper with a long handle terminating in a duck's head and a strainer (the holes in the central perforated disc are done with dilute glaze). There is an accidental splash of added red on his left shoulder. Up on the right a food basket with red ties is suspended by a red loop and above it is written ΗΟΓΑΙΣΚΑΛΟΣ. At the foot of the left-hand couch a woman sits on a plain stool with a plain cushion, playing the pipes. She is dressed in chiton (dilute glaze folds on the sleeves) and himation (black border) and has a red wreath around her short cut blond hair (dilute glaze). On the couch a bearded man reclines to the left. He has twisted his head and torso round to the right and holds out a skyphos in his right hand (little finger extended). He wears a dotted himation with a black border and has a red wreath in his hair. He leans against a striped cushion. Over his knee is hung a *chelys* lyre and under his couch rests a pair of boots (one in profile, one back view). Over his head is written his name: ΔΙΓΙΛΟΣ (for Diphilos). Further to the right, beyond a spotted flute-case hanging in the field is written ΚΑΛΟΣ. On the right hand couch are a hetaira and a youth. On the right is the youth, his dotted himation in disarray and his right foot raised. He has grasped the hetaira by her left wrist and has put his right hand on her left shoulder. He has a red wreath in his hair and leans against a striped cushion. His mouth is slightly open. The hetaira, who wears a chiton, girt at the waist with a black girdle, has her right hand under the youth's right elbow. Her right heel rests on the end of the couch; her left foot dangles beside it. Her hair has two wavy dilute lines below the main mass. Above and behind their legs a food basket with red ties hangs from a red loop; on the floor under the couch is an animal-legged footstool decorated with two stars – against it rests a pair of sandals (that in the centre seen from under the sole, that at the right hand end seen edge-on). Over their two heads is the inscription: ΝΙΚΟΓΙΛΕ ΚΑΛΕ (for Nikophile).

Ground line: double reserved line.

Relief line contour throughout (except hair); dilute glaze for minor interior markings; thick reserved line inside lip, thin outside; added red for inscriptions.

c. 490 BC.

Comment: Attributed by K. Wernicke (*Die griechischen Vasen mit Lieblingsnamen* [Berlin 1890] 15) to Hieron, by F. Dümmler (*Berliner philologische Wochenschrift* 8 [1888] 20) to Brygos. Dümmler was followed by Hartwig and Hoppin; Beazley gave it to his Brygos Painter. It is an early mature work of the Brygos Painter and may be compared with pieces like the Louvre Iliupersis cup and the Würzburg *komos* cup (*ARV*² 369, 1; 372, 32). The potting has been attributed by Bloesch to Brygos.

Relatively few straightforward symposium scenes by the Brygos Painter have survived (*ARV*² 372, 25, 26 and 28): on a Louvre fr. the symposium merges into love-making (*ARV*² 372, 30) and on the other London cup it devolves into a komos (**41** [E 71]), while on a Cabinet des Médailles piece Herakles makes an entrance (*ARV*² 370, 8). The figure of the boy with dipper and strainer next to the column on side B closely recalls the figure of a boy on a cup by the Foundry Painter (*ARV*² 401, 11: see *VA* 93). It also recalls the servant of Achilles on the Vienna skyphos (*ARV*² 380, 171) and the servant at the symposium on a cup by Makron (*ARV*² 478, 316).

For the *barbiton* and the *chelys* lyre see Maas and McIntosh Snyder 79–112 and 113–38. For the *plektron* see most recently F. Jurgeit in *Dohrn Festschrift* 53–62. For the head-post of the couches on the exterior cf. the Chiusi cup (*ARV*² 389, 24), which may well be a work of the Brygos Painter himself. For food baskets with a small flat base see E.R. Knauer in *Getty Vases* 3, p. 95 fn. 12.

For Kallisto as a hetaira's name cf. Aelian *Var. Hist.* 13, 32; see further Peschel *HSK* 183–4. *Diphilos kalos* and *Nikophile kale* are so-called tag-*kaloi* (cf. Beazley *ARV*² 1574 and 1614; Peschel 396 note 245). For the name Nikophile see Peschel 184.

For the lack of aspiration (*P* for *PH*) on this cup see Hartwig *M* 319–21; P. Kretschmer, *Die griechischen Vaseninschriften ihrer Sprache nach untersucht* (Gütersloh 1894) 81; Cambitoglou *Brygos Painter* 11 with note 37; Immerwahr *Attic Script* 88. Immerwahr's suggestion that the lack of aspiration may have been intended to indicate that the symposiasts were drunk (more clearly on *ARV*² 376, 90) is to be preferred to the idea that the painter was a foreigner. On the status and origins of potters and painters see most recently D. Williams in A. Verbanck-Pierard and D. Vivier (eds.), *Culture et Cité. L'avènement d'Athènes à l'époque archaique* (Brussels forthcoming).

44 (pls. 60–1 and fig. 11a)

Cup: GR 1843.11–3.11 (*BM Cat Vases* E 69)
From Vulci; Canino collection.
Bought of the Principessa di Canino, 1843.

Bibliography: *Mus. Étrusque* no. 645; S. Birch, *Archaeologia* 32 (1847) pls 8 (I), 9 (A), 11 (B), with p. 150–67; Murray *DGV* no. 47; Klein *Euphronios*[2] 238; Hartwig *M* 359 with fig. 49, 688 no. 49; Tonks *Brygos* 108 no. 17; Hoppin i, 132 no. 63; *AV* 176, 7; *ARV* 246, 2; Bloesch *FAS* 82 no. 10; *ARV*[2] 369, 2; *Para* 365; Robertson *HGA* 232, pl. 76 b; Wegner *Brygosmaler* 83–90, pl. 9 (I and A); *Beazley Add*[2] 224; Schefold *Sagen* 260 fig. 236 (I); Carpenter *Art and Myth* fig. 330 (A–B); Robertson *Art of Vase-painting* 88, 91 fig. 82, 95.

Dimensions: width 41.5; diam. 32.7; diam. of tondo 16.4; ht. 13.8; diam. of exterior ground line 16.0; diam. of foot 12.0.

Condition: made up from frr.: two rim frr. and four small wall frr. missing, together with other chips.

Description

INTERIOR: man leading a woman (Odysseus and Briseis?).
On the left a young woman, head lowered, is being led to the right. She wears a chiton and a himation (horizontal battlement border, dilute glaze vertical band, rows of dilute glaze dots) which is pulled up over the back of her head. She has a disc earring and a stephane with a row of sigmas. Her hair has a wash of dilute glaze and one long curly tress falls down behind her ear. Her mouth is slightly open and she must be exchanging words with the bearded man on the right, who similarly has his mouth open. Dressed in short chiton (dilute glaze folds), himation (rows of dots; battlement upper border) and petasos with red ties, he moves to the right, but turns his head back to look at the girl whom he leads, gripping her left wrist and hand in his right. He holds a spear in his left hand across his body, so that the point is above her head. There is dilute shading on his petasos at the top and above the beginning of the brim. His hair and beard are done with a dilute glaze wash and there are rows of dilute glaze dots on his neck.
Border: stopt maeander (five-stroke, anticlockwise).

EXTERIOR: the Arms of Achilles.

Side A (U): quarrel over the arms of Achilles.
On the far left a male in dotted chlamys holds the right arm of the figure in front of him (his head and part of his draped lower torso are missing). In front is a bearded man, probably Ajax, in boots (dilute glaze wash) with horizontal rolls and red ties and a dotted himation with a black border loosely draped over his arms, who attempts to move forward to the right. He holds a sword back in his right hand and a striped scabbard in his left. His pectorals and mid-line are enhanced with dilute glaze to indicate hair. A youth tries to push him back to the left. He has a chlamys with rows of dots in dilute glaze over his upper arms and turns his head back to the right. His hair is painted with dilute glaze. In the centre is a man in a long chiton (folds in dilute glaze) and a dotted himation with a battlement upper border; he is presumably Agamemnon. He moves to the left, but his arms are outstretched to left and right; his head, which is missing, was turned to the right, as the red ties from his headband on the left indicate. On the right a youth pushes to the right at a bearded man. The youth has a himation (black border, rows of dots) loosely draped over his shoulders; his hair is combed up in plait over his neck and he has a double red hair-band. The bearded man, probably Odysseus, in front of him endeavours to move to the left. In the struggle his himation (black border, rows of dots) has slipped from his right shoulder; he has just drawn his sword from its striped scabbard, which he holds in his left hand (hand and top of scabbard missing). He wears boots like those worn by Ajax: rolls above the ankles, red ties and dilute wash. His pectorals and mid-line are enhanced with dilute glaze to indicate hair and his lips are slightly parted. On the far right a bearded man moves to the left, a dotted himation (black border) over his shoulders, his right hand gripping the left shoulder of the man in front, his left hand probably the man's left wrist (both missing). His hair is combed up into a stiff fringe and his pectorals and mid-line are enhanced with dilute glaze to indicate hair.

Side B (L): the vote for the arms of Achilles.
On the far left stands Odysseus, dressed in a dotted himation with a battlement border (all the himatia on this side have such a border) and shoes. He leans on a knotty stick, his right hand on his hip under the drapery, his left hand up in front of his chest. His pectorals and mid-line are enhanced with dilute glaze to indicate hair. His mouth is open and he has a red apicate fillet. In front of him stands a youth, dressed in a himation with rows of dots and leaning on a knotty stick. He reaches down to the right with his right hand to place his pebble (not shown) on the plain block (dilute wash) in the centre. His hair is tied up in a plait over his neck and he has a double red fillet. His left hand is to be thought of as on top of his stick, near his right armpit. In front of him stands Athena who wears a chiton, himation, scaly snake-fringed aegis (dilute wash inside) and Attic helmet (dilute wash for caul; black neck-guard). She holds a spear upright in her right hand and gestures with her left hand. Her head (hair done with dilute wash) is turned to the right, but her right knee is bent and the leg is to be thought of as facing to the left. Her lower legs are obscured by the corner of the block. On the corner in front of the folds of her chiton are two rows of black pebbles, totalling twenty. In the centre stands a bearded man to the left, wearing a dotted himation and a red fillet. He twists his right shoulder in order to place a pebble (not shown) on the block which hides his lower legs. His left hand is on a knotty stick, which goes under his left armpit (lower part of stick not drawn). At the right corner of the block stands a youth in a himation with rows of dots and double red hair-band leaning back on a knotty stick. He also holds his right hand down to cast his vote. On the corner of the block in front of the folds of his himation are two rows of black pebbles, totalling eleven. On the right a bearded man in a dotted himation and shoes moves forward to the left to vote, but turns his head back to the right. He holds a knotty stick in his left hand across his body and holds his right hand out to vote (pebble not shown). He has a reserved head-band. On the far right stands Ajax, his dotted himation with its battlement border framing his head. He leans on a knotty stick (with groups of horizontal lines

in dilute glaze on it), his head lowered in despair, his right hand to his forehead. He wears a red fillet.
Under handles: B/A, Corinthian helmet (dilute glaze on cheek-piece; black on neck-piece; dilute glaze wash for fur frontlet; chequer-board pattern on caul) on top of a shield (dilute glaze hatching before rim); A/B, pair of greaves (dilute glaze wash, elaborate modelling around knee-caps and a scroll on the calf, red ties above).
Ground line: two reserved lines.

Relief line contour throughout (except hair); dilute glaze for minor interior markings; thick reserved line inside lip, thin outside.

c. 490–485 BC.

Comment: Attributed to Brygos by Klein, who was followed by Hartwig and others. Beazley gave it to his Brygos Painter. It is an early mature work of the artist and may be compared with the Louvre Troilos cup and the Vatican arming cup (*ARV*^{2} 369, 3; 373, 48). These seem to be slightly later than **43** (E 68) and they lead on to fully mature works such as the Vienna skyphos (*ARV*^{2} 380, 171). There is both vitality and power in the drawing and a fine range of moods in the narrative. Bloesch has attributed the potting to Brygos.

The quarrel between Ajax and Odysseus for the arms of Achilles has been discussed recently by O. Touchefeu in *LIMC* i *sv* Aias I p. 324–7; D. Williams, *AntK* 23 (1980) 137–45; Schefold *Sagen* 259–61. See also H.A. Shapiro, *BABesch* 56 (1981) 149–50; G.F. Pinney and R. Hamilton, *AJA* 86 (1982) 581–4; and M. Tiverios, *Mia "Krisis ton Oplon" tou zographou tou Sulea* (Athens 1985); but contrast D. Williams in F. Lissarrague and F. Thelamon (eds.), *Image et céramique grecque* (Rouen 1983) 139 f.n. 60. For a possible early representation of the quarrel see A.-N. Malagardis in *Ancient Greek and Related Pottery, Copenhagen* 390–406. See also now Beazley in *Beazley Lectures* 91–2 and Robertson *Art of Vase-painting* 87–9.

Various suggestions have been offered as to the identity of the two figures on the interior: see *ARV*^{2} 369, 2; Robertson *HGA* 232; D. Williams, *AntK* 23 (1980) 140; Schefold *Sagen* 261; Robertson *Art of Vase-painting* 95–6. The petasos worn by the man recommends an identification as Odysseus; the girl might be Chryseis, as D.S. Robertson suggested following *Iliad* i 439–45 (quoted in *ARV*^{2} 369, 2), but this would remove any close connection with the scenes on the exterior. Martin Robertson (*HGA* 232) suggested Tekmessa with either Teukros leading her away after the death of Ajax or Ajax himself with his newly won concubine. Schefold, however, has recently suggested Briseis, an additional prize that went to Odysseus with Achilles' arms. The pair seem to be conversing and the angle of the spear recalls that held by Patroklos on the Getty Iliupersis cup by Onesimos (D. Williams, *Getty Vases* 5 [1991] 58): it surely symbolises possession. As a result, Schefold's solution is perhaps the best. A very similar pair, only the man lacks the petasos, occurs on a fine cup by the Foundry Painter in Tarquinia (*ARV*^{2} 405, 1), which Beazley identified as Agamemnon and Briseis.

For the chequer board pattern on the caul of the helmet cf. the Vienna skyphos (*ARV*^{2} 380, 171) and see Beazley in C.B. iii, 36, where he suggests that on such helmets a patterned fabric might have been attached to the metal, although it now seems more likely that the bronze was actually painted (cf. H. Bron in M. True and J. Podany [eds.], *Small Bronze Sculpture from the Ancient World* [Malibu 1990] 189–94). The horizontal bands on the boots worn by Ajax and Odysseus on side A are probably caused by tying additional thongs around the soft boots to try to stop them sliding down: cf. Morrow *Greek Footwear* 65: she notes the same effect on the Parthenon Frieze, North XXXIX 122 (her pl. 45).

45 (pls. 62–4 and fig. 11b)

Cup, type C: GR 1873.8–20.376 (*BM Cat Vases* E 65)
From Capua.
Bought of Alessandro Castellani, 1873.

Bibliography: W. Helbig, *BdI* 1872, 39–41; F. Matz *AdI* 1872, 294–308; Klein *M*^{2} 183–4 no. 8; Murray *DGV* no. 43 (I); Klein *M*^{2} 183 no. 8; L. Urlichs, *Der Vasenmaler Brygos* (Würzburg 1875) 5–6; Hartwig *M* 687 no. 6; Hoppin i, 110–11 no. 4; *VA* 89; *AV* 176, 5; F.R. i 238–44, pl. 47 (A–B); Tonks *Brygos* 104 no. 8; *ARV* 247, 13; Bloesch *FAS* 134 no. 4, pl. 36, 2; *ARV*^{2} 370, 13 and p. 1649; Cambitoglou *Brygos Painter* 20–3, pls. 8, 1 (I), 9 (A–B), 1, 4–5 (profile); *Para* 365 and 367; Wegner *Brygosmaler* 28–31, pls. 6–7, 16b, 34a, 38a and 40g; Boardman *ARFV Archaic* fig. 252 (A–B); Schefold *GkhK* 123–5, figs. 155–6 (A–B); E. Simon in Kurtz and Sparkes *Eye of Greece* 125–9, figs. 30 a–b; D. Williams *Greek Vases* 46 fig. 50 (I) and 47 fig. 51 (A); K. Schefold in *LIMC* iii *sv* Chrysippos II, pl. 228 (I); I.Th. Kakrides (ed.), *Ellenike Mythologia* (Athens 1986) I, 57 fig. 19 (B) and 189 fig. 64 (A); R. Hägg, N. Marinatos and G.C. Nordquist (eds.), *Early Greek Cult Practice* (Stockholm 1988) 58 figs. 11 a–b; Immerwahr *Attic Script* 88–9 no. 551; Robertson *Art of Vase-painting* 96–7 with fig. 90; D. Williams, *AJA* 96 (1992) 622–624.

Dimensions: width 36.6; diam. 27.5; diam. of tondo 17.1; ht. 12.3; diam. of exterior ground line 12.5; diam. of foot 11.2.

Condition: intact.

Description

INTERIOR: Warrior and girl.
On the left a warrior sits on a stool with fringed cushion decorated with rows of dots and rows of two-tailed blobs. He is dressed in short chiton (dilute glaze folds on shoulder), dotted himation (battlement upper border, black lower border), cuirass, Corinthian helmet and red greave-pads (upper band crenellated, lower plain). His hair and beard are done with dilute glaze; a long curl falls down over his shoulder. He holds a spear upright in his left hand (a group of dilute glaze lines on upper shaft; point breaks the border pattern) and holds out a bossed phiale in his right. The bosses are done with raised clay and then gilded by using red miltos as a bole. His mouth is open and his name is written as if issuing from it: +PV≶IΓΓO≶. On the right stands

a girl in chiton (folds of second overfold and sleeve done in dilute glaze; ends of red girdle show over her right knee) and himation. Her blond hair (done with dilute glaze) is tied up at the back with a double reserved cord with three tassels that fall on her shoulder and a hair slide or clip. She supports the rim of a black shield (reserved line at joint with rim) with her left hand and holds up a dipper with a long handle that terminates in a very schematic duck's head: she is about to pour wine into the warrior's phiale. Over her back is written her name: ΙΕVΧΣΟ. Her disc earring is done with raised clay and was gilded, like the phiale.
Border: dotted saltire cross (blobs at ends of arms) alternating with three units of stopt maeander (five- to six-stroke, anticlockwise: reversed behind helmet crest and woman's head, and only two units at two o'clock).

EXTERIOR: satyrs threaten Hera and Iris.

Side A: Hera threatened by satyrs
Creeping out from under the handle root on the extreme left is a satyr, named ΤΕΡΓΟΝ. His left knee is almost on the ground, his right is doubled up under him; both hands are on the ground. Like all the other satyrs on the cup, he has his mouth slightly open, his hairline is receding, he has an erection and he wears a red wreath of ivy leaves. In addition, however, his long hair falls down in curls over his back. Almost alongside him walks another satyr, named ΒΑΒΑΚ+ΟΣ. His fists are clenched (the preliminary sketch shows that the left arm was originally raised by *c.* 90 degrees: see fig. 1,h). In front of him is a third satyr, named ΗVΔΡΙΣ (the first letter is cramped and may be a mistake for *K*), who moves forward, but the way he spreads his hands suggests he may be hesitating (his erection is obscured by the tail of the next satyr). In the centre is a fourth satyr, named ΣΤVΟΝ, who stoops as he moves forward. He is almost in three-quarter back view. Facing these satyrs stands Hermes (ΗΕΡΜΕΣ retr., except final sigma). He wears a dotted chlamys with a black border tied at the neck (circular brooch), petasos (dilute hatching along the curve before the brim, to indicate shadow) with red ties and winged boots and carries a *kerykeion* (four raised dots for gilding on finial) in his left hand. His right hand is raised with thumb and forefinger together. Behind Hermes, Hera (ΗΕΡΑ retr.) moves rapidly away to the right, her head turned back to the left and her right arm outstretched. She wears a chiton (dilute glaze folds on sleeve) with a red tie under the overfold, a himation with a battlement border, a stephane, a snake bracelet and disc earring (stephane and bracelet are done with raised clay and were gilded). She has gathered some of her chiton in her left hand to aid her flight. On the far right Herakles (ΗΕΡΑΚΛΕΣ retr., except final sigma) moves rapidly to the left: his left foot is off the ground. He is dressed in a striped jacket, trousers decorated with stripes, rows of dots and double tailed blobs, a short chiton and his lion-skin. The upper folds of his chiton are done with dilute glaze. He holds a bow (red string) and arrow out in his left hand and a club, which is done with raised clay and was gilded, back in his right hand. A quiver with two arrows in it hangs from a red strap at his left hip. He is shown in three-quarter back view.

Side B: Iris caught by two satyrs, Dionysos and a satyr.
On the left a satyr, named ΔΡΟΜΙΣ, runs past a plain block: both his feet are off the ground and his arms are outstretched. The preliminary sketch lines indicate that the artist had once intended to draw a folding stool covered with an animal skin on this block (see fig. 1f). In front of him stands Dionysos (ΔΙΟΝVΣΟΣ) with his legs crossed, the left frontal, the right on tip toe behind. He is dressed in a long chiton with a red girdle and a himation and has an animal skin (*pardalis*) tied around his neck and a red ivy wreath in his hair. He has a striped sceptre in his left hand and a black kantharos in his right. The preliminary sketch indicates that a regular vine branch was once intended. In the centre is an altar with volute finials and an ovolo pattern. At the centre of either volute is a lump of raised clay that was gilded. The altar is wreathed with ivy and has three splashes of red, either blood or wine. A satyr, named Ε+ΟΝ, is climbing over the altar to reach Iris. He is seen in three-quarter back view and has his right foot on top of the altar, next to the fire-brick, his left leg trails behind. He has gripped Iris' right wrist with his left hand and tugs at the upper folds of her chiton with his right. Iris (ΙΡΙΝ) runs away to the right, left foot off the ground, but turns her head back towards Echon. She has scaly wings and is dressed in a chiton (dilute glaze folds for second overfold), a plain sakkos and disc earring (raised clay for gilding). In her right hand she holds a *kerykeion*. In her left hand she has an elongated object filled with a dilute glaze wash: it continues in dilute glaze without relief line contouring up in a high curve with a slight blob at the end (see fig. 1g). On the right a third satyr, named ΛΕΦΣΙΣ, stops Iris' flight. He has caught her left elbow with his right hand and endeavours to wrench the object from her with his other hand. He is seen in three-quarter back view; his left foot is off the ground.
Ground line: single reserved line.

On edge of foot: ΒΡVΛΟΣ ΕΓΟΙΕΣΕΝ, in glaze, spaced and divided so that *Brygos* is under side A, *epoiesen* under side B (see fig. 3g).

Relief line contours throughout (except hair); dilute glaze for minor interior markings; added red for inscriptions; thin reserved line outside at juncture of offset lip and wall.

c. 485–480 BC.

Comment: Signed by Brygos as potter; attributed by Beazley to his Brygos Painter. It is a masterpiece of his fully mature period and may be compared with such pieces as the Vienna skyphos, the Berlin Gigantomachy cup, the Acropolis Circe frr., the Tarquinia cup of type C, the Getty Ajax cup, and the Munich and Cab. Méd. Dionysiac cups (ARV^2 380, 171; 370, 10; 369, 5; 369, 4; *Para* 367 add as 1 *bis*; 371, 15; 371, 14).

Bloesch placed this cup of type C in his Kalliades-Brygos Class. The Getty now has a huge type C cup signed by Euphronios as potter which may be placed in this class. The form of the feet of one cup decorated by the Brygos Painter (Tarquinia RC 6846: ARV^2 369, 4) and one by the Castelgiorgio Painter (**47** [E 67]) suggest that they should be moved from Bloesch's general list (*FAS* 131–3) to his Kalliades-Brygos group. The form of the foot of the cup in Vienna decorated by Makron (*ARV*^{2} 467, 127) reveals that Makron's other lipped cups are also close to the Kalliades-Brygos Class (*ARV*^{2} 465, 94–5; 467, 128–9; 472, 211), as, indeed, does the form of the foot of the London cup by his follower, the Clinic Painter (E 66: *ARV*^{2} 808, 2), although it should be noted that the decoration under the foot remains Macronian. It may well be that Euphronios' essay into type C cups set the pattern for Brygos, with Kalliades and the potter of Makron's Cs (unless he is Kalliades) also following suit.

The arrangement of Brygos' signature on the foot seems quite deliberate. The splitting of name and verb occurs in the signatures of Euphronios (e.g. **6** [E 44], on a handle; perhaps also on the Getty Iliupersis cup; cf. also the wide gap in Euthymides' potter signature on the foot of New York 1981.11.9). On the arrangement and placing of signatures see D. von Bothmer in *Eye of Greece* 45–8 and B. Cohen, *MetrMusJ* 26 (1991) 49–95.

The subject of the tondo is obscure. Schefold has noted that one of the Oceanids was named Zeuxo and that the name Chrysippos appears on a couple of late fifth-century pieces centring around Aphrodite (Schefold in *LIMC* iii *sv* Chrysippos I and IV, p. 289–90). Immerwahr suggests a connection between Chrysippos' name and his golden phiale. For the form of the greave pads (split in two, upper band crenellated) cf. the Triptolemos Painter's skyphos: Berlin 1970.9, E.R. Knauer, *Ein Skyphos des Triptolemosmalers* (Berlin 1973) fig. 122.

The scenes on the exterior are most fully and recently discussed by E. Simon in *Eye of Greece* 125–9, who suggests a link with a satyr play, perhaps called 'Iris' and possibly by the writer Pratinas. For the subject see also, however, J.D. Beazley, *JHS* 30 (1910) 57; Haspels, *Attic Black-Figure Lekythoi* (Paris 1936) 20; and now two articles by A. Kossatz-Deissmann, *LIMC* iv 696–7 (Hera) and *LIMC* v 751–2 (Iris), and D. Williams, *AJA* 96 (1992) 624. The scene is set as the sanctuary of Dionysos by the altar and the raised step for a throne. Iris has been sent by Hera to interrupt the sacrifice to Dionysos, but the satyrs, at the god's behest, have caught her and still others are threatening Hera herself. Hermes tries to halt them, but it is probably the imminent arrival of Herakles, dressed in the costume of the Scythian police of Athens, that will save Hera.

The object in Iris' hand is the tail and spine (*osphus*) of the sacrificial victim (*pace* Simon 126 n. 21), see most recently F. van Straten in R. Hägg, N. Marinatos and G.C. Nordquist (eds.), *Early Greek Cult Practice* (Stockholm 1988) 51–68. For the fire-brick (*epipyron*) on the altar see J.D. Beazley, *JHS* 59 (1939) 21.

The names of the satyrs are particularly descriptive. On side A they are connected with the characters or physical attributes of satyrs or their regular activities (Babakchos – reveller; Terpon – joyful; Kydris – lusty [rather than Hydris – watery?]; Styon – erect). On side B the names are connected with the actions of the chase and capture of Iris (Dromis – rushing; Edon – holding; Lephsis – catching): Iris as the object of the chase has her name in the accusative (Immerwahr *Attic Script* 89; Simon 127 n. 24, links the names with those of dogs). For names of satyrs and maenads see most recently A. Kossatz-Deissmann, *Getty Vases* 5 (1991) 131–99. For the satyr under the handle compare a cup by Makron (*ARV*^{2} 462, 45); cf. also the komast under the handle on a cup by the Dokimasia Painter (*ARV*^{2} 373, 46 with *Para* 372).

Gilding of areas of raised clay seems to occur first in the circle of the Pioneers, on Euphronios' Acropolis cup (*ARV*^{2} 17, 18), the Sosias Painter's cup in Berlin (*ARV*^{2} 21, 1) and Acropolis 9 fr. (B. Graef and E. Langlotz, *Die antiken Vasen von der Akropolis zu Athen* ii [Berlin 1933] pl. 1). It remains extremely rare until the latter part of the fifth century, when it suddenly becomes quite common (many collected in O. Jahn, *Ueber bemalte Vasen mit Goldschmuck* [Leipzig 1865]).

Found in a tomb by Simmaco Doria, probably during the winter of 1870/71, on the northern side of Santa Maria di Capua Vetere. The tomb had a single interment but had been plundered in antiquity. The vases found in it were all Attic. For excavations during this period in Capua see J. Beloch, *Campanien* (Berlin 1879) 357. For the particular tomb, the so-called Brygos Tomb, see W. Helbig *BdI* 1872, 39 (tomb II); J.D. Beazley *AJA* 1945, 156–8; D. Williams *British Museum Society Bulletin* 49 (July 1985) 33; Williams *Greek Vases* 45–8; D. Williams, *AJA* 96 (1992) 617–36.

46 (pl. 65 and fig. 11c)

Cup: GR 1950.1–4.10
Gift of Mr. L.J.E. Hooper, 1950.

Bibliography: M. Robertson, *British Museum Quarterly* 16 (1951–2) 19–21, pl. 9; *ARV*^{2} 379, 146.

Dimensions: diam. 21.4; diam. of tondo 13.6; ht. 8.1; diam. of foot 8.8.

Condition: made up from frr.; right handle missing with a section of rim; two other rim fr. and some chips missing.

Description

INTERIOR: warrior advancing.
A warrior in Corinthian helmet, chlamys (black border), greaves and red greave-pads charges to the right, a shield on his left arm and a spear held low in his right. He has long straggly hair in front of his ear done with dilute glaze. The shield is seen in three-quarter view: it has a crescent between two circles as a device and a leather apron decorated with dotted spirals and dots, and with key-hole cut-outs (vandykes) along the bottom edge. On the left, an arrow (three dots on the shaft by the feathers) flies past at knee level, unless it is to be thought of as stuck in the ground; on the right, a small reserved stone is about to strike the middle of his shield.

INSCRIPTION: HEΓAIΣ KAΛE
Border: complex stopt maeander (seven-stroke, anticlockwise) interrupted by four blackened cross-squares; odd man at 10 o'clock.

Relief contours throughout; dilute glaze for minor interior markings; added red for inscription.

c. 480 BC.

Comment: Attributed to the Brygos Painter as a late work by Martin Robertson. The blackened cross-squares are not usually so dark in the works of the Brygos Painter and the complex stopt maeanders are usually clockwise not anticlockwise, but there are parallels (*ARV*² 377, 106; 379, 145; 379, 147).

Martin Robertson associated the cup with Bloesch's 'Conefoot' Class (cf. Bloesch *FAS* 128–9: 'Kegelgruppe'). These conefoot cups seem to continue on from Brygos' small type B cups. Bloesch listed 14 decorated examples, all but two decorated inside only. Of these, Beazley gave eight to the Brygos Painter or his manner, while also adding more (*ARV*² 376, 90 [Bloesch no. 5]; 377, 107 and 115 [8]; 378, 130 and 135 and 137; 379, 148 and 150 [12] and 156 [10]; 380, 165 [6] and 168 [9]; manner sundry 389, 28 [14]; 390, 40 and 44 [1]), one to the Painter of Munich 2676 (392, 6), one to the Briseis Painter (407, 13 [3]) and two to the Painter of Agora P 42 (415, 7 [15]; 416, 8 [11]). In addition, Beazley placed two of Bloesch's list in the manner of Onesimos (*ARV*² 332, 26 [13] and 30 [7]), but both these are very probably the work of the Foundry Painter. The two decorated outside as well as inside are by followers, not by the Brygos Painter himself (*ARV*² 407, 13 and 415, 7). All seem to be fairly late in the production of the Brygan group. In addition to these Brygan conefoot cups, there are two decorated by Onesimos (*ARV*² 328, 122; 329, 131), thereby illustrating contact between the painter Onesimos and the potter Brygos.

For a warrior under fire from arrows compare the warrior in retreat on a Proto-Panaetian cup (Berlin 2304: *ARV*² 1563, Antias kalos 4); the fight scene on the Onesiman kyathos (*ARV*² 333, upper); compare also Makron's slinger cup in Japan (*Ninagawa Museum* 79–83, no. 34). On two later pieces, one showing a fight between a Greek and a Persian (*ARV*² 631, 38), the other an Amazonomachy (*ARV*² 613, 1), an arrow is also seen in mid flight. Rocks are often to be seen in the hands of warriors and monsters, when they probably represent a last desperate resort, snatched up from the ground (cf. a giant on **5** [E 47] and the Minotaur on **18** [E 48]). Rocks in mid flight are rarer (e.g. thrown by Ajax, *ARV*² 434, 74; thrown by a centaur, *ARV*² 187, 58). Rocks were clearly also suitable missiles during sieges (Getty 84.AE.38 – W.A.P. Childs, *Getty Vases* 5 [1991] 27–40; Centre Island, private fr., white rocks in flight, attributed by Bothmer to the Swing Painter) . For shield-aprons see J.K. Anderson, *Military Theory and Practice in the Age of Xenophon* (Berkeley 1970) 17 with note 18.

Nos. 47–57: The Brygan Circle

Beazley (*ARV*² 368 and 400, with 386–424) divided the imitators and followers of the Brygos Painter into four main sections. The first consists of a small, loose group of minor imitators who span the mature and late phases of the Brygos Painter, but also go beyond, into the Early Classical period. Here belongs, amongst others, the Castelgiorgio Painter. The second section consists only of the Foundry Painter, a particularly lively artist who also has strong and important connections with Onesimos. The third section is called by Beazley the Mild Brygan Group and consists of the works of four artists, including the Briseis and Dokimasia Painters, pupils of the Brygos Painter, but whose work tends to be less spirited. Both the Briseis Painter and the Dokimasia Painter, like the Brygos Painter, also decorated large vessels. Finally, there is the Painter of the Paris Gigantomachy, who has something in common with the Foundry Painter, but is much more mechanical and never made the move to a grander scale.

No recent study has been made of the Brygan Circle as a whole; remarks on the painters represented in the British Museum collection are made here in the commentary to individual cups.

47 (pls. 66–7 and fig. 11d)

Cup, type C: GR 1836.2–24,131 (*BM Cat Vases* E 67)
From Vulci; Durand collection.
Bought at the Durand sale, 1836.

Bibliography: *Cabinet Durand* lot 395; Hartwig *M* 361–2, 688 no. 51; Murray *DGV* no. 45; Hoppin i 131 no. 61; Tonks *Brygos* 113, no. 48; *AV* 184, 2; *ARV* 258, 3; Bloesch *FAS* 132 no. 15, pl. 35, 3 (B and foot); *ARV*² 386, 3; *LIMC* i *sv* Achilleus no. 836; *LIMC* vi pl. 236, Memnon no. 53 (A).

Dimensions: width 37.4; diam. 29.0; diam. of tondo 16.4; ht. 11.3; diam. of exterior ground line 15.0; diam of foot 11.1.

Condition: Made up from frr.: many chips at breaks and one small rim fr. missing.

Description

INTERIOR: seated man and woman with jug.

On the left is seated a bearded man dressed in a long chiton, dotted himation with a black border and shoes. He wears a double red headband with a loop and ties at the back. On his chair is spread an apparently circular or oval textile decorated with dotted cross-hatching and with a border of stopt maeanders. He holds a phiale in his right hand and gestures with his left. Facing him stands a woman in chiton, himation (black battlement upper border, plain lower) and headscarf, whose jewellery consists of a disc earring and a snake bracelet on the left wrist. She holds an oinochoe up in her right hand, with her left she fingers some folds of her chiton down by her side. Her rather awkward pose with upper body to left and lower body to right is presumably to be explained by imagining that she has just finished pouring wine into the man's phiale and is turning to walk away. Between and behind the figures is a fluted column with a plain block base and a Doric capital with architrave above (*viae* and *guttae* done in silhouette). Reserved exergue below.

Nonsense inscription: ΟΛΙΛΛΗΙ

Border: stopt maeander (four-stroke, anticlockwise).

EXTERIOR: Achilles and Memnon; Assembly of deities.

Side A (L): duel between Achilles and Memnon.
On the left a winged female wearing chiton, himation and disc earring moves forward to the right, her right arm raised, seemingly touching her double red hair-band, perhaps in a gesture of anxiety, her left arm outstretched. In the centre is the fight between Achilles and Memnon. Achilles, on the left, strides forward, a shield on his left arm (seen from the inside) and a spear held low in his right. He is clad in a fringed short chiton with wavy folds decorated with dots, cuirass, greaves and helmet. Memnon, dressed in short chiton, cuirass, black scabbard (with relief dots down the middle), double crested helmet with a red palmette on the back (circumscribed in dilute glaze) and greaves, sinks backwards braced by his big round shield. His legs face to the right, but his head and body are in back view. He still holds a *machaira* in his extended but drooping right hand, while his left hand has loosened its grip on the shield. On the right a winged female, who must be Eos, moves to the left. She wears a chiton, a himation, a sakkos, a snake bracelet and a disc earring. Her right arm is outstretched and her left (drawn with a right hand by mistake) is raised to the back of her head, in a gesture of dismay. Nonsense inscription (non-letters).

Side B (U): Assembly of deities.
On the left is seated a bearded male, presumably Zeus, who wears a long chiton and a dotted himation. He has a reserved fillet (decorated with two lines) in his hair. He holds a bossed phiale (with relief dots) in his right hand and his left rests on the shaft of a striped sceptre. There is an apparently circular or oval textile decorated with a dotted chequer pattern over his backless throne, which has volute finials (relief dot in the centre of each volute; dilute glaze strokes for wood grain). In front of him is a fluted column with a simple block base and a Doric capital. Next to the column stands a youth, dressed in a himation, who faces to the left. He is probably Ganymede. He proffers an oinochoe in his right hand. His hair, done up in segments at the back, is bound with a red apicate fillet. Behind him, in the centre, stands a bearded warrior, presumably Ares. He faces to the left and his left leg is frontal. He is equipped with a Corinthian helmet, shield (device: snake; sparse dots around rim), greaves and a spear and wears a short dotted chiton with wavy folds and a himation. Next to him, on the right, stands a winged woman in chiton, himation (black border) and headscarf (relief dots in hair over brow): she may be Nike or Iris. She holds an oinochoe in her right hand and gestures with her left, ready to wait on the goddess, probably Hera, who is seated on a stool on the far right, facing left. She holds a striped sceptre in her left hand and a phiale in her right. She wears a chiton and a dotted himation with a black border and her hair is held up at the back with the aid of a stephane with peaks (relief dots in hair over brow). Her throne is like that of Zeus (dilute glaze strokes for wood grain), the seat covered with an apparently circular or oval rug, decorated with dotted cross-hatching pattern. Under the handle behind Zeus is a leopard. Imitation inscription (non-letters).

Ground line: border of stopt maeanders (four-stroke, anticlockwise).

Relief line contour throughout (except for the hair); dilute glaze for minor interior markings; narrow reserved line at junction of offset lip and bowl outside; added red for inscriptions.

c. 490–480 BC.

Comment: Attributed by Hartwig to Brygos and by Beazley to his Castelgiorgio Painter. This artist, named after the find-spot of one of his cups, is a rather weak imitator of the Brygos Painter. The London cup is particularly close to the cup in Palermo (*ARV*[2] 386, 4); and these two pieces bear some relation to Beazley's Painter of Agora P. 42 (*ARV*[2] 415–6) a 'Mild Brygan'. For a discussion of the shape see **45** (E 65), which is probably of the same time.

On Achilles and Memnon see A. Kossatz-Deissmann *LIMC* i 180–1 and vi 448–461; Schefold *Sagen* 195–6. For the scene of the departure of Ares, cf. D. Williams in E. Böhr and W. Martini (eds.), *Studien zur Mythologie und Vasenmalerei* (Festschrift for K. Schauenburg; Mainz 1986) 78. For the rear view of a helmeted head see D. Williams in *New Perspectives* 291 with note 23 (listing *ARV*[2] 8, 9; 149, 14; 653, 1). For the leopard see **11** (E 57). For the chitons with wavy folds see on **3** (E 45). For circular or oval textiles over chairs or thrones cf. also three pieces by Douris (*ARV*[2] 431, 43 and 44; Getty 81.AE.213, 85.AE.18 and 185, 88.AE.30 etc. frr. [phiale], M. Robertson, *Getty Vases* 5 [1991] 75–98, esp. fig. 1x).

48 (pls. 68–9 and fig. 12a)

Cup: GR 1850.3–2.2 (*BM Cat Vases* E 78)
From Vulci; Braun collection.
Bought of Mr. Farrer, 1850.

Bibliography: *Sale Catalogue of the Emil Braun Collection* (Christie's) February 21 1850 no. 40; Hartwig *M* 392–4, 689 no. 9; Murray *DGV* no. 55; Tonks *Brygos* 109 no. 21; Hoppin i 457 no. 13; *VA* 94; *AV* 186, 1; *ARV* 263, 3; Bloesch *FAS* 73 no. 20; *ARV*[2] 401, 3 and p. 1651; Beazley *RG* 55–6, figs. 6–8; Poliakoff *Combat Sports* 55 fig. 53 (detail of A); Sweet *Sport and Recreation* 82 fig. 28 (A); E. Spathari (ed.) *Ellada Athletismos Politismos* (Athens 1988) 50 fig. 33; R. Jackson, *Doctors and Diseases in the Roman Empire* (London 1988) p. 35 fig. 5 (A); *Beazley Add*[2] 230–1; *Beazley Lectures* 80, pl. 50, 2 and 51.

Dimensions: width 39.6; diam. 31.5; diam. of tondo 19.6; ht. 12.0; diam. of exterior ground line 12.3; diam. of foot 12.3.

Condition: made up from frr.; ancient rivet holes (6 pairs, holding left handle and part of rim).

Description
INTERIOR: Trainer and boxer.
A bearded trainer stands to the right, but looks back over his shoulder to the left. He wears a himation (black border; battlement border around shoulder only), shoes and a red apicate

fillet in his hair (tails at back). The hair down the median line of his stomach is done with irregular short strokes in dilute glaze. He holds a forked stick out in his right hand; his left is within a bunch of drapery behind his back. On the right stands a naked athlete tying a thong (drawn in relief lines) around his raised right hand and wrist. His left leg is frontal, his right leg flexed behind his left with only the toes touching the ground. He has a red apicate fillet in his hair (tails at back). Preliminary sketch reveals that the trainer's arm was originally intended to have been bent up at 90°, holding his stick vertically (see fig. 1i).

Nonsense inscriptions: O[...]EO≶E≶EO≶N, NENONNOEO (Es with their three strokes facing downwards).

Border: dotted cross-squares alternating with three units of stopt maeander (anticlockwise); additional maeander unit at 10 o'clock.

EXTERIOR: athletes.

Side A (U): boxers and pancratiasts.

On the left is a pair of boxers in a bout. The boxer on the left has his left arm bent up in front, his right arm back, and there is a dilute line on his cheek. His opponent, facing to the left, is seen in three-quarter back view, his left arm out in front, his right drawn back for a blow. His cheek is heavily marked with relief lines, under the eye and along the cheekbone, to denote swelling. The thongs of both boxers around their hands and wrists are painted in red. In the centre is a pair of pancratiasts down on the ground. On the left, the youth has his torso frontal, his right leg tucked up under resting on the ball of the foot and partially obscuring his genitals, his left leg outstretched to the right. His head is turned to the right, his right arm is out to the left, fist clenched to deliver a blow, his left holds his opponent's head in an armlock, his fingers seeming to claw at his opponent's right eye and the palm and heel of his hand covering his mouth. He has a relief line marking his cheekbone and two dilute creases on his brow. His opponent has a frontal face. His legs are wrapped round the first youth's left leg and he has both hands to that youth's face, his thumbs probably searching for his right eye. Above them hangs a discus in a bag – the discus is decorated with a cross and the mouth of the bag with dots – and a pair of thongs. On the right a bearded trainer steps forward, his forked stick raised over his head to stop the fouls and the fight. He is dressed in a himation (black border) and shoes; his left arm is under the himation. On the far right is a column with a plain one step base and a plain termination at the top.

Side B (L): hoplitodromos and boxers.

On the left a hoplitodromos moves to the right, wearing greaves and a thick reserved fillet round his head. He carries a shield on his left arm and holds a helmet down in his right hand (missing fr. had part of crest and calf of this figure and, on the inside, part of the maeander border). In front of him stands a trainer, whose torso and left leg are fully frontal, but his inclined head is turned to the right. He wears a himation (black border) and a red wreath and holds a forked stick in his right hand, his left arm akimbo under the himation. In the centre a pair of boxers fight with open hands. They both have red thongs around their hands and wrists and the outlines of the cheeks are marked with dilute lines. The boxer on the left has both legs frontal. His left arm is extended in a defensive position, while with his right he wards off the left arm of his opponent. The boxer on the right has his left arm out in front and his right arm bent up over his head; part of his back is visible. Behind him hangs a pair of thongs. On the right stands a boxer holding a red thong stretched between his two hands. His right leg is frontal and his left is turned to the right, but his head faces back to the left. On the far right is a pillar with fluting done in dilute glaze, a plain single step base and plain termination on top, on which rests a pair of thongs.

Ground line: two closely set reserved lines.

Graffito under foot: see fig. 3k.

Relief line contour throughout (except hair); dilute glaze for minor interior markings; thick reserved line lip, thin outside; added red for inscriptions.

c. 490 BC.

Comment: Given by Hartwig to his Diogenes Master (although he did group together the first three pieces in Beazley's later list of the Foundry Painter; cf. Buschor *GV* 176), by Murray with some reservation to the style of Brygos and attributed by Beazley to his Foundry Painter. The potting has been attributed by Bloesch to Euphronios.

For the Foundry Painter see, in addition to Beazley's lists and lecture (Beazley *RG* = *Beazley Lectures* 78–83), Knauer *Foundry Painter* and Robertson *Art of Vase-painting* 107–9. He decorated mainly cups, but also a skyphos (*ARV*^{2} 403, 37), a phiale (with coral red inside: Getty frr.), a kantharos of type C (*ARV*^{2} 1651 add as 37 *bis*), a kantharos with applied masks (Getty 85.AE.263), a head vase (*ARV*^{2} 382, 184) and a pyxis (Brauron Mus. frr.). The earliest works of the Foundry Painter derive from Onesimos' Lykan cups: the Foundry Painter was a pupil of Onesimos (e.g. *ARV*^{2} 331, 17 [manner of Onesimos]; *Para* 361, 131 *bis* [Onesimos]; *Para* 370 add as 33 *bis*; *ARV*^{2} 1651 add as 18 *bis*; Bloomington see Knauer *Foundry Painter*, 402, 19). The London athletic cup is an early mature work. Its tondo border ties it to a number of other works by the painter (*ARV*^{2} 401, 2; 402, 12–13; *Para* 370, add as 12 *bis*) and to the Brygos Painter's early mature phase (cf. **42** [E 68]).

The open-handed boxers on the exterior recur on a fr. by the Foundry Painter (*ARV*^{2} 401, 6) and on an unpublished cup in a New York private collection (Spears) by the Dokimasia Painter (cf. also *ARV*^{2} 340, 73, Antiphon Painter). They are perhaps engaging in preliminary feints or sparring: see Gardiner *AAW* 205–6, *akrocheirizesthai*. On boxing techniques in general see now Poliakoff *Combat Sports* 80–5.

The pancratiasts on side A demonstrate one of the two forbidden actions of pancratiasts (cf. Aristophanes *Birds* 442 and *Peace* 899), namely gouging. We cannot be sure if the pancratiast with the frontal face was biting his opponent, the other outlawed practice, but given the opportunity provided, it seems most likely that he would have done so. For a full discussion of the pankration see Gardiner *AAW* 212–21 and, most recently, Poliakoff *Combat Sports*.

For the Foundry Painter's nonsense inscriptions cf. now Immerwahr *Attic Script* 89: writing 'without bothering to turn the cup'. This is most noticeable in the production of the Es. The retrograde graffito is perhaps more Greek than Etruscan.

49 (pls. 70–1 and fig. 12b)

CUP: GR 1895.5–13.1
From Vulci.
Bought of Miss McCracken, 1895.

Bibliography: Hartwig *M* 349–54, 688 no. 42; Hoppin i 142 no. 110 (ii 490); *AV* 178, 25; *ARV* 257, upper; Bloesch *FAS* 85 no. 24; *ARV*^{2} 405, 2; *Para* 370 and 371; Knauer *Foundry Painter* 16, with figs. 25 (detail A) and 26 (detail B); *Beazley Add*^{2} 232; Robertson *Art of Vase-painting* 109 and figs. 106–7 on p. 110.

Dimensions: width 37.0; diam. 29.6; diam. of tondo 19.6; ht. 11.2; diam. of exterior ground line 12.8; diam. of foot plate 11.6.

Condition: made up from frr.: three bowl frr. and four areas of rim missing.

Description

INTERIOR: man listening to a youth playing pipes.

On the left sits a bearded man on a plain stool. He leans back, nonchalantly gripping his left knee with both his hands so that his foot is off the ground. A plain stick rests between his legs and a himation with a black border is casually draped over his thighs. He has a long thick red fillet around his head with a large loop at the back and triple tassels. His mouth is open and he may be supposed to be singing. On the right stands a youth playing the pipes (relief line indicates puffed cheeks). He is supported by a knotty stick under his left armpit. A himation with a black border is loosely draped over his right shoulder, round his back and is tucked up on top of the crook of the stick. He wears a pair of high boots and also has a long thick red fillet with loop and tassels in his hair. Above and behind the pair a food basket (partly missing) is hung from red ties.

INSCRIPTION: HOΓAIΣKAΛOΣ

Border: dotted saltire squares alternating with three units of stopt maeander (anticlockwise, mostly five-stroke).

EXTERIOR: komasts and women.

Side A (U): three males, a woman and a door.

On the far left is hung a spotted flute-case. In front of it stands a youth playing the pipes. His weight is carried on his right foot, his left rests behind it, the toes curled over so that their tops touch the ground. He wears a himation (black border) loosely draped over his arms and has a red wreath in his hair. In front of him hangs a food basket with red ties above and tassels below. Next is a male to the right: the whole of the upper part of this figure is missing. He wears a himation (black border) and leans heavily on a knotty stick; his right leg is frontal. In front of him is a doorway with one leaf open (dilute strokes for the grain of the wood; black discs for the metal studs). Beyond the doorway is a couple shown making love. On the left are the slightly bent lower legs of a man, who wears a himation (black border) which falls loosely behind his legs. He was probably about to penetrate (perhaps anally) the naked hetaira, who bends forward, supporting herself with the aid of a knotty stick that she grips in her left hand and bracing herself with the right hand on her right knee, her left elbow on her left thigh. Her hair is cut short, she has a red wreath in her hair and she wears a disc earring. The small rounded object against her thigh near her bottom seems to be a drapery weight.

INSCRIPTION: HOΓA[IΣ...

Ground line: two closely set reserved lines.

Side B (L) : two men, a woman and a youth.

On the left a man playing the pipes (relief line to indicate puffed cheek) wears a himation (black border) over his shoulders and a pair of shoes (waist and thighs missing). He stoops slightly and has his left leg forward. His hair is receding and he has a red fillet round his head with three leaves at the front. Before him dances a naked woman: she moves to the right but looks back at the piper, her arms extended as she plays the krotala, one in either hand. Her hair is cut short and there is a thin red fillet with three leaves at the front in her hair. This pair is preceded by a bearded komast, also dancing, for his left foot is off the ground in front of him. He has a himation (black border) over his arms and shoulders that is pulled over the back of his head and holds a skyphos out in his left hand and a stick down in his right. He has a red fillet with three leaves at the front. In front of him is hung a spotted flute-case. On the far right a youth observes their approach, leaning on a stick. He is dressed in a himation that is pulled up over the back of his head and covers both his arms (part of his middle is missing). He has a red wreath around his head. Behind him is suspended a food basket, of which only the upper right hand corner, part of the red ties above and the red tassels below are preserved.

INSCRIPTION: HOΓAIΣKAΛ[OΣ]

Relief line throughout (except for the hair); dilute glaze for minor interior markings; thick reserved line inside lip, thin outside; added red for inscriptions.

c. 490–485 BC.

Comment: Attributed by Hartwig to Brygos and, after much reflection, given by Beazley to his Foundry Painter. At first, Beazley had followed Hartwig, although he did comment 'nicht sicher eigenhändig' (*AV* 178). In *ARV* he placed the piece in the Manner of the Brygos Painter, together with a cup in Tarquinia (already given in *VA* 94 to the Foundry Painter, but removed again in *AV* 188–9), and by *ARV*^{2} he had moved both into the sphere of the Foundry Painter with the comment 'close to the Brygos Painter at his height, but hardly from his hand. They might be by the Foundry Painter at the point in his career when he was nearest to the Brygos Painter' (*ARV*[2] 405). By the time of his Feltrinelli lecture (*RG*; delivered in 1965) Beazley had clearly refined his position, for here he selected a small group of vases by the Foundry Painter, among which the Tarquinia cup played a special role (see *RG* 59 = *Beazley Lectures* 82), and both cups are added to the list of works by the Foundry Painter in *Para* (370–1 add as *ARV*[2] 402, 14 *bis*: the Tarquinia cup as 23 *bis*).

Alongside this pair of cups in particularly polished style one may place a fragmentary piece in Cahn's collection in Basel (inv. 714): interior, male and girl moving to right, she plays the pipes; exterior, komos and youths with flute girls – two frr. in the collection of Miss E.D.B. Vermeule in Boston join the Cahn frr. All these rather more refined and even works of the Foundry Painter continue on from the Toledo *komos* cup (64.126: *Para* 370, add as 12 *bis*; *CVA Toledo* 1, pls. 55–6) and represent the painter's fully mature work. They stand side by side with the Brygos Painter's fully mature middle work. The Foundry Painter's late works are not numerous: they seem rather stiffer than his mature works (e.g. *ARV*[2] 401, 10; 405, lower – Berlin inv. 3240; 401, 10 *bis* – *Beazley Add*[2] 231; London market [inside only, pair of acontists]).

Bloesch attributed the potting of the London cup to Brygos, as a later work.

The motif of the door occurs on a number of pyxides, see S. Rutherfurd Roberts, *The Attic Pyxis* (Chicago 1974) 181–3; it is more fully discussed in a Roman context in B. Haarlov, *The Half-Open Door: A common Symbolic Motif within Roman Sepulchral Sculpture* (Odense 1977). A very similar door appears on a lekythos by the Brygos Painter (*ARV*[2] 384, 210). The Foundry Painter also depicts the open gates of Troy on his ambitious cup in Boston (*ARV*[2] 402, 23).

The leaves attached to some of the fillets are often referred to as vine leaves, but it has been argued that since wreaths of vine are not referred to in ancient sources, but ones of celery are, such leaves may really be of celery (see M. Blech, *Studien zum Kranz bei den Griechen* (Berlin 1982) 51–2 and 69). On anal intercourse see E.C. Keuls, *The Reign of the Phallus* (New York 1985) 176–9; cf. also K.J. Dover, *Greek Homosexuality* (London 1978) 100–1.

50 (pls. 72–3 and fig. 12c)

Cup: GR 1843.11–3.92 (*BM Cat Vases* E 76)
From Vulci; Canino collection.
Bought of the Principessa di Canino, 1843.

Bibliography: *Mus. Étrusque* no. 1984; Hartwig *M* 426–9, 689 no. 2, pls. 42, 1 and 41; Murray *DGV* no. 53; *VA* 109 and 110 no. 7; Hoppin i, 101 no. 6; *AV* 194, 1; *ARV* 266, 1; Bloesch *FAS* 88, below no. 3; *ARV*[2] 406, 1 and p. 1651; *Para* 371; *LIMC* iv *sv* Eurybates 1, no. 5, pls. 49–50 (details of heralds on left of B and right of A); I.Th. Kakrides (ed.), *Ellenike Mythologia* (Athens 1986) V, 96 figs. 73–4 (A–B); *Beazley Add*[2] 232; Carpenter *Art and Myth* fig. 302 (A).

Dimensions: width 38.2; diam. 30.0; diam. of tondo 17.5; ht. 12.0; diam. of exterior ground line 12.0; diam. of foot 11.2.

Condition: made up from frr.: one rim fr. and two small wall chips missing.

Description

INTERIOR: seated old man and man.

On the left an old man with beard and receding hair is seated on a simple stool with a striped cushion. He is dressed in long chiton and himation and has a red wreath in his hair. He holds a plain stick in his left hand and gestures towards the bearded man facing him with his right hand. This man wears a himation and shoes and has a red wreath in his hair. He leans to the left on a knotty stick and is seen in three-quarter back view. His left arm, covered in drapery, is bent back to hold the top of his stick which supports him under his left armpit. He gestures with his right hand towards the seated man.

Nonsense inscription: ΛVIOSKIOSVIS

Border: dotted cross square alternating with five units of running maeander (five-stroke, clockwise); irregularities at 7 o'clock (three and a half maeander units) and at 8 and 9 o'clock (only four units).

EXTERIOR: Briseis.

A (L): Briseis being led away from Achilles.

On the far left a bearded herald in short chiton, chlamys, *pilos* hat with red ties and boots with horizontal divisions (dilute glaze) starts to move away to the left but turns back his head and torso so that his right leg is also seen from the back (dilute glaze wash in hair and beard). He holds a *kerykeion* up in his left hand; his right hand grips the draped hand or wrist of a woman behind him. She is Briseis and wears a chiton and a himation pulled up over the back of her head, faces to the left, a double red band around her head. Behind her is a second bearded herald (dilute glaze wash for beard). He wears a *pilos* hat with red ties, horizontally striped boots (dilute glaze) and a chlamys that covers the short chiton that he is presumably wearing beneath it. In the centre a bearded man in a himation leans on a knotty stick to the right, his right hand on his hip, his left arm hidden in his drapery. He has a red fillet in his hair. He faces the tent of Achilles which takes the form of four (only two shown) plain posts with simple block bases with a large striped textile with a fringed edge draped over them. Up in the folds of this marquee are, on the left, a Corinthian helmet with a long crest on a square hook or shelf and, on the right, a scabbard with a red strap. Next to the scabbard is planted a spear. In the centre of the tent sits Achilles on an elaborate folding stool (animal legs) with a cushion decorated with zigzags. He wears shoes and a himation which envelops all but the upper part of his face. He has a red fillet in his hair and dilute wash in his wavy hair. His left arm is wrapped around a knotty stick. Behind the tent, on the extreme right, stands a bearded elder in long chiton, himation and shoes; he also has a red hair-band. He holds a staff or sceptre in his right hand.

Nonsense inscription: ΛVIOSL

Side B (U): Briseis being led back.

On the left a bearded man, wearing a himation pulled up over the back of his head and a red fillet, leans on a knotty stick, his

right leg frontal: he is presumably Agamemnon. In front of him stands a bearded elder to the left. He is dressed in long chiton (dilute glaze border), himation, shoes and a red fillet and rests his right hand on top of a plain stick. Behind him stands a second bearded elder similarly dressed and accoutred but facing to the right. In the centre is a fluted column with a plain block base but a Doric capital with architrave above. To the right of the central column a herald in *pilos* hat with red ties, chlamys and red thonged high sandals moves to the right. In his right hand he holds a *kerykeion*; his left hand is raised inside his chlamys; at his hip is a scabbard. In front of him is Briseis in chiton (upper folds done with dilute glaze) and himation pulled up over the back of her head. She has a double red band around her head. In front of her is a second herald who leads her by the hand – hers within its drapery. He is moving right but has turned back to look at her, his head to the left, torso and right leg frontal. He is dressed in short chiton, chlamys and *pilos* hat with red ties and holds a *kerykeion* up in his left hand. In front of him, on the extreme right, is a second column, as the first. These two columns are probably intended to be the entrance porch to Agamemnon's more palatial tent, out through which the two heralds are leading Briseis.
Nonsense inscription: ΛVIOVIO≶KI
Under either handle: a solid stone seat with dilute glaze strokes.
Ground line: single reserved line.

Relief line contour throughout (except for hair); dilute glaze for minor interior markings; added red for inscriptions.

c. 485–480 BC.

Comment: Given by Hartwig to his 'Bald-headed Master' (Meister mit dem Kahlkopfe), it became the name-piece of Beazley's Briseis Painter.

On the Briseis Painter see in addition to Beazley's lists: *VA* 109–11; Richter and Hall 71–2 (no. 51); C.B. ii 39–41 (no. 86); Boardman *ARFV Archaic* 137; M. True, *Getty Vases* 1 (1983) 76–9; D. von Bothmer in *Festschrift Schauenburg* 65–70; Robertson *Art of Vase-painting* 115. The cup attributed by True is, in fact, a late work by Onesimos. Bothmer publishes a lekythos with the *kalos* name Lykos (*ARV*[2] 1596, once Nicole), but the date suggests that the Lykos is not the same Lykos as is praised on Onesimos' later works. It is possible to isolate three Lykoi among Beazley's list (*ARV*[2] 1595–6): Lykos I appears on a work by Euphronios (*ARV*[2] 1596 bottom = 13, 1); Lykos II is praised by Onesimos, the Antiphon Painter, the Foundry Painter and the painter of the Boston hydria (*ARV*[2] 1596 middle), and is named by the Triptolemos Painter; Lykos III is praised on works by the pupils of the Antiphon Painter (*ARV*[2] 1596 nos 19 and 21) and greeted on a vase by the Copenhagen Painter (*ARV*[2] 1596 middle = 257, 14).

The painter's earliest phase has perhaps not been identified yet, for nothing in Beazley's lists seems appreciably earlier than apparently mature works such as the London pair of cups. The Briseis cup should also be compared with the artist's other major mythological cups (*ARV*[2] 406, 7–8) and with some of his other elaborate works (e.g. *ARV*[2] 407, 16; *Para* 372, add as 8 *bis*, with *Beazley Add*[2] 232). These all belong beside fully middle works of the Brygos Painter. A series of slighter cups may reflect the artist's later years. The Basel cup (BS 442, ex Schweizer; *Para* 372, add as 32 *bis*; *CVA Basel* 2, pl. 13, 3 and 16 and 17 1–2) has been rightly reattributed to the Painter of the Fourteenth Brygos.

The Briseis Painter also decorated several neck-amphorae, lekythoi, an oinochoe, pyxides, an alabastron, dishes and a plate, all of which shapes can be found elsewhere in the Brygan workshop. In addition, there are an amphora of Panathenaic shape and two column-kraters (J.R. Guy has attributed one from Gravina with an Anacreontic scene to the Briseis Painter): these shapes reveal contact with other painters of larger shapes that are less often connected with the Brygan workshop, such as the Triptolemos Painter and the Flying-angel Painter. His work on larger shapes carries him fully into the Early Classical period.

Bloesch placed the London cup with three other cups decorated by the Briseis Painter as being in the neighbourhood of the potter Brygos.

For the iconography of the exterior see A. Kossatz-Deissmann *LIMC* iv *sv* Briseis, p. 157–166, especially 166; Schefold *Sagen* 181–2; and D. Williams in *Getty Vases* 5 (1991) 56–9. The two heralds on both sides are presumably Talthybios and Eurybates. On side A the painter has combined the leading away of Briseis with the embassy to Achilles and the man in front of Achilles' tent is presumably Odysseus (or Ajax) and the elder behind it Phoinix (as Beazley suggested: *ARV*[2] 406, 1). Makron's roughly contemporary depiction of the Briseis scene has the embassy on one side and the leading away on the other: *ARV*[2] 458, 2. On the embassy to Achilles see on **28** (E 56). On side B the two elders who watch the sending back of Briseis are not easily identified. This is the only occurrence of the return of Briseis (unless the tondo of **44** [E 69] shows an excerpt – see on **44** [E 69]).

It is not certain whether the scene on the interior belongs in the sphere of *genre* or mythology. If mythological and linked with the exterior, it might be Odysseus' embassy to Chryses. See also on **51** (E 75).

On the Briseis Painter's nonsense inscriptions see most recently Immerwahr *Attic Script* 89 with footnote 38 (this cup his no. 557). For the boots of the two heralds on side A cf. on **44** (E 69); those worn by the herald on side B are *krepides*. For the dilute glaze border to the chitons and the fringe of the tent see Bothmer in *Festschrift Schauenburg* 68.

51

(pls. 74–5 and fig. 12d)

Cup: GR 1843.11–3.54 (*BM Cat Vases* E 75)
From Vulci, Cucumella area C ('fam. Fepia') March 1829; Canino collection.
Bought of the Principessa di Canino, 1843.

Bibliography: *Mus. Étrusque* no. 1436; Hartwig *M* 429–33, 689 no. 3, pl. 42, 2 and 43; Murray *DGV* no. 52; Hoppin i 101 no. 5; *VA* 110 no. 9; *AV* 194, 3; Beazley *ARV* 267, 2; Bloesch *FAS* 88, below no. 3, pl. 24, 4; *ARV*^{2} 406, 2; *Para* 371; Boardman *ARFV Archaic* fig. 271 (parts of A and B); *Beazley Add*^{2} 232.

Dimensions: width 38.4; diam. 30.4; diam. of tondo 19.0; ht. 12.0; diam. of exterior ground line 11.5; diam. of foot plate 11.2.

Condition: made up from frr.; two rim frr. missing.

Description

INTERIOR: guard at a door and old man.

On the left a youth wearing a pair of boots with horizontal bands, a red band in his hair and a chlamys (black border) draped over his shoulders stands to the right, a spear held vertically in his left hand (the point is painted over the border). He gestures with his right hand. He stands in front of a door with one leaf open. The door has a central post and threshold, while lines of dilute glaze have been used to simulate the grain of the wood and black dots for the heads of the metal bolts that hold the cross-pieces in place. There is also a porch-like roof extension to protect the guard. An old man approaches the youth from the right. He is bald, but for a shock of streaky hair on the back of his neck; his beard is reduced to a stubble on his chin. He wears a long chiton (dilute glaze for upper folds; lower folds alternately relief line and dilute glaze) with a continuous maeander border and a tasseled fringe, a himation (black border), a pair of shoes and a red fillet around his head. His left hand rests on top of a stick and he gestures with his right hand as if asking permission of the guard to enter the building.

Border: running maeander (five-stroke, anticlockwise) interrupted in nine places by a dotted cross square; joint next to the spear head which overlaps the border.

EXTERIOR: Dionysos with satyrs and maenads.

Side A (L): Dionysos with two satyrs and two maenads.

On the left a satyr moves to the right, right hand above and behind his head, left arm outstretched. He has a red ivy wreath in his hair. In front of him is a maenad (her shoulders and head are missing). She wears a chiton: the belt shows and there is only one kolpos, thus enabling her to have 'wing sleeves'. There is a spotted animal skin over her shoulders (with cloven hoof, so a deer). In front of her a satyr with hair along the median line of his chest and stomach plays the pipes for Dionysos, who dances in the centre. Dionysos wears a short, belted chiton and high skin boots (cut like greaves, laced at front, long and pointed spotted flaps). He has an ivy wreath (red band and reserved leaves) in his hair and has a chlamys (black border) draped over his left shoulder. He holds a thyrsos out in his left hand and a snake back in his right. His right leg is raised off the ground behind him and his upper body and head bent down. On the right a maenad moves to the right, but turns her head back to the left. She has a wineskin (nonsense inscription in dilute glaze) held in her left hand and resting on her shoulders. She wears a chiton with 'wing sleeves' and a droplet earring. There is an ivy wreath (red band and reserved leaves) in her hair. On the extreme right is a tall, stylized rock formation.

Side B (U): three maenads and two satyrs.

On the left a maenad dances to the right, but she twists her upper body round to the left and her head is back and down to the right. She wears a chiton, a crossed reserved band in her hair and a droplet earring. Her arms are enclosed in 'wing sleeves'. In front of her stands a large thyrsos. Next is a satyr playing the pipes to the right. He has an ivy wreath (red band and reserved leaves) in his hair and has hair down the median line of his torso. In front of him stands a large thyrsos (no head shown). In the centre a maenad dances to the right, her head (back of head missing) to the left and thrown back, her right foot off the ground. She wears a chiton with 'wing sleeves' and has an animal skin about her waist. In front of her dances a satyr, an ivy wreath in his hair (red band and reserved leaves) and hair running down his median line from below his pectorals. He has his right foot off the ground behind him and gestures with his arms in front of him. His head is turned back to the left. Between him and the central dancing maenad a thyrsos tumbles to the ground. On the far right a maenad in belted chiton and 'wing sleeves' dances more somberly to the right, her head down. She has a reserved crossed band around her head and wears a droplet earring. On the extreme right is a tall, stylized rock formation.

Ground line: single reserved line.

Relief line contour throughout (except hair); dilute glaze for minor interior markings; reserved line inside lip only.

c. 485–480 BC.

Comment: Given by Hartwig to his 'Bald-headed Master' (Meister mit dem Kahlkopf), but attributed by Beazley to his Briseis Painter. On the painter see further on **50** (E 76). Placed by Bloesch with three other cups decorated by the Briseis Painter as being in the neighbourhood of the potter Brygos.

Beazley suggested that the scene on the interior showed Priam at the door of Achilles' 'tent' (*ARV*^{2} 406, 2), presumably asking entrance of a young guard. It is almost as if the tondo of this cup should have been on **50** (E 76). The head of Priam is repeated almost exactly on the fr. in the Vlasto-Serpieri collection, now in the National Museum, Athens (*ARV*^{2} 408, 35).

For stubble chins, and heads, see D. Williams in *Amsterdam Colloquium* 275–81. A similar old man is also found on frr. by the same painter in Bryn Mawr (*ARV*^{2} 407, 17). For the boots worn by the guard see on **44** (E 69); also **50** (E 76).

The lively thiasos on the exterior is similar to that on the Oxford cup (*ARV*^{2} 406, 3), where there are maenads with wing-sleeves and one with her head thrown back. The explanation of the 'wing sleeves' is Beazley's (C.B. ii, 40). A fr. from a closed vase with the head of a maenad in Turin, attributed to the Dokimasia Painter by Beazley (414: *ARV*^{2} 414, 35; Wegner pl. 39 c), is very close to the London cup. The figure of Dionysos has been compared by Beazley with the figure on a stamnos in London showing Dionysos *mainomenos* (see *ARV*^{2} 298 on E 439). For his boots see Morrow *Greek Footwear* 65, who calls them *embades*, the flaps possibly being extensions of felt socks (*piloi*); and J. Boardman and D.C. Kurtz, *Getty Vases* 2 (1986) 61, who simply call them *kothornoi*. The dance on side B seems to involve weaving around thyrsoi that have been driven into the ground – that on the right has probably been knocked over by the satyr. A maenad dances next to a 'planted' thyrsos on a kantharos by the Nikosthenes Painter (*ARV*² 126, 27) as Dionysos takes part in a ceremony at an altar.

52

(pl. 76 and fig. 13a)

Cup: GR 1896.6–21.1
From Vulci; Canino collection.
Presented by Miss Agnes F. Pariss, 1896.

Bibliography: *Notice d'une collection de vases peints tirés des fouilles faites en Étrurie par feu le Prince de Canino* (Paris 1845) no. 116; *VA* 110, 12; Hoppin i 102 no. 9; H.B. Walters, *JHS* 41 (1921) 124–5 fig. 5; *AV* 194, 4; *ARV* 268, 25; *ARV*² 409, 42; Ginouvès *Balaneutikè* 81 and 83.

Dimensions: diam. 22.5; diam. of tondo 11.8; ht. 9.0; diam of foot 8.8.

Condition: made up from frr.: right handle missing and much of rim.

Description

INTERIOR: naked woman at a basin.
A naked woman, wearing a sakkos, a thigh band with a pendant and a twin disc earring, stoops over a large basin, her hand and wrists obscured by its rim. On the upper wall of the basin are faint traces of a nonsense inscription in dilute glaze (ΛΙΟΣΙ); on the lower wall are dilute glaze strokes for shading. The basin rests on a low fluted shaft with an ovolo-type moulding at the top. The curving of the flutes into the top of the base is greatly exaggerated. The base rests on a simple block, at the front of which is a vertical stone with a curved edge on the front of its upper edge.
Nonsense inscription: ΛΛΟΛ
Border: stopt maeander (five-stroke, clockwise), with the joint at one o'clock.

Relief line contour throughout; added red for inscription.

c. 480 BC.

Comment: Attributed by Beazley to his Briseis Painter. It is a slight, later work corresponding to the period of the Brygos Painter's later works.

The naked woman is presumably having a complete wash in the privacy of a house. She may or may not be a hetaira. For the type of basin see Ginouvès *Balaneutikè* 77–99; for women washing 163–174. Actual examples of such basins on fluted stands have been found both in sanctuaries and in domestic contexts (Ginouvès *Balaneutikè* 84–6). Ginouvès (*Balaneutikè* 83 n. 8) suggests that the vertical edging stone on the London cup may have served to collect spillage. It is found again in a scene of athletes washing on a kantharos with applied plastic masks painted by the Foundry Painter, now in the Getty Museum (85.AE.263).

53

(pls. 77 and 78 a-b, fig. 13b)

Cup: GR 1836.2–24.173 (*BM Cat Vases* E 818)
From Vulci; Durand collection.
Bought at the Durand sale, 1836.

Bibliography: *Cabinet Durand* lot 667; Hartwig *M* 373 no. 8; Hoppin i 134 no. 69; *ARV* 271, 9; *ARV*² 412, 10; V. Olivova, *Sports and Games in the Ancient World* (London 1984) 103 (A); Sweet *Sport and Recreation* 31 fig. 7 (A); *Beazley Add*² 233.

Dimensions: width 31.0; diam. 22.6; diam. of tondo 12.1; ht. 8.8; diam. of exterior ground line 7.8; diam. of foot 9.0.

Condition: made up of frr.: three large rim frr. missing, along with two areas of wall and other chips; fr. missing from foot plate.

Description

INTERIOR: love-making.
A bearded, naked man kneels to the right, his back resting against a large folded cushion decorated with pairs of black bands with a line between, his fingertips reaching for the ground to help his balance. A naked hetaira stands on the right and slowly eases herself backwards and downwards onto the man's erect penis, one hand resting on his ribs, the other on his hip, steadying her progress. Her hair is cut short.
Border: stopt maeander (clockwise; joint at 7 o'clock).

EXTERIOR: athletes.

Side A (L): wrestlers and a trainer.
On the left is a fluted column on a simple block base (the top is missing). Both of the wrestlers bend forward, their arms interlocked (the face of the male on the left is missing as is most of the upper part and parts of the legs of the wrestler on the right). On the right stands a bearded trainer, leaning on a knotty stick. He wears a himation with a black border and shoes. He holds a forked stick out over the pair of wrestlers.

Side B (U): two hoplitodromoi and a trainer.
On the left a youth wearing a himation (black border) stoops to the right, his right hand resting on the upper shaft of a knotty stick, his left holding a forked stick down towards the ground. In the centre a bearded man in greaves and thick reserved headband runs to the left but looks back to the right. He holds a Chalcidian helmet (frontlet imitating hair) out in front in his right hand; the shield on his left arm has a five-lobed leaf device. His penis is infibulated. On the right a youth in greaves and a helmet runs quickly to the left. Behind him a shield, seen in profile and decorated with an arc (part of a large circle) and two dotted circles, leans against a fluted column. The column rests on a simple block base and has no capital.
Ground line: two reserved lines.

Relief line contours throughout (except hair); dilute glaze for minor interior markings; reserved line inside and outside lip.

c. 485–480 BC.

Comment: Placed near Brygos by Hartwig; attributed by Beazley to his Dokimasia Painter.

On the Dokimasia Painter see, in addition to Beazley's lists: E. Vermeule, *AJA* 70 (1966) 1–22; M. Schmidt, *Festschrift Bloesch* 100–4; H.A. Cahn, *RA* 1973, 3–22; Boardman *ARFV Archaic* 137; C. Isler-Kerenyi, *Stamnoi* (Lugano 1976–7) 59–64; Robertson *Art of Vase-painting* 115–18. He can be very close to the Brygos Painter. Indeed, Beazley changed his mind over the attribution of some three pieces that he initially gave to the Brygos Painter (see *ARV*[2] 1649 and *Para* 372–3). In general, the Brygan spirit is somewhat diluted, but his figures have a good deal of presence. He takes his name from the scene on a cup in Berlin (*ARV*[2] 412, 1). This and his other grand cup (*ARV*[2] 413, 25) are representative of the artist's mature work: they belong beside the Brygos Painter's middle phase. The painter's earliest surviving cup seems to be that formerly on the Paris Market (*ARV*[2] 413, 12; now Getty Mus. 82.AE.121). Two further pieces precede the main body of the painter's mature *oeuvre* (*ARV*[2] 413, 15; *Para* 372, add as 25 *ter*). The Copenhagen hunting cup seems particularly late (*ARV*[2] 413, 16).

The painter also decorated a series of stamnoi in an Early Classical style that belong at the end of his career (*ARV*[2] 414, 34; 415, 4; *Para* 373, add as 34 *bis*, with *Beazley Add*[2] 233; *Para* 373, add as 34 *ter*, with *Beazley Add*[2] 234. Add *ARV*[2] 814, 100 – now *CVA Edinburgh* pl. 18). The shape of the first two of these stamnoi has been loosely connected with some by the Kleophrades Painter (B. Philippaki, *The Attic Stamnos* [Oxford 1967] 55), the two in Switzerland and the one in Edinburgh are placed in the Class of the Late Stamnoi of the Berlin Painter (Philippaki *op. cit.* 42 and 153, addenda to p. 42). The Boston calyx-krater (*ARV*[2] 1652; *Para* 373, add as 34 *quater*) is very different and surely by the Brygos Painter himself. Robertson suggests that the Munich kalathoid-psykter (*ARV*[2] 385, 228) might be moved to the Dokimasia Painter, but this, too, seems out of place next to the Dokimasia Painter's stamnoi. Beazley also placed an amphora of Panathenaic shape near the Dokimasia Painter (*ARV*[2] 415 3): this shape was also decorated by the Briseis Painter.

The love-making on the interior of the London cup involves an unusual pose, making the cup difficult to poise correctly. Something similar recurs on three fragmentary cups in the collection of Herbert Cahn in Basel (inv. 1666 [ex Greifenhagen], exterior, attributed to Onesimos by Bothmer; inv. 1665 [ex Greifenhagen], tondo, U. Gehrig, *Antiken aus Berliner Privatbesitz* [Berlin 1975] no. 232; inv. 1662 [ex Olivia Curtius and Greifenhagen], tondo, ph. R.I. 37.885). On a cup by the Tarquinia Painter a girl climbs backwards onto a seated youth (*Para* 427, add as 869, 63 *bis*); on a cup attributed to the Boot Painter by J.R. Guy a girl is already in place, but has her head turned away (Getty 83.AE.321 [ex Raubitschek]: Reinsberg fig. 60); and on an oinochoe by the Shuvalov Painter a hetaira climbs forwards onto the knees of a youth (Berlin 2414: *ARV*[2] 1208, 41). Such passive poses by men are not common. For a homosexual version cf. London F 65 (*ARV*[2] 1154, 35) and P.H. von Blanckenhagen in L. Bonfante and H. von Heintze (eds.), *Essays in Archaeology and the Humanities: In Memoriam Otto J. Brendel* (Mainz 1976) 37–41.

Athletic scenes seem to be rare in the *oeuvre* of the Dokimasia Painter, but add a fragmentary early cup in Greifswald (294: A. Hundt and K. Peters, *Greifswalder Antiken* [Berlin 1961] pl. 27). On infibulation by athletes see most recently Sweet *Sport and Recreation* 129–33. For the shield device of a leaf see J.D. Beazley, *BSA* 46 (1951) 13–14; cf. also **3** (E 45).

54 (pl. 78 c and fig. 13c)

Cup, type C: GR 1952.12–2.12
E.P. Warren collection.
Bought of Mrs. G. Redfern-Loades, 1952.

Bibliography: *ARV* 271, 15; *ARV*[2] 413, 17.

Dimensions: diam. *c.* 30.0; length at rim 7.0; height 5.1.

Condition: single rim fr.

Description
Offset lip inside and outside.
EXTERIOR: bearded man in a pilos (with roughly vertical dilute glaze lines) slashes down to the left with a machaira. There is a skin tied at his neck (dilute wash), under which he wears a chiton. A branch with tiny red leaves projects up to the left of his pilos and down below his hand (a row of red dots over the knuckles and a trace of the branch below the fingers of the hand). An object coming up to the branch at the extreme left corner of the fr. might be a spear or, as Bothmer suggests, the tip of an antler.

Relief contours throughout.

c. 490–480 BC.

Comment: Attributed by Beazley to the Dokimasia Painter. The figure probably comes from a complex hunting scene, as on the later Copenhagen cup (6327: *ARV*[2] 413, 16); for the head compare the Leningrad Dolon cup (*ARV*[2] 413, 23). The Dokimasia Painter decorated a number of lipped cups: *ARV*[2] 413 nos. 16, 22 and 22 *bis*, and 373, 46 with *Para* 372. The first, the Copenhagen hunting cup, is of type C, the second is preserved only in frr. and the latter two are Acrocups (Bloesch *FAS* 141–4).

The drawing is very fine and it must have come from an important cup, comparable to fully mature works of the Brygos Painter, such as **45** (E 65) and the Tarquinia type C (*ARV*[2] 369, 4).

This fragment was listed by Beazley in 1942 (*ARV* 271, 15) as on the Market.

55 (pl. 78 d-e)

Cup: GR 1952.12–2.10
From Vulci. E.P. Warren collection.
Bought of Mrs. G. Redfern-Loades, 1952.

Bibliography: *ARV*^{2} 414, 2.

Dimensions: diam. c. 24.0; (a) length at rim 4.0; (b) gt. dim. 4.3.

Condition: two separate frr., one wall, one rim.

Description

EXTERIOR: hetairai.

Fr. a) – rim. Head and shoulders of a naked woman to right, her arms outstretched to left and right, her breasts everted. She wears a plain necklace with a central pendant (dilute glaze) and a red band in her short-cut hair. Touch of a vertical form at the right hand corner of fr. (her arm bent up?).

Fr. b) – mid wall. Hips and thighs of a naked woman to the left. The contour of a hand or arm is just visible crossing her body at the level of her hips: it might be hers or another's.

Relief line contour throughout (except hair); reserved line inside and outside lip.

c. 490–480 BC.

Comment: Placed near the Dokimasia Painter by Beazley with the further comment 'may be by the painter himself'. It is very difficult to be sure of the attribution of these frr. The necklace recalls jewellery worn by hetairai on cups by Onesimos (e.g. *ARV*^{2} 320, 10 and 12; 326, 90; 328, 114; 1645–6, add as 320, 9 *bis*). The possibility that these frr. might be by the Foundry Painter should be considered. Indeed on the right hand side of the exterior of a cup in the White/Levy collection (*Glories of the Past* no. 119) the woman bending over for intercourse has very similar face and hair.

The find-spot is provided by Beazley. Bothmer notes that Vulci is also the find-spot for GR 1952.12–2.7 (*ARV*^{2} 29, 19), which was listed by Beazley in 1942 as being on the Italian Market (*ARV* 26, 18).

56 (pls. 79 and 80 a-b, fig. 13d)

CUP: GR 1836.2–24.212 (*BM Cat Vases* E 70)
From Vulci; Durand collection.

Bibliography: *Cabinet Durand*, lot 809; Murray *DGV* no. 48; Hartwig *M* 330, 688 no. 26; *VA* 96 no. 26, fig. 64 (I); Hoppin i 133 no. 64; Tonks *Brygos* 109 no. 20; *AV* 191, 40; *ARV* 277, 71; *ARV*^{2} 421, 78.

Dimensions: width 40.8; diam. 33.0; diam. of tondo 18.6; ht. 13.0; diam. of exterior ground line 14.5; diam. of foot plate 12.4.

Condition: made up from frr.; two pairs of ancient rivet holes; reserved surface eroded in places (especially side B).

Description

INTERIOR: symposium – two youths share a couch, a boy.

The youths recline to the left. The one on the left of the couch turns his head to the right. He holds a black skyphos in his left hand and holds up his empty right hand as if playing kottabos. The youth on the right holds a black skyphos with a reserved band at handle level in his left hand and holds out a cup by one handle in his right, ready to flick it in the game of kottabos. His mouth is open. Both youths wear a dotted himation with a black border and have a red band with five large leaves at the front in their hair; they recline against cushions decorated with groups of three stripes separated by rows of dots. The couch's legs are cut off by the border, as are the first youth's legs. Below the couch is a three-legged table with two spare red fillets with leaves trailing from it. In front of the table a naked boy moves to the right, but turns his head back to the left.

Nonsense inscription: ΛΙΕΣΜΙ

Border: stopt maeander units (four-stroke, anticlockwise).

EXTERIOR: symposium.

Side A (U): a man and four youths, one with his hand behind his head.

Each of the symposiasts wears a dotted himation with a black border and a red apicate fillet in his hair and reclines against a cushion decorated with groups of three stripes separated by a row of dots. The youth on the left turns his head to the right as he holds a cup up in his right hand by one handle for a *kottabos* throw; his left arm is stretched out to the right. His lower left leg is tucked under so that only the top of the thigh is shown under the drapery. The second youth holds up a cup in his right hand in a similar fashion, but holds a black skyphos in his left hand close against his chest. Behind him is a food basket hanging from red ties and, beyond, a spotted flute-case. The youth in the centre tilts his head back and wraps his right arm round it, as he sings. In his left hand he holds against his chest a black skyphos with a reserved band at handle level. Behind him is a plain stick. On the right is a bearded man who holds out a cup in his right hand by its handle for kottabos, as he turns his head back to the right. Above him a small cup (foot black; perhaps a stemless cup), seen from underneath, is hanging on the wall. On the far right is a youth holding in his left hand a black skyphos with a reserved band at handle level. Behind him a food basket hangs from red ties. The symposiasts seem to divide into two pairs flanking the central singer.

Nonsense inscription: ΑΣΙΡΙ

Side B (U): a man and four youths.

On the far left a youth holds a cup up by its handle in his right hand for a *kottabos* throw and a black skyphos with a reserved band at handle level in his left against his chest. Behind him is a plain stick. Next is a bearded man who turns his head back to the right, as he holds a black skyphos in his left hand. Behind him is a knotty stick. In the centre is a youth who holds a cup up by its handle in his right hand for a *kottabos* throw. His left arm is missing below the elbow: it must have been raised at right angles. His left knee, covered in drapery, is brought round to the right in a strongly foreshortened view. Behind him there was a small cup hung on the wall, seen from underneath (as on side A; only the edge of it is preserved). On the right a youth turns back to the right as he holds a cup up by one handle in his right hand for a *kottabos* throw. On the far right a youth also holds a cup up in his

right hand by one handle for a *kottabos* throw, as he grips in his left hand a black skyphos with a reserved band at handle level (the base of the skyphos and part of his hand and drapery are missing). Behind him hangs a food basket.
Nonsense inscriptions.
Ground line: a frieze of silhouette vessels set between two black lines (a glaux, three skyphoi, two oinochoai resting on their sides, a kantharos of Sotadean type and three pairs of boots).

Relief line contour throughout (except hair); dilute glaze for minor interior markings; thick reserved line inside lip, thin outside; added red for inscriptions.

c. 485–480 BC.

Comment: Given by Hartwig and Murray to Brygos, attributed by Beazley to his Painter of the Paris Gigantomachy.

On the Painter of the Paris Gigantomachy see, in addition to Beazley's lists, his *VA* 94–6 and D. von Bothmer in *Glories of the Past* no. 120. The London cup is a large work by the painter in his mature phase. Beazley said of the painter (*ARV*[2] 400) that he 'has vigour, but no subtlety, and most of his work is mechanical and repetitive.' Beazley marked three cups as early (*ARV*[2] 418, 25–6 and 420, 60). The last of these is really a work of the Foundry Painter (see *CVA Amsterdam* pl. 30, 2 and 31, 1 with text p. 52; *Glories of the Past* 167), but one may add three more early pieces (*ARV*[2] 417, 7; 420, 67; *Para* 374, add as 41 *bis*). The damaged Innsbruck komast cup (ii.27.2: *ARV*[2] 420, 61) is even earlier. His major mythological cups (*ARV*[2] 417, 1–3) belong to his mature phase. They reflect, through the medium of the Brygos Painter, iconographic ideas developed by Onesimos. The mature cup with Greeks fighting Persians, once on the Rome Market (*ARV*[2] 417, 4), is now New York 1980.11.21. Several cups are labelled by Beazley as 'late' (*ARV*[2] 420, 59; 421–2, 90–6; *Para* 374, add as 94 *bis*): they are already Early Classical (add also *ARV*[2] 418, 19 and 22; 419, 48–9; 872, 12) and represent his latest phase. It seems clear that he did not enter into a monumental phase like his companions, the Brygos, Briseis and Dokimasia Painters.

The scheme of the interior recalls that of the Leningrad cup where the boy is replaced by a woman playing the pipes (*ARV*[2] 418, 22); compare also three other cups where the third figure is omitted (*ARV*[2] 420, 62 and 421, 85; Lugano market [Studer]). Three further pieces by the Painter of the Paris Gigantomachy repeat the frieze of vessels on the exterior: Lugano market; Basel, Cahn inv. 620; Chamay frr. The Florence frr. (*ARV*[2] 421, 80 have been reattributed by J.R. Guy to the Triptolemos Painter). For further examples of such a frieze see **8** (E 64). For cups hung up on the wall and seen from underneath, cf. especially the works of Douris (see on **20** [E 49]).

The so-called Sotadean kantharos, shown in the frieze (also on the Lugano market cup), has been identified by J. Boardman with Herakles' *karchesion*, see *JHS* 99 (1979) 149–51; for an alternative identification see M. Pfrommer, *Studien zu alexandrinischer und grossgriechischer Toreutik frühhellenistischer Zeit* (Berlin 1987) 3–4. The Apulian rhyton in the Petit Palais combines a ship's prow with a *karchesion* of the type sketched by Boardman (Petit Palais 411: J. S. Morrison and R.T. Williams, *Greek Oared Ships* (Cambridge 1968) pl. 26, c).

The potting was not attributed by Bloesch and Seki (*U* 48 no. 204: he calls the foot alien!). The narrow black band under the foot is a late feature; the thickness of the foot plate can be paralleled in the workshop of Brygos.

57 (pl. 80 c)

Cup: GR 1934.11–5.3 ('XY.2')
From Orvieto.
Bought of P. Hartwig, 1893.

Bibliography: *AV* 192, 54; *ARV* 277, 80; *ARV*[2] 422, 104.

Dimensions: gt. dim. 5.9; 0.4 thick.

Condition: single fr. from wall.

Description
EXTERIOR: athlete.
Hips, groin and upper legs of a naked male moving to right.
All contours done with relief line; dilute glaze for minor interior markings.

c. 490–480 BC.

Comment: Attributed by Beazley to the Painter of the Paris Gigantomachy. It is a mature work of the artist. The figure may have been a boxer like those on a number of other cups (*ARV*[2] 419, 32–4 and 46; Kyoto, Hashimoto coll. 75, *CVA Japan* 1, pl. 2; Athens, Goulandris 271, L.I. Marangou, *Ancient Greek Art: The N.P. Goulandris Collection* [Athens 1985] no. 142), a fact that illustrates well the repetitive nature of his work.

Found unregistered in the British Museum in 1934, but a drawing in the Beazley Archive in Oxford, done for Hartwig, shows the fr. in the same batch as the Makron cup **31** (E 63) and so it should also be from Orvieto.

No. 58: The Kleophrades Painter

Predominantly a pot-painter, the Kleophrades Painter did, however, occasionally turn his hand to the decoration of cups (see below). The bibliography on his *oeuvre* is considerable, see in particular: J.D. Beazley, *JHS* 30 (1910) 38–68; 36 (1916) 123–8; *VA* 40–4; Beazley *Kleophrades-Maler*, J.D. Beazley, *The Kleophrades Painter* (Mainz 1974: original English text revised by Beazley in 1944); G.M.A. Richter, *AJA* 1936, 100–15; J. den Tex, *AM* 62 (1937) 38–40; L. Schnitzler, *OpAth* 2 (1955) 47–60; R. Lullies, *Die Spitzamphora des Kleophrades-Malers* (1957); Richter *Survey*[2] 66–8; J.D. Beazley, *AntK* 1 (1958) 6–8; Robertson *GP* 102–3; Shefton in Arias and Hirmer *HGVP* 328–31; *ARV*[2] 181–95; U. Knigge, *AM* 85 (1970) 1–22; A. Greifenhagen, *Neue Fragmente des Kleophrades-malers* (Heidelberg 1972); F.W. Hamdorf, *Pantheon* 32 (1974)

219–24; J. Boardman *GettyMusJ* 1 (1974) 7–14; Boardman *ARFV Archaic* 91–4; Robertson *HGA* 231–6; J. Boardman, *AntK* 19 (1976) 3–18; J. Boardman and U. Gehrig, *AA* 1981, 329–32; M. Robertson, *Getty Vases* 1 (1983) 51–4; D. von Bothmer, *The Amasis Painter and His World* (Malibu 1985) 230–1; S.B. Matheson, *Getty Vases* 4 (1989) 95–112; F. Lissarrague in F. Beri (ed.), *Dionysos Mito e Mistero* (Comacchio 1992) 257–76; Robertson *Art of Vase-painting* 56–66.

The relative chronology of his career has been well set out by Beazley. This remains unchallenged, although a variety of attempts have been made at isolating very early works or phases (e.g. M. Robertson in B.K. Lambrinoudakis [ed.], *Stele. Tomos eis mnemen Nikolaou Kontoleontos* [Athens 1978] 125–9, suggesting a cup from the Agora; M. Ohly-Dumm in *Amsterdam Colloquium* 165–72, arguing for the identity of Euthymides and the Kleophrades Painter; J.R. Guy, unpublished lecture, New York 1991, pressing Beazley's comparison with the Pezzino Group [*ARV*² 32]; Robertson *Art of Vase-painting* 59, suggesting that the Berlin Sosias cup [*ARV*² 21, 1] is a very early work of the Kleophrades Painter).

58 (pls. 81–3 and fig. 13e)

Cup, type B or C: gr 1864.10–7.1685 (*BM Cat Vases* E 73)
Excavated on Rhodes, Kamiros Tomb F 81.

Bibliography: E. Gerhard, *Archäologischer Anzeiger, zur Archäologischen Zeitung* 24 (1866) 203*; P. Gardner, *The Journal of Philology* 7 (1877) 215–26, pls. A and B; Hartwig *M* 585 note and 623–4 no. 17; J.D. Beazley, *JHS* 1910, 63 no. 32; *AV* 76, 72; Hoppin ii, 143 no. 20; *ARV* 128, 94; *ARV*² 192, 106; Bloesch *FAS* 137 no. 4; Beazley *Kleophrades-Maler* 6, 16 and 29 no. 80, pl. 32, 1 (detail of B); *Para* 341; J. Boardman, *GettyMusJ* 1 (1974) 7–14; *LIMC* iv *sv* Glauke I no. 3, pl. 159 (detail of zone) and *sv* Galene I no. 2; *Beazley Add*² 189; *LIMC* vi *sv* Nereus no. 71, pl. 524 (detail of zone).

Dimensions: width 42.4; diam. 32.0; diam. of zone 26.0; diam. of tondo 12.0; diam. exterior ground line 14.0.

Condition: made up from frr.; foot missing, together with large sections of the bowl and part of the rim. Small holes have been drilled in to the edges of some frr. to key the earlier plaster restoration.

Description

INTERIOR: tondo and zone.
Tondo: Peleus and Thetis.
Thetis (ΘΗΤΙϟ) is moving to the right, but turns her head back to the left. She wears a chiton and a cloak over her shoulders. There is a red tie in her hair that ends in a loop at the back, the ends trailing over her left shoulder. She also has an elaborate white stephane in her hair that has a chequerboard pattern at the front (some of the added white has been chipped away to form the darker squares) and lotus blossoms attached to the upper contour. Her right arm was bent down towards Peleus (now missing), her left holds up her long black hair (done with additional relief lines on the black) over her left shoulder. Peleus must have been wrestling her about the middle: all we have of him is perhaps a reserved area beneath Thetis' chiton hem and the end of his name ([ΓΕΛΕV]ϟ). On the right was an altar with a black ovolo moulding at the top and a single step base. On top of the altar is the forepart of a *ketos*. The spiky ruff, an ear and part of the body with flippers and dorsal fin are preserved: the upper section of its body is covered with scales bounded below by a dotted stripe. On the left is part of the body of a snake, its skin provided with a row of dots on one side of the median line: this represents one of Thetis' transformations. The ground line takes the form of a small reserved exergue.

Zone: Nereids fleeing to Triton and Nereus.
At the left handle is Triton (ΤΡΙΤΩΝ). He has a white beard and long white hair tied in a pony-tail at the back; his hair has receded at the front, but there is a little tuft of three curls on top. He wears a short chiton over his human part and a red fillet in his hair. Little is preserved of his piscine part, but it was scaly with an ovolo-like lower edge and there was a fringed fin at the top. He holds a dolphin up in his left hand and, across his body in his right hand, a sceptre with a lotus finial, striped shaft (groups of dilute glaze lines) and a pointed end. Running up to him from the right comes a Nereid (ΚVΜΑΘΕΑ) in chiton and himation (black border). Her right hand is outstretched in appeal for help, her left fingers her long hair over her left shoulder in the manner of Thetis on the tondo. Her hair is tied with a red loop, and she has a reserved stephane with a battlement peak and an earring. Behind her sits Nereus (ΝΗΡΕVϟ) on a high-backed chair with a leather cover over it (zigzag decoration; key-hole fringe). He wears a long chiton and a himation (black border) and his long white hair is tied up at the back with a red band (the red has smudged over the top of the white in the area of the tuft at the back). He holds a dolphin up in his left hand and in his right hand a sceptre with a lotus head, striped shaft (pairs of relief lines) and square end across his body. Running up to him are two Nereids. The first wore a chiton and had her left hand stretched out in front and her right hand back behind her. Her chiton has a decoration of crosses and a border of small vertical lines. Of the second Nereid, only a foot under a long garment and an outstretched hand are preserved. Her name was written behind her, Galene ([Γ]ΑΛΕΝΗ). Continuing clockwise, around the lower part of the zone run three more Nereids, away from Nereus and towards Triton's back. Only part of the head and one shoulder of the first, perhaps Pasithea ([...]ΘΕΑ), are preserved. She wore a chiton and a himation. Her hair is tied up with a red loop (triple tails fly out behind) and she has a stephane with a battlement peak and an earring. In front of her runs Kymo (ΚVΜΩ). Her chest is frontal and so was her head, as the remains of her jaw line indicates. Part of the hair framing her head is visible on the left. She wore an elaborately decorated chiton enriched at the bottom by trefoils linked in an arcade pattern and a border of reserved circles, which at the bottom are dotted and at the neck are almost squares). She also has a cloak

draped around her shoulders and a necklace with a central pendant. The last figure, behind Triton, is Glauke (written ΓΛVΚΗ) of whom only part of the head and the tips of the toes of her backward right foot are preserved. She had a red tie in her hair and wears a reserved stephane with a battlement peak and an earring.
Border between tondo and zone: alternating blackened cross-squares and three units of stopt maeander (anticlockwise, five-stroke).
Below the offset lip is a reserved band.

EXTERIOR: Herakles and Kyknos; Diomedes and Aineas.

Side A (U): Herakles and Kyknos.
On the far left stood Athena to the right: only a foot and the lower part of her chiton and himation (dilute glaze band at hem) are preserved, together with the end of her spear. In front of her wide-eyed Herakles (ΗΡΑΚΛΕΟΣ) storms to the right, clad in belted lion-skin and short chiton. The lion-skin is knotted at the neck and has a band of dilute glaze along its edges. He has a Boeotian shield on his left arm and thrusts down with a spear into the shoulder of his opponent. His left foot is in mid air, only two of the toes of his right foot, seen frontally, make contact with the ground. His opponent, Kyknos (ΚVΚΝΟΣ), clad in short chiton, cuirass, greaves and Corinthian helmet is down on his left knee, his right leg outstretched and seen in three-quarter view. He has attempted an overhead thrust with his spear at Herakles' waist, but the spear has broken on the invulnerable lion-skin. He bleeds from wounds to his chest and right thigh and his grasp on the shield on his left arm is slipping. Behind Kyknos, Ares (ΑΡΗΟΣ) presses forward. He is clad in short chiton, cuirass, greaves and Corinthian helmet and has, at his left hip, a sword in a scabbard around which is entwined a snake. He is seen in three-quarter back view, the right leg seen fully from behind. He has a shield (device: bull's head) and thrusts forward with a spear, held in his right hand, at Herakles.

Side B (L): Diomedes and Aineas.
On the far left stands the calm figure of Athena (ΑΘΗΝ[Α]). She wears a chiton (dilute glaze folds) and himation and is equipped with an Attic helmet, shield and spear, which she holds vertically. In front of her is Diomedes (ΔΙΟΜΗΔΗΣ) in short chiton, cuirass and Corinthian helmet. He has a red baldric crossing from his right shoulder to his left hip and holds a sword low in his right hand, his left arm is protected by a shield seen from the inside. There is part of what seems to be a fold of drapery between the sword hilt and his leg; if it is from a chlamys, the artist has forgotten to paint any of it at shoulder level. Aineas (ΑΙΝΕΑΣ) is down on his left knee and his right leg was stretched out to the left (cf. Kyknos on side A). He is clad in short chiton, cuirass, greaves and Corinthian helmet. He has a spear stuck in his chest, the upper part of the shaft has snapped. His right arm is raised over his head, as if attempting to chop off the spearhead with his sword. The shield on his left arm begins to slip from his grasp (cf. Kyknos on side A). The pupil of his eye has slid upwards and his head droops. In the background behind him is Aphrodite (ΑΦΡΟΔΙΤΗΣ), dressed in chiton, himation, sakkos (black stripe) and earring. She has appeared suddenly to rescue Aineas, and the tail folds of her cloak still bear the imprint of her passage to the left, although she is already beginning to move back to the right, as the heel of her left foot (below Aineas' greaved knee) reveals. She has her right hand under Aineas' right armpit and her left reaches for his left armpit, as she endeavours to lift him, her head slightly bowed with the effort.
Under the handles: floral complex of three palmettes with tendrils ending in spirals; the palmette under the handle has an elongated central frond (rounded in one case, pointed in the other).
Ground line: blackened cross-square alternating with six units of stopt maeander (five-stroke, anticlockwise).

All contours done with relief line (including hair); dilute glaze for minor interior markings.

c. 480 BC.

Comment: Attributed to Douris by Hartwig and to Kleophrades by F. Hauser (in F.R. ii 228); Beazley gave it to his Kleophrades Painter as a 'later' work, comparing it with the amphora with Ajax and Hektor in Würzburg (*ARV*[2] 182, 5; *Kleophrades-Maler* 16). The fullest discussion of the cup is Boardman's, which comments on all iconographic matters as well as the drawing.

Beazley attributed four other cups (*ARV*[2] 191–2) to the Kleophrades Painter, two as early works (potted by Kleophrades), two as 'later' works and one as a 'late' piece. M. Robertson has suggested that a sixth cup (Agora P 2754: *Stele* 125–9) might be a very early work by the Kleophrades Painter, but this seems improbable. Beazley asked whether the Boot Painter (*ARV*[2] 192 and 821) might not be a late phase of the Kleophrades Painter. There are clearly strong connections (note especially the figure of Athena on side B of this cup), but it seems more likely that the Boot Painter was a pupil of the Kleophrades Painter in his later years (cf. M. Robertson *op. cit.* 128 note 22). There also appear to be potting connections between both painters and the late products of the Brygan Circle.

The cup has an offset lip inside only: the stem may have been of type B or type C. Bloesch placed the cup in his 'Eleusisgruppe'. For another cup by the same painter with an offset lip inside only see Getty 77.AE.21,18: M. Robertson, *Getty Vases* 1 [1983] 53 fig. 6. One of the 'later' cups (*ARV*[2] 192, 105; Bloesch *FAS* 132 no. 14) is of type C cup with a fully offset lip. Euphronios' giant type C cup with fully offset lip in the Getty, decorated by Onesimos, also has a zone around the tondo, and a reexamination of such type C cups suggests that Euphronios potted an early series and was followed by Brygos, who may have been the potter of the Kleophrades Painter's cups with offset lips, both inside only and fully offset (see further D. Williams, *Getty Vases* 5, 1991, 47–9; and above on **4** [D 1] and **44** [E 65]).

On Peleus and Thetis see X. Krieger, *Der Kampf zwischen Peleus und Thetis in der griechischen Vasenmalerei* (Diss. Münster 1973); Schefold *Sagen* 95–102. On the *ketos* see J. Boardman in L. Kahil, C. Auge and P. Linant de Bellefonds (eds.), *Iconographie Classique et Identites Regionales* (*BCH Supplement* xiv, Paris 1986) 447–53; J. Boardman in *Monsters and demons in the ancient and medieval worlds. Papers presented in honor of E. Porada* (Mainz 1987) 73–84. For a frontally-headed Nereid at the seizing of Thetis compare a stamnos by the Berlin Painter (*ARV*² 209, 161). Frontal faces are not very common in the work of the Kleophrades Painter (*ARV*² 182, 6; 188, 67; 191, 102; and perhaps Atlas on the volute-krater, now Getty Mus. 77.AE.11 – see A. Greifenhagen, *Neue Fragmente des Kleophradesmalers* [Heidelberg 1972] pl. 25). For elaborate stephanai compare Makron's skyphos: London E 140 (*ARV*² 459, 3).

The arrangement of the figures in the zone is, it would seem, not carefully worked out. The placement of Triton at the left and Nereus at the top works well, but the other two cardinal positions are not significantly stressed (contrast the Getty Onesimos potted by Euphronios: D. Williams, *Getty Vases* 5, 1991, 49–56 and 61).

On Herakles and Kyknos see Schefold *GuH* 136–8 and *Urkönige* 176–7. On Diomedes and Aineias see Schefold *GuH* 218–9; F. Canciani in *LIMC* i *sv* Aineias esp. 384–5 and 394; J. Boardman and C. Vafopoulou-Richardson in *LIMC* iii *sv* Diomedes I esp. 400 and 408; Schefold *Sagen* 187–9. For a broken spear cf. a lekythos in Cleveland (W.G. Moon and L. Berge [eds.], *Greek Vase-Painting in Midwestern Collections* [Chicago 1979] no. 105). On the idea of trying to chop off a spearhead with a slashing blow of the sword see B.F. Cook, *MetMusJ* 24 (1989) 57–8.

For the tomb-group see *BM Cat Terracottas* 26 and *BM Cat Glass* i 157. The sepulchral chamber contained three glass vessels (*BM Cat Glass* 133 and 261; and GR 1864.10–7.59, now in Istanbul), five terracottas (*BM Cat Terracottas* 232, 267, 281, 282 and 926) and three black glaze vessels (GR 1864.10–7.1612 and 1620; and 1949.2–20.23). Higgins refers to the vase as a 'family heirloom'.

CONCORDANCES

BM Cat Vases numbers with new CVA running numbers

BM Cat Vases	*CVA* number
D 1	4
E 23	9
E 25	12
E 39	18
E 43	10
E 44	6
E 45	3
E 46	2
E 47	5
E 48	19
E 49	20
E 50	23
E 51	26
E 52	21
E 53	22
E 54	24
E 55	27
E 56	28
E 57	11
E 58	31
E 59	41
E 60	29
E 61	37
E 62	38
E 63	32
E 64	8
E 65	45
E 67	47
E 68	43
E 69	44
E 70	56
E 71	42
E 73	58
E 75	51
E 76	50
E 78	48
E 99	17
E 134, 3	39
E 816	7
E 818	53

Register numbers with new CVA running numbers

Register number	*CVA* number
GR 1836.2–24.25	6
GR 1836.2–24.101	3
GR 1836.2–24.131	47
GR 1836.2–24.173	53
GR 1836.2–24.212	56
GR 1836.2–24.230	11
GR 1836.2–24.231	9
GR 1843.11–3.4	24
GR 1843.11–3.10	29
GR 1843.11–3.11	44
GR 1843.11–3.13	19
GR 1843.11–3.15	20
GR 1843.11–3.16	27
GR 1843.11–3.44	38
GR 1843.11–3.45	22
GR 1843.11–3.53	21
GR 1843.11–3.54	51
GR 1843.11–3.61	28
GR 1843.11–3.92	50
GR 1843.11–3.94	26
GR 1848.3–20.1	12
GR 1848.6–19.7	43
GR 1850.3–2.2	48
GR 1864.10–7.81	17
GR 1864.10–7.1685	58
GR 1865.11–18.46	7
GR 1866.8–5.4	42
GR 1867.5–8.1012	41
GR 1867.5–8.1060	18
GR 1867.5–8.1061	8
GR 1867.5–8.1063	37
GR 1873.8–20.376	45
GR 1883.12–8.1	31
GR 1888.6–1.757 and 758	4
GR 1892.5–18.1	23
GR 1892.7–18.6	10
GR 1892.7–18.7	2
GR 1893.11–15.2	32
GR 1893.11–15.2, 14	33
GR 1893.11–15.2, 15	34
GR 1893.11–15.2, 16	35
GR 1893.11–15.2, 17	36
GR 1893.11–15.3	39
GR 1894.3–14.1	5
GR 1895.5–13.1	49
GR 1896.6–21.1	52
GR 1897.10–28.1	13
GR 1901.5–14.1	16
GR 1901.7–11.2	1
GR 1905.1–26.1	4
GR 1924.7–18.1 and 2	2
GR 1934.11–5.3	57
GR 1950.1–4.10	46
GR 1952.12–2.6	14
GR 1952.12–2.8	30
GR 1952.12–2.9	40
GR 1952.12–2.10	55
GR 1952.12–2.11	25
GR 1952.12–2.12	54
GR 1993.4–5.1	15

INDEXES

Find spots

Collectors and Dealers

Painters, Potters, Groups and Classes

Mythological Subjects

Kalos Names

LIST OF ILLUSTRATIONS

Plates

46. (a) **31** (E 58): Exterior, side A
(b) **31** (E 58: Exterior, side B

47. (a) **32** (E 63): Interior
(b) **32** (E 63): Tondo

48. (a) **32** (E 63): Exterior, side A
(b) **32** (E 63): Exterior, side B

49. (a) **32** (GR 1893.11–15.2,1): Exterior, side A
(b) **32** (GR 1893.11–15.2,2): Exterior, side A
(c) **32** (GR 1893.11–15.2,3): Exterior, side B
(d) **32** (GR 1893.11–15.2,4): Exterior, side B
(e) **32** (GR 1893.11–15.2,5): Exterior, side B
(f) **32** (GR 1893.11–15.2,6): Exterior, side A/B
(g) **32** (GR 1893.11–15.2,7): Exterior, side A/B
(h) **32** (GR 1893.11–15.2,8): Exterior, side A/B
(i) **32** (GR 1893.11–15.2,9): Exterior, side A/B
(j) **32** (GR 1893.11–15.2,10): Exterior, side A/B
(k) **32** (GR 1893.11–15.2,11): Exterior, side A/B
(l) **32** (GR 1893.11–15.2,12): Exterior, side A/B
(m) **32** (GR 1893.11–15.2,13): Exterior, side A/B
(n) **33** (GR 1893.11–15.2,14): Exterior
(o) **34** (GR 1893.11–15.2,15): Exterior
(p) **35** (GR 1893.11–15.2,16): Exterior
(q) **36** (GR 1893.11–15.2,17): Exterior

50. (a) **37** (E 61): Interior
(b) **37** (E 61): Tondo

51. (a) **37** (E 61): Exterior, side A
(b) **37** (E 61): Exterior, side B

52. (a) **38** (E 62): Interior
(b) **38** (E 62): Tondo

53. (a) **38** (E 62): Exterior, side A
(b) **38** (E 62): Exterior, side B
(c) **39** (E 134, 3): Interior
(d) **40** (GR 1952.12–2.9): Exterior

54. (a) **41** (E 59): Interior
(b) **41** (E 59): Tondo

55. (a) **41** (E 59): Exterior, side A
(b) **41** (E 59): Exterior, side B

56. (a) **42** (E 71): Interior
(b) **42** (E 71): Tondo

57. (a) **42** (E 71): Exterior, side A
(b) **42** (E 71): Exterior, side B

58. (a) **43** (E 68): Interior
(b) **43** (E 68): Tondo

59. (a) **43** (E 68): Exterior, side A
(b) **43** (E 68): Exterior, side B
(c) **43** (E 68): Exterior, side B, detail
(d) **43** (E 68): Exterior, side B, detail

60. (a) **44** (E 69): Interior
(b) **44** (E 69): Tondo

61. (a) **44** (E 69): Exterior, side A
(b) **44** (E 69): Exterior, side B
(c) **44** (E 69): Exterior, side B, detail
(d) **44** (E 69): Exterior, side B, detail

62. (a) **45** (E 65): Interior
(b) **45** (E 65): Tondo

63. (a) **45** (E 65): Exterior, side A
(b) **45** (E 65): Exterior, side B

64. (a) **45** (E 65): Exterior, side A, detail
(b) **45** (E 65): Exterior, side B, detail
(c) **45** (E 65): Exterior, side A, detail

65. (a) **46** (GR 1950.1–4.10): Interior
(b) **46** (GR 1950.1–4.10): Tondo

66. (a) **47** (E 67): Interior
(b) **47** (E 67): Tondo

67. (a) **47** (E 67): Exterior, side A
(b) **47** (E 67): Exterior, side B

68. (a) **48** (E 78): Interior
(b) **48** (E 78): Tondo

69. (a) **48** (E 78): Exterior, side A
(b) **48** (E 78): Exterior, side B
(c) **48** (E 78): Exterior, side A, detail

70. (a) **49** (GR 1895.5–13.1): Interior
(b) **49** (GR 1895.5–13.1): Tondo

71. (a) **49** (GR 1895.5–13.1): Exterior, side A
(b) **49** (GR 1895.5–13.1): Exterior, side B
(c) **49** (GR 1895.5–13.1): Exterior, side A, detail
(d) **49** (GR 1895.5–13.1): Exterior, side B, detail

72. (a) **50** (E 76): Interior
(b) **50** (E 76): Tondo

73. (a) **50** (E 76): Exterior, side A
(b) **50** (E 76): Exterior, side B
(c) **50** (E 76): Exterior, side B, detail

74. (a) **51** (E 75): Interior
(b) **51** (E 75): Tondo

75. (a) **51** (E 75): Exterior, side A
(b) **51** (E 75): Exterior, side B

76. (a) **52** (GR 1896.6–21.1): Interior
(b) **52** (GR 1896.6–21.1): Tondo

77. (a) **53** (E 818): Interior
(b) **53** (E 818): Tondo

78. (a) **53** (E 818): Exterior, side A
(b) **53** (E 818): Exterior, side B
(c) **54** (GR 1952.12–2.12): Exterior
(d) **55** (GR 1952.12–2.10): Exterior

79. (a) **56** (E 70): Interior
(b) **56** (E 70): Tondo

80. (a) **56** (E 70): Exterior, side A
(b) **56** (E 70): Exterior, side B
(c) **57** (GR 1934.11–5.3): Exterior

81. (a) **58** (E 73): Interior
(b) **58** (E 73): Tondo

82. (a) **58** (E 73): Zone
(b) **58** (E 73): Zone
(c) **58** (E 73): Zone
(d) **58** (E 73): Zone

83. (a) **58** (E 73): Exterior, side A
(b) **58** (E 73): Exterior, side B
(c) **58** (E 73): Exterior, side A, detail
(d) **58** (E 73): Exterior, side B, detail

Drawings

Fig. 1 (Sketches)
(a) **5** (E 47): Interior
(b) **5** (E 47): Exterior, side A
(c) **26** (E 51): Interior
(d) **27** (E 55): Interior
(e) **27** (E 55): Exterior, side A
(f) **45** (E 65): Exterior, side A
(g) **45** (E 65): Exterior, side A
(h) **45** (E 65): Exterior, side B
(i) **48** (E 78): Interior

Fig. 2 (Palmettes under handles)
(a) **19** (E 48)
(b) **20** (E 49)
(c) **21** (E 52)
(d) **22** (E 53)
(e) **24** (E 54)
(f) **26** (E 51)
(g) **27** (E 55)
(h) **28** (E 56)
(i) **29** (E 60)

Fig. 3 (Palmettes, signatures and graffiti)
(a) **8** (E 64)
(b) **17** (E 99)
(c) **37** (E 61)
(d) **38** (E 62)
(e) **6** (E 44)
(f) **37** (E 61)
(g) **45** (E 65)
(h) **6** (E 44)
(i) **38** (E 62)
(j) **20** (E 49)
(k) **48** (E 78)
(l) **21** (E 52)

(Figs. 4–13: profiles)
Fig. 4:
(a) **1** (GR 1901.7–11.2)
(b) **2** (E 46)
(c) **3** (E 45)
(d) **4** (D 1)
(e) **5** (E 47)
(f) **6** (E 44)

Fig. 5:
(a) **7** (E 816)
(b) **8** (E 64)
(c) **9** (E 23)
(d) **10** (E 43)
(e) **11** (E 57)

Fig. 6:
(a) **12** (E 25)
(b) **13** (GR 1897.10–28.1)
(c) **16** (1901.5–14.1)
(d) **17** (E 99)
(e) **18** (E 39)

Fig. 7:
(a) **19** (E 48)
(b) **20** (E 49)
(c) **21** (E 52)
(d) **22** (E 53)

Fig. 8:
(a) **23** (E 50)
(b) **24** (E 54)
(c) **26** (E 51)
(d) **27** (E 55)
(e) **28** (E 56)

Fig. 9:
(a) **29** (E 60)
(b) **31** (E 58)
(c) **32** (E 63)
(d) **37** (E 61)

Fig. 10:
(a) **38** (E 62)
(b) **41** (E 59)
(c) **42** (E 71)
(d) **43** (E 68)

Fig. 11:
(a) **44** (E 69)
(b) **45** (E 65)
(c) **46** (GR 1950.1–4.10)
(d) **47** (E 67)

Fig. 12:
(a) **48** (E 78)
(b) **49** (GR 1895.5–13.1)
(c) **50** (E 76)
(d) **51** (E 75)

Fig. 13:
(a) **52** (GR 1896.6–21.1)
(b) **53** (E 818)
(c) **54** (GR 1952.12–2.12)
(d) **56** (E 70)
(e) **58** (E 73)

Note on the illustrations

All profile drawings are half actual size.

All other drawings are actual size.

All fragments are reproduced actual size.

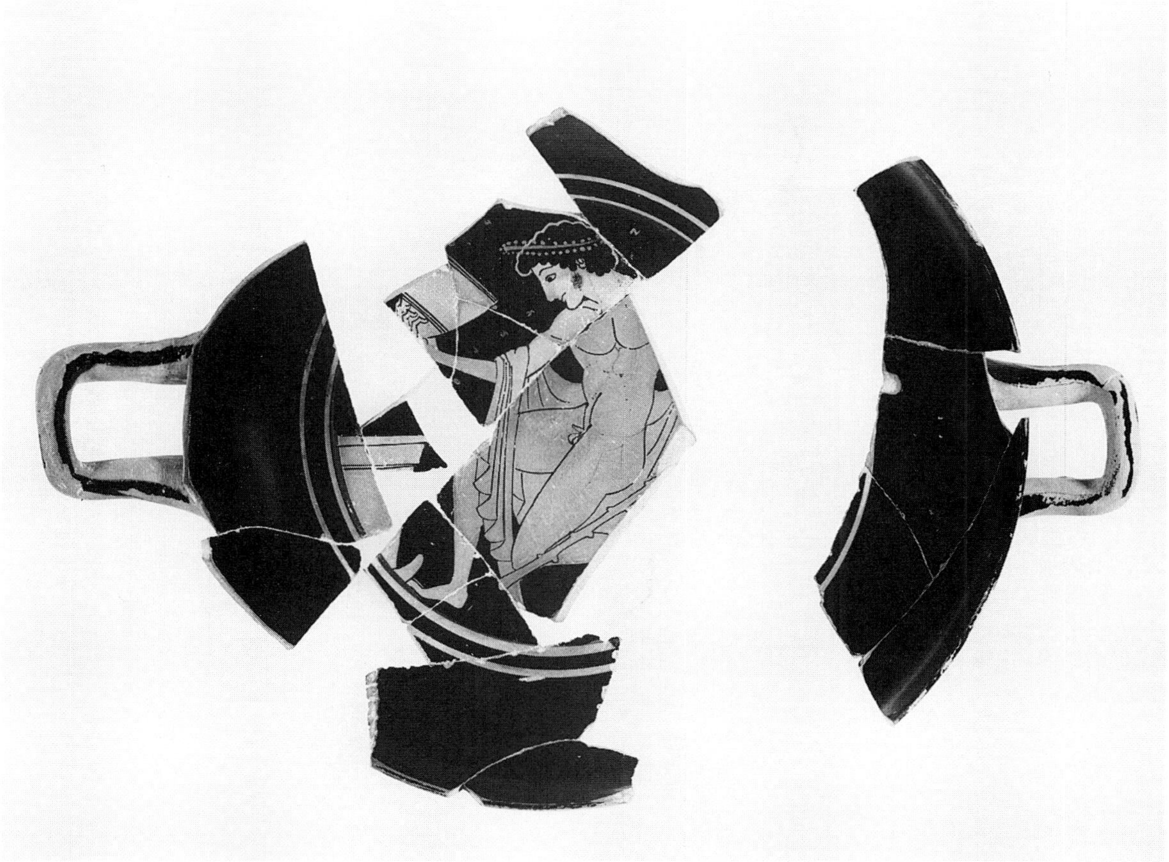

(a) 1

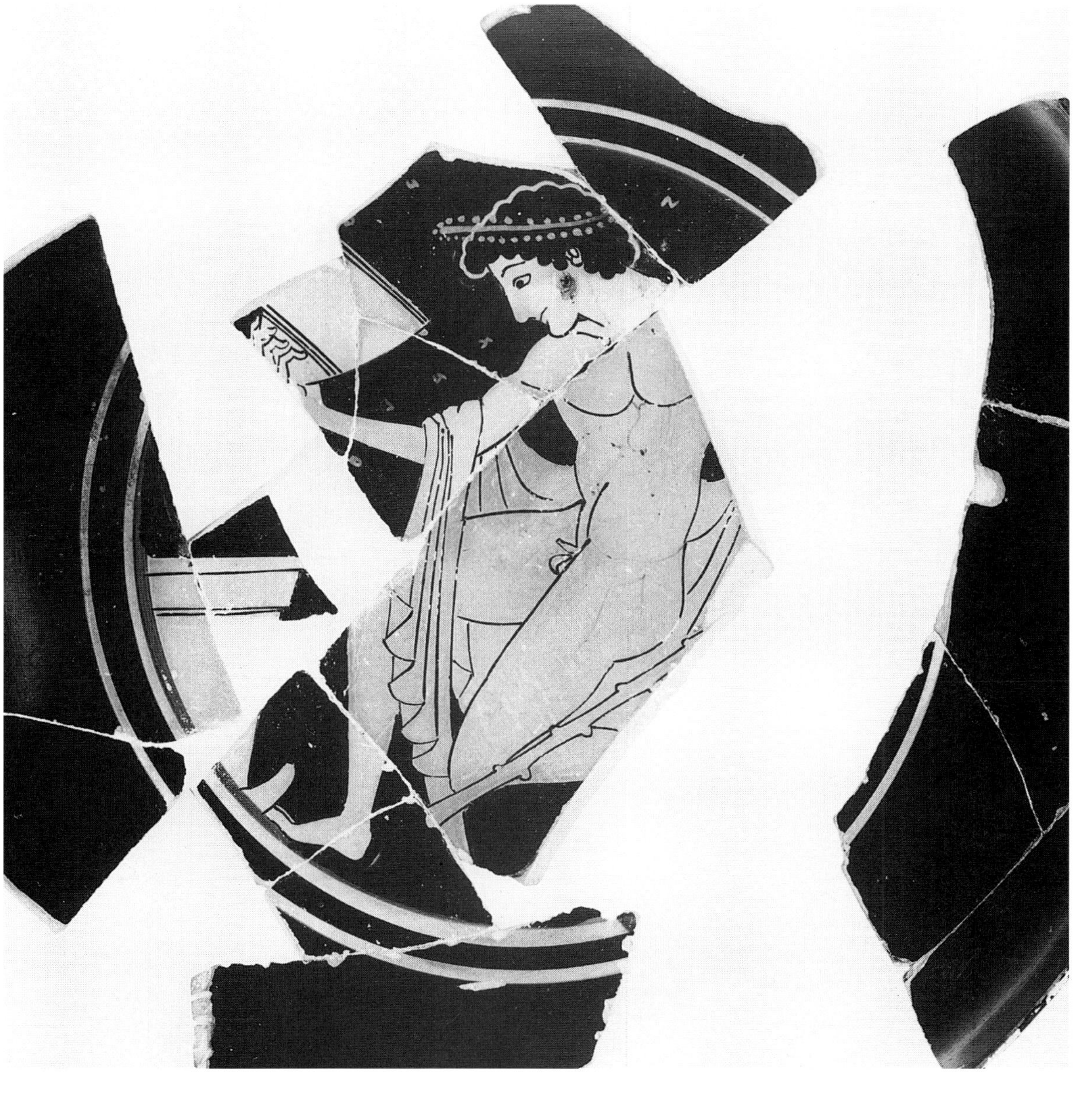

(b) 1

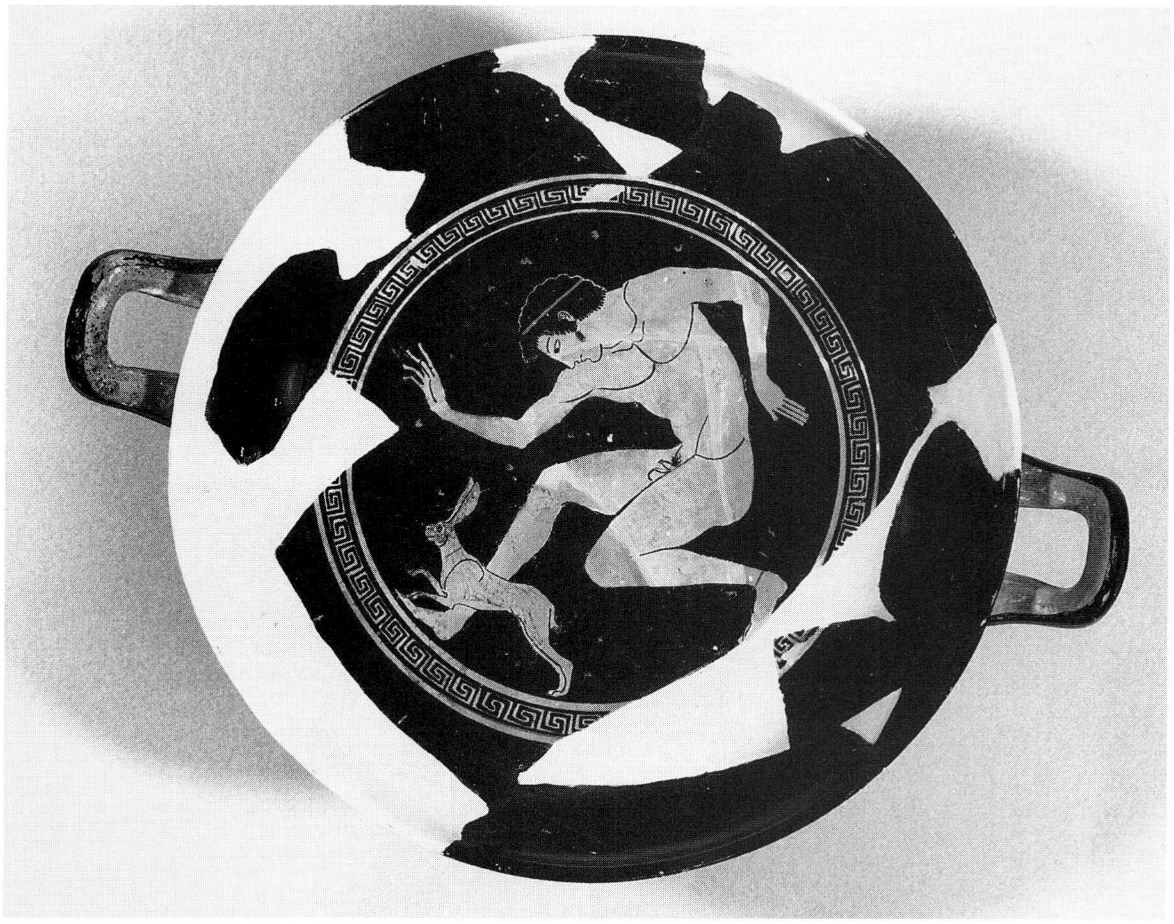

(a) 2

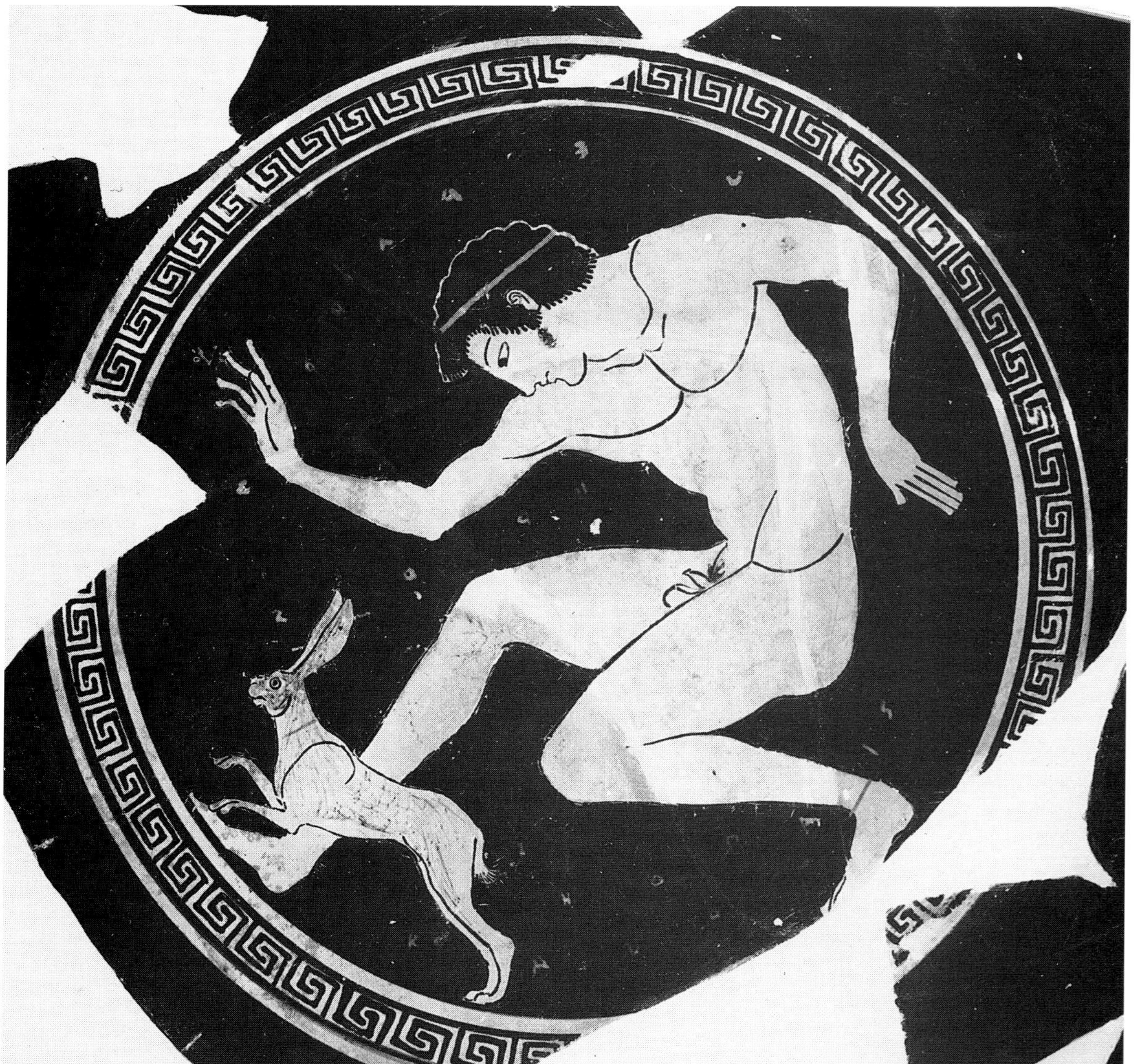

(b) 2

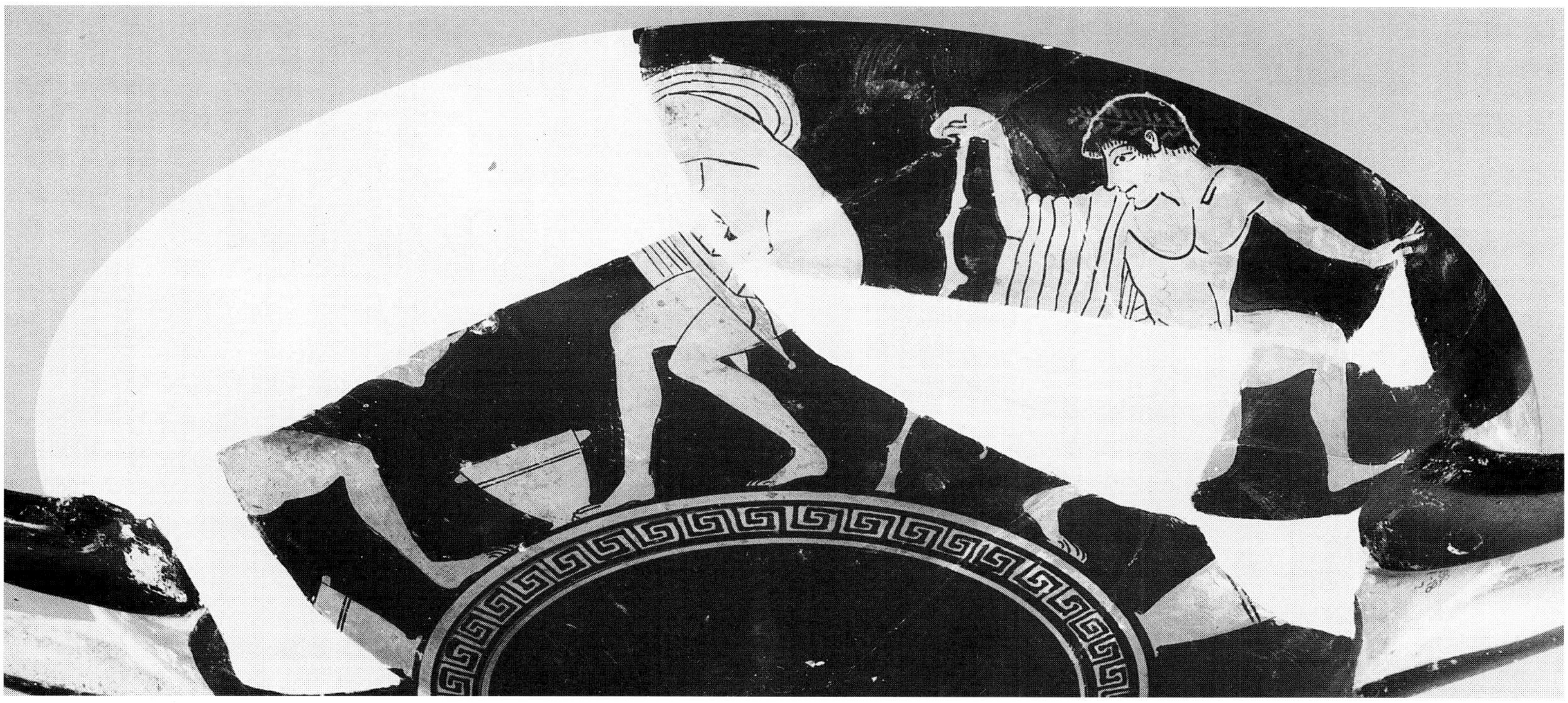

(a) 2

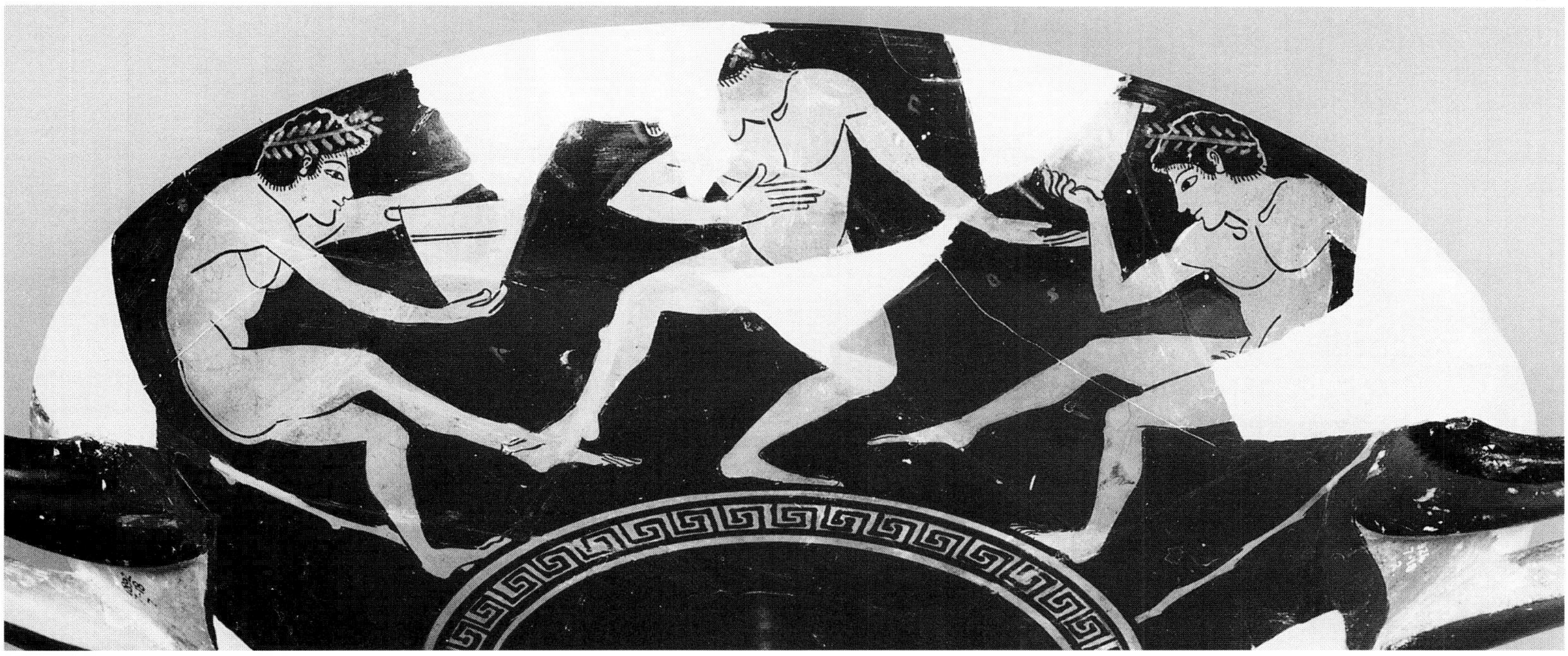

(b) 2

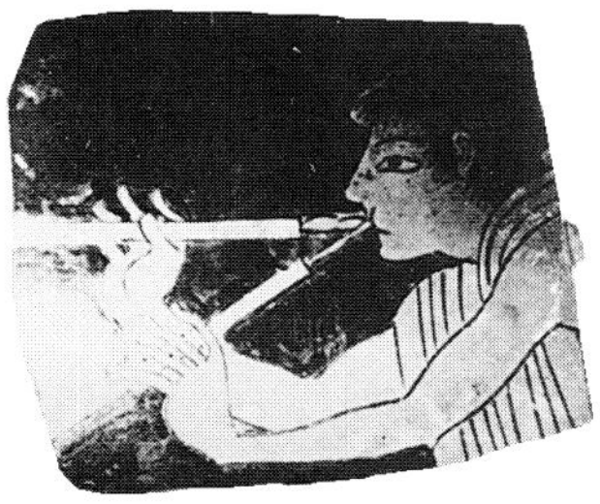

(c) 2

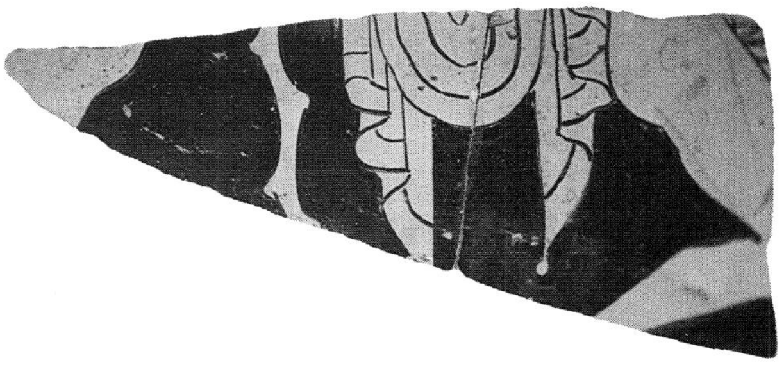

(d) 2

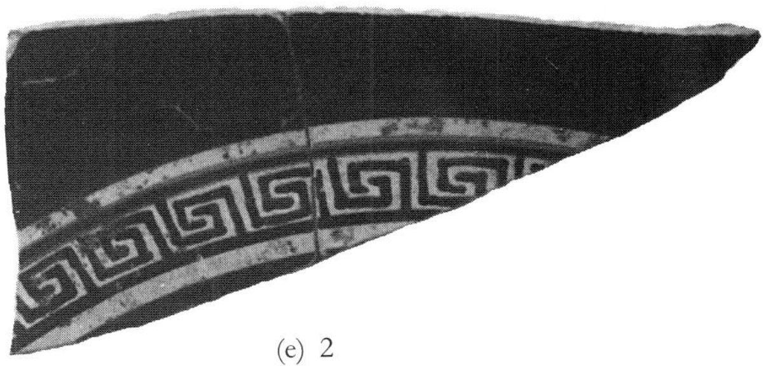

(e) 2

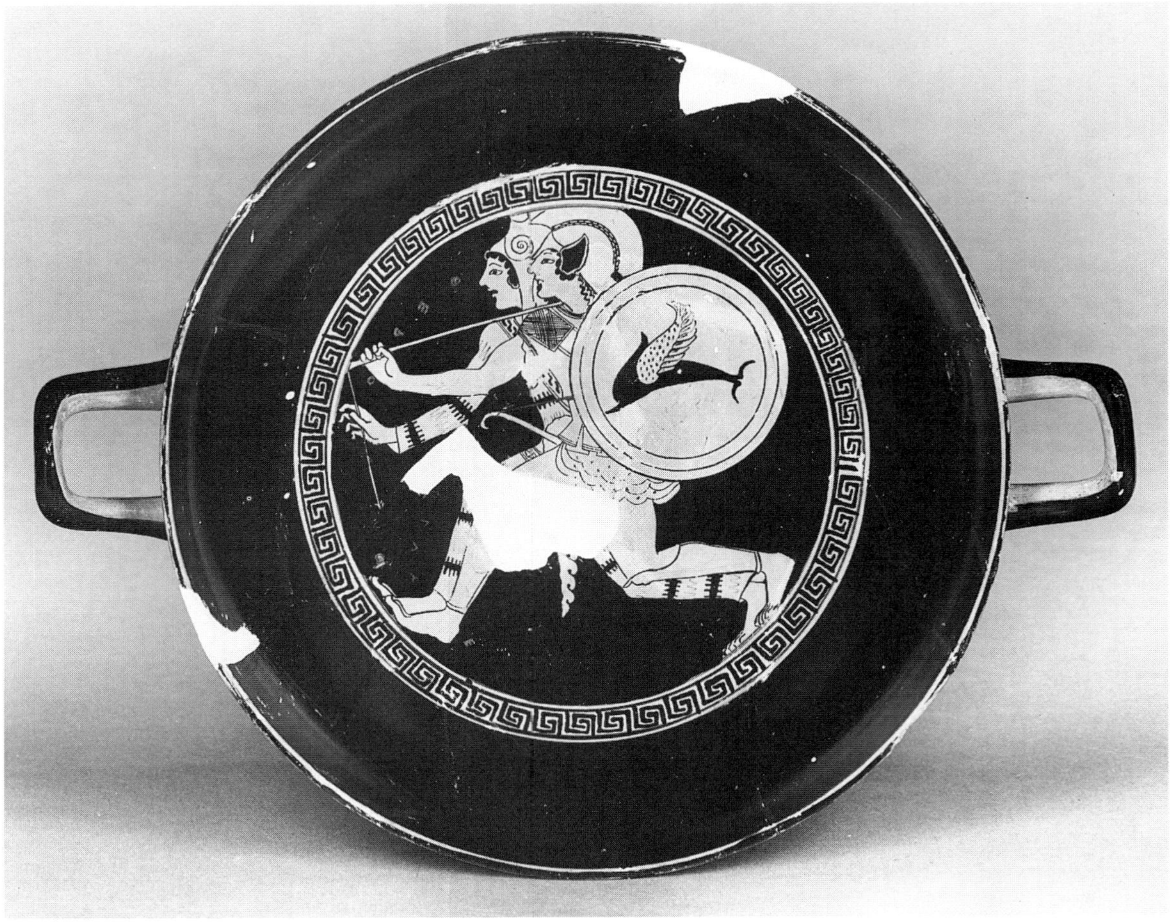

(a) 3

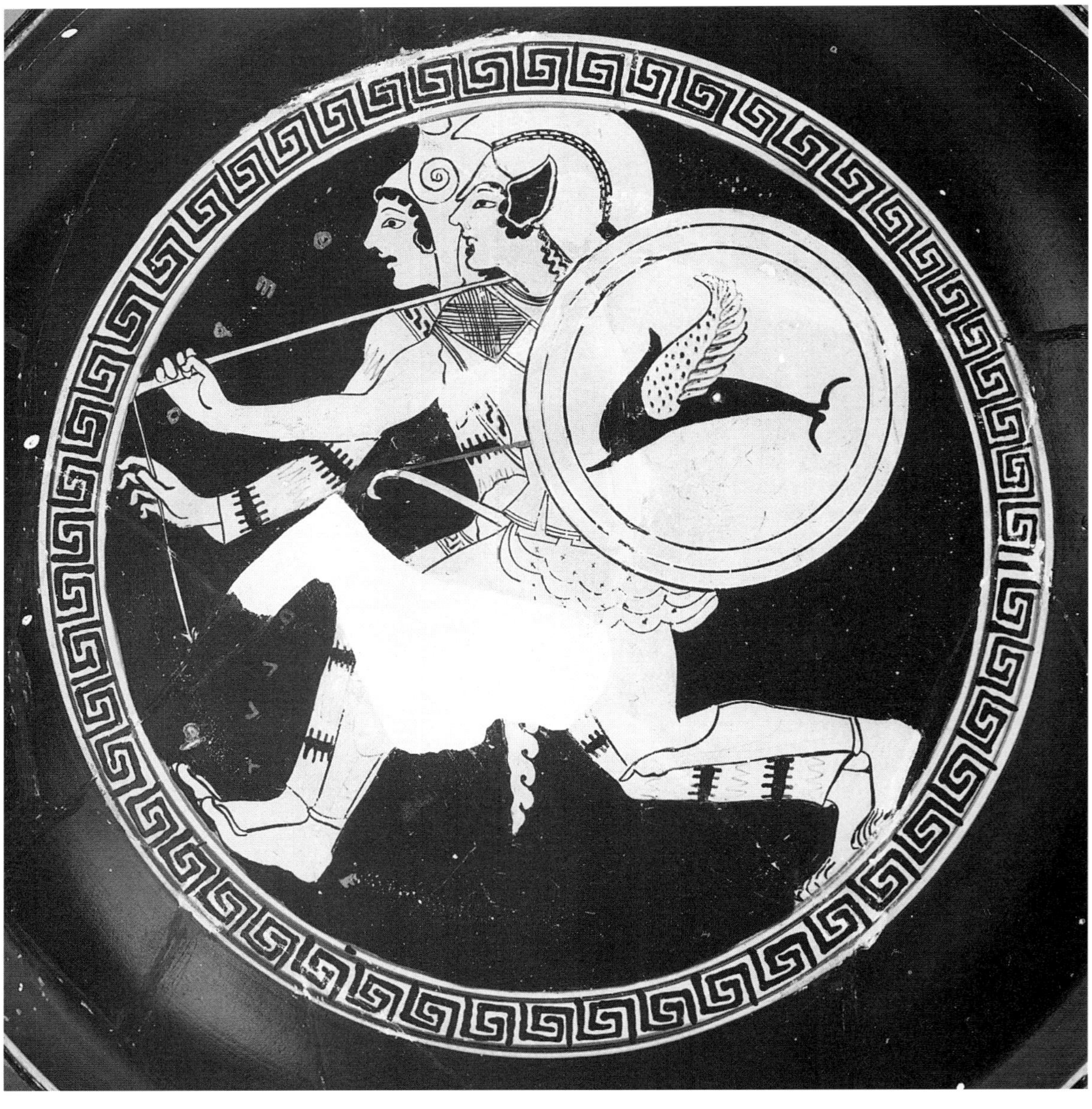

(b) 3

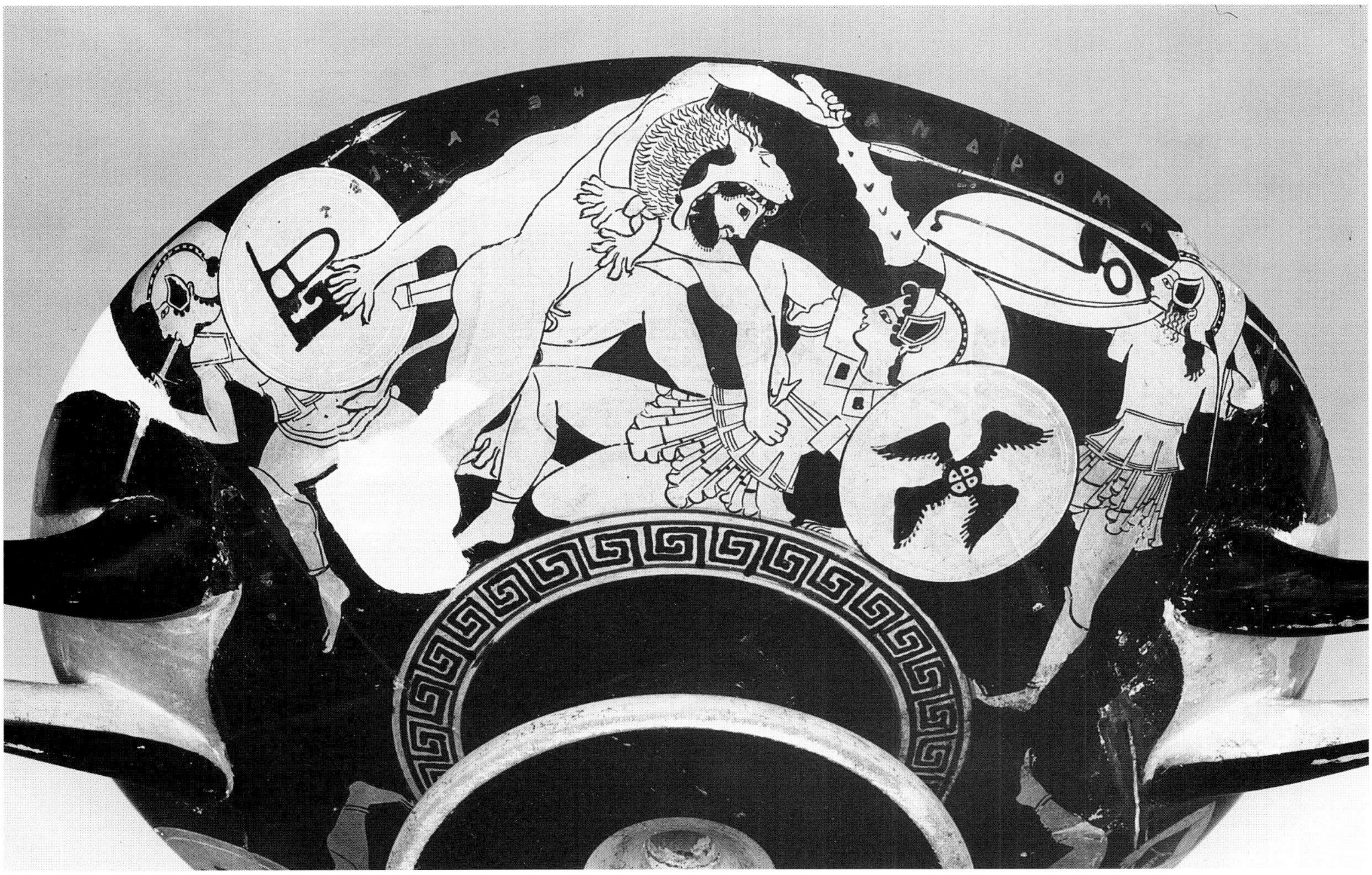

(a) 3

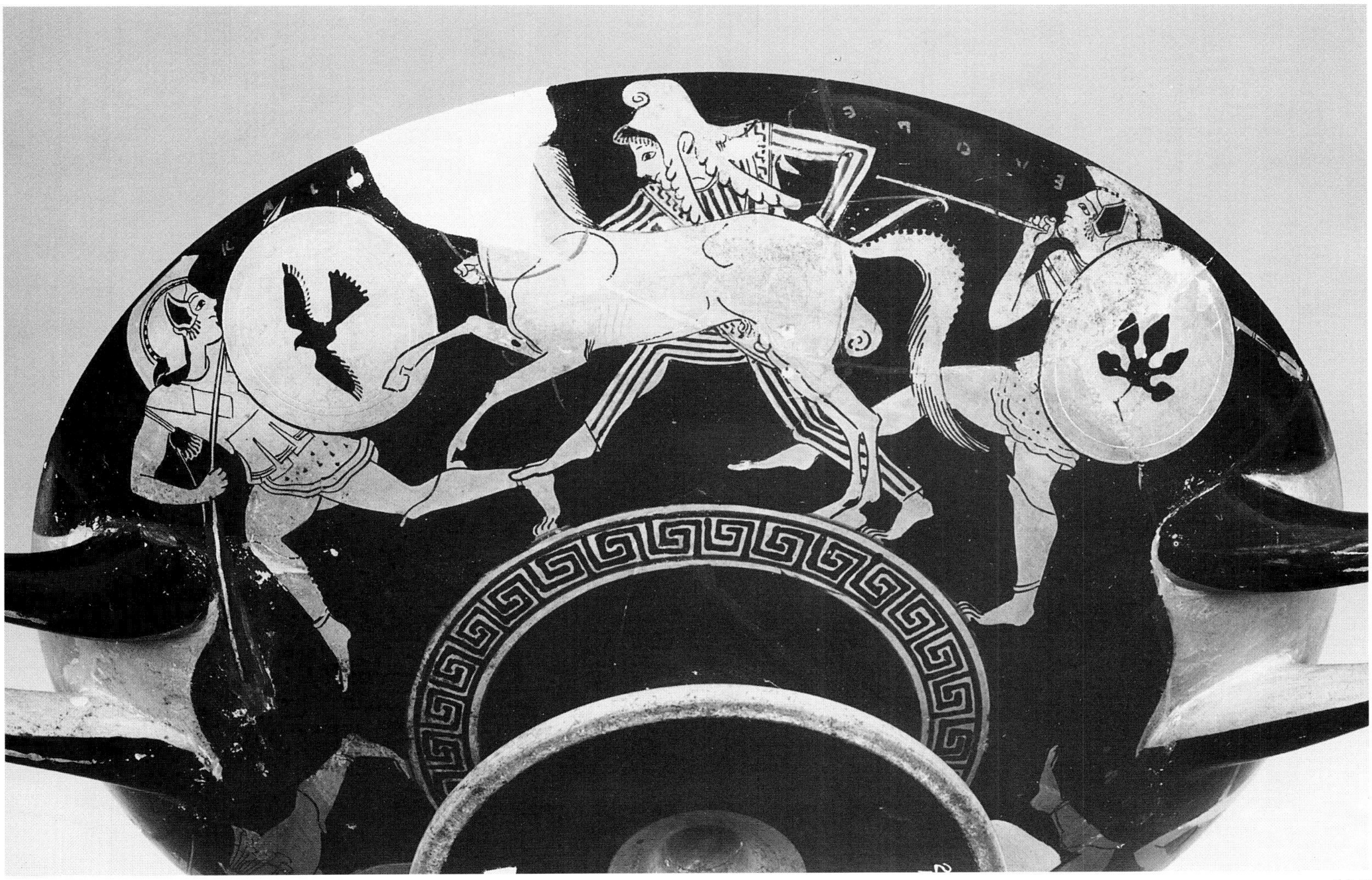

(b) 3

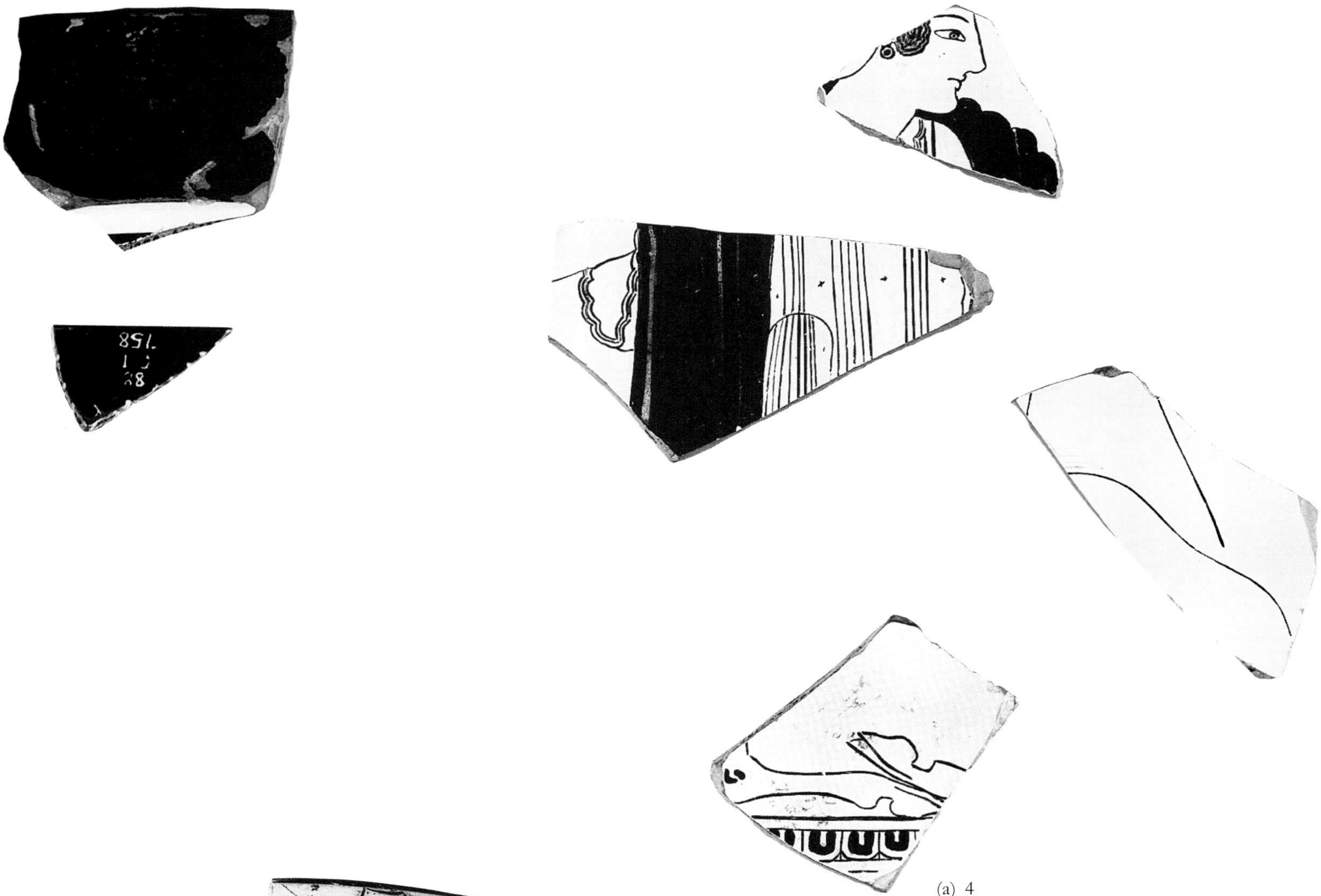

(a) 4

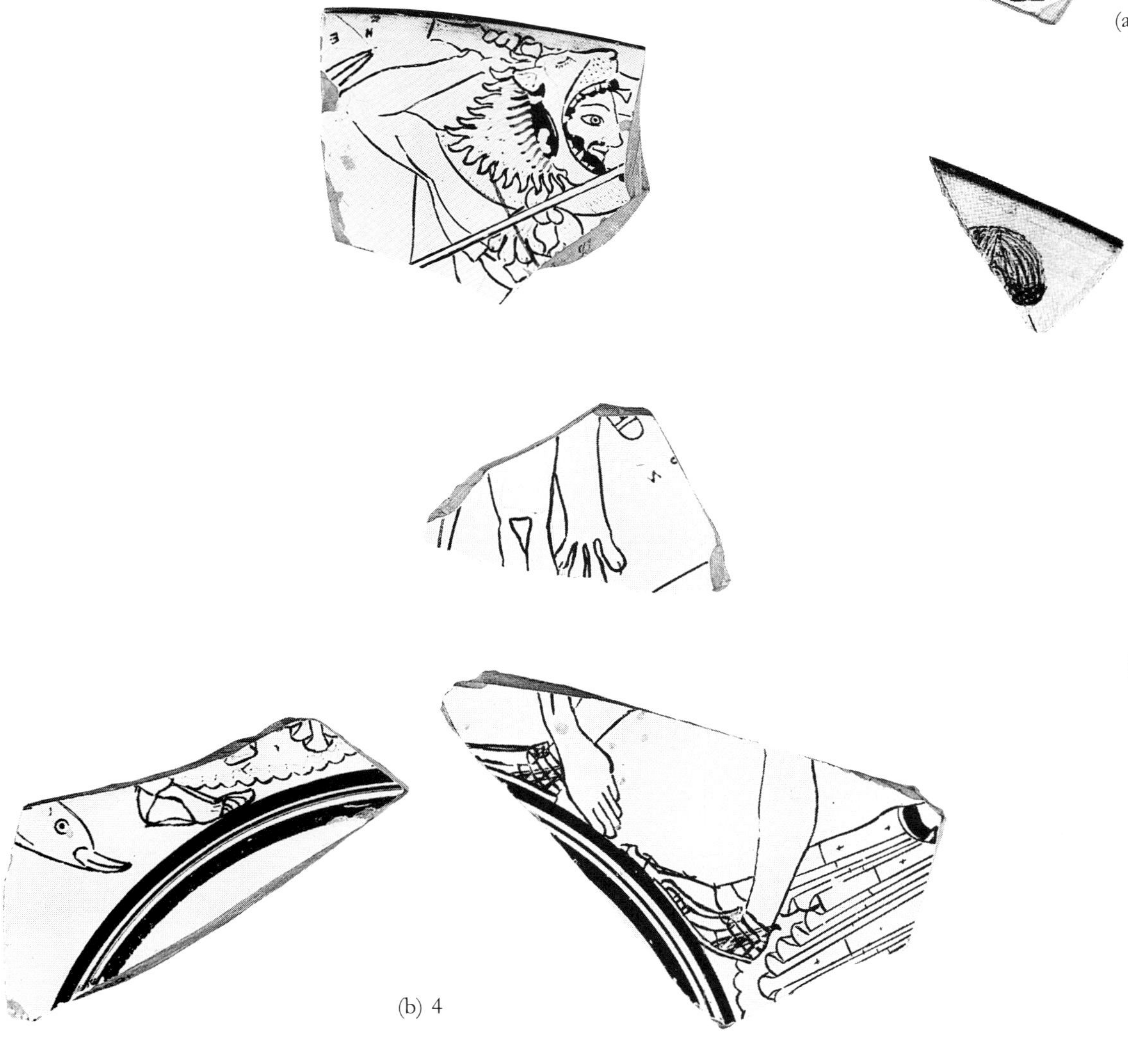

(b) 4

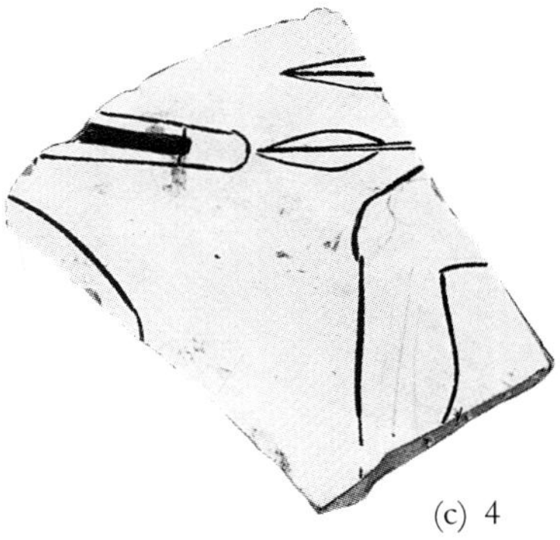

(c) 4

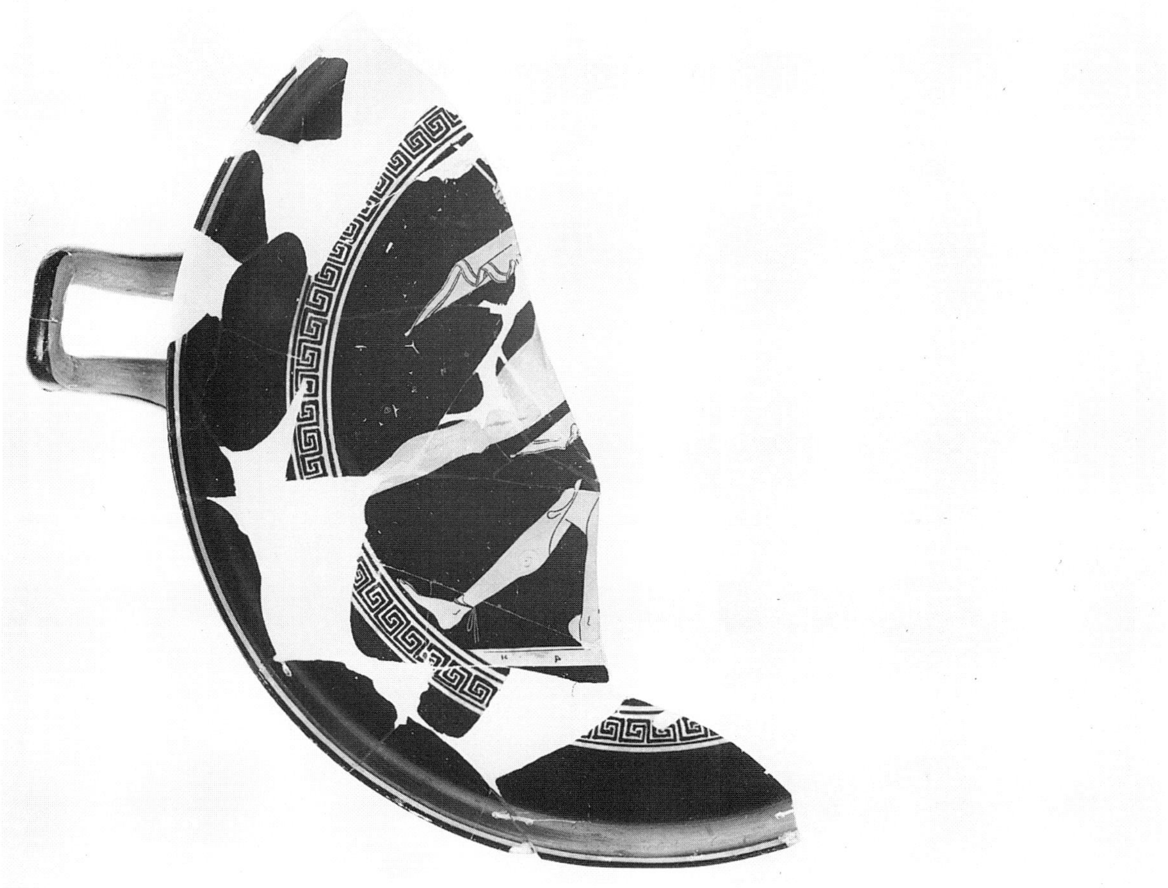

(a) 5

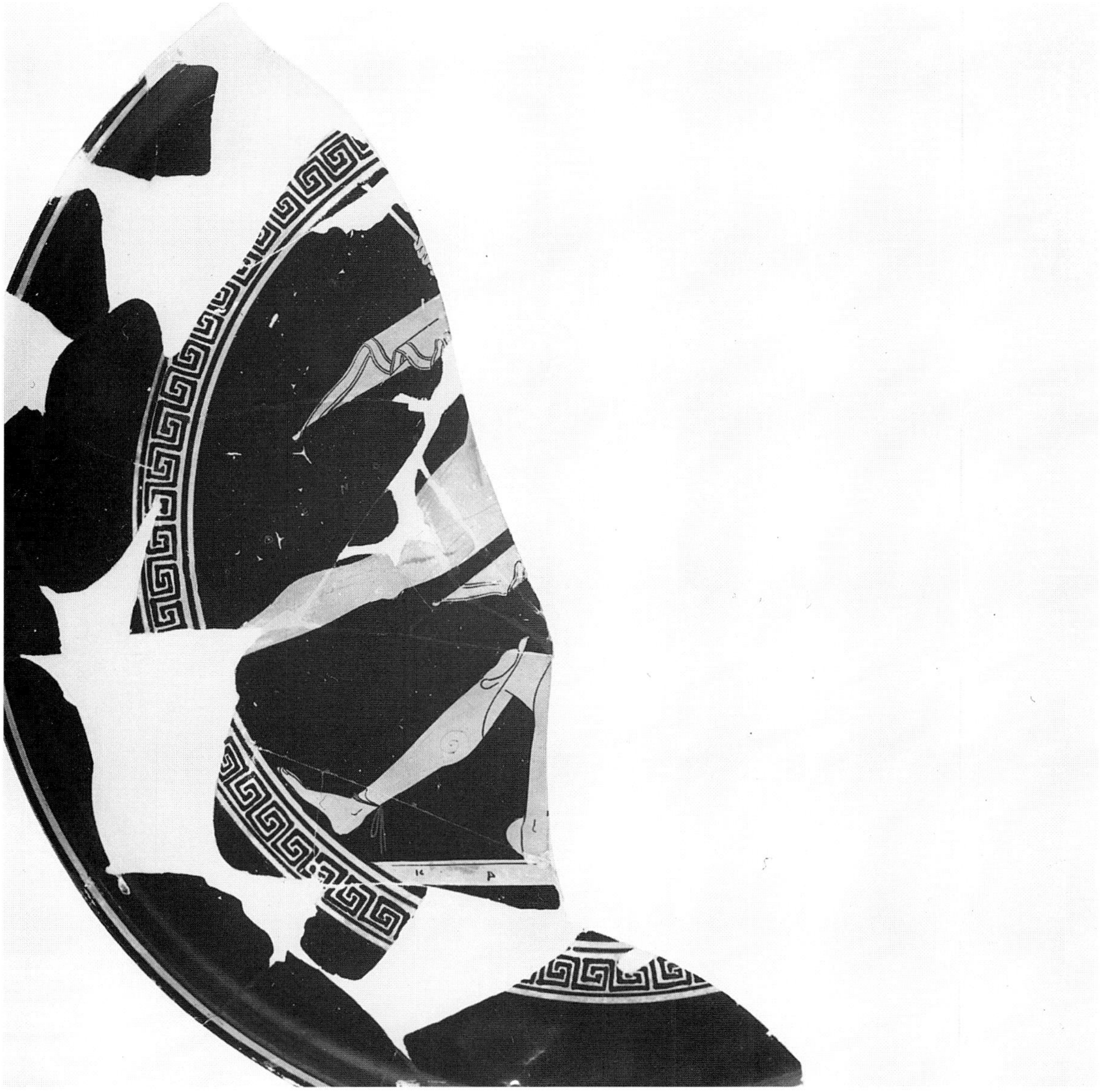

(b) 5

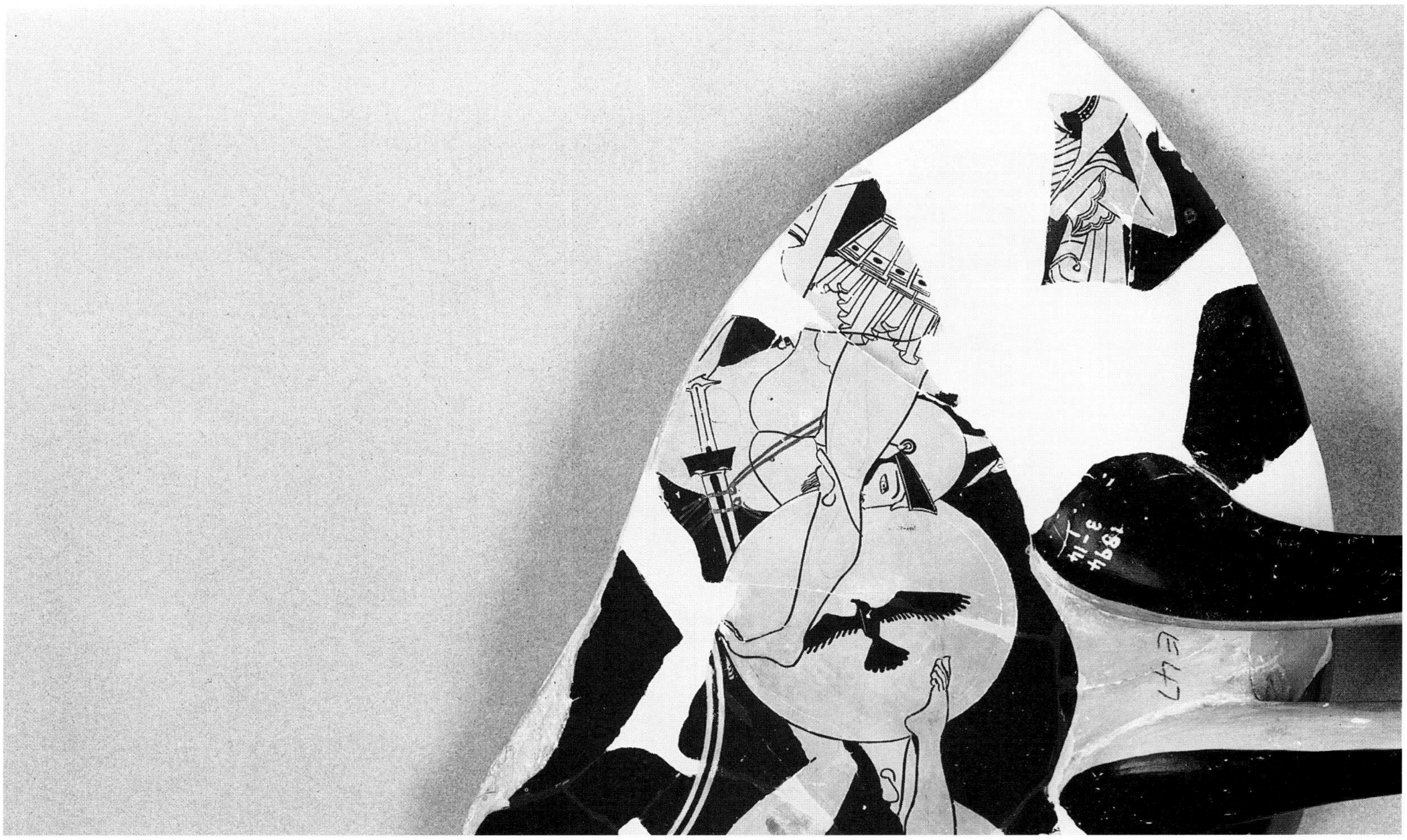

(a) 5

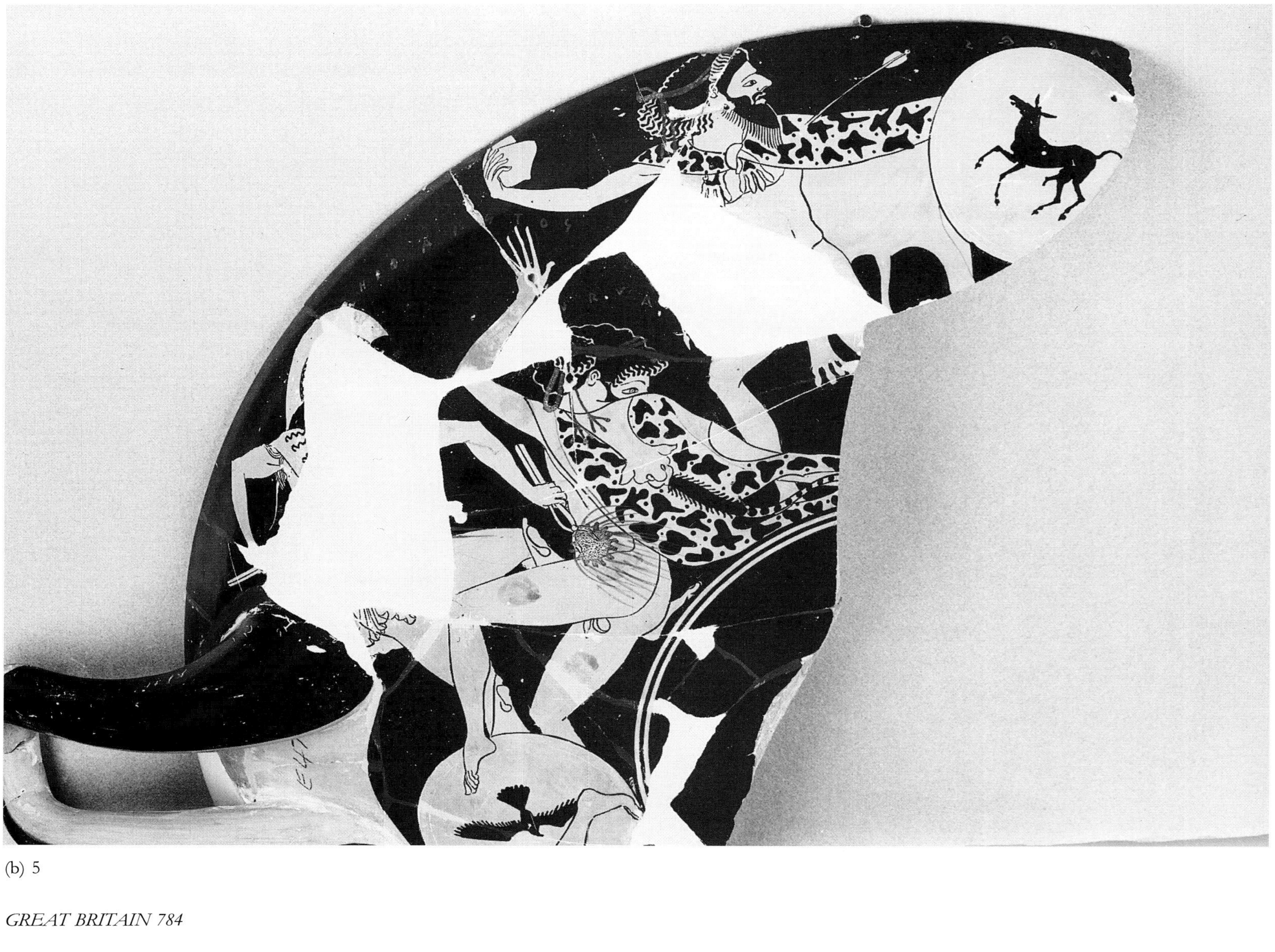

(b) 5

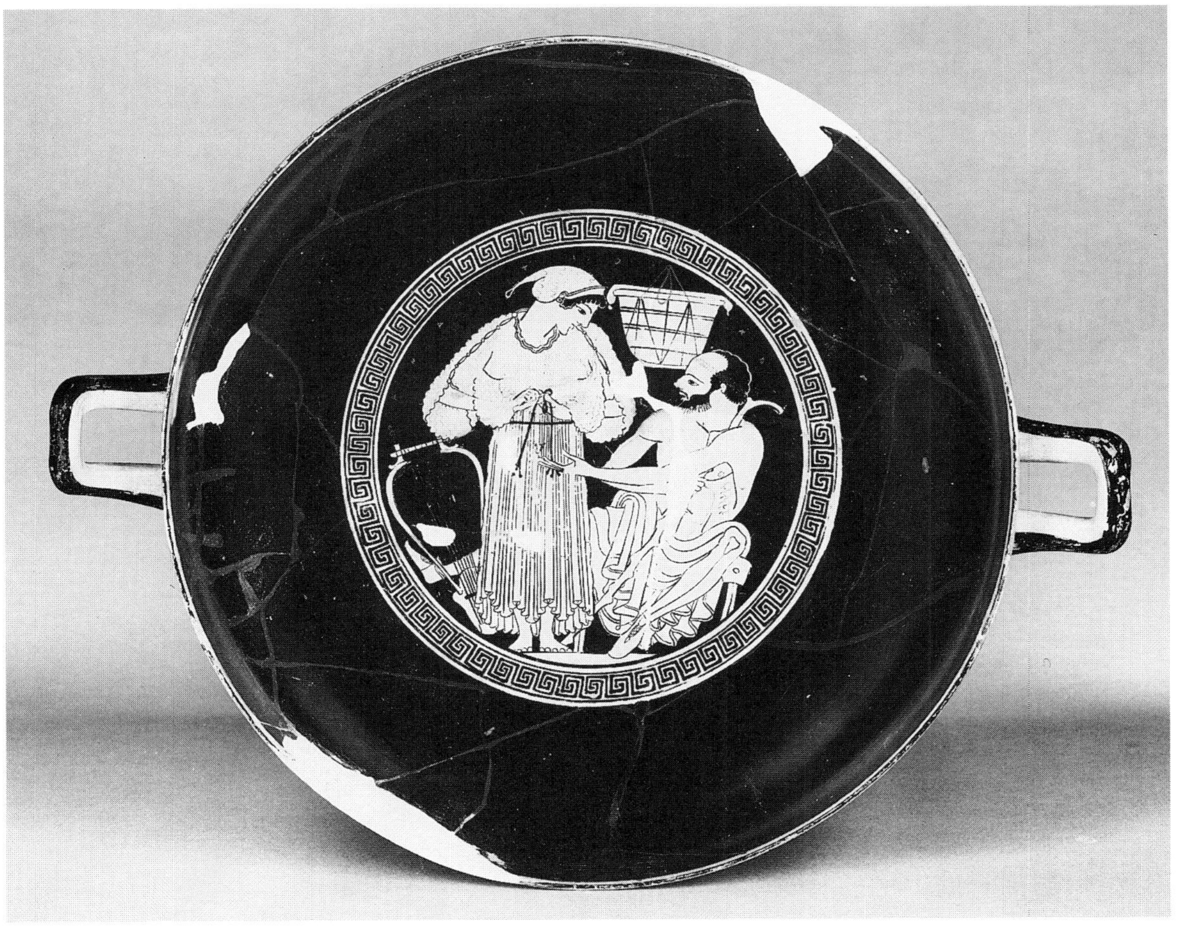

(a) 6

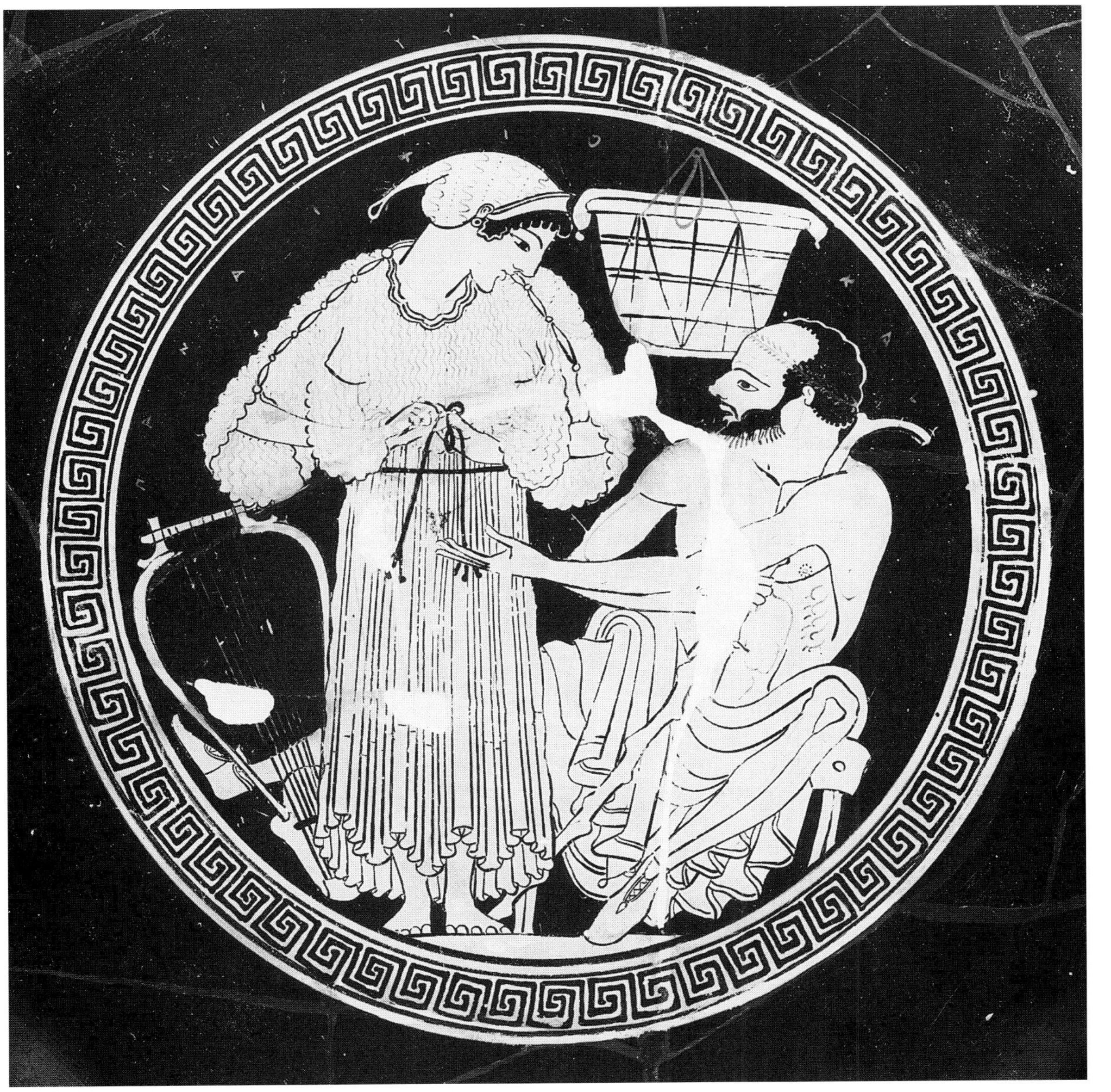

(b) 6

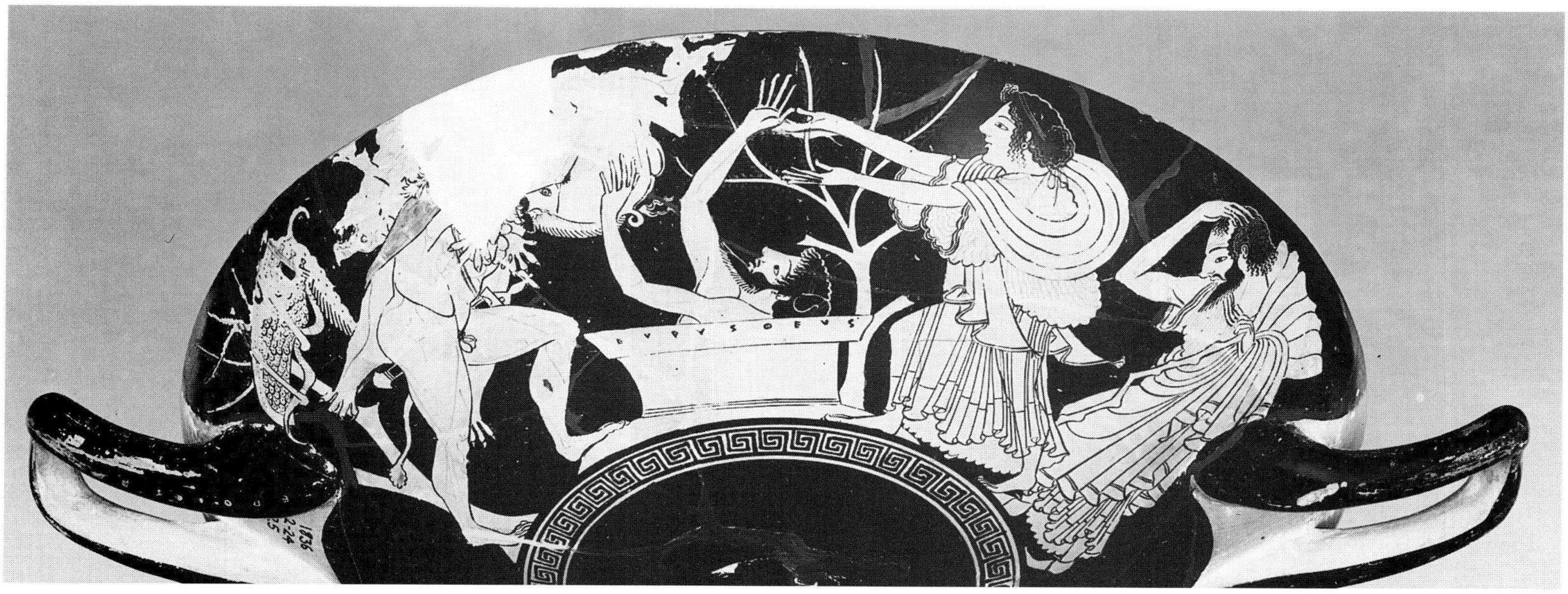
(a) 6

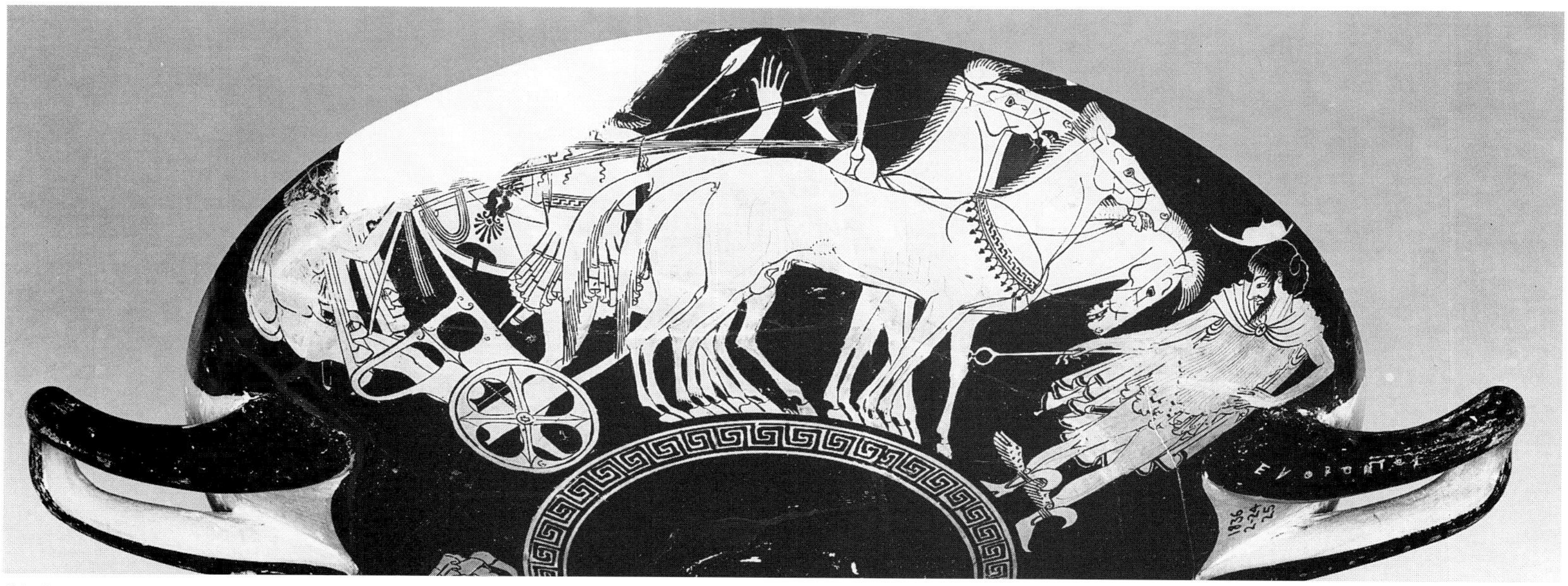
(b) 6

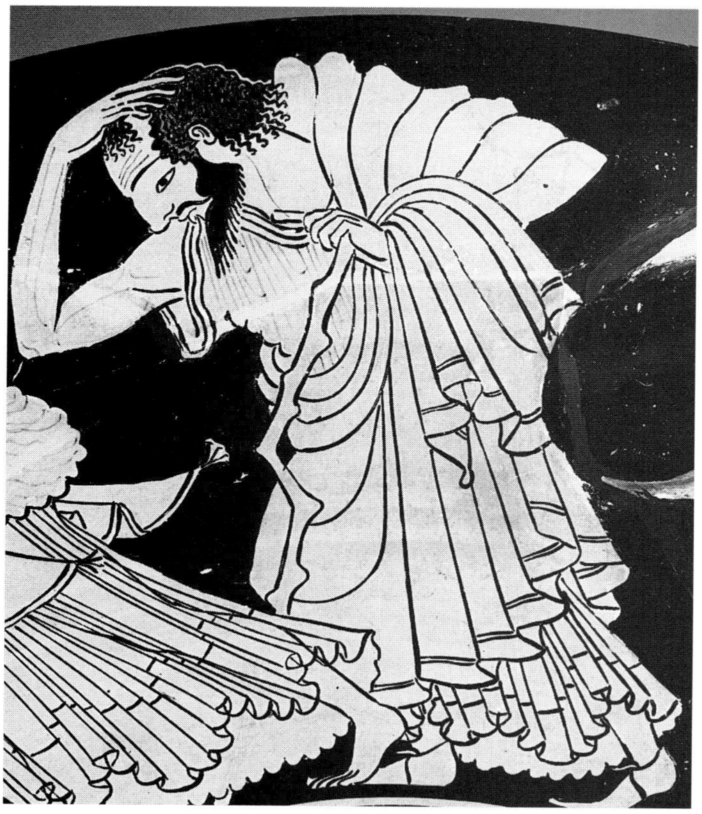
(c) 6

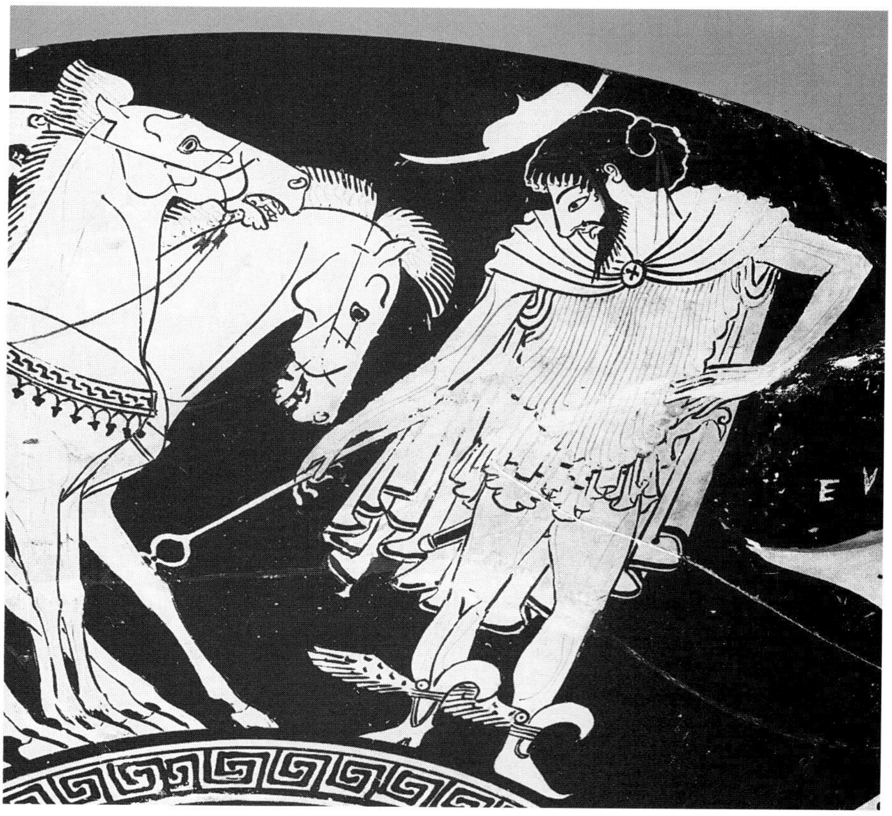
(d) 6

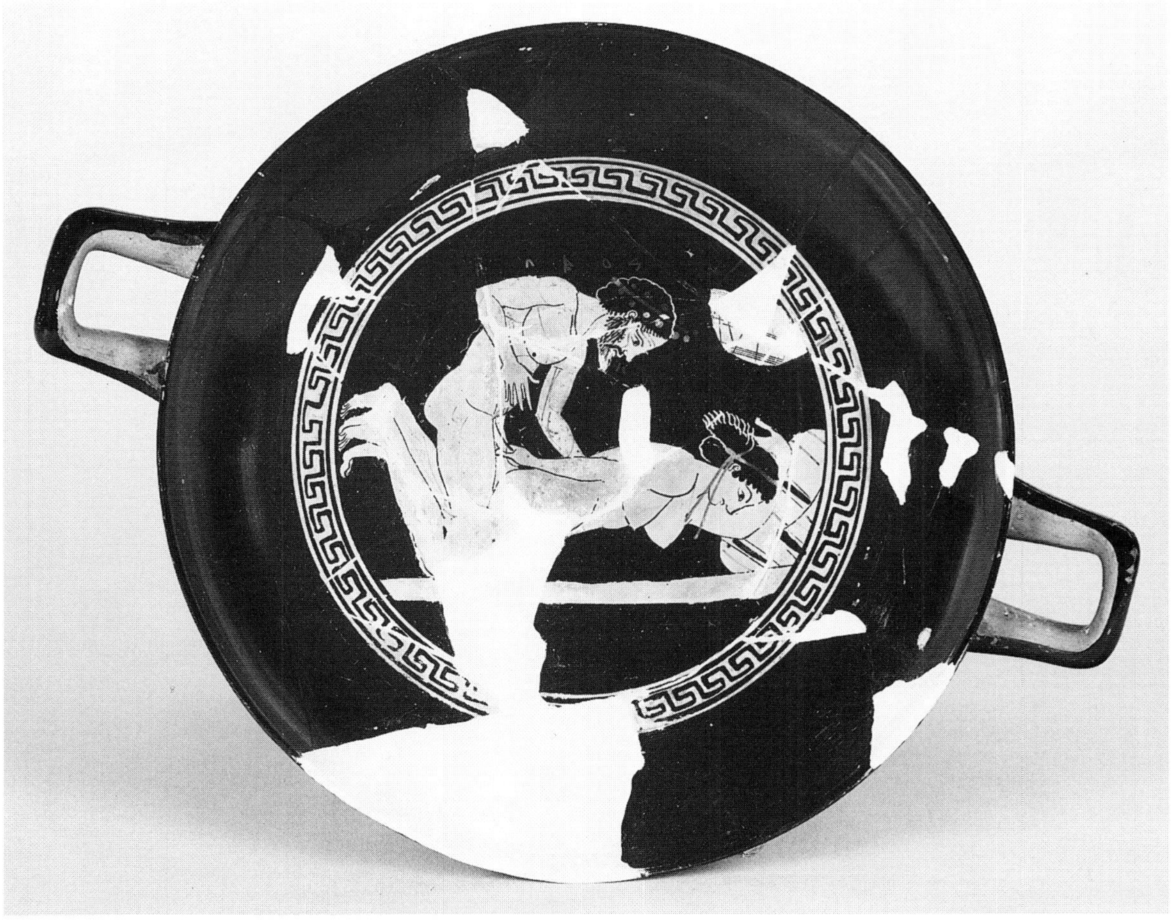

(a) 7

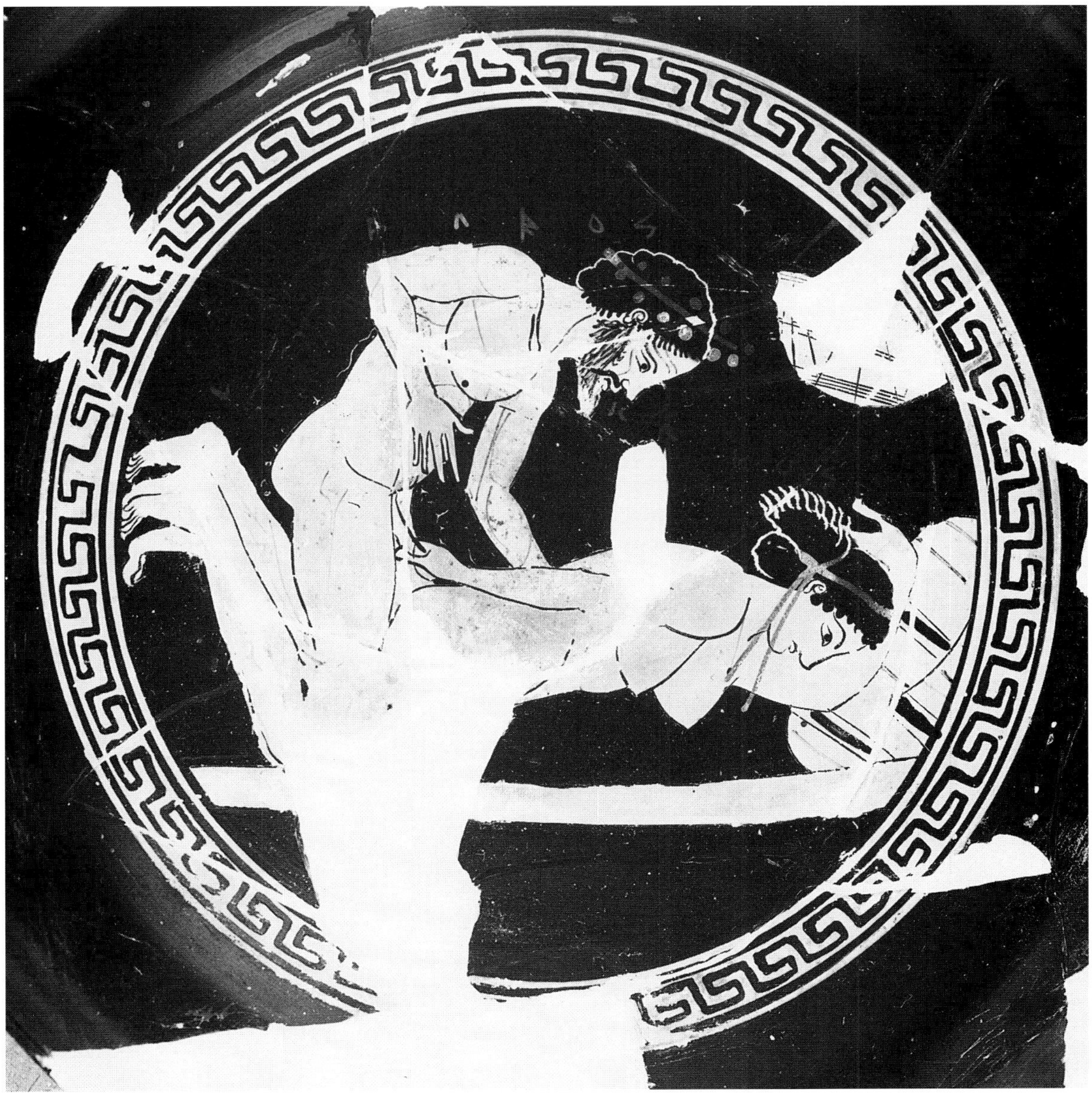

(b) 7

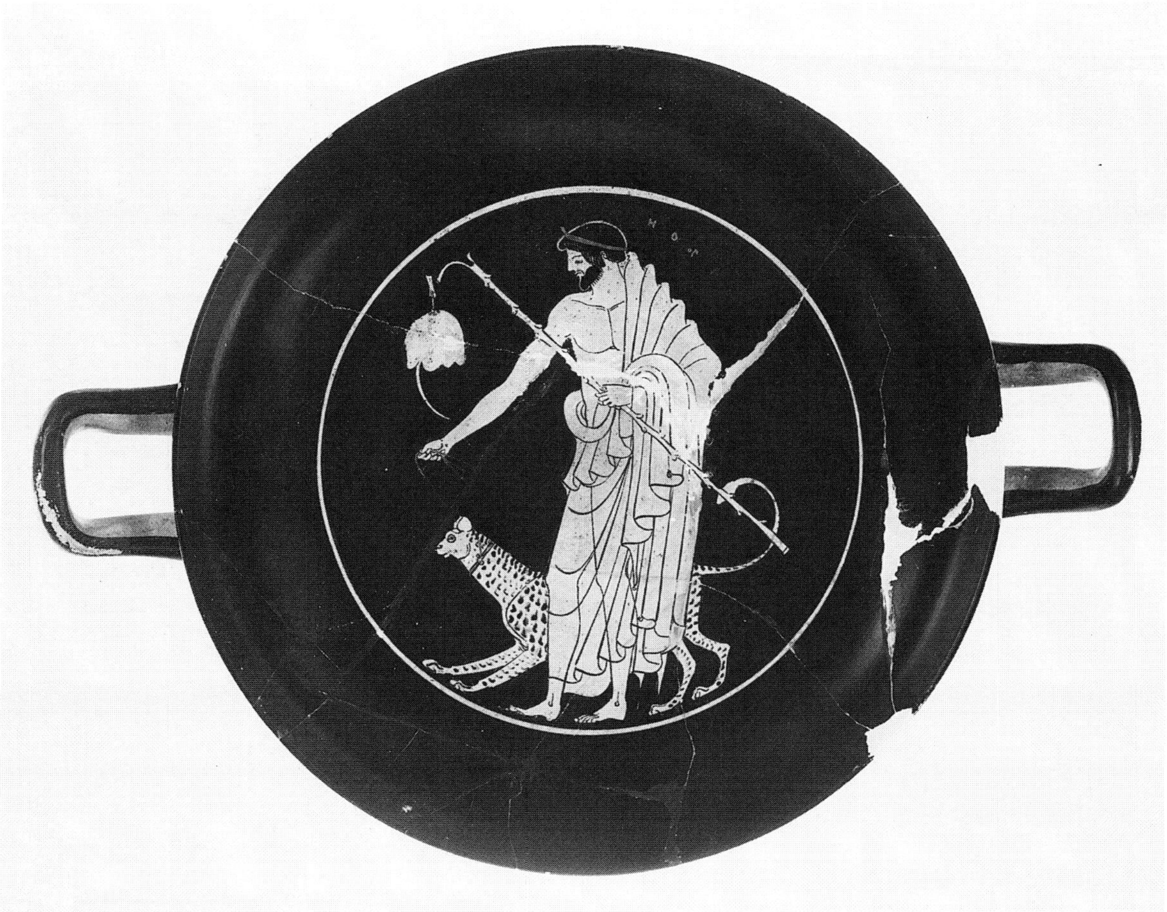

(a) 11

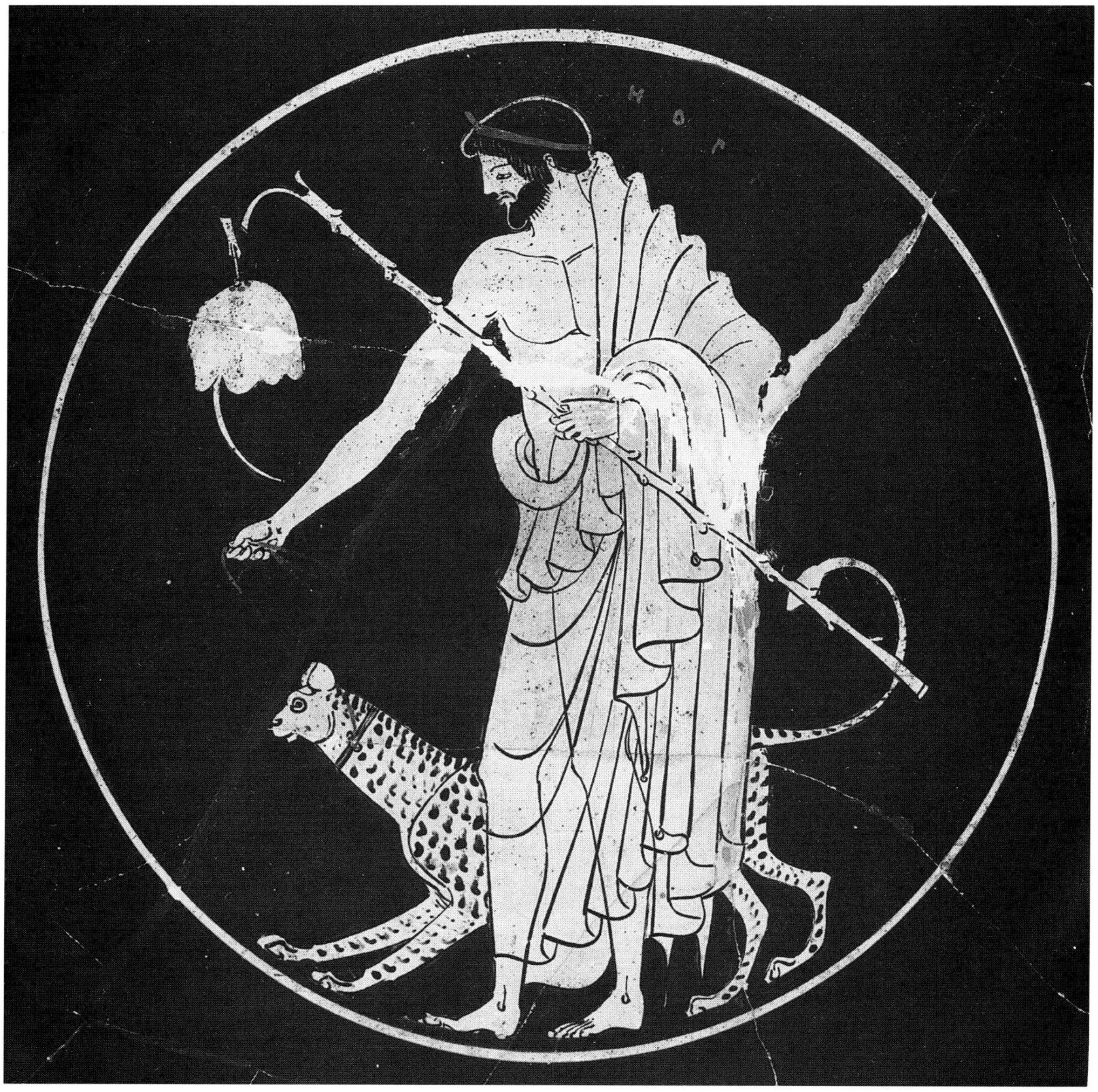

(b) 11

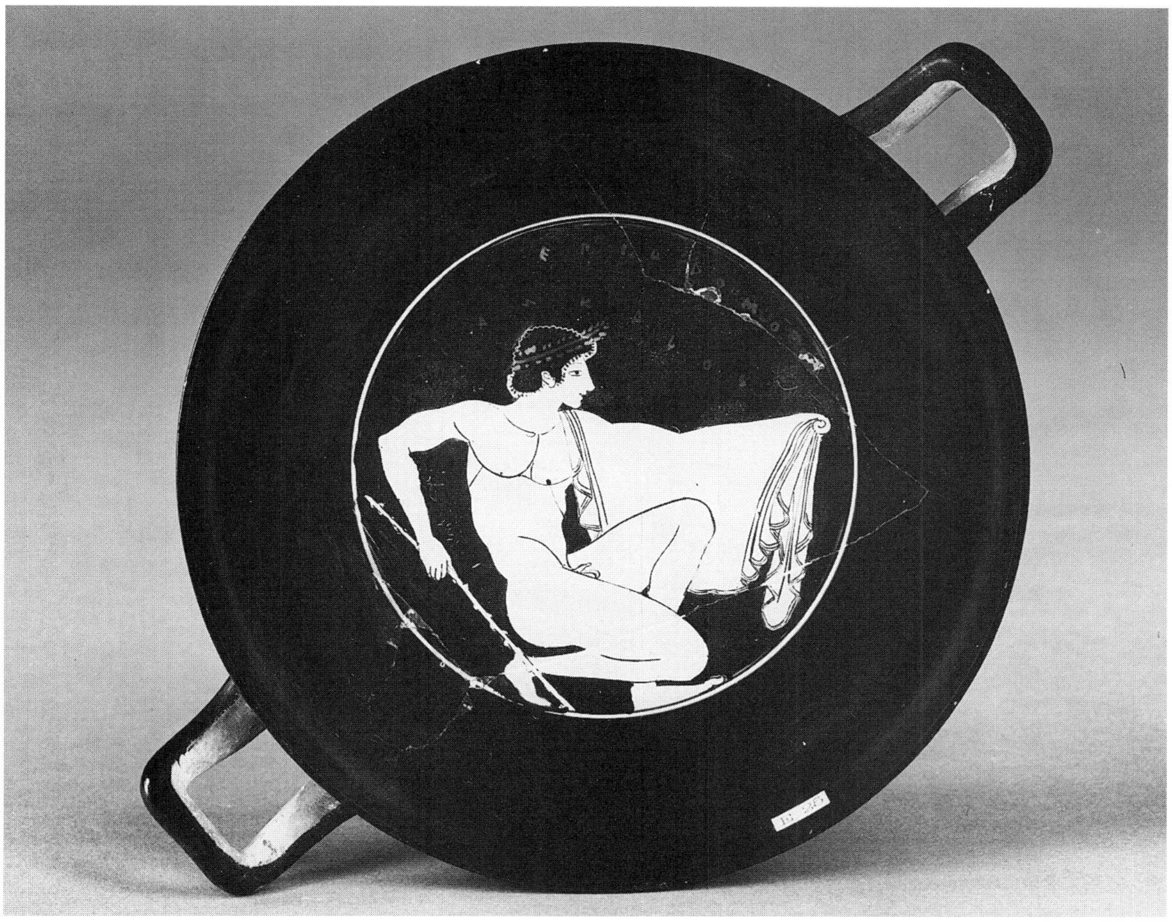

(a) 12

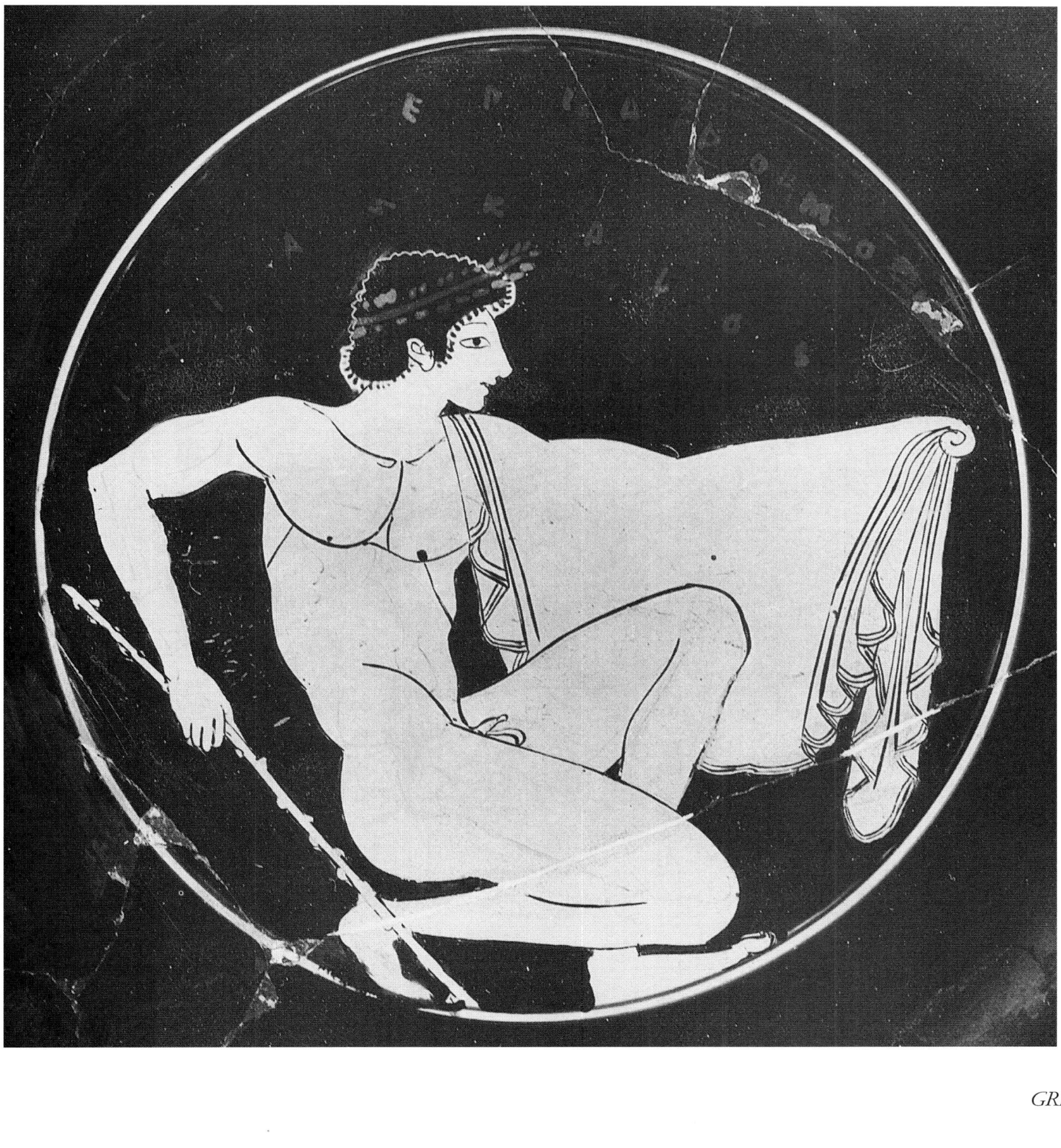

(b) 12

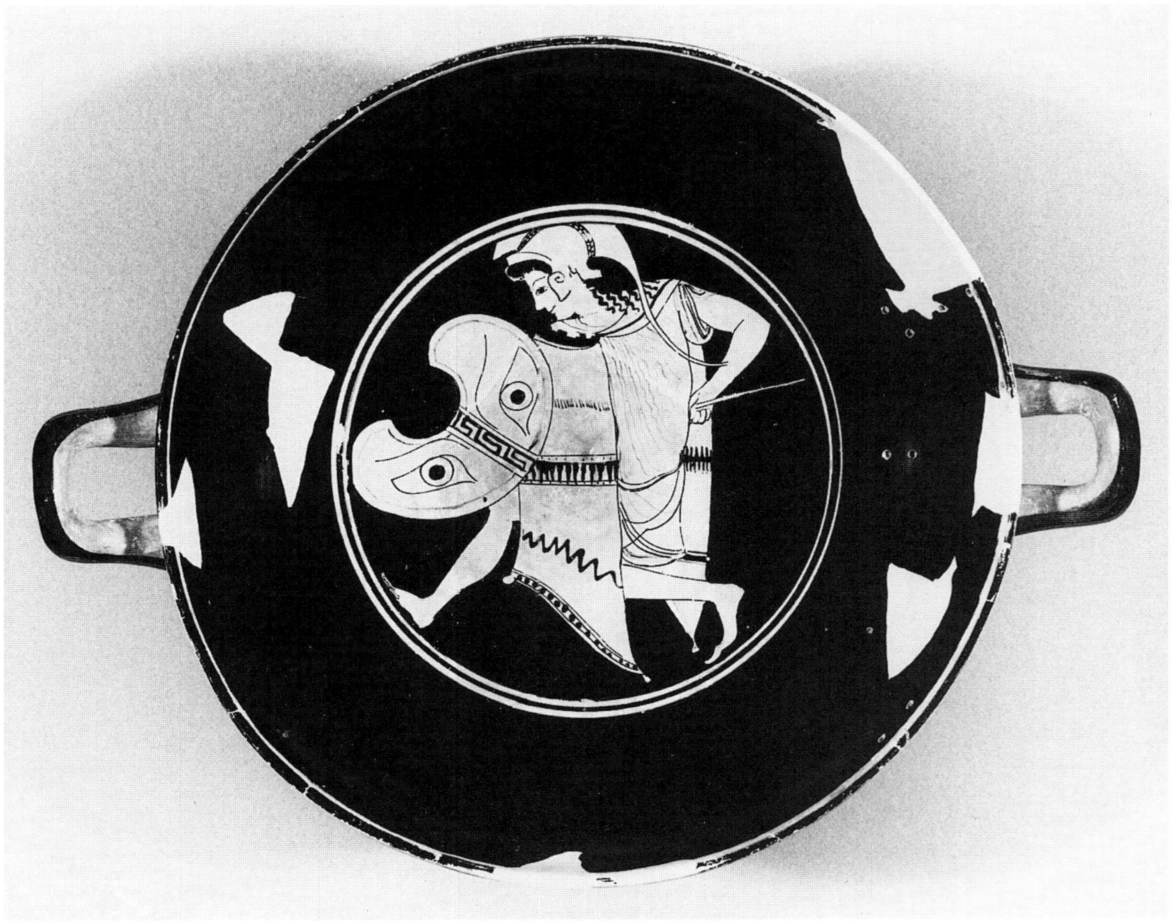

(a) 13

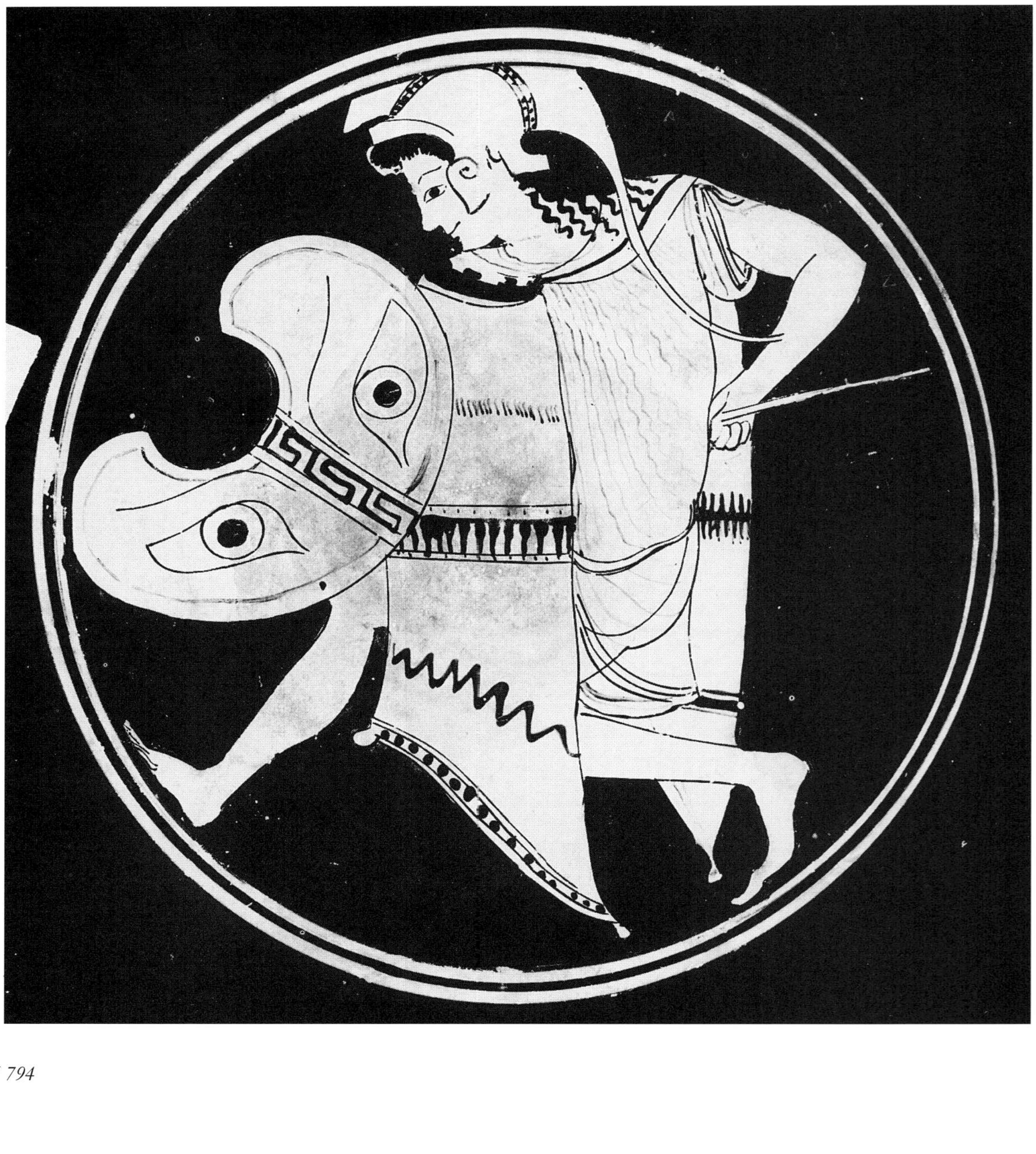

(b) 13

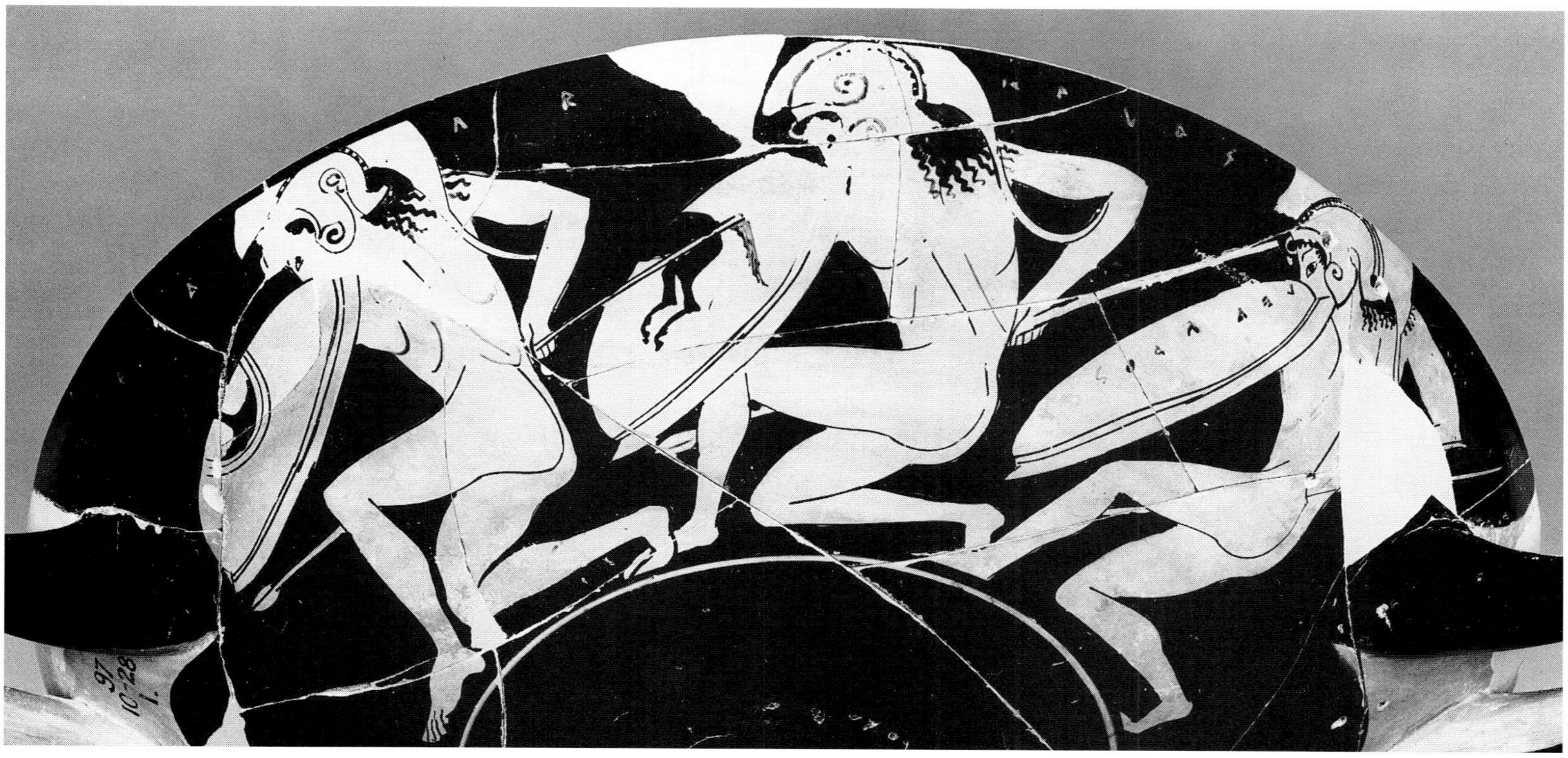

(a) 13

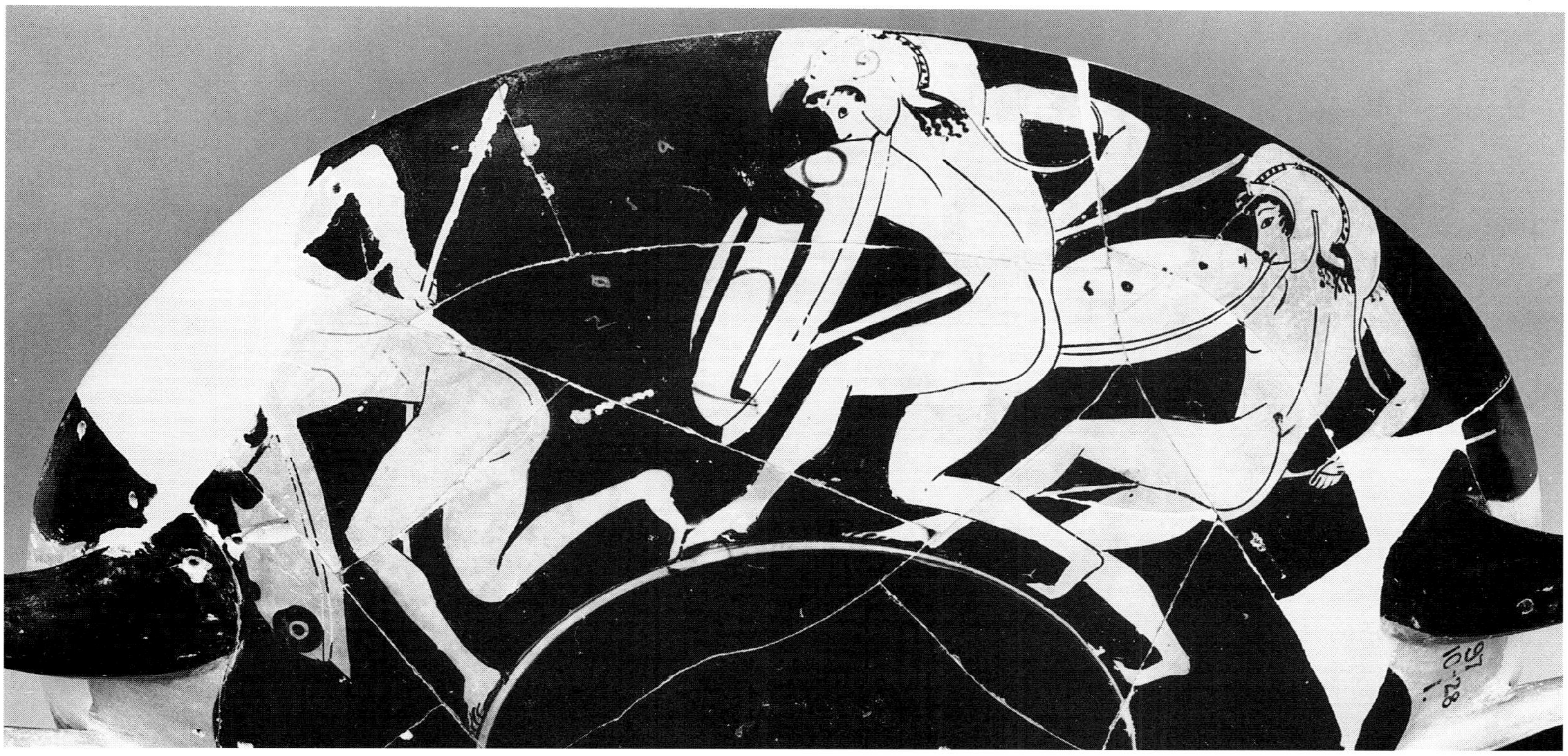

(b) 13

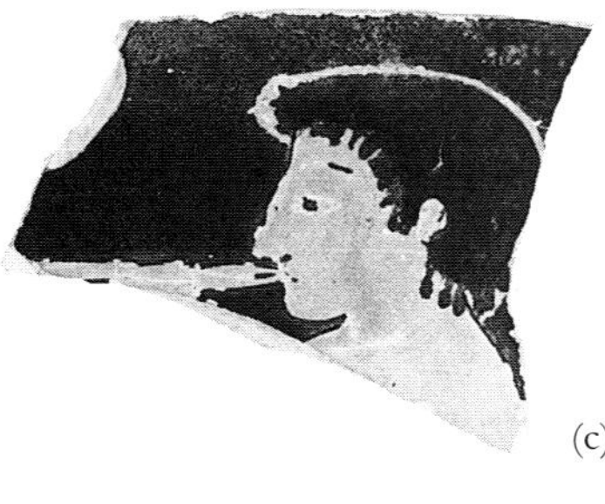

(c) 14

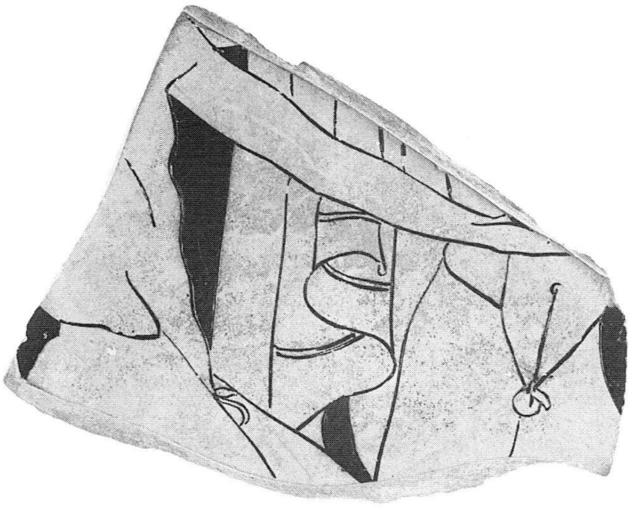

(d) 15

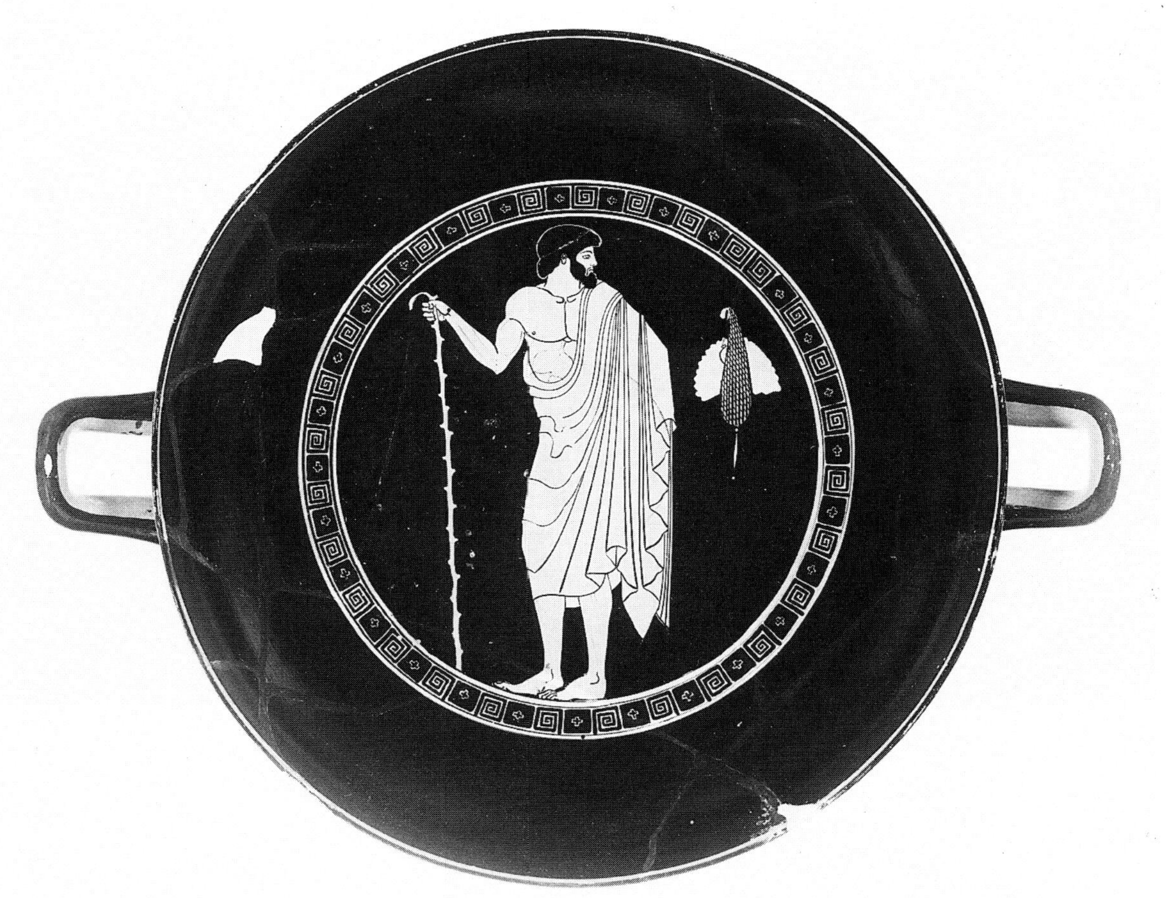

(a) 21

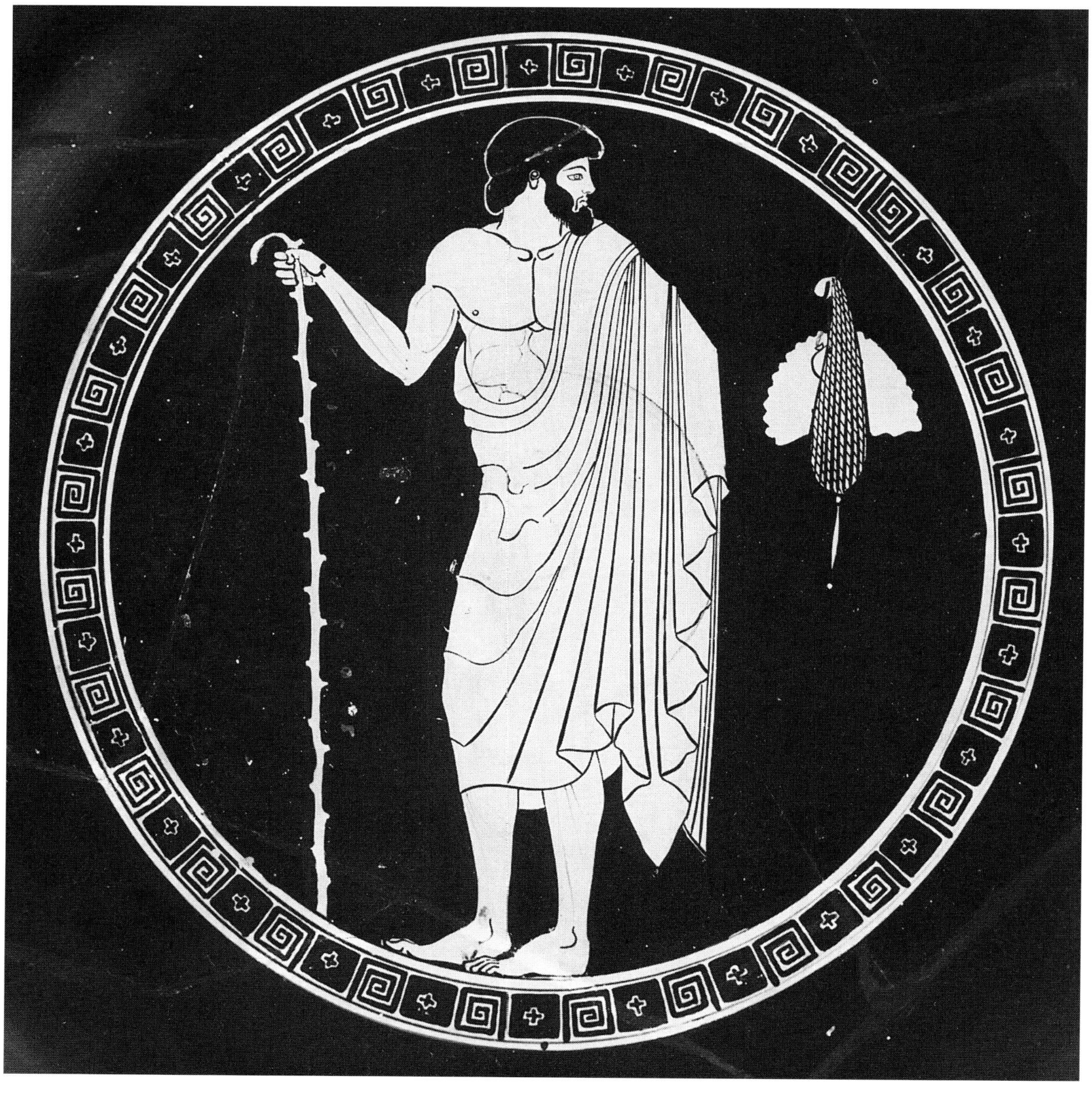

(b) 21

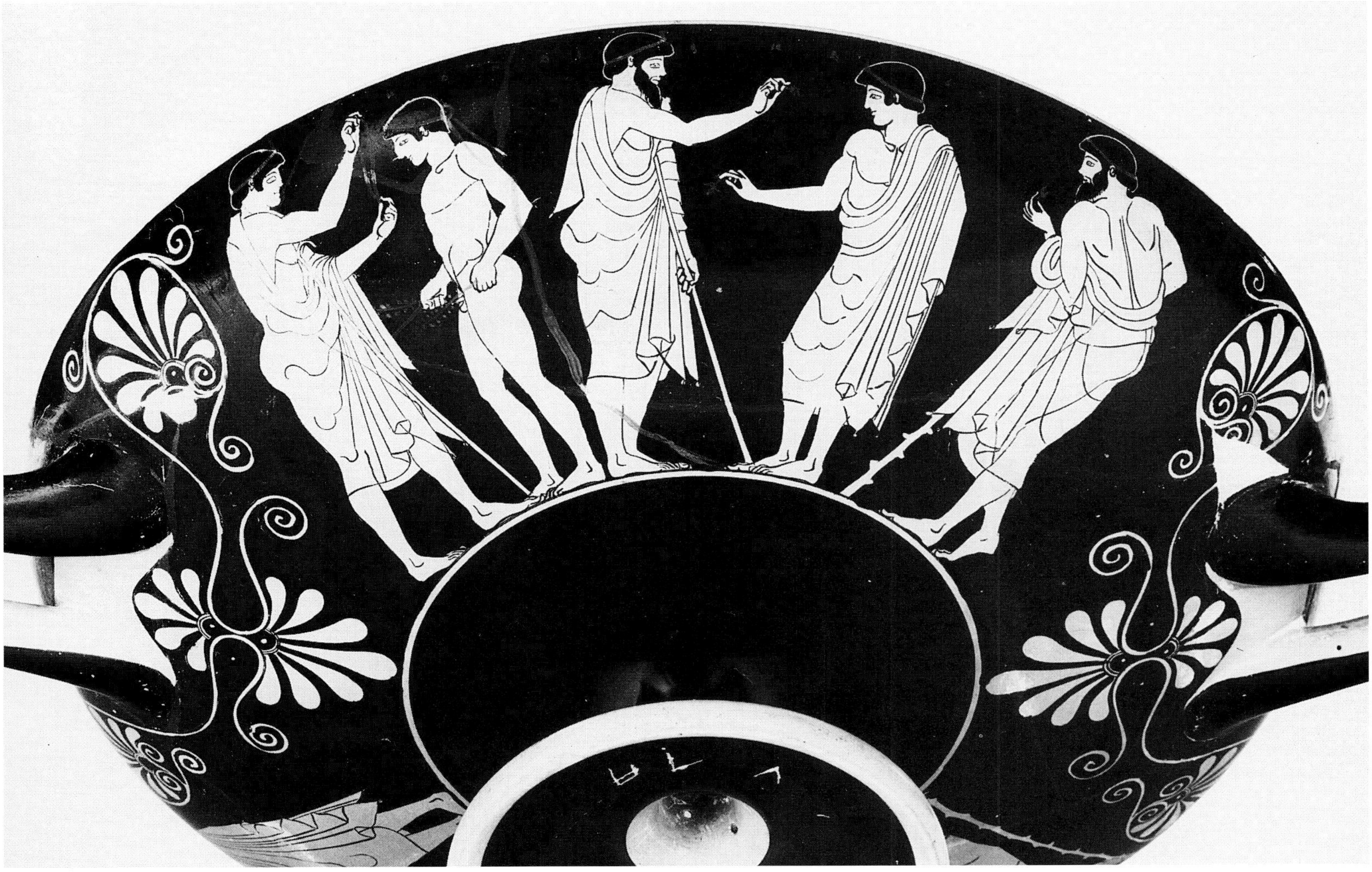

(a) 21

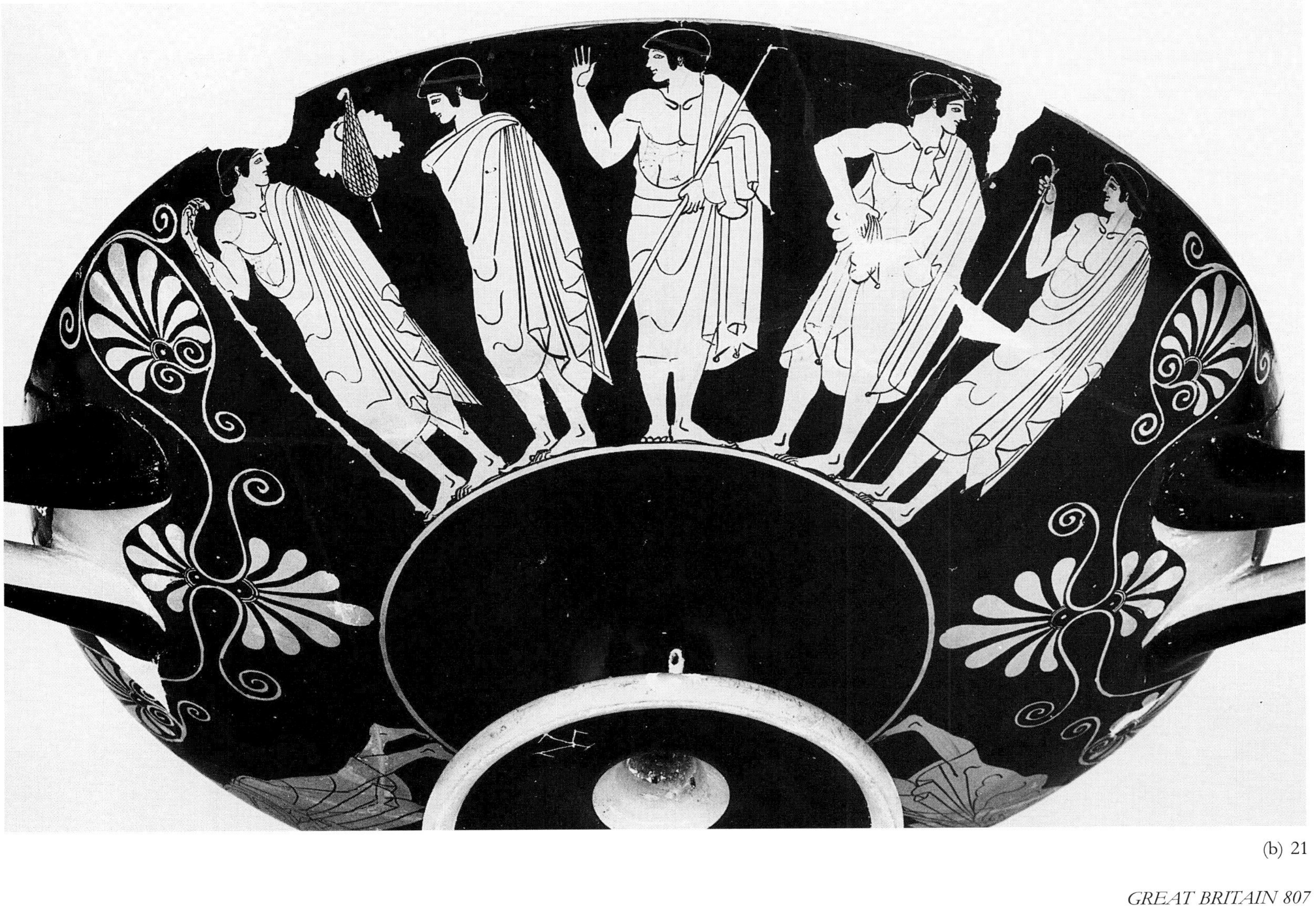

(b) 21

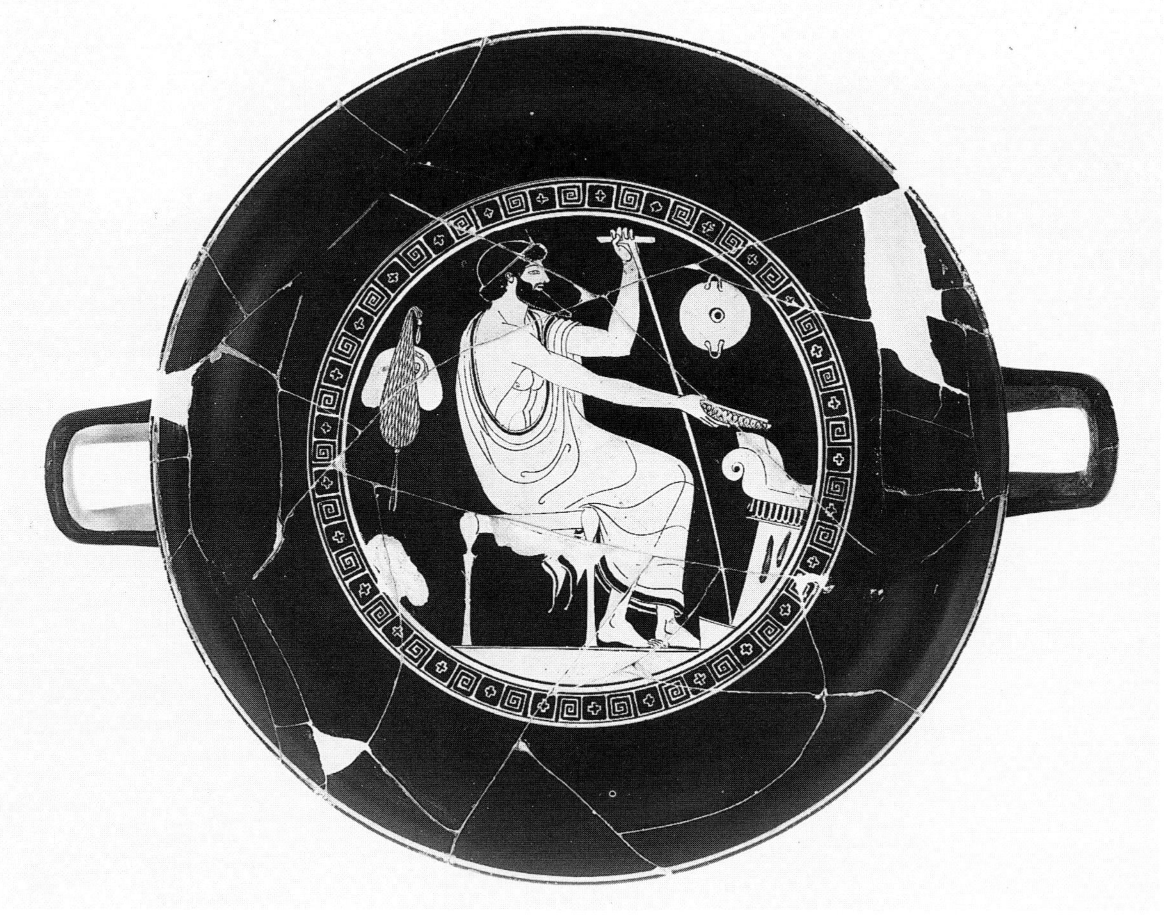

(a) 22

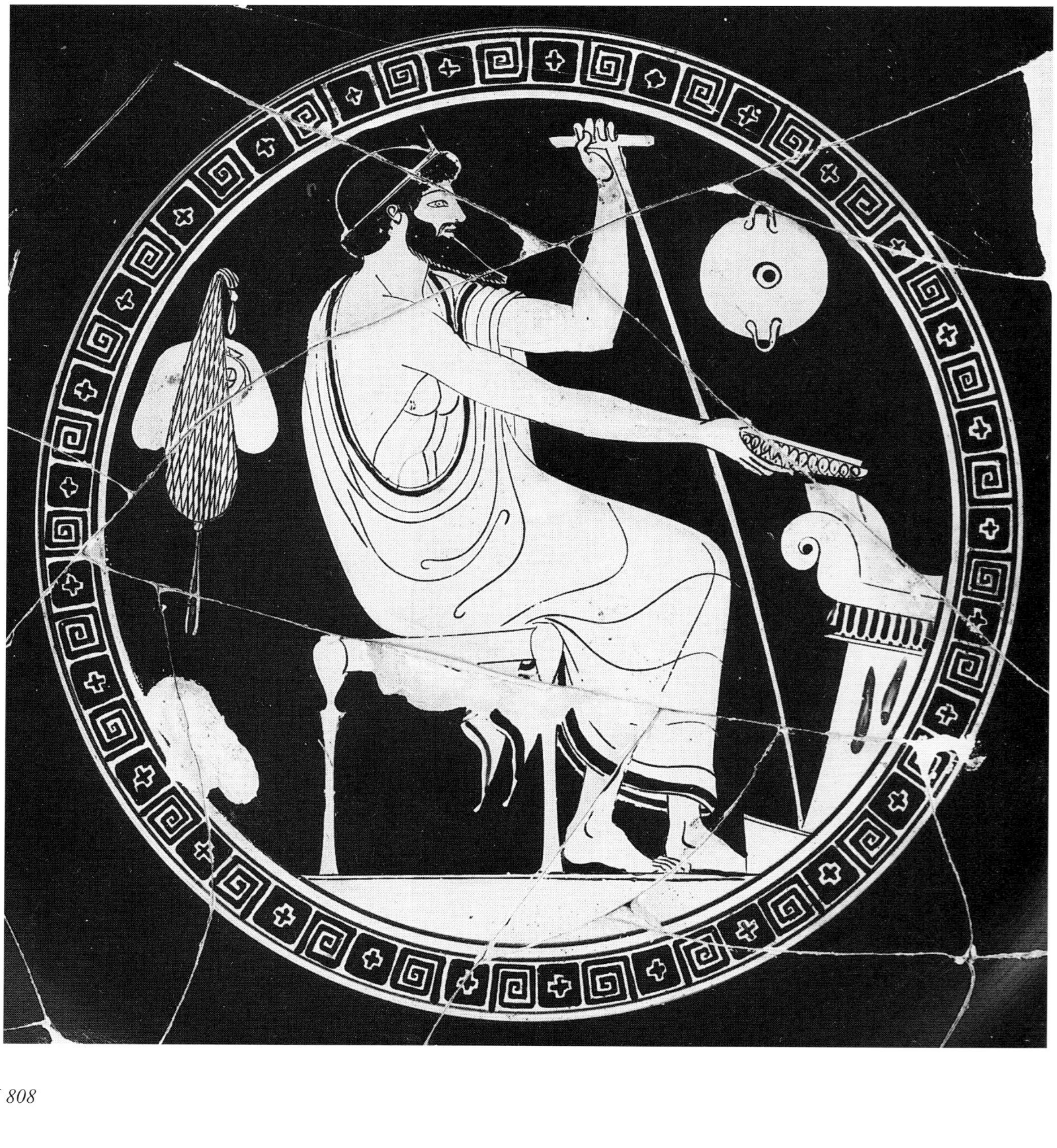

(b) 22

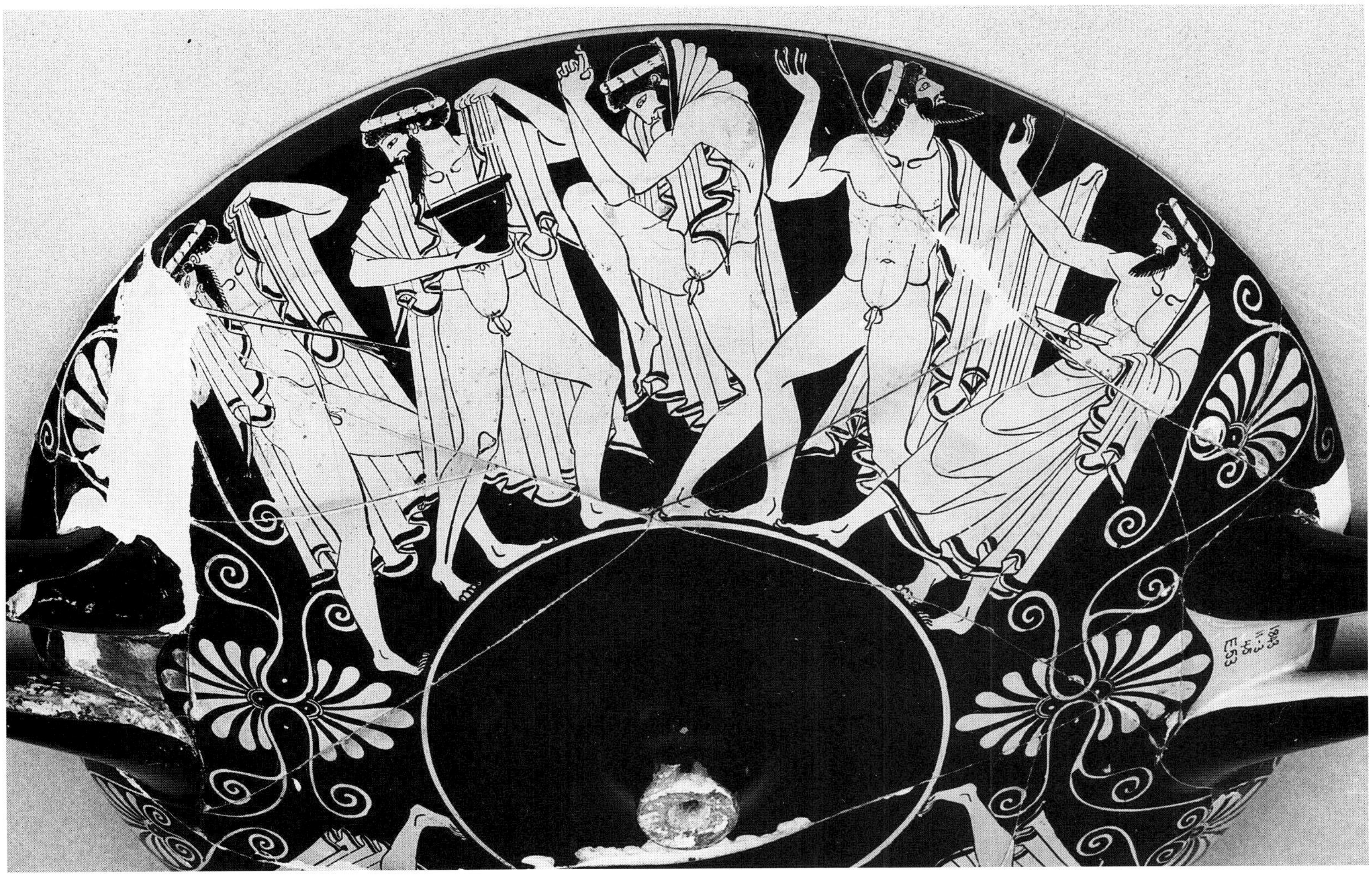

(a) 22

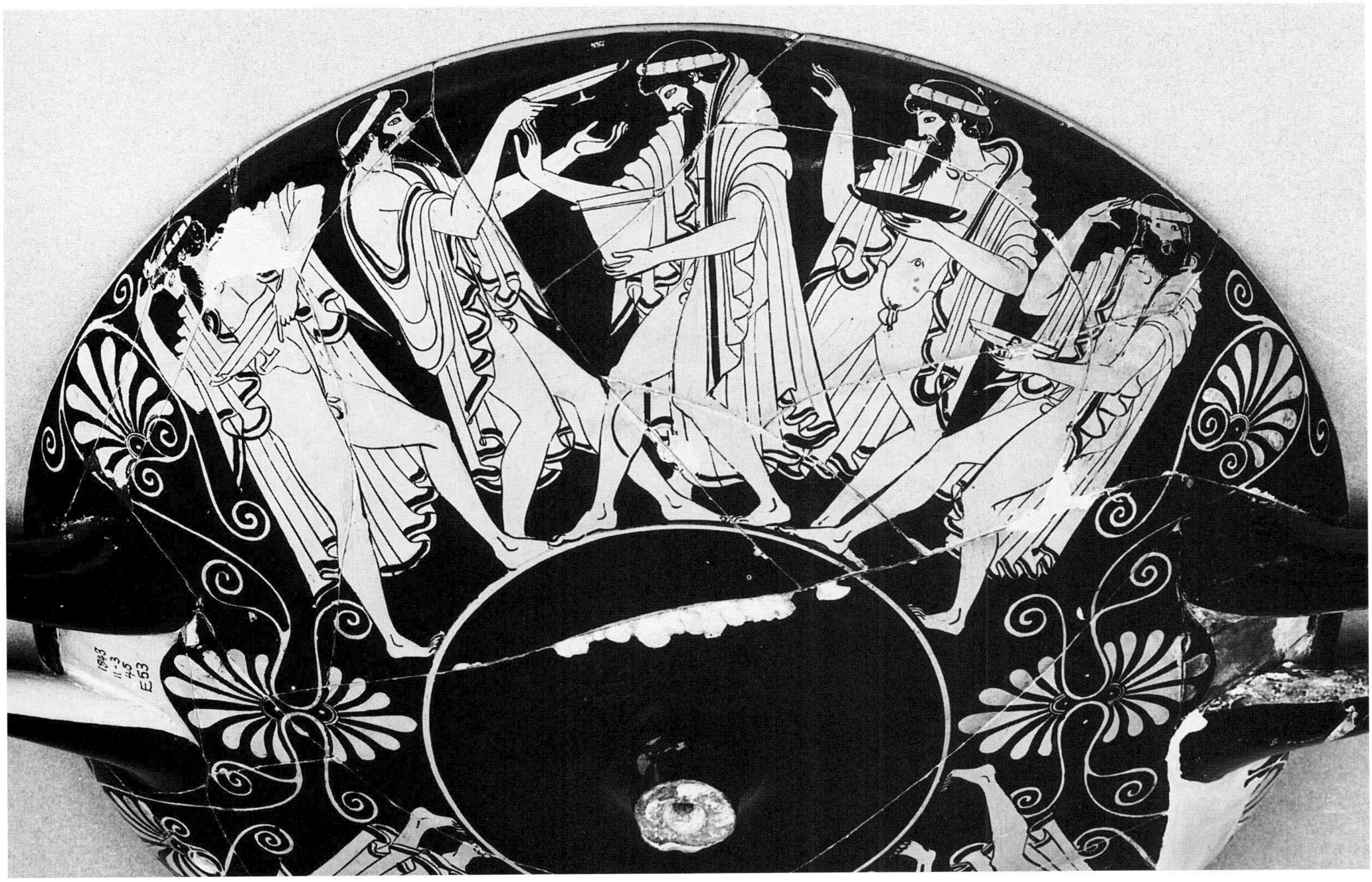

(b) 22

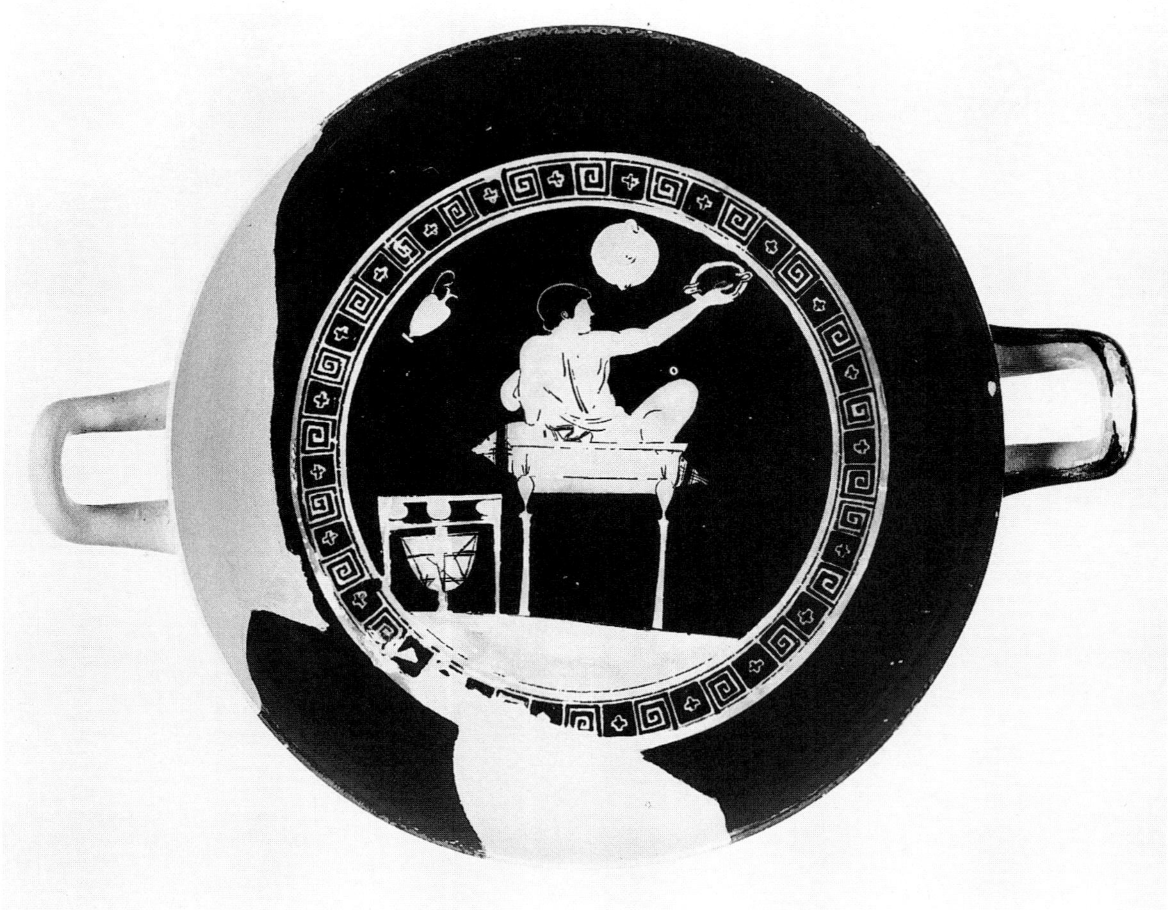

(a) 23

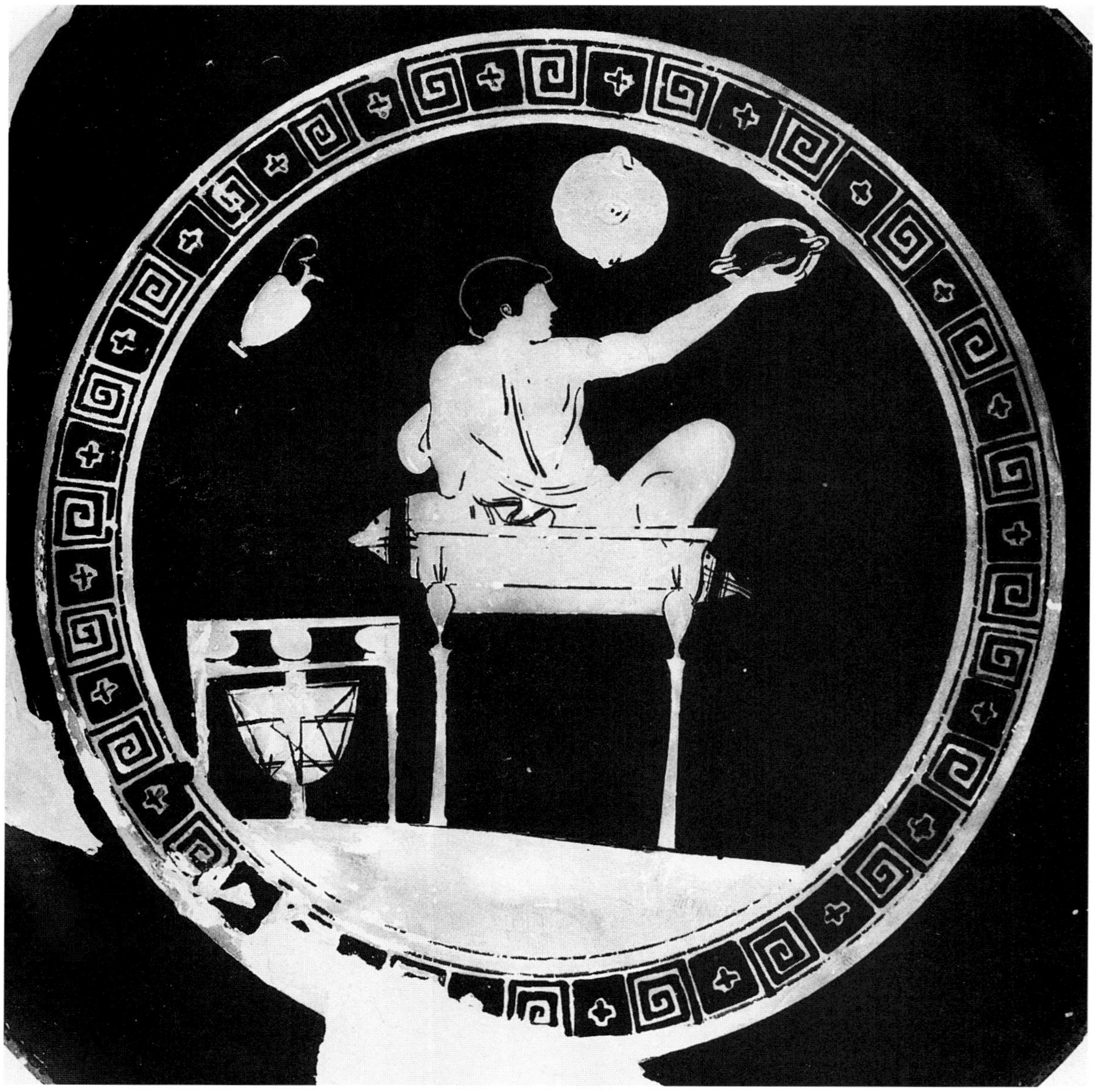

(b) 23

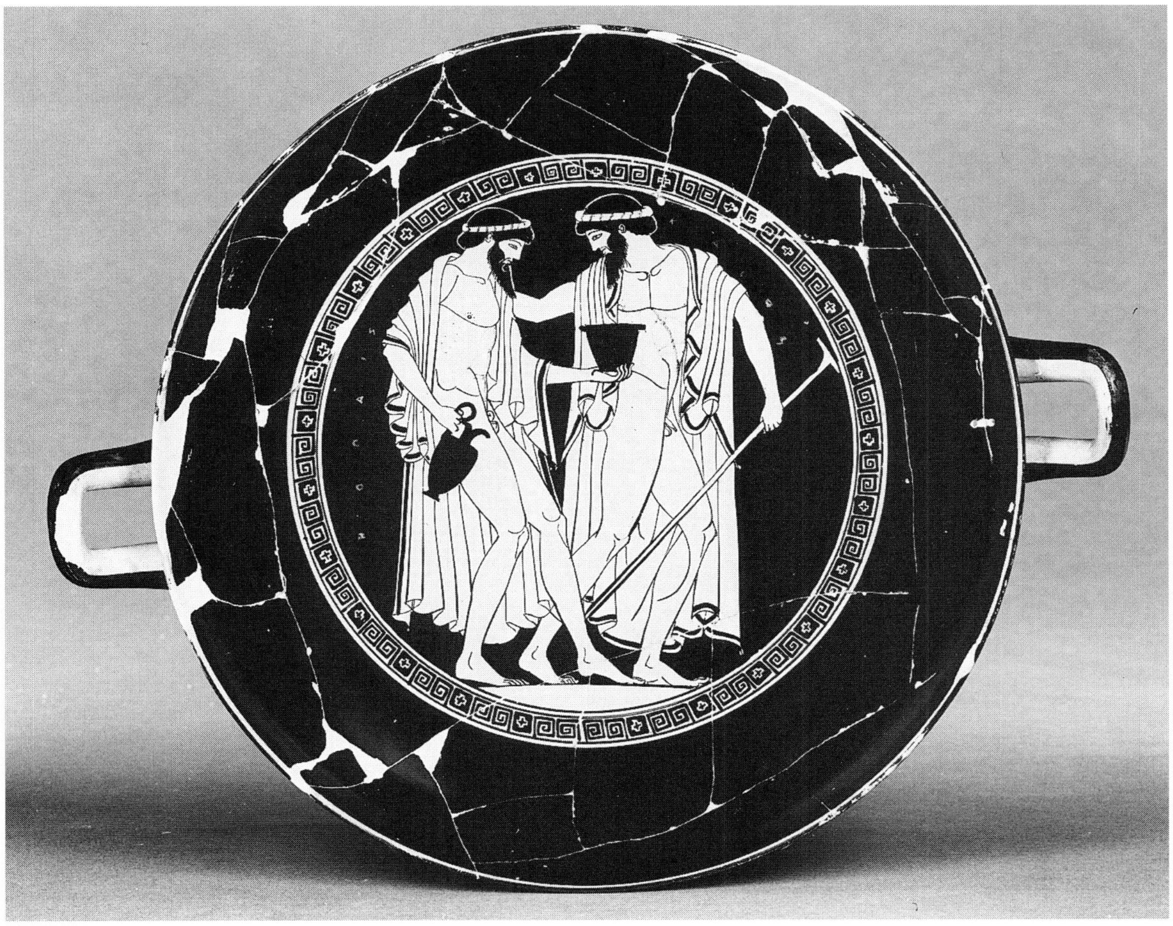

(a) 24

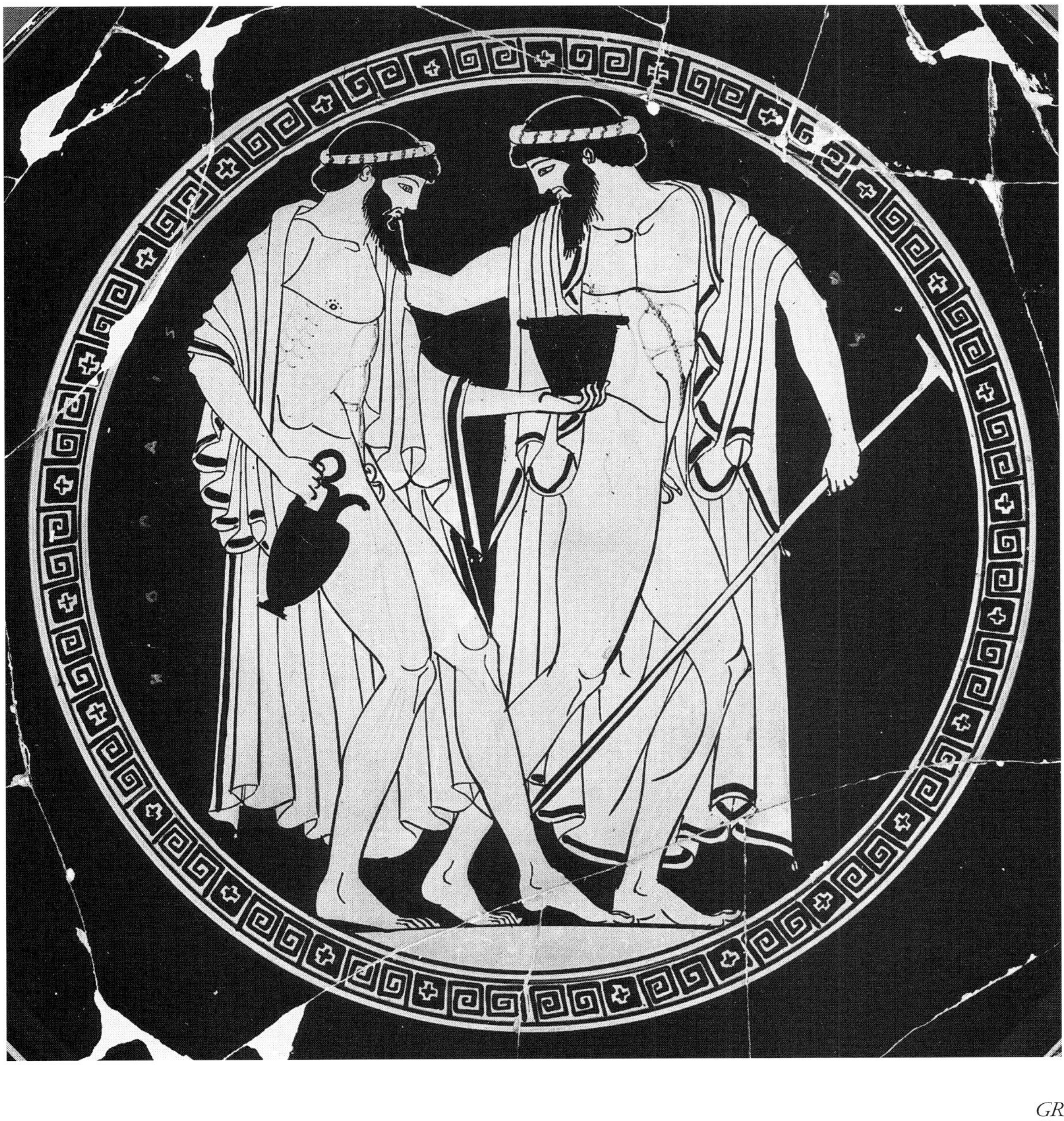

(b) 24

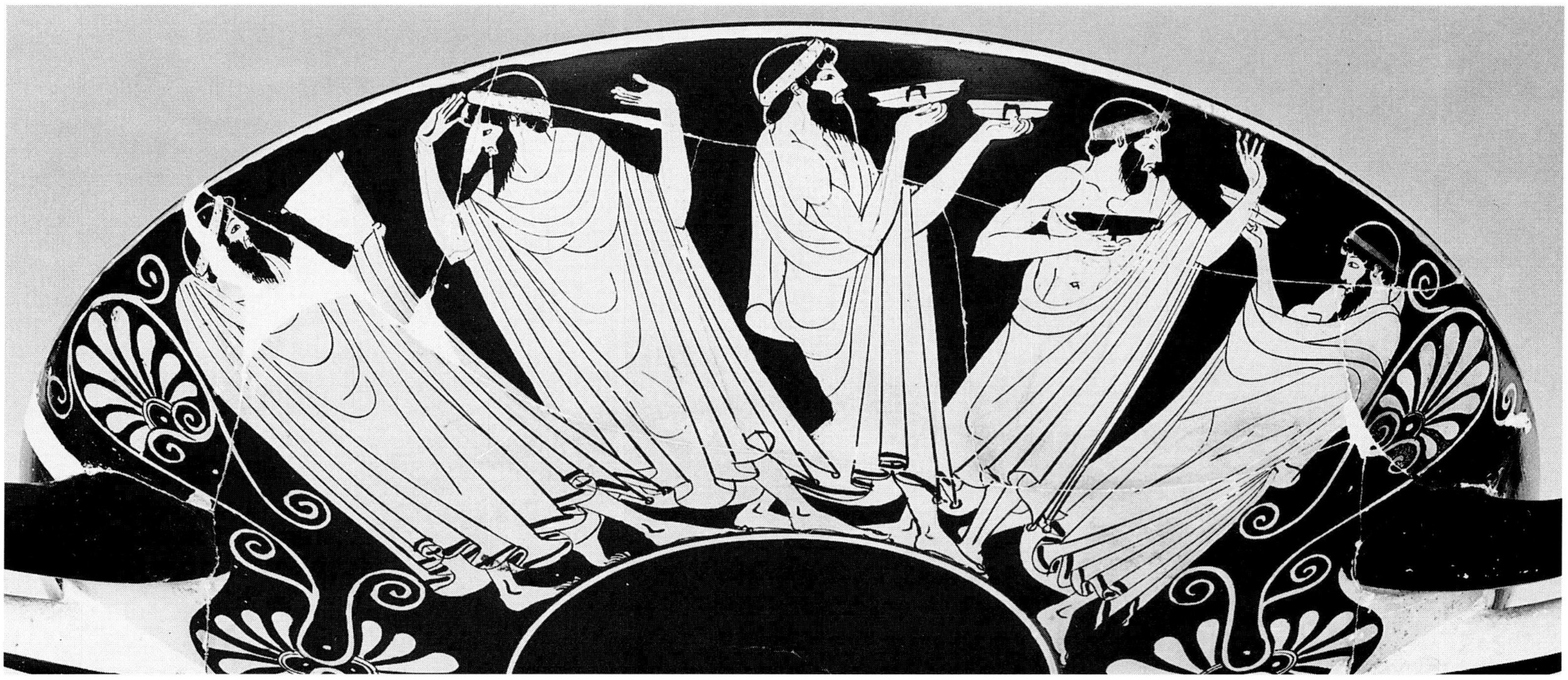

(a) 24

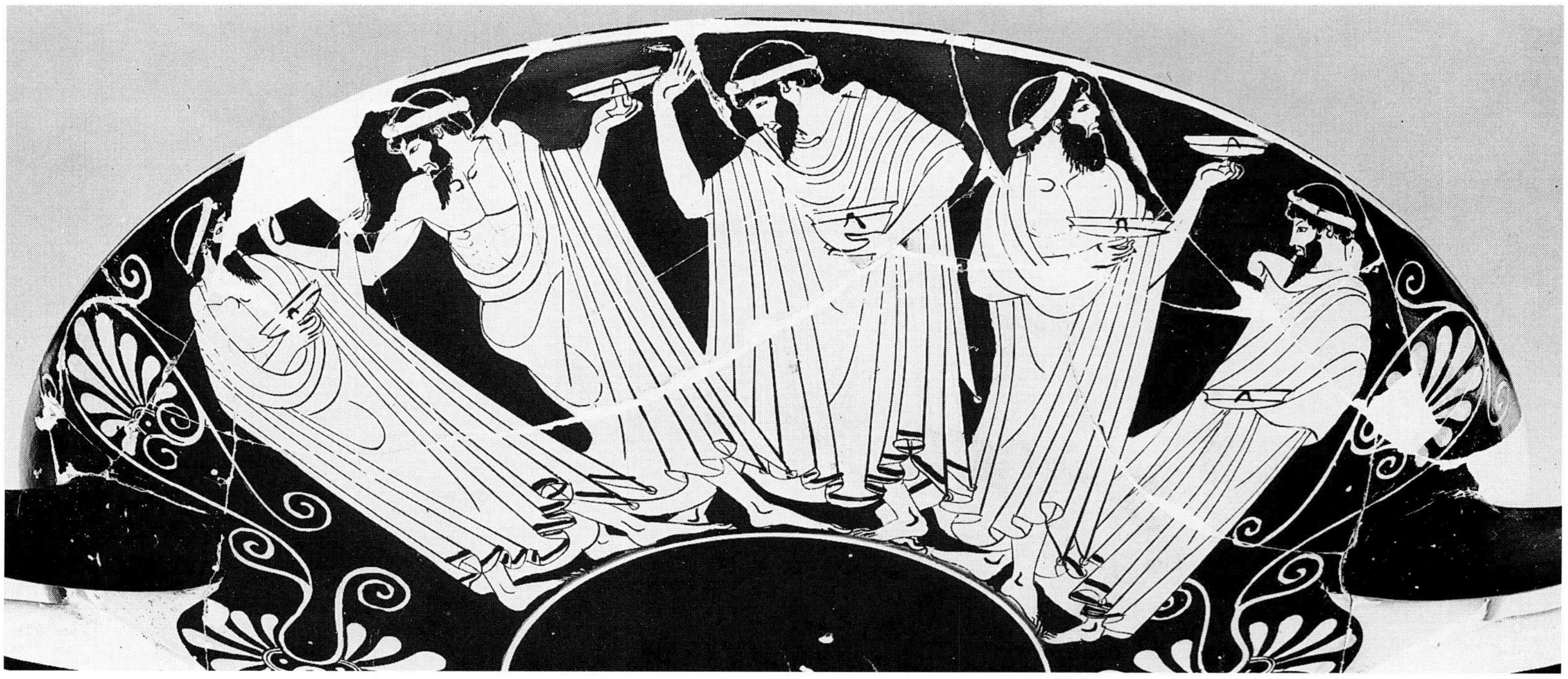

(b) 24

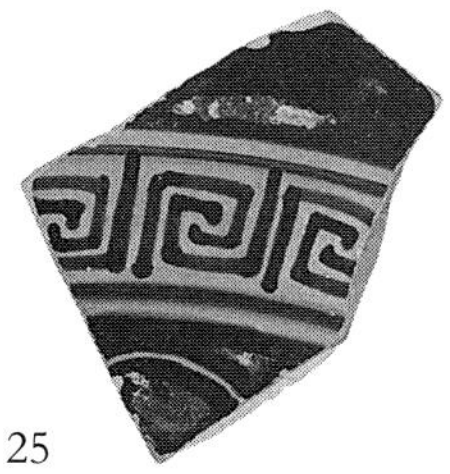

(c) 25

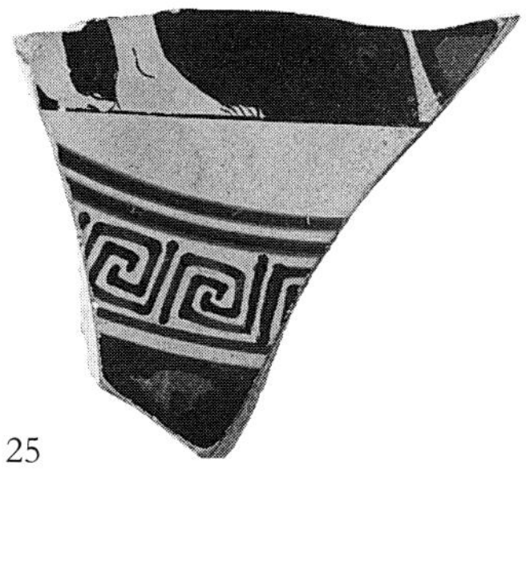

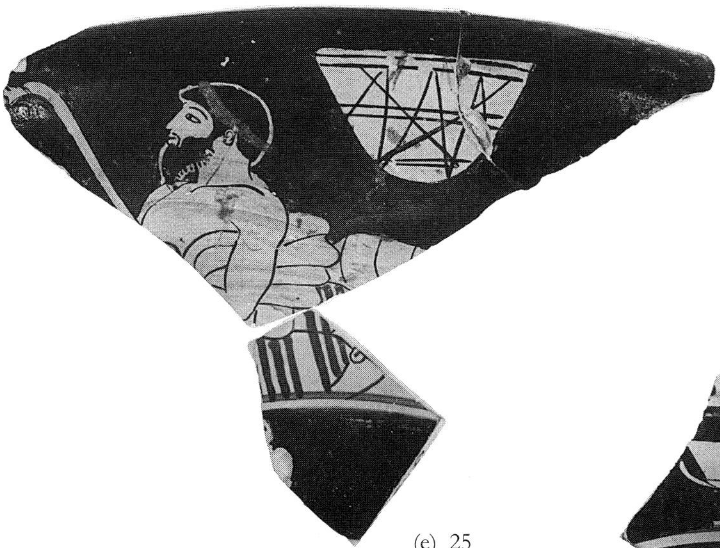

(e) 25

(d) 25

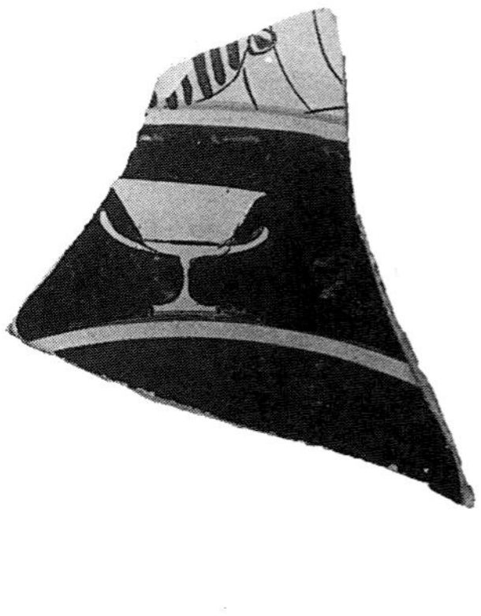

(f) 25

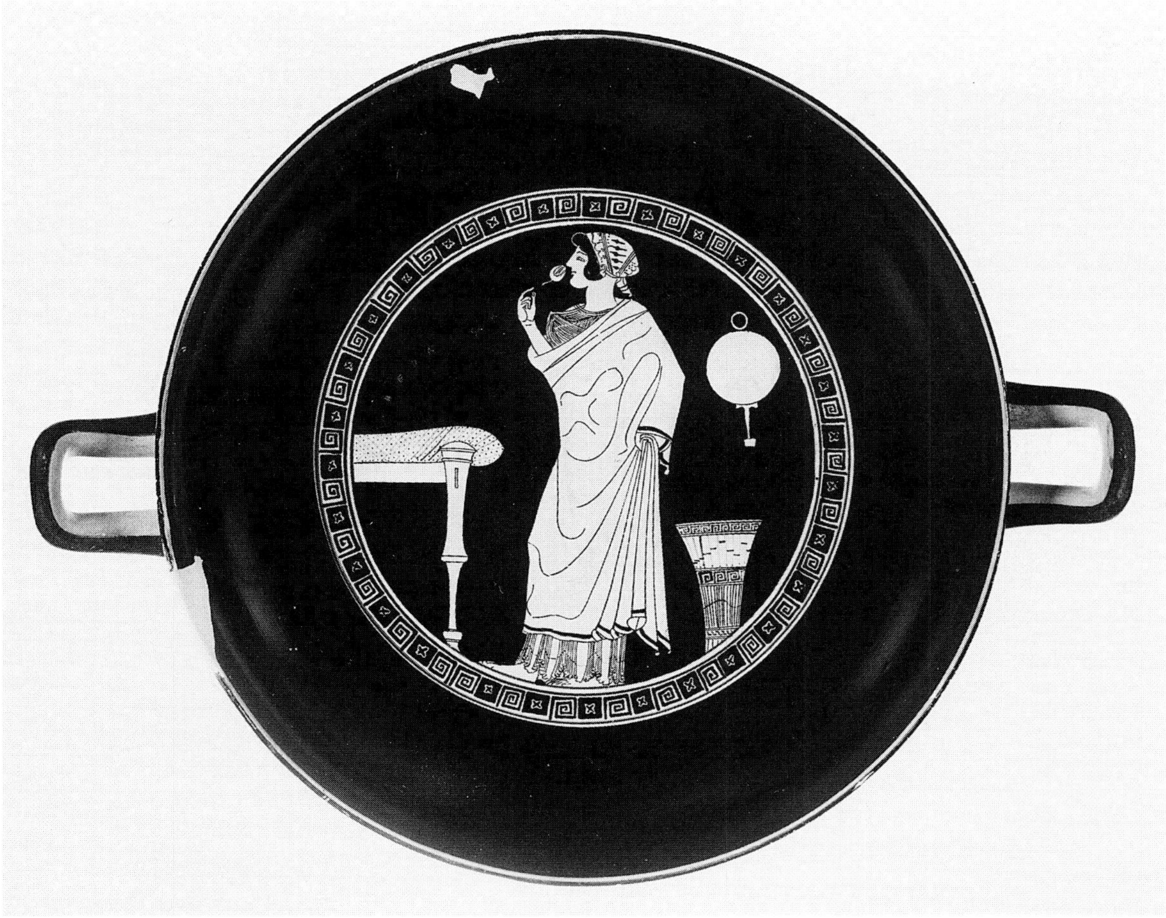

(a) 26

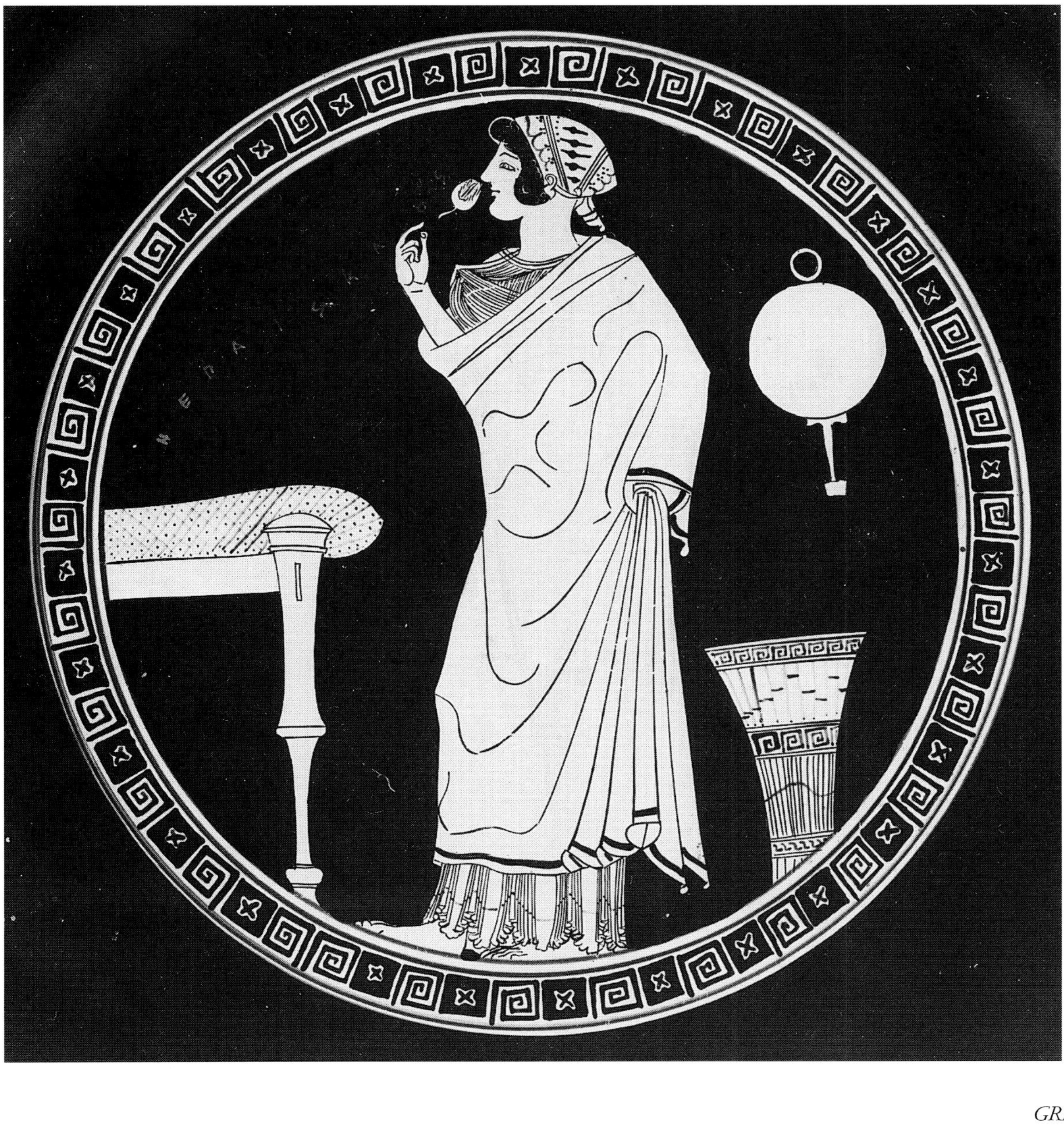

(b) 26

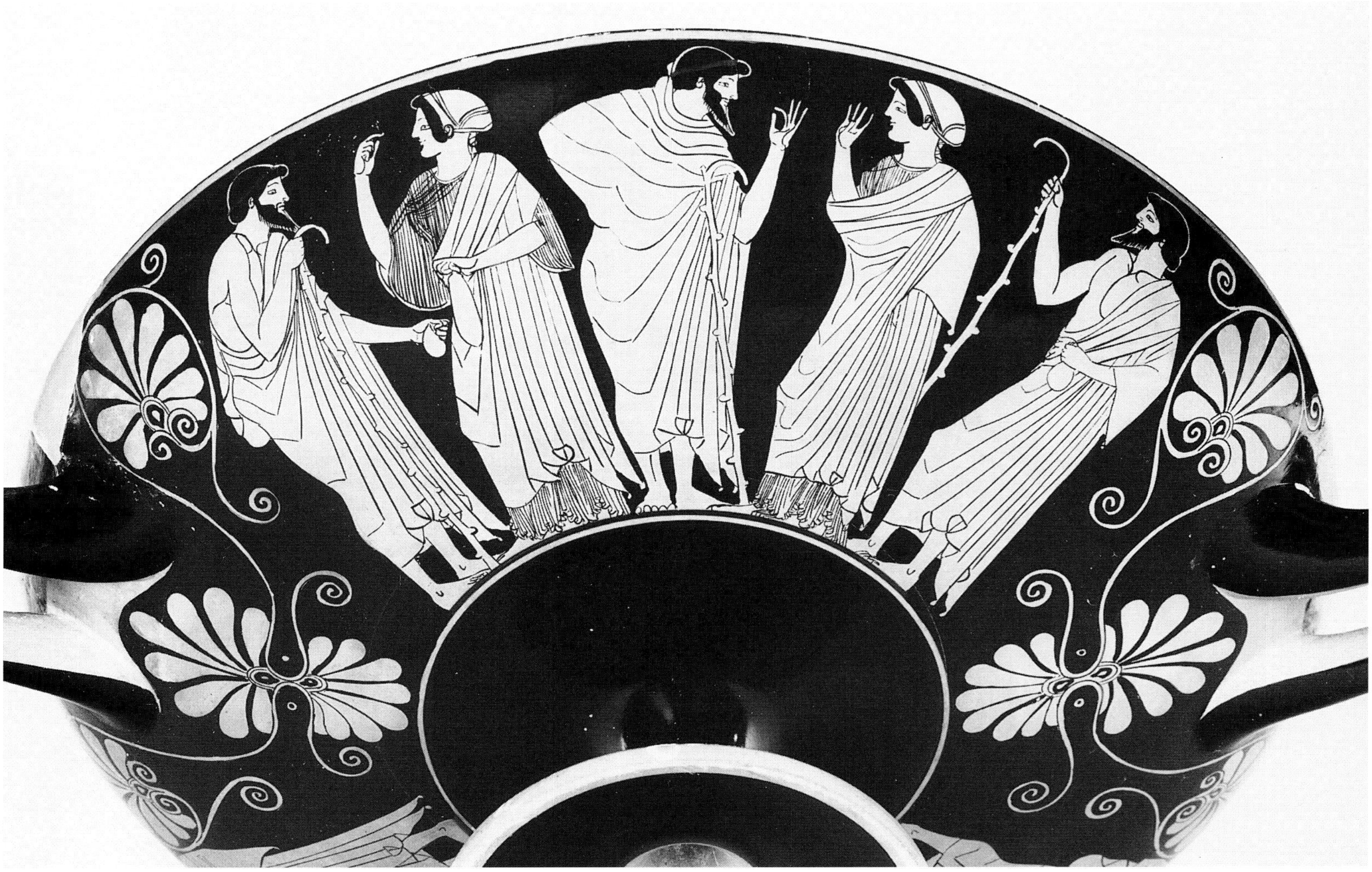

(a) 26

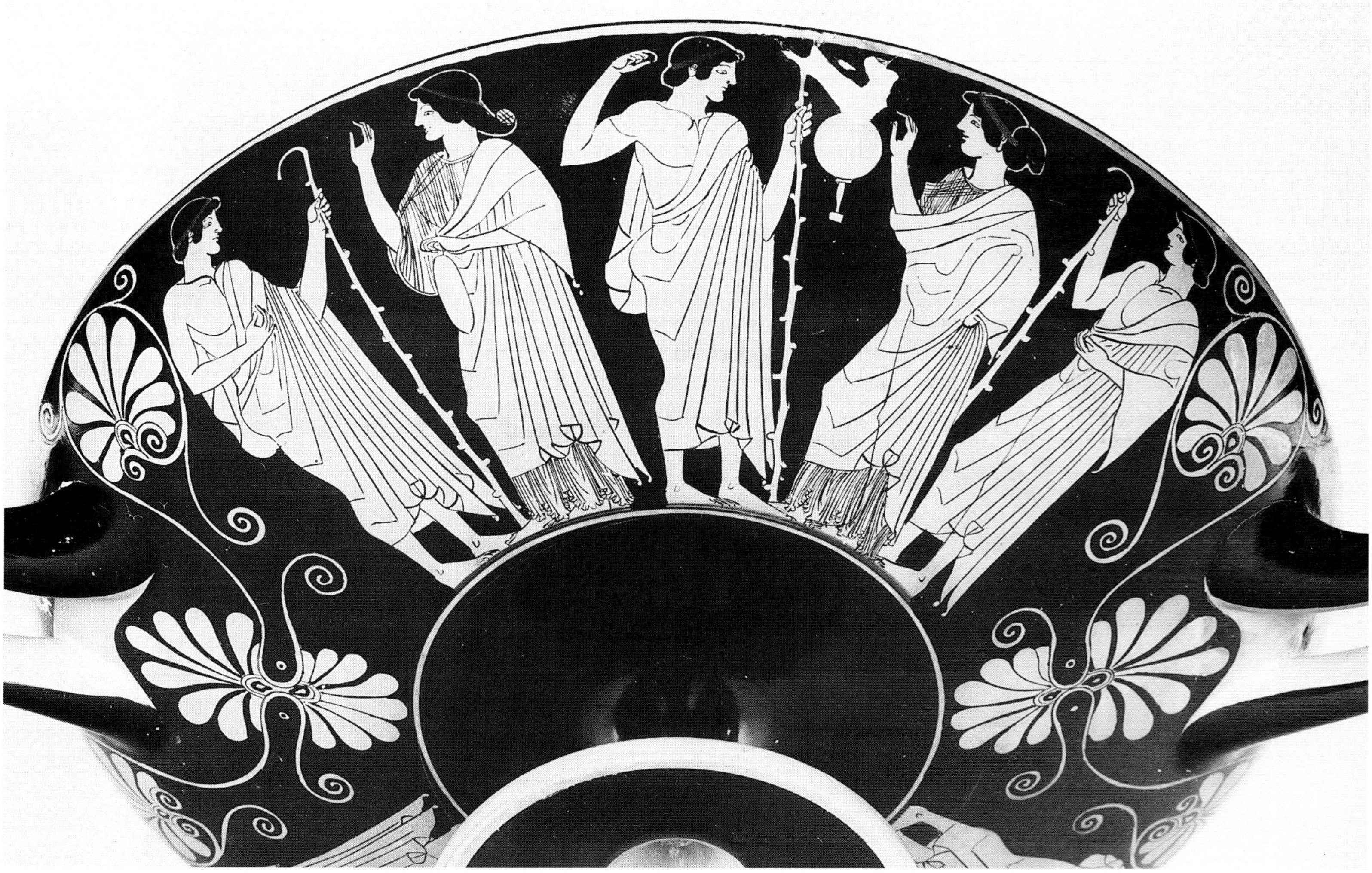

(b) 26

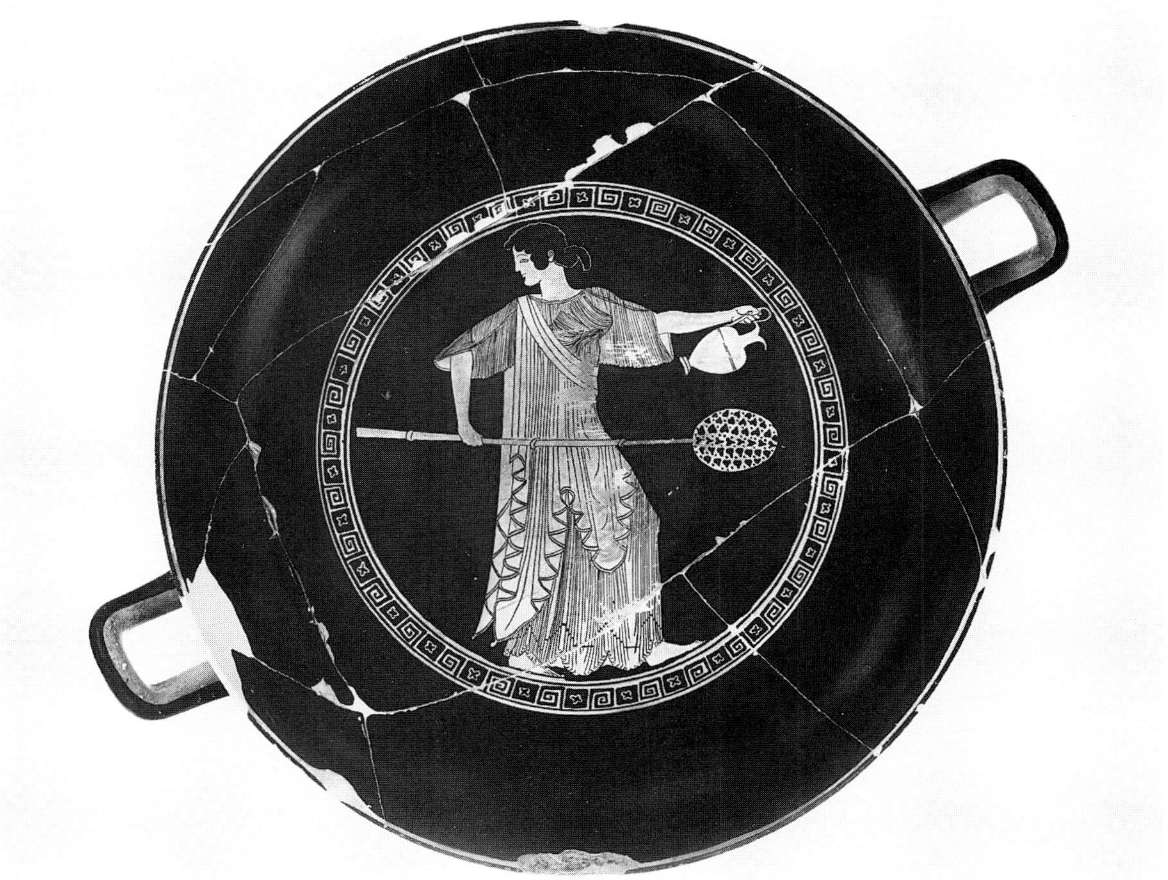

(a) 27

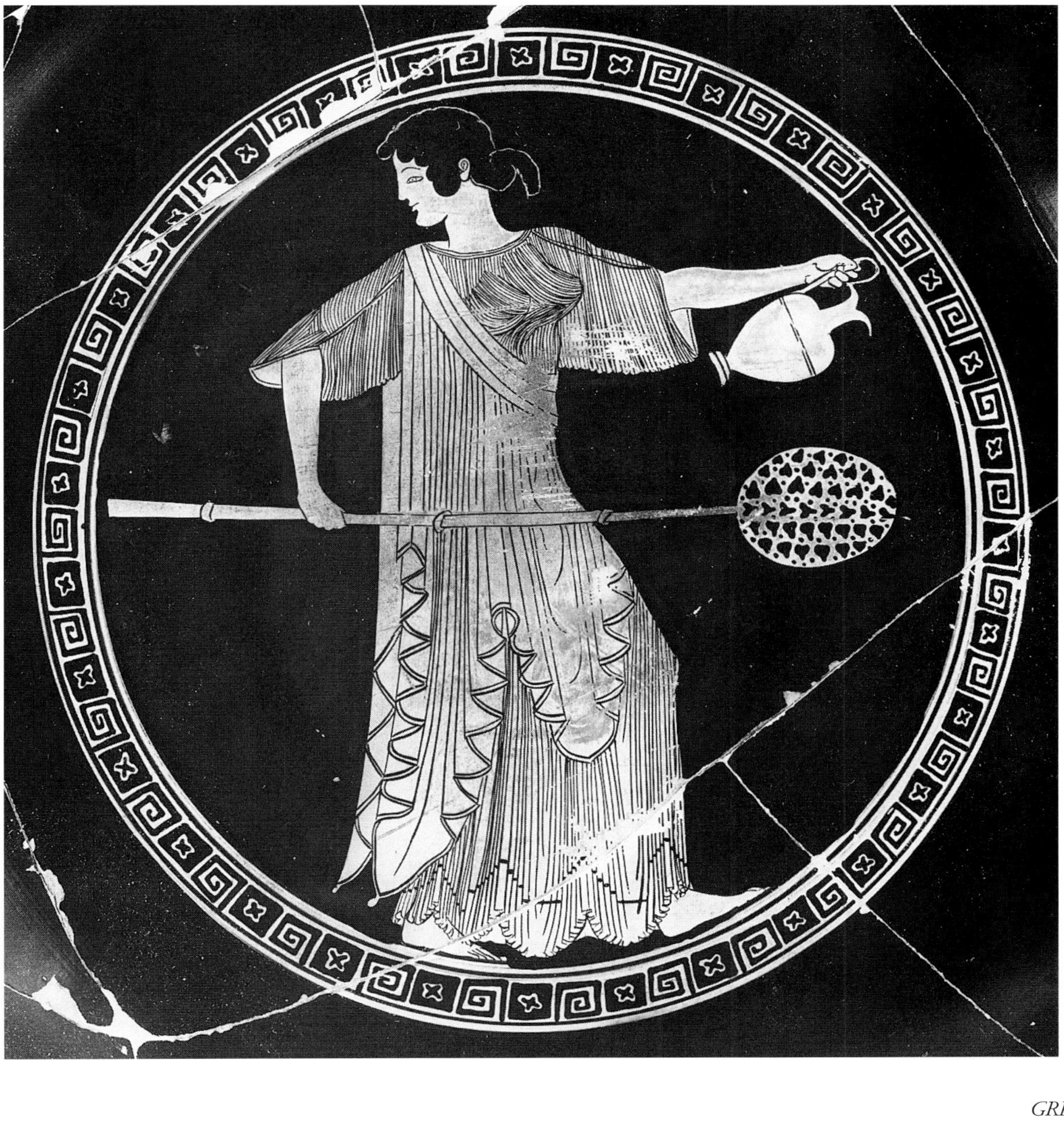

(b) 27

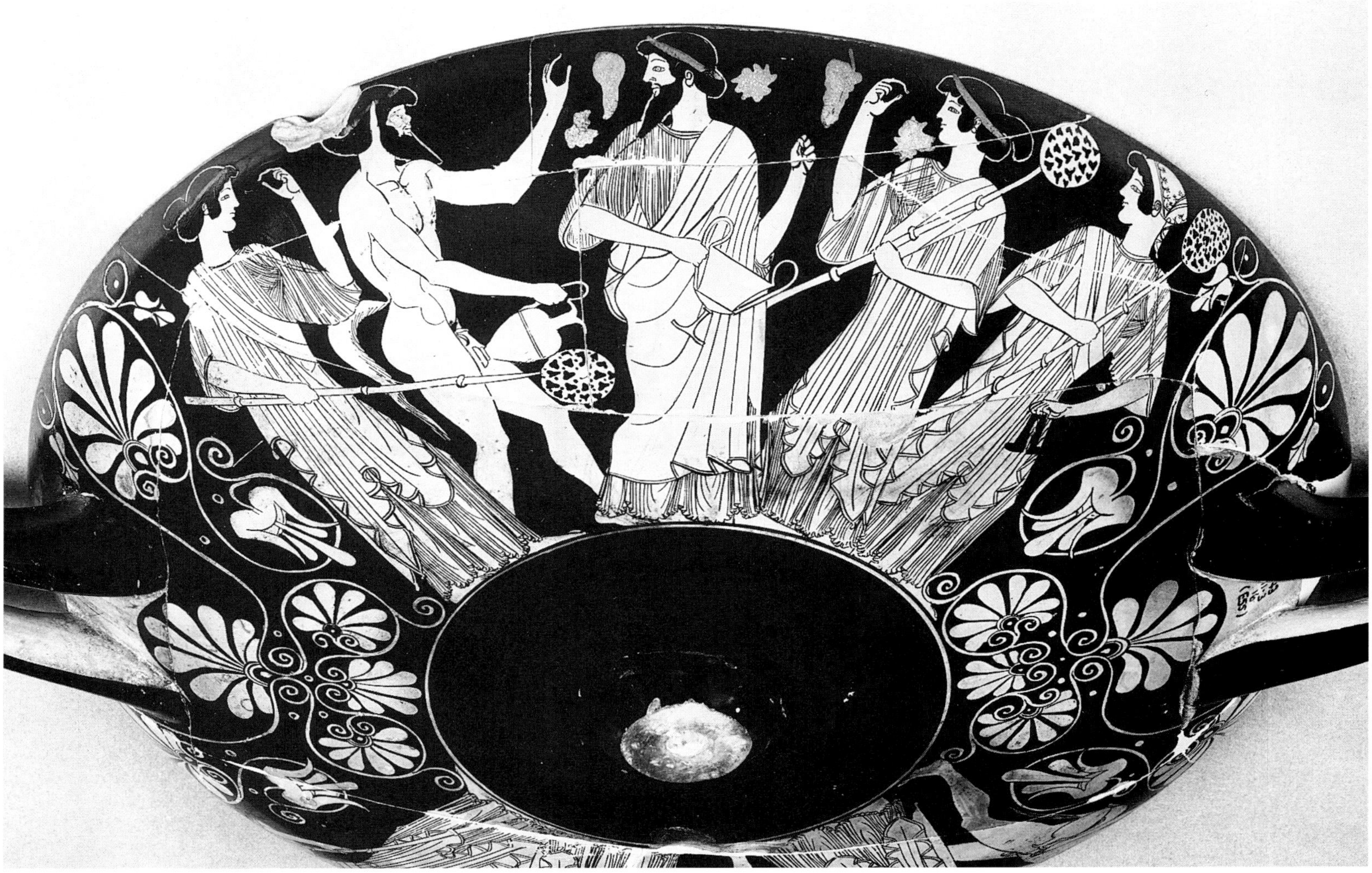

(a) 27

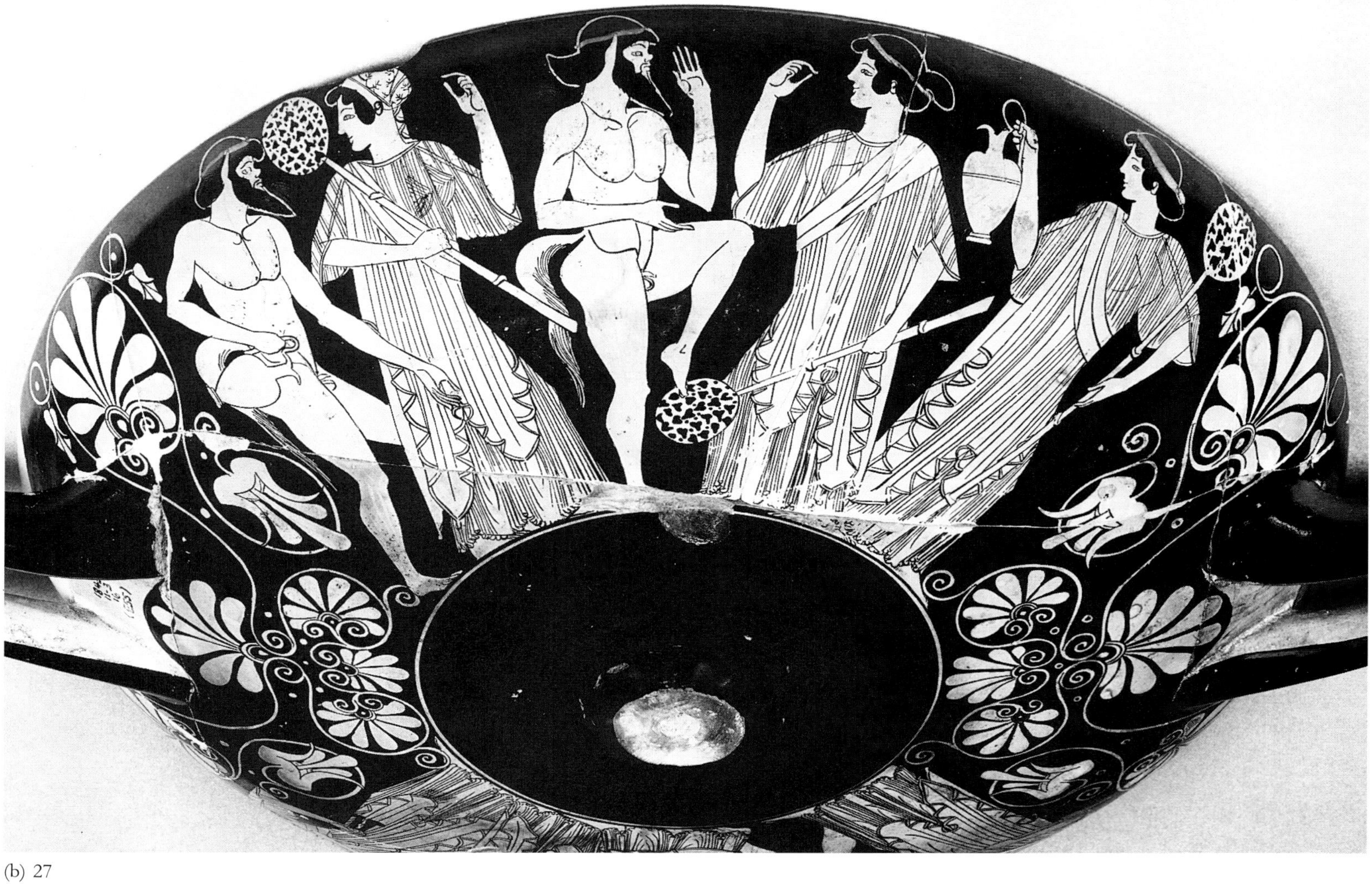

(b) 27

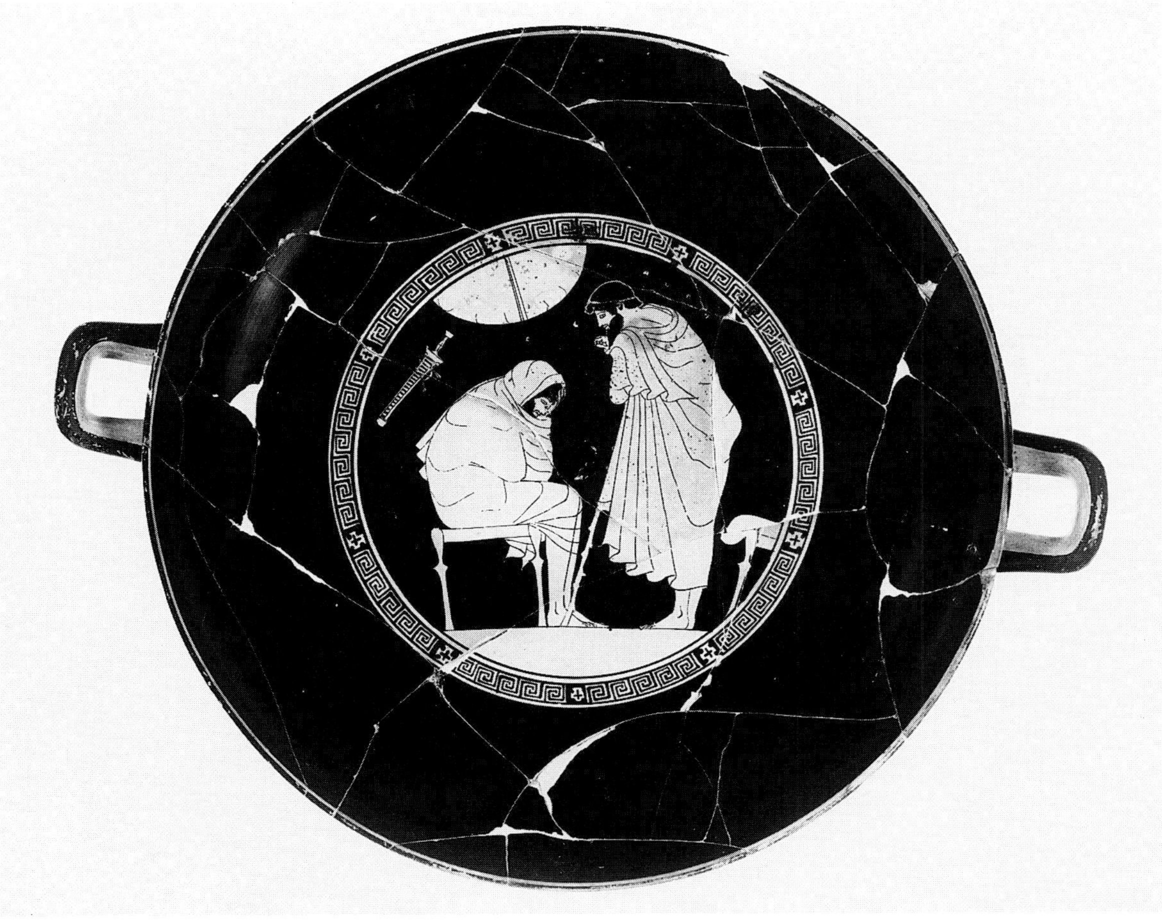

(a) 28

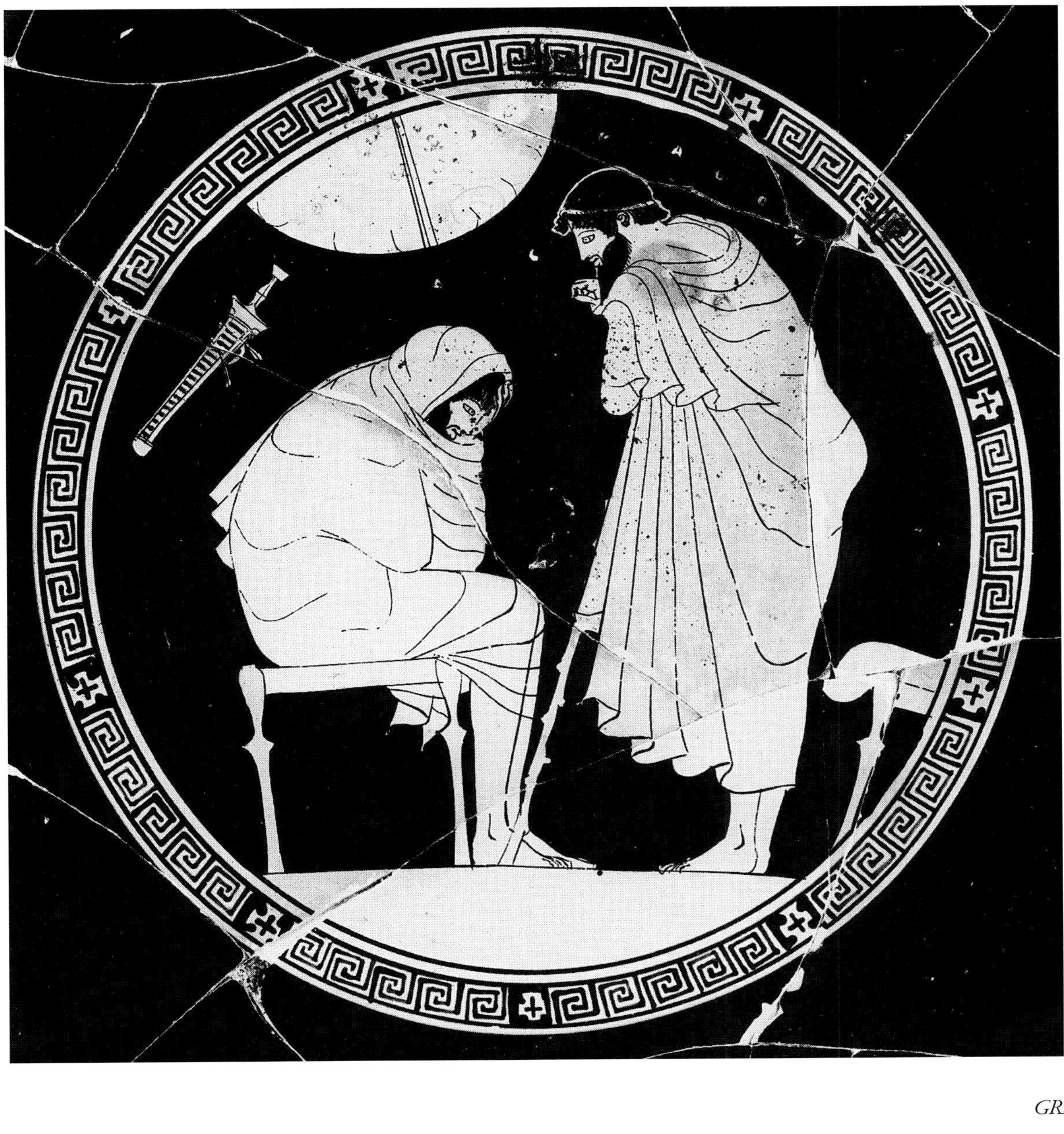

(b) 28

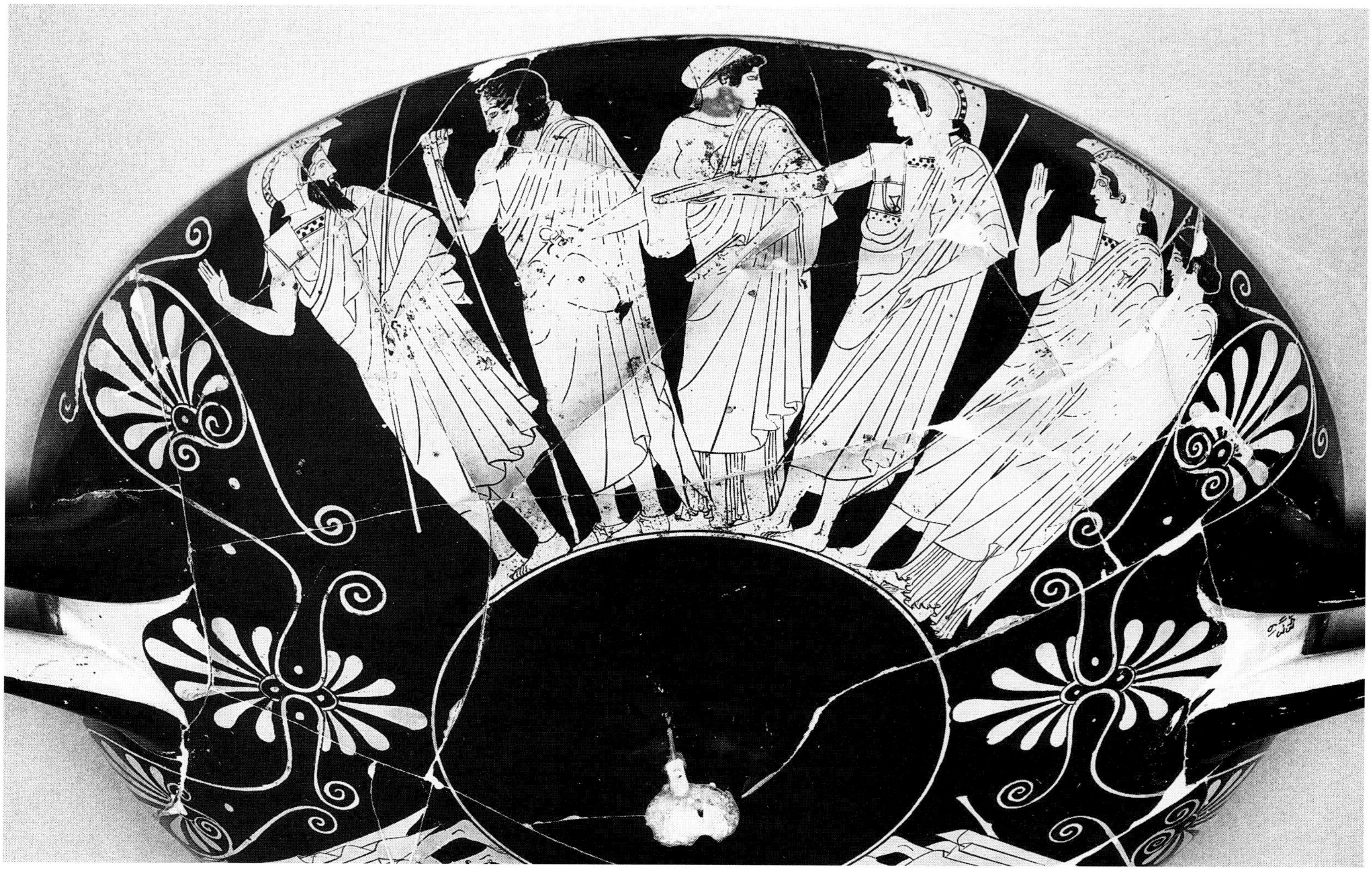

(a) 28

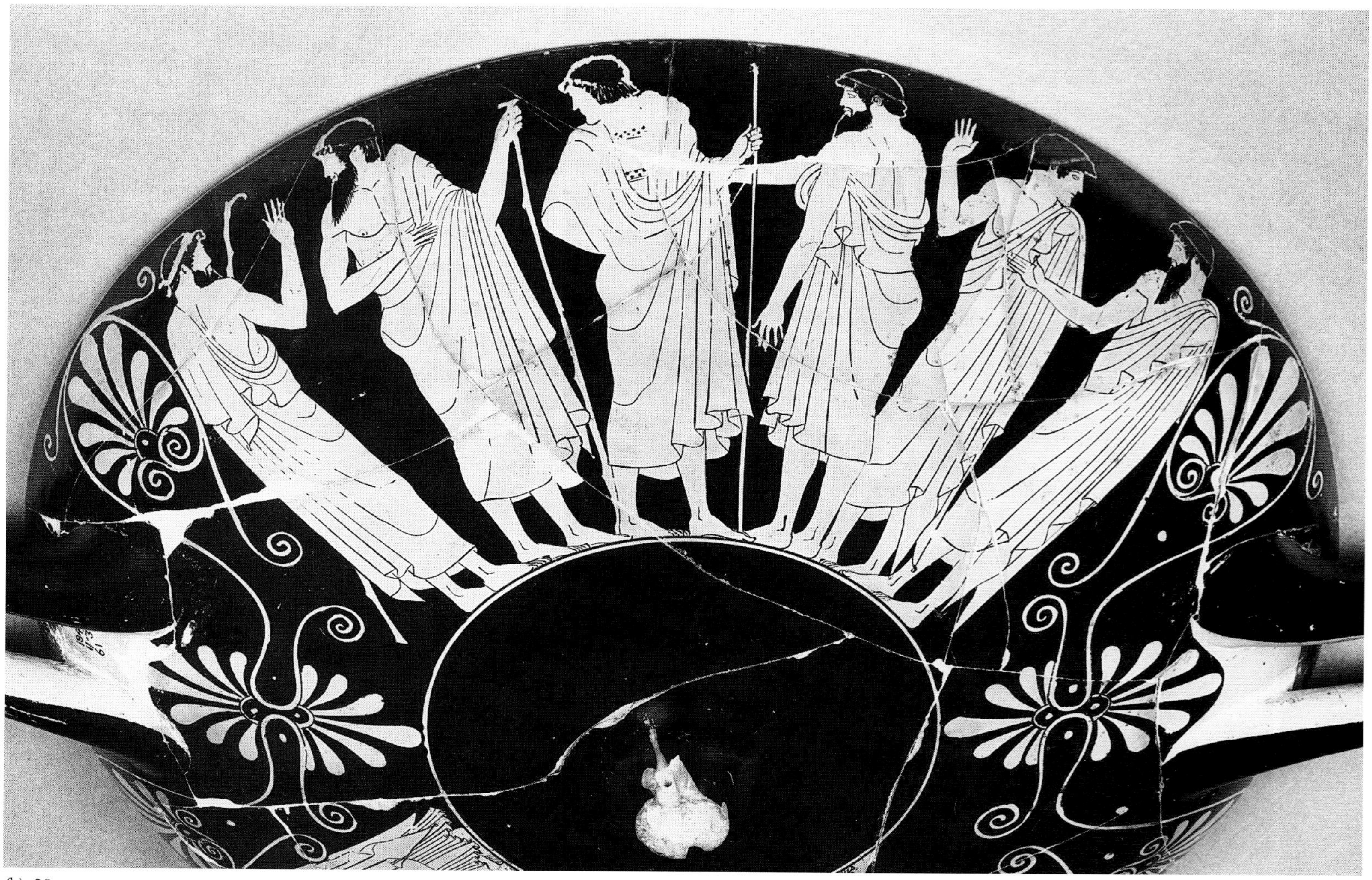

(b) 28

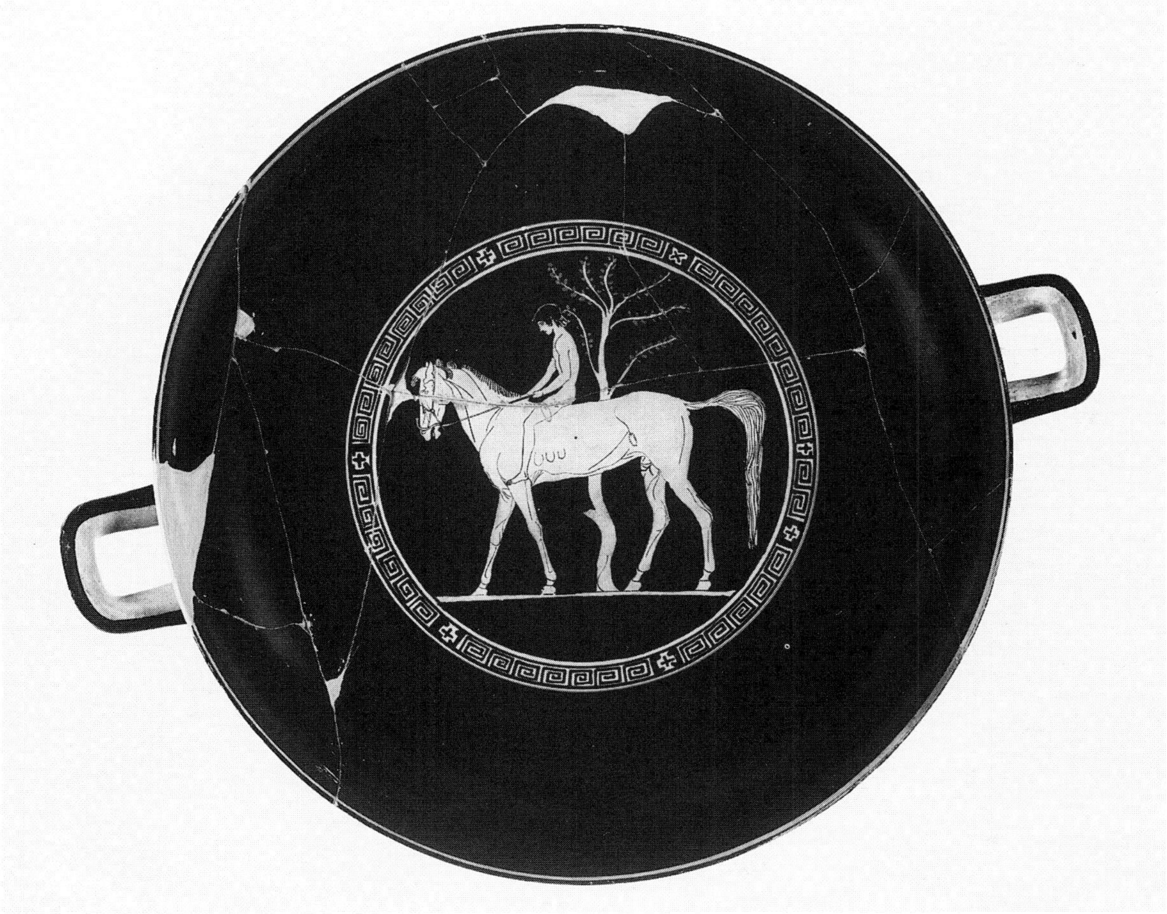

(a) 29

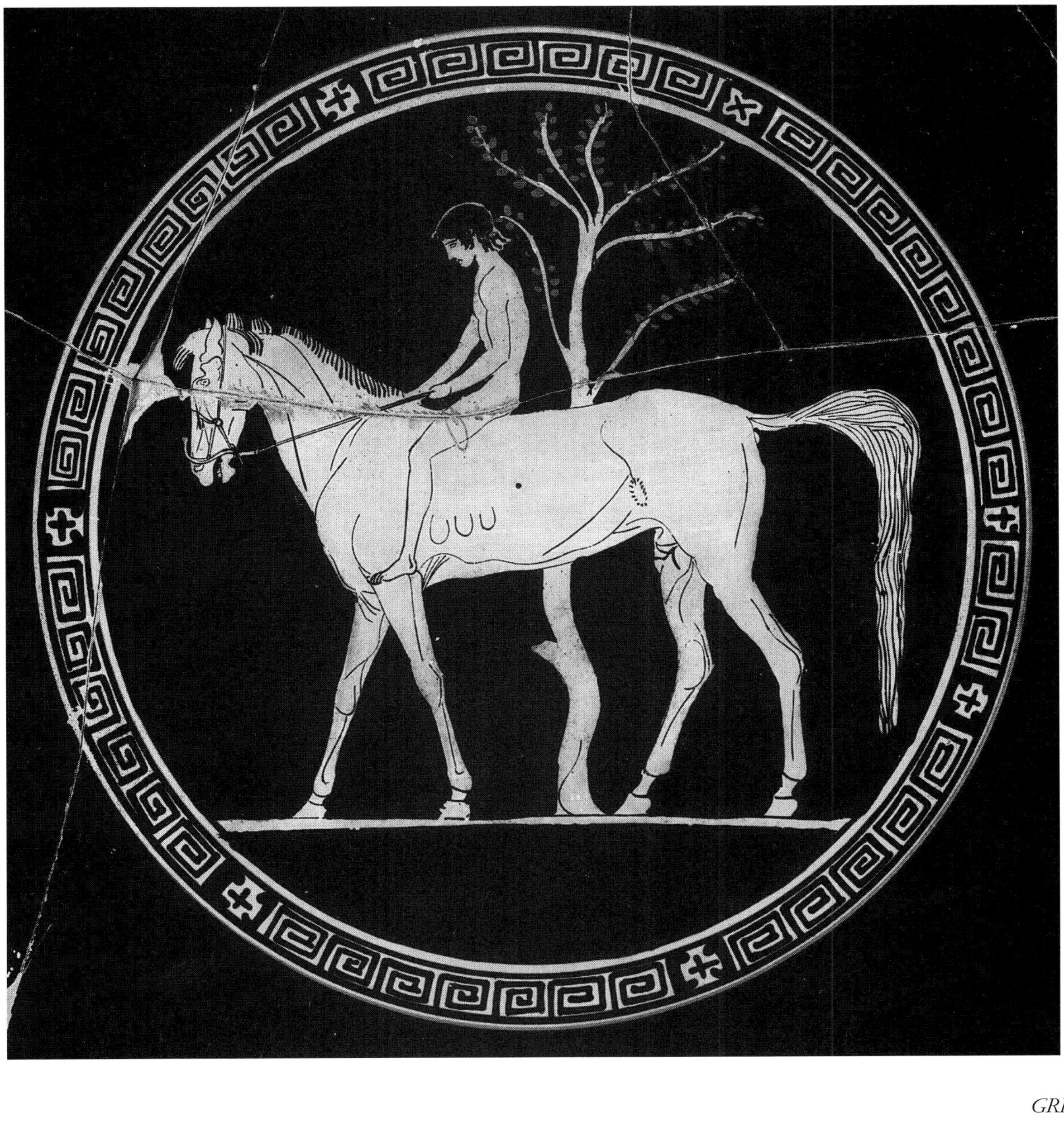

(b) 29

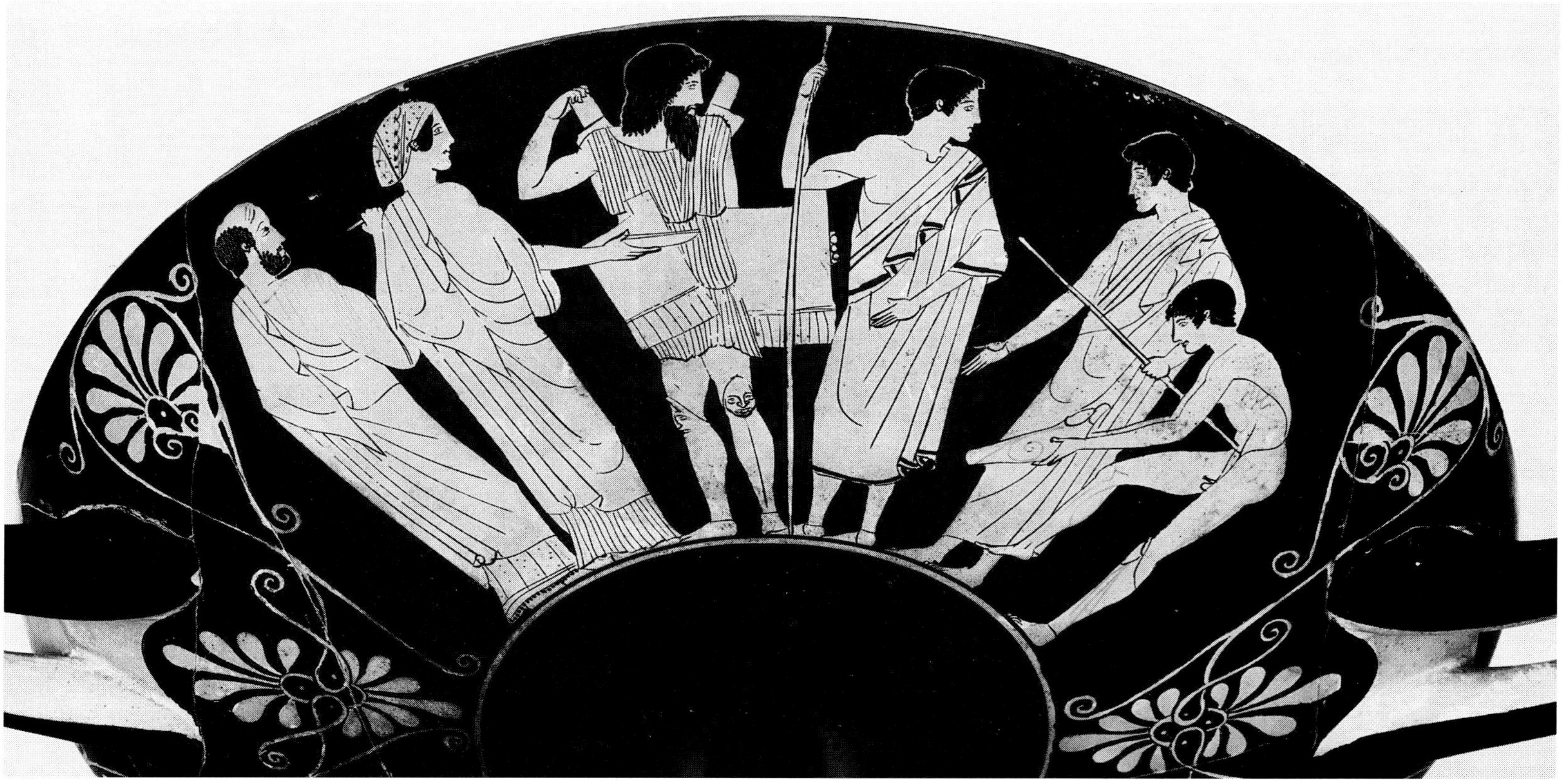

(a) 29

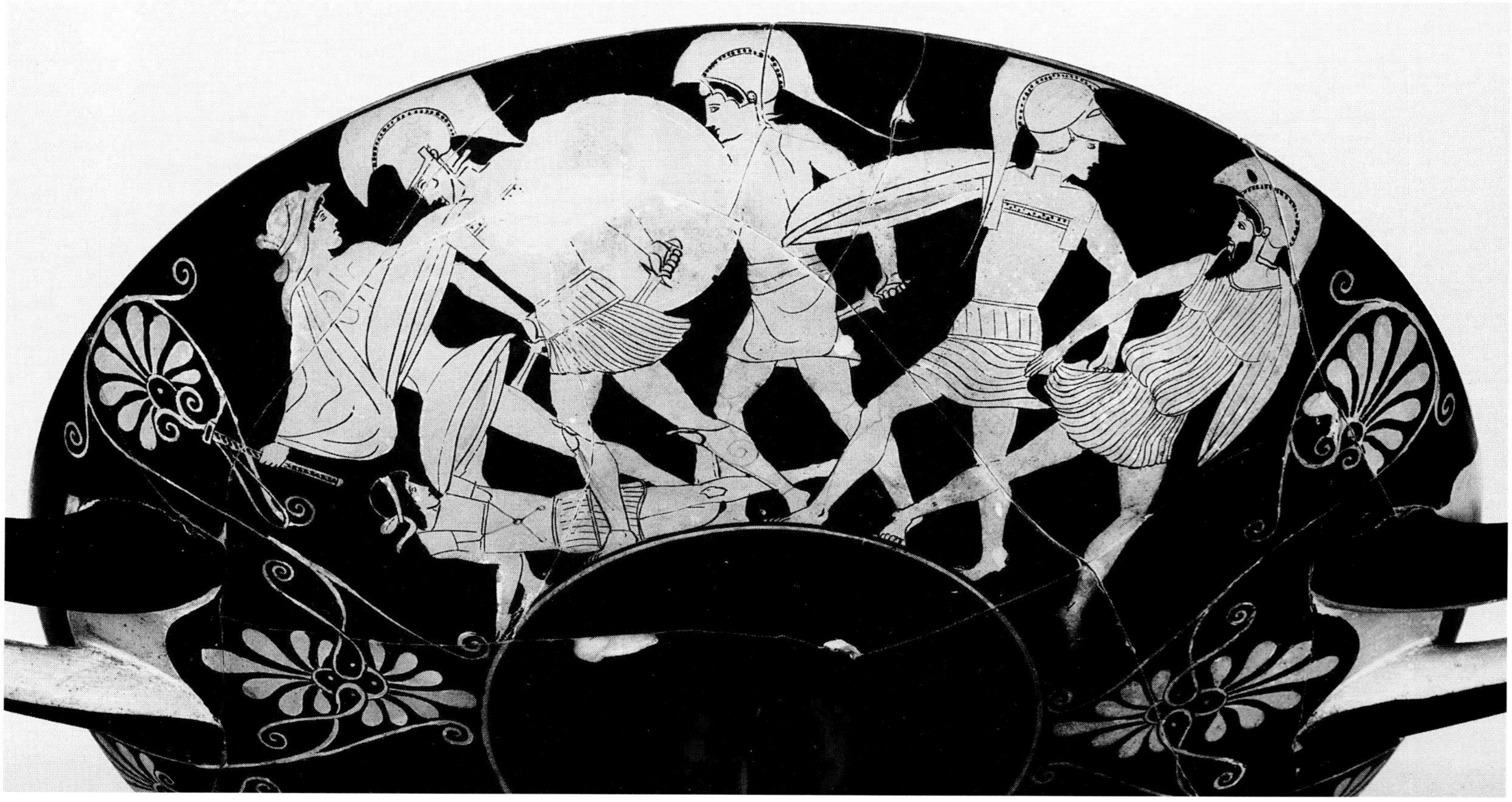

(b) 29

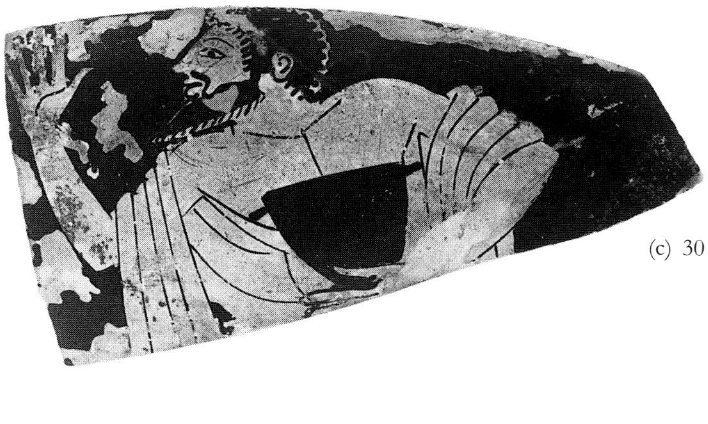

(c) 30

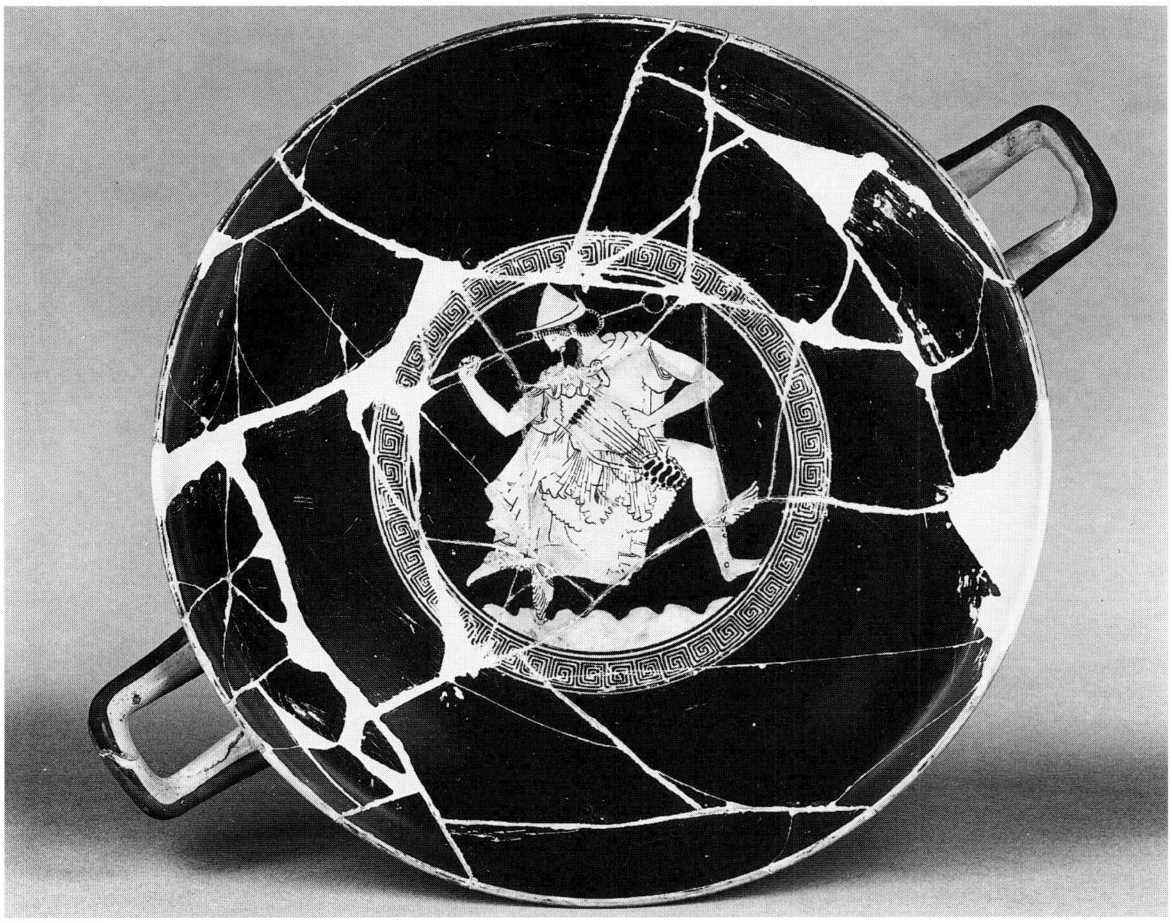

(a) 31

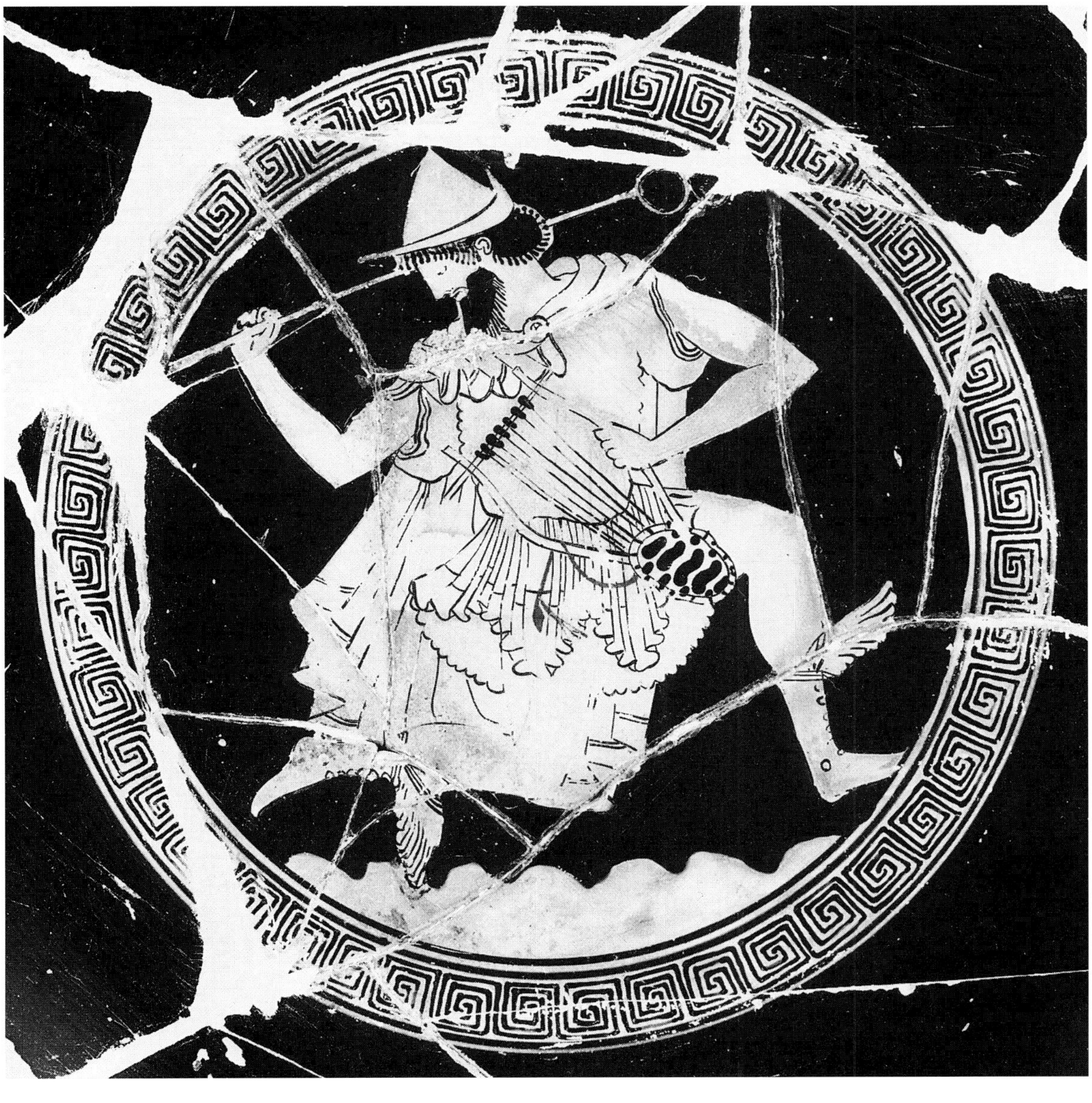

(b) 31

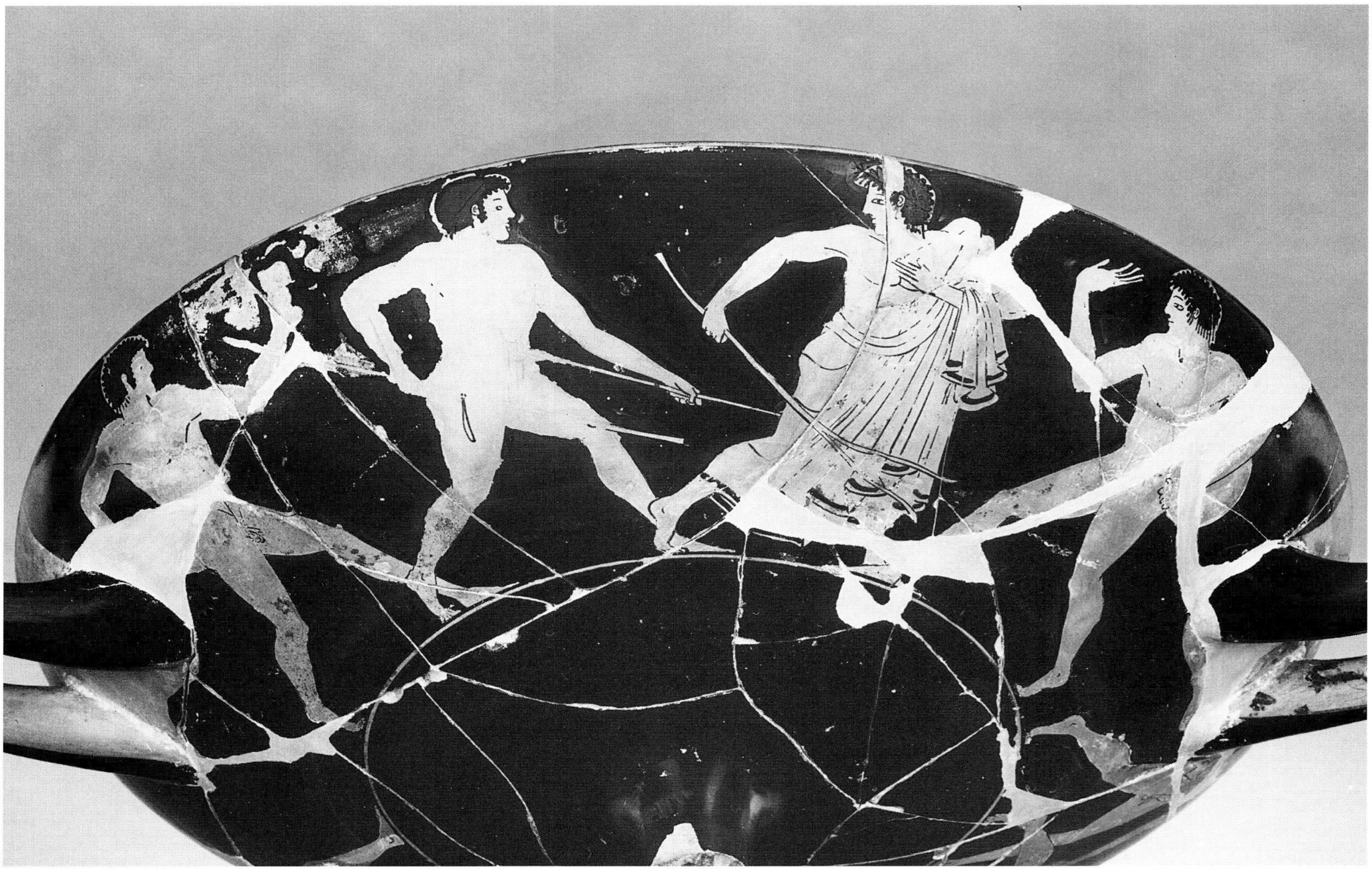
(a) 31

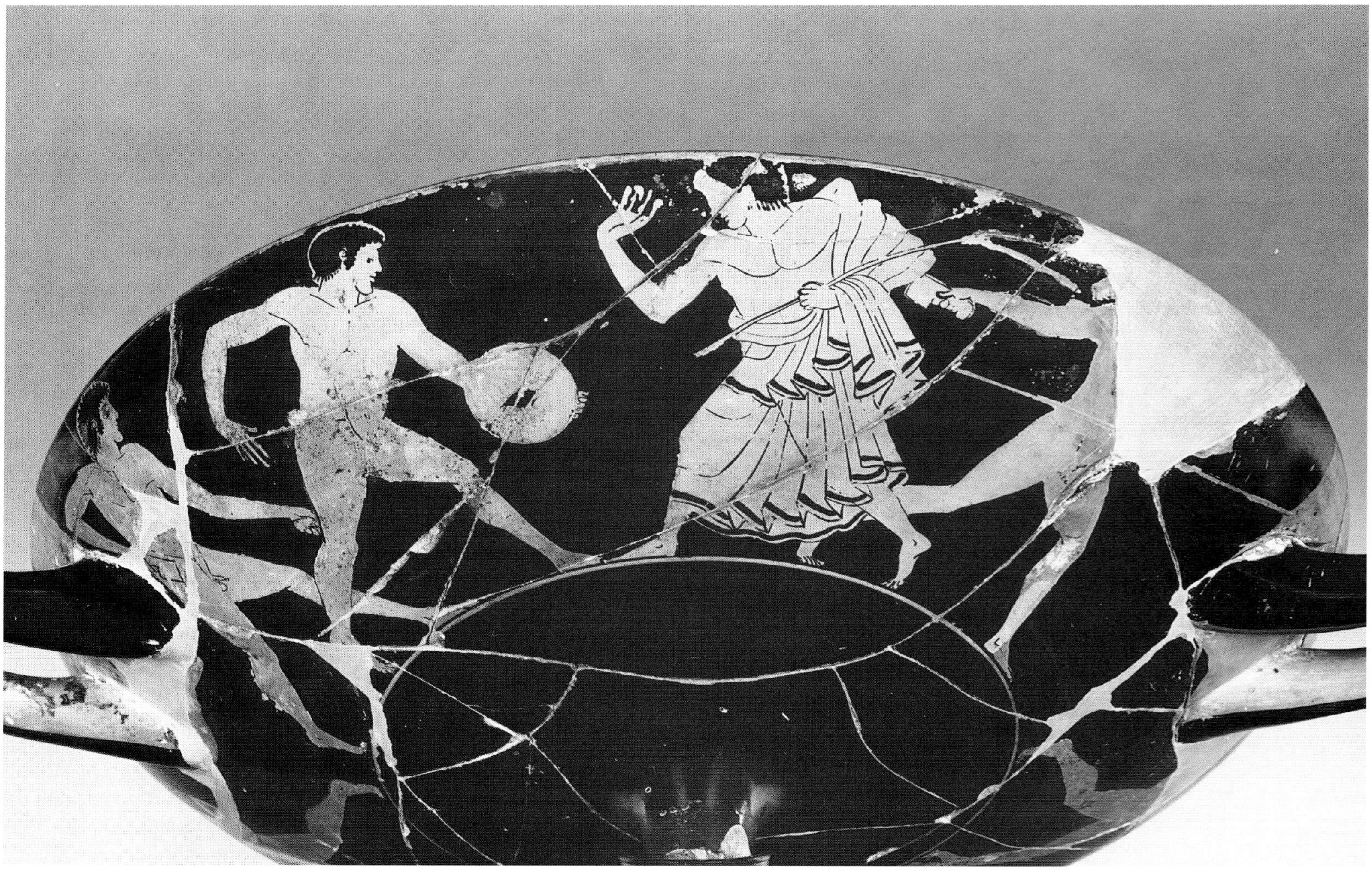
(b) 31

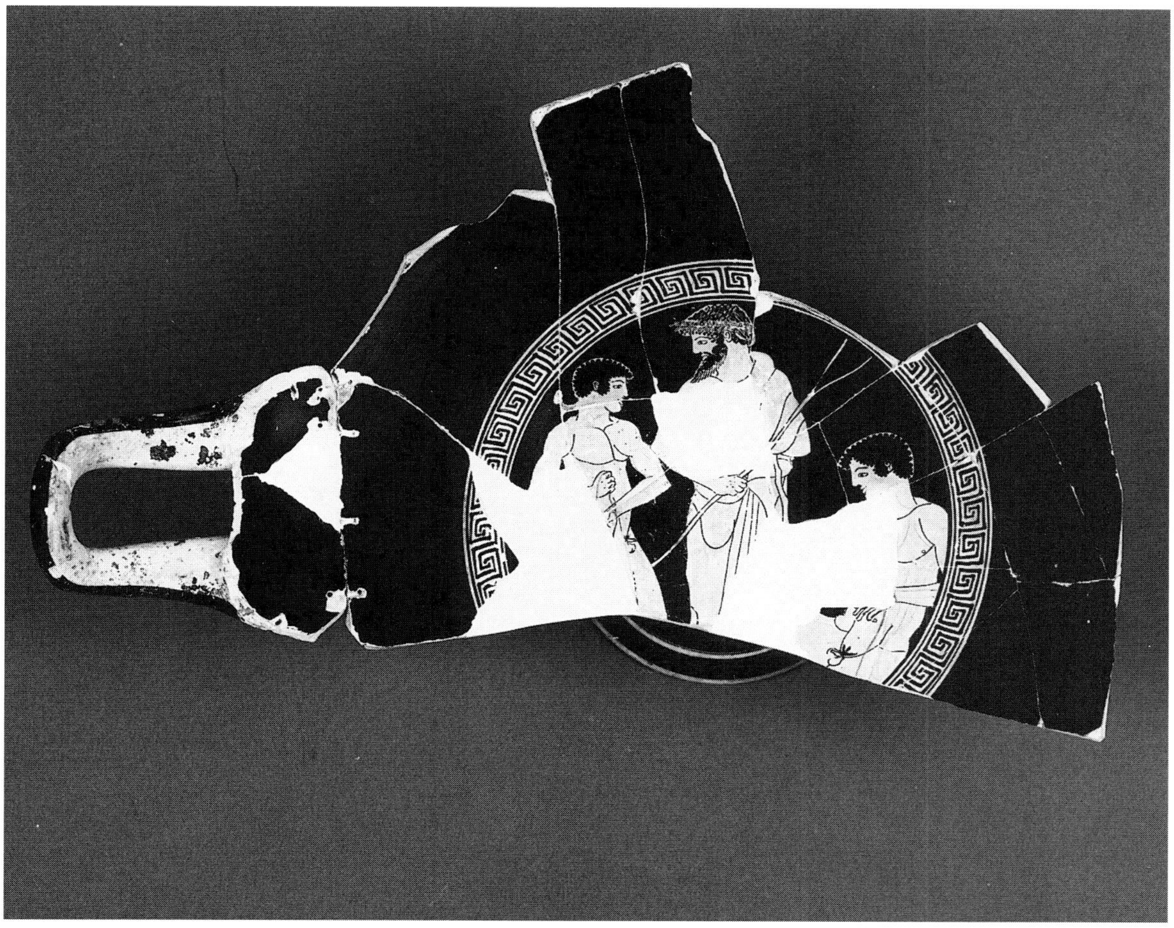

(a) 32

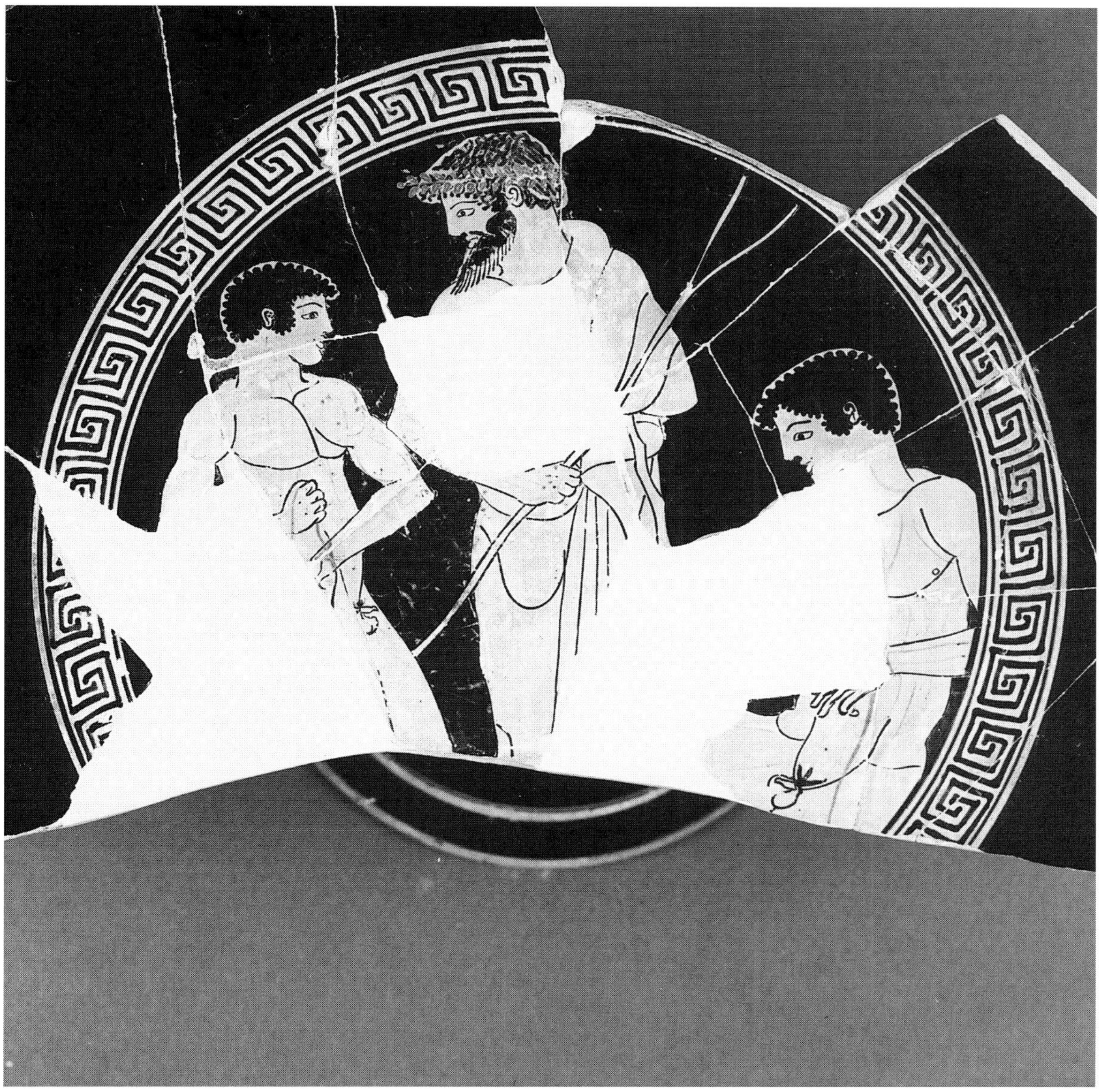

(b) 32

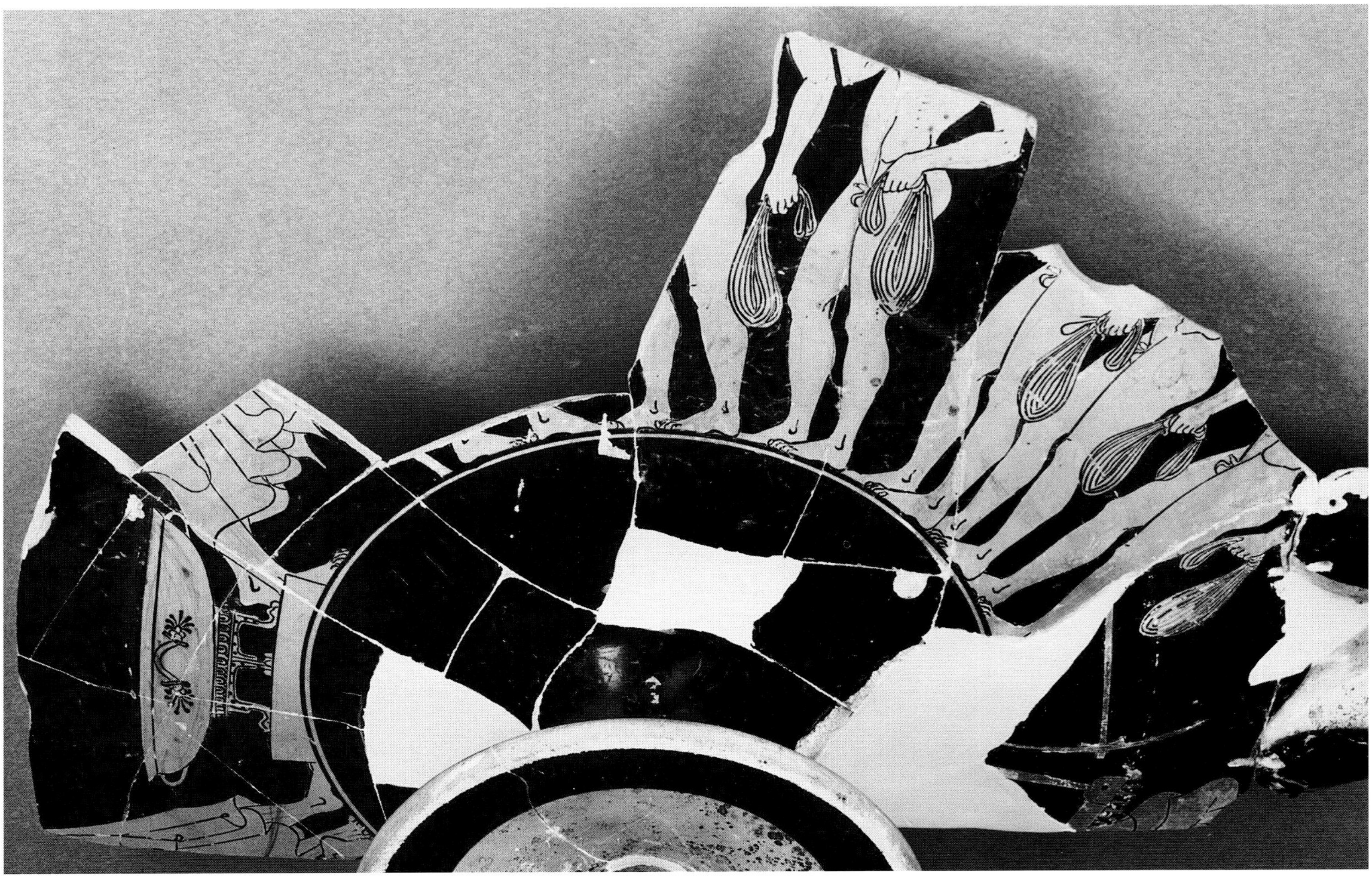

(a) 32

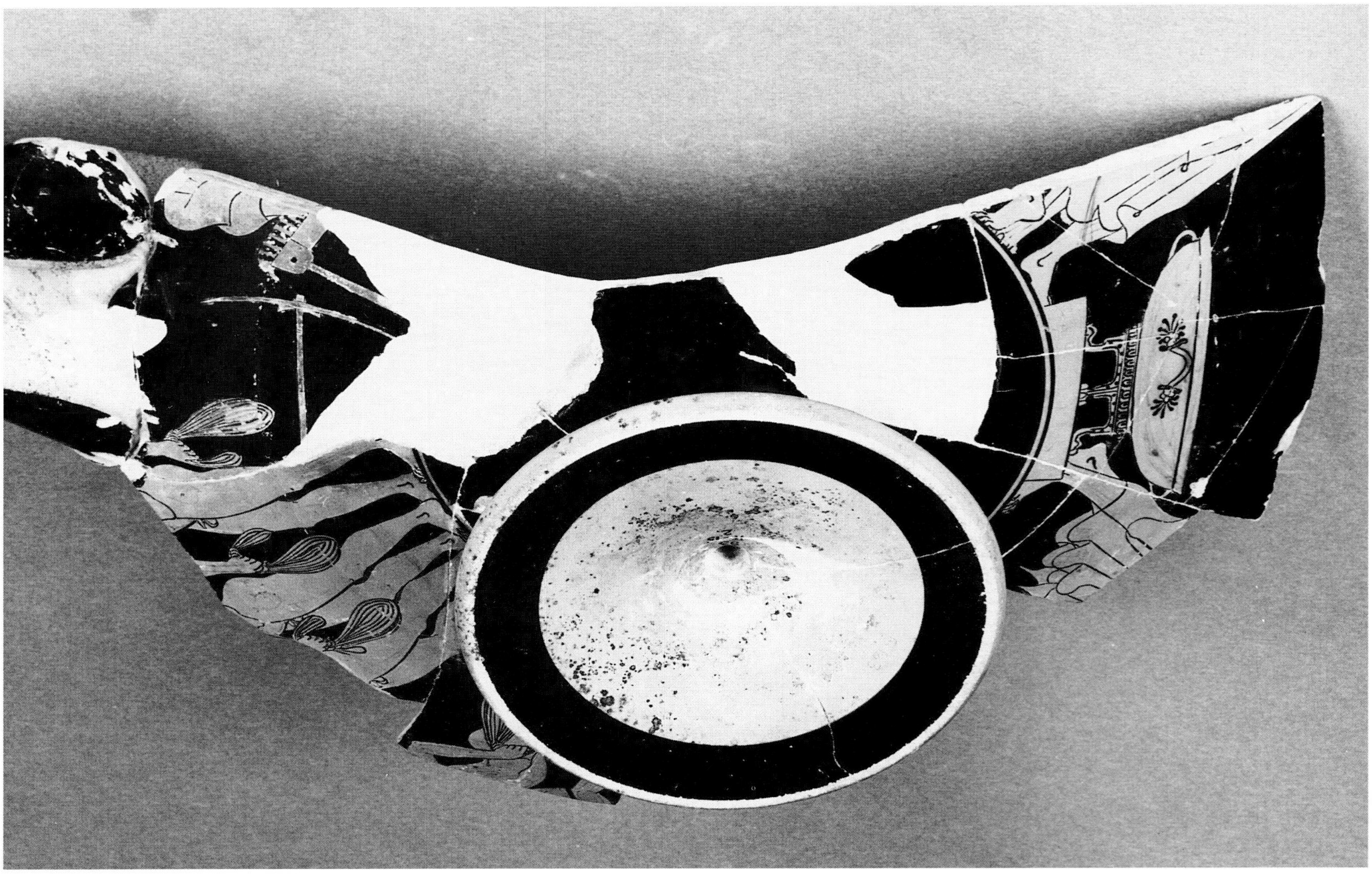

(b) 32

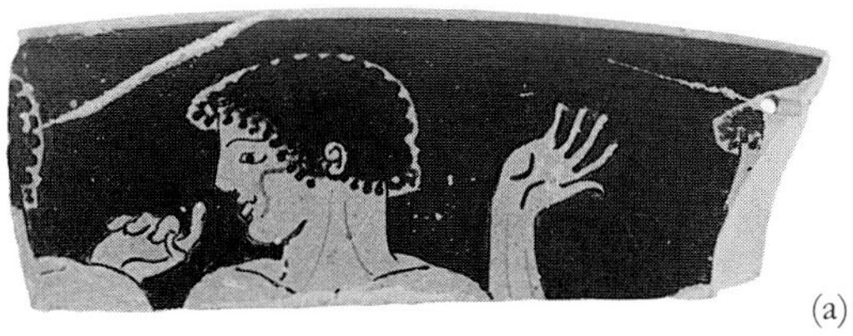
(a) 32

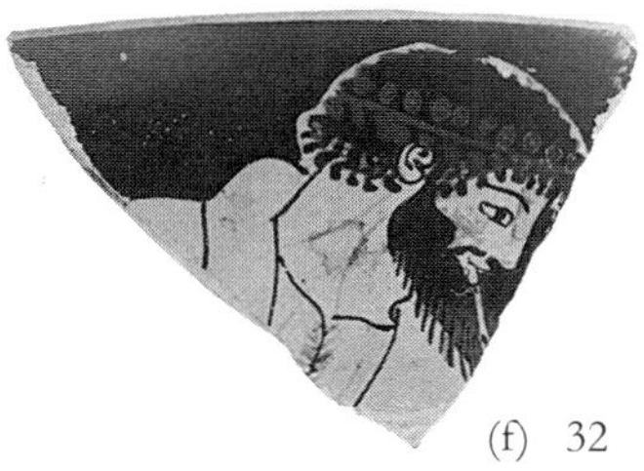
(f) 32

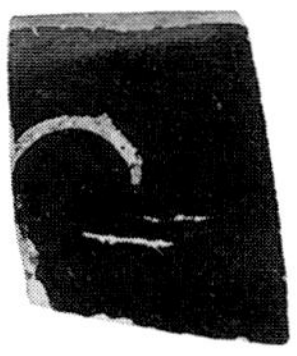
(g) 32

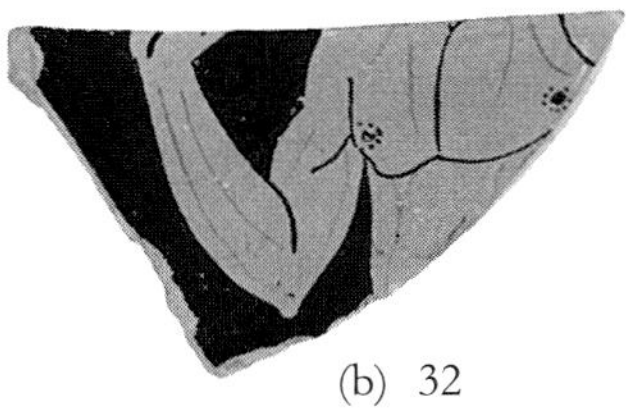
(b) 32

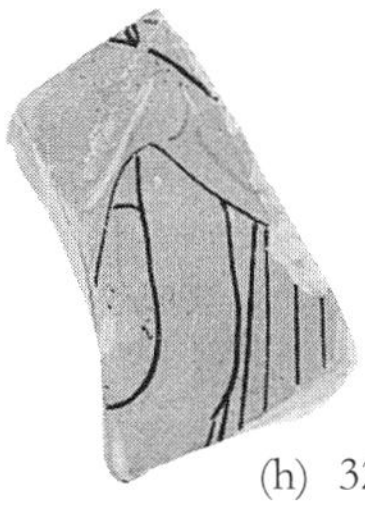
(h) 32

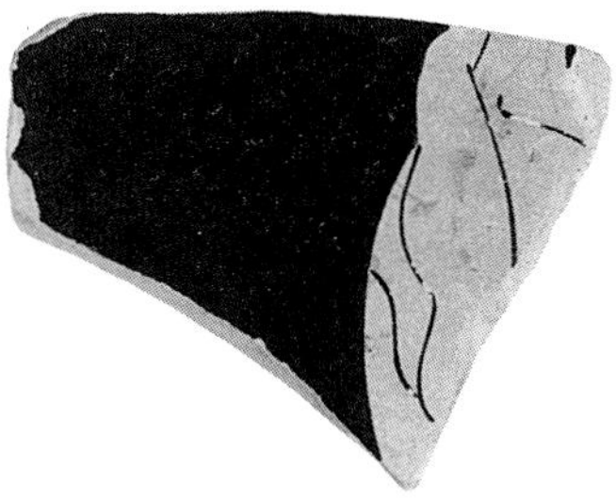
(i) 32

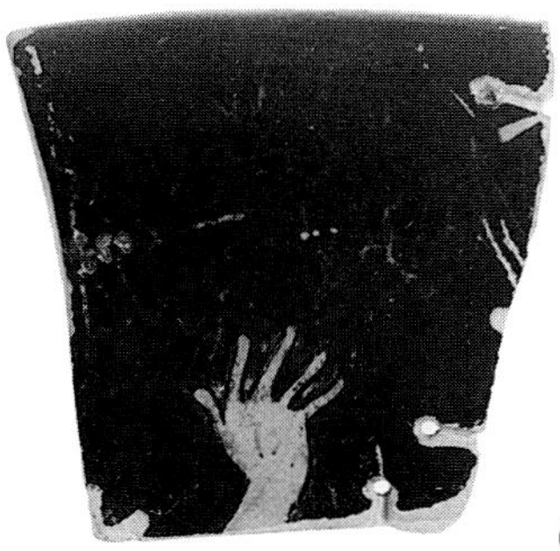
(c) 32

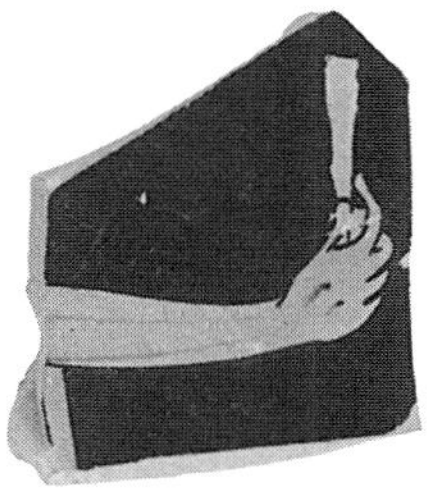
(j) 32

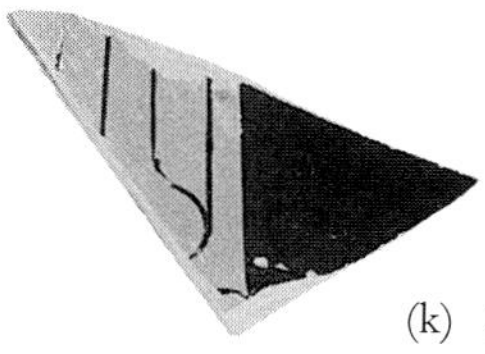
(k) 32

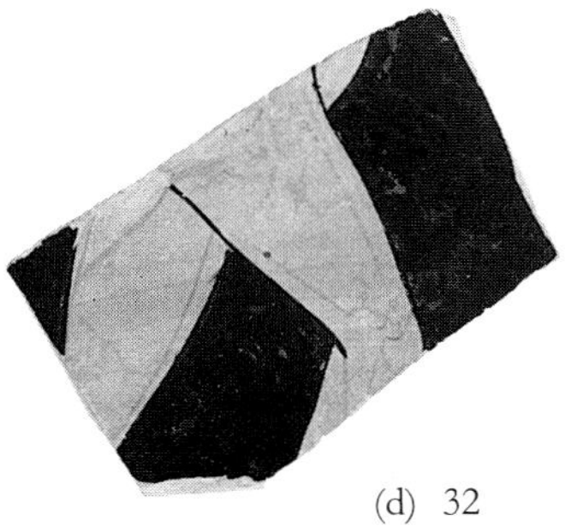
(d) 32

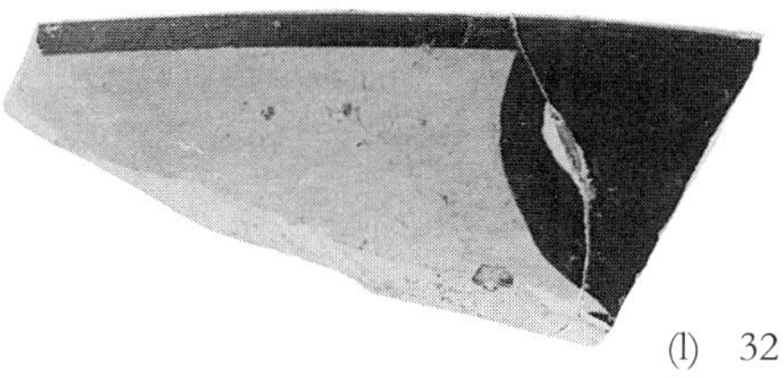
(l) 32

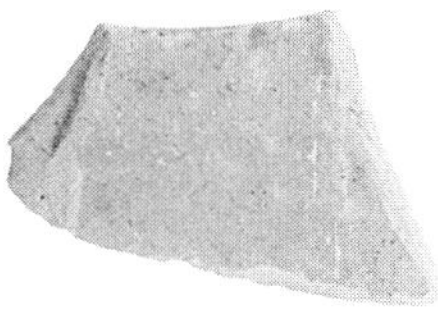
(m) 32

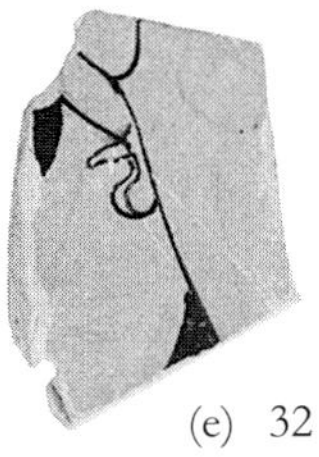
(e) 32

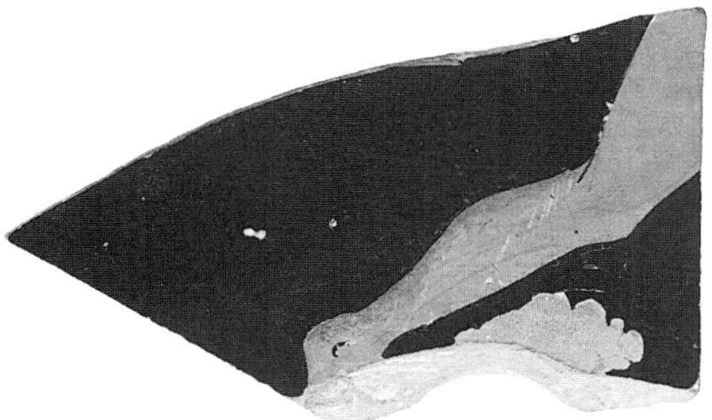
(n) 33

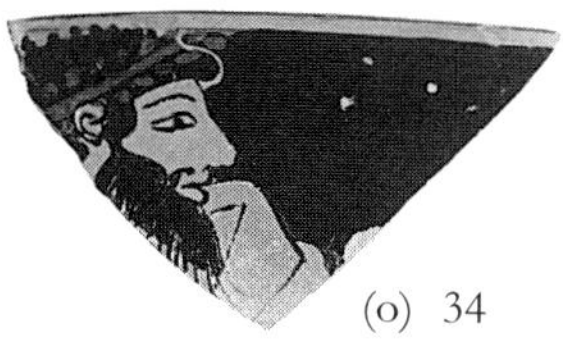
(o) 34

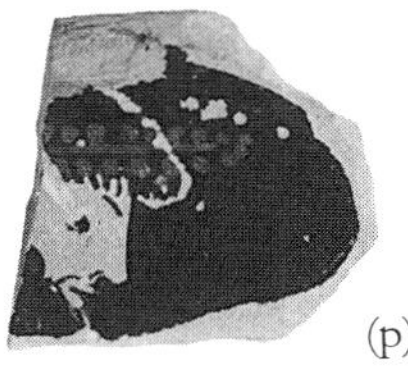
(p) 35

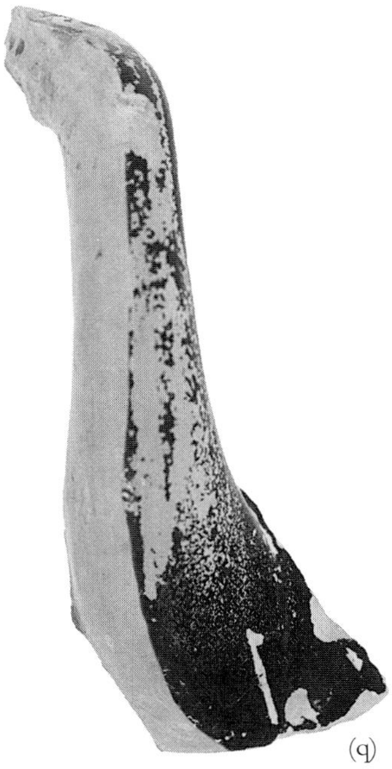
(q) 36

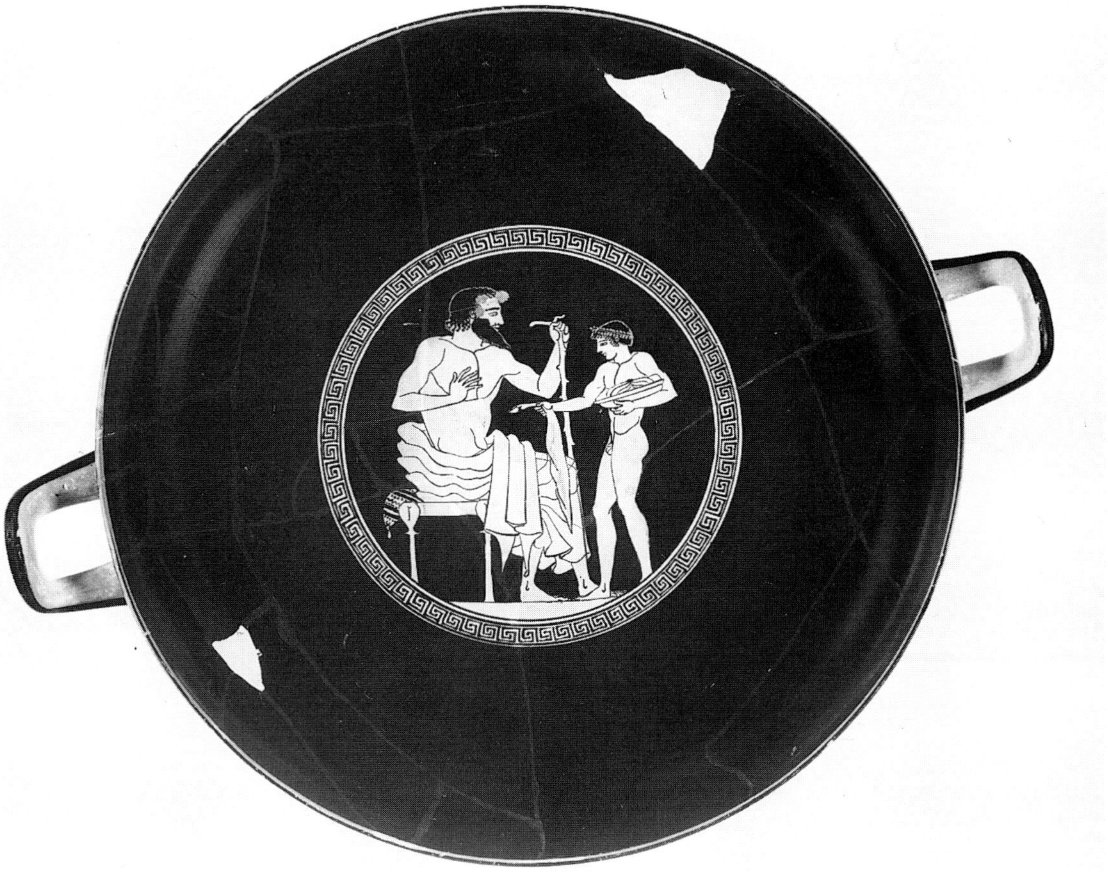

(a) 38

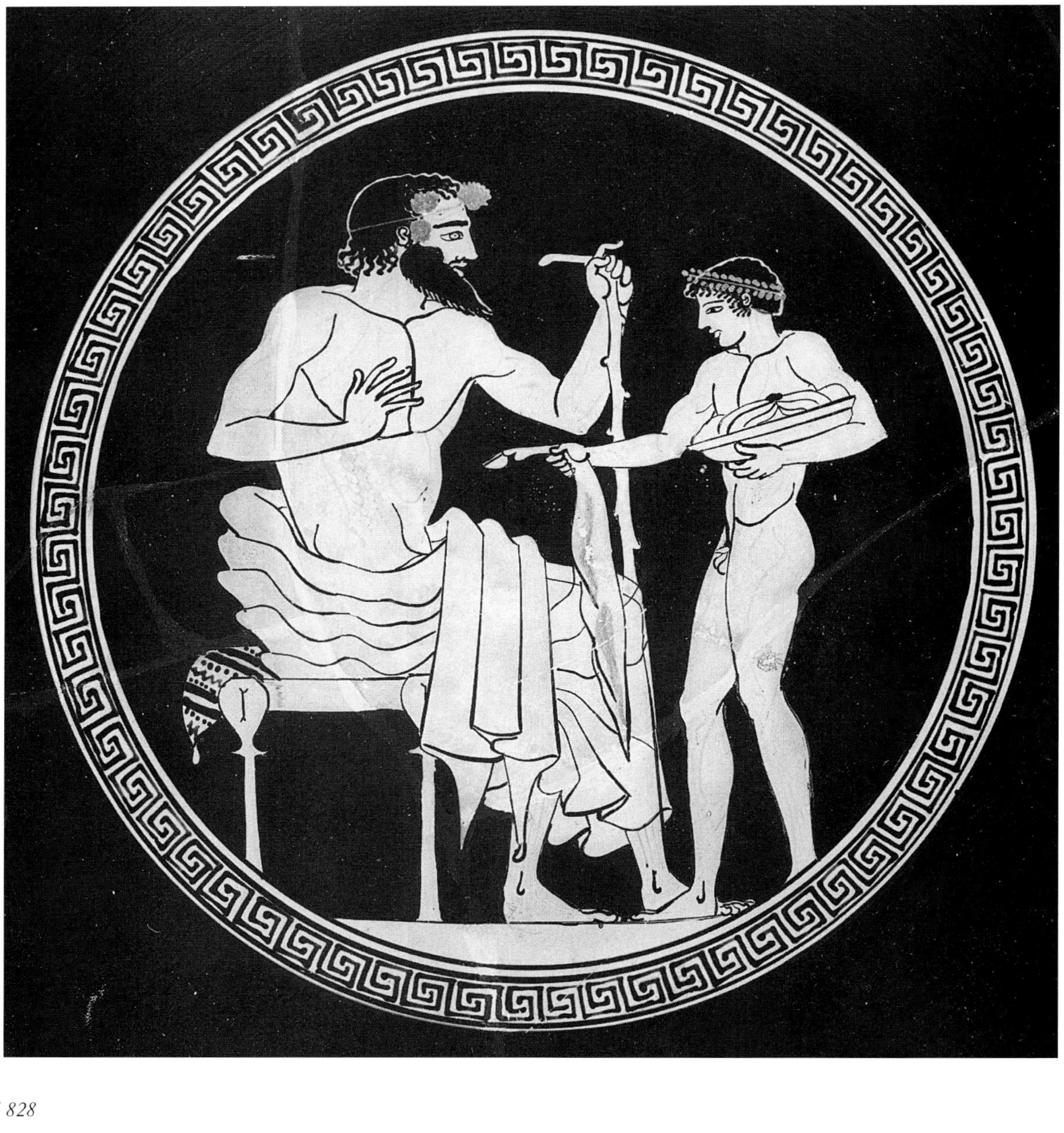

(b) 38

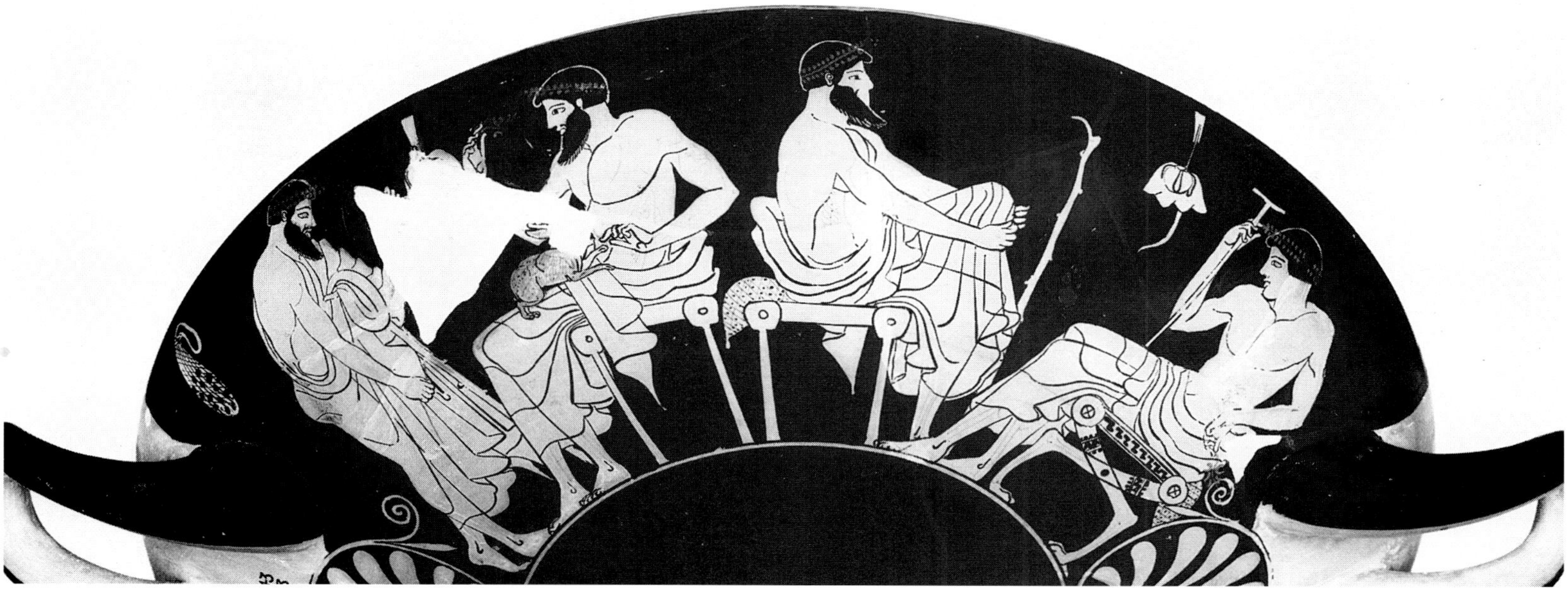

(a) 38

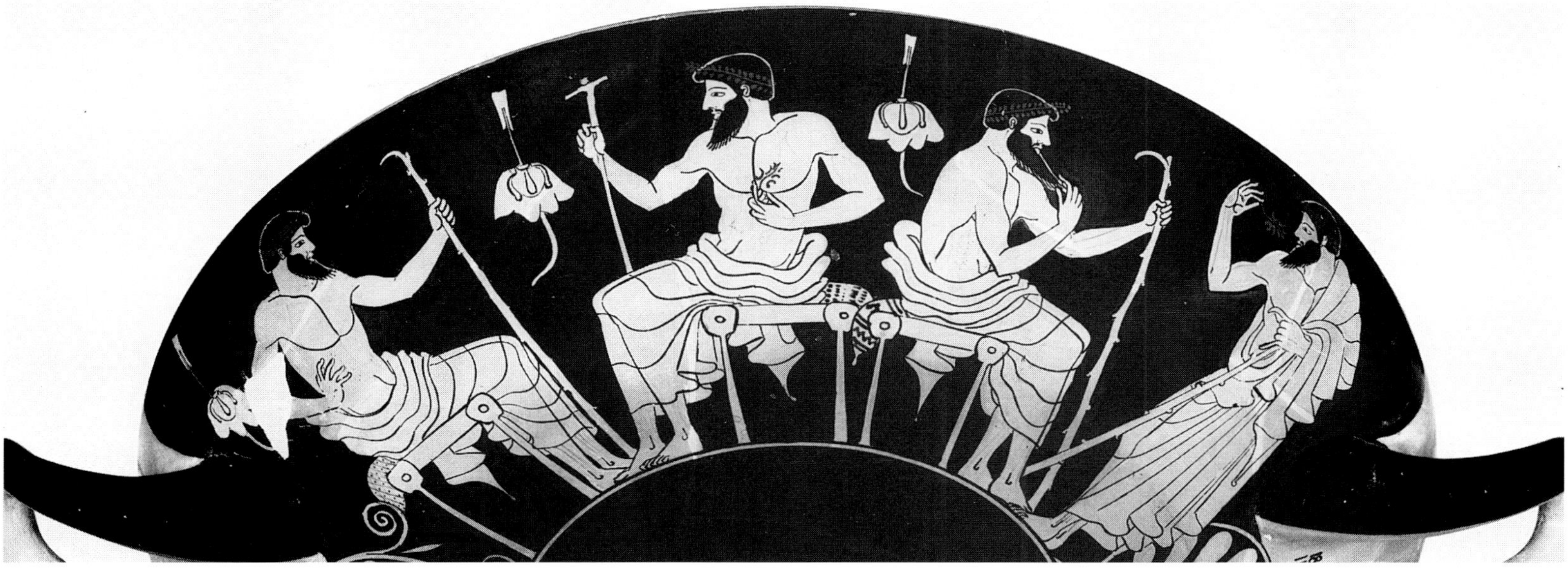

(b) 38

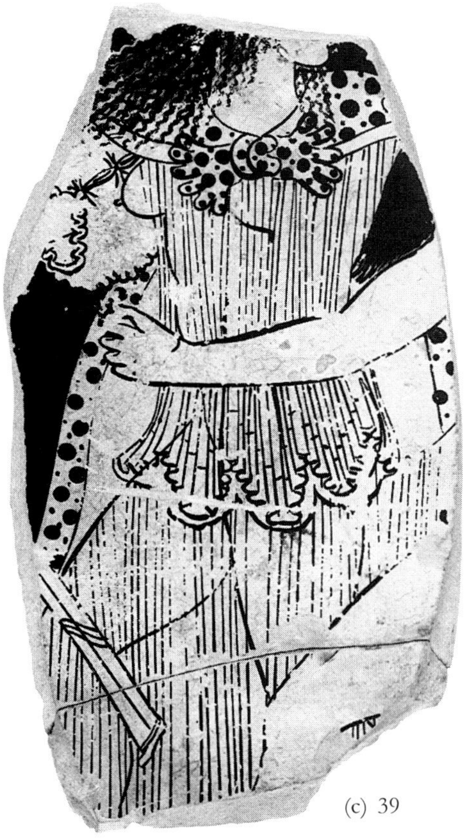

(c) 39

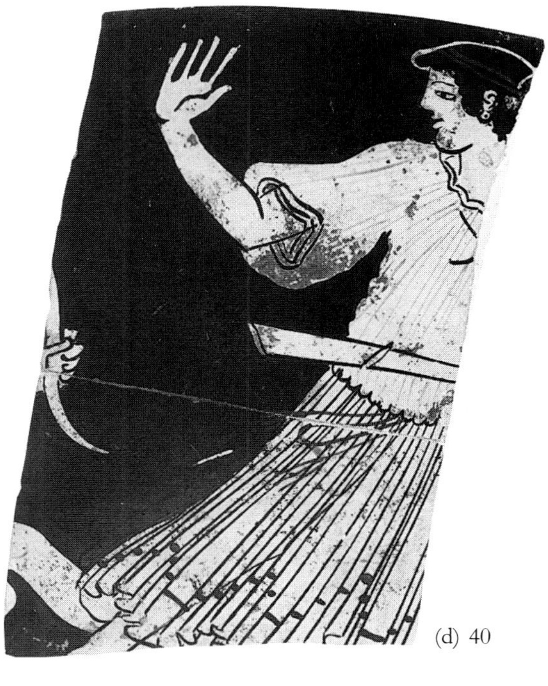

(d) 40

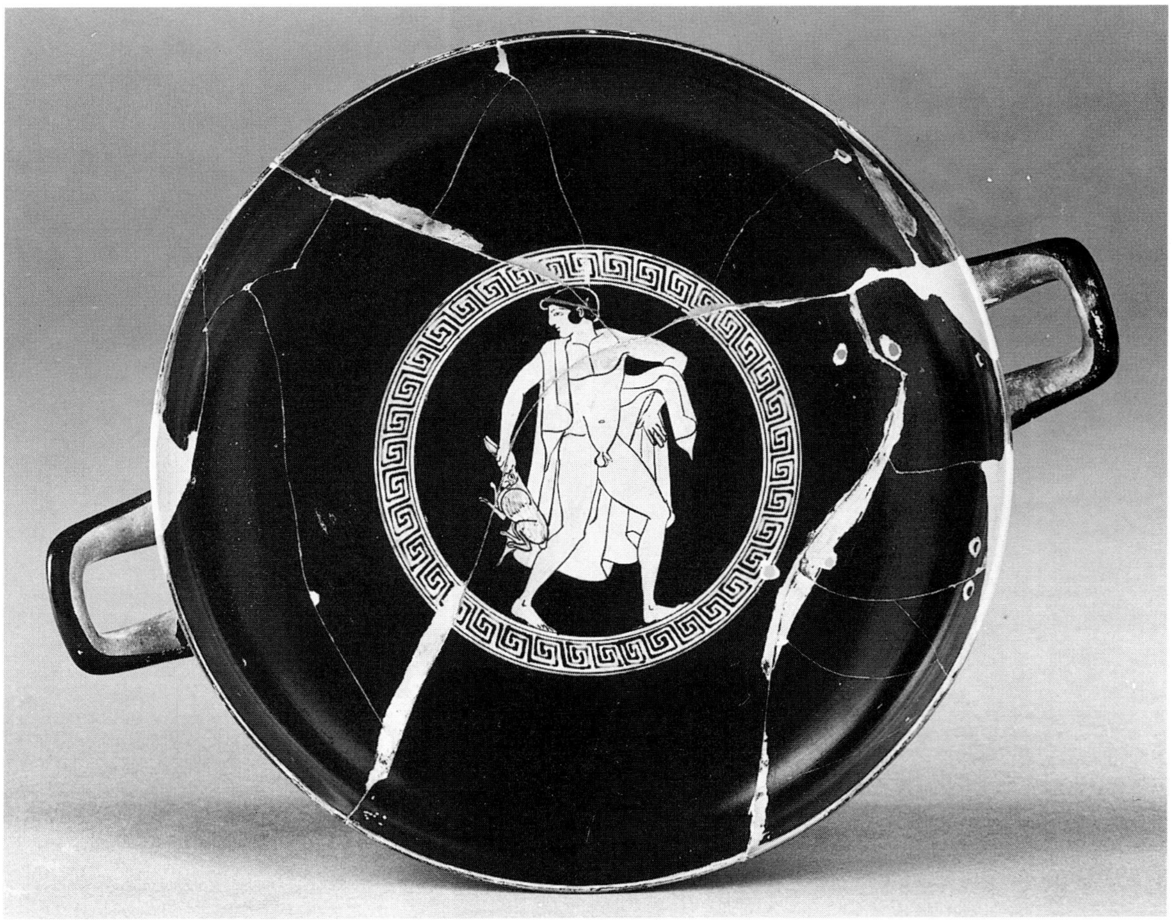

(a) 41

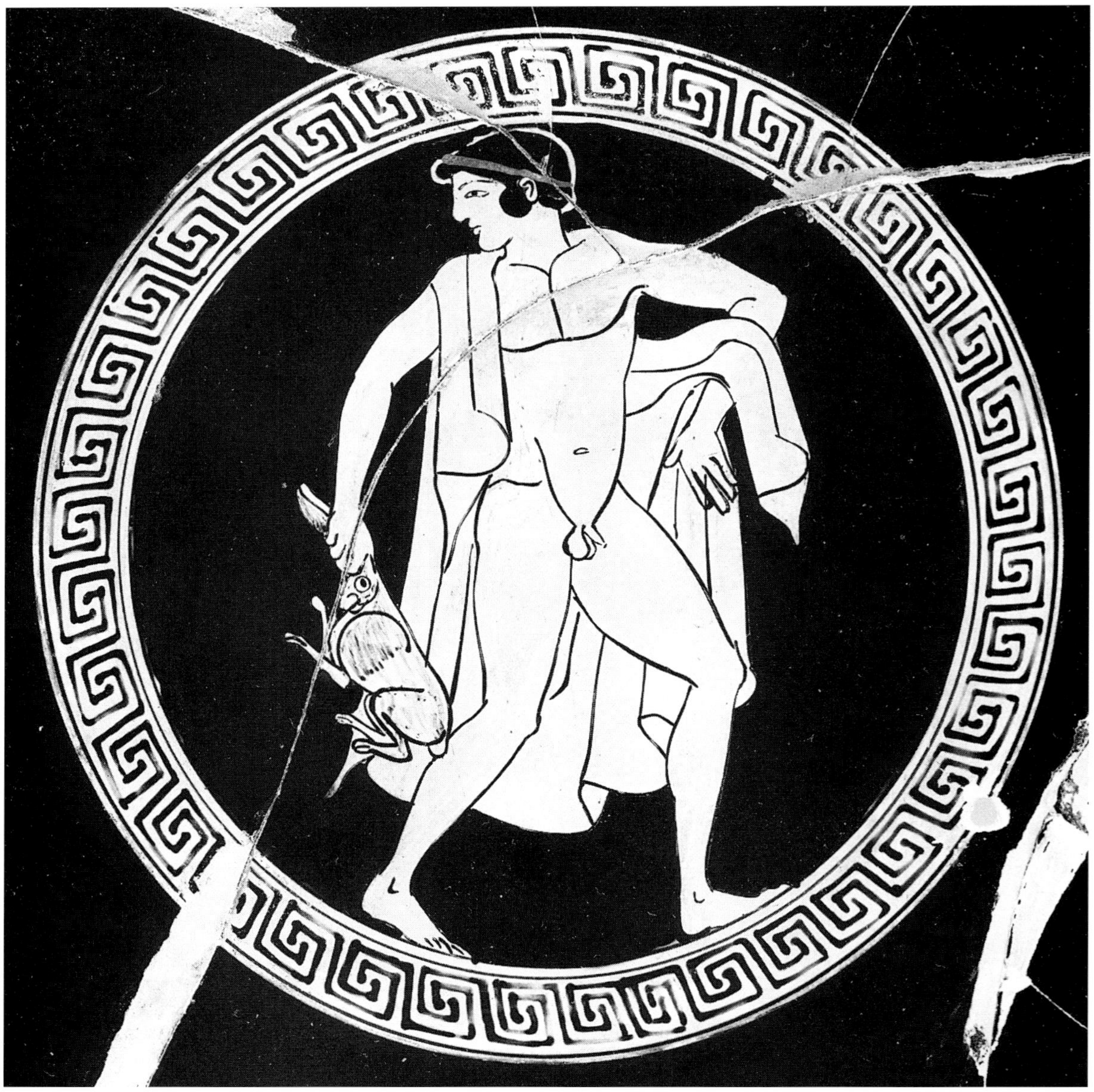

(b) 41

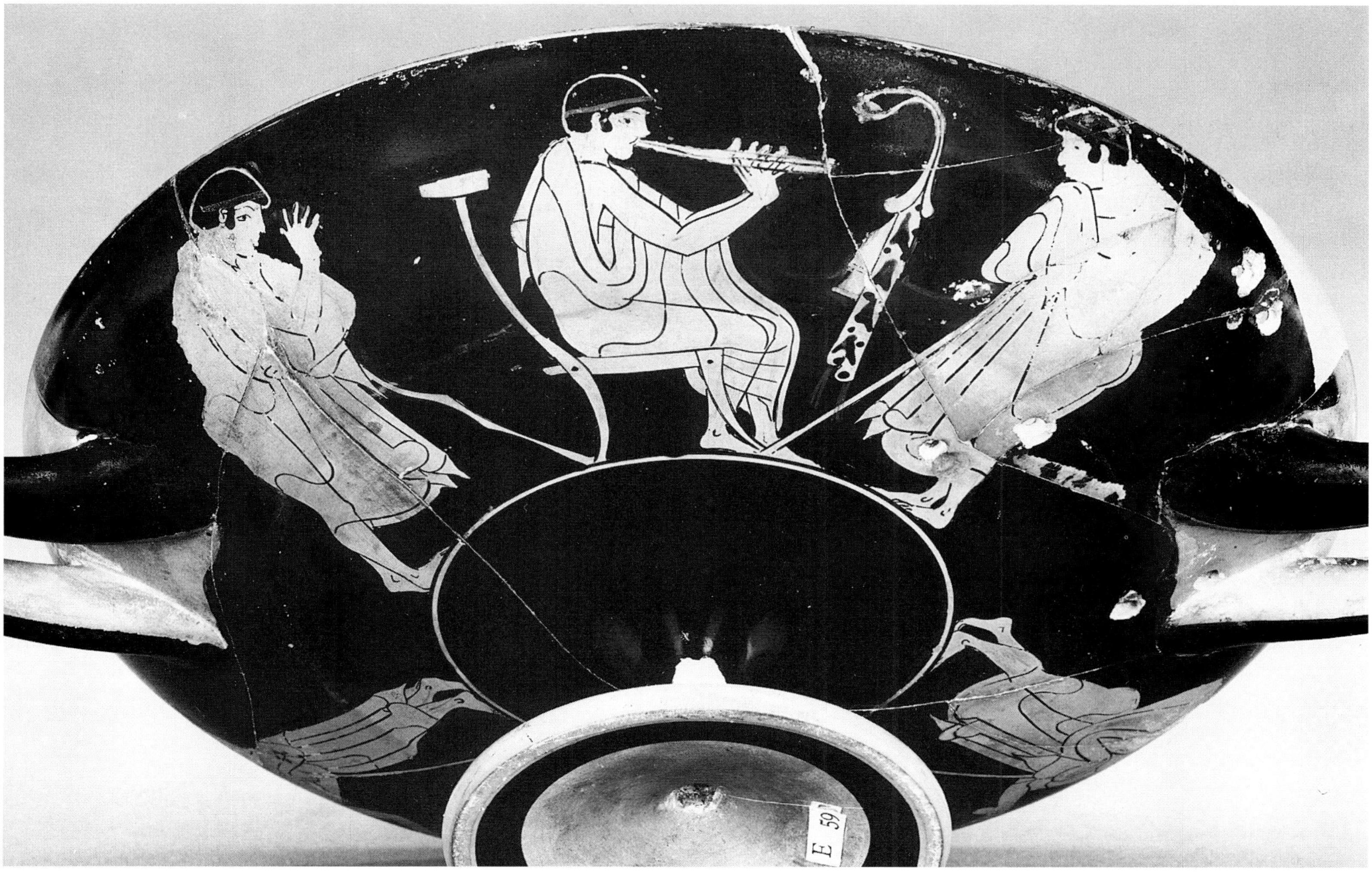

(a) 41

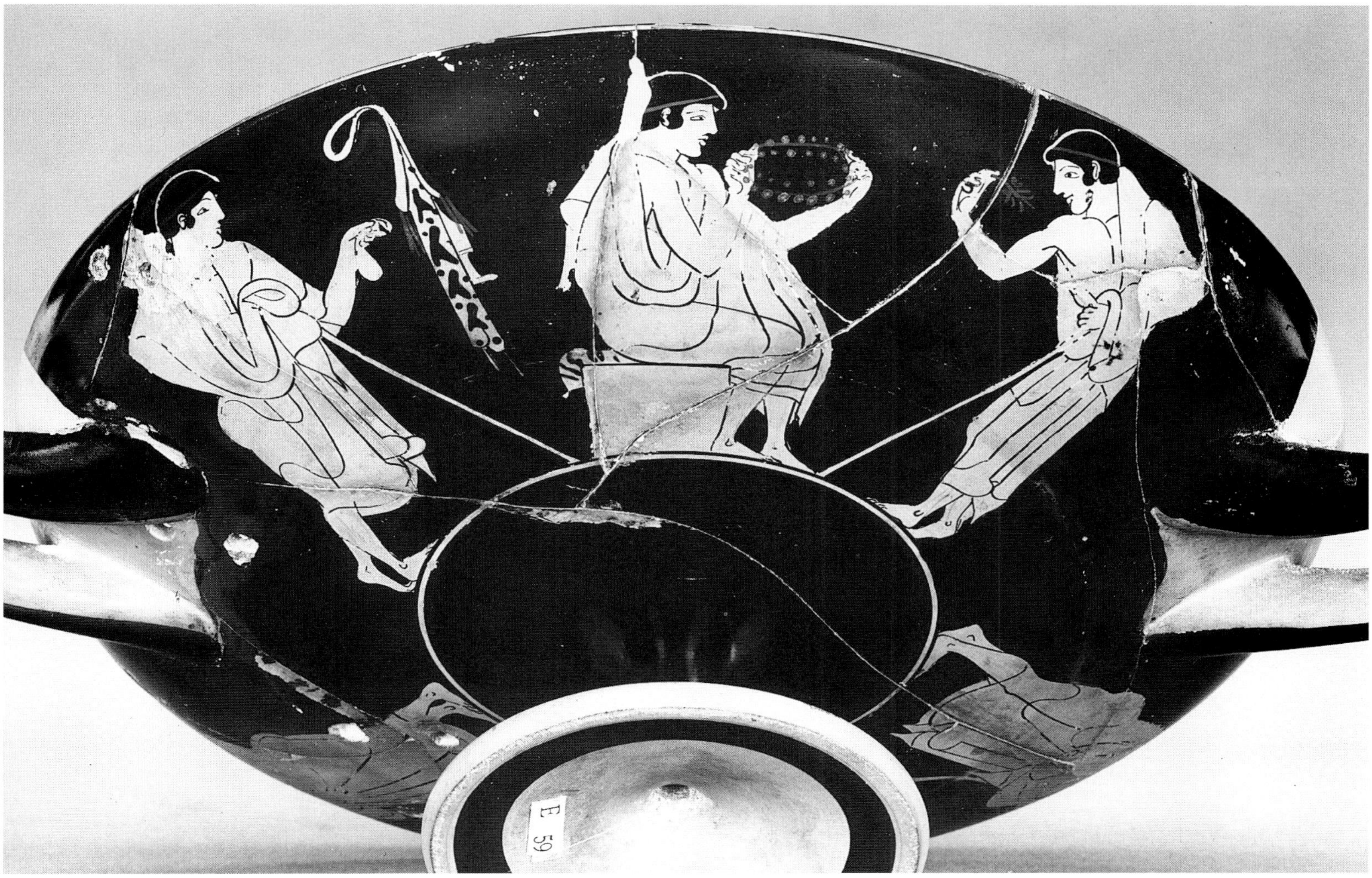

(b) 41

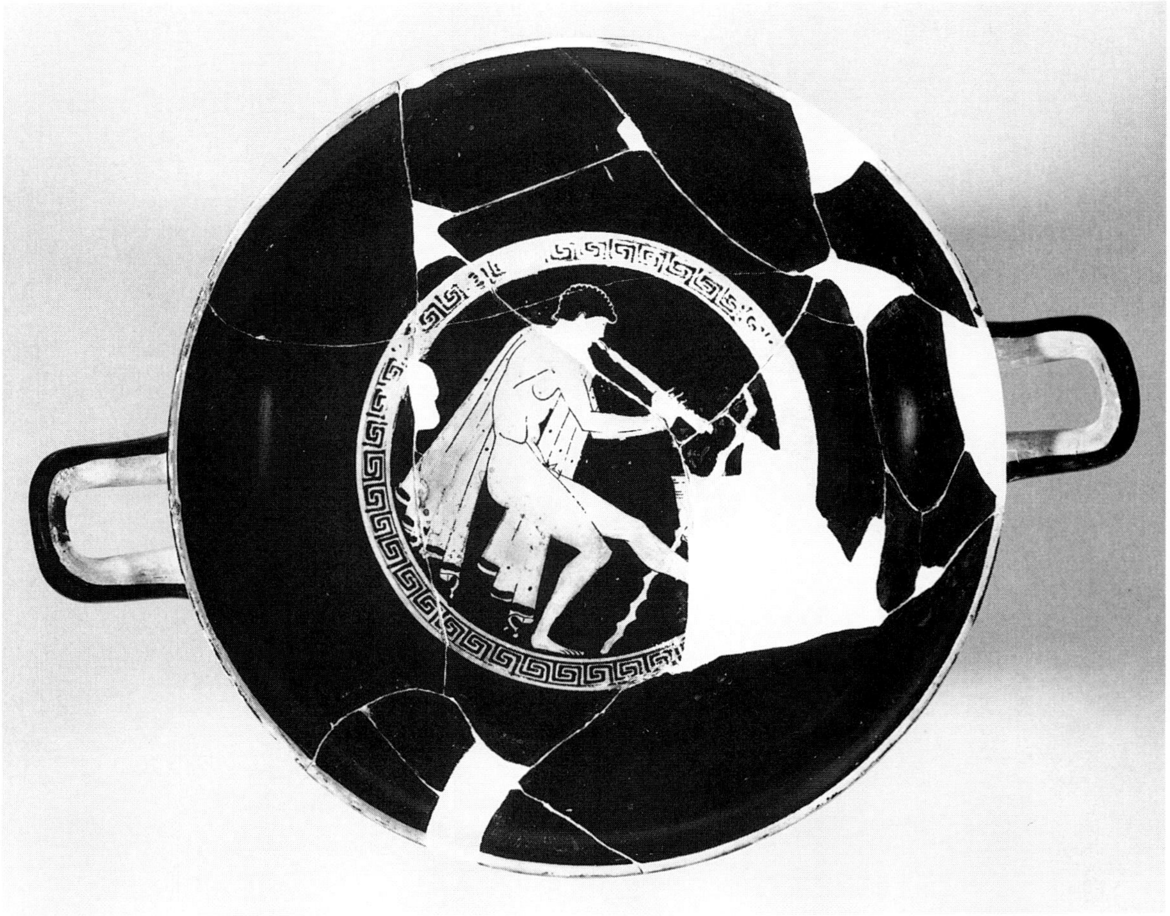

(a) 42

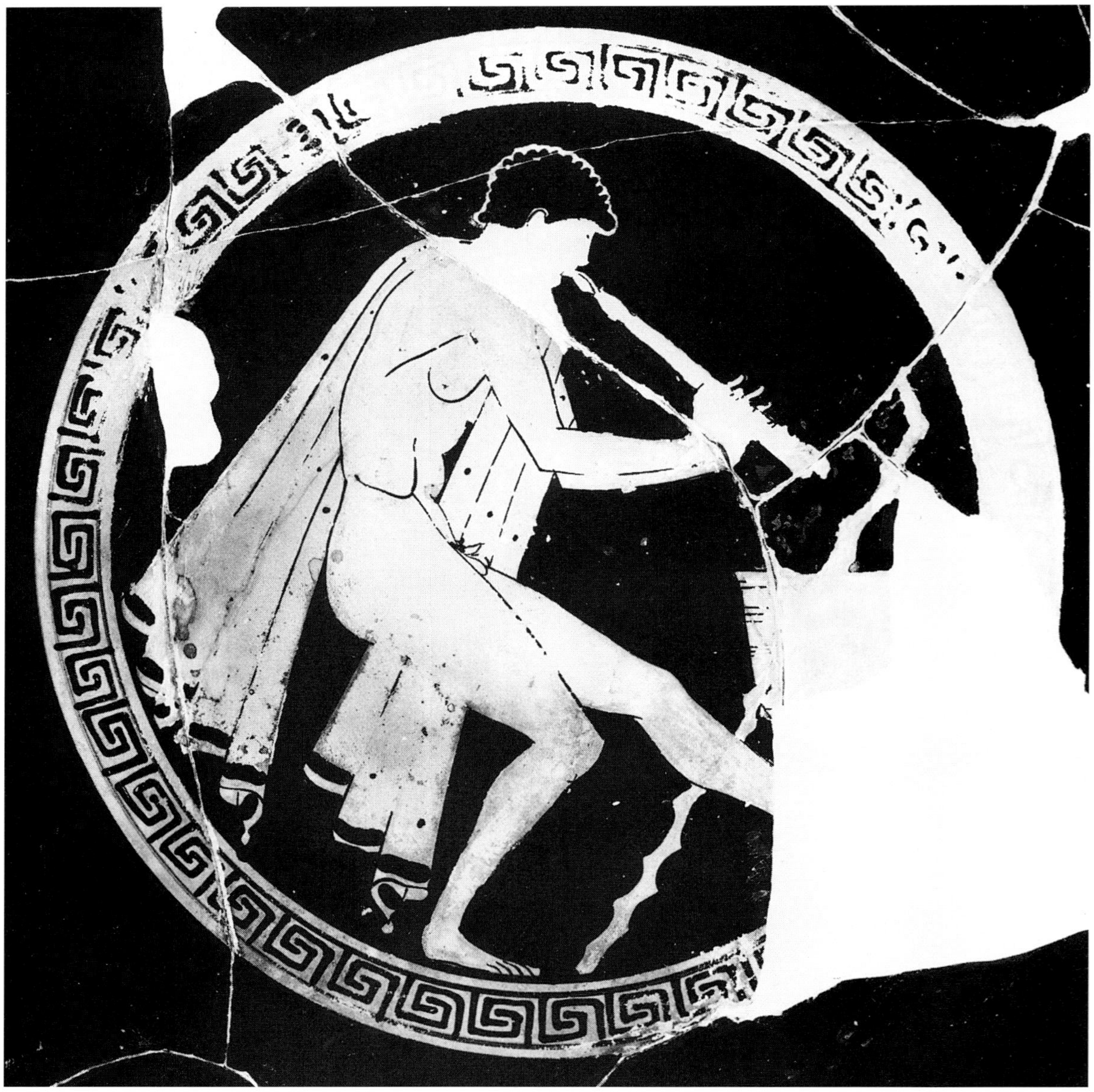

(b) 42

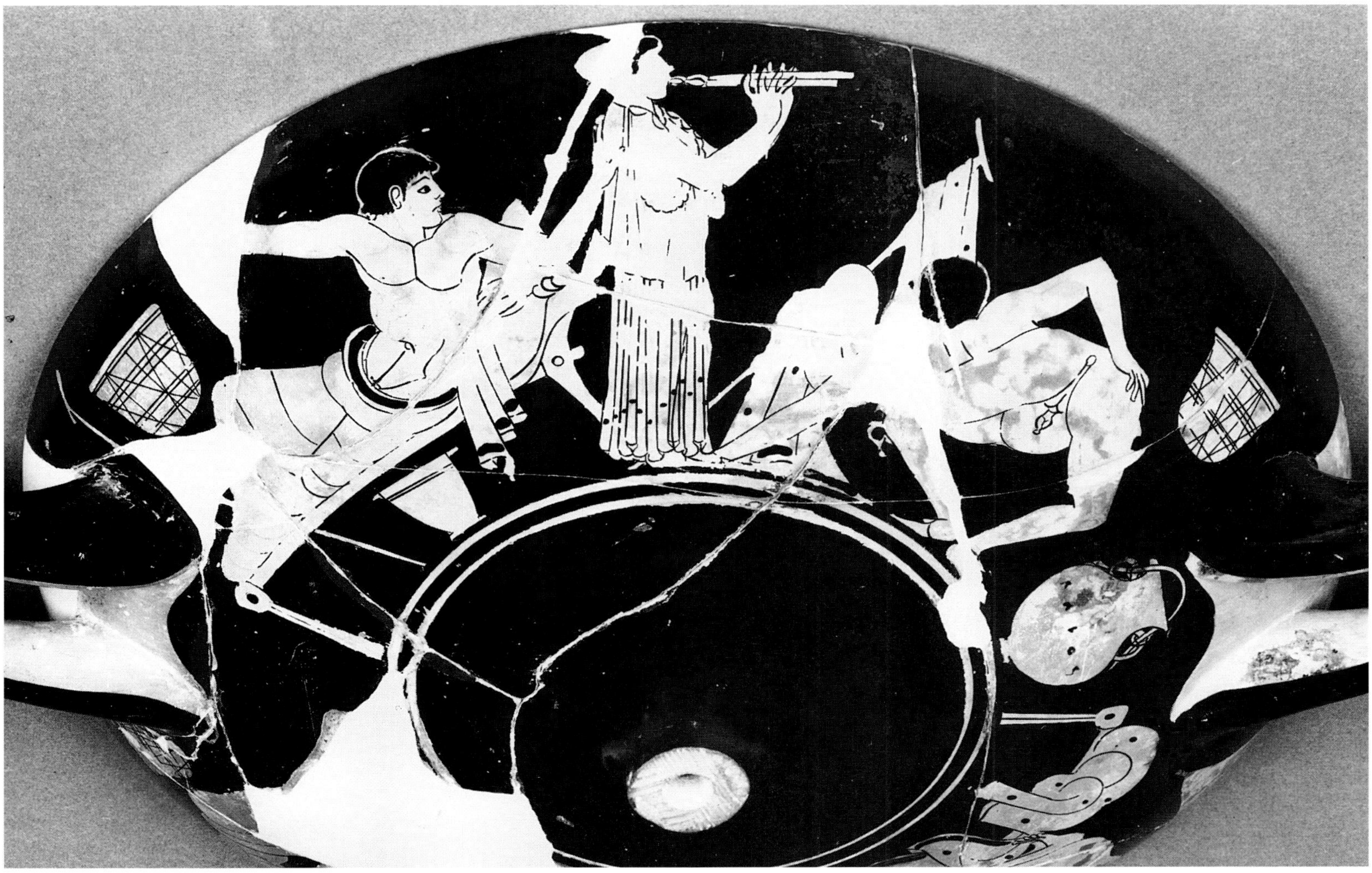

(a) 42

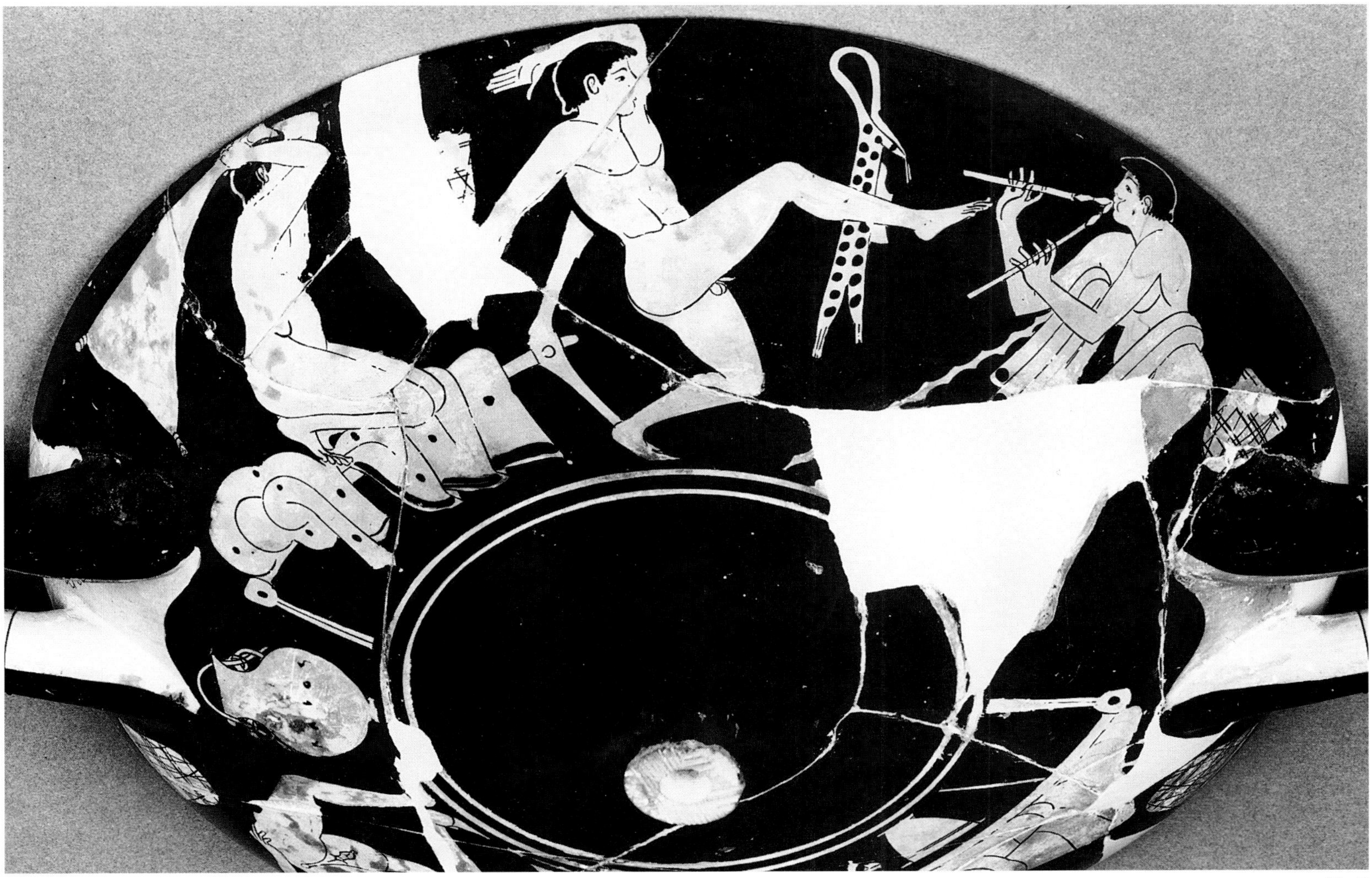

(b) 42

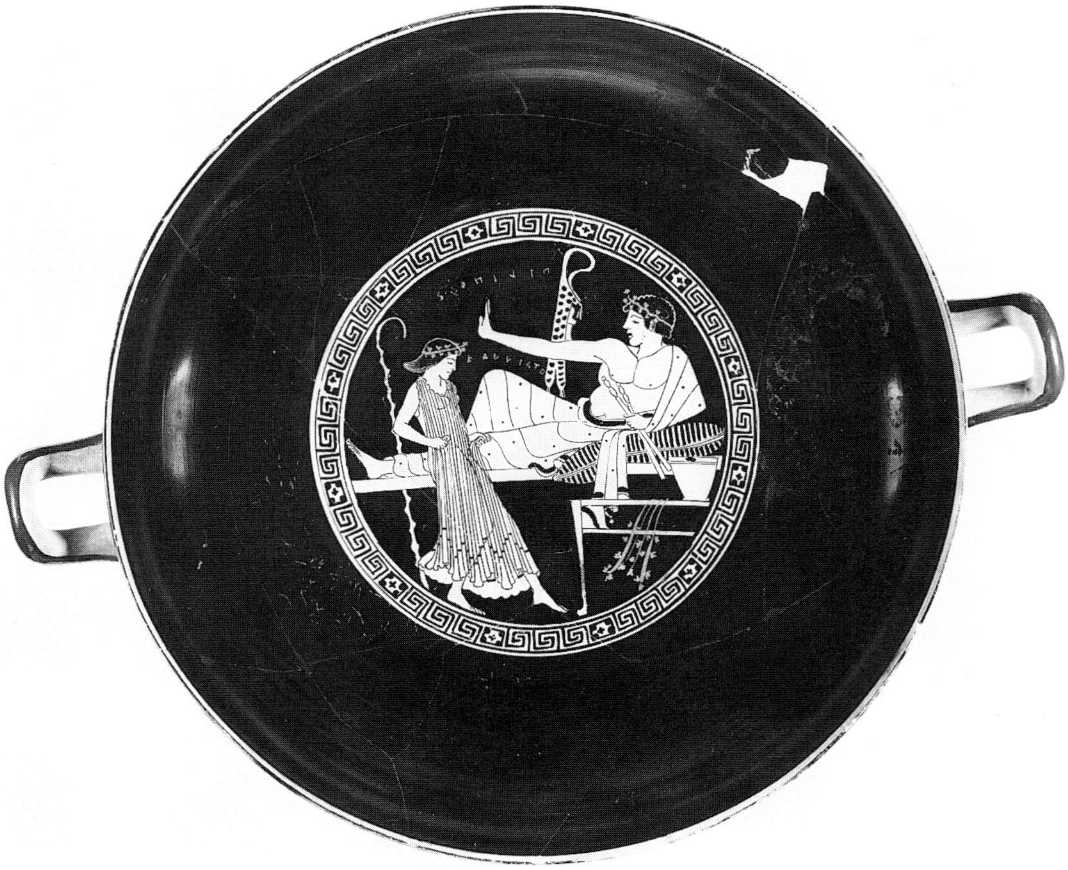

(a) 43

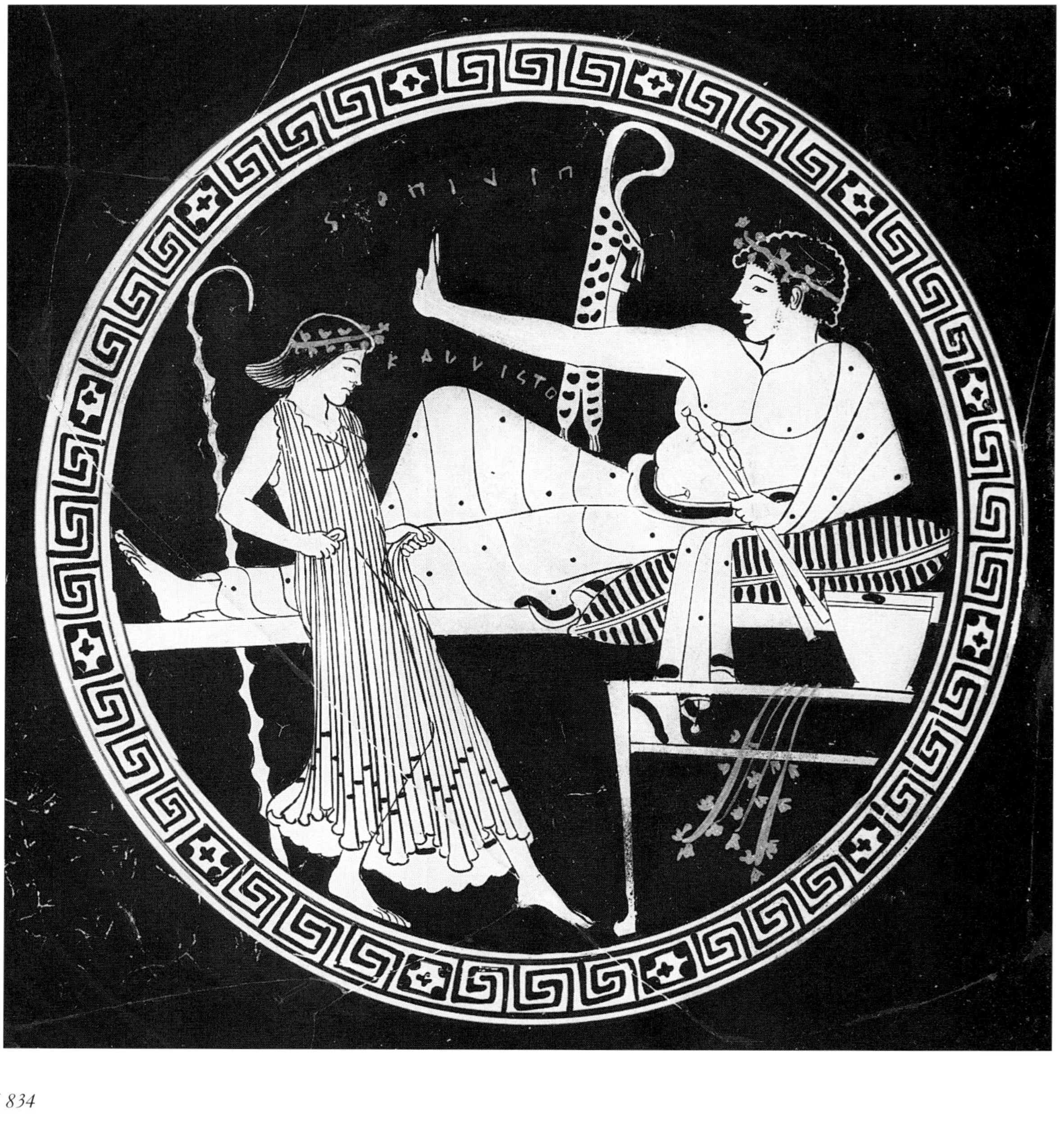

(b) 43

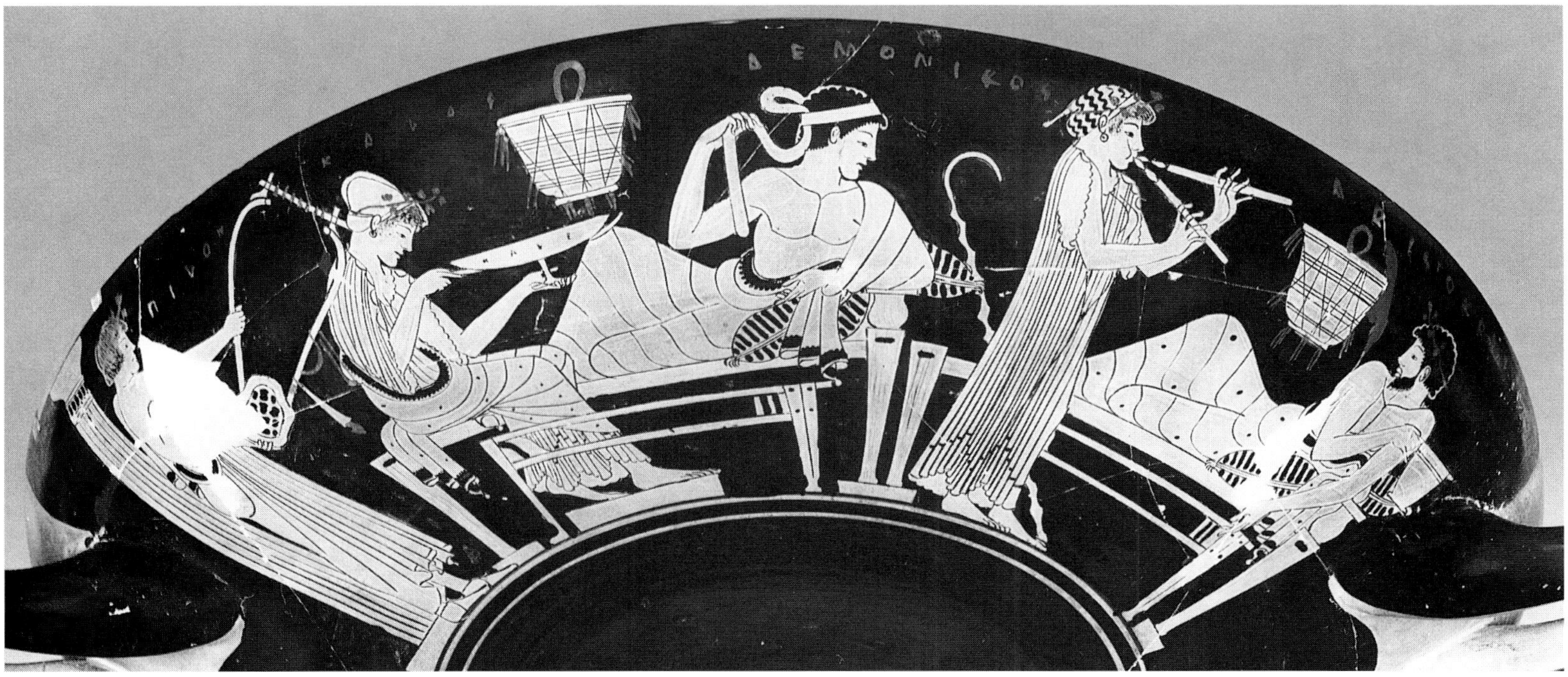

(a) 43

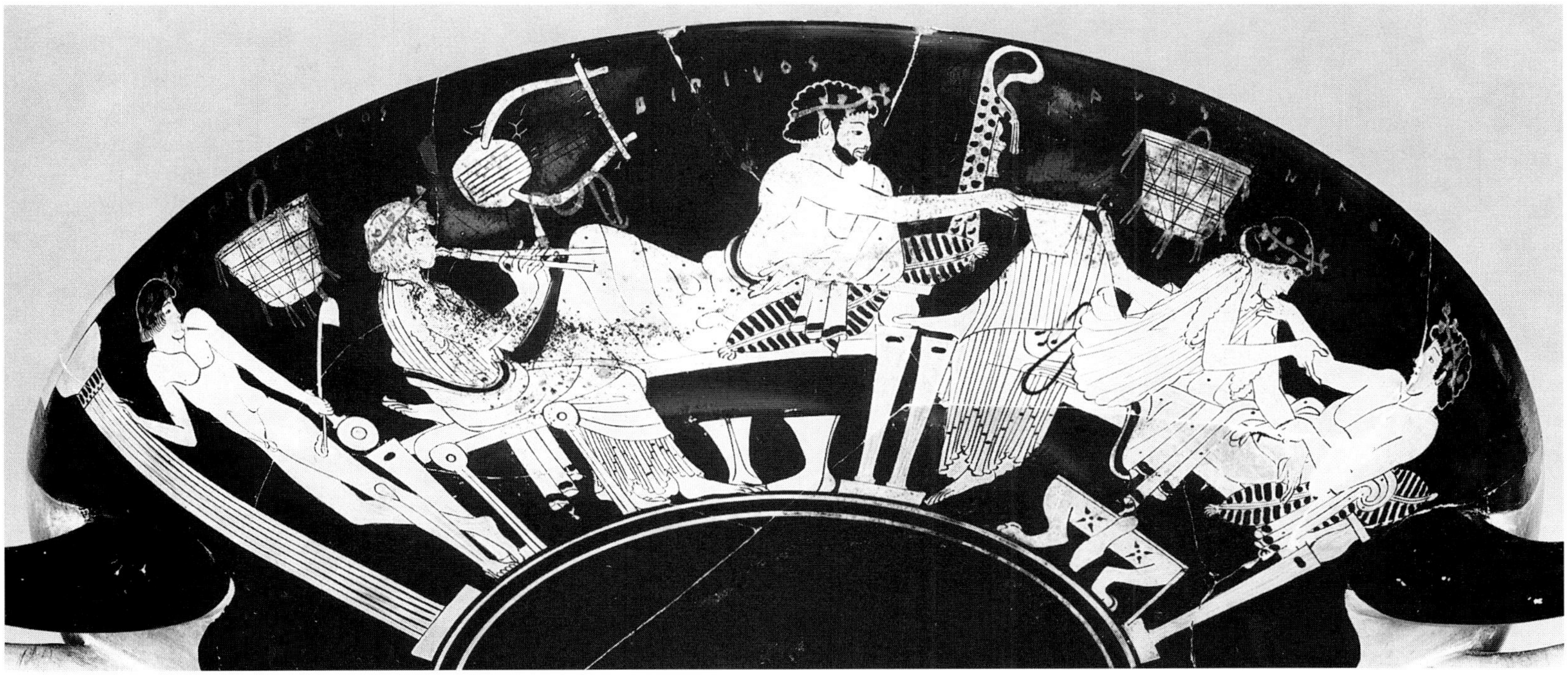

(b) 43

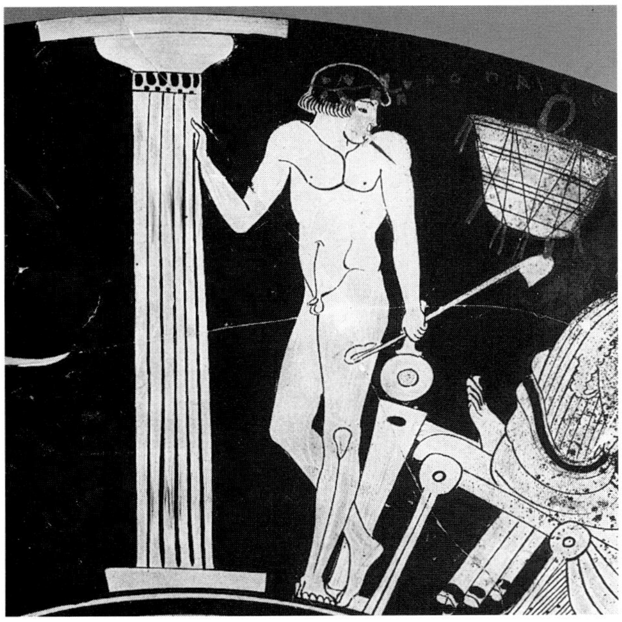

(d) 43

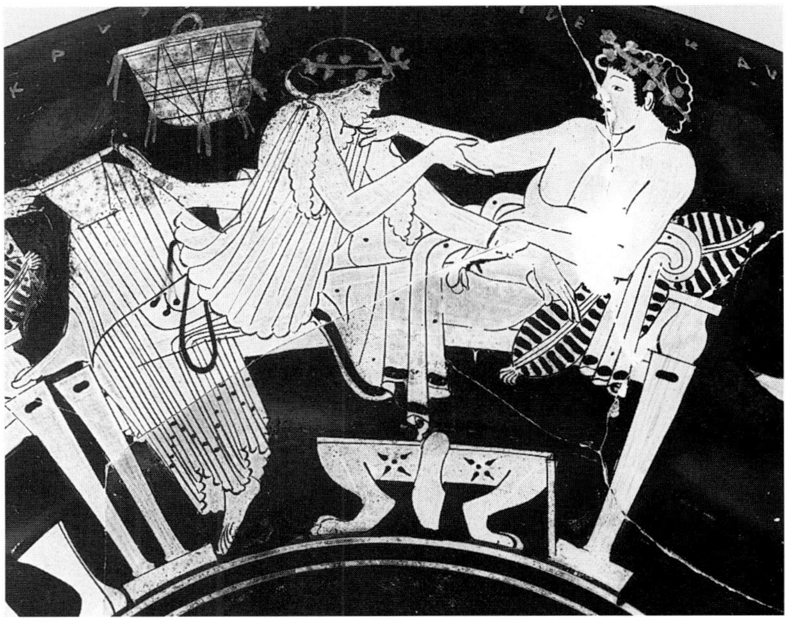

(c) 43

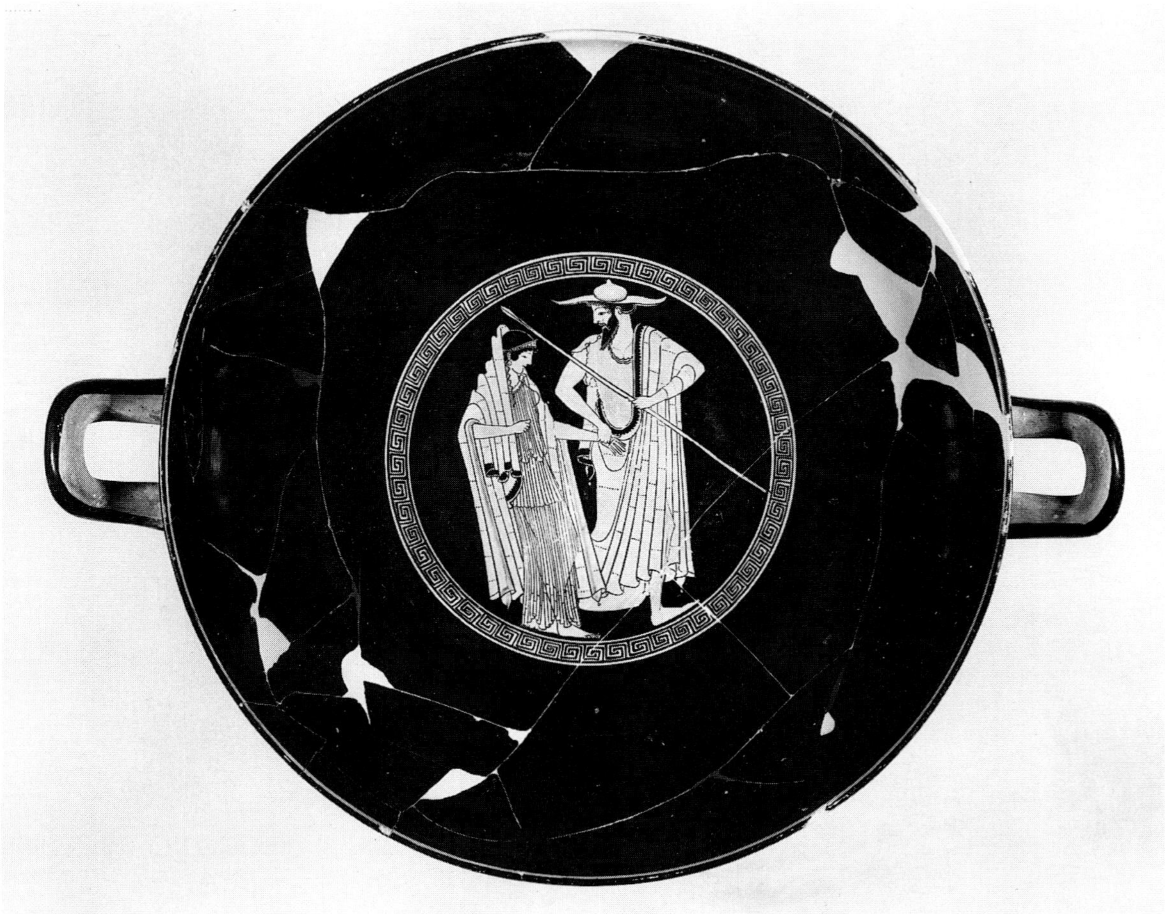

(a) 44

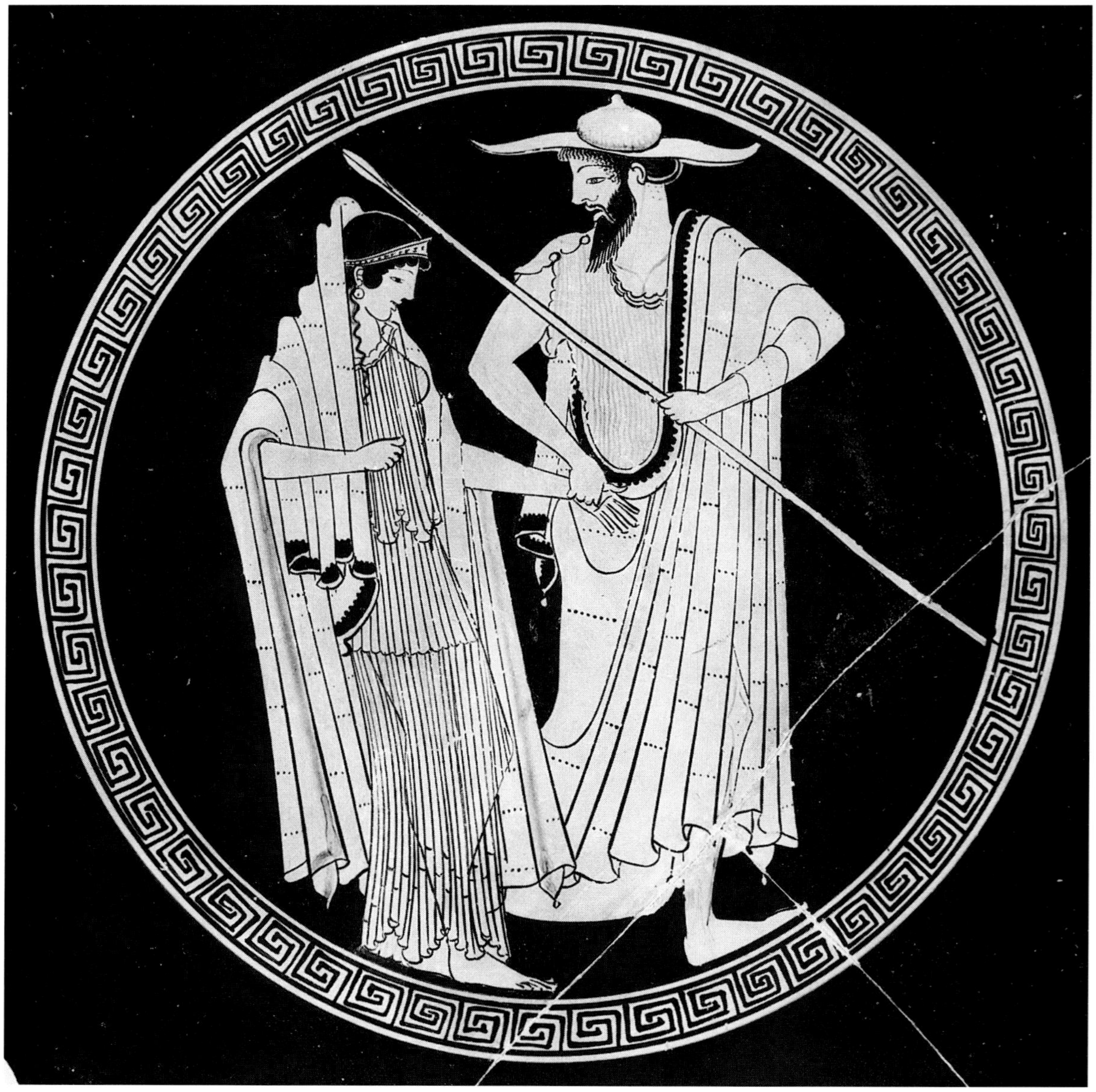

(b) 44

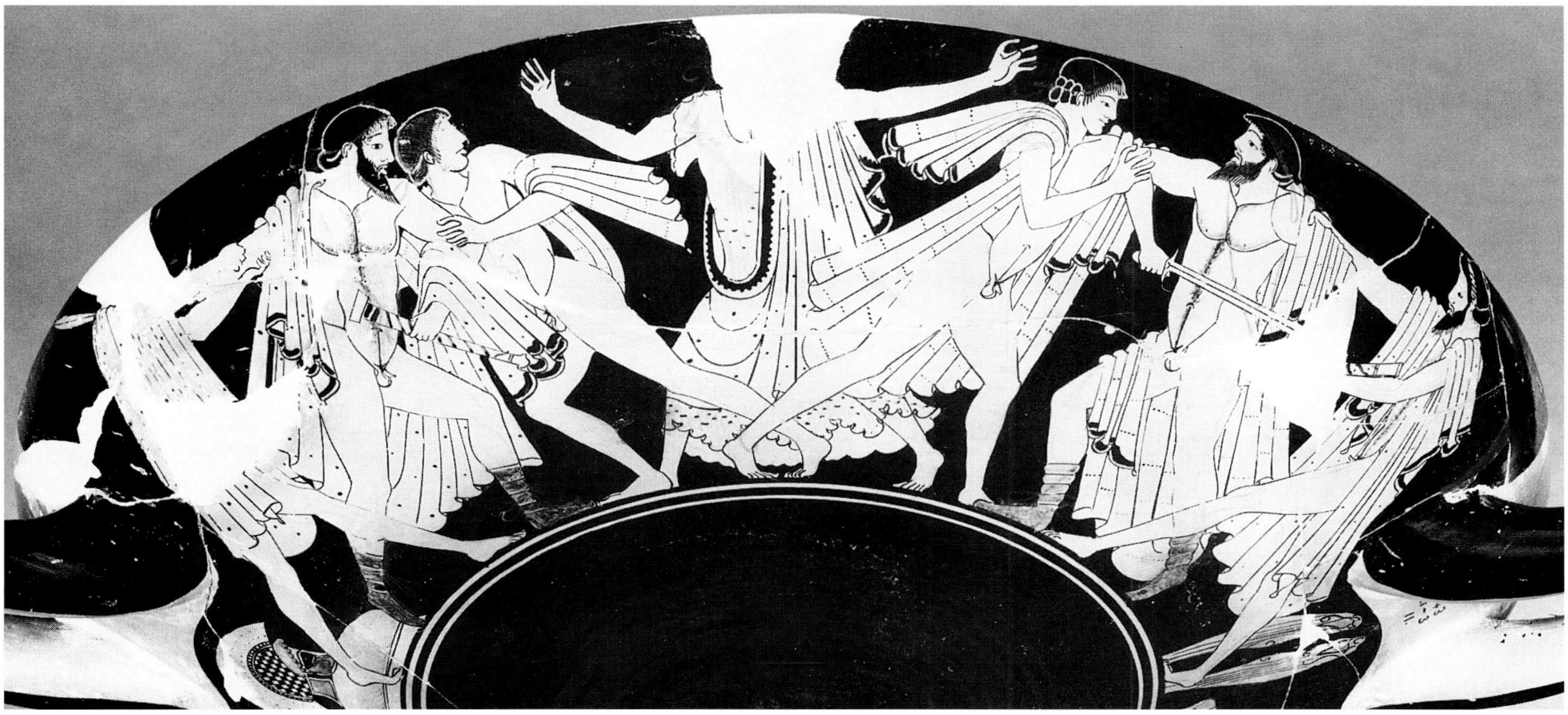

(a) 44

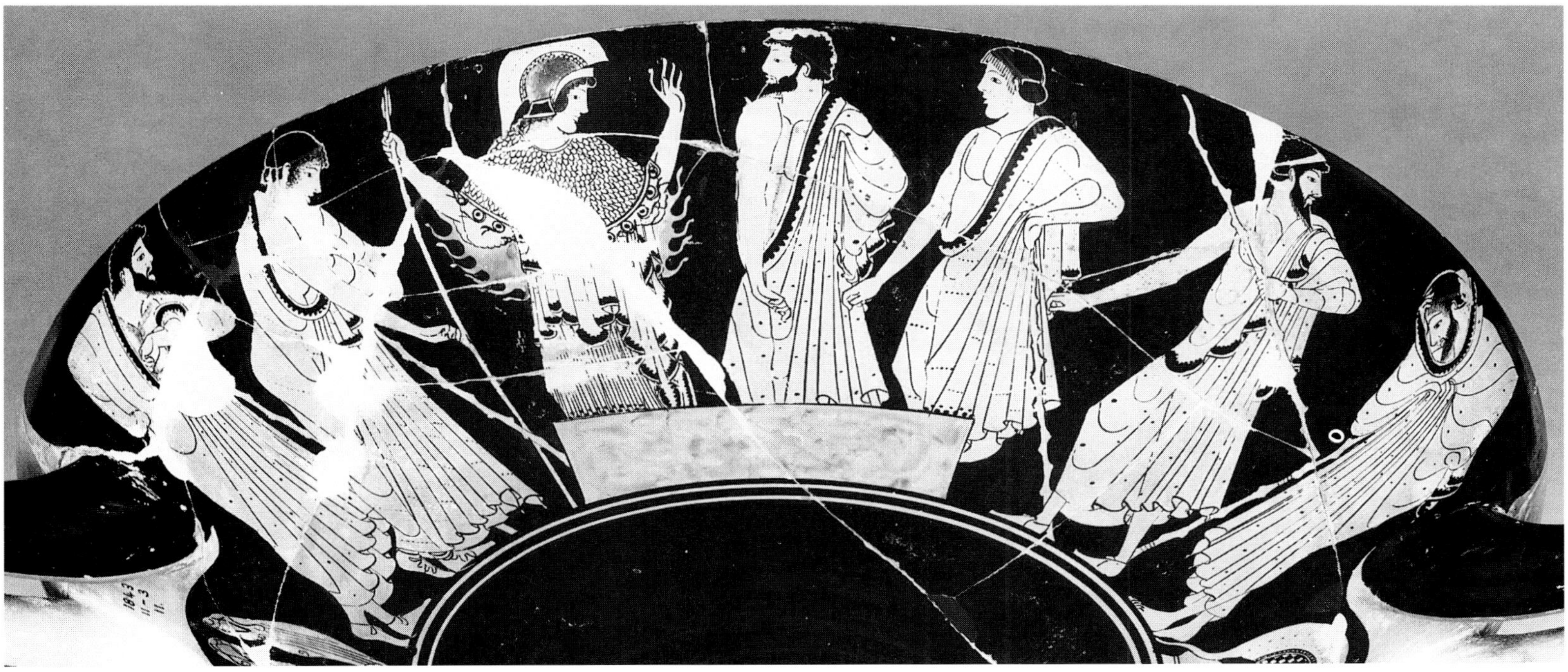

(b) 44

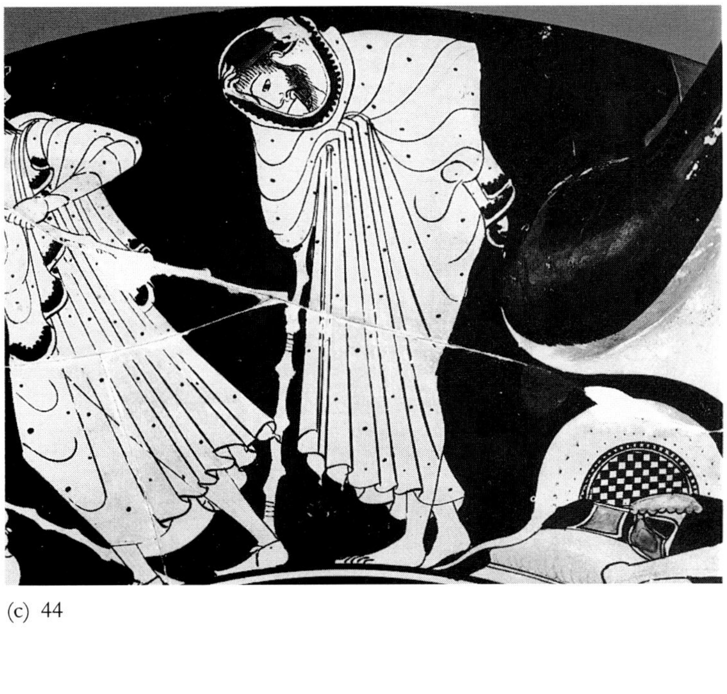

(c) 44

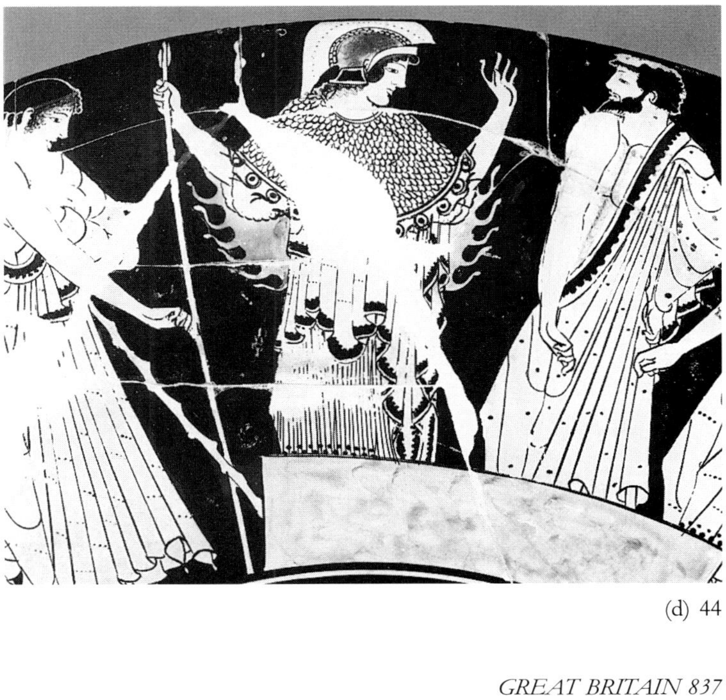

(d) 44

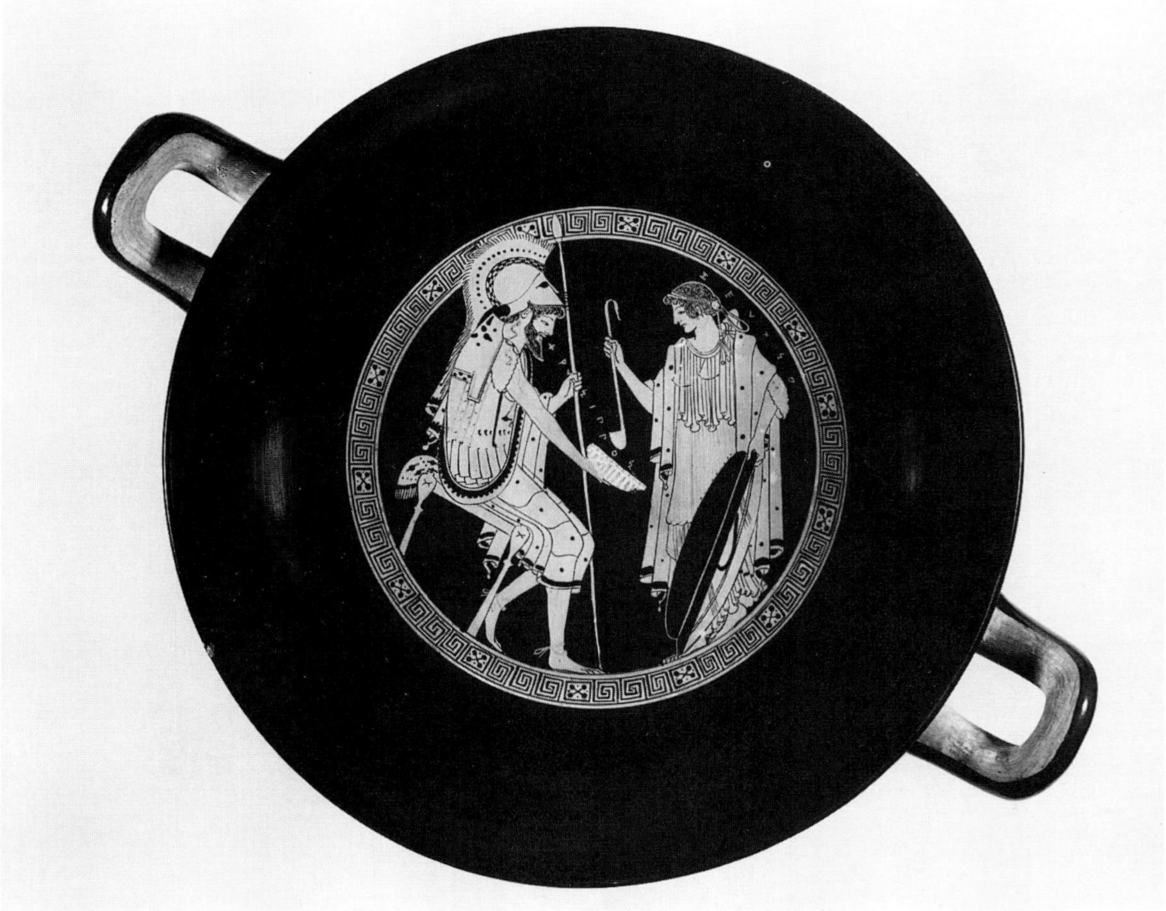

(a) 45

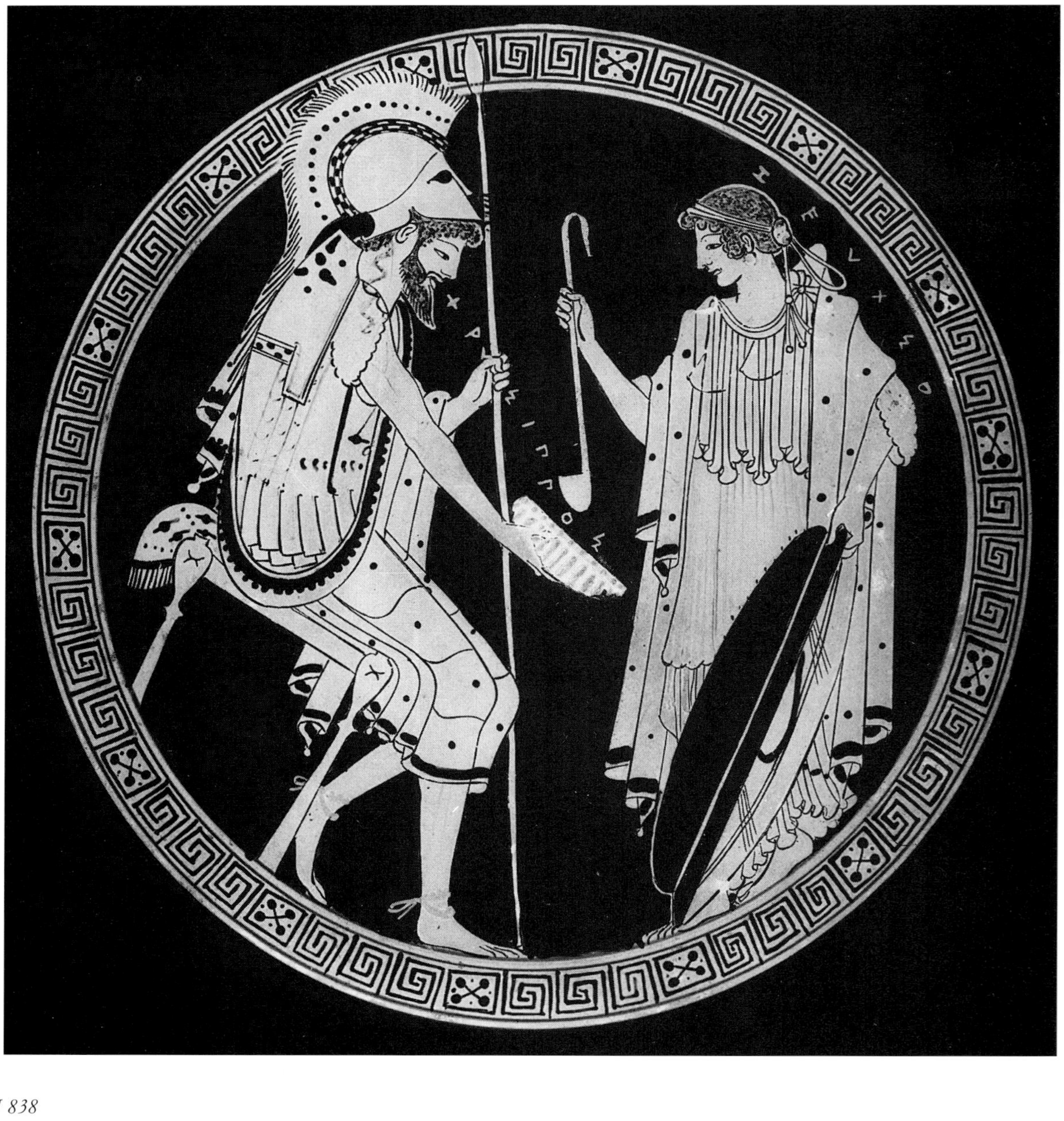

(b) 45

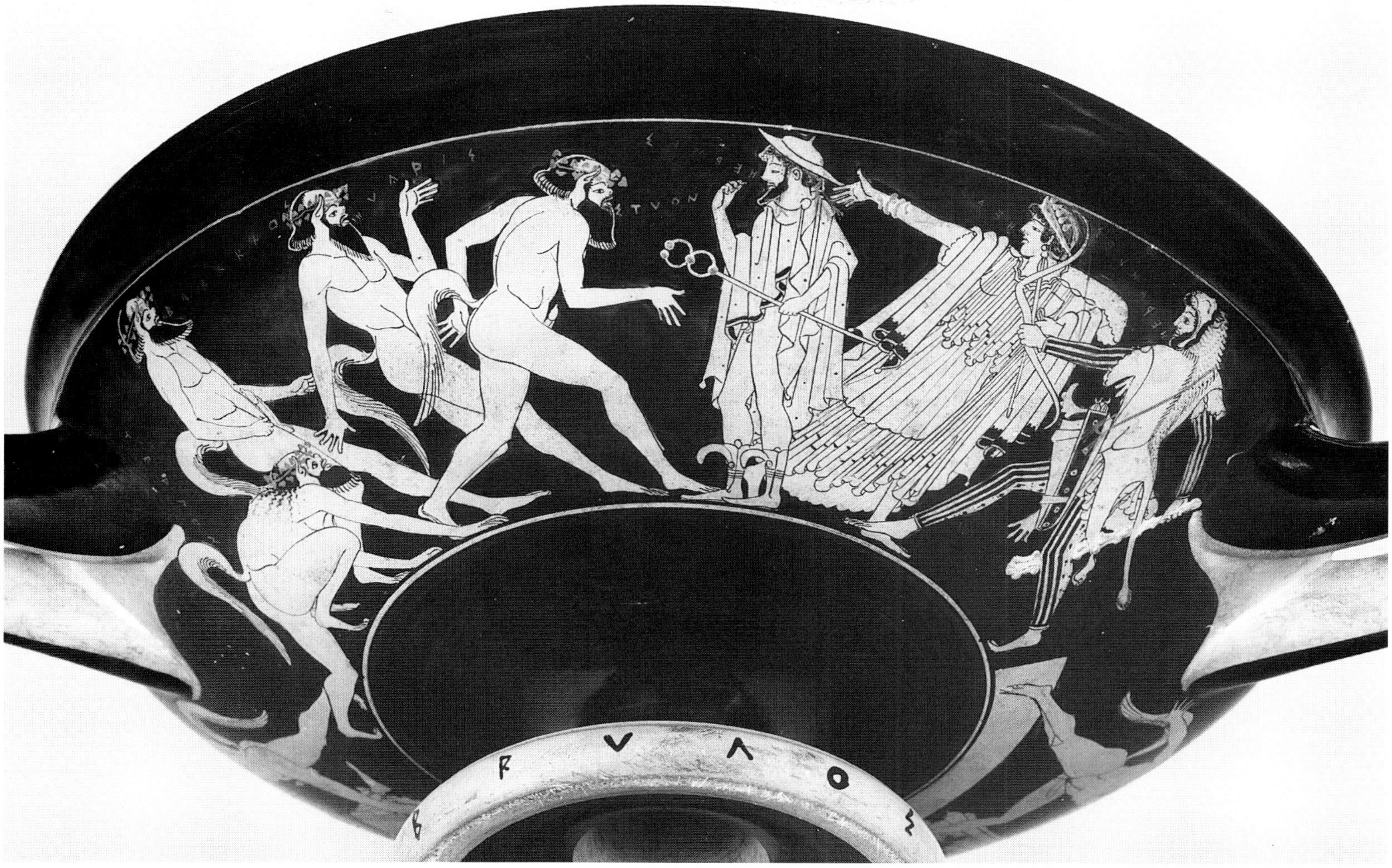

(a) 45

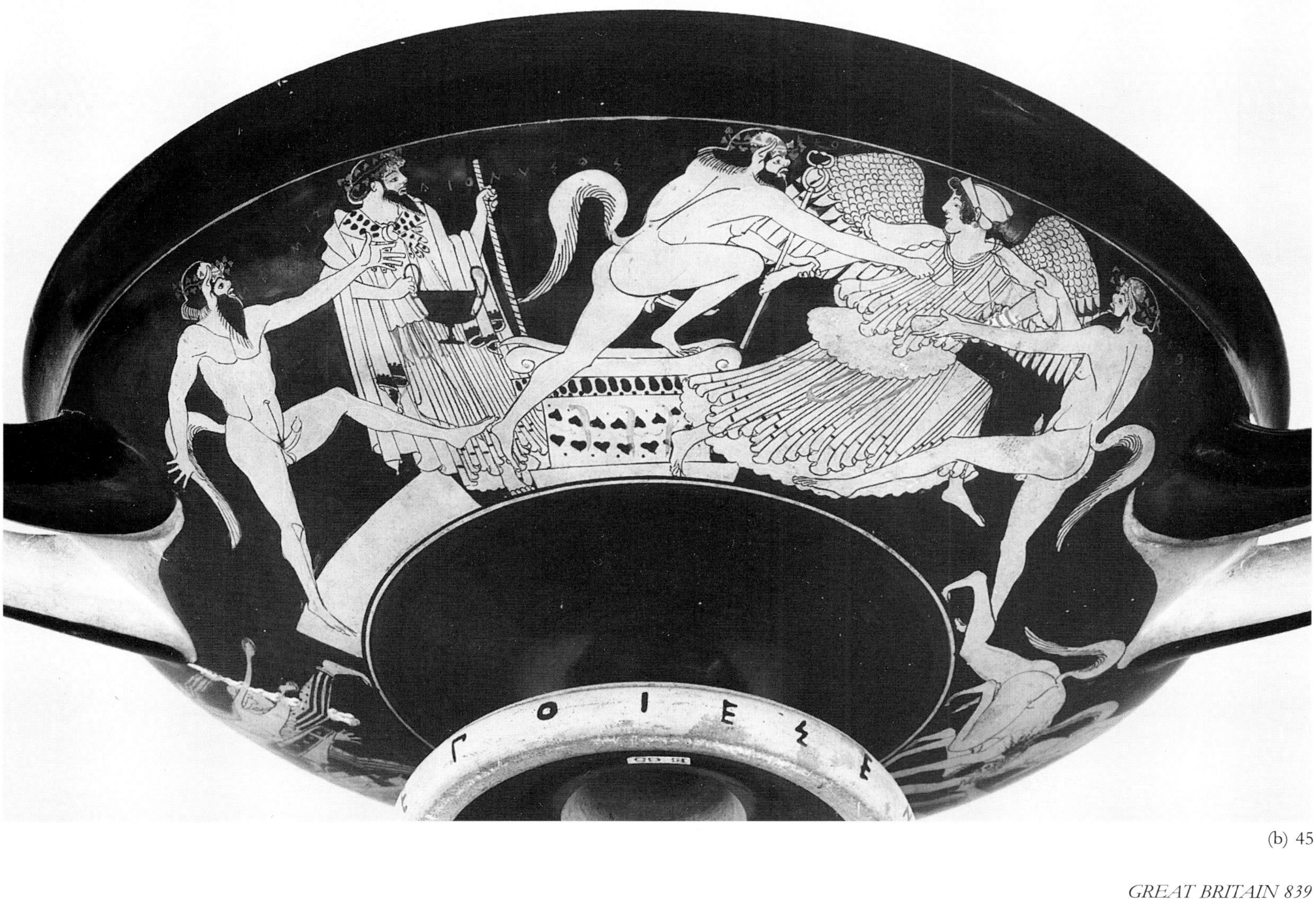

(b) 45

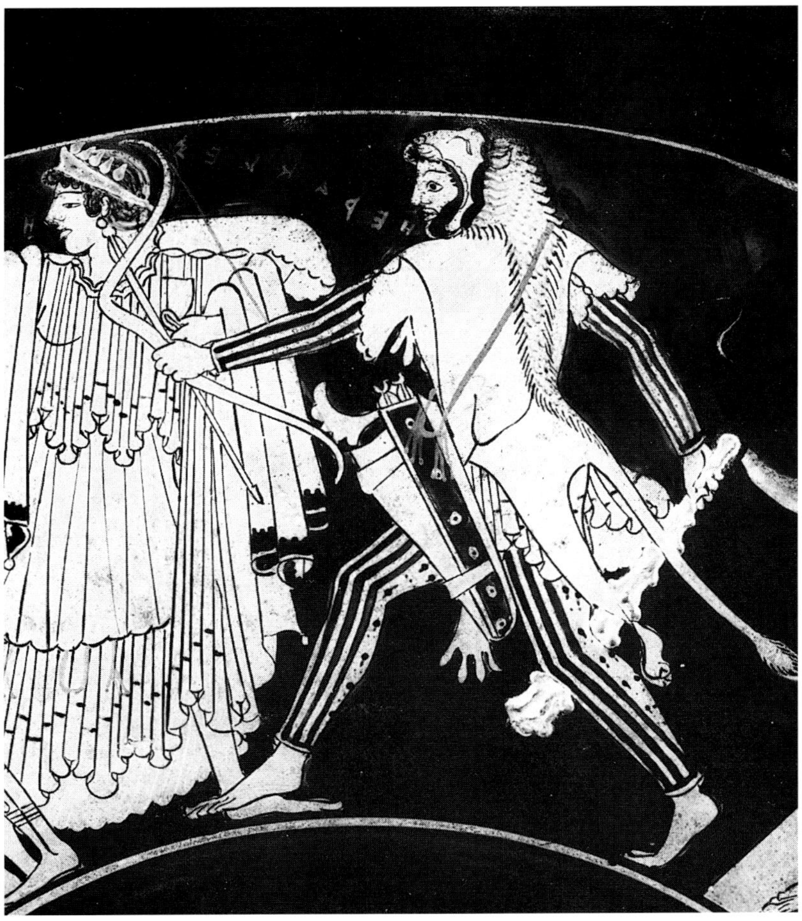

(a) 45

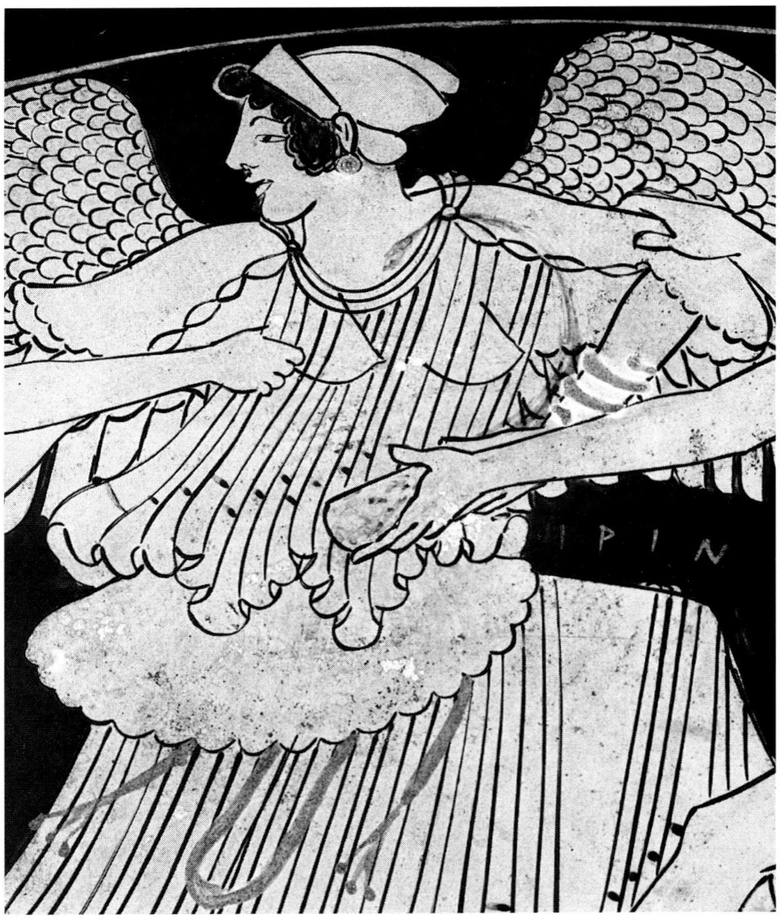

(b) 45

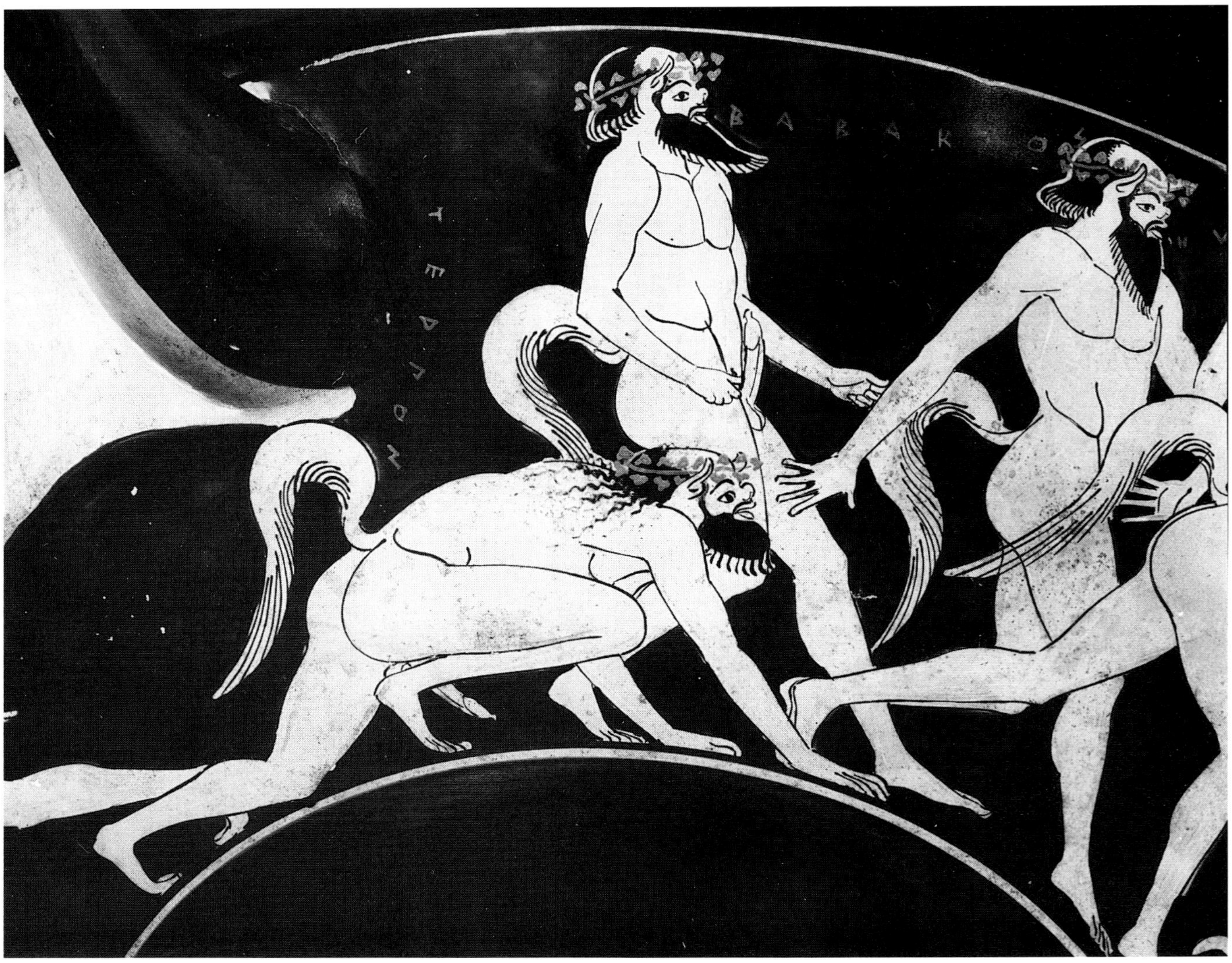

(c) 45

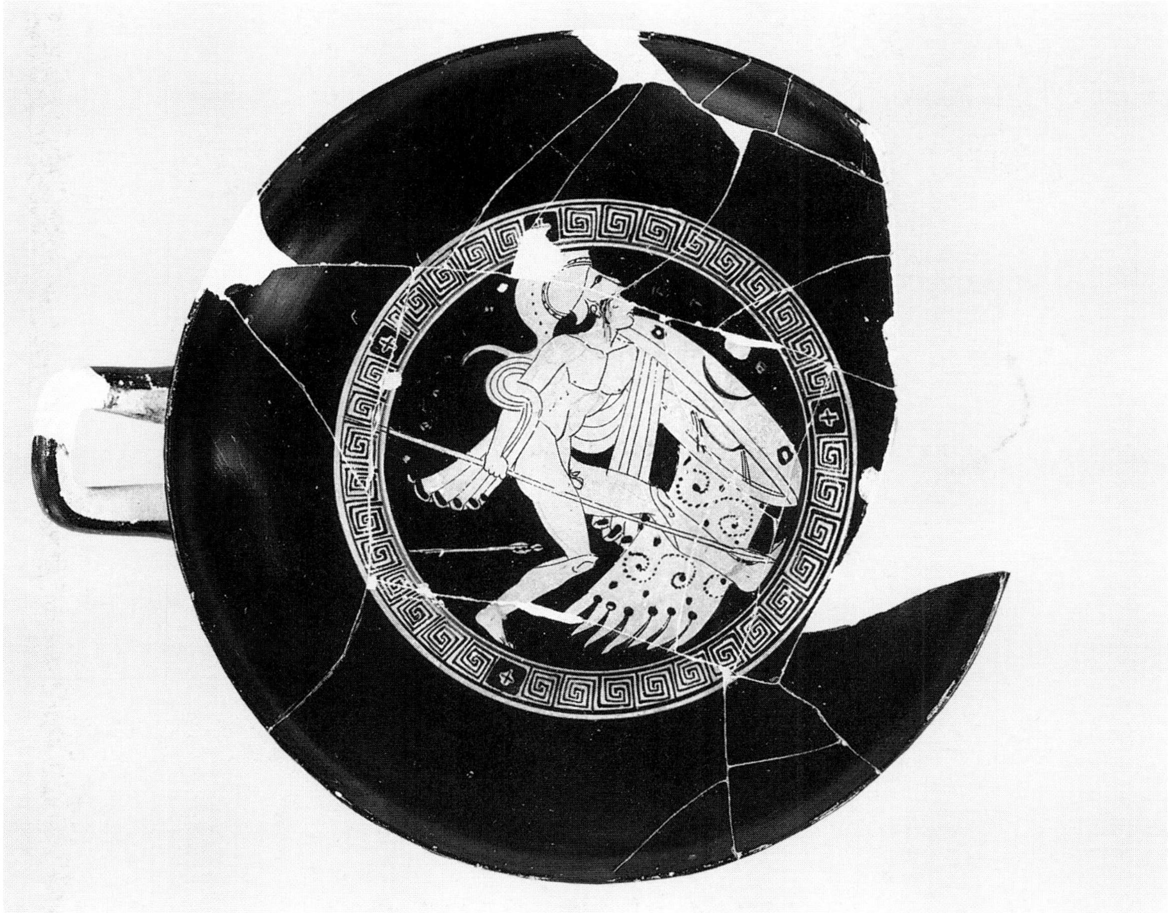

(a) 46

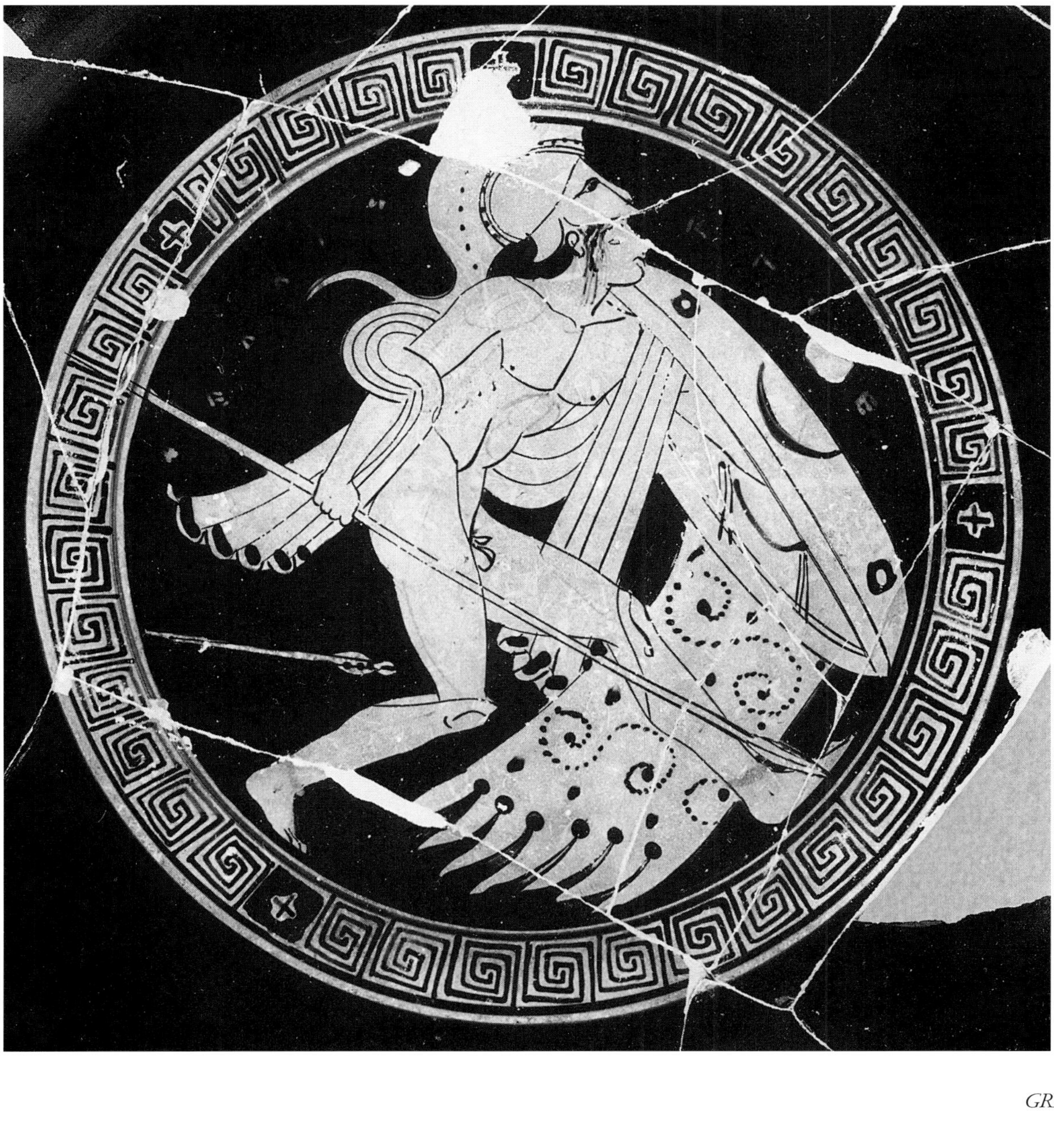

(b) 46

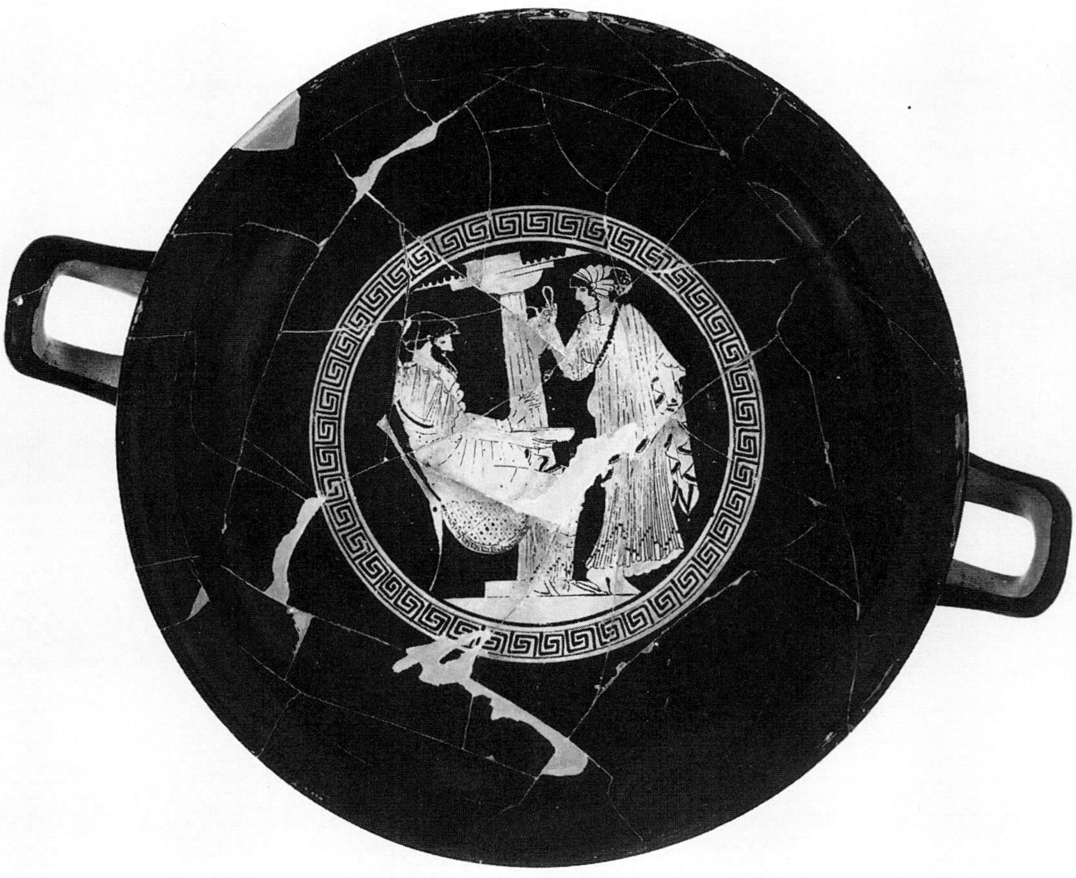

(a) 47

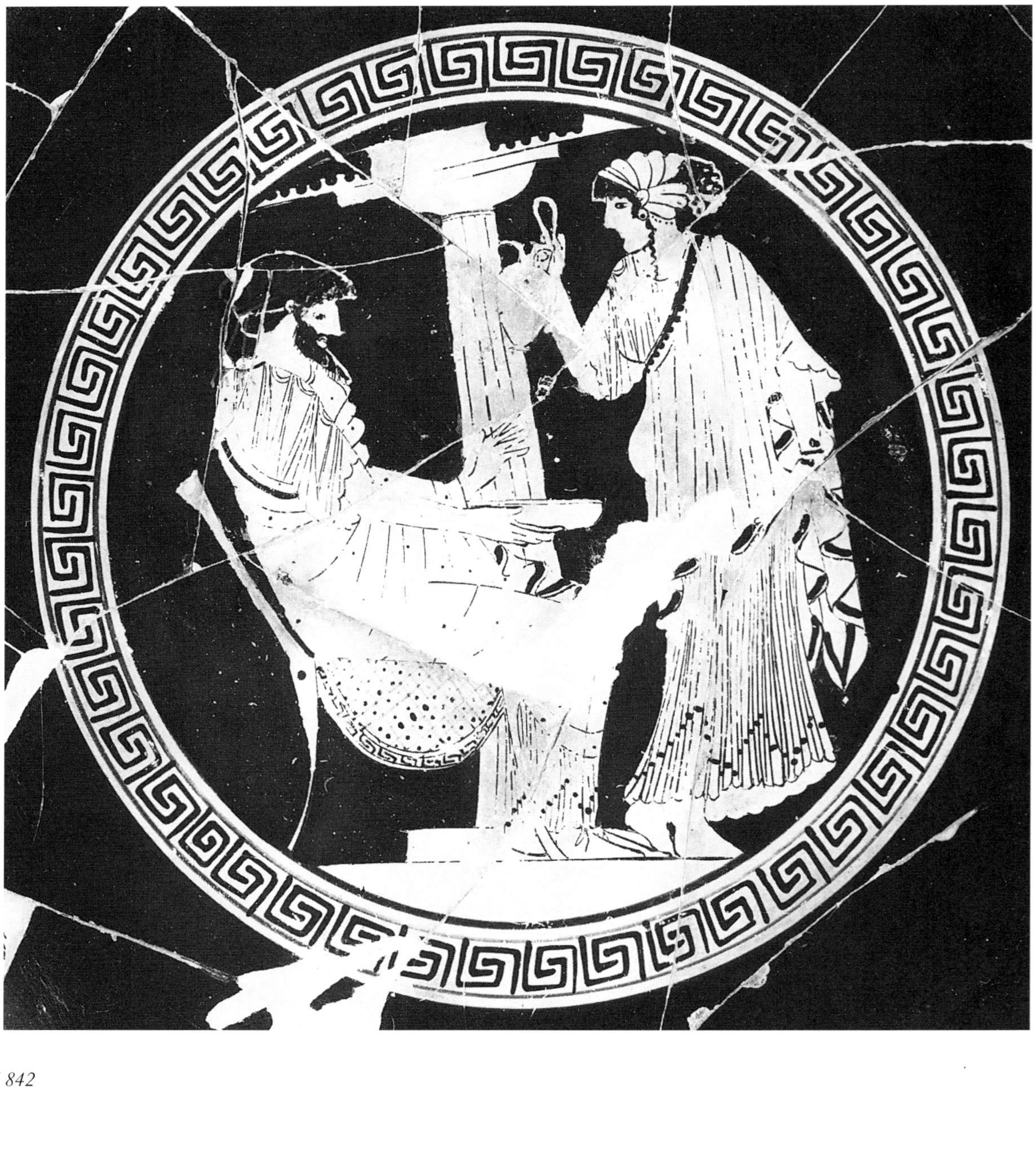

(b) 47

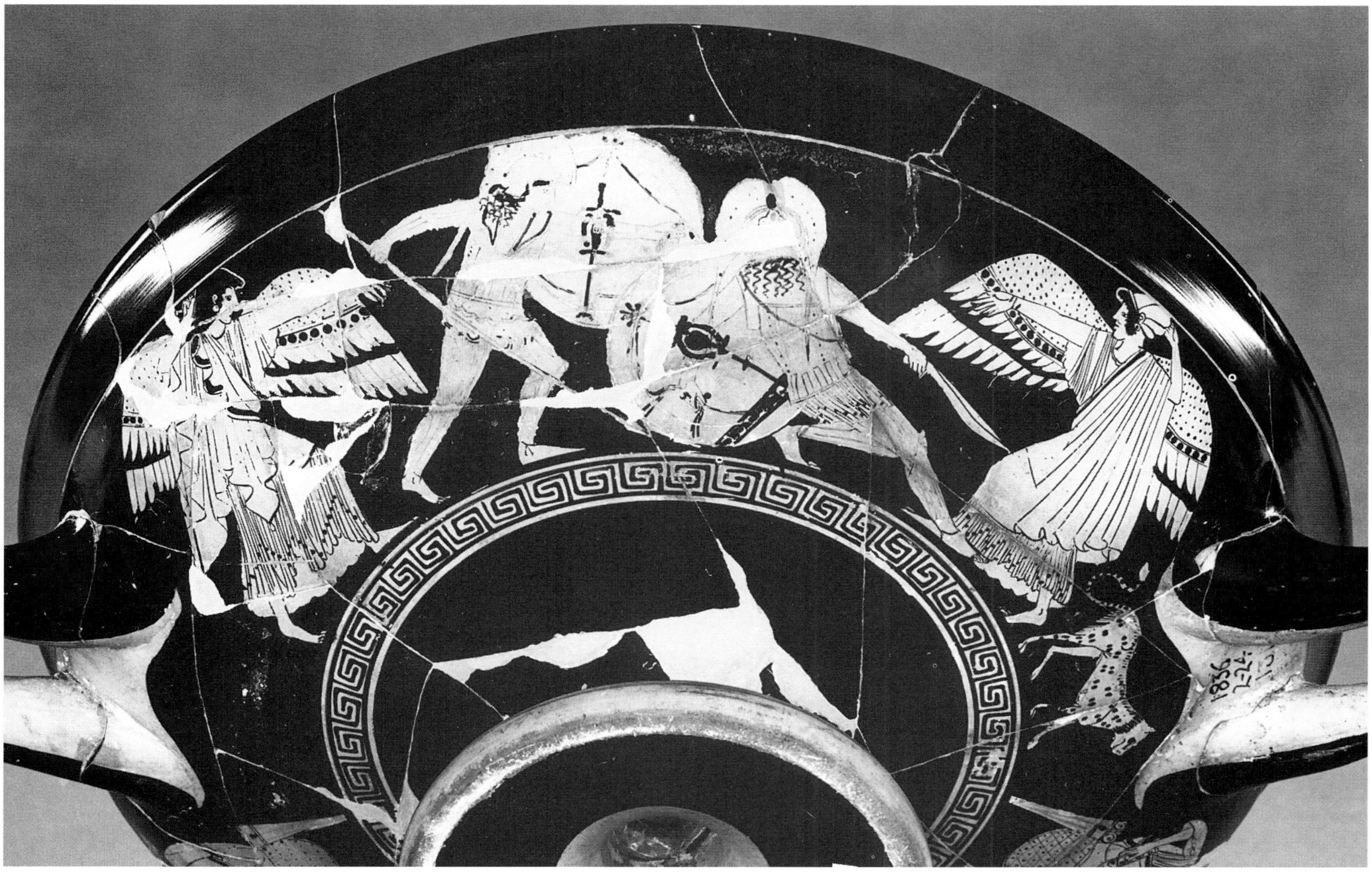

(a) 47

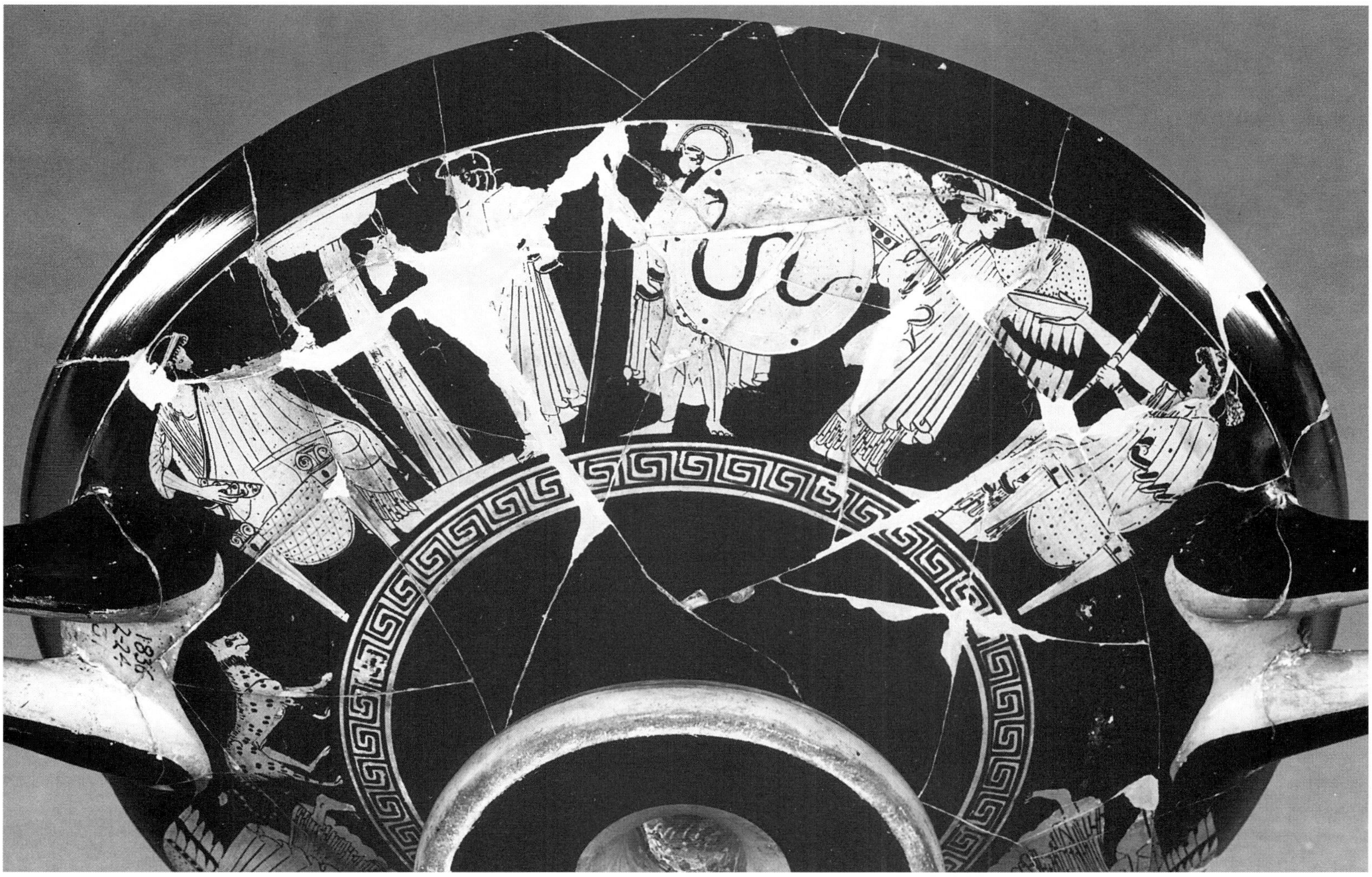

(b) 47

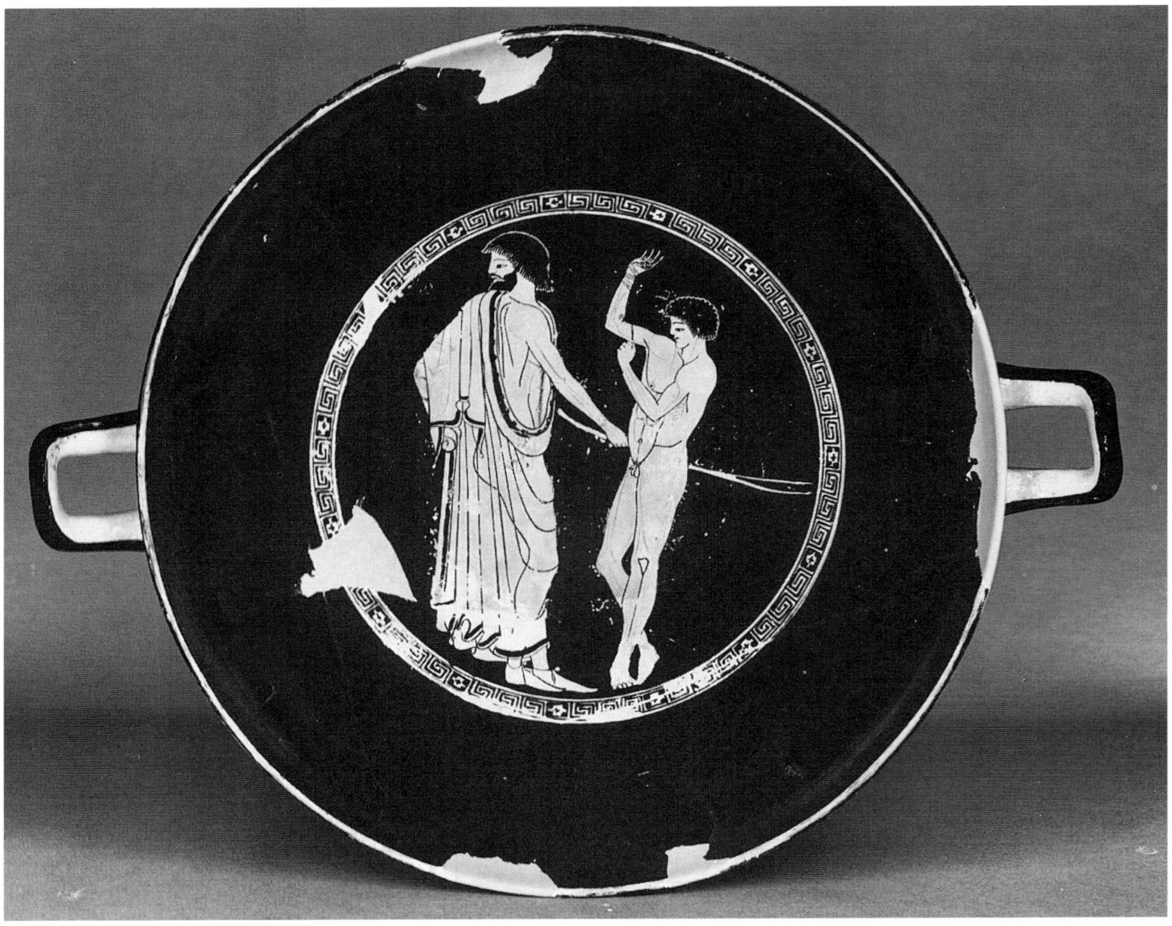

(a) 48

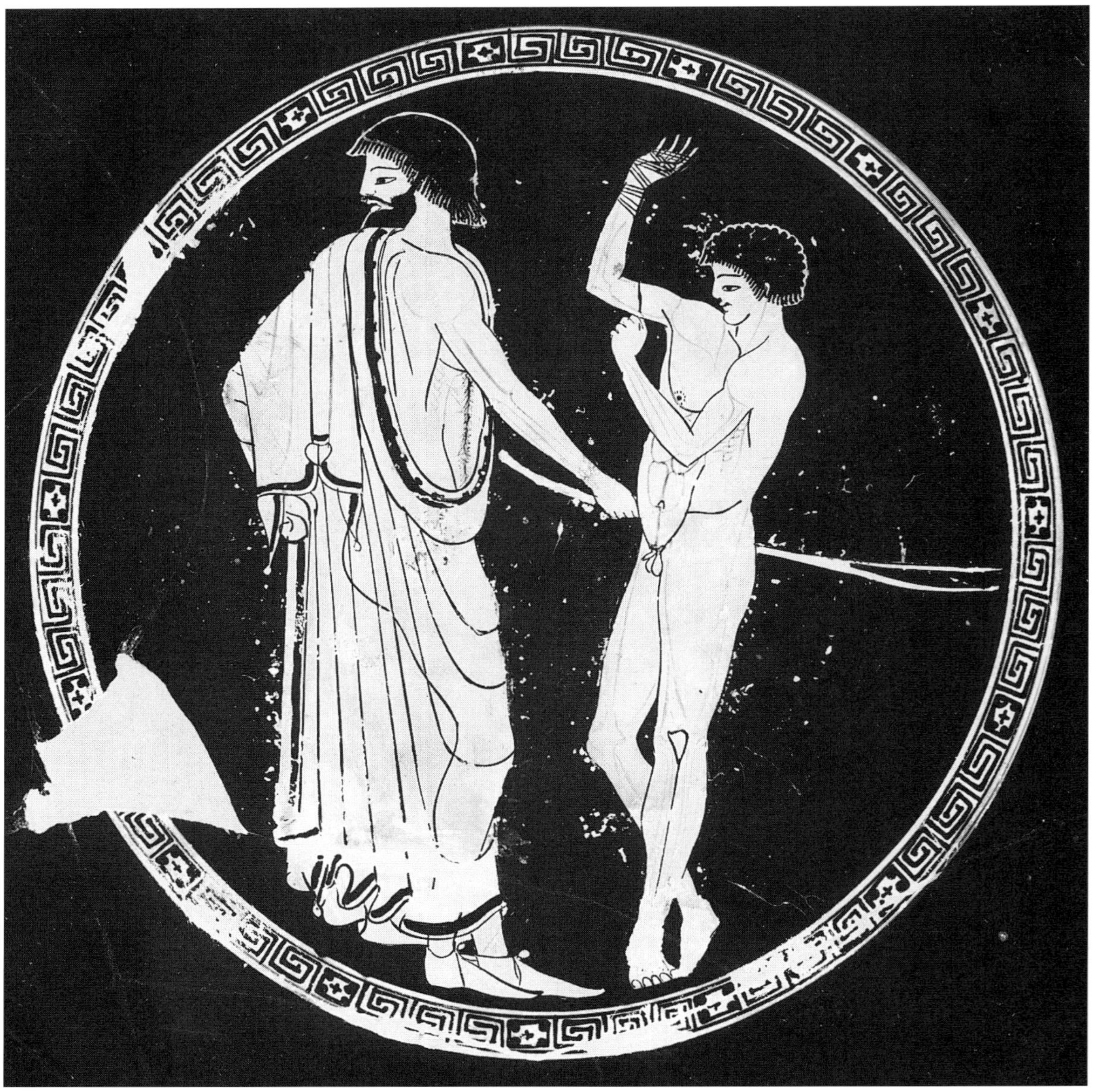

(b) 48

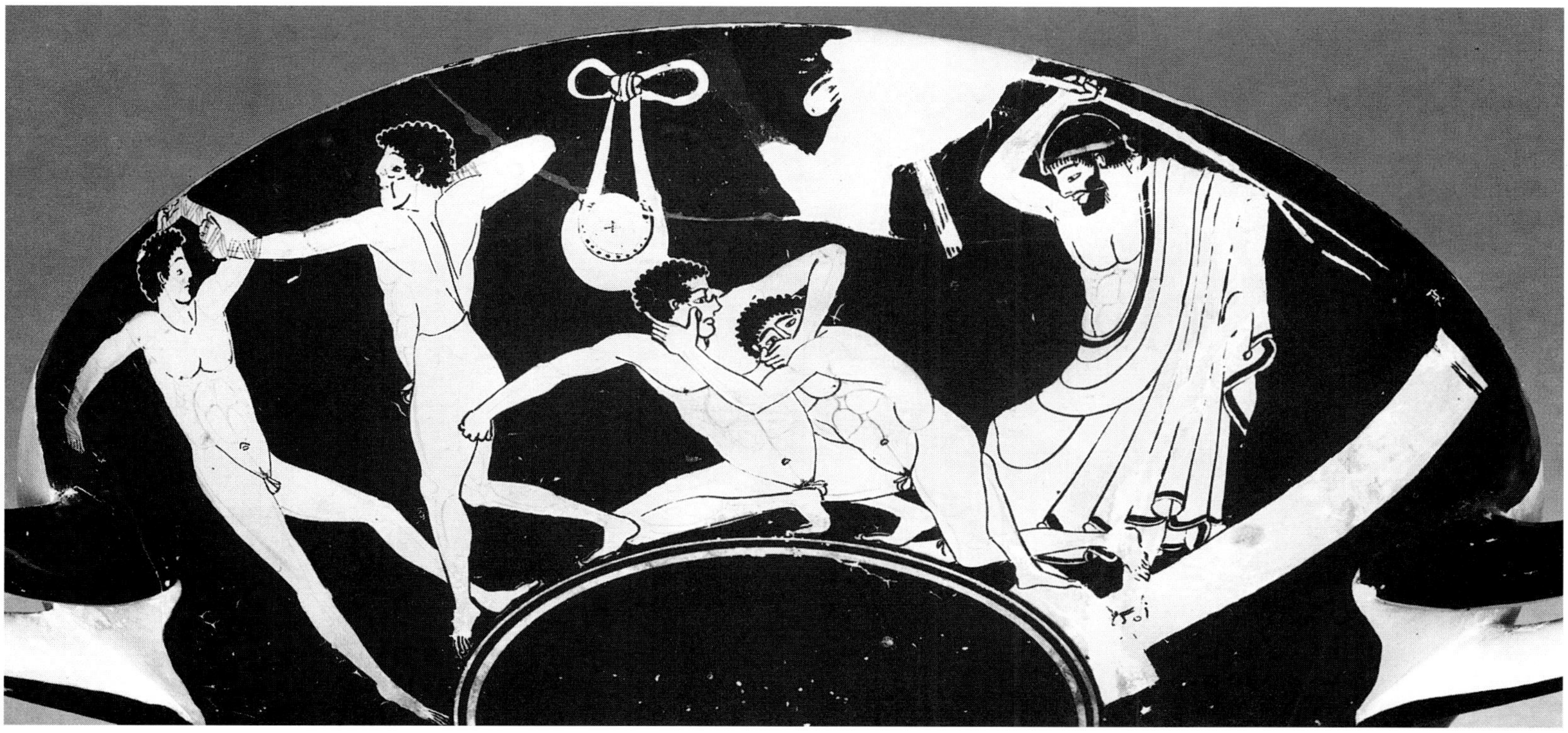

(a) 48

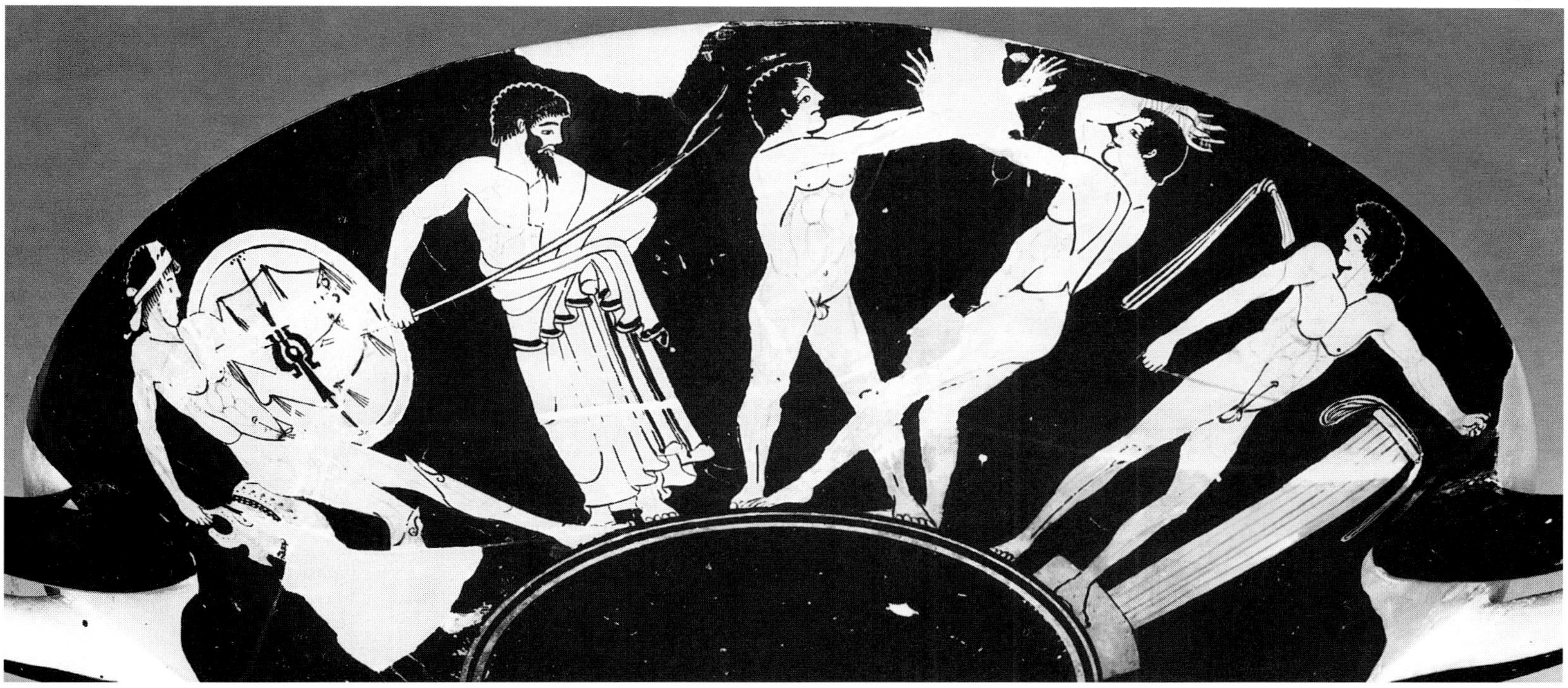

(b) 48

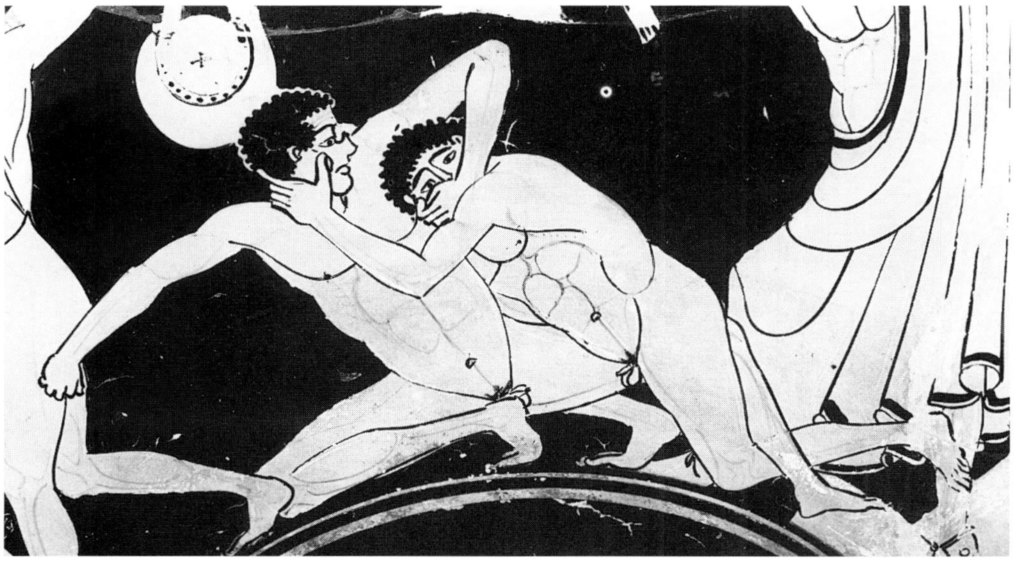

(c) 48

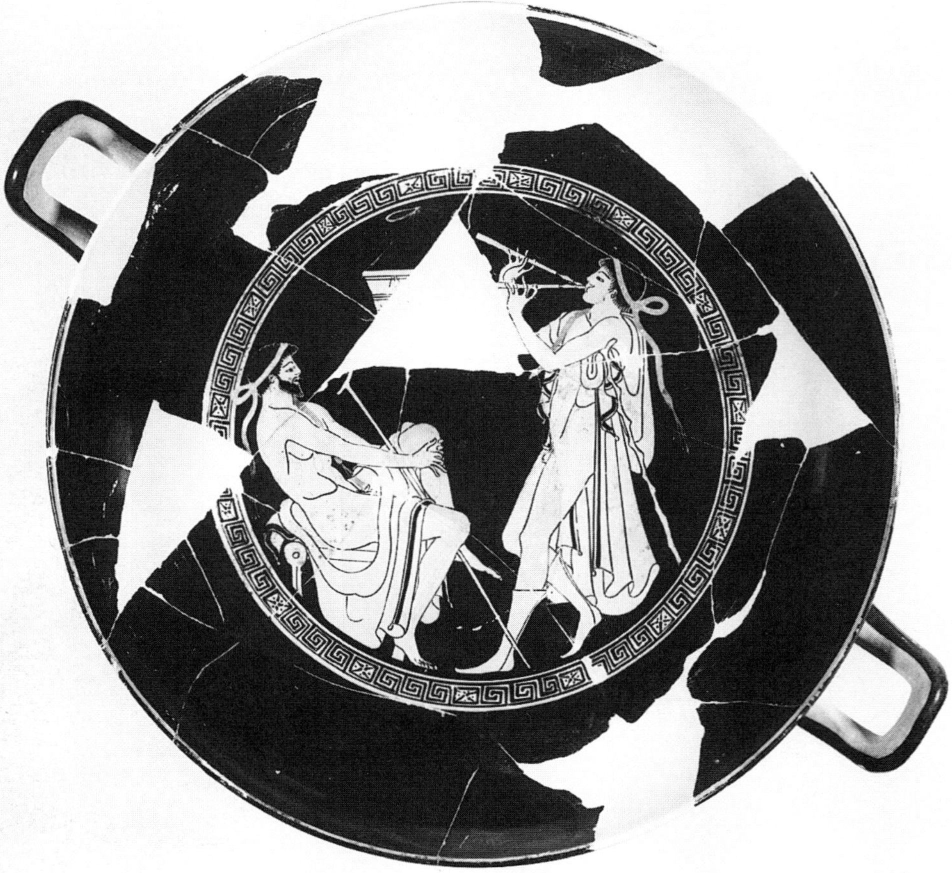

(a) 49

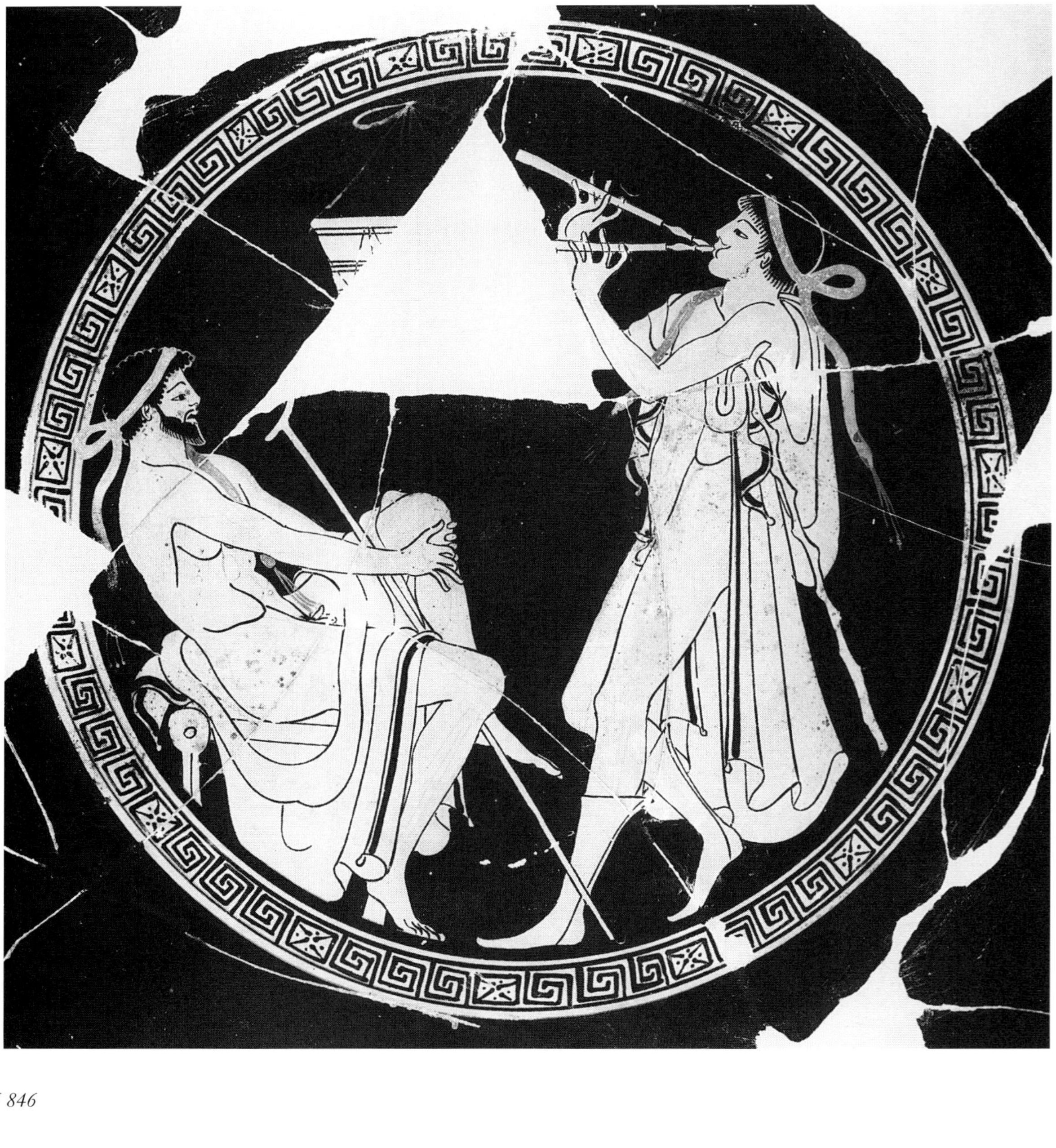

(b) 49

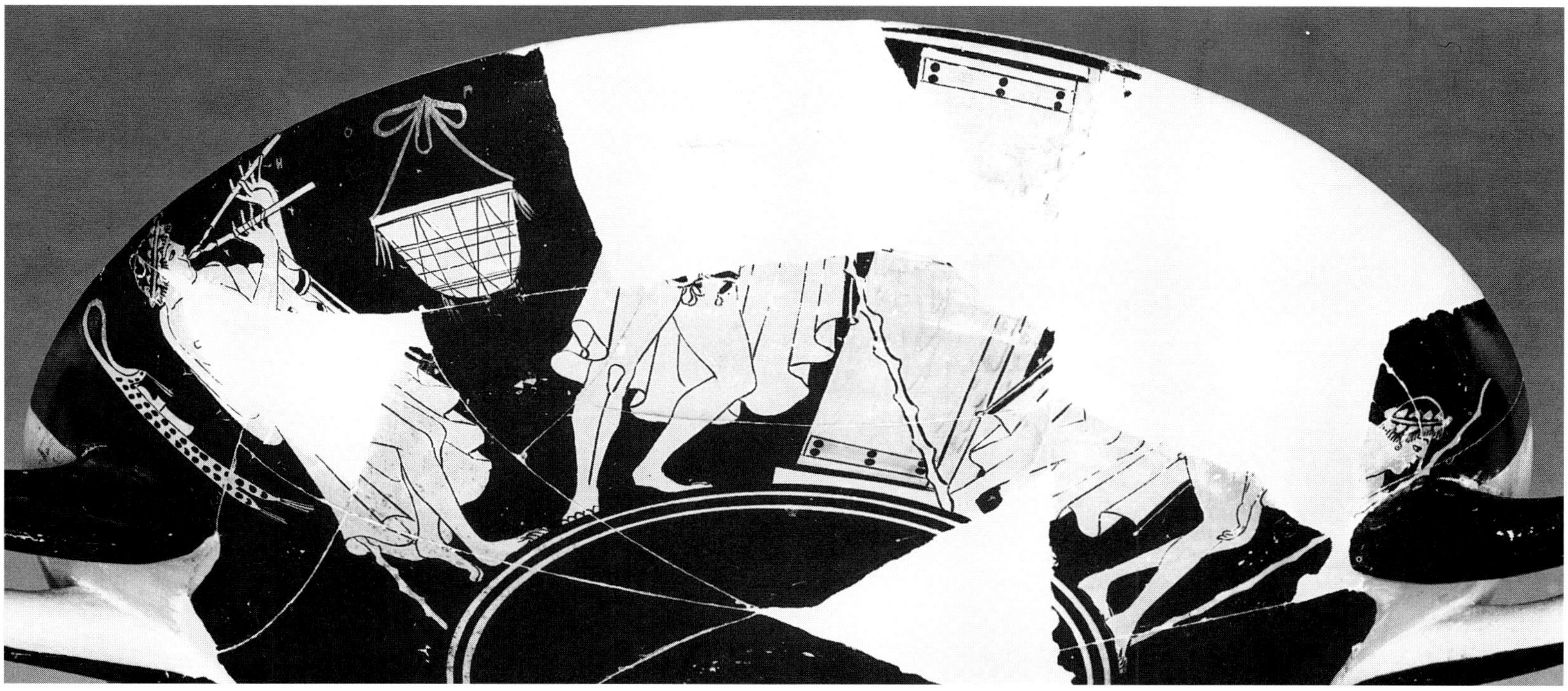

(a) 49

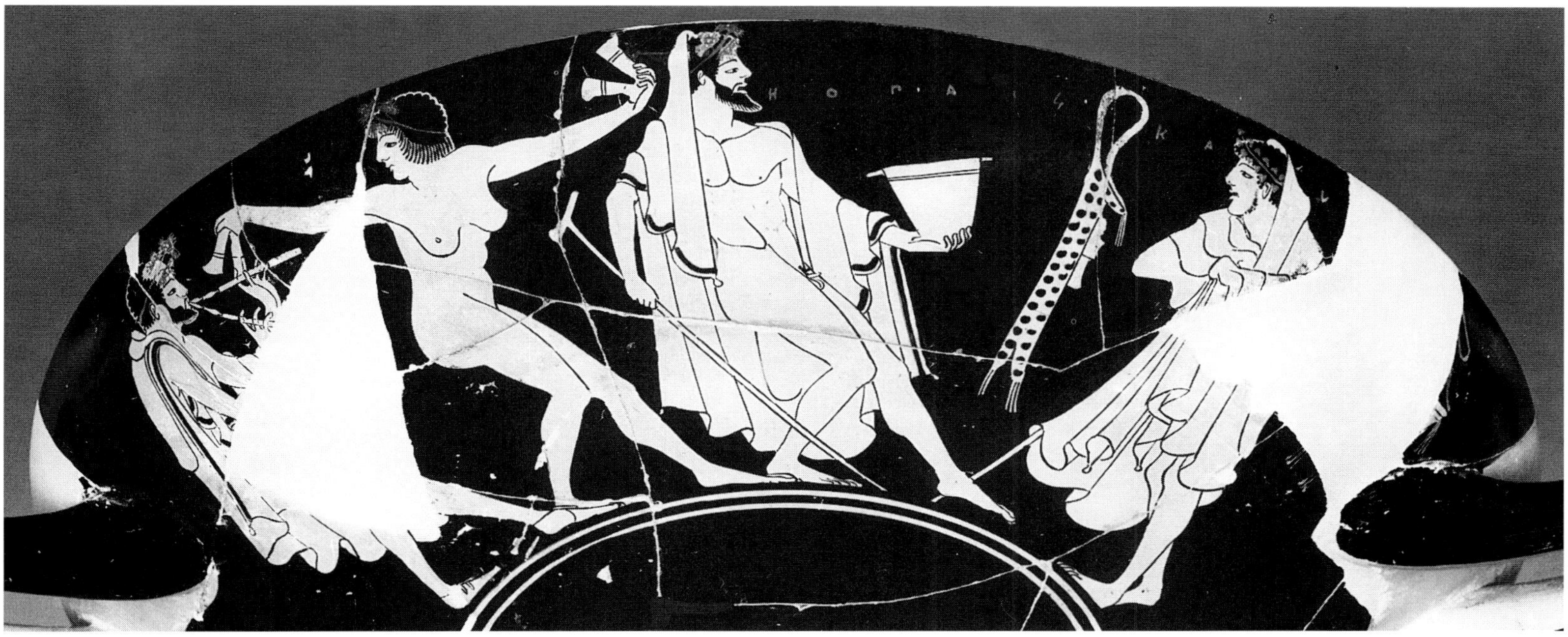

(b) 49

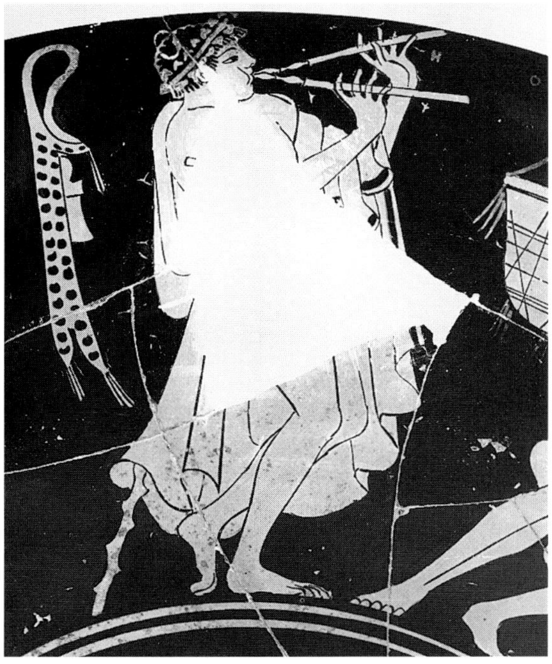

(c) 49

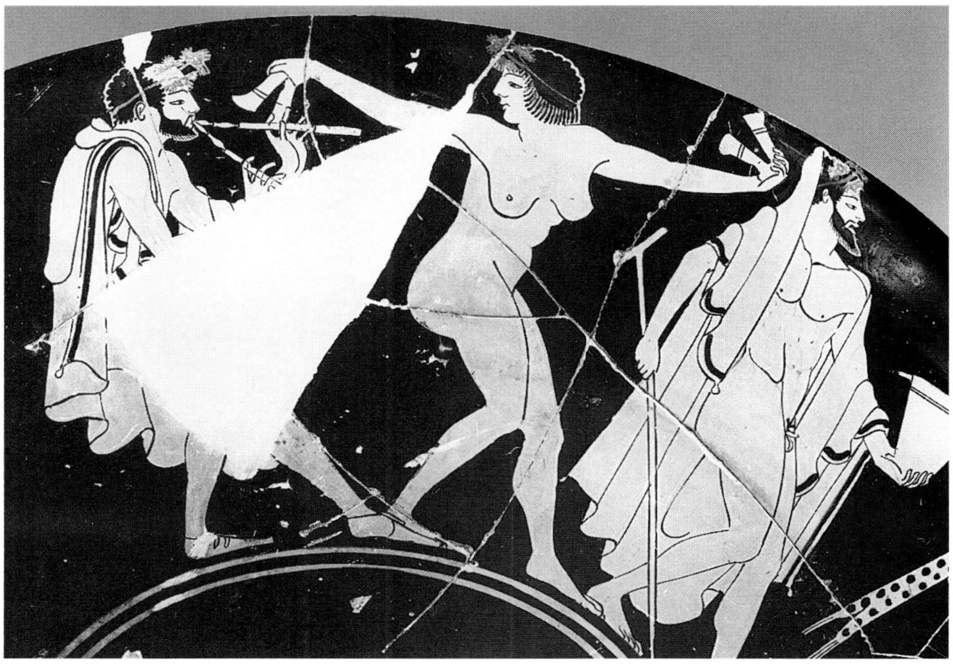

(d) 49

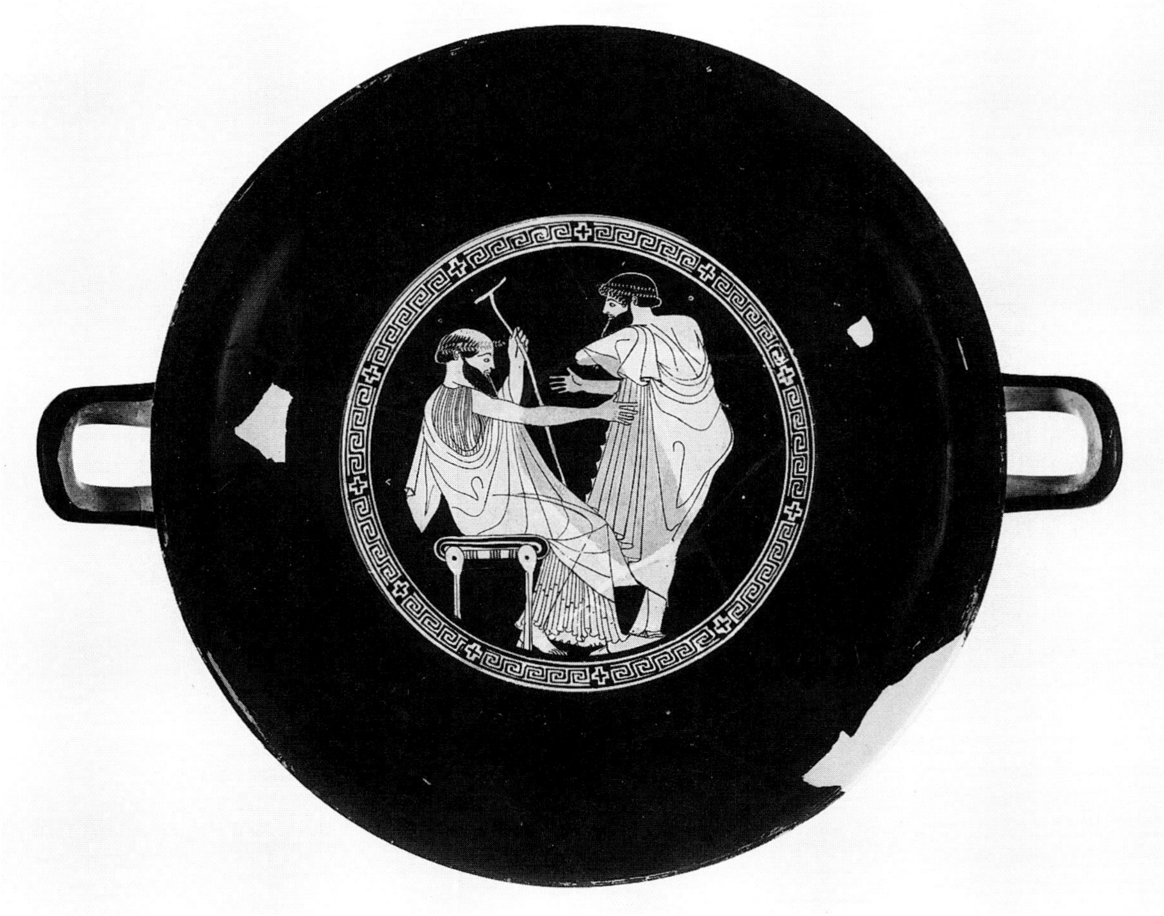

(a) 50

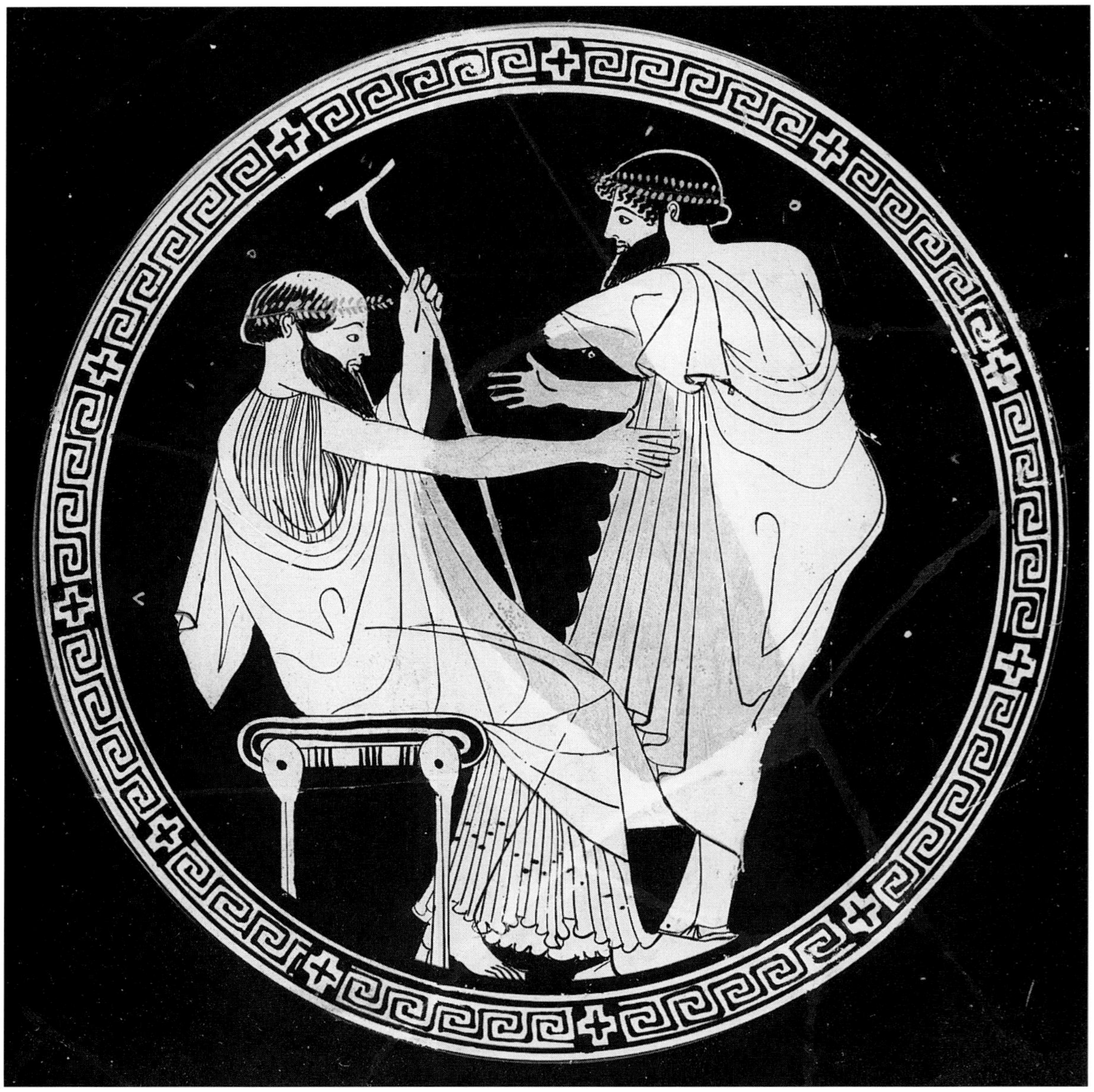

(b) 50

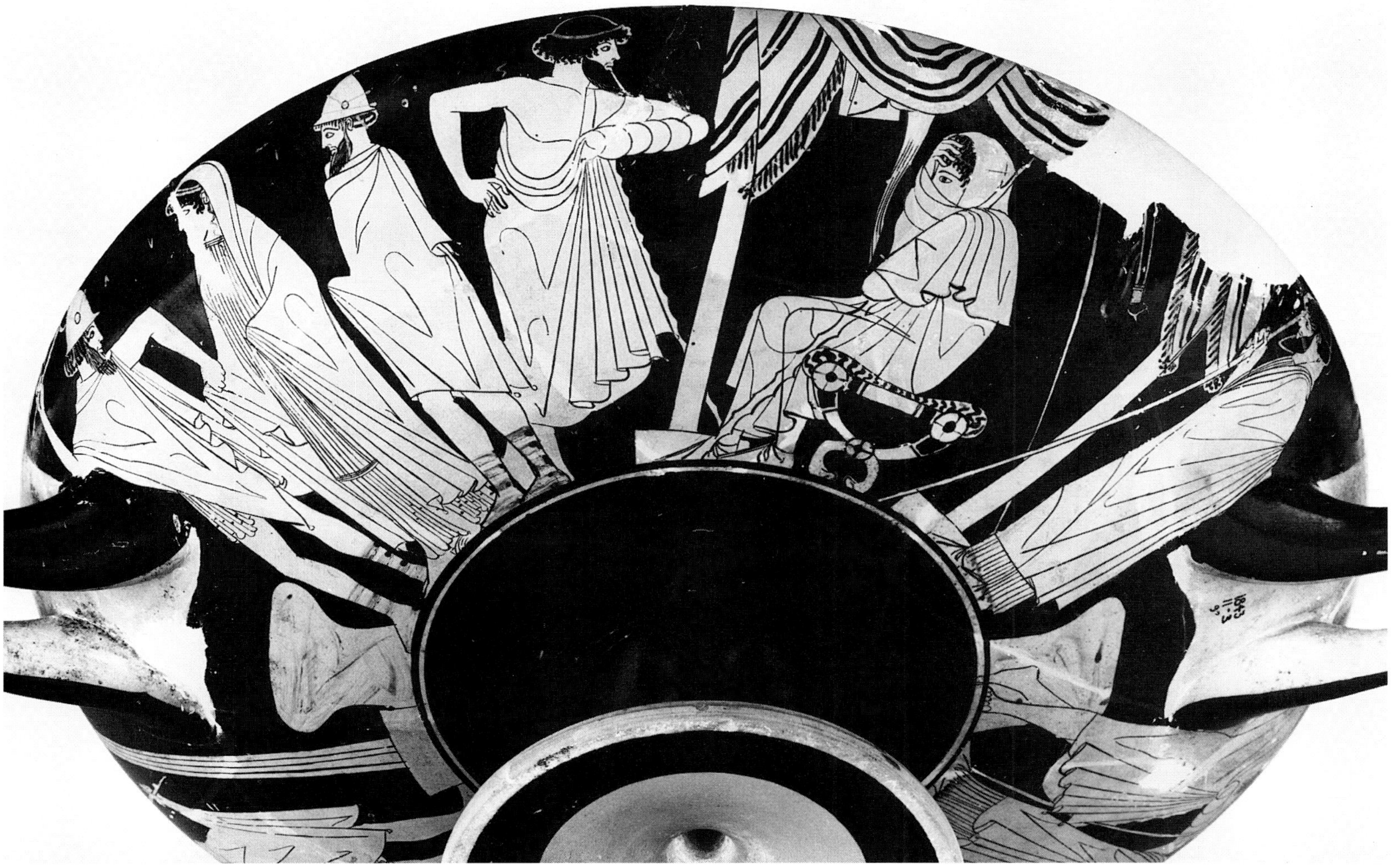

(a) 50

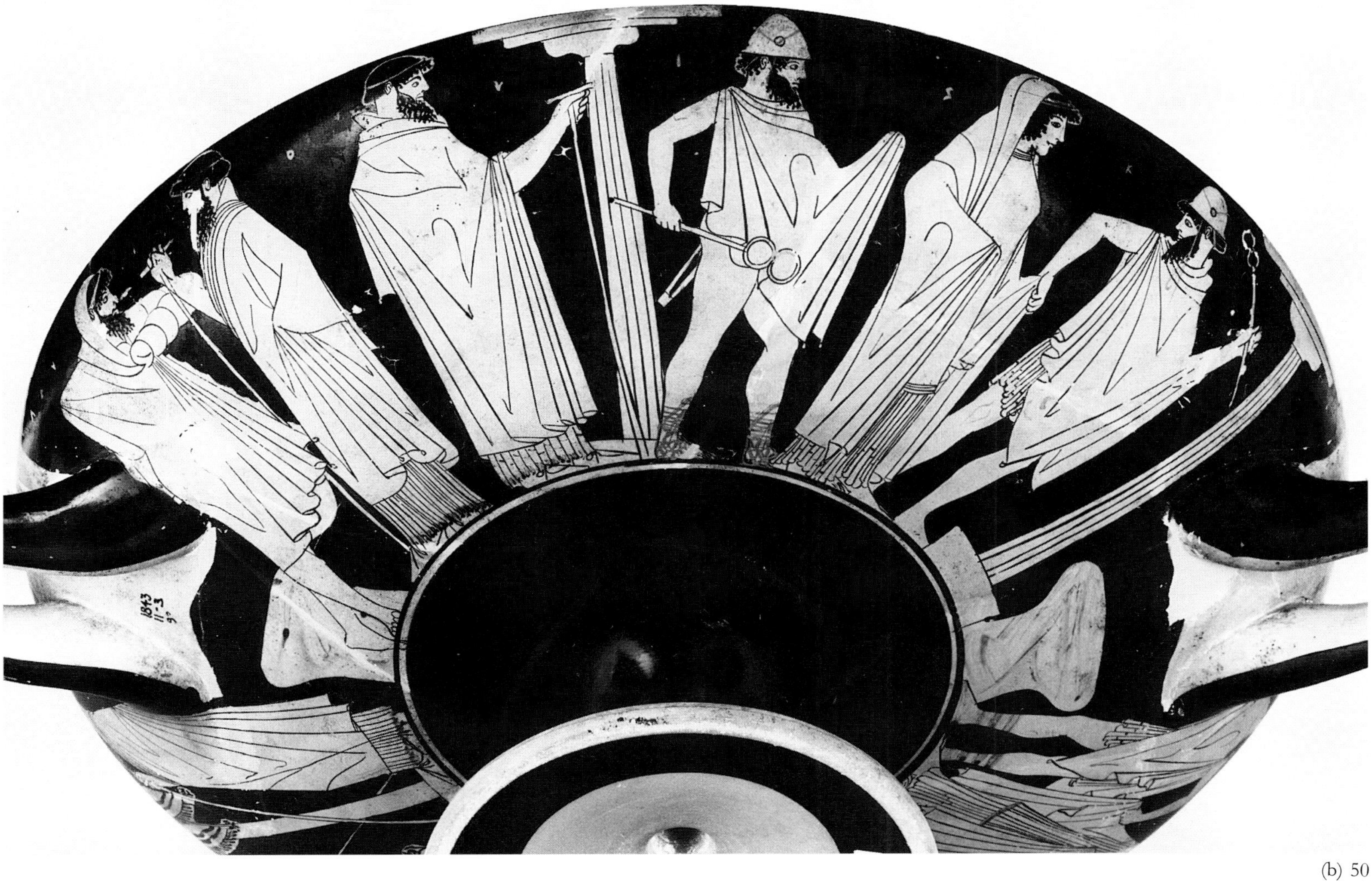

(b) 50

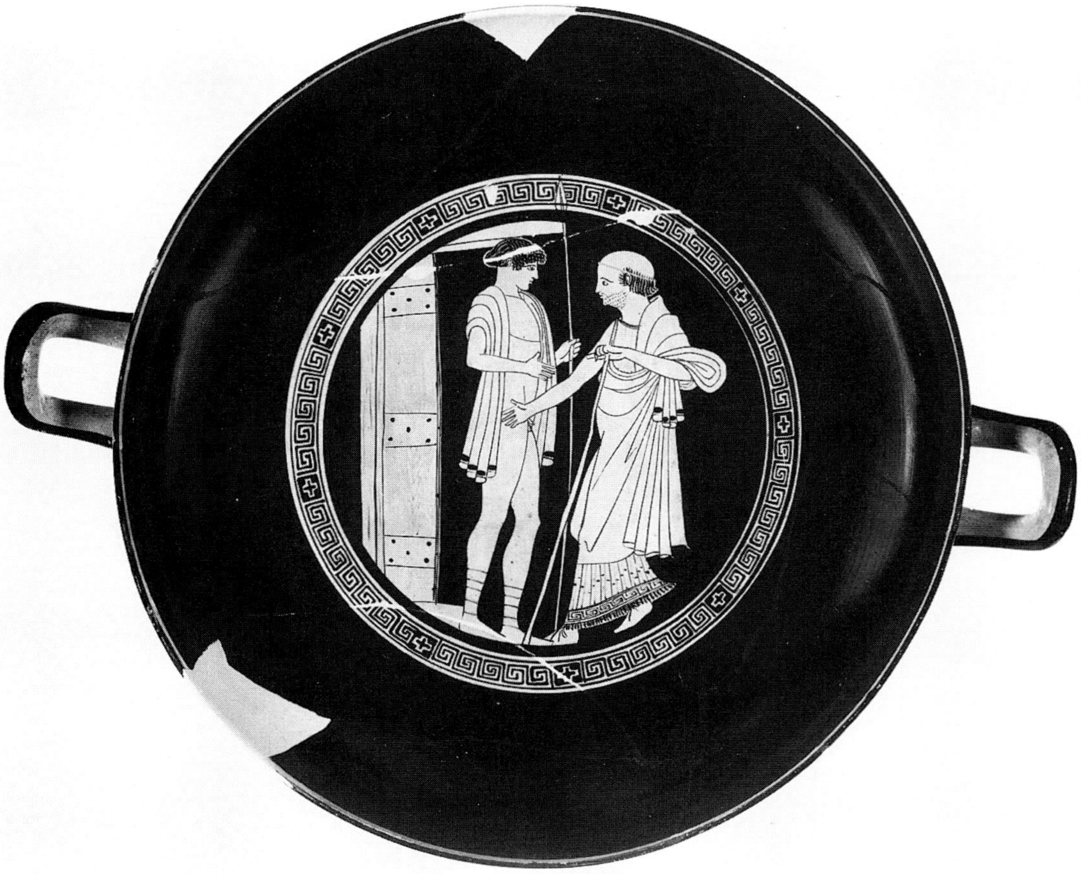

(a) 51

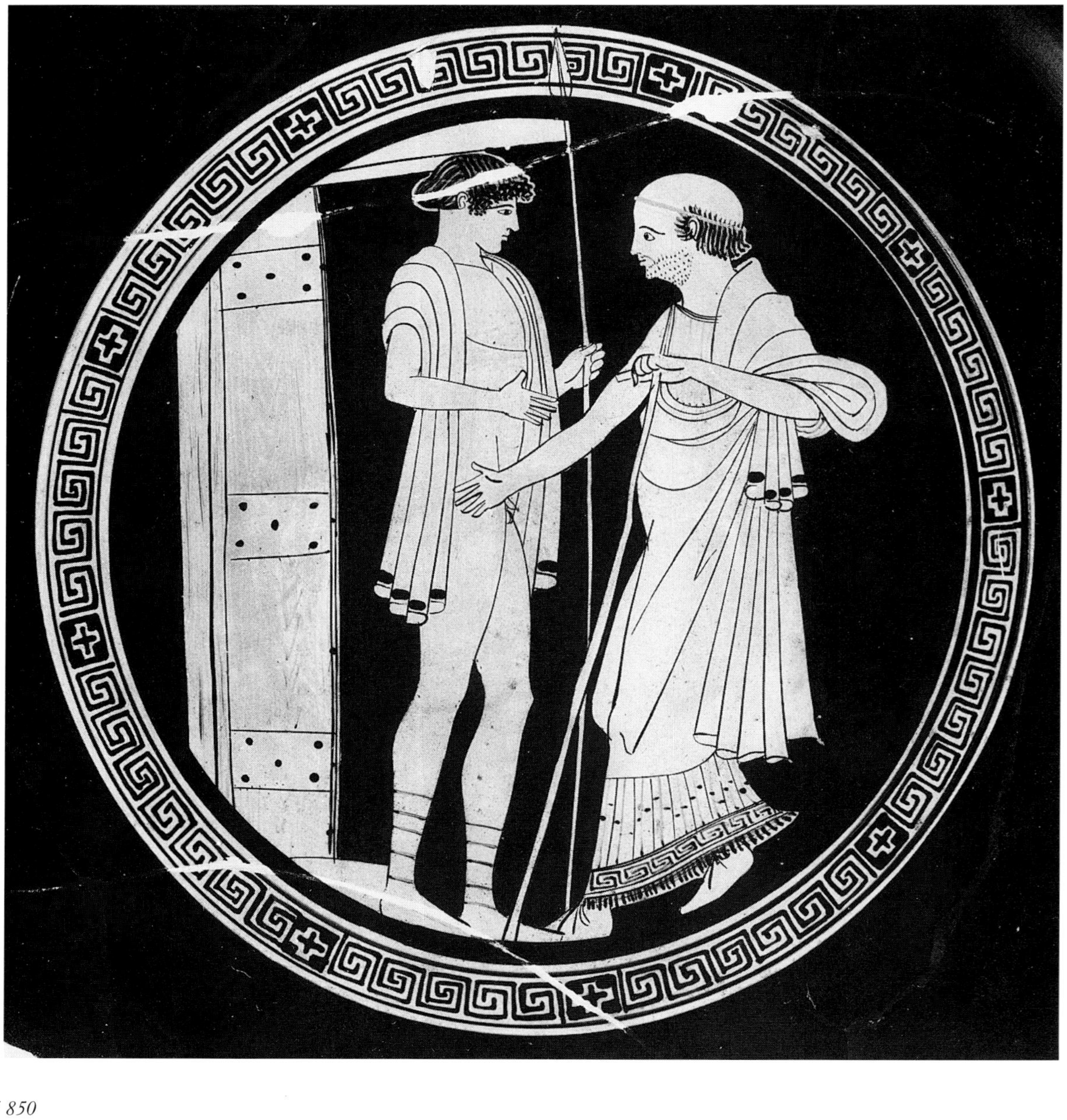

(b) 51

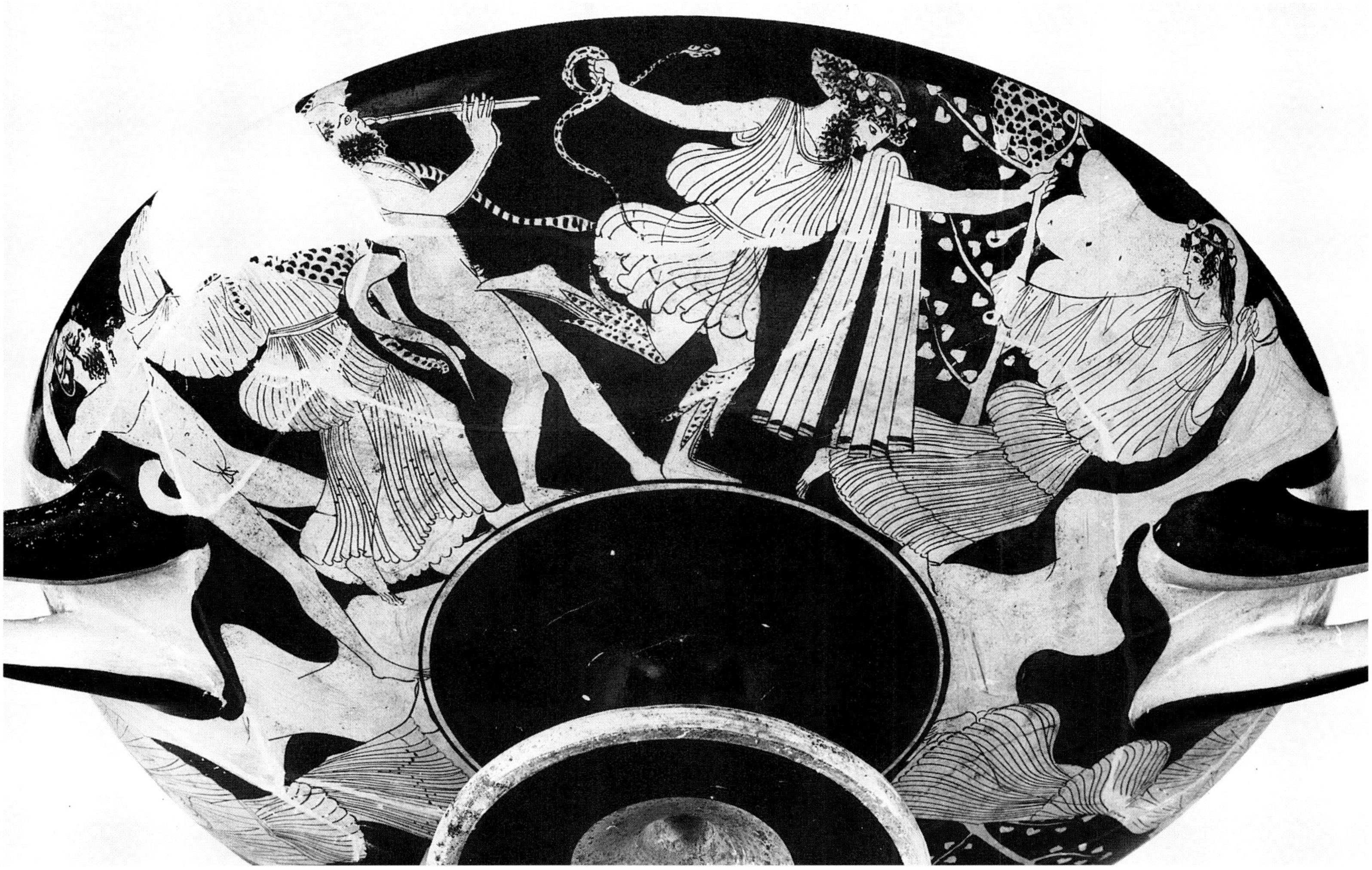

(a) 51

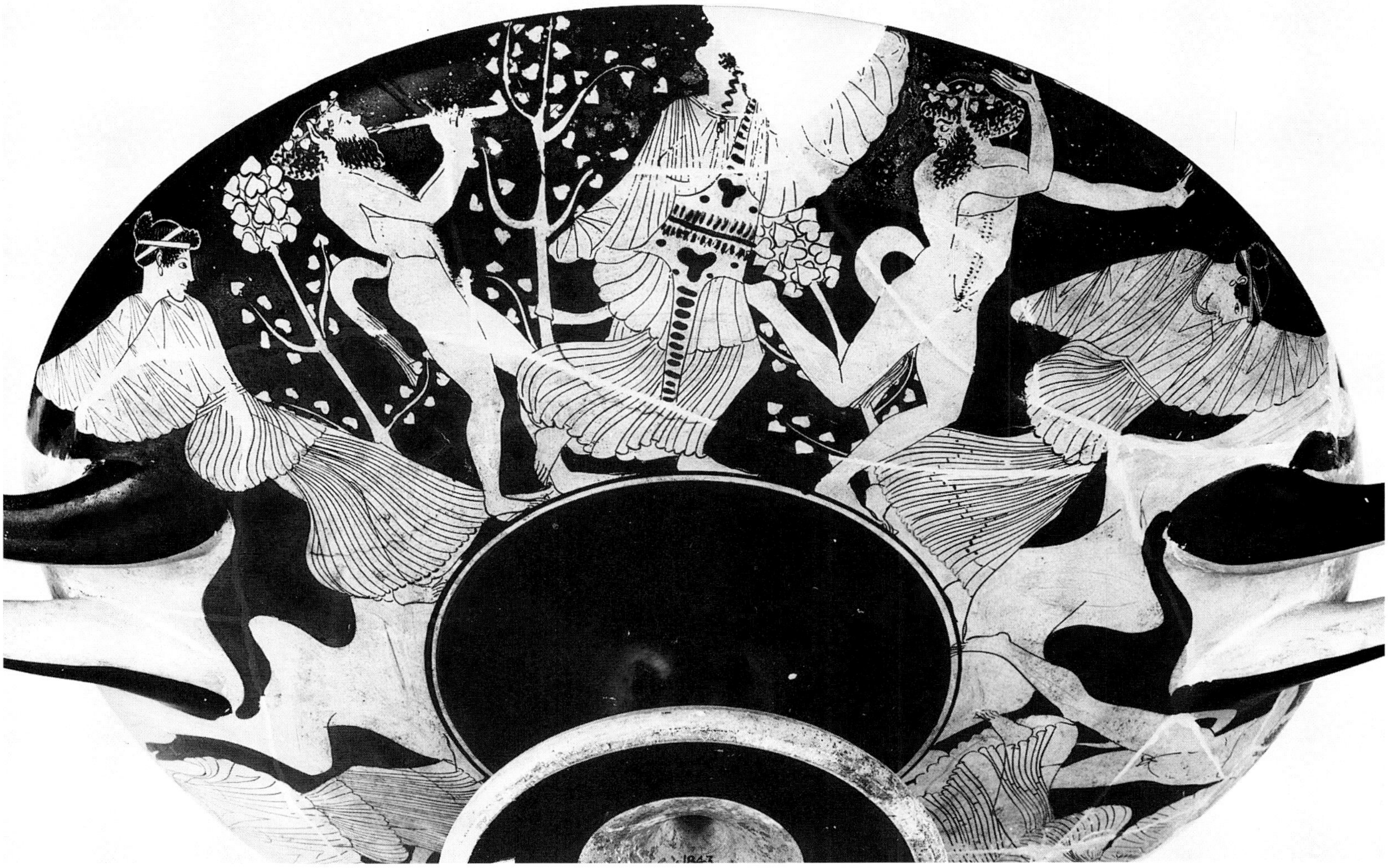

(b) 51

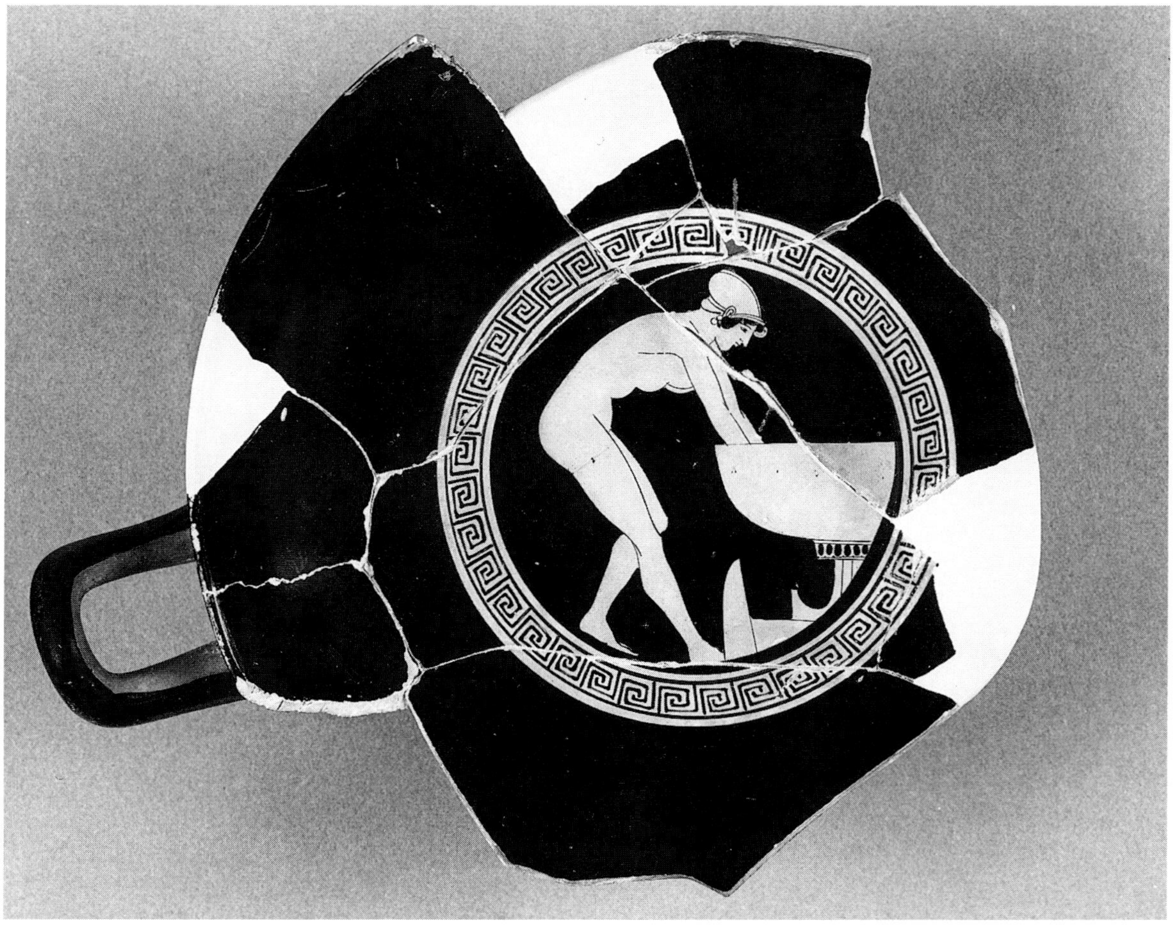

(a) 52

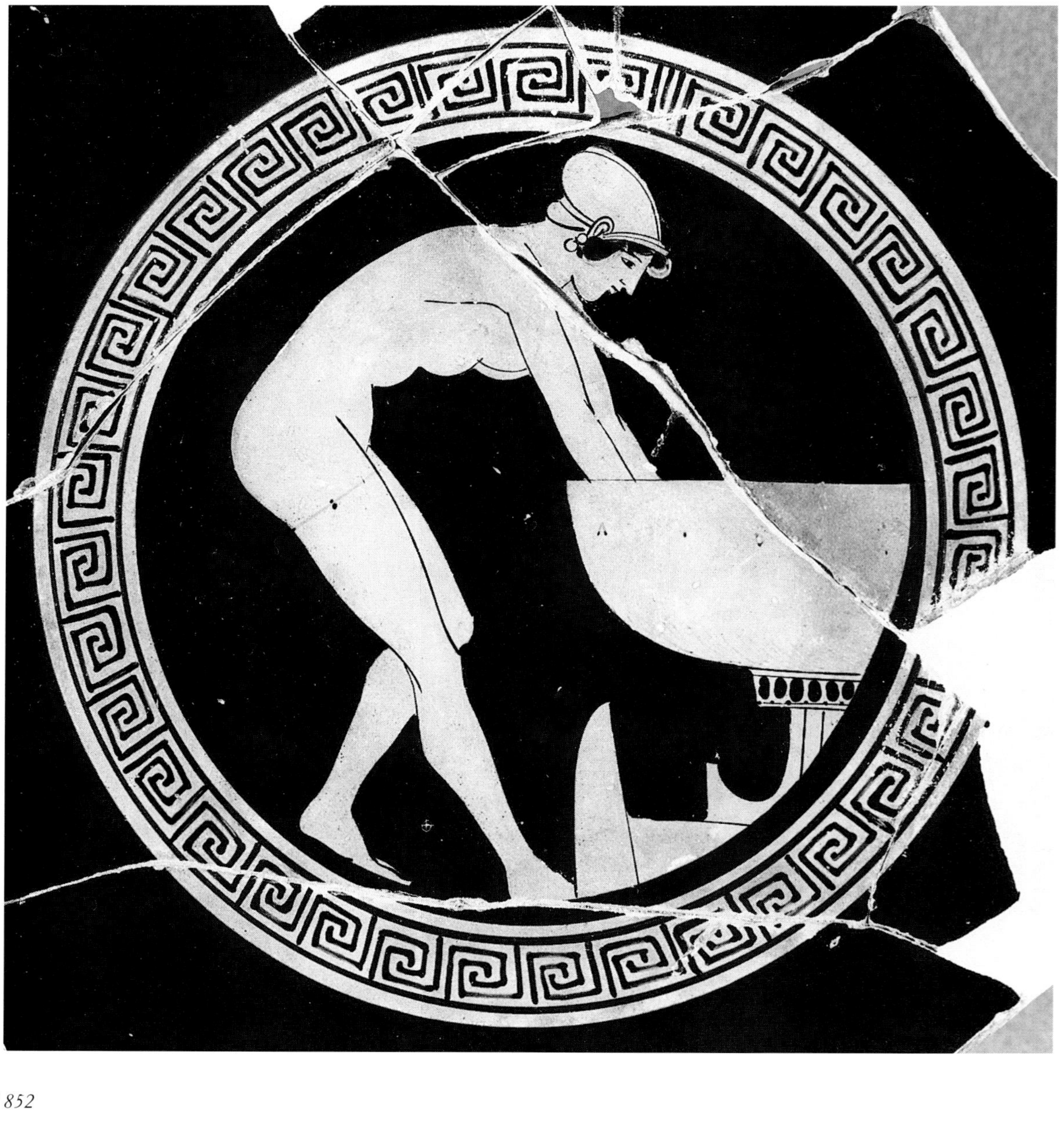

(b) 52

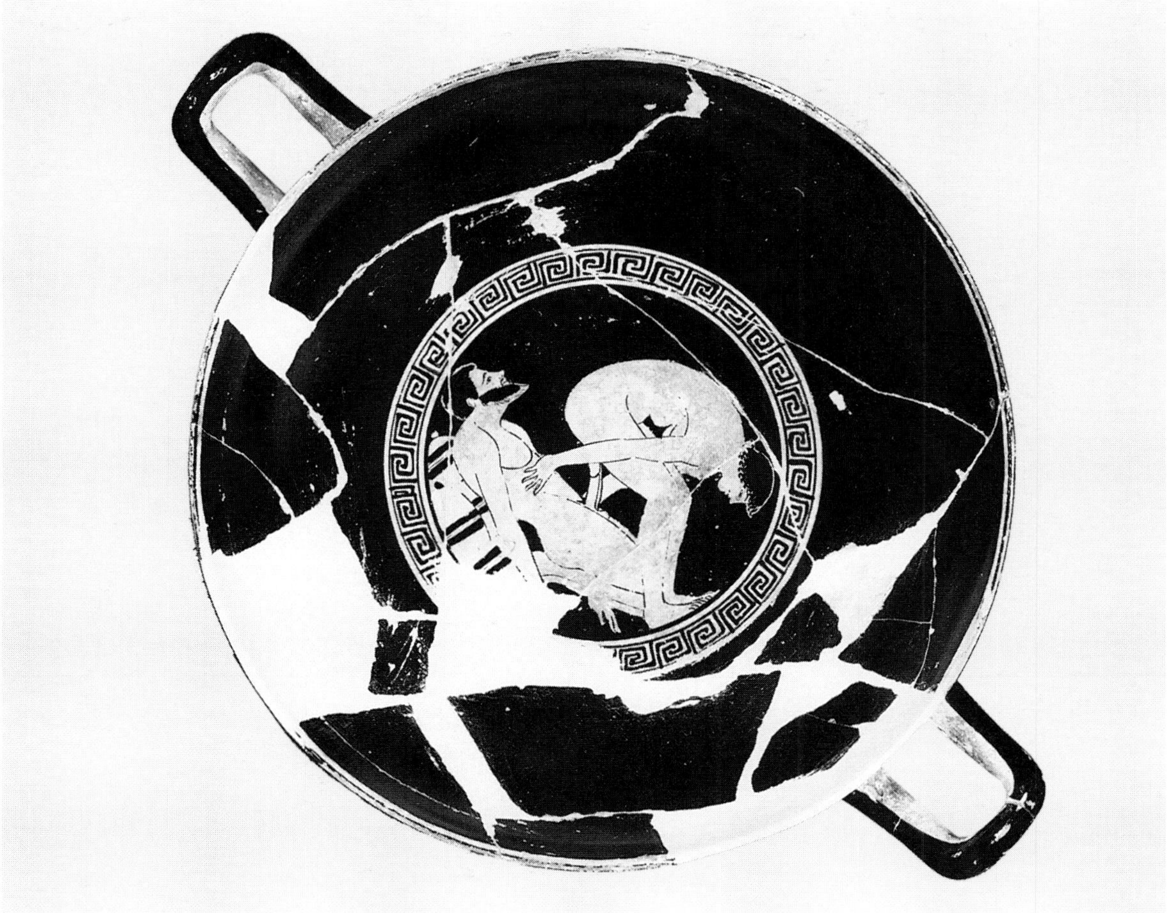

(a) 53

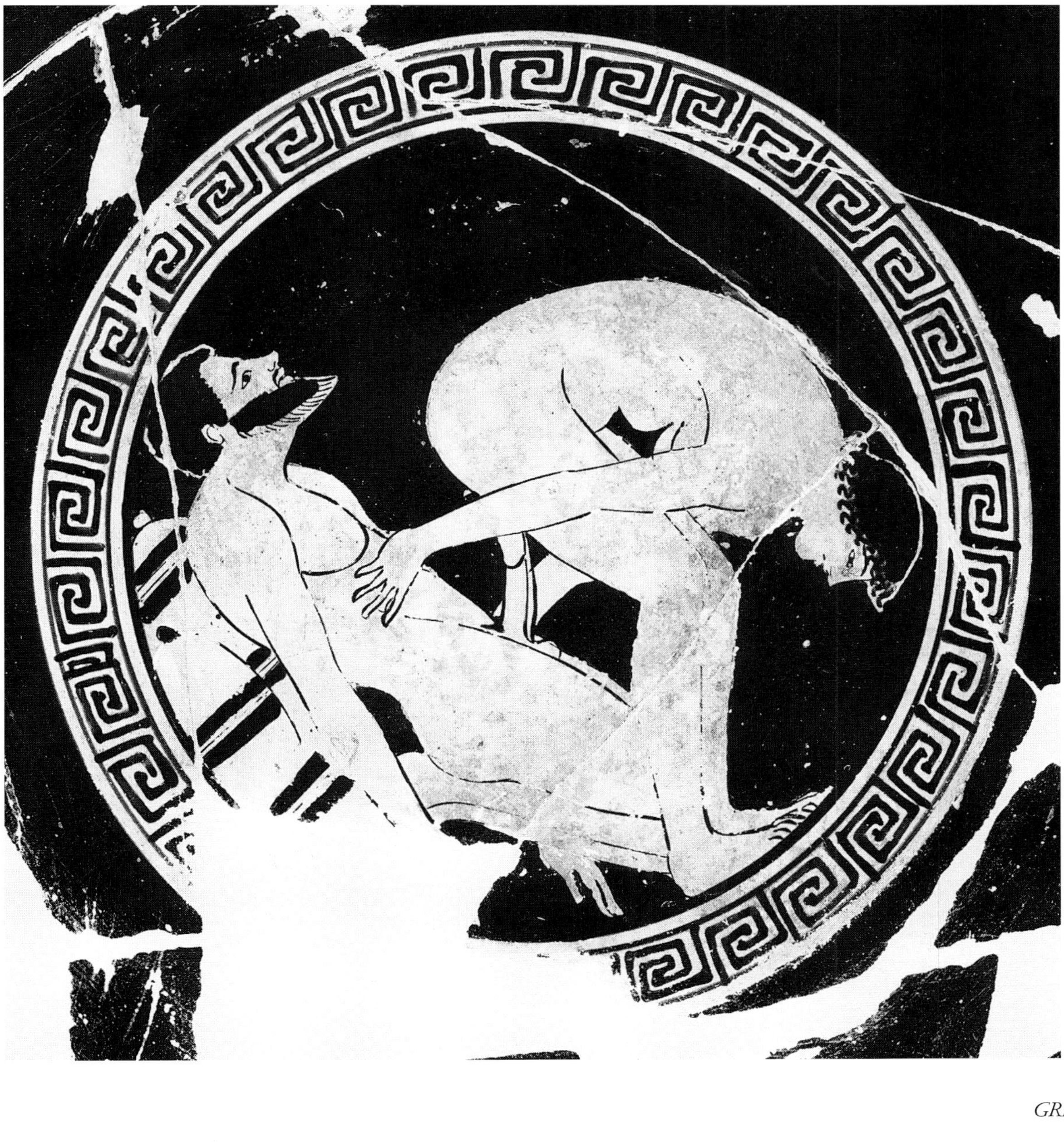

(b) 53

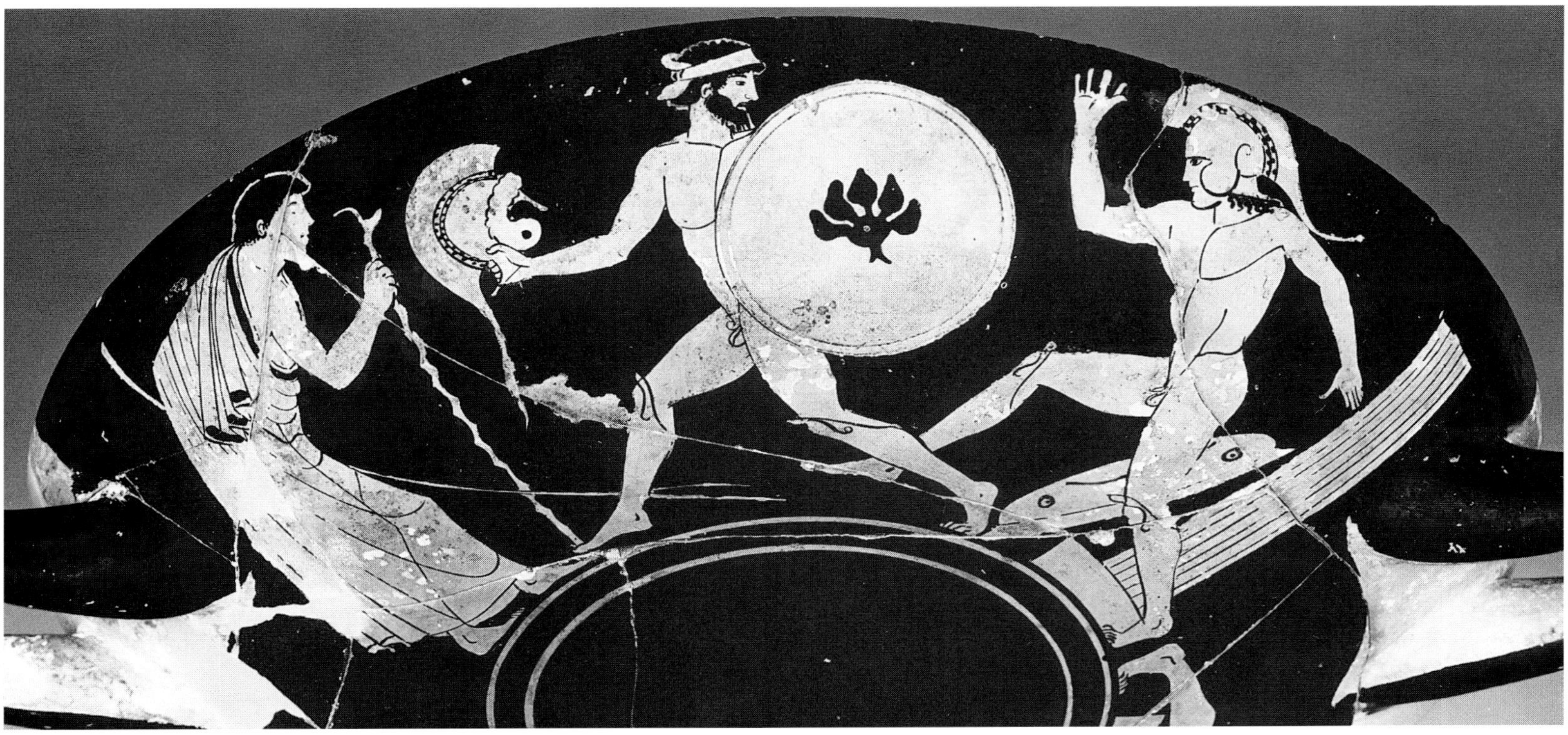

(a) 53

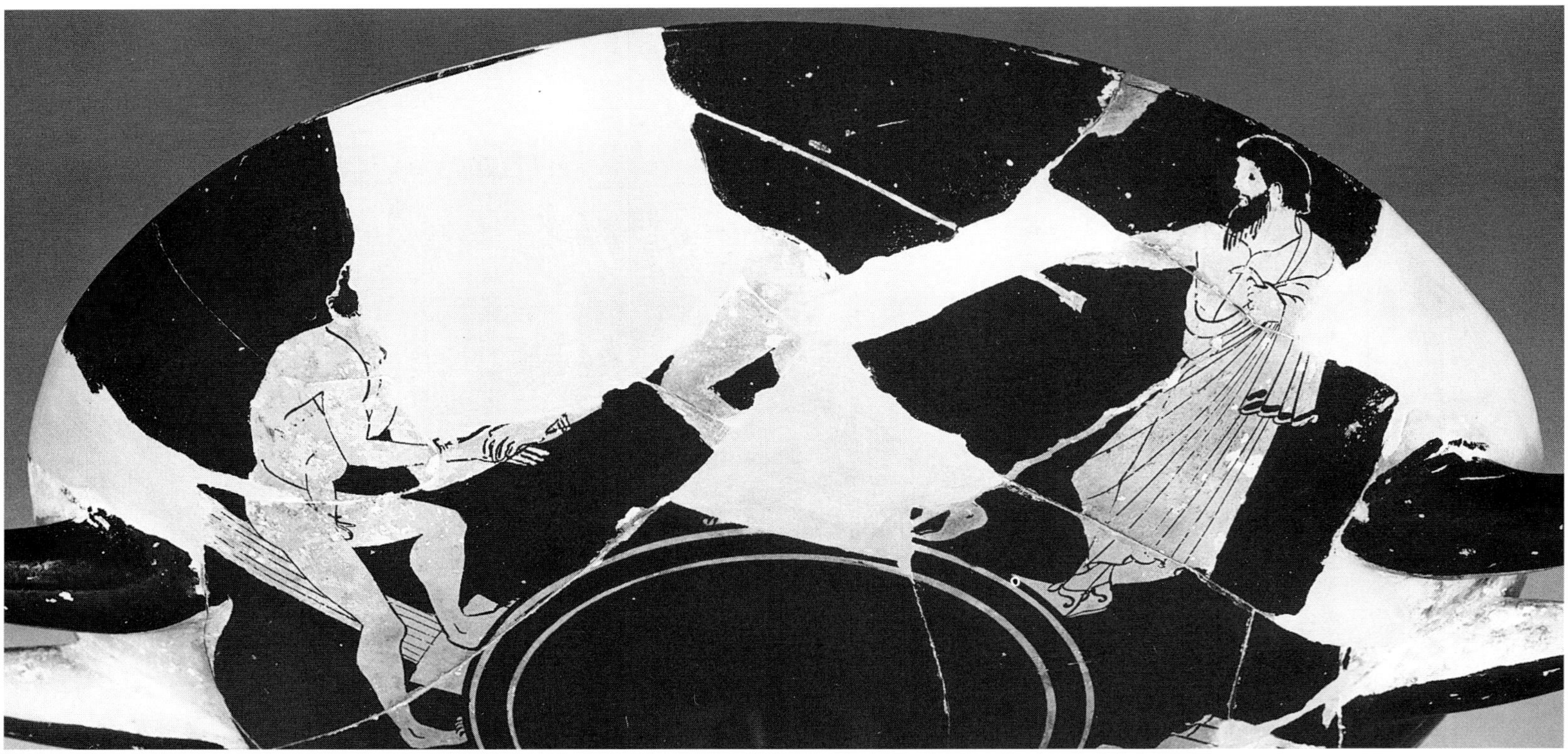

(b) 53

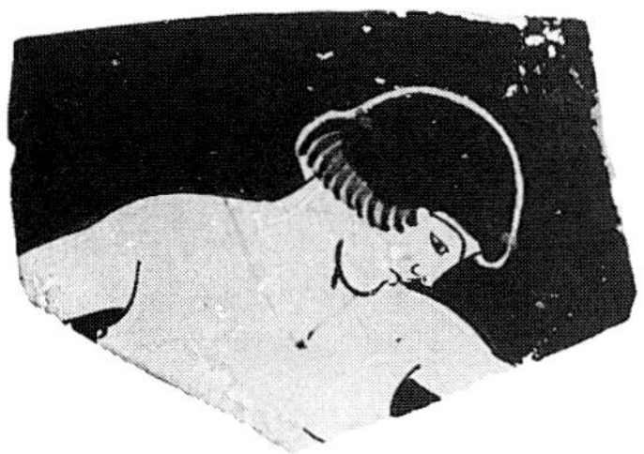

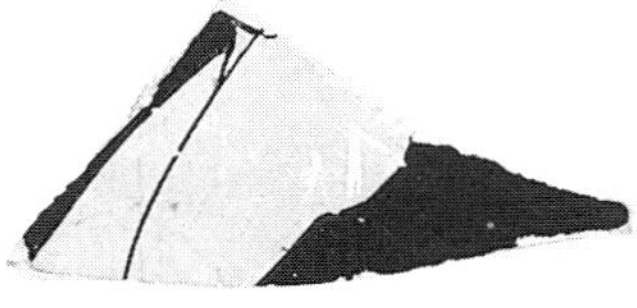

(c) 54

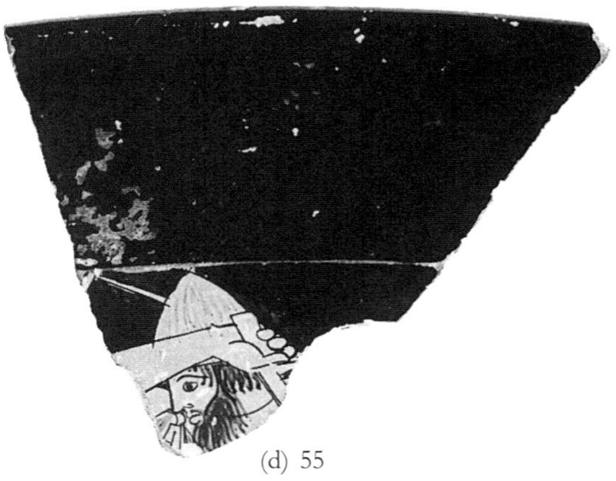

(d) 55

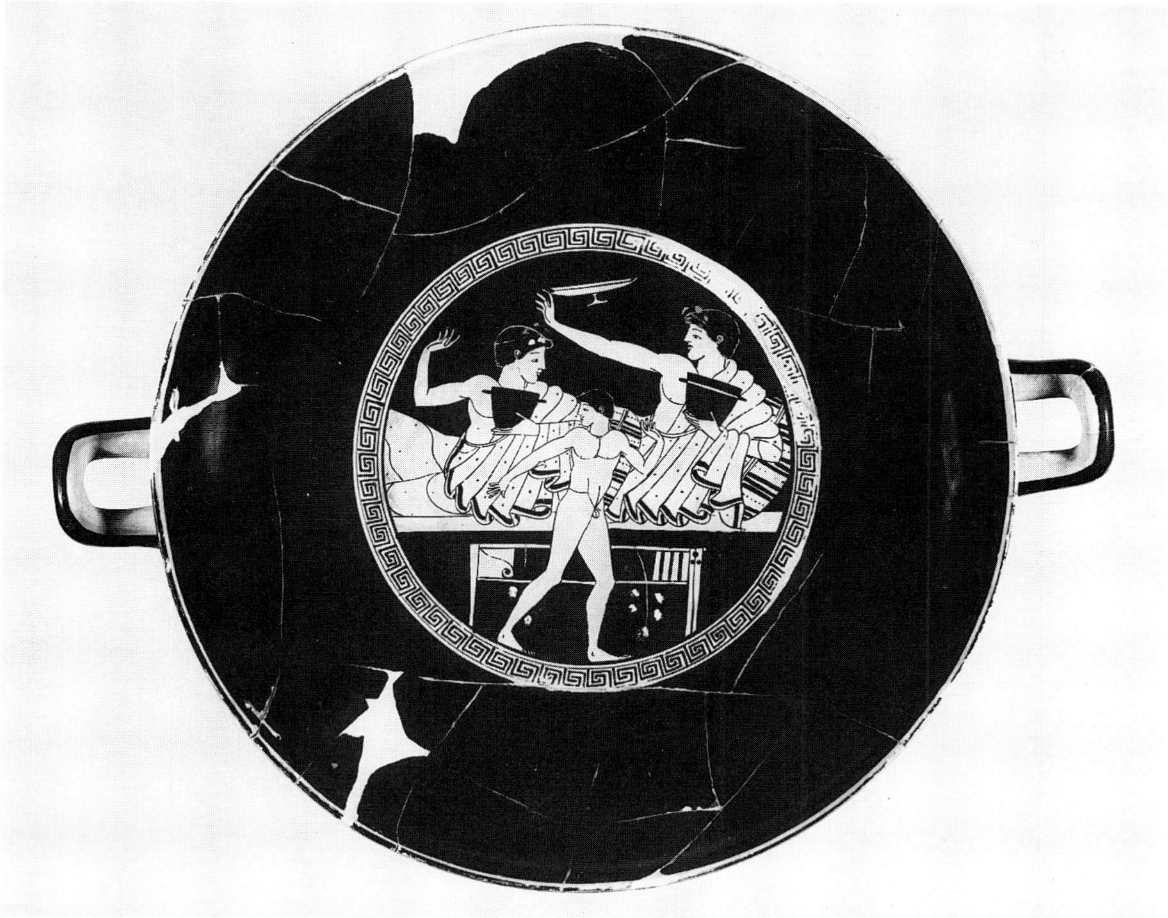

(a) 56

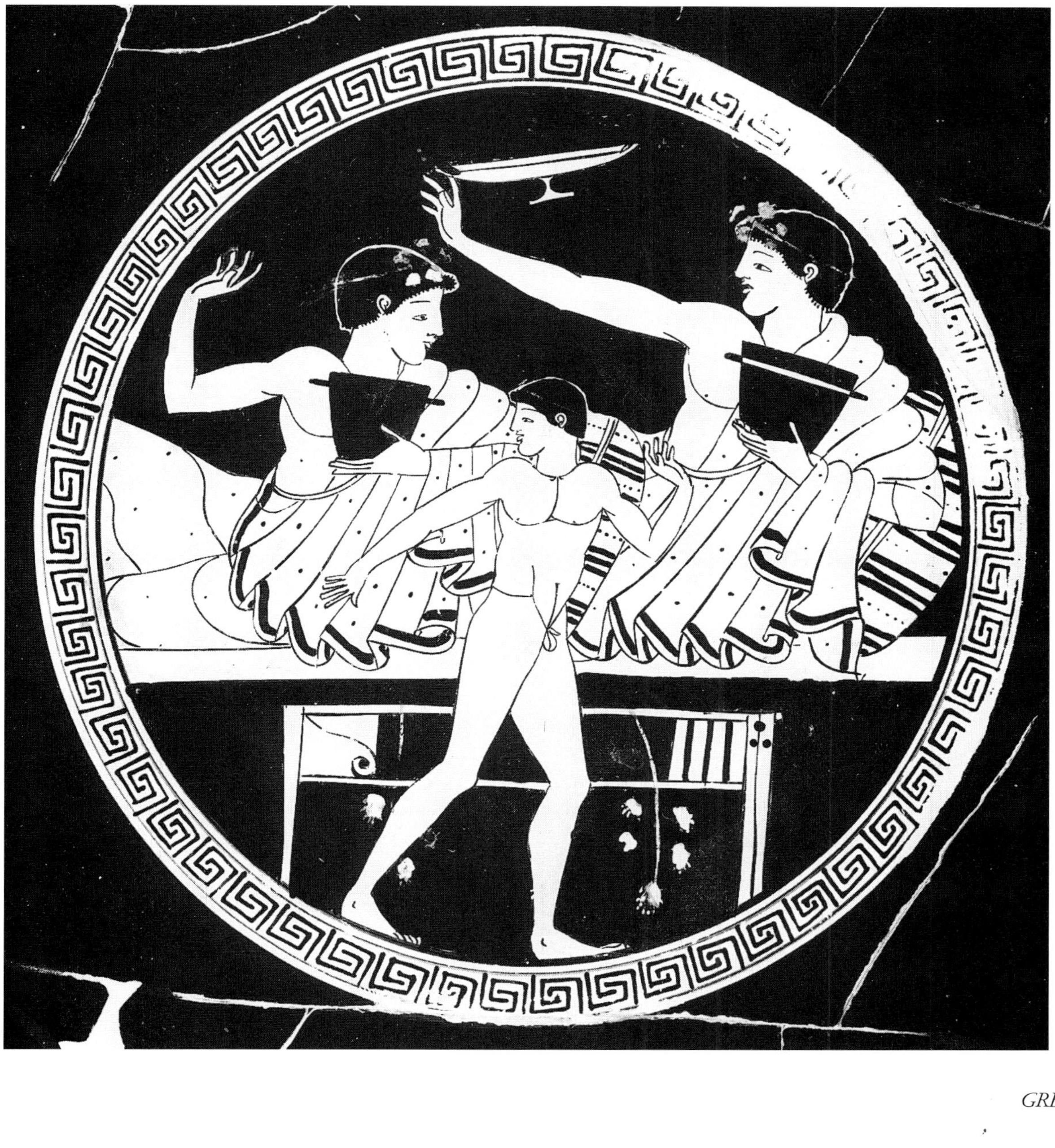

(b) 56

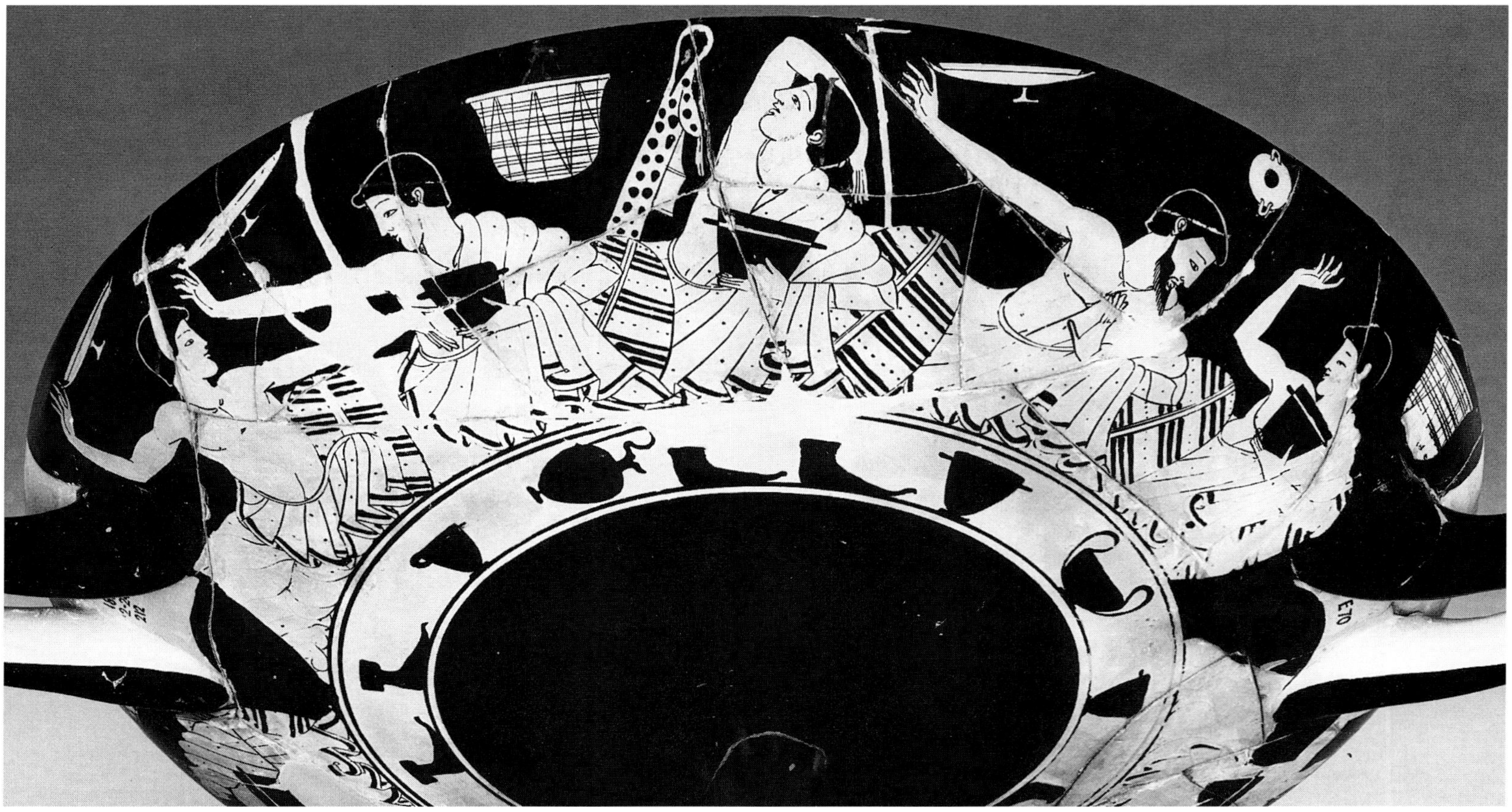

(a) 56

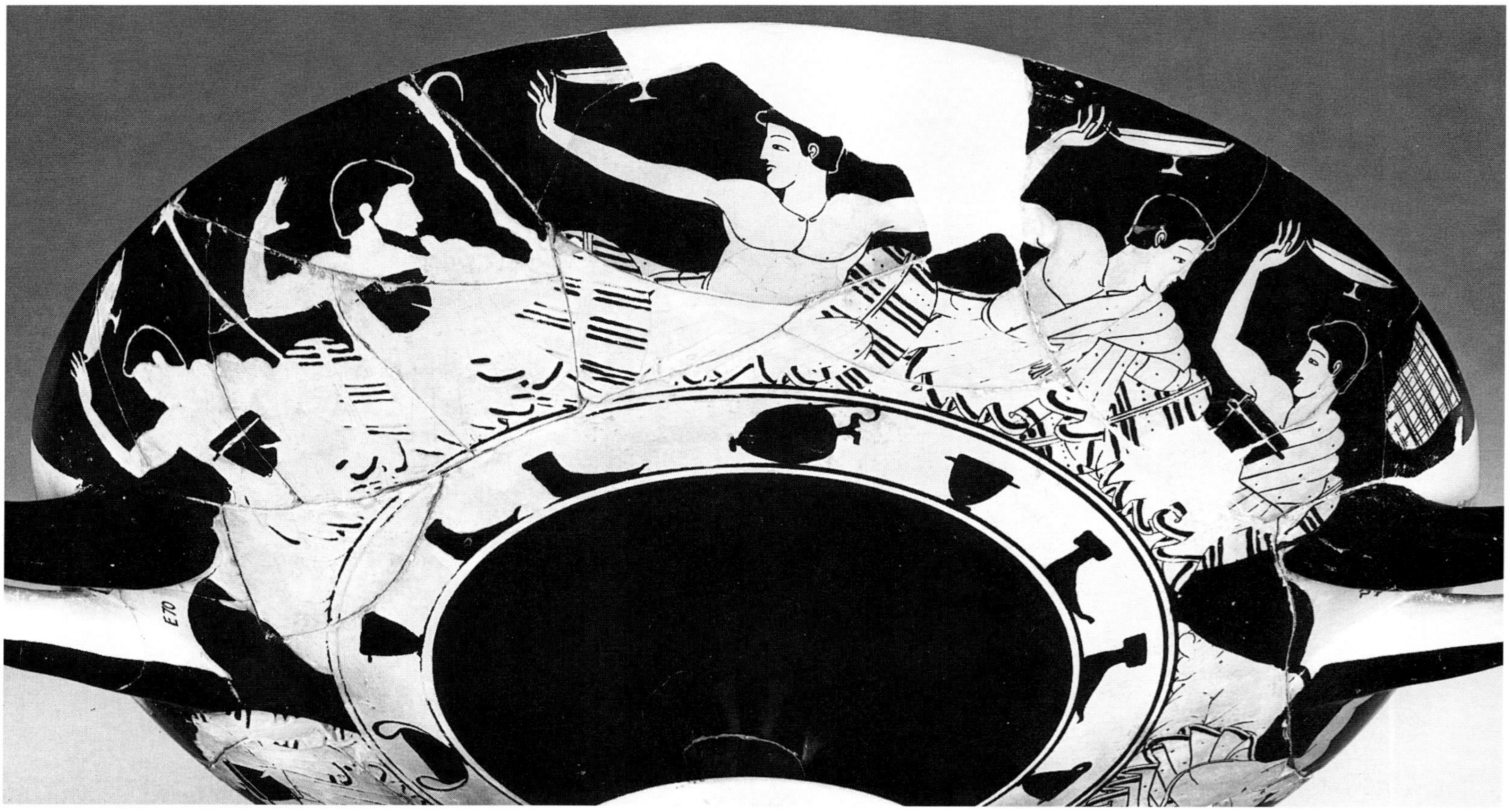

(b) 56

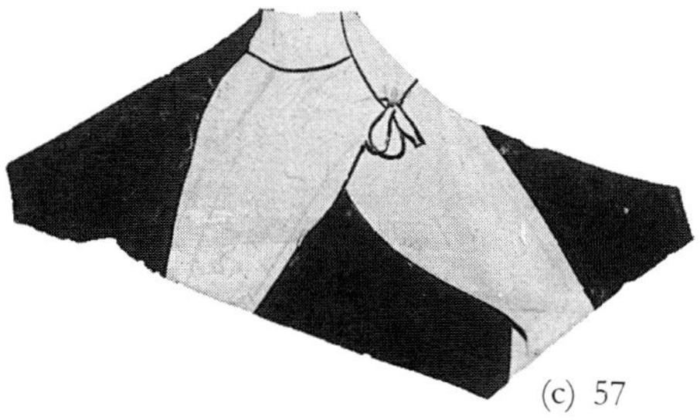

(c) 57

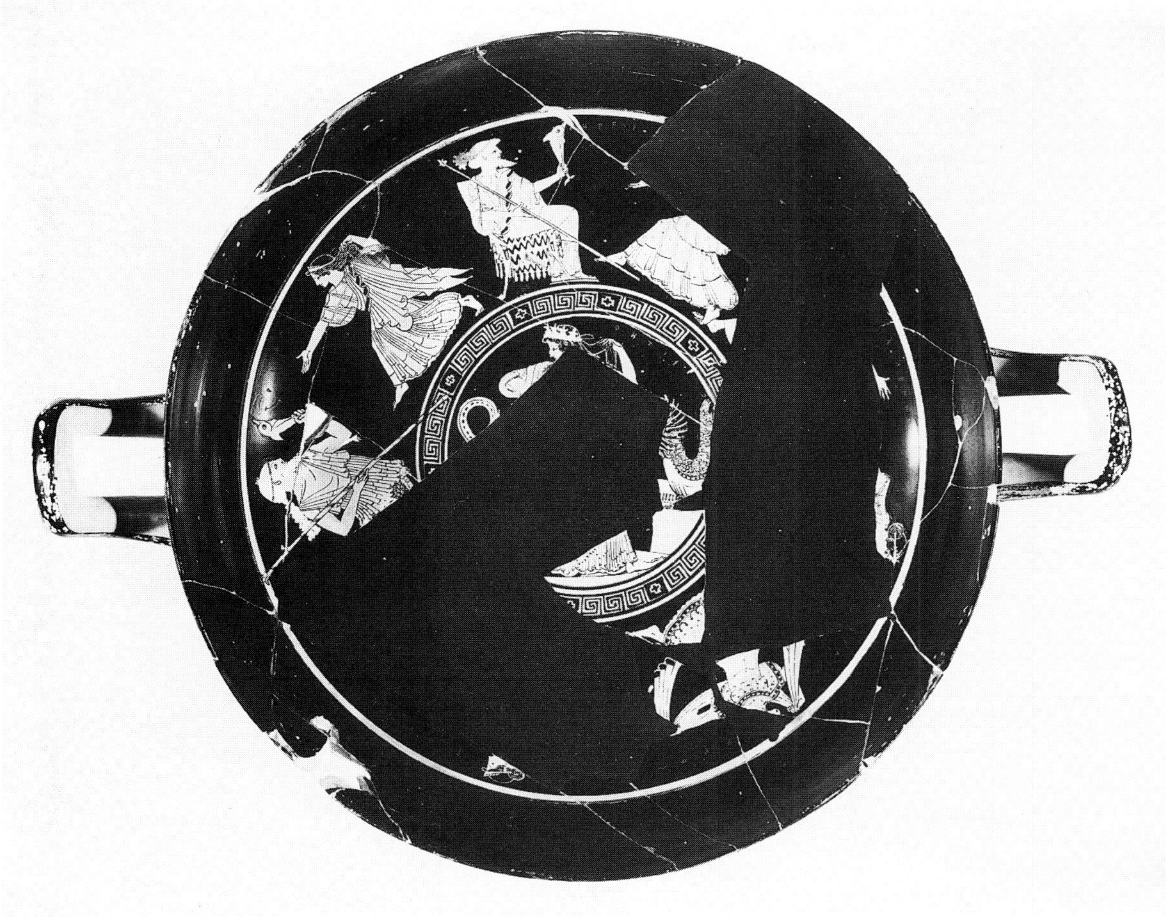

(a) 58

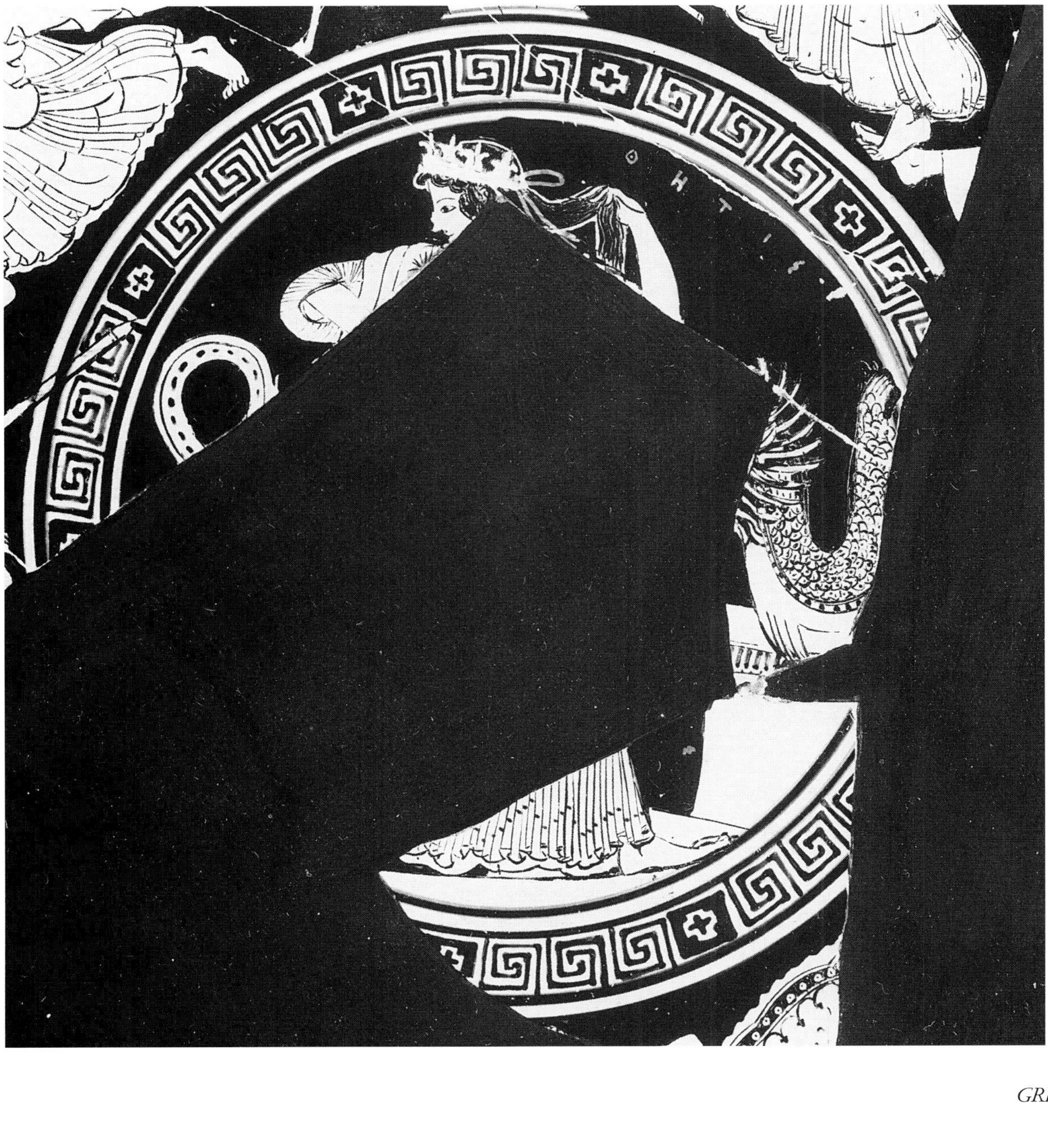

(b) 58

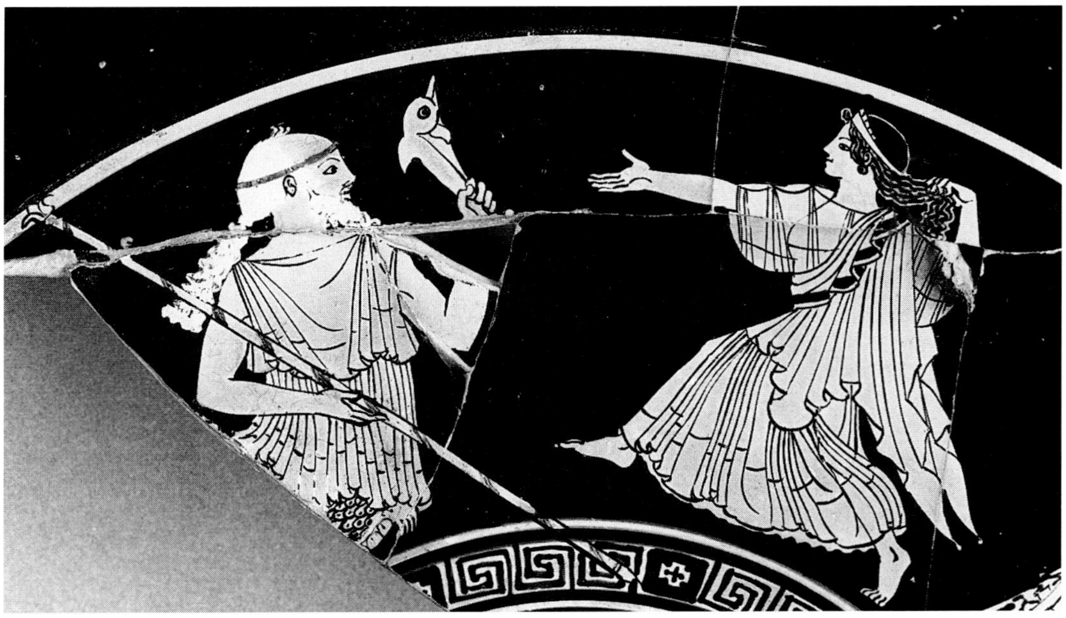

(a) 58

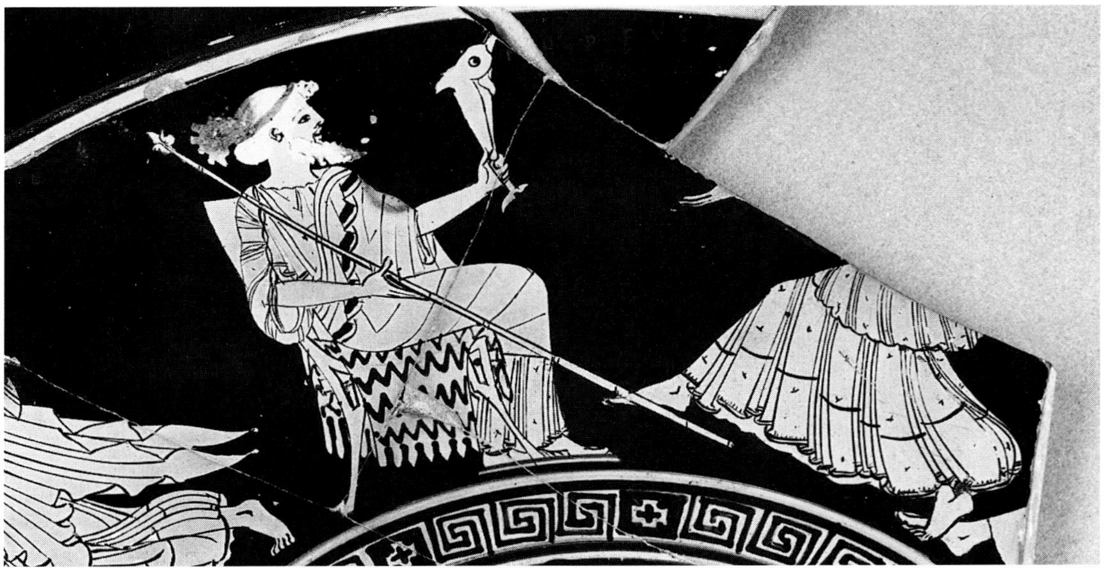

(b) 58

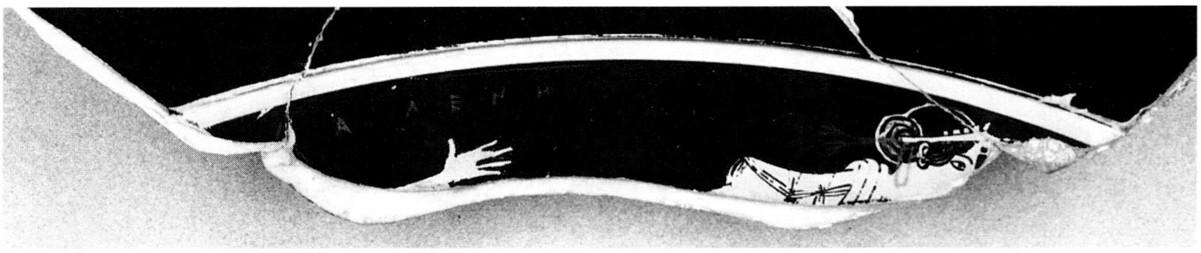

(c) 58

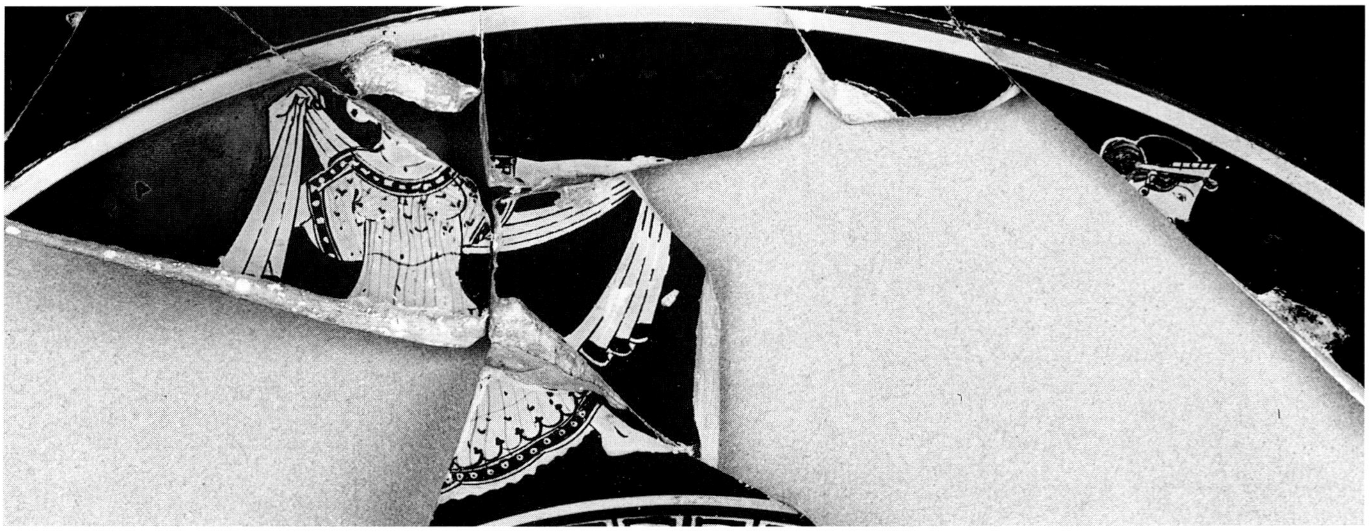

(d) 58

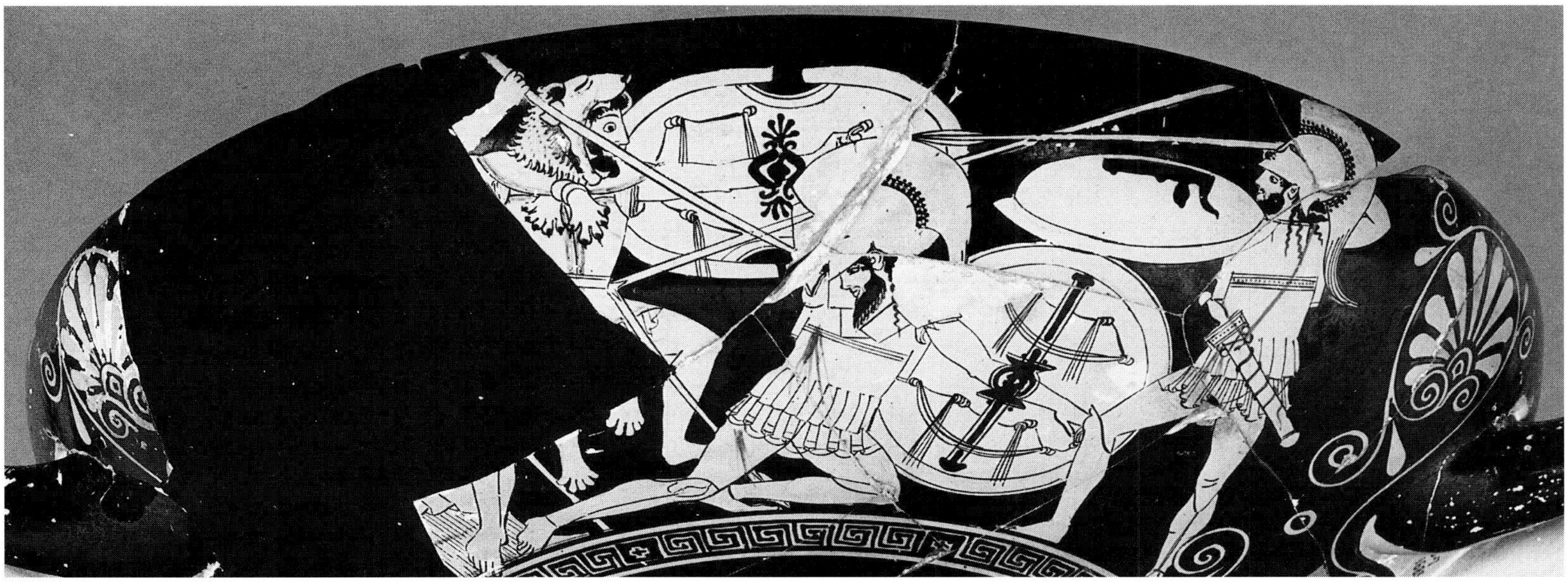

(a) 58

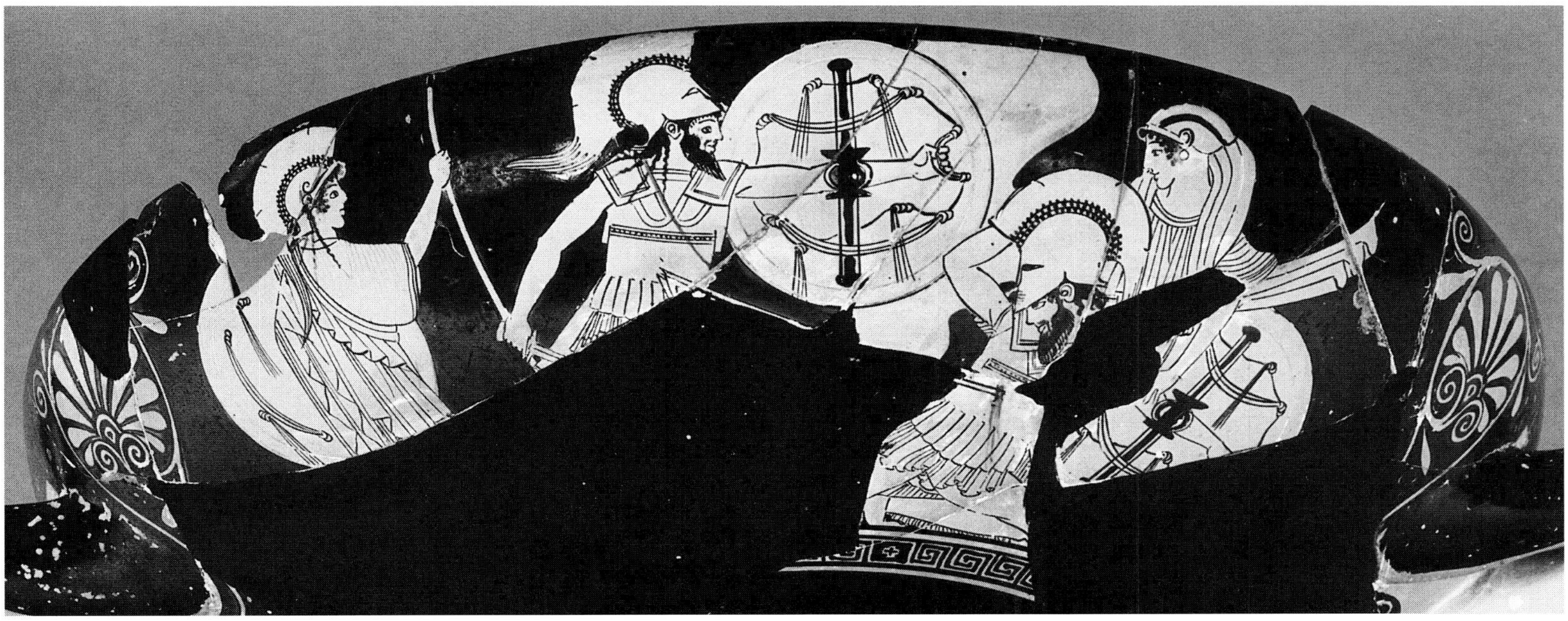

(b) 58

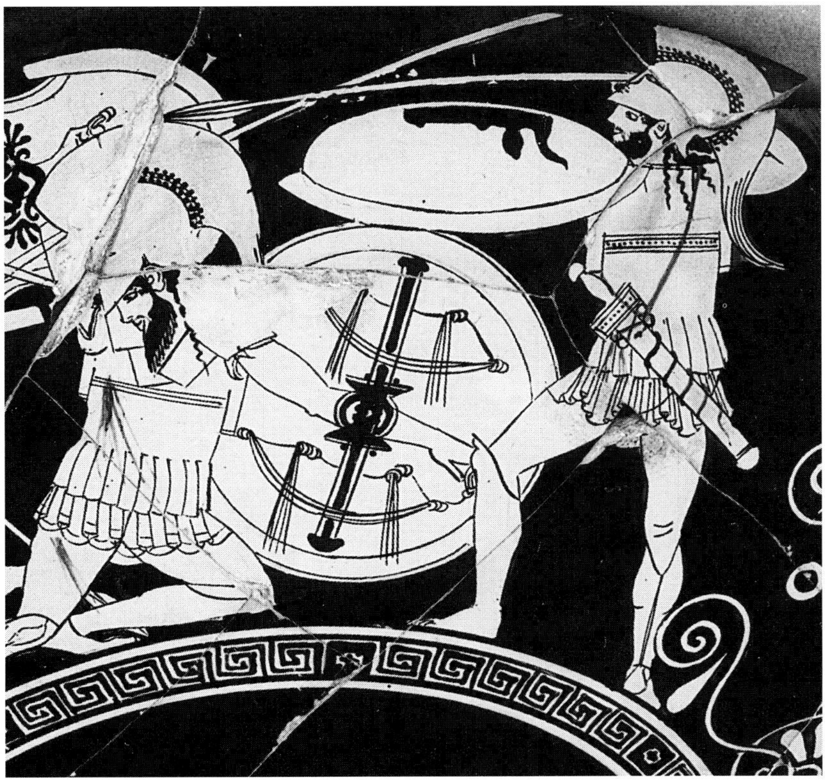

(c) 58

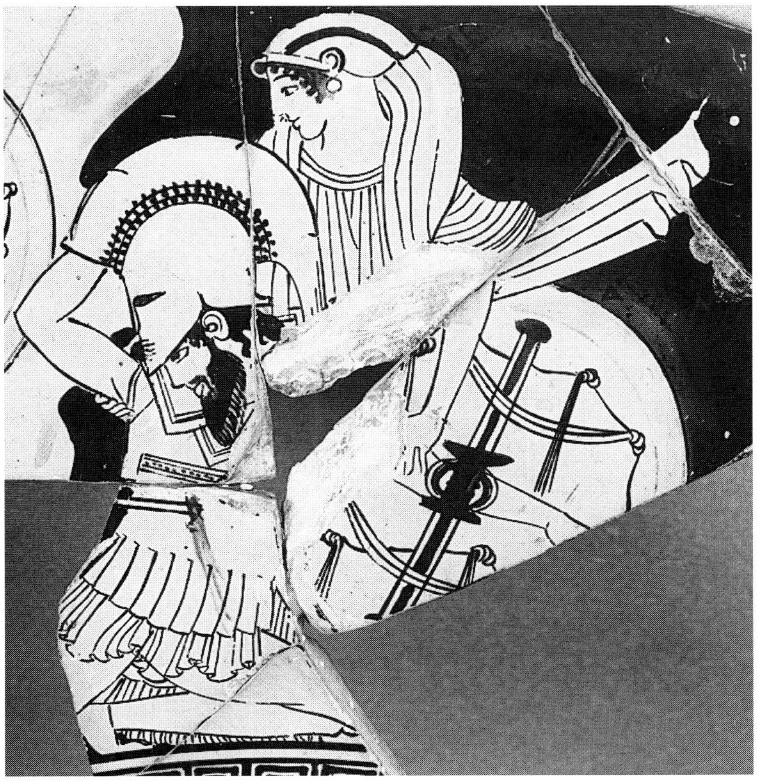

(d) 58

FIGURE 1

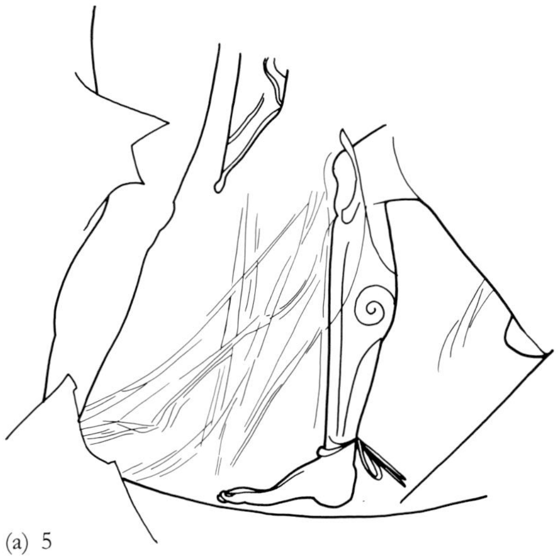

(a) 5

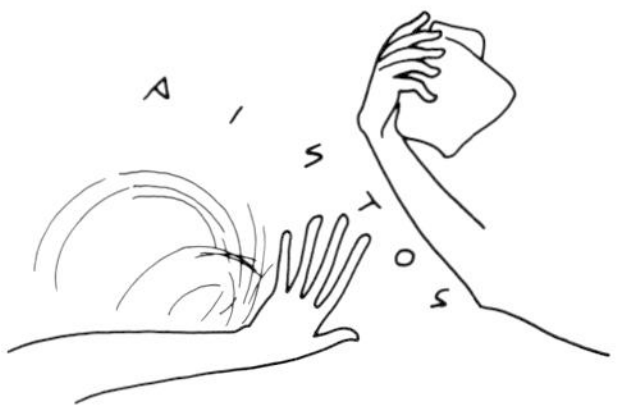

(b) 5

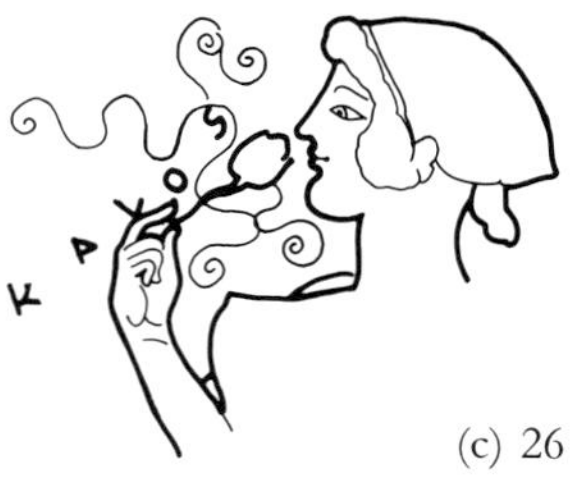

(c) 26

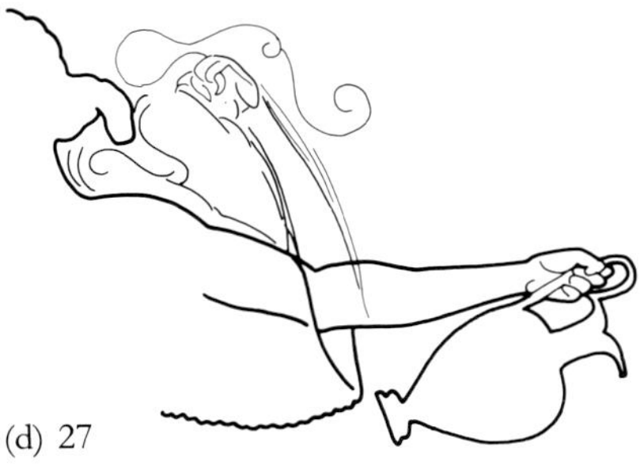

(d) 27

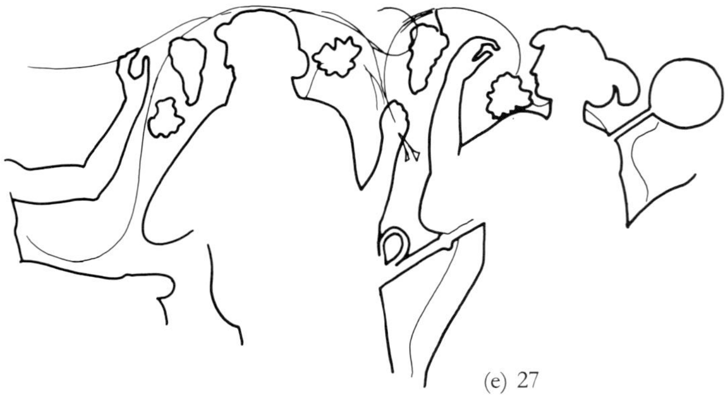

(e) 27

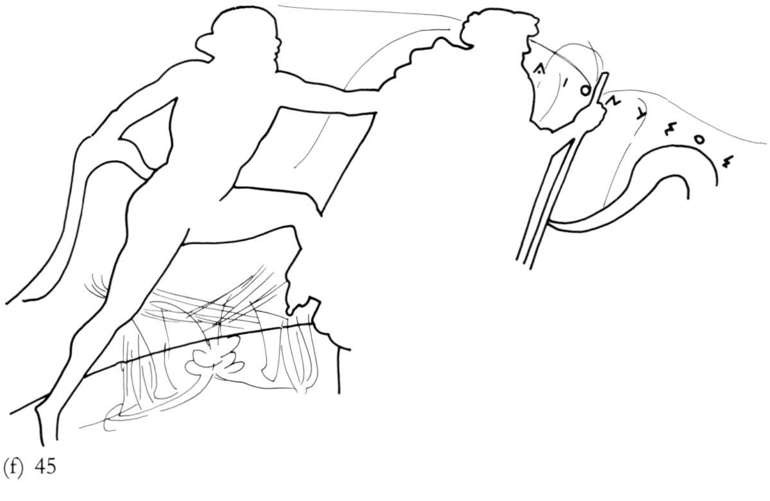

(f) 45

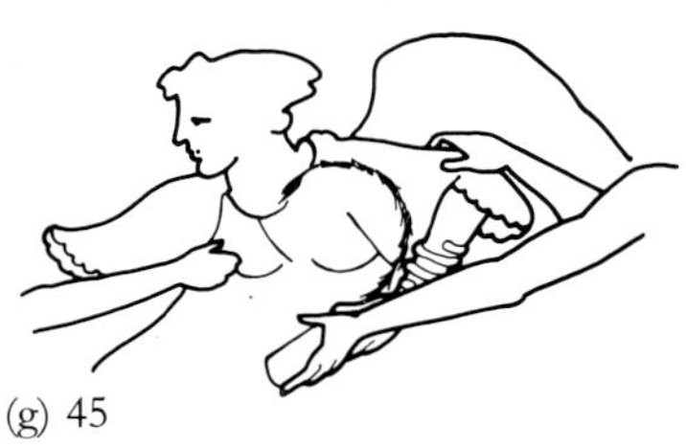

(g) 45

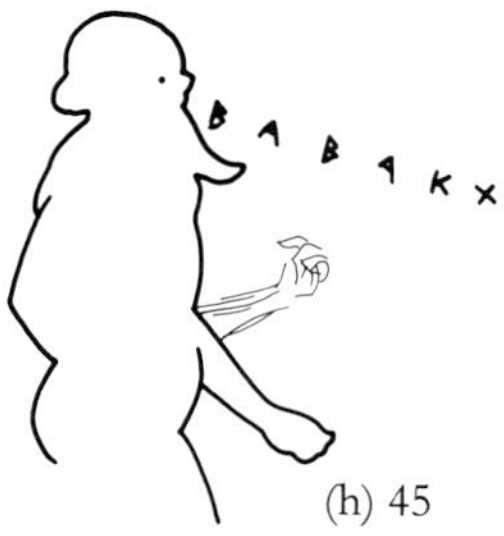

(h) 45

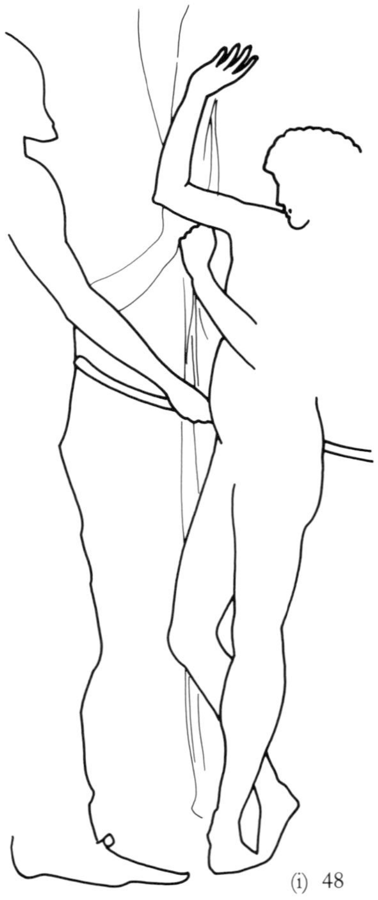

(i) 48

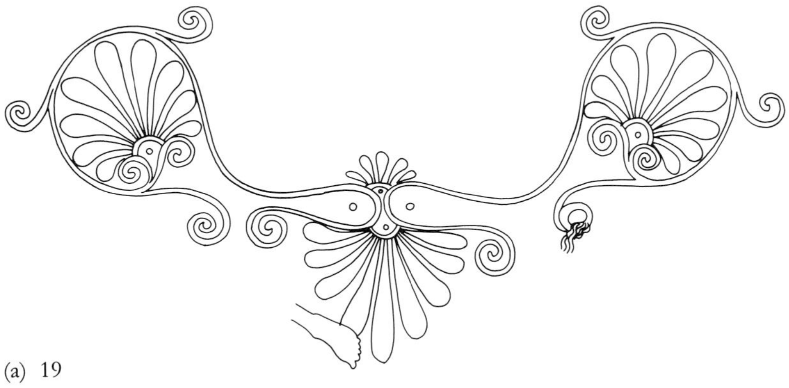

(b) 20

(a) 19

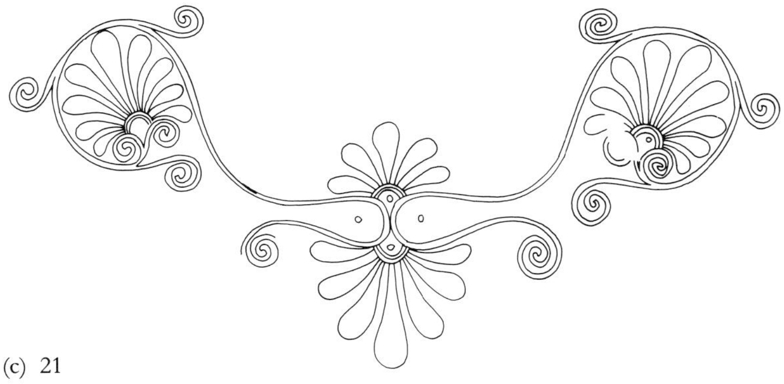

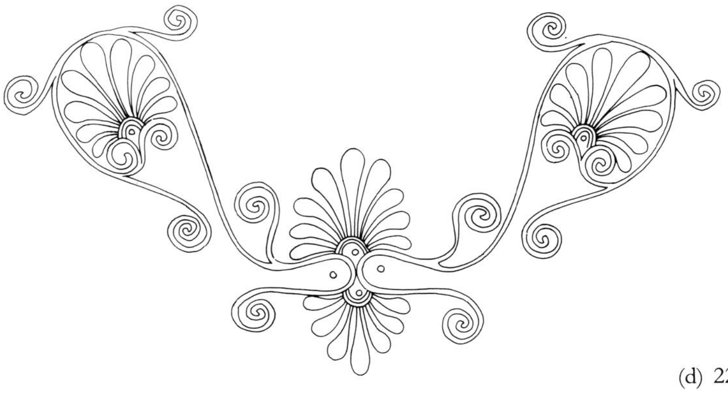

(c) 21

(d) 22

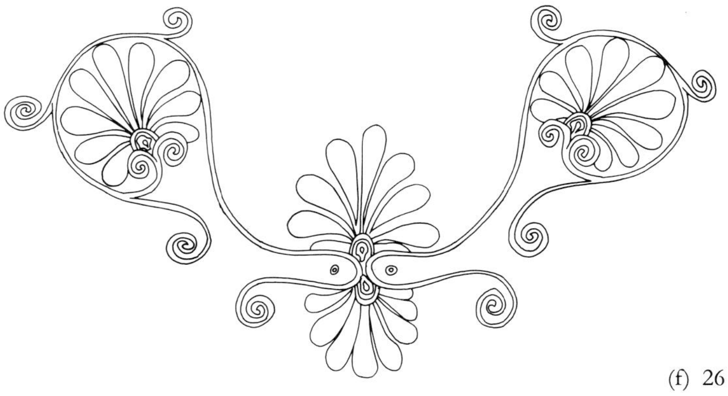

(e) 24

(f) 26

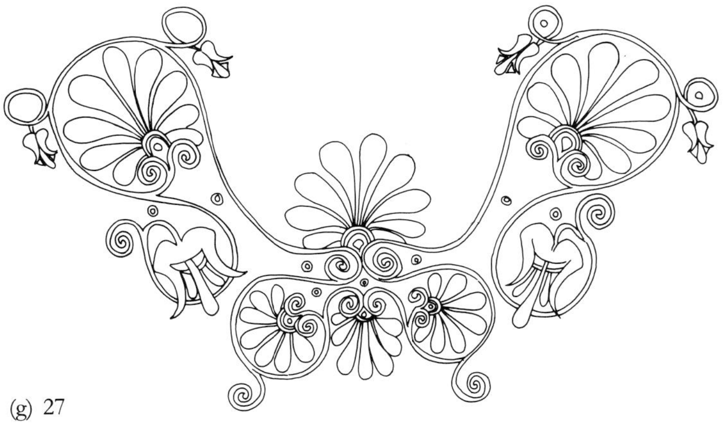

(g) 27

(h) 28

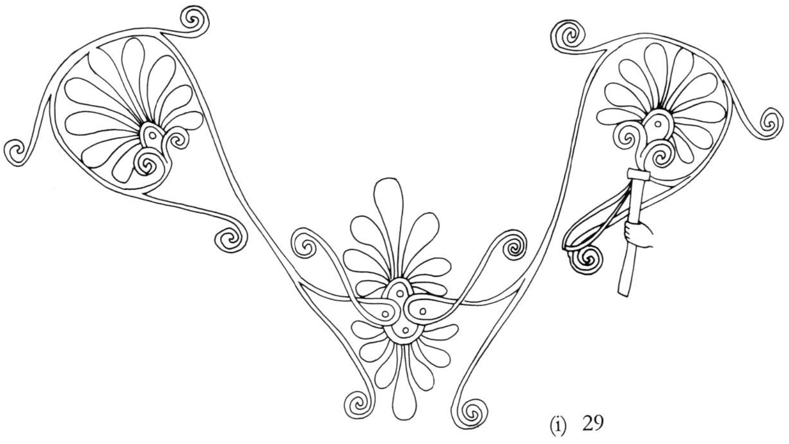

(i) 29

FIGURE 3

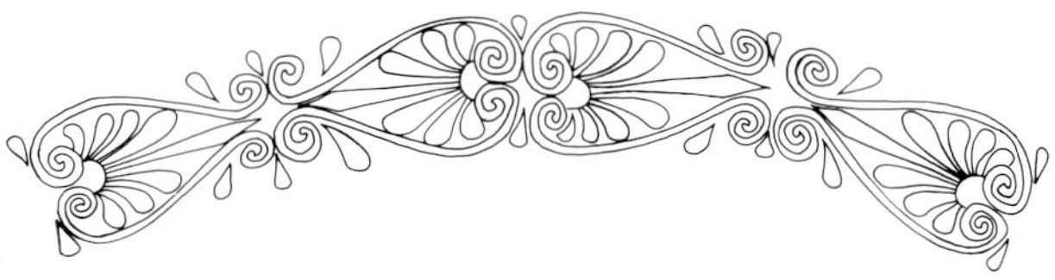

(a) 8

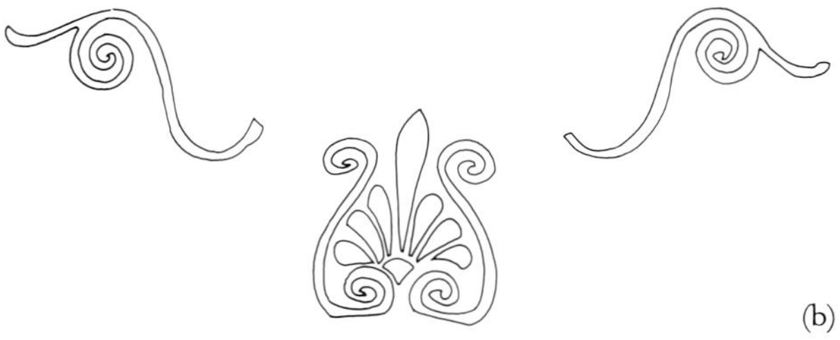

(b) 17

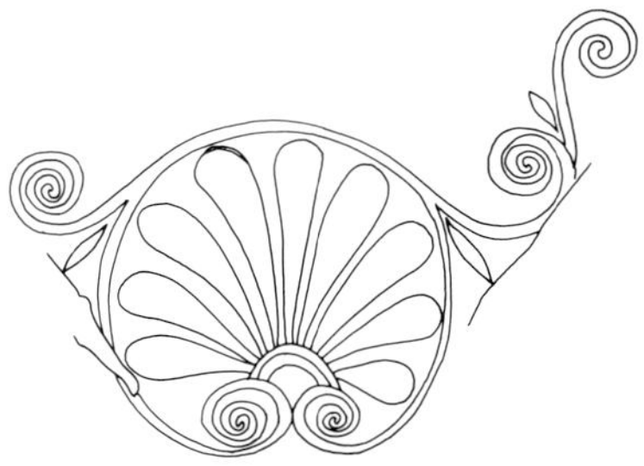

(c) 37

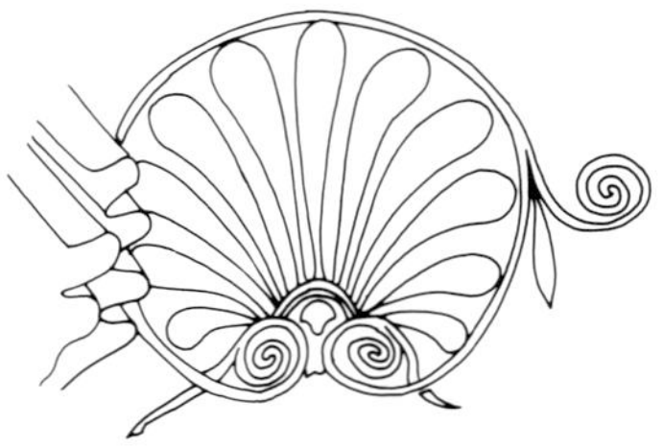

(d) 38

(e) 6

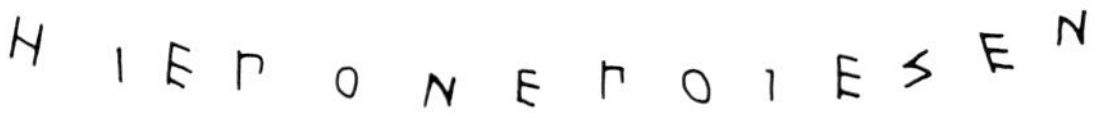

(f) 37

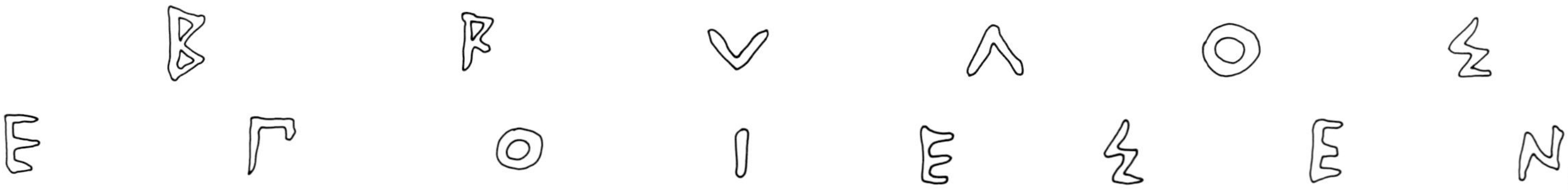

(g) 45

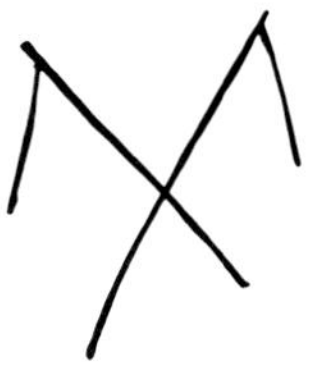

(h) 6

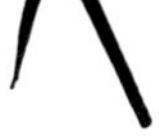

(i) 38

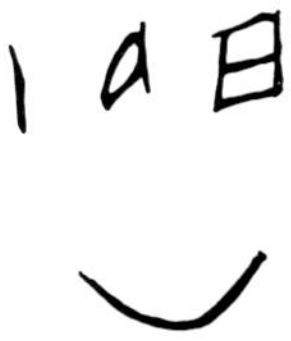

(j) 20

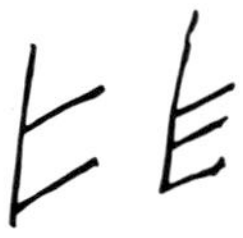

(k) 48

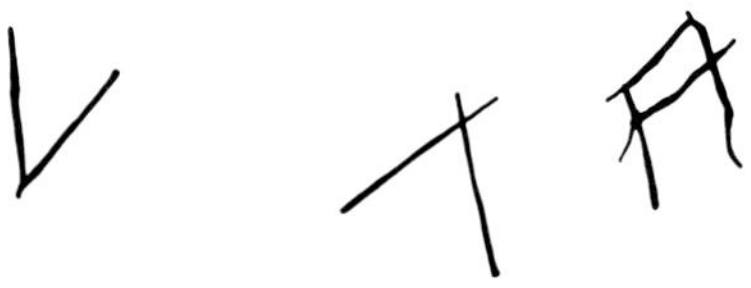

(l) 21

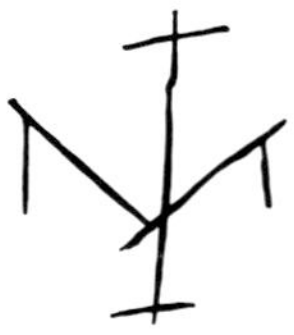

(l) 21

FIGURE 4

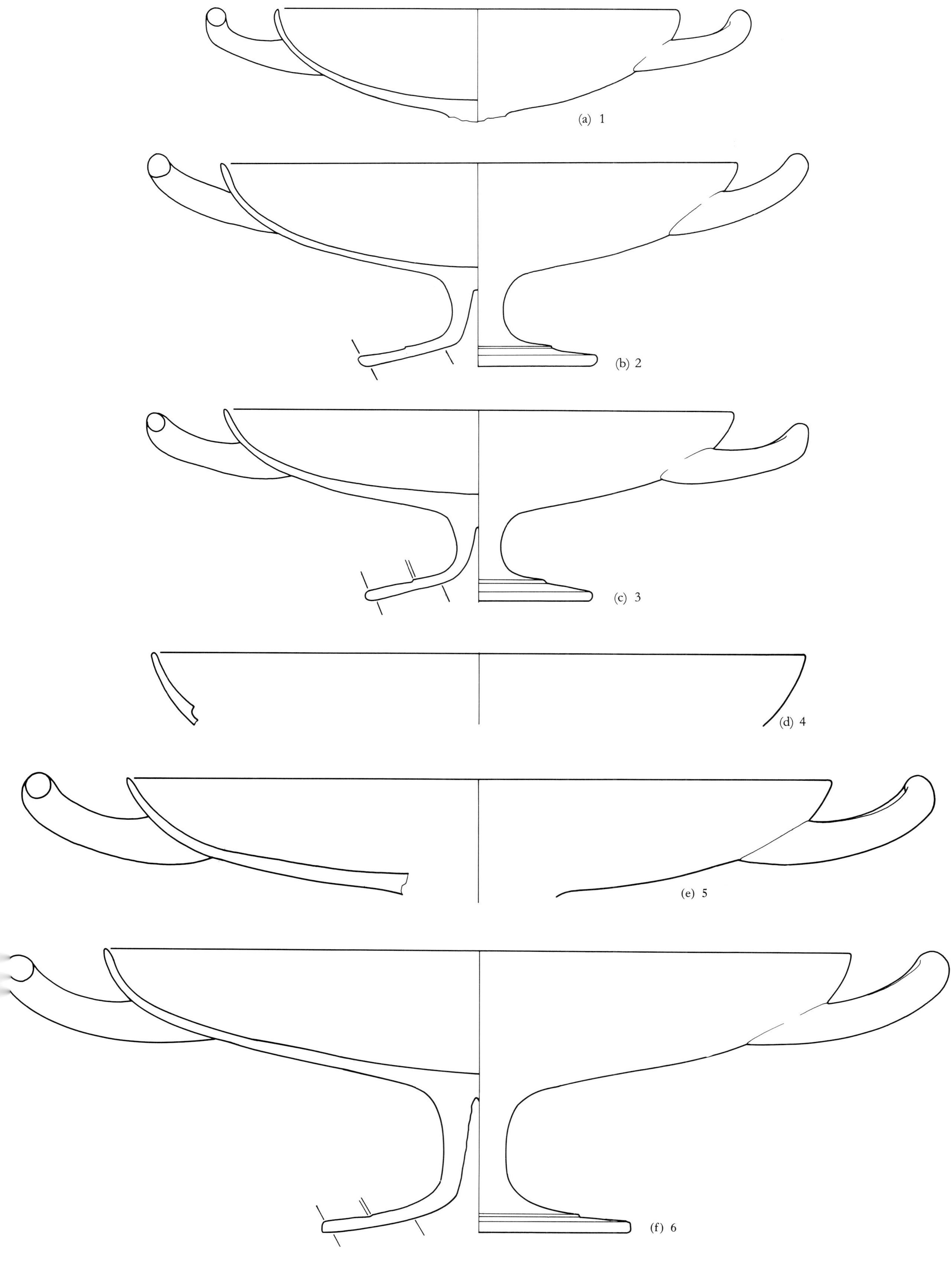

FIGURE 5

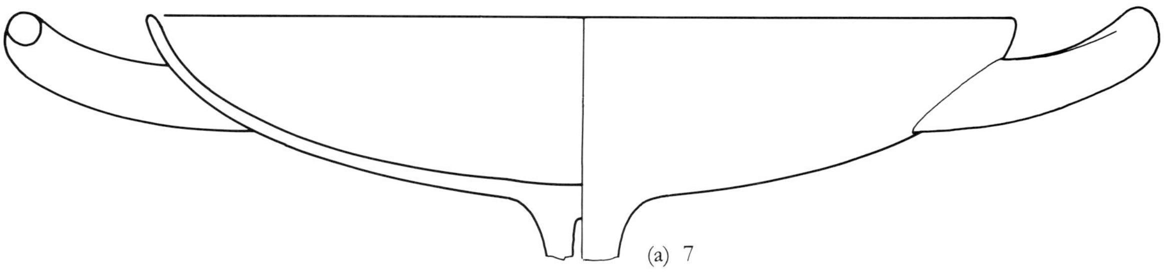

(a) 7

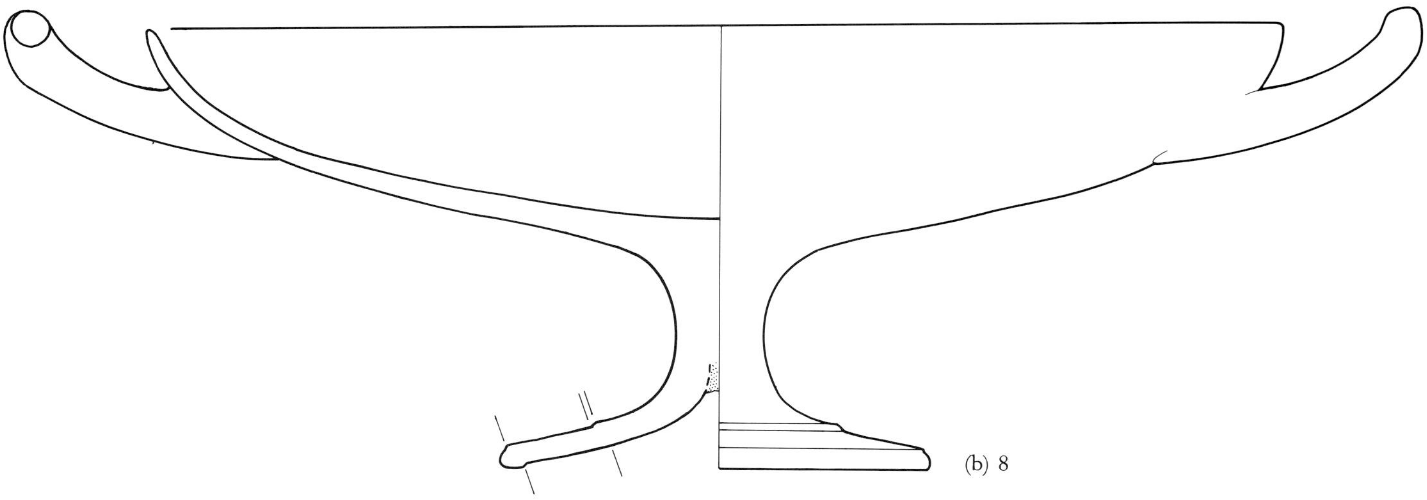

(b) 8

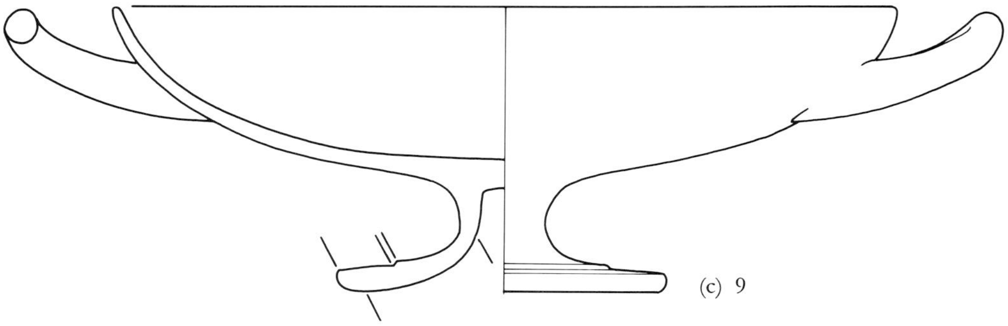

(c) 9

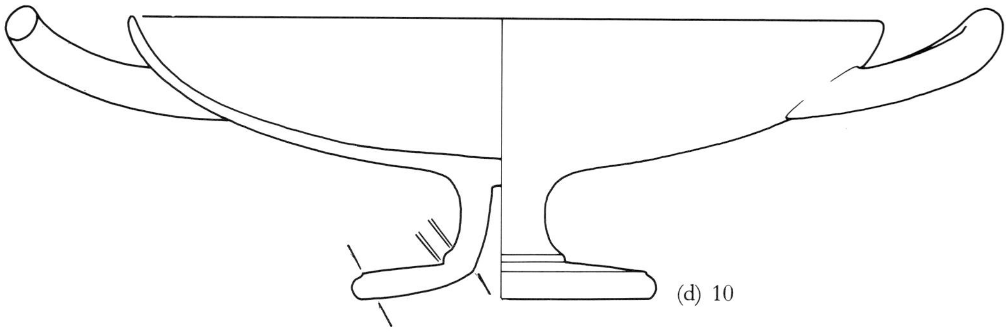

(d) 10

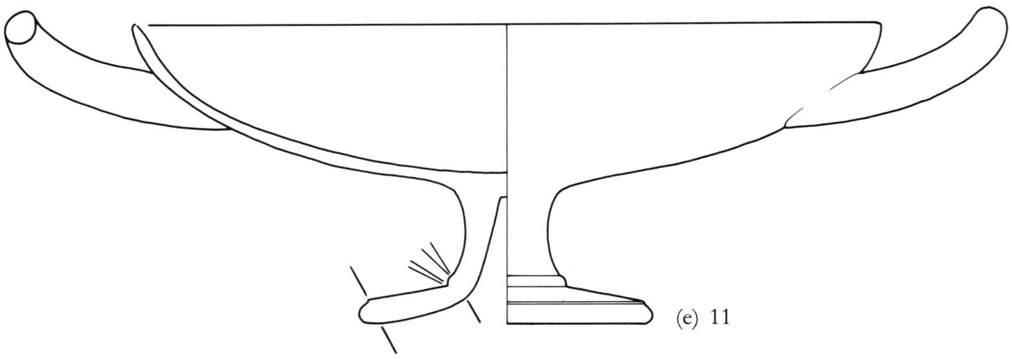

(e) 11

FIGURE 6

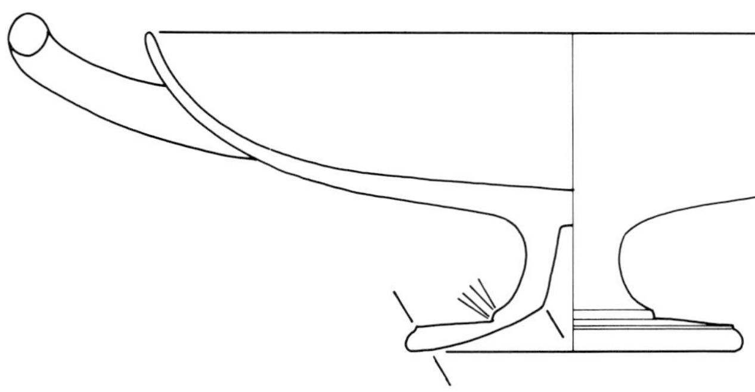

(a) 12

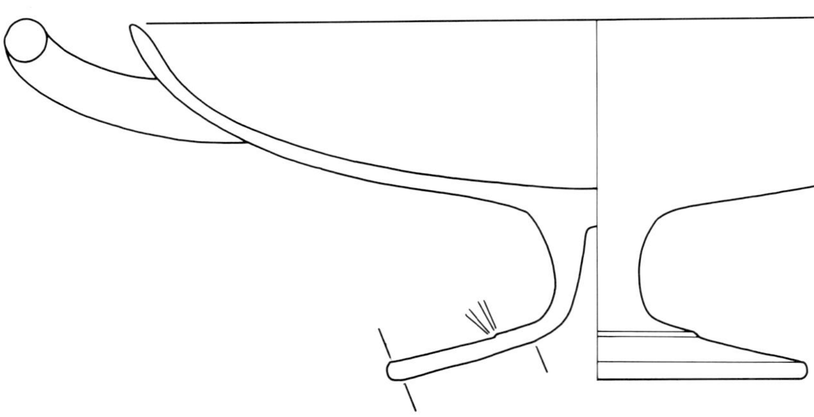

(b) 13

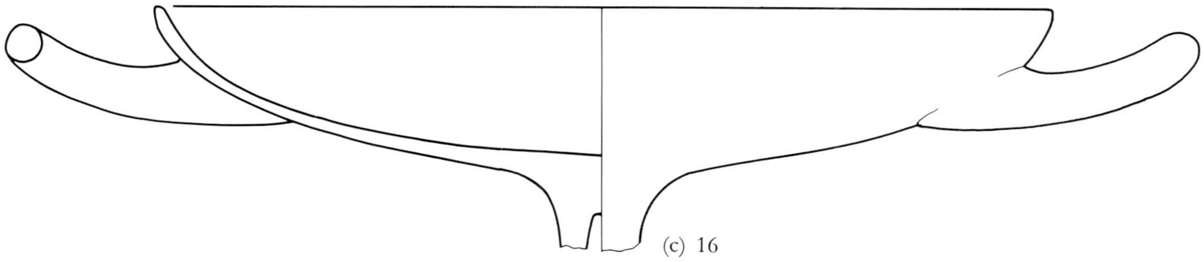

(c) 16

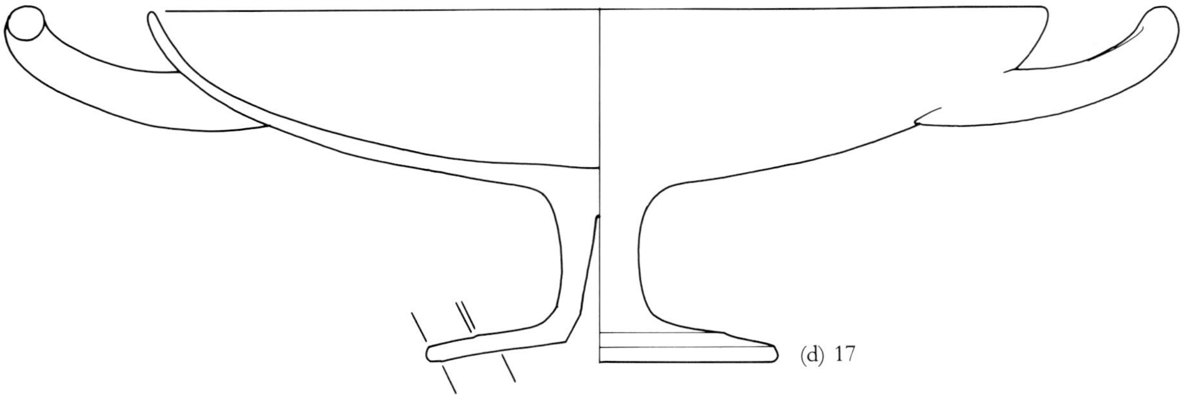

(d) 17

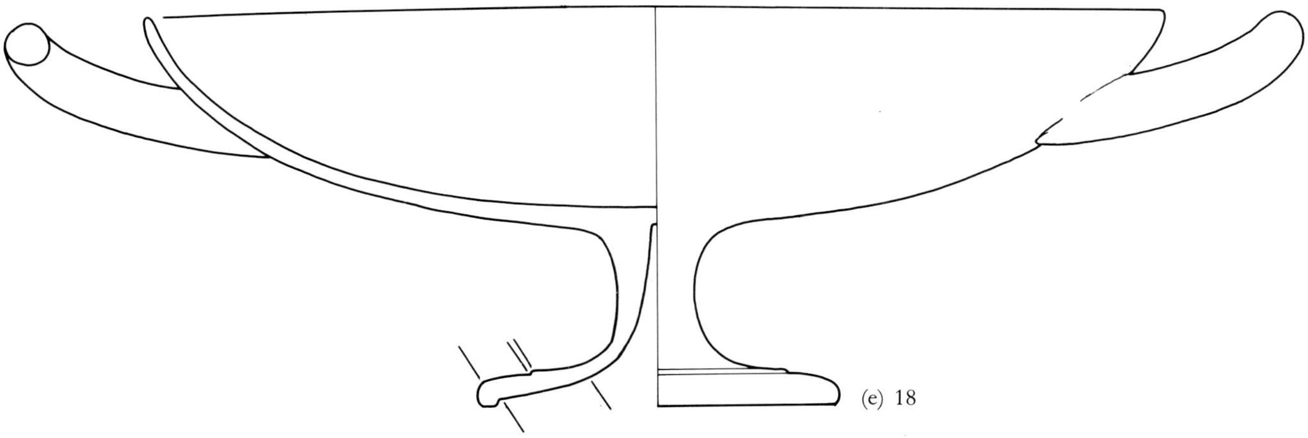

(e) 18

FIGURE 7

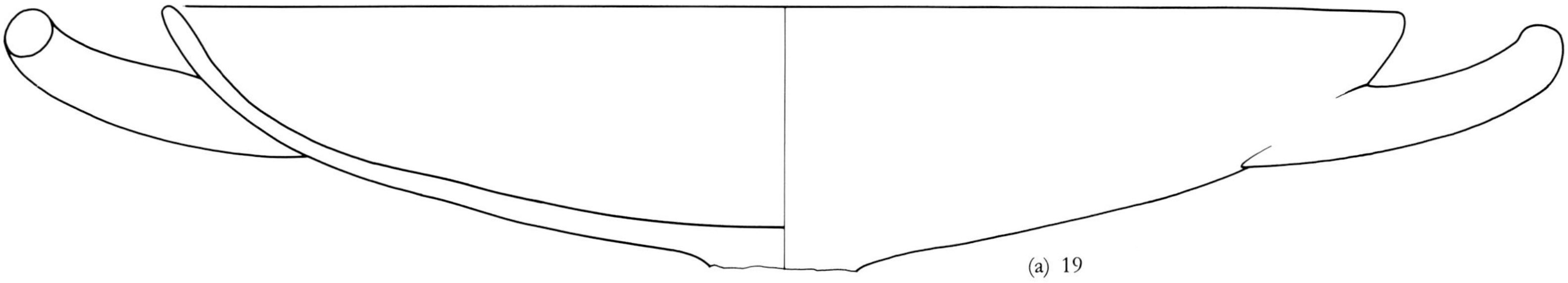
(a) 19

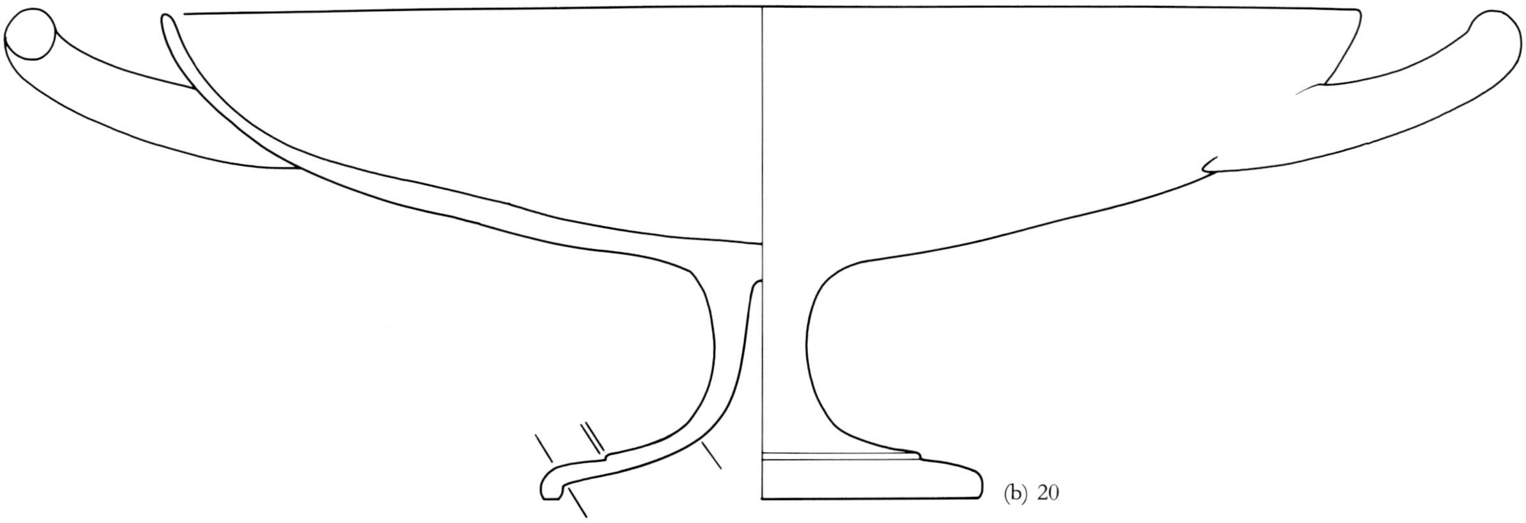
(b) 20

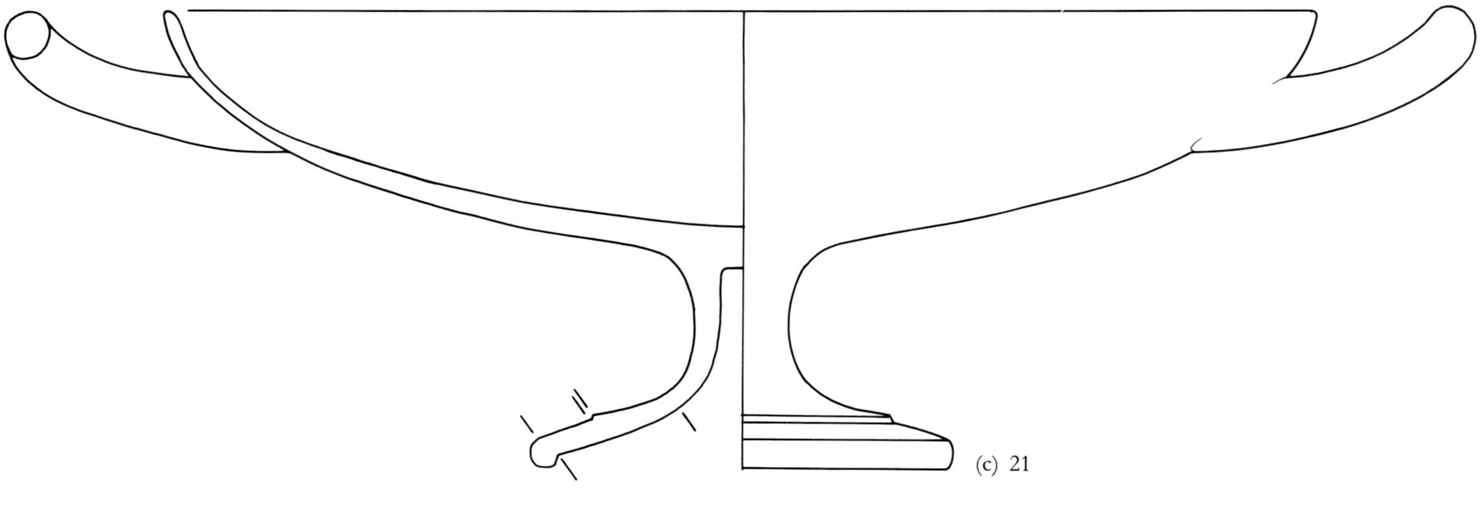
(c) 21

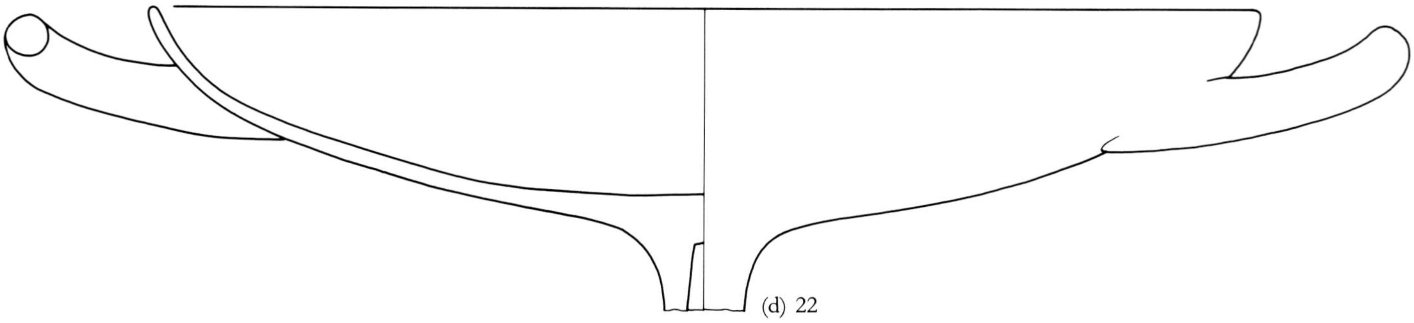
(d) 22

FIGURE 8

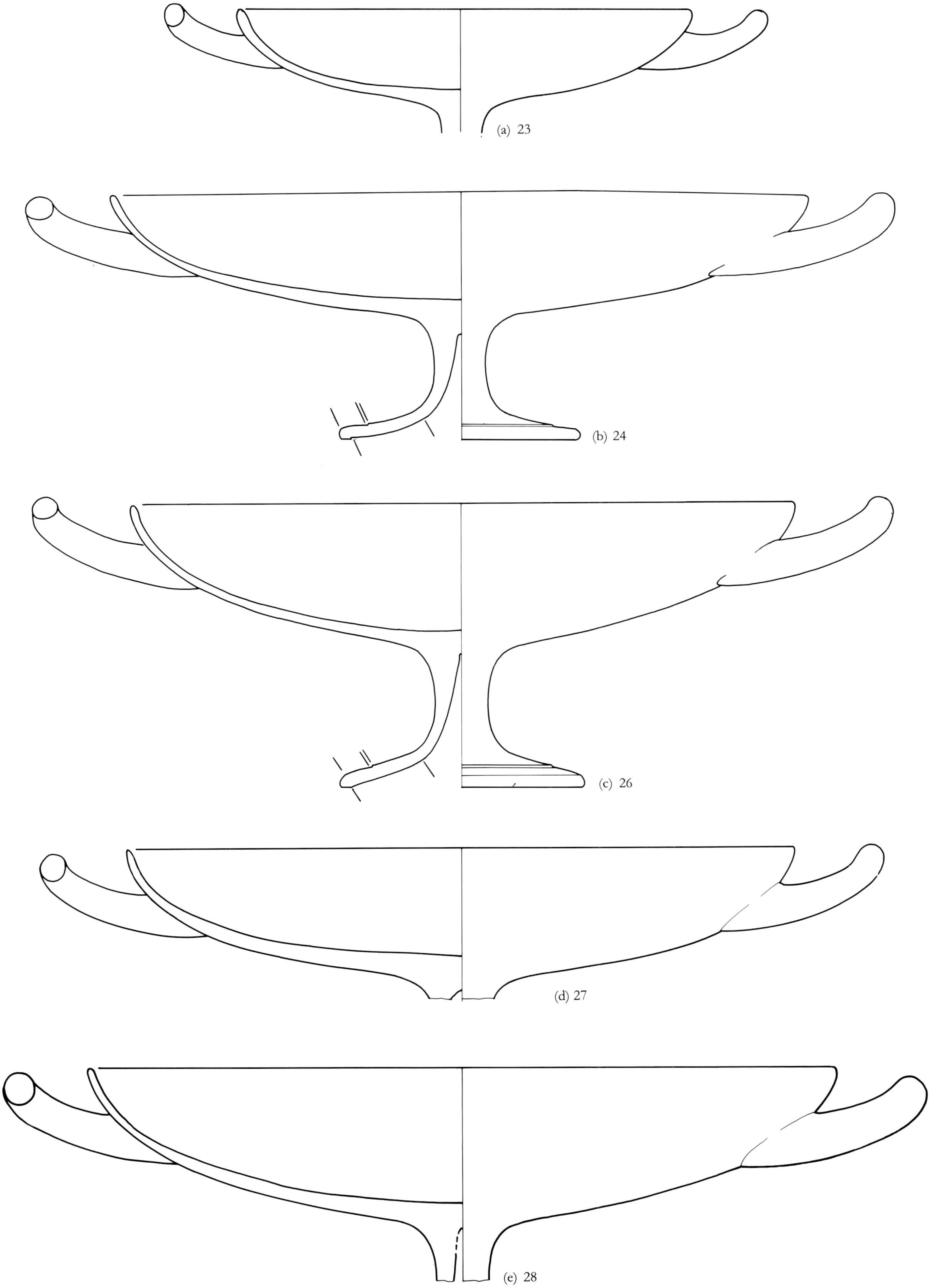

FIGURE 9

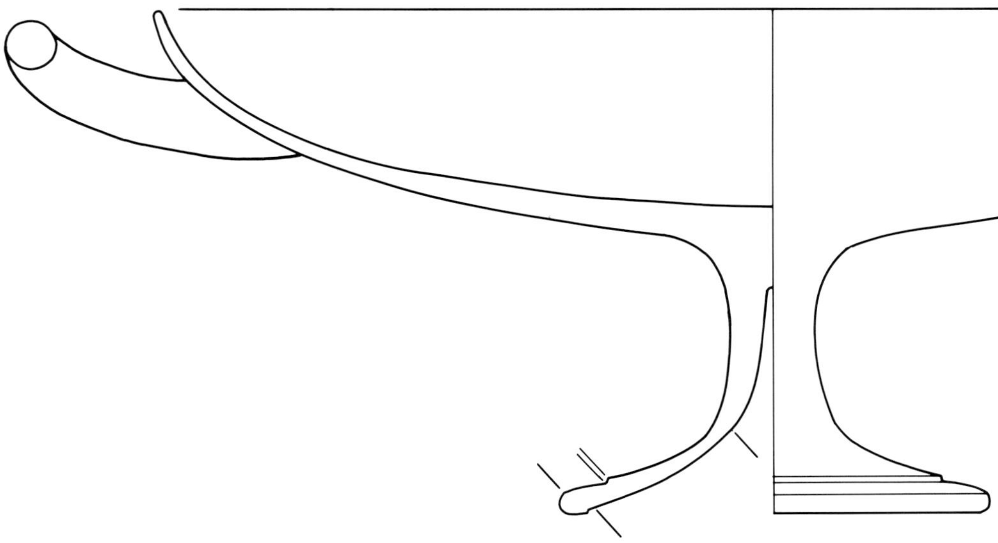

(a) 29

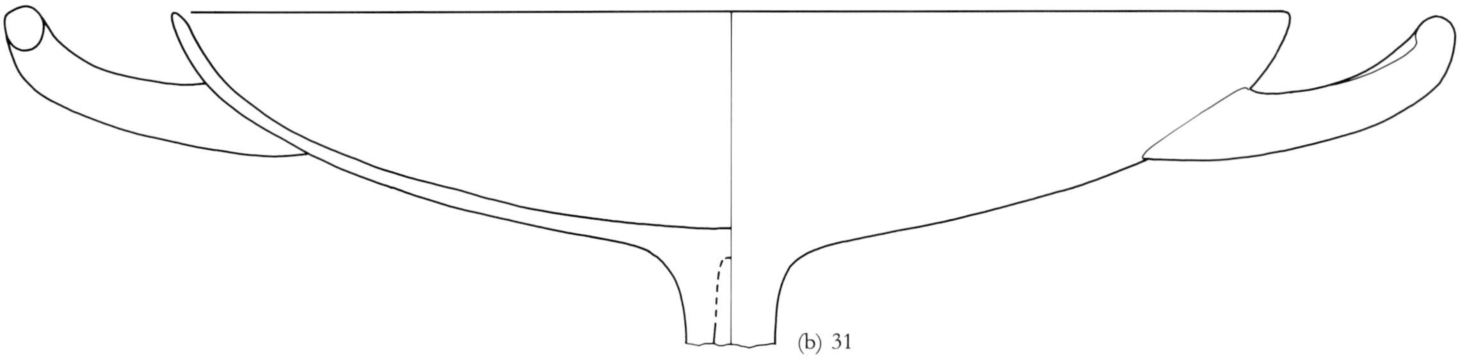

(b) 31

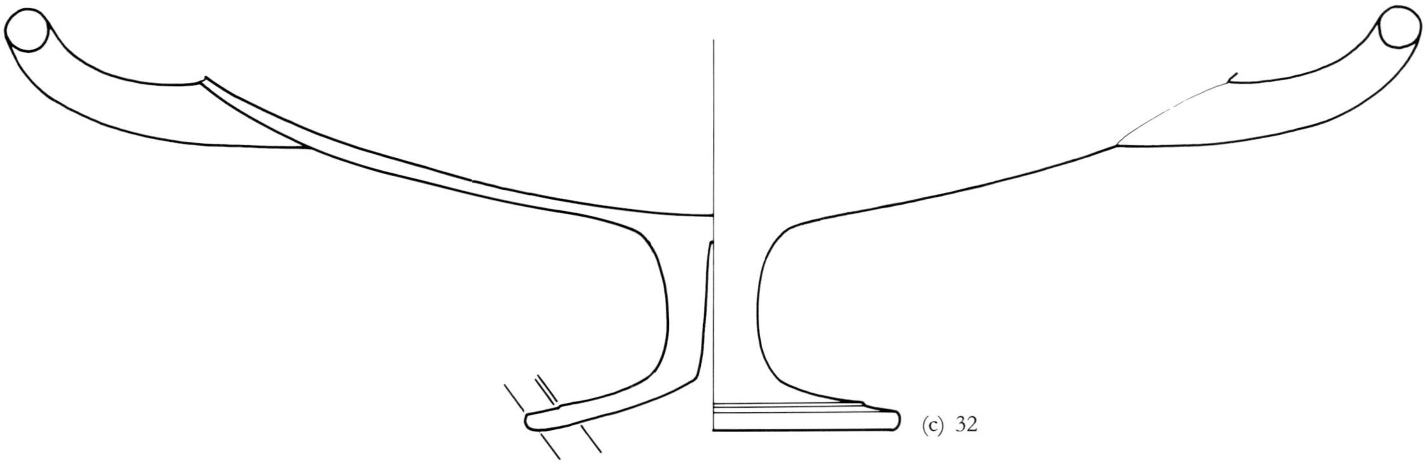

(c) 32

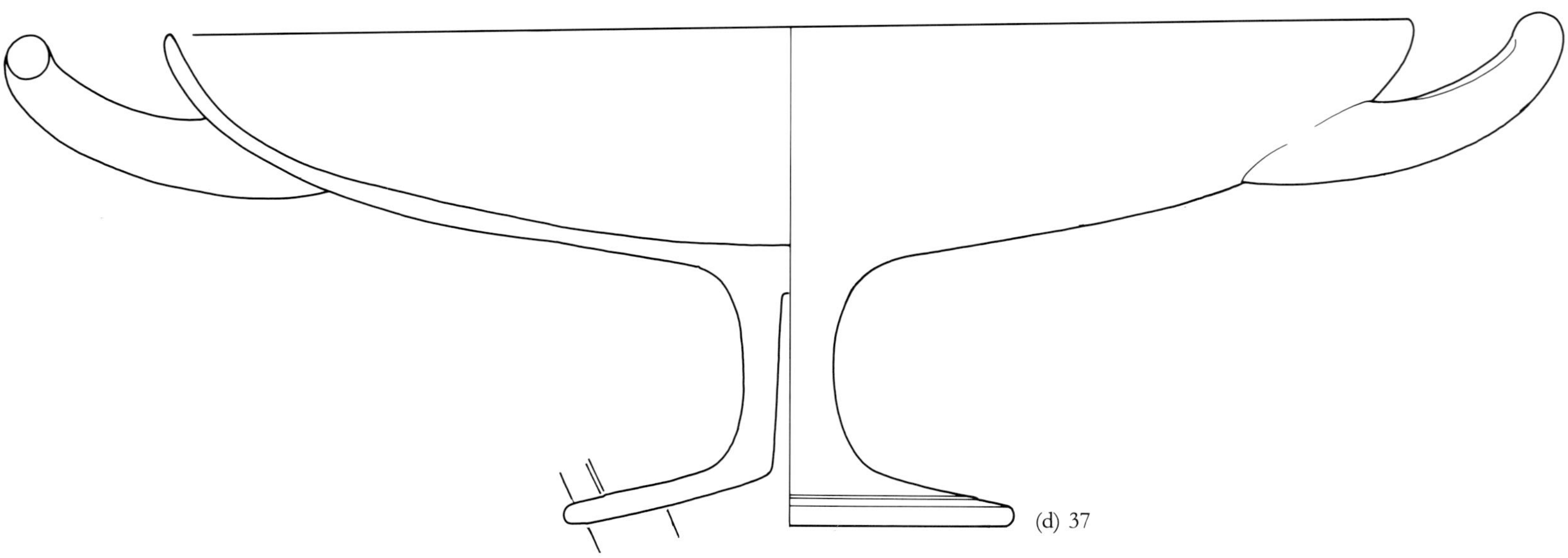

(d) 37

FIGURE 10

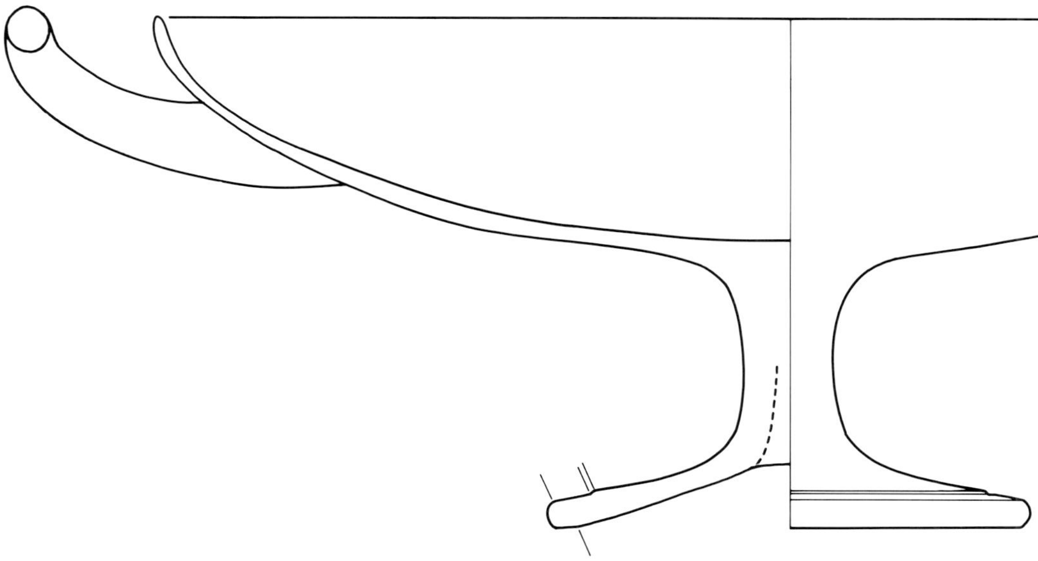

(a) 38

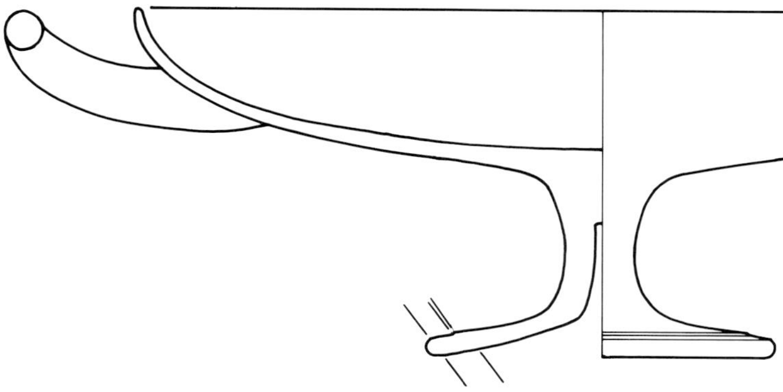

(b) 41

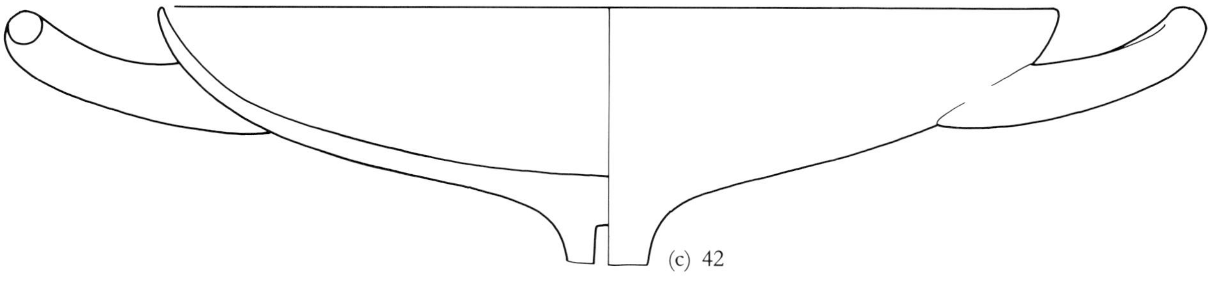

(c) 42

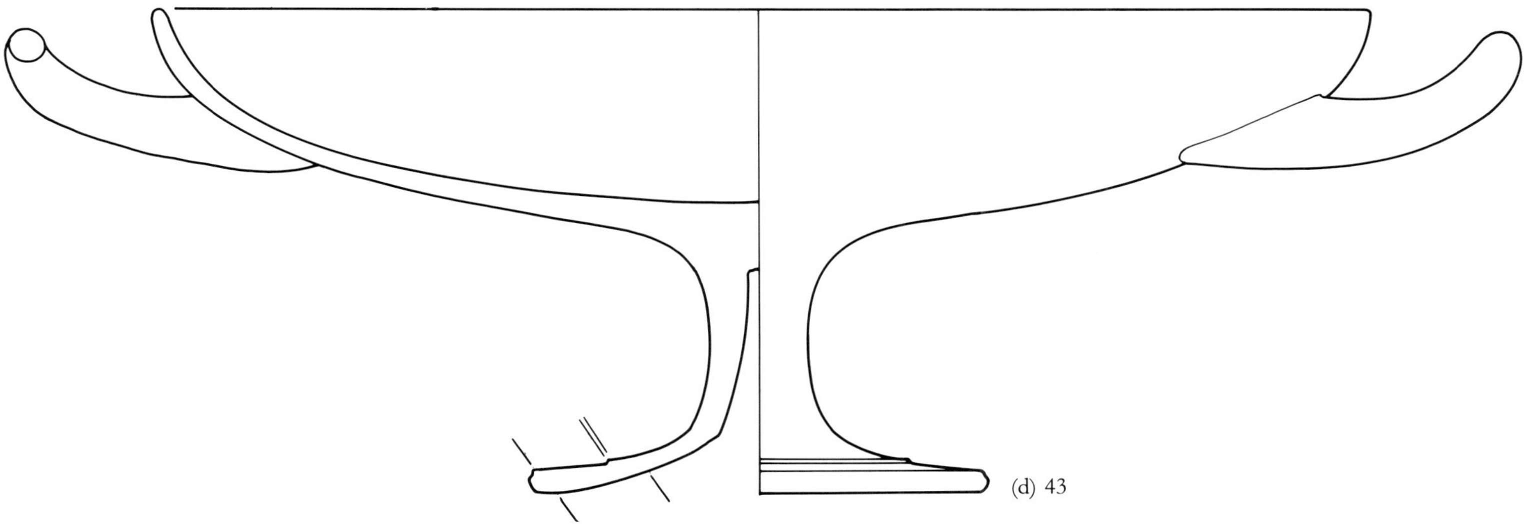

(d) 43

FIGURE 11

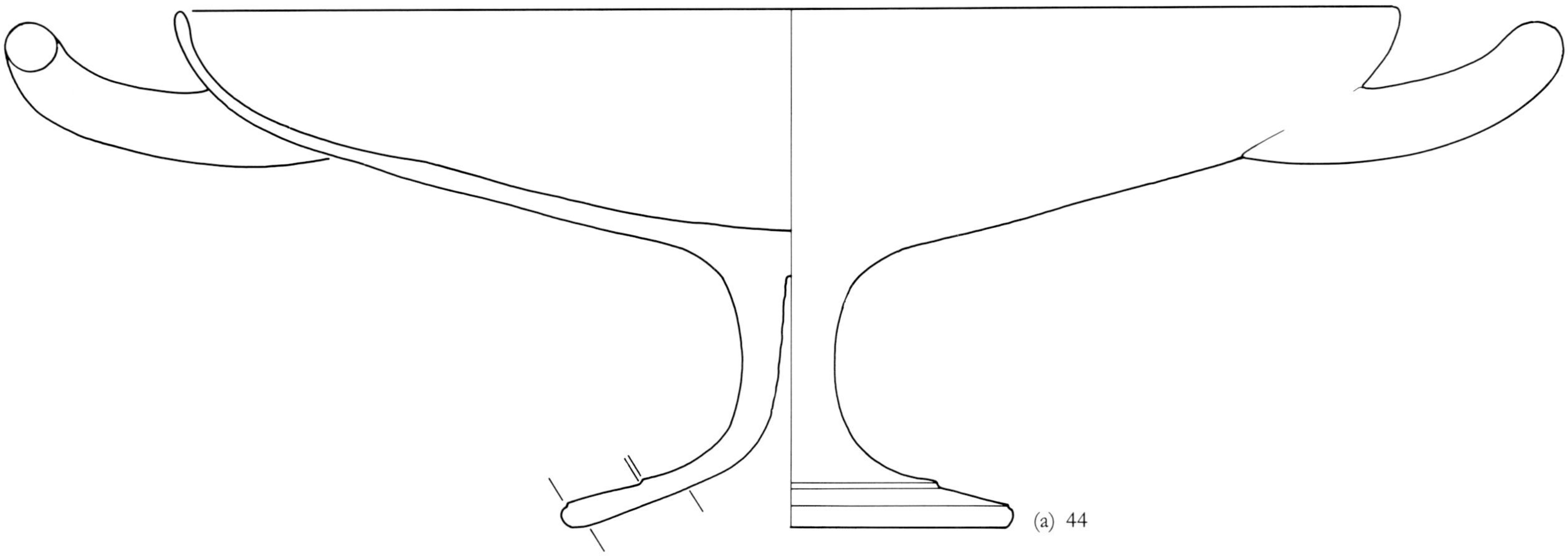

(a) 44

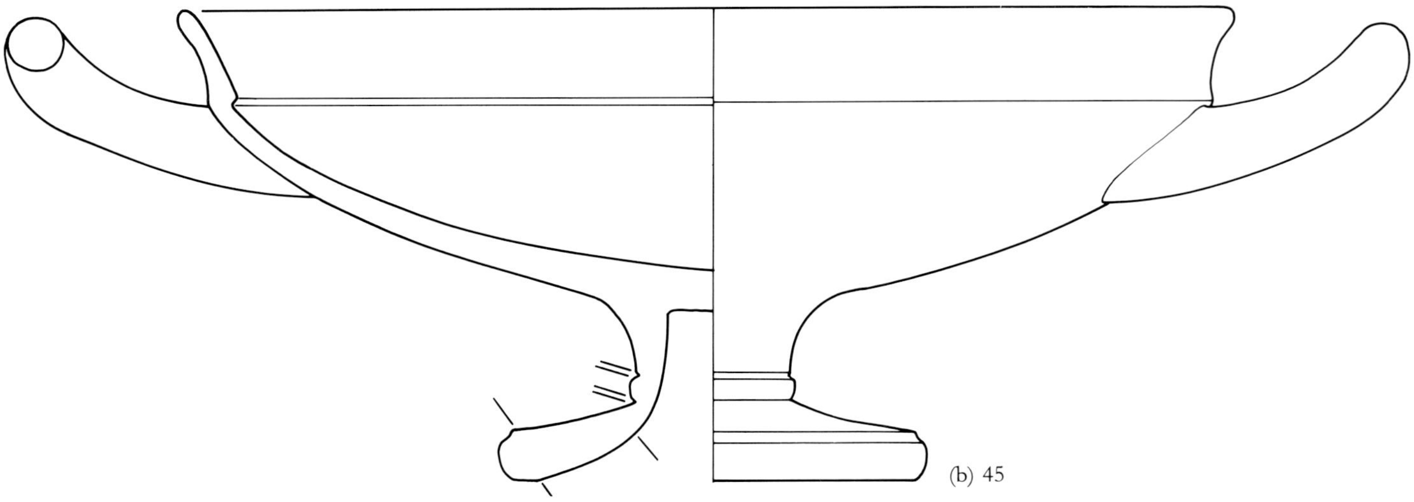

(b) 45

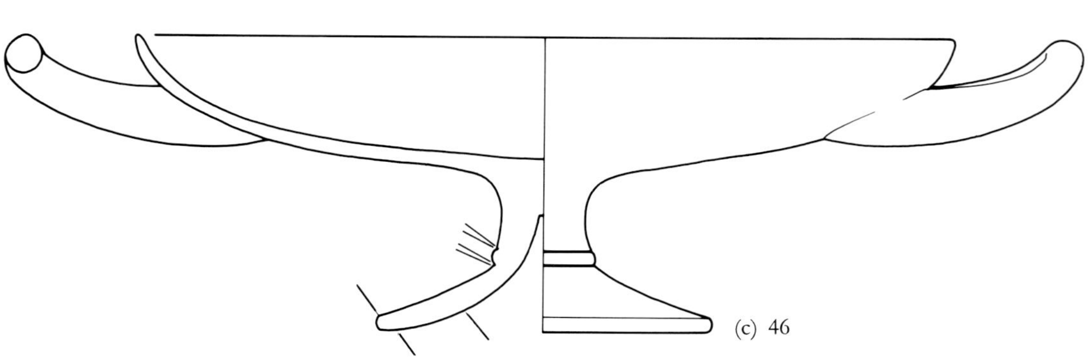

(c) 46

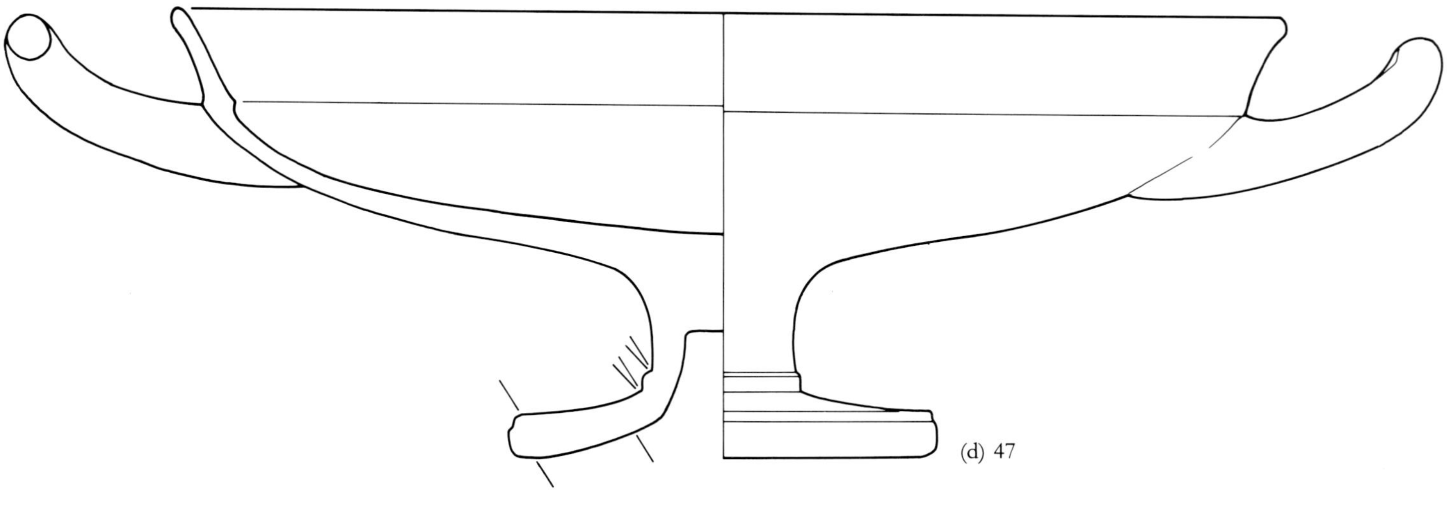

(d) 47

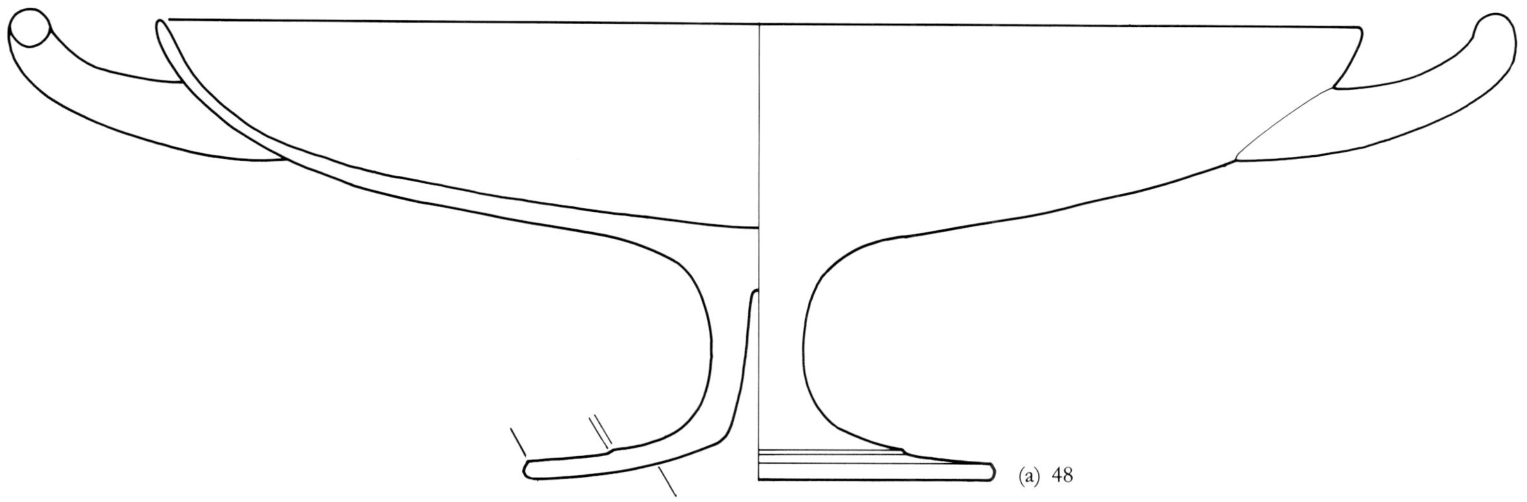

(a) 48

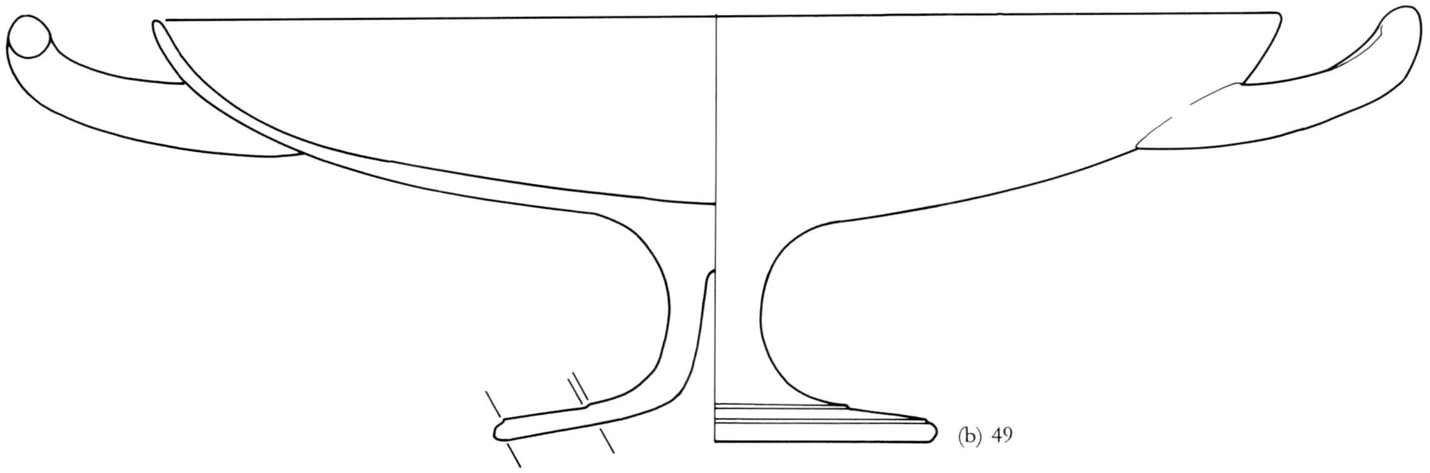

(b) 49

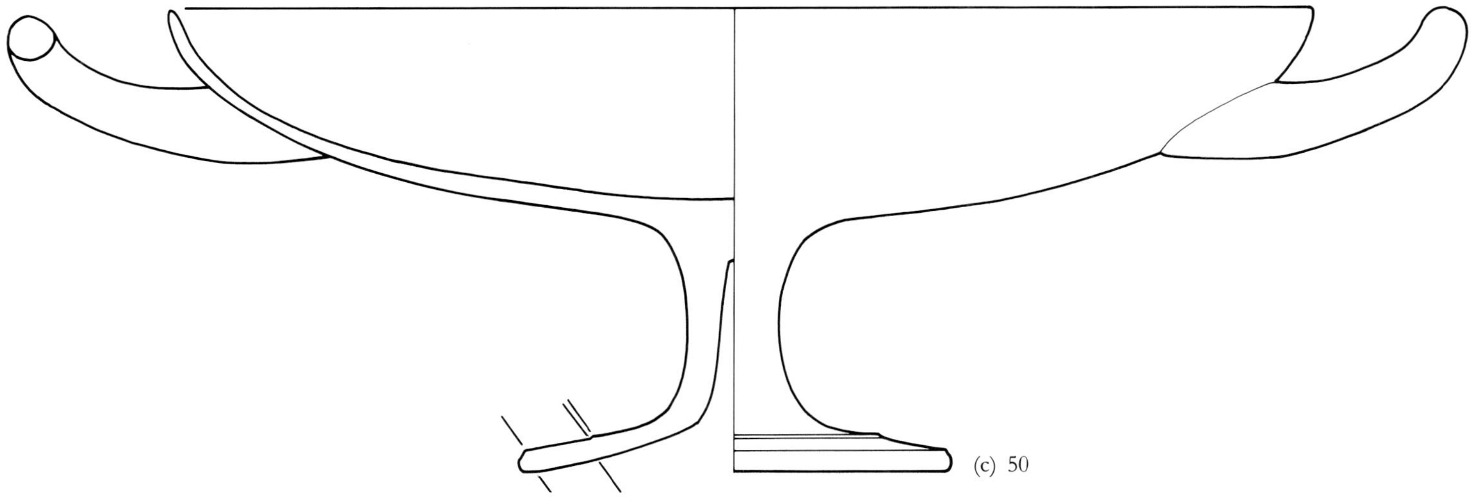

(c) 50

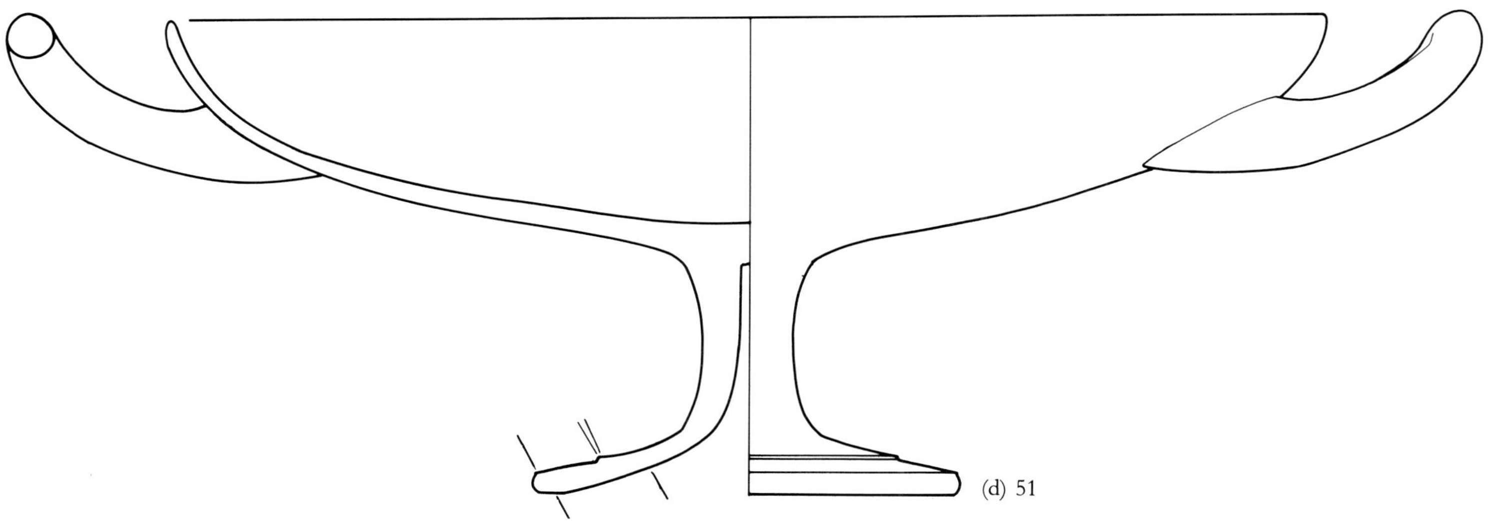

(d) 51

FIGURE 13

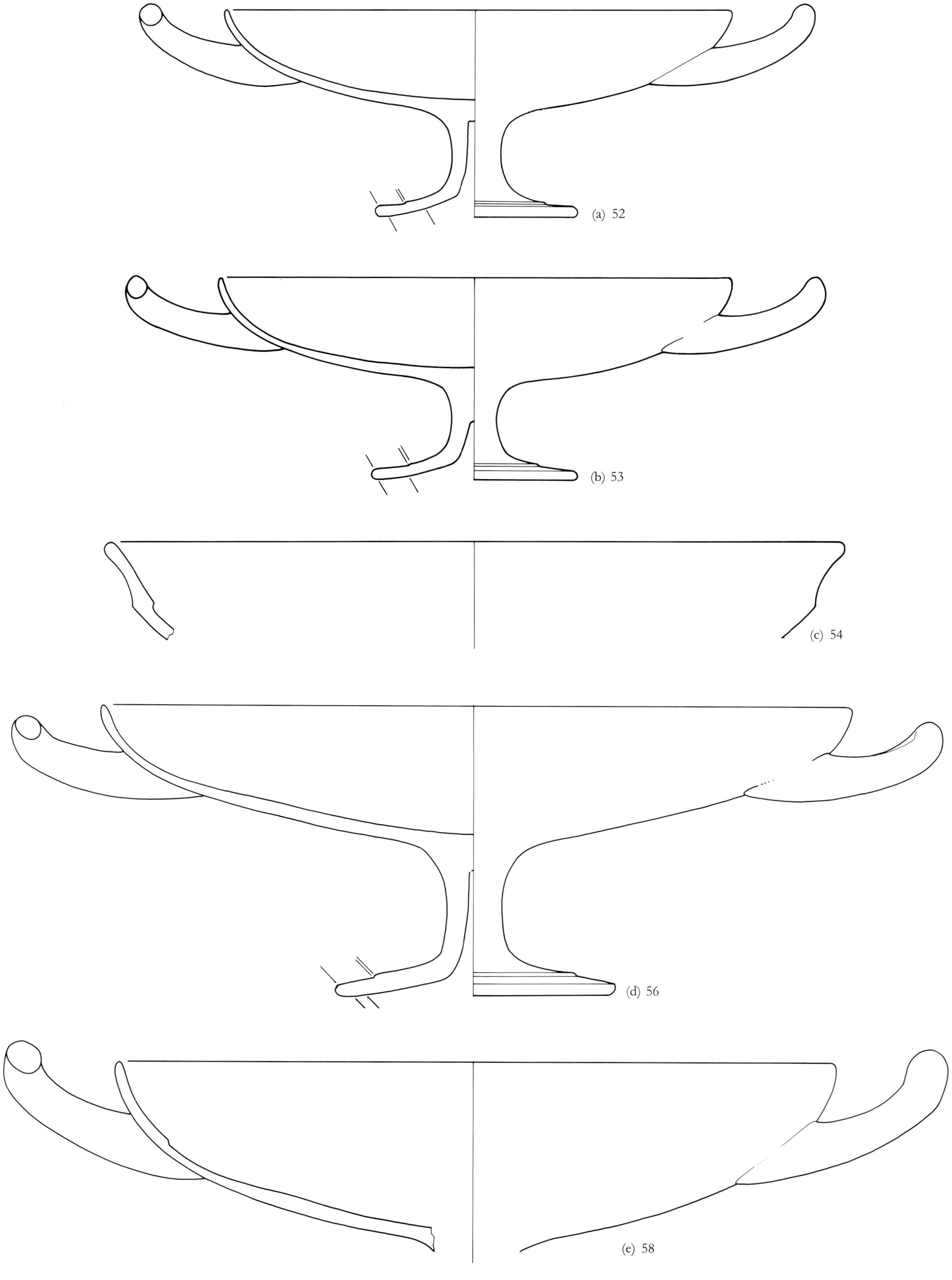